ESSAYS ON WITTGENSTEIN

ESSAYS ON WITTGENSTEIN

Edited by

E. D. Klemke

UNIVERSITY OF ILLINOIS PRESS
URBANA, CHICAGO, LONDON

To Gulliume Moor

Contents

Preface, ix

PART THREE: PHILOSOPHY OF LOGIC AND MATHEMATICS

Preface

LUDWIG WITTGENSTEIN has been
described as "without doubt one of the greatest philosophers of our
time."[1] G. J. Warnock writes that "there can be no serious doubt
that the most powerful and pervasive influence upon the practice
of philosophy in this country [Great Britain] today has been that of
Ludwig Wittgenstein."[2] Judging by the number of articles and
books which have appeared,[3] it is apparent that this influence has
extended to the United States and to other countries as well.

Ludwig Josef Johann Wittgenstein was born in Vienna on April
26, 1889. In 1908 he registered as a student in the engineering department at the University of Manchester. After having decided to
give up his studies in engineering and to study logic and the philosophy of mathematics, he went to Cambridge University in 1911
(apparently on the advice of Frege) in order to study with Bertrand
Russell. At Cambridge, he also met (among others) A. N. White-
head and G. E. Moore. His *Tractatus logico-philosophicus* was
completed in 1918 and published in 1922. After having given up
philosophy for a period he returned to Cambridge in 1929, received
his Ph.D. that year, and was made a Fellow of Trinity College in

---

[1] K. T. Fann, ed., *Ludwig Wittgenstein: The Man and His Philosophy: An Anthology* (New York: Dell Publishing Co., 1967), p. 11.

[2] G. J. Warnock, *English Philosophy Since 1900* (London: Oxford University Press, 1958), p. 64.

[3] See Selected Bibliography.

ix

1930. During the 30's and 40's, he lectured, although not continuously, at Cambridge. He completed the *Philosophical Investigations* in 1948–49, although the work was not published until 1953. After visits to the United States, Oxford University, and Norway, he returned to Cambridge and died on April 29, 1951.[4]

Since I had already edited a collection of *Essays on Frege*,[5] and a collection of *Essays on Bertrand Russell*,[6] it was suggested that I compile a companion volume on Wittgenstein. But this time I faced a problem. There already existed several books and anthologies on Wittgenstein. Upon investigation, I found that a number of philosophers were working on papers on Wittgenstein, or had devised topics for such essays, and were willing to contribute them to the present collection. Thus, whereas the Frege volume contained only two new essays, and the Russell volume ten, this volume contains eleven previously unpublished (and in some cases long) essays. These are essays 5, 6, 7, 8, 15, 16, 17, 18, 19, 22, 23.

I would again like to express my gratitude to all of the writers, editors, and publishers who kindly granted permission to allow essays to be reprinted in this volume, and to the writers who contributed new papers for the book. I would also like to express my appreciation to all who gave advice and helped with the selection of items and topics to be included or with the task of getting the manuscript prepared for publication. I am especially indebted to Professors Gustav Bergmann, Lee Brown, K. T. Fann, Newton Garver, Moltke S. Gram, Herbert Hochberg, and Farhang Zabeeh; to Mr. G. Moor for his advice and help; to Mr. Truman Metzel; to Mr. Edward Nilges, who assisted in preparing the bibliography; to Mrs. Mary L. Facko, who worked hard at typing the manuscript and other tasks; to Richard Fleming, who compiled the index; to the staff of the University of Illinois Press; and to President Rolf Weil,

---

[4] For further details see G. H. von Wright, "A Biographical Sketch," and Malcolm's memoir, in Norman Malcolm, *Ludwig Wittgenstein: A Memoir* (London: Oxford University Press, 1958).

[5] E. D. Klemke, ed., *Essays on Frege* (Urbana: University of Illinois Press, 1968).

[6] E. D. Klemke, ed., *Essays on Bertrand Russell* (Urbana: University of Illinois Press, 1970).

Dean Paul Olscamp, and Dean George Watson, of Roosevelt University, for granting me a reduced teaching load so that I could work on this project.

E. D. Klemke
Evanston, Illinois
June, 1970

PART ONE
Wittgenstein's Ontology

I

Ineffability, Ontology, and Method

GUSTAV BERGMANN

THIS paper[1] has three parts. The first could very well stand by itself. "Ineffability" would be an appropriate title for it. The third part could almost stand alone, too. If it did, "Some Remarks on Ontology" would be an appropriate title; these remarks are not unconnected with what is said in the first part. The second part connects the other two by explicating some of the philosophical uses of 'form'. There is no part corresponding to the third noun in the title of the whole. What I believe to be the right method in philosophy distinguishes between the commonsensical and the philosophical uses of words, insisting that the latter all require commonsensical explication. Though by no means the whole of the method, which is a many-faceted thing, that is indeed one of its basic ideas. Also, it can be shown at work in relative isolation. As the paper proceeds, this idea comes gradually to the fore. Hence the third noun of the title.

I

Each of us is *acquainted* with some things and facts (states of affairs). Synonymously, these things and facts are *presented* to us.

Reprinted with the kind permission of the author and the editor from *The Philosophical Review*, 69 (1960):18–40.

[1] Some of this material I presented first during the summer of 1958 at Northwestern University in a joint seminar with Herbert Hochberg, to whom I am indebted for many stimulating discussions. Since then I have benefited also from discussions with Edwin B. Allaire.

What one is acquainted with he knows. Each of us also knows much else. These things and facts, however, he knows only *by means of* what is, or has been, presented to him. A very large number of philosophers past and present either explicitly or implicitly accept these propositions. Some of those who now accept them explicitly call them a Principle of Acquaintance (PA). How are we to understand the italicized phrase in its last clause? That is a very large question or, rather, a group of questions. Proponents of a PA may still reasonably disagree on the answers to all or some of them. For what I am about, however, the last clause does not matter at all. So I shall ignore it. Notice next that I spoke of *a* rather than *the* PA. I did this in order to indicate that what I stated is merely a schema which one may reasonably call a principle only after he has specified what he takes himself to be acquainted with. Again, there is disagreement. In philosophical discussions some use their words so (and thereby choose their philosophical gambits) that they are, at some times, presented with (some) physical objects and some of the characters they exemplify. According to others, the things presented to us are all phenomenal, such as, say, colored spots in a visual field, in such contexts also called sensa, and their colors, in such contexts also called phenomenal colors. For my purpose the disagreement does not matter. I shall take us to be acquainted with such things as colored spots in visual fields. In fact, I shall talk about no others. But I make this "choice" only because, without as far as I can see introducing any bias, it will simplify the exposition, and not because it happens to be the one I would make where it does matter.

Some hold that there are things so *simple* that if we want to speak about them directly, all we can do is name them—that is, attach words to them as mere labels. The qualification "directly" is meant to brush aside what is familiar as well as irrelevant for my purpose; for example, reference by definite description. The phrase 'mere label' indicates that there is not and could not be anything about a linguistic expression serving as a name that provides a cue for what it is the label of. In so-called ideal languages (another controversial subject that I shall keep out, although a bit later I shall for convenience's sake use a few symbols and, still later, even the idea of an improved language) this shows itself in the circumstance that an expression serving as a name is (in the written case) a sign no (geometrical) part of which is itself a sign. It follows, or very nearly so, that one can name only what he is or has been presented with. All this is indeed part of the relevant notion of 'simplicity', which I do not propose to examine in this paper. Whether this special use of 'simple' can be satisfactorily clarified may be controversial. Surely it is now again controversial whether there are in any language any expressions that are, in the sense specified, names. I shall proceed as if there were. What I want to say could be said even if there were not. But it might have to be said very differently. I shall therefore not claim that this "choice" of mine, the second I am making, merely simplifies the exposition. On the other hand, the simplification achieved by my first choice should by now be obvious. Everyone can agree that *if* it makes sense to speak about sensa and *if* there are things so simple that they can only be named, then sensa are among these things.

Notice that I said sensa are among those simple things and not, as might have been expected, sensa and some of their characters. Thereby hangs another controversy, the last one I must mention and show to be irrelevant, though only in a peculiar way, in order to clear the air and set the stage.

Consider a green spot. Call F the fact of its being green. It is as "simple" a fact as I can think of. Yet, being a fact, F, like any other fact, has constituents which are things. In this sense no fact is "simple." (The familiar difference thus revealed between the uses of 'simple' as applied to facts and to things, respectively, will play a role in the last part.) Which thing or things are the constituents of F? Some answer that they are two, namely, an *individual* (the spot) and a *character* (the spot's color). The answer seems obvious; to me it is obvious. But, then, it has not been and still is not obvious to many. Up to a point, of course, everyone agrees that in being presented with F he is presented with the color. Beyond that point, though, some try to make distinctions. They might claim, for instance, that the individual and the character are not presented in quite the same way, only the former but not the latter being "wholly presented." Objections against calling the character a thing, as well as against calling an expression directly referring to it a name, as either unusual or confusing, may be a linguistic symptom of this attempt to distinguish. An extreme and explicit variant of it is to insist that F has only one constituent (which is a thing) and that this constituent is neither the spot nor its color but, rather, the "colored spot." We have come upon the root of the realism-nominalism controversy, a disagreement so fundamental that one might expect it to be relevant to almost any question a philosopher is likely to raise. I shall take it for granted that F has two constituents which are things and which are presented to us whenever F is presented, namely, the individual and the character. But I shall also argue that F has three further constituents which *in some sense* are presented to us whenever F is. The accent in this paper is on these additional three—this excess, as it were, over either one or two constituents. This is the peculiar way in which, fundamental as it is, the difference between one and two, if I may so express myself, does not matter for my purpose.

When I know that this is a green spot, I know also that (1) the spot is an individual, (2) the color is a character, and (3) the former exemplifies the latter (and not, perhaps, the latter the former). How could I know all this if it were not, in some sense, presented to me? To grasp the idea more firmly, consider for a moment a visual field containing two spots, one red, one green. When this field is presented to me, I also know which spot exemplifies which color and, for that matter, also that no spot or color exemplifies the other spot or color. How, to repeat, could I know all these things if they were not presented to me? The three additional constituents of F are, accordingly, the two "properties" of (1) individuality and (2) universality, and the "nexus" of (3) exemplification.

Three brief comments before I continue should clear the air. First, I did not call exemplification a relation but, noncommittally, a "nexus." Unfortunately, I cannot think of an equally noncommittal word to take the place of 'property'. So I used the latter, with tongue in cheek, and on paper with quotation marks around it. Second, there is a sense in which the three additional constituents are not quite independent of each other. As we ordinarily think of it, the nexus of exemplification is asymmetrical. The distinction between individuality and universality introduces this asymmetry a second time. In the lower functional calculus (LFC), the dependence shows itself as follows. After we have distinguished between x- and f-variables (and the constants that can be substituted for them), the parentheses and the order in the conventional notation '$f(x)$' are redundant. '$.fx.$' and '$.xf.$', with the pair of dots indicating that the string is a sentence and without any attention paid to order, would do as well. (The case of relations is different, of course; but we need not bother with it.) Third, *if* the three additional constituents could be named, some (including myself) would insist that their names belong to a "type" different from that of either of the two names of the two constituents which are things. Whether or not this distinction is both sound and important makes no difference for my purpose. So, once more, we need not bother.

I refrained from calling the three crucial constituents "things." Even so, some may feel that, merely by insisting on their being in some sense presented in F and therefore calling them constituents of F, I am opening the door to confusion by blurring fundamental distinction. If I were to stop now, these critics would be right. The distinction they wish to defend is fundamental indeed. Nor is anything I have said or shall say meant to weaken it. Rather, I wish to make it more accurately, in order to avoid some confusions that may beset us if we do not make it accurately enough. For this purpose I turn to language. Specifically, I would say that I turn to the LFC. But if someone wants to think of what follows as a "language game," he may do so. In a "game" as limited as the one I shall play, the difference makes no difference.

My calculus (or game) has two kinds of names or prospective names: lower-case letters ('a', 'b', . . .) for individuals, upper-case letters ('G', 'H', . . .) for characters. A sentence is a string consisting of one name of each kind. I shall continue to write it conventionally, for example, '$G(a)$'. Looking at a name of this game, I know, therefore—even if I do not know *which thing* it has been attached to as a label (or whether it has been attached at all)—the *kind of thing*, whether individual or character, to which it has been or could be attached. We have come upon a confusion lurking behind the phrase 'mere label'. In one obvious sense a name is a mere label. In another sense it is not. In this latter sense there are indeed no mere labels. Who sees that clearly also sees how the distinction between the two constituents of F which are things and the three further ones which are not appears in my game. The individual and the character are represented by "labels." Individuality and universality are represented by the shapes of these "labels," exemplification by two "labels" being strung together into a sentence.[2]

The critic I just mentioned may grant that as long as I play this game the distinction he watches over is safe. But then what is to keep me from obliterating it by "labeling," in a different game, the three crucial constituents? He has a point. He adds that sooner or later I am even likely to play this different sort of game, since it is often part of the relevant use of 'presented' that what is presented can be labeled. Again, he has a point. The proper way to meet it and, by meeting it, to safeguard the fundamental distinction is to show that any attempt at labeling the three additional constituents either leads to disaster or, at least, is futile. This I shall do next.

Let '*a*', '*G*', '*I*', '*U*', '*E*' be the labels one may try to attach to the spot, its color, individuality, universality, and exemplification, respectively. What I controversially claim to be presented when *F* is presented would be expressed by

$$(1)\ I(a), \qquad (2)\ U(G), \qquad (3)\ E(G, a).$$

The roughness due to the fact that two capital letters occur in both (2) and (3) and altogether three letters in (3) I said before I would ignore. Notice, first, that in this game, too, the marks are of two kinds of shapes. For, if they were not, how would I know which go with which to make a string that is a sentence? Notice, second, that in order to understand (1), (2), and (3), I would therefore have to understand first that exemplification and kind of object exemplifying or exemplified are represented by the juxtaposition of "labels" and the shapes of the labels, respectively. This is the heart of the matter. It shows what I meant by saying that any attempt to label the three crucial constituents is futile. I am also convinced that, if made uncritically, it sooner or later will lead to disaster. This, however, I shall not show.[3]

'Ineffable' has been put to several philosophical uses. Philosophical uses require commonsensical explications. A proposition is philo-

---

[2] There is a blur here as obvious and, alas, annoying as the failure to distinguish between *type* and *token*. Two tokens are two individuals exemplifying the same type. Juxtaposition, representing exemplification, is exemplified by the individuals in the tokens. All other representing features are constituents of the types.

[3] Reinhardt Grossmann reminds me that, according to Meinong, who

sophical if it contains at least one word used philosophically. I offer what has just been said about the futility of introducing '*I*', '*U*', and '*E*' into our game as the explication of the philosophical proposition, "Individuality, universality, and exemplification are ineffable." Clearly, one may agree (as I do) that these three constituents of *F* are ineffable in this sense without agreeing (as I do not) that they are ineffable in some other sense, or that certain other things are also "ineffable," either in this or in another unexplicated and philosophical sense. For that matter, one may wish to offer the claim that all philosophical uses require commonsensical explications as the explication of the paradoxical philosophical proposition that what philosophers try to say is "ineffable." If I may so explicate it, then I, for one, accept that proposition. It is indeed one of the mainstays of my method. But, then, this is not the way that paradoxical proposition was meant and used.

So far I have attended to the thing itself, without any mention, except for a passing reference to the realism-nominalism controversy, of the huge body of dialectical argument that has grown up around it. Accordingly, I have not used any technical word, such as 'ontology'. I even avoided the nontechnical words, such as 'form', which in these arguments have been used philosophically. Nor have I mentioned any names. One is on the lips of every likely reader. *Absentiā fulget.* I shall not mention it, simply because I do not on this occasion wish to make assertions about the proper reading of a notoriously difficult text and, still less, about what was in the mind of its author when he wrote it. One other name I shall mention. Much of what I have said is not new, of course. What is new, if anything, is the use I made of a certain argument pattern to explicate one philosophical use of 'ineffable' by demonstrating the "futility" of labeling, as we label some "things," the three crucial constituents of *F*. This pattern, though of course with a different

---

thought about these things carefully and often profoundly, exemplification is the only "real relation," while such relations as, say, being to the left of (i.e., the kind I call descriptive) are merely "ideal." There is a general awareness that for some such reasons Meinong, in spite of his care and profundity, bogged down. Grossmann is engaged upon a study designed to show accurately why and how Meinong and some others who played similar gambits met their defeat.

twist, is that of a famous argument proposed by Bradley. Since his name is not now on everybody's lips, I think that I should mention it.

II

The key word of the dialectic is 'form'. 'Structure' is sometimes used synonymously, or very nearly so. I shall stay with 'form'. The key phrase is 'logical form'. 'The ontological status of logical form' or, briefly, 'the ontological status of logic' is the tag for the issue I am considering. My critic was apprehensive lest the line I took lead to the "reification of logical form." Had he used the phrase, he would have used 'form' philosophically. The thing to realize before tackling this use is that 'form' has three relevant commonsensical meanings. They are all syntactical. That is my cue for another effort to avoid controversy.

I promised to keep out the issue of ideal languages. I shall keep the promise. But I shall henceforth use the LFC (with the "label" constants I added to it) as an improved language, that is, as a calculus syntactically constructed and interpreted by interpreting its undefined signs only. Whether such a "language" is a suitable tool for philosophical analysis is now again controversial. But, again, the controversy does not affect us. For *if* I have committed myself to the "reification of logical form," then, *because* of the tool I use, the commitment should be even easier to spot in my argument than it would be if I did not use that tool. Thus, if a bias is introduced, it is one against the point I am arguing.

Form$_1$ refers to the shape of the signs and to the rules, based on their shapes and nothing else, by which they may be strung together into sentences. This is the first relevant commonsensical meaning of 'form'. If all sentences were atomic, my critic could be answered conclusively and exhaustively as follows. Signs are labels (though not mere labels) representing (simple) "things." Individuality, universality, and exemplification, the three "formal" or "logical" constituents of facts, cannot, except at the price of futility, be so represented. They are represented by form$_1$. The quotes I have put around 'formal' and 'logical' mark philosophical uses. The very sentence in which they occur explicates them. (About the philosophical use of 'thing' presently, in the third part.) Thus I safeguard the ontological distinction. Yet I need not, in order to safeguard it, deny that logical form (philosophical use) is like "things" *in one respect*, namely, that it, too, is presented to me. For indeed, if it were not presented, how could it be represented by form$_1$? And, if it were not presented, why do I use a language of just this form$_1$? Notice, too, that there is something ineffable, in the sense explicated, in any possible language, as long as by language we mean—and I do not know what else we could mean—something having signs and sentences as well as rules by which the former may be strung into the latter. I speak of possible languages rather than of possible worlds because the use of 'possible' in the latter phrase is patently philosophical, while in the former, as long as one thinks of an uninterpreted calculus, it is not.

In our language (LFC) not all primitive (undefined) signs are labels. Those which are not are called logical. What can be said about them, commonsensically, contributes to the explication of the philosophical use of 'form'. Instead of calling these signs logical—as for the most part I shall, in order not to strain the usage—I would therefore rather call them formal$_2$. Lest this seem artificial, consider that, to say the least, the unexplicated uses of 'formal' and 'logical' quite often blur into each other. We just came upon an instance in the synonymy of 'logical constituent' and 'formal constituent'. The synonymy of 'logical truth' and 'formal truth' is another. The only reason the redundance of 'logical form' is not more apparent is that the adjective serves to set off the philosophical context from such very different ones as those in which we speak of, say, the form of a symphony or a vase.

The logical signs are either variables or connectives or operators. A variable as such (that is, technically, a free variable) merely marks form$_1$. Since no more needs to be said about form$_1$, we are left with connectives and operators. For what I am about, though surely not otherwise, there is no difference between these two kinds. Thus nothing will be lost if for the sake of both brevity and simplicity I ignore operators and make my case for connectives.

Like form$_1$, the connectives (form$_2$) represent something which in some sense is presented to us. They represent an aspect of what some philosophers, using the word philosophically, call the world's "form." This is the gist of the argument. My critic at this point finds his worst fears exceeded. I began by claiming *some sort* of "ontological status" for exemplification and so on, which to him seemed bad enough. Now I am about to do the same for negation, disjunction, and so on, which to him seems even worse. Some of his dismay is due to the particular flavor of philosophical talk. The rest is properly dispelled by the commonsensical observations and distinctions that follow.

What form₂ represents is different from "things." This comes out in at least three ways. First, the nonlogical primitive signs, also called descriptive, are all labels; the connectives are not. Second, having constructed LFC syntactically, one may start its interpretation by attaching its descriptive primitives as labels to things. In principle, one must do that. Practically, one may instead make these signs "stand for" some words of our natural language, which, in an obvious sense, is the only one we speak and understand, just as a moment ago I made 'G' stand for 'green'. For the connectives the latter alternative is the only one available. We make '~', 'V', and so on, stand for 'not', 'or', and so on. Third, the use of the connectives is completely and accurately regulated by the so-called truth tables, that is, by an algebraic machinery with two counters which can be made to stand for 'true' and 'false'. On this 'completely and accurately' hangs the current controversy about improved languages. *What form₂ represents is different from what is represented by form₁.* In the written case the difference appears, trivially, in the (geometrical) differences between form₁ and form₂. Much less trivially, it appears in the circumstance that while, as we saw, form₁ *cannot*, except at the price of futility, be represented by primitive signs of the language, form₂ *must* be so represented by at least one primitive logical sign. *Yet form₂ represents something.* Consider a calculus which is like LFC in being of the same form₁ but unlike it in that the algebraic machinery associated with its "connectives" has three counters instead of two. Technically, it is a lower functional calculus with a three-valued non-Aristotelian logic. I do not know how to interpret this calculus so as to make an artificial language out of it. Nor does anyone else. And there is one and only one reason why this is so. We do not know how to interpret the "connectives." This shows that form represents something. Or, if you please, it shows what is meant by saying that it "represents" something (though of course not any "thing"), which is, in some sense, "presented" to us. Nor is that all. Still another very important point can and must be made in order to secure the distinctions and allay the fears. As I arranged the exposition, this point must wait for the third part.

Form$_3$ is a property of expressions. Take an expression, eliminate first all defined terms, then substitute appropriate variables for all descriptive primitives. Two expressions have the same form$_3$ if and only if this procedure, applied to both of them, either yields different tokens of the same type or can be made to yield them by applying to the variables of one the procedure known as "rewriting." This is the third relevant commonsensical use of 'form'. Notice in passing that it leads immediately to a fourth, which appears in the proposition that a sentence expresses a "formal" truth or falsehood (is analytic or contradictory) if and only if its truth or falsehood depends only on its form$_3$.

Form$_3$, too, represents something. After what has been said, this need not be argued separately. I have argued that form$_1$ and form$_2$ each represent something. Form$_3$ is compounded of form$_1$ and form$_2$. What it represents is correspondingly compounded of what is represented by form$_1$ and form$_2$. If someone pointed out that the use of 'compounded' in the preceding sentence is at least tinged with metaphor, I would not fuss. But I would observe that the unpacking of the rudimentary metaphor, after what has been said, is merely tedious. So I turn instead to three comments.

1. If the language contains *defined* signs, then the form$_3$ of expressions which are sentences may be given a representative (not: be represented) in the language. Take '$G(a) \lor H(a)$'. Substitution of variables for the (primitive) constants yields '$f(x) \lor g(x)$'. Write '$R(f, g, x)$' as an abbreviation for the latter expression. 'R' is a defined ternary predicate. (I continue to ignore types.) For every sentence a "corresponding" relation R can be defined. Two sentences are of the same form$_3$ if and only if the constituents which are things of the facts which they represent exemplify the same relation R. In this sense R is a representative of (not: represents) form$_3$. What it represents (or expresses, but not: is a representative of) is of course what is represented by form$_3$ (not: form$_3$).

2. 'Thing', it must have been noticed, I use so that a thing is what either is or by the rules of the language could be labeled. Defined signs are not labels. '*R*' is a defined sign. Moreover, '*R*' is a defined logical sign, that is, all the primitive signs in its definiens are logical and, therefore, not labels. These are two good reasons why introducing '*R*' into the language is not a back-handed way of giving the wrong kind of ontological status to form$_3$. The fundamental distinctions are still safe.

3. Test what is being said now against what was said in the first part about exemplification by so defining '*Ex*' that '*Ex(f, x)*' stands for '*f(x)*'. Notice that, unlike '*E*', '*Ex*' is a defined logical sign. Notice, too, that the possibility of introducing it does not in the least militate against what has been said about the futility of *labeling* exemplification. What one may wonder about is, rather, whether this futility does not infect all '*R*'. In a sense it does. Only, if the expression is complex enough, then '*R*' is of some technical use.

Those who distrust the distinction between the commonsensical and the philosophical uses of words more often than not want to be shown the exact point of transition. I would remind them of what James once said. One cannot light a candle so quickly that one sees what the dark is like. But I would add that in some cases one can do better than in some others. In the case of '(logical) form' one can do rather well. Sentences, it has been said, manage to express facts because they are "logical pictures" of the facts they express. In this context 'logical picture' is expendable. What is intended can be said without the phrase as follows. (*S*) *A sentence manages to express because, taken as a fact, it shares logical form with the fact it expresses.* Take once more our paradigm, *F*, and the sentence expressing it, '*G(a)*'. Here is what in this case I take *S* to mean: '*a*' and '*G*' represent the spot and the color, respectively; their shapes, the spot and the color being an individual and a character, respectively; their juxtaposition, the exemplification of the color by the spot. Generally, it seems, the idea of "shared logical form" is that of a one-one correspondence between the constituents of the fact expressed and geometrical features of the sentence expressing it, such that constituents of the same kind correspond to features of the same (geometrical) kind. If that is what *S* means, then I understand it. Of course I do, since it is exactly what I said myself. Only I said it without using 'logical form'. Thus I have shown, not surprisingly, that like all philosophically used words and phrases, the phrase is expendable. Now I shall show two more things; namely, first, that if the phrase is used as in S it leads to immediate catastrophe and, second, that in certain other contexts it invites confusion and makes falsehood seem plausible.

First, write '$G(a)$' without brackets, as I did before, and assume the two letters to be things. The assumption is in the spirit of the dialectic. Considered as a fact, a token of the sentence then consists of two things of different kinds standing in a certain (geometrical) relation. The constituents of this fact are, therefore, two individuals (the letters), two nonrelational (the letters' shapes) characters, and one relational (the letters' juxtaposition) character, and, if I may so express myself, individuality twice, universality three times, in addition, of course, to (relational) exemplification. Everything else apart, clearly they are too many for a one-one correspondence with the constituents of the fact expressed. It follows that if 'logical form' is explicated in the only way I can think of, the sentence and the fact do not "share" the same "logical form." Rather, we stand here at the beginning of an infinite regress. This is disaster indeed. The regress, by the way, though of course again with a different twist, is not unrelated to another part of Bradley's famous pattern.

What philosophers try to say is always ineffable. This, we remember, is the general ineffability thesis. As it was meant, though not as I suggested it might be explicated, it is vague and indefensible. Yet it has come to stand for quite a few things that are neither vague nor indefensible. The related distinctions between language as "part" and "picture" of the world and between speaking and speaking about speaking are two such things. Those who held the general thesis held it, in part, because they thought "logical form" to be "ineffable." That is why they used 'logical form' as they did in S. As was shown in the last paragraph, the disaster that befell them is due to an implicit neglect of the two distinctions.

Second, form$_1$, form$_2$, and form$_3$, I argued, each represent something that in some sense is presented to us. What they represent I now call *logical form*. This explicates the use I shall henceforth make of the phrase. Nor am I the only one who, either implicitly or explicitly, uses the phrase in this way. That explains in turn the dismay of my critic. He takes me to assert that logical form "exists," which to him is absurd. So far I avoided 'exist', leaving it deliberately to the last part. At this point, though, I wish to say that had I cared to indulge, I could have borrowed a soothing word from the tradition. I might have said that logical form, though it does not "exist," yet "subsists." Of course, the tag merely dignifies the distinctions I made commonsensically and without using any tag, between the two kinds of "ontological status." But, then, sometimes tags are convenient. Right now I find this one handy for building a verbal bridge.

If logical form does not even "subsist," that is, if it has no ontological status whatsoever, then it is nought. Nought is nought, unchanged and unchangeably, in all "possible worlds." This is one pillar of the bridge. The occurrence of 'formal' in 'formal truth' provides the other. Remember that formal truths are also called logical; infer speciously that logical truths are nought; and you are in sight of the philosophical proposition the bridge leads to. (*A*) *The logic of our world is that of all possible worlds.* For example, '$p \vee \sim p$' is formally true in all possible worlds. The word used philosophically in *A* is 'possible'. One such use of 'possible' is easily explicated as follows. In our world a state of affairs is possible if and only if it is expressed by a sentence (of our language) that is not a formal falsehood (contradictory). Clearly this is not the way the word is used in *A*. As it is used there, the phrase 'possible world' is inseparable. I find it difficult to explicate. Or, rather, in the one explication I can think of the phrase sounds rather inflated. One can, as we saw, construct calculi which are in some fundamental respects like and in some others unlike the calculus we can make into an improved language by interpreting it. Such calculi are possible (commonsensical use). The illustration I used was a three-valued lower functional calculus. If one wishes one may, with some bombast, speak of such a calculus as the language of a "possible world." If one does that, then *A* is patently false. I say patently because in the purely syntactical sense of 'formal truth'—and there is in this case no other—'$p \vee \sim p$' is not a formal truth, or, as in this case one says, rather, is not a theorem of the three-valued calculus. Thus I have kept my promise to show that in some contexts the unexplicated use of 'logical form' leads to confusion and falsehood. The context is

that of *A*. The confusion is that between the two suggested explications of 'possible'. The falsehood is *A* itself, which asserts what I
call the *absolutist* conception of analyticity.

III

Ontology asks what "exists." This use of 'exist' is philosophical. I
couldn't possibly here explicate it fully. I shall merely state two
basic ideas, calling them basic because I believe that either explicitly
or implicitly they have shaped the whole ontological enterprise.
Then I shall point out a few of their implications. The connection
with the first two parts is twofold. One of these ideas involves that
of names or labels. For another, it will be remembered that, when
discussing form₂, I promised an important further argument to allay
the apprehensions aroused by its being given any sort of ontological
status. This argument concludes the paper.

From now on, when I mention 'exist', I shall surround it with
single quotes. When I report its philosophical uses, I shall surround
it with double quotes. When I use it commonsensically, I shall not
use quotes. And I shall presently treat 'thing' and 'fact' in the same
way. The practice saves space and avoids tedium. But, of course, it
should be kept in mind.

Ontologists do not just either catalogue or classify what exists.
Rather, they search for "simples" of which everything that exists
"consists." These simples, and nothing else, they hold to "exist," or
to be the only existents. (I shall use 'existent' in no other way.) If,
for instance, the tones in a symphony were simples, they would
"exist"; the symphony, though of course it exists, would not "exist."
This is the first basic idea. It amounts to an explication of the
ontologists' philosophical use of 'exist'. Consider the classical phenomenalist. His tones are such things as sensa and, if he is not a nominalist, some of the characters they exemplify. His symphony is the
physical object. And we know him to assert that physical objects do
not "exist." That shows in one important case the adequacy of the
explication. Notice, though, that it explicates one philosophical use
('exist') in terms of another ('simple'). Everything therefore still
depends on whether an adequate explication can be found for this

use of 'simple' (and of 'consist'). I do not propose to answer the
questions that raises. I merely wish to state one idea which I believe
to be a part of the philosophical idea of simplicity and which, therefore, no adequate explication of the latter can ignore. What is "simple" is so simple indeed that, in speaking about it (directly), the
best or the most one can do, put it any way you wish, is to name it,
that is, attach a label to it (though not necessarily, as we saw, a mere
label). This is the second basic idea. It reveals a connection, not surprising from where I stand, between the ontological enterprise and
language. The way I deliberately presented this connection shows
that it does not at all depend on the idea of an improved, and still
less of course on that of an ideal language. Once more, therefore, no
vitiating bias is introduced if I avail myself of one of the advantages
of improved languages. A name or label is simple in some linguistic
sense of 'simple'. The idea of linguistic simplicity, though surely not
philosophical, is yet not obvious. Thus it needs explanation. Improved languages, to say the least, provide us with models of what
one might reasonably mean by 'linguistically simple'. This is the
advantage of which I wish to avail myself.

Like all languages, our paradigm, the LFC with constants, contains signs (words) and sentences. That opens two possibilities: simple signs and simple sentences. (Perhaps it would be better to say
simplest; but I shall stay with 'simple'.) A simple sign is one no
(geometrical) part of which is a sign (for example, '*a*', '*G*', '∨'). A
simple sentence is one no geometrical part of which is a sentence;
for example, '*G*(*a*)'. Such sentences are called atomic. But an atomic
sentence contains at least two simple signs. In this sense not even an
atomic sentence is simple. Thereby hangs a tale.

What sorts of entities (I must avoid 'thing') have been held to
"exist"? The tradition has two streams. At times they intermingled.
Also, one is so much broader that it may be called the main stream.
Yet the two are clearly discernible. According to some philosophers
all existents are "things"; according to some others they are all
"facts." The former I call thing ontologists; the latter, fact ontologists. These uses of 'thing' and 'fact' are of course philosophical. But
their explication seems by now obvious. A "thing" is what is named
by a descriptive primitive sign; for example, '*a*' and '*G*', but not '∨'.
A "fact" is what is referred to (I avoid 'named') by an atomic sen-

tence. It is important to keep in mind how much narrower these (explicated philosophical) uses are than the commonsensical ones. We may and do call an entity a thing and say that it exists even though, in a certain ontology, it may not be a "thing" and therefore not "exist." As for 'thing', so for 'fact'. We naturally call what a sentence refers to a fact (state of affairs) and, if the sentence is true, say that it exists. But again, in a certain ontology it may not be a "fact" and therefore not "exist." An ontologist unaware of the ambiguity is likely to get into trouble. Of this presently; now for four brief comments.

First, in the first two parts I was concerned with securing *some* sort of ontological status for logical form, arguing that while it does not "exist," it yet "subsists." Naturally, therefore, I was not particularly concerned with what "exists." Yet one may infer from the way I proceeded and, in particular, from how I used 'name', that I am a thing ontologist and not a nominalist. The inference is correct.

Second, what I had in mind when I said that at times the two streams mingled are the several philosophies of substance. Every such philosophy is a heroic attempt to reconcile the irreconcilable. To grasp that firmly, consider the philosophical uses of 'substance'. They all share three features. First, "substances" are the only (independent) existents. Second, a "substance" is a "thing." Third, a "substance" is a thing that, by virtue of being this thing, has certain characters. But a thing having a certain character is expressed by a sentence; and sentences refer to facts!

Third, if the two ideas I singled out are basic, then fact ontologists would have to hold, either explicitly or implicitly, that some sentences at least are names. Many philosophers cannot make any sense out of the idea that a sentence may be the name of something. Thus they reject it as absurd; so do I. An analytical philosopher does not, however, just express his opinions but presents and examines arguments for and against all sorts of positions, including those he rejects. It is my next purpose to state correctly and accurately, which among other things also means as parsimoniously as possible, a difficulty on which any fact ontology must bog down.

Fourth, fact ontologies have been attractive to philosophers. Had they not been, why all the ingenious substance philosophies which, we just saw, try to have the best of both worlds? Whence the attraction? The clue—I planted it in the second comment—is a certain philosophical use of 'independent'. This idea of "independence" is also part of the idea of "existence." What truly exists ("exists"), exists "independently." None of us is ever presented either with an individual that is not qualified or with a character (quality) that is not exemplified by an individual. *In this sense*, "things" are not independent. An individual exemplifying a certain quality, on the other hand, or a certain quality being exemplified by an individual, which is the same, is a fact expressed by a sentence. This, I believe, is the deepest structural root of the attraction fact ontologies have had and perhaps still have for some philosophers.

I turn to the difficulty no fact ontology can overcome. To state it effectively, it will be best to state first two very general conditions. I speak of conditions rather than of principles or presuppositions because of the blur that has gathered around the latter notions. What I mean is that hardly any philosopher would consider his analysis adequate if it were pointed out to him that it fails to meet these "conditions."

Every sentence is about something. To separate what can be separated, consider for the moment only *true* sentences. To keep out what is irrelevant, consider only sentences not mentioning entities a philosopher may think problematic on grounds that have nothing to do with the issue. Translation into ontological talk of the commonsensical 'being about something' yields the condition that there must be some existents (at least one) such that since they (it) are there (exist) the sentence is true, while if they were not there, it would be false. This is the first condition. 'Meaning' has several meanings (uses). In one use, sentences are said to have meanings. What one calls the meaning of a sentence must not depend on whether the sentence is true or false. That is the second condition.

Return to F expressed by '$G(a)$'. Let '$\sim H(a)$' stand for the true sentence that the spot is not red. What is it about? The commonsensical answer is, of course, that it is about (expresses, refers to) the fact (not "fact"!) of the spot not being red. But, then, '$\sim H(a)$' is surely a sentence of the kind to which the first condition applies. Thus the fact ontologist must find an existent, that is, a "fact" the sentence is about. He presents us, as I believe he must, with the "negative fact" of the spot not being red. But, if this is a "fact," then he must by the rules of his own game be able to "name" it, that is, he must be able to produce an atomic sentence that refers to it. If he cannot, then he violates the second basic idea. '$\sim H(a)$' is not atomic. Nor of course can he produce an atomic sentence that by any stretch of the imagination could be said to be about the fact in question. This most parsimonious way of stopping him in his tracks has not, as far as I know, been noticed in the huge literature about "negative facts." Failure to grasp explicitly the two basic ideas and, just as important, failure to distinguish between the two uses of 'fact' are three plausible reasons for this oversight.

In a fact ontology, what would *false* sentences be about? Once the barriers are down, the obvious answer is "false facts." The false atomic sentence '$H(a)$', for instance, would "name" the "false fact" of the spot being red. (The double quotes around 'name' mark my own reluctance, but I am playing someone else's game.) Some philosophers willing to put up with "negative facts" boggled at "false facts." At this point, something called a robust sense of reality is usually invoked. We must not have the world cluttered with such existents as the "false fact" expressed by 'The moon is made of green cheese'. Economy, in some such sense, does guide the ontological enterprise. This, however, is not the point I wish to make. The point is, rather, that the crowding or cluttering is not really as great as it might seem to one who fails to appreciate the distinction between the two uses of 'fact'. If, for instance, the sentence 'The moon is made of green cheese' upon analysis turns out not to be atomic, then even a fact ontologist would not have to put up with the fact that it refers to as a "fact" of his world. He need merely count among his existents those "false facts" to which false atomic sentences refer. One may wonder whether, had this been clearly seen, those who swallowed "negative facts" would have strained at "false facts."

Consider for a moment a fact ontologist who holds fast to the second basic idea. In other words, he understands that by the rules of his game only atomic sentences can be "names." He has two alternatives. Either he accepts "false facts" or he holds that only true atomic sentences are "names." The second alternative is repugnant to him. The structural reason for this repugnance can be stated in four steps. *One.* A true atomic sentence is a name. *Two.* A false atomic sentence, therefore, at least purports to be a name. *Three.* But a name that does not name anything is nonsense (has no meaning). *Four.* Yet false sentences have meaning. Notice that, in the fourth step, the second condition is operative. At this point our philosopher, unwilling to accept "false facts," thinks of another expedient. Reifying 'meaning', he makes sentences name "meanings." But what, then, becomes of "facts"? Obviously the "fact" of this being green cannot be identified with the meaning of 'this is green'. Otherwise, the difference between its being and its not being green, respectively, would be lost. The only way out is to reify 'true' and 'false' and make a "true" (or "false") fact a compound, in some obscure sense of 'compound', of "meaning" and "truth" (or "falsehood"). In this case, though, even a true atomic sentence refers no longer to a "simple" but to a "compound." Thus the first basic idea is lost.

The imaginary fact ontologist whose predicament I just exhibited reminds me of two important philosophers. Frege is close in both time and resemblance. Aquinas is more remote in both respects. Yet the resemblance to me is unmistakable. Frege modifies the pattern by means of his double semantic tie. A sentence expresses its meaning (he calls it sense) and refers (he uses the word technically) to one of the two existents 'True' and 'False'. In Aquinas' world, individual substances, which are the only existents, are created by God endowing "natures" with "being." That makes Being and Not-being correspond to True and False. *Ens, verum, res,* and *unum,* some will remember, are in a peculiar scholastic sense synonymous. *Unum,* I think, can here without strain be made to correspond to "simple."

I am ready to turn once more to that aspect of logical form which is represented by form$_2$. For reasons which I believe are obvious, the arguments have not centered on conjunction but, rather, on negation and disjunction. So I shall do two things. In the case of *negation* many thing ontologists thought they had come upon a difficulty of the kind one would call epistemological rather than ontological. I shall show that the supposed difficulty disappears if one grants that logical form is in some sense presented to us. In the case of *disjunction* I shall dissect and, by dissecting it, dispose of an objection against granting some kind of ontological status (in traditional terms, subsistence) to logical form.

Take a true negated atomic proposition, say, '$\sim H(a)$', asserted when F is presented. The "things" presented are the spot and its actual color (G). Those who think that there is a difficulty also seem to think that whenever we assert truly and in the presence of the best evidence available anything as "simple" as '$\sim H(a)$', what we assert should be presented to us. They solve their difficulty by concluding that we "deduce" '$\sim H(a)$' from '$G(a)$', which refers to what is presented to us, in conjunction with another proposition, of which we have knowledge of a special and privileged kind, to the effect that the two colors $(G$ and $H)$ are incompatible. The troubles this gambit leads to are notorious. To say the least, the price one pays for it is very high.[4] Fact ontologists of course may try to remove the alleged difficulty, consistently within their game, by introducing a "negative fact" as what is presented to us on such occasions. Perhaps that is one of the attractions of a fact ontology. On the other hand, I do not see the original difficulty. When I am presented with F, I am, among other things (not "things"), presented with the spot and its actual color. On some earlier occasions I have been presented with the color red. In some sense I am also presented with logical form. That is all that need be said about how I come to know that the spot is not red. In fact, it is part of what one may reasonably mean by saying that in some sense logical form is presented to us.

Assume for the sake of argument that 'This road leads to Oxford' and 'This road leads to Cambridge' are both atomic. The objection based on disjunction runs as follows. What exists is fully determinate. There is, therefore, or there may be, the fact that this road leads to Cambridge as well as the fact that this road leads to Oxford. For these are fully determinate. But there is in the world no such inde-

---

[4] See "On Nonperceptual Intuition," *Philosophy and Phenomenological Research*, 10 (1949):263–64. A fact ontologist willing to pay the price might hope thereby also to get rid of "negative facts" by "analyzing," say, the fact of this being not red into the two "positive facts" of this being green and green being incompatible with red. The hope fails on the obvious ground that, of the two sentences 'This is not red' and 'This is green, and green is incompatible with red', the latter says more than the former. Ontologically, therefore, and this is the relevant context, I do not know what it means to "analyze" the fact expressed by the former into the latter. The reason for that not having always been obvious is probably that in certain discussions the ontological and epistemological contexts were improperly mixed.

terminate *fact* as a road leading either to Cambridge or to Oxford. More dramatically, there is no "or" in the world. I have shown in the second part that one may grant some sort of ontological status to logical form, without thereby being committed to the belief that there is "or" in the world in the same sense in which there are "things." But I also promised on that occasion a further argument, which I am now ready to make. Return to the sentence in which the word 'fact' is italicized. Everything depends on whether it is taken commonsensically or philosophically. If it is taken commonsensically, then of course there are such facts. They exist. At least we say it every day and do not by saying it get into any trouble as long as we continue to speak commonsensically. If, on the other hand, that word in that sentence is taken philosophically (ontologically), then two things need to be said. First, a thing ontologist must not take it ontologically, for he knows no "facts." For him no fact, whether or not the sentence expressing it is atomic, is an existent. Nor, second, would a fact ontologist with a firm grasp of the two basic ideas have to worry about the indeterminateness of the fact expressed by a disjunction. In his world some "facts" do "exist." But these are all expressed by atomic sentences and are, therefore, determinate in the relevant sense. A disjunction, however, is not an atomic sentence. What it refers to, though a fact, for the fact ontologist as well as for anyone else, is therefore not even for him a "fact." Hence it need not be determinate. It may well be, by the way, that this determinateness of "atomic facts" is still another cause of the lure of fact ontologies. Perhaps such "determinateness" is an ingredient of "independence." However that may be, I conclude, first, that, irrespective of whether one is a thing or a fact ontologist, the objection collapses. This is as it should be. For whether or not logical form "subsists" *should not* depend on what kind of entities "exist." That, as I explicated the ideas, it actually *does not* should further blunt the suspicion that I unduly reify logical form. I conclude, second, that a thing ontologist, merely by raising the objection, accepts without noticing it the basic gambit of the fact ontologist. This, however, is the sort of thing a philosopher must not do without noticing it.

2

The Glory and the Misery of
Ludwig Wittgenstein*

GUSTAV BERGMANN

THE *Tractatus logico-philosophi-
cus* appeared in 1921; the *Philosophical Investigations*, posthu-
mously, in 1953. Wittgenstein will live through these two books.
The contrast between them is striking. In the author's view, and not
in his alone, the second repudiates the first. As his epigones see it,
his glory is the second. The first they consider, however tenderly
and reverently, a relative failure. As I see it, Wittgenstein's glory is
the *Tractatus;* his misery, the *Philosophical Investigations*. The disagreement could not be more complete. Yet I agree with the epigones that the connection between the two books is very close
indeed. I see in the second the reaction, dictated by the council of
despair, to the relative failure of the first.

The *Tractatus*, then, if I am right, is a glorious failure. It is also,
I am deeply convinced, an achievement of the first rank. Nor is that
paradoxical. None of our predecessors achieved more. No one
among us and our successors will do better. The fundamental
metaphysical problems are too difficult for this to be otherwise.
Fortunately, their number is small. Even the secondary ones, though
quite a few, are not too many. Good philosophers therefore do not

Reprinted with the kind permission of the author and the publisher
from Gustav Bergmann, *Logic and Reality* (© 1964 by the Regents of
the University of Wisconsin, Madison), pp. 225–41.

* This essay appeared in Italian translation in *Rivista di Filosofia*, 52 (1961):
387–406. Printed by permission.

pursue many questions. Rather, they are pursued by a few which they articulate ever more richly and explore ever more deeply, down toward the fundamental ones. The few great among the good can rethink a fundamental problem on their own. Such a problem always consists of a group of dialectically connected questions. To rethink it is either to discover a new dialectical connection within the group or, at the very highest, to affect these connections even more radically by discovering a new question to be added to the group. The new question permits and requires new answers. The glorious failures are those who knew how to ask the new question but did not find the new answer.

Wittgenstein all through his philosophical life was obsessed by two fundamental problems. What is the nature of logical truth? Call this the first. What is the nature of mind? Call this the second. Both have shaped both books. The first dominates the *Tractatus;* the second, the *Philosophical Investigations.* On the first, he asked the decisive new question, led a part of the way toward the new answer. On the second, he merely misled, lending specious plausibility to a stale old answer.

(1) There are no philosophical propositions. Those passing for such are neither true nor false but, literally, nonsense. (2) The illusion that keeps us from seeing through this sort of nonsense is linguistic. (3) To destroy the illusion, or, in a phrase that has become famous, to show the fly the way out of the bottle, is to direct attention to the ineffable, which language shows but cannot say. That is Wittgenstein's conception of the philosophical enterprise. (1) states his nihilism; (2) is the root of the linguistic turn; (3), that of the therapeutic approach. I reject (1) and (3). There are philosophical propositions. Nor is there anything ineffable. Wittgenstein's insistence on the linguistic turn, more radical and more profound than Russell's, is the other half of his glory. But he executed it wrongly, herostratically. That makes (2) his other glorious failure, which, since our questions as well as our answers depend on our conception of the philosophical enterprise, made the other two, the glorious as well as the miserable one, inevitable. So I shall next execute the right linguistic turn.

(1) Words are used either *commonsensically* or *philosophically.* A proposition in which at least one word is used philosophically is

a philosophical proposition. As such, philosophical uses are unintelligible. But they can and must be made intelligible by explicating them, i.e., by talking commonsensically about them. Thus explicated, a philosophical proposition says something about the world, which, as the case may be, is either true or false. (2) Every systematically constructed language *shows* some things which cannot without futility be *expressed* in it. These things, though, far from being ineffable, can and for certain purposes must be expressed by talking about the language and what it talks about. Jointly, (1) and (2) are the gist of the right linguistic turn. Technically, they are equally fundamental. Nontechnically, (1) is the heart of the matter. So I leave (2) until later and comment next on (1).

"Bodies don't exist, only minds do" is a classical philosophical proposition. "Minds don't exist, only bodies do" is another. "Characters don't exist, only individuals do" is a third. If the words are all taken commonsensically, such propositions are not at all nonsensical. Rather, they are patently and blatantly false; so patently and blatantly indeed that only a madman could assert any of them. Yet each has been asserted by some philosophers. According to Wittgenstein, these men either futilely tried to express the ineffable, or, confusingly and themselves confused, presented as an assertion about the world what is at best one about the way we use language. I believe that these men often succeeded very well in directing attention to certain pervasive, or, as one says, categorial features of the world. Only, I also insist that these features can and must be talked about commonsensically.

Classical ontology is dominated by the several ontological uses of 'exist' and 'existence'. Since the core of all fundamental problems is ontological, I shall next indicate the explications of two such uses.

(*a*) If *something is presented to me, so is its existence.* The formula explicates the use. To have "existence" in this sense and to have "ontological status" is one thing and not two. The idea is commonsensical. Yet some comments will be helpful. *One.* Something may exist without being presented. If converted, the formula is no longer commonsensical. *Two.* Perception is one kind of presentation. Direct awareness is another. Do both kinds make the formula the truism it must be if it is to serve its purpose? By this question hangs a huge body of dialectic. For my purpose here the answer does not matter. *Three.* In such sentences as 'There is a coffee house around the corner' existence is represented by the phrase 'there is'. Existence(*a*) or ontological status can always be so expressed. But we also say, commonsensically, that there is a prime number between 4 and 6. Are we then prepared to grant some ontological status to such "entities" as numbers? Wittgenstein, we shall see, is not. I am. The way I just used 'entity' is ontologically neutral. It will be convenient to have this neutral word available.

(*b*) *What exists is simple.* The formula explicates another philosophical use of 'exist', provided only we understand this very special, though commonsensical use of 'simple'. An entity is thus simple if the only way of directly referring to it, in any language, is by naming it. A *name*, in this very special sense, is also called a label. That conveys the idea that a name can only be attached to what is or has been presented. There is also the idea that a label as such does not tell us anything about what it labels except, of course, that it exists(*a*). This, though, we shall see, is not quite correct in the case of linguistic labels or names. In a systematically constructed language a name is, of course, a primitive descriptive sign. Notice that an equivalent formula has become available: An entity exists(*b*) if and only if, provided it is presented, it can be named. Notice, too, that an entity which could not be named, or, more precisely, as we shall presently see, an entity which could not be named without futility, may yet be presented and even be represented in the language by something which is not a name. Such an entity would exist(*a*) without existing(*b*).

The sentential tautologies so-called are familiar instances of logical truth. What is the structure of such truths? We are ready for Wittgenstein's first fundamental problem. Rethinking it, he discovered the new question which is his glory. How does any sentence, whether or not it expresses a logical truth, manage to express what it does? In appearance the new question is unduly linguistic, in an obvious bad sense of 'linguistic'. In substance, it points to the ontological core of the problem. Even better than that, the right answer provides an invaluable lesson, teaching us how to do ontology after the linguistic turn. That is why the glory of the one who first asked the question is great, even though his answer went wrong. Here is what we are told. Take the (written) sentence itself as a fact. This (linguistic) fact shares with the fact it expresses a "logical form." That is how the former manages to express the latter. 'Logical form' is used philosophically and, unhappily, remains unexplicated. So we are not surprised when we are also told that "logical form" is ineffable, merely shows itself. There is an easy transition, noticed, or, more likely, unnoticed, from being ineffable to being nothing, or, what amounts to the same, not having any ontological status, not existing(*a*). This sort of transition I call a verbal bridge. The original question Wittgenstein answered as follows. A truth is logical if and only if the sentence expressing it is true by virtue of its "logical form" alone. But, then, we are also told that a sentence expressing a tautology (logical truth) really says nothing and is therefore not really a sentence. This supports my belief that, unwittingly, Wittgenstein walked that bridge. Whether or not he did, his answer does not recognize the ontological status of what, speaking philosophically, he calls "logical form." That is the fatal flaw. The right answer, conversely, crucially recognizes the ontological status (existence[*a*]) of what I call the world's *form*. And, of course, it provides an explication for this use of 'form'. Notice, for later reference, that I suppress the adjective, 'logical', and speak of the world's form instead.

These are the bare bones of my thesis. Putting some flesh on them, I shall first state the right answer. But, of course, if that needs to be said at all, without Wittgenstein's glorious failure, there would be no right answer today.

Suppose that, being presented with a green spot, I say, truly, 'This is green'. Limiting ourselves to true sentences merely avoids problems which, though most weighty in themselves, can at this point be avoided. What an (indicative) sentence expresses is a fact. The fact in the example is the spot's being green. Call it *F*; the sentence, *S*. *S* or *F*, each in its way, is as simple as a fact or a sentence can be, though of course neither is simple(*b*). Now if *S* is true, there must be something else that makes it true. Or, as one says, the truth of *S* must be grounded ontologically. On this first move idealists and realists agree. The only difference between them is that for the realist the ground is independent of the mind to which *F* is presented, while for the idealist *F* depends on, or even more strongly, is the activity of this mind. But, then, don't minds and their activities have ontological status in the idealist's world?

S thus is true because it expresses F, and F exists(a). If, therefore, we want to know how S manages to express F, we must first find out what there is to be expressed. In other words, we must begin with an ontological assay of F.

I hold that there are individuals and characters, all of the former and some of the latter being simple(b). Calling them both *things*, I also hold that, when presented with F, I am presented with two things, an individual named 'This' and a simple character named 'green'. Hence, my assay of F yields *at least* two simples. That raises two questions. (1) Is this assay complete? More strongly, could it possibly be complete, or must it yield something else? (2) Is it correct as far as it goes? (2) may be controversial; (1), to my mind, is not. As it happens, my main point hangs on (1).

Simples enter into complexes. F, for instance, on any assay I can think of, is a complex. Take now two spots, one green and square, the other blue and round. If my assay is correct as far as it goes, there are thus six things "tied" into two complexes. You see already the deeper point. There must be "something" which ties anyone's simples (or, for that matter, things, if there should be no simples) into complexes. Also, this "something" must be presented. For, if it were not, how could I know that in the example, say, green goes with square but not with either blue or round? It follows that there must be ties, having ontological status, which tie the simples into complexes. What then, one may ask, ties the ties to the simples? There are only two possibilities. One is, paradoxically, an infinite regress, which is the way Bradley took to monism. The other is my solution. There are *fundamental ties*, I also call them *nexus*, which tie without themselves being tied to what they tie.

The nexus which ties an individual and a character into a fact I call *exemplification*. It follows that the ontological assay of F yields at least three constituents, two simples and exemplification. Notice, too, that a fundamental tie is not a relation. In the complex 'This is louder than that', for instance, there are three simples, this, that, and the relational character louder-than, held together by (relational) exemplification.

Further analysis, which I cannot now reproduce, shows that the complete assay of *F* yields two further nonthings, individuality and universality. When I am presented with an individual, I am also presented with its individuality. For, if I were not, how would I know that it is one? As for individuals, so for characters. As I use 'form', these three nonthings, exemplification, individuality, universality, are constituents of the world's form. As I use 'subsist', their peculiar ontological status is *subsistence*.

Does Wittgenstein agree with what has been said so far? There are very, very many passages in the *Tractatus* which seem to make it crystal clear that he, too, so assays *F* that 'This' and 'green' in *S* name two simples in *F*. I say "seem" because there are also many passages, such as 3.1432, which have been much written about recently, that cannot be reconciled with those very, very many others. On the nominalism-realism issue—for that is, of course, what the matter amounts to—the *Tractatus* is confused. Historically, I believe, that has something to do with the great impact Frege's views had on its author. Concerning exemplification, turn to 2.03: *Im Sachverhalt haengen die Gegenstaende ineinander wie die Glieder einer Kette.* That is exactly what they don't do.[1] If they did, there would be no need for a nexus. The image, admirably clear, leaves no doubt that Wittgenstein is radically wrong, making exemplification a part of that "logical form" which is "nothing."

How does *S* manage to express *F*? In a systematically constructed language *S* becomes '*Ga*', i.e., in essence, the juxtaposition of two marks of different shape (capital and lower case). '*a*' names or labels the individual; its shape represents, without naming it, the individuality of the thing named. As for '*a*', so for '*G*'. Names are thus not pure labels. Their shapes, which are geometrical characters, represent, without naming them, ontological categories. Exemplification, finally, is represented, though, again, not named, by the relational geometrical character of juxtaposition. *S* is a geometrical fact. Between certain geometrical features of *S* on the one hand and the constituents of *F*, there is a one-one coordination of the

[1] Or, if you care to put it this way, things are *independent*. The philosophical uses of 'independent' are crucial. The formula "Only what is independent exists" controls indeed several philosophical uses of 'exist'. E. B. Allaire (*Philosophical Review*, 69 [1960]: 485–96) has very ingeniously distinguished four relevant commonsensical uses of 'independent'. If I am not mistaken, I just identified a fifth.

kind called isomorphism. To understand a language is to know the
rules of this isomorphism. Or to say the same thing differently, *S*
manages to express *F* by virtue of this isomorphism. This is my
answer. Let us confront it with Wittgenstein's.

S manages to express *F* by virtue of a shared "logical form,"
which is ineffable. That is his answer. The isomorphism mentioned
in mine is anything but ineffable. I just stated it by speaking commonsensically *about F* and *S*. Now this isomorphism is also the only
explication I can think of for Wittgenstein's philosophical use of
'logical form'. The explication makes his answer intelligible. Rather
strikingly, it also makes it false. Nor is that difficult to show. Assume for the sake of the argument that the two marks in *S* are individuals. Then the geometrical fact *S* has five constituents which
are things, namely, the two marks, the two geometrical characters
which are the shapes, the relational geometrical character of juxtaposition; and, in addition, individuality twice, universality thrice,
exemplification thrice. That makes 13. *F*, we remember, has all together 5 constituents. And there is of course no one-one coordination between 5 and 13. Such are the bitter fruits of using words
philosophically, without explication.

The ontological distance between, say, an individual and individuality is tremendous. Wittgenstein safeguards it without effort. For
him, the individual exists; individuality, being part of "logical form,"
is nothing. For me the two are alike in both having ontological
status (just as they are both presented). The difference so far is
merely that in the language I constructed the individual is named
while its individuality is otherwise represented, namely, by the
shape of its name. That is not yet enough to secure that tremendous
distance. I secure it by showing that the subsistents could *not without futility* be named. Take individuality. Let us try to name it. If
it is a thing, then it is of course a (simple) character. Name this
alleged character by '*I*'. That makes '*Ia*' the crucial sentence. The
point is that it says what it says, namely, that *a* is an individual, only
because the shapes of *a* and *I* and their juxtaposition represent, without naming them, individuality, universality, and exemplification,
respectively. That shows what I mean when I say that the introduction of '*I*' is futile.

If one wishes, one may put the last point as follows: *a*'s being an individual is *shown* in the language by the shape of its name; but one cannot without futility *say* in this language that it is one. Remember now the second part of the right linguistic turn: Every systematically constructed language shows some things which cannot without futility be expressed in it. When first stating this part, I postponed comment. Now, without further comment, we understand. We have recovered all that is recoverable from Wittgenstein's famous ineffability thesis. The rest is nonsense, not because it is metaphysics, but because it is bad metaphysics.

There is of course much more to the world's form than is represented in *S*, just as there are many more facts than can be expressed by sentences as simple as *S*. We have had no more than a glimpse. And, of course, we cannot pursue. So I must venture to state the idea. Philosophy is a dialectical structure that rests on a phenomenological base. What is presented to us is a matter of phenomenology. If certain entities were not presented to us, we could not know what commonsensically we do know, e.g., that this is red, that green, this to the left of that, and so on. That is the dialectical twist. What must be presented to us must also be represented in our language, otherwise it could not express what it does. That is how language may be brought in. Then we are ready for the linguistic turn. 'Ontological status' has been used philosophically. I explicate this use by the formula: What must be represented has ontological status. That, though, is only the beginning. The furniture of the world is not all of one kind. The different kinds, even the glimpse we had taught us that, are represented very differently, i.e., in the written case, by very different geometrical features of the language. Or, rather, that is how I explicate the traditional ontological vocabulary. Enough has been said to support a claim made earlier. The right answer to Wittgenstein's new question is the key to the new ontology.

We are ready for the original question. What is logical truth? It is nothing. Nor is the sentence expressing it really a sentence. That, succinctly, is Wittgenstein's answer. I answer that it is a fact of (in) the world's form and that the sentence expressing it is a sentence like any other, except, of course, that its truth depends only on those of its geometrical features which represent constituents of the world's form. Lest the difference between the two answers seem slight, let me point out two consequences which loom large.

(1) The connection between the philosophical uses of 'logical' and of 'necessary' is very close. "A logical truth is a necessary truth, and conversely." We all know this classical proposition. Partly because of it, I avoid 'logical' wherever I can and speak instead of formal truth (instead of: logical truth) and of the world's form (instead of: logical form). And I explicate the philosophical use of 'necessary' in that classical proposition so that a truth is necessary if and only if it is formal. That turns the proposition into a tautology. Wittgenstein disagrees. According to him, the formal truths of our world are also the formal truths of all possible worlds. Replace 'formal truth' by 'logical form' and you will see the verbal bridge. "Logical form" is nought; and nought, as it were, is the same in all possible worlds. But, then, what shall we make of that phrase, 'all possible worlds'? Clearly, it is used philosophically. So it must be explicated. I can think of two explications. One turns the proposition into a tautology: every world which has the same form as ours has the same form as ours. With the other explication, the proposition says that any word *must* have the same form as ours. I simply do not understand this *must*. If the logical is to be identified with the necessary, in some unexplicated and inexplicable sense of 'necessary', then, if you permit me an aphorism, there is nothing logical about logic. Technically, upon the explication which does not trivialize it, Wittgenstein's thesis, that the logic of our world is that of all possible ones, is simply false. I must not be technical here. But I can identify for you another bridge he walked on this as well as on many other occasions, all through his work. It leads from 'possible' to 'conceivable'. That is his psychologism. For it puts into the act what, if it is what it is supposed to be, must be a feature of the act's intention. Historically, Wittgenstein inherited this fateful mistake from Kant.

(2) There is a class of truths, Kant calls them synthetic a priori, which are clearly not formal. 'Nothing is (at the same time all over) both red and green' is a familiar example. Many philosophers tried to secure for these truths a special status, in the same boat with formal truths. In Wittgenstein, throughout his philosophical life, the

urge was very strong. (In this, too, he shows the influence of Kant.) In the *Tractatus* he satisfies it by the claim that the sentences expressing those truths are, like tautologies, true by virtue of their "logical form" alone. That clashes with the very numerous passages according to which only tautologies can be true by their "logical form" alone. There is in the *Tractatus* one lonely passage (6.3751) which shows unmistakably that Wittgenstein himself was not wholly at ease. In the short paper of 1929, the only other publication during his lifetime, he returned to the attack; but again, alas, to no avail. This dissatisfaction may well have been one of the major intellectual motives for his eventual repudiation of the *Tractatus*.[2]

This chair's being brown is a physical fact. That water if heated boils is another. Your perceiving that the chair is brown is a mental fact. So is my wondering whether this speech is too long, his remembering something, and so on. That there are both physical and mental facts, or, for short, both minds and bodies, is common sense. Perceiving something, remembering something, thinking of something, are mental facts of the kind called *acts*. There are also others, but we can safely ignore them. The fundamental task is the ontological assay of the act. In this task Wittgenstein failed. His way out was to reject it. There is nothing to be assayed; there are no minds. The failure is foreshadowed in the *Tractatus*. The *Philosophical Investigations* are virtually materialistic. Materialism is absurd. That makes the failure so miserable. We shall understand it better if I first tackle the task.

What one perceives when perceiving something, what one knows when knowing something, and so on, is the act's *intention*. To perceive something, to know this thing, to remember it, are different acts with the same intention. What they differ in I call the act's *species*. Acts thus may differ in species and intention. Acts are mental, of course; intentions, either physical or mental. What we perceive is physical; that is part of what perceiving means. No thing is both physical and mental. In perceiving, therefore, the act and its intention have no thing in common. (I say no thing, rather than

---

[2] E. B. Allaire has argued this point very convincingly in the first of two short but very weighty papers he has already published on Wittgenstein (*Analysis*, 19 [1959]:100–5 and 21 [1960]: 14–16). Frequent discussion with him during the last years has been invaluable to me.

nothing, because the world's form is pervasive and neither physical nor mental.) This, by the way, is true for all acts. But we can presently stay with perception, where the distinctness of act and intention is, if anything, even more obvious.

The perceptual complex has three constituents, (1) the act, (2) the intention, (3) the body, i.e., the relevant physical facts about the perceiver's body. 'Complex' I use advisedly, to remind you that if there is to be a complex, its constituents must be tied together. Now for three constituents to make a complex there must be at least two and there may be three ties. (2) and (3) are both physical. (2) causes (3). This is the tie the scientists investigate. The tie between (1) and (3) is that between a mind and its body. This tie I take to be parallelistic. The third tie, call it the *intentional tie*, connects (1) and (2), the act and its intention. Its nature is the heart of the problem.

Do not confuse the intentional tie with the mind-body tie. When I perceive a landscape I perceive a landscape, not the relevant facts it causes in my body. Since the landscape is causally tied to the body and the body in turn parallelistically to the mind, there would still be a complex even if there were no intentional tie. To say the same thing differently, one may try to replace the direct intentional tie by a chain with two links, one causal, one parallelistic. For two weighty reasons that will not do. (*a*) I perceive the square tower to be round. More dramatically, I have a hallucination. In the first case, the physical fact invoked differs from the intention. In the second, there is none. (*b*) Some sentences are compounded of others. A language is called truth-functional or extensional if and only if the truth value of a compound depends only on the truth values of its components. Consider now the compound 'Smith believes that Caesar was murdered'. Assume it to be true. Replacing the true component 'Caesar was murdered' by the equally true 'The husband of Calpurnia was murdered', one obtains 'Smith believes that Calpurnia's husband was murdered'. Unless Smith knows that Caesar was Calpurnia's husband the new compound will be false. As for believing, so for all species. Statements expressing the intentional tie are not extensional. The causal tie, on the other hand, as well as the parallelistic one can be expressed in an extensional language. So, therefore, can the two-link chain. It follows that the intentional tie is a direct tie between the act and its intention. What, then, is its nature? Before I answer, one more idea must be introduced. But notice first that the author of the *Tractatus* was profoundly committed to the thesis that everything can be expressed in an extensional language.

None of the three constituents of the perceptual complex is a simple. Thus they, too, must be ontologically assayed. Crucial, of course, is the assay of the act. The tradition is dominated by one idea. Its formula is: A mind can only know what is *in* it. Everything depends on what the 'in' stands for. The tradition thinks of the mind as an individual of a very special kind, called a *substance*, and of its properties and only its properties being in it. What the mind knows is in it as its color or its shape are in the flower. That makes what I call the species a case of exemplification, or of whatever comes closest to it in these ontologies. The trouble is that in all of them, except perhaps the Aristotelian-Thomistic one, the intentional tie cannot be accounted for. In the perceptual case, for instance, the intention is itself a substance with properties. *And how can a substance be a property of another substance?* Dialectically, this is the deepest root, much deeper than the relatively shallow skeptical one, of the development from Descartes to idealism. Be that as it may, I am now ready for the answer.

An act is an individual exemplifying two simple characters. This individual is not at all a substance—there are none in my ontology— but momentary and bare, a bare particular so-called. One of the two properties is the species. The other I shall here call a *thought*. The intentional tie is between the thought and the intention. When we say, for instance, that the thought that Peter is tall *means* that Peter is tall, 'means' represents this tie. I say represents rather than names and also speak of the *meaning tie* because it is a nexus and, as such, belongs to the world's form. So, by the way, do the causal and the parallelistic ties. Only they also belong to the form of a world otherwise like ours but without mind. In this sense, intentionality is the essence of mind.

How does this assay account for those cases, false belief, imagination, and so on, in which the fact S intended by the thought $\ulcorner S \urcorner$ does not exist (a)? Or, synonymously, if 'S' is false, how can '$\ulcorner S \urcorner$ means S' be true? If the meaning nexus were a relation, it couldn't.

Since it is a part of the world's form, there is no difficulty. To get a glimpse of the idea, consider 'S or not-S', where the nexus is "or." Either S or not-S does not exist (a).[3] Yet, 'S or not-S' expresses a truth in the world's form. So does 'ᴿSᐧ means S'.

Turn now to *Tractatus* 5.542. 'A believes that p', 'A thinks that p', and so on, all mean no more nor less than 'The sentence 'p' means p'. That is the gist of this passage. The sentence, here as always, is for Wittgenstein a physical fact. Substituting the sentence for the thought, he thus substitutes a physical fact for one that is mental. That is the decisive step toward materialism. Abstract thought is indeed, as one says, largely verbal. Properly understood, though, that means merely that such thought consists largely of awarenesses of words and sentences! Wittgenstein's 'says', if it means anything at all, stands for my 'means'. If so, then, even with the substitution of the sentence for the thought, ' 'p' says p' is no longer extensional. Nor is that all. The sentence 'p' "says" p only by virtue of a shared "logical form," which is ineffable. Hence, ' 'p' says p' is not really a sentence. The only thing that makes sense to me in all this is that the intentional nexus is indeed part of the world's form. For Wittgenstein, being part of "logical form," it is nothing. Once more, therefore, the act and its intention have fallen apart. The two ways out are idealism and materialism. Husserl took the first; Wittgenstein, the second.

This is the place to call attention to an ambiguity in the use of 'express'. A sentence as such does not "express" anything. We express a thought by means of it. This can be done because of the isomorphism between certain geometrical features of the sentence and what it "expresses." The ambiguity, if unnoticed, leads to disaster in the philosophy of mind. Outside of it, no harm is done. That is why I let it pass until now.

Materialists replace philosophy by science. Or they mistake the latter for the former. The later Wittgenstein is no exception. Not surprisingly in one as preoccupied with language as he was throughout his career, the key science is the psychology and sociology of language, or, if you please, of communication. Not that the *Philo-*

---

[3] More precisely, one of the two exists merely in the mode of possibility. This point, though of the greatest importance in some other contexts, may be safely ignored in this essay.

sophical Investigations is a conventional scientific book. It is merely a medley of comments. Some are very keen; some others, more or less obvious; the rest, standard armchair psychology in the standard behavioristic style. Underneath, and not just underneath, there is always the effort to convince us—or should I perhaps say to convince himself?—that philosophy is all a mistake. The author was nevertheless a profound philosopher. So one comes every now and then upon a profound philosophical insight. The buzzing of the fly intrigues.

Assume that one tries to teach his language to one with whom he cannot talk at all. To teach the color words, he may use color charts, will do a good deal of pointing, and so on. As for the color words, so, with two differences, for the words referring to mental things. For one, the physical aspects of behavior will be much more prominent among the cues given by the teacher and taken by the pupil. (I put it this way because pointing is also behavior.) For another, the pupil could not learn unless he knew, from his own mind and body, which states of the two typically go with each other. The important truism that basically language must be learned and taught this way is characteristic of methodological behaviorism. Metaphysical behaviorism is materialism. The former makes sense, the latter doesn't. The transition from the one to the other is fallacious. The Wittgenstein of the *Philosophical Investigations* makes it. Or he nearly makes it. Here and there a tortured qualification betrays the uneasy conscience and the inner struggle.

How does the teacher know that the lesson has been learned? When the pupil comes to use the words correctly, thus showing by his behavior that he knows what they mean. That is the root of the formula before which the epigones prostrate themselves: (1) meaning is use. 'Meaning' itself, of course, has many uses. Its use in the *Tractatus* may be epitomized by two formulae: (2) meaning is reference, and, (3) the meaning of a sentence is the method of its verification. Each of the two transitions, from (2) and (3) to (1), relates to a philosophical problem. Had Wittgenstein been able to solve these problems, or, what amounts virtually to the same, had he been able to make the required dialectical distinctions, he would not have made the transitions.

Take an individual and its name. By (2) the former is the meaning of the latter. Imagine that you are with only two persons in a room: one is your friend; the other you have never seen before. In this "context" your friend says, with or without pointing, "This is Peter." Because of the context you understand what he says. The next time you meet Peter you will recognize him. But you will recognize him only by the combination of characters he exemplifies. We do not recognize individuals as such, whether you use 'individual' as I just did or so narrowly that only sensa and their like are individuals. Thereby hangs an important philosophical point. Much less importantly, it follows that, first, communication depends on context, and, second, since a design of marks or noises not relying on context would have to contain names of individuals, we could not by means of it communicate. (That is the heart of the overblown quarrel about "ideal languages.") The epigones, convinced that there are no names, are in danger of convincing themselves that there are no things to be named. There is only language. Hence, in spite of the materialistic substitution of words for thoughts, the idealistic structure is so clearly discernible in so much of what they say.

One knows what a sentence means if and only if one knows what to look for in order to decide whether it is true or false. If one can look, he must inspect what he finds. Then he can actually decide. Negatively, a sentence is meaningless, not really a sentence, unless it can in this sense be "reduced" to what can be inspected. Much detail apart, this is the gist of (3). 'Inspect', which I use advisedly, has two connotations. By one of these hangs a fundamental philosophical problem. 'Inspection' may connote public inspection, i.e., not only by myself but also by others. With this connotation, since obviously we cannot inspect each other's minds, (3) obviously entails philosophical behaviorism. Statements about minds, to be meaningful, must be construed as statements about bodies. With the other connotation, one can inspect only what can be checked and rechecked. But one can only check and recheck what persists more or less unchanged. In this sense, mental individuals cannot literally be inspected, not because they are private, but because they are momentary. Yet there is a substitute. The mind within one specious present often shifts back and forth between an awareness and the awareness of this awareness. Assume three such shifts to have occurred. Then there are six awarenesses, two groups of three, the members of each group of the same kind. This is the substitute. Dialectically pursued, it leads to the fundamental problem of time and identity. For all other problems, the substitute will do. Wittgenstein, I believe, did not start out a materialist. But it seems that in the fashion of the phenomenalists he always thought of mental facts as sense data, or something like sense data, and always completely missed the act. Sense data are awarenesses, of course. But the awareness of an awareness is always an act. Hence, if there were no acts, there would not even be the substitute for the inspection of mental things. This, I suggest, is the structural root of that underground affinity between phenomenalism and materialism which causes some to seesaw between the two. One cannot but think of Russell.

Remember, finally, that festering dissatisfaction about the synthetic a priori. The formula that meaning is use offers a specious way out. One who knows the rules for the use of language knows that 'this is both red and green' violates these rules. Or, as it is now put, nothing being both red and green is part of the meaning of the words 'red' and 'green'. Still differently, 'nothing is both red and green' is true not because the world is what it is but because we use language as we do. I merely ask two questions. Is every true (general) sentence true by virtue of the meanings of the words that occur in it? If not, where and how do you draw the line? The second question has no answer. One may try to answer the first by admitting, or even insisting, that the meaning of a word changes as we discover what is true and false about what it represents. There is of course *a* meaning of 'meaning' for which this is true. If, however, this were *the* meaning of 'meaning' in which we must first know what a sentence means before we can even ask whether it is true or false, then we could never know whether any single proposition containing a word is true without first knowing the totality of propositions which contain the word and are true. The holistic and idealistic structure of the doctrine is unmistakable. The ultimate subject of all predications is the Absolute. John Dewey, another structural idealist, propounds substantially the same doctrine of meaning. His Absolute is the sociopsychological process of inquiry. The epigones' Absolute is language.

Wittgenstein is a philosopher of the first rank. So we must study his work for its own sake. But we also may and should relate it to that of his peers, particularly if they are his contemporaries. So far, this century has seen four philosophers of the first rank. The other three are Husserl, G. E. Moore, and Russell. Moore, for whom I have a very special affection, was an *éminence grise*. Either one says very much about his contribution, or one better says nothing. Here I shall say nothing. Russell's lasting achievements are easily identified. Tremendous as they are, they lie all in the area of logic, in the narrower sense of 'logic'. If asked to list four, I would mention his analysis of relations, the theory of types, his analysis of definite descriptions, and the logization of arithmetic. If asked to select among these four the one of greatest philosophical import, I would without hesitation point at the first. No one before Russell really understood relations. Wittgenstein has learned much from Russell and Moore. The most interesting confrontation is nonetheless with Husserl.

The world of my ontology, or, for short, my world is structured. The entities structuring it all have ontological status. Otherwise there would be no structure. No structure and no world is perhaps not quite the same. But the difference, if any, is not great. Among the entities which provide the structure there is one major division. Some are relations. Some belong to the world's form. Relations are things, and they share the ontological status of nonrelational characters. That is Russell's epochal insight. The Husserl of the *Untersuchungen*, who was still a realist of sorts, did see that the world's form has ontological status. Unfortunately, he located it, together with all characters, in a realm of Platonic essences. That is one seed of his later tragedy.

Most of my world is physical. Some of it is mental. Through the intentional tie, minds may know the world. In this sense, minds may also know themselves. In another sense, they don't. The awareness of an awareness is always a second awareness, never a part of the first. From this one point, which he took from Husserl, Sartre spun his philosophical fable.

The minds of my world do not create its structure. Nor do they impose it on what is without structure presented to them. Rather, it is presented to them. Our minds are of course active and even creative in many commonsensical ways. Or, alas, some minds are at some times. But, just as there are in my world no substances, there is nothing in it which, in this philosophical sense, is either creative or even active. Nor is that a coincidence.

The minds or Selves of the great tradition are not bare individuals. They are individual substances. If an image will help, think of such a Self as the inner of a sphere; of its properties, which you remember are the only things it can know, as coatings of the surface. The inner either actively creates these everchanging coats; or, at least, it actively imposes a structure upon what is, without one, impressed on the surface from without. Just think of Kant's synthetic unity of apperception! One who sets his feet into this path and walks it steadily will arrive at idealism.

Husserl's incomparable glory is the ontological assay of the act in the *Untersuchungen*. Yet, he understood neither relations, nor the need for fundamental ties, nor the difference between them. That is the other seed of the tragedy. Had he understood these things, he would not have said that the constituent of the act which I call the thought is "intrinsically relational." Nothing is intrinsically relational. The very phrase is a contradiction in terms. In particular, act and intention remain unconnected. Eventually, therefore, one or the other will be lost. That makes even the *Untersuchungen* a glorious failure. Eventually, deeply rooted in the Leibniz-Kant tradition as he was, the master dialectician of the *Untersuchungen* became the idealist of the *Ideen*.

Wittgenstein came as close to the correct ontological assay of the extensional part of the world's form as Husserl came to that of the act. Yet he shrank away from giving ontological status to what he was the first to see so clearly. Nor did he countenance active minds which might have provided that status. The possibility of minds which can know the world without being active in that certain philosophical sense he did not see. Thus mind was lost and the world left without form. Such a world is not much of a world. Thus, eventually, the world was lost. The epigones talk about language.

3

Stenius on the Tractatus

GUSTAV BERGMANN

A biographer's subject almost al-
ways becomes his hero. Only the exceptional biographer knows how
to avoid this trap. As with biographers, so with commentators. Only
the exceptional commentator will not twist and bend his chosen
text to make it say what he himself believes. At least, he will try to
make it consistent. Stenius' book[1] on Wittgenstein's *Tractatus* is
exceptional in this admirable sense. Nor is it just a commentary
but, rather, less as well as much more. It is less because it is selective.
The principle of selection is again admirable. Stenius selected those
passages concerning a few fundamental and controversial issues out
of which he believed he could make sense. Trying to find this sense,
he thought for himself. The task he set for himself, the sense he
sought and found, are thus philosophical, not merely exegetic or
biographical. That makes the book much more than just a commentary. It is itself a philosophical treatise, and a very considerable one
indeed.

Stenius knows and shows that there are two groups of crucial
passages in the *Tractatus* which cannot be reconciled with each
other. Then he opts for one. Thus he "corrects" Wittgenstein.
(The word is his, not mine.) The idea of, or behind, the correction

Reprinted with the kind permission of the author and the editor from
Theoria, 29 (1963):176–204.

[1] Erik Stenius, *Wittgenstein's Tractatus. A Critical Exposition of Its Main
Lines of Thought* (Oxford: Blackwell, 1960).

is the central idea of the book, its major contribution. I judge it to be original and ingenious as well as radically mistaken, in a way that is extraordinarily illuminating. To justify these judgments is the task I set myself in this study. To solve it properly Stenius' ideas must of course be presented, which cannot be done without also presenting Wittgenstein's. Nor can a judgment be justified without some exposition of the ideas on which it rests. That makes three sets of ideas. To present them completely takes three books, Stenius', the *Tractatus*, and the one I haven't written. The only way out is selection. The first selection determines the other two. Pride of place belongs to Stenius, of course. I select his central idea, the "correction."

Since I must justify my judgments, considerable space will have to be allowed to my views. Yet I shall be most succinct in stating them. Hans Hahn, who was a great teacher as well as a great mathematician, once said to a seminar of which I was a member: "Just knowing how a proof goes, you know nothing. When you know why it goes this way rather than that or that other way, then you begin to know something." I must state what I believe to be the right answers to some philosophical questions. But I shall achieve that extra succinctness by not arguing that just these and not those or those other answers are right. Those who care for the argument I refer to six recent essays[2] as well as to five others, by Allaire[3] and Grossmann,[4] discussion with whom has become so indispensable to me that sometimes I cannot tell who first said what.

How does a sentence manage to say what it says? The question dominates the *Tractatus*. Stenius rejects its answer. So let us take our bearings from the question. As Stenius and I use 'sentence', a

[2] "Ineffability, Ontology, and Method," *The Philosophical Review*, 69 (1960): 18–40; "The Ontology of Edmund Husserl," *Methodos*, 12 (1960):359–92; "Acts," *Indian Journal of Philosophy*, 2 (1960):1–30, 96–117; "Generality and Existence," *Theoria*, 28 (1962):1–26; "Meaning and Ontology," *Inquiry*, 5 (1962): 116–42; "La gloria e la miseria di Ludwig Wittgenstein," *Rivista di Filosofia*, 52 (1961):387–406. The present study elaborates a few of the many points rather briefly touched upon in the Italian piece on Wittgenstein.

[3] "Tractatus 6.3751," *Analysis*, 19 (1959):100–5; "Existence, Independence, and Universals," *The Philosophical Review*, 69 (1960):485–96; "Tractatus 3.333," *Analysis*, 21 (1961):14–16.

[4] "Conceptualism," *Review of Metaphysics*, 13 (1960):243–54; "Frege's Ontology," *The Philosophical Review*, 70 (1961):23–40.

sentence is a physical fact. Physical facts do not *say* anything. As it stands, the question is blurred. Replace 'says' by 'expresses' and the blur remains. Physical facts don't *express* anything. It is we who express our thoughts. More precisely, one expresses a thought by uttering a sentence which represents the thought's intention, i.e., the fact which the thought is about. That splits the question into three. (1) How does a sentence manage to represent a fact? (2) What is the connection[5] between a thought and its intention? (3) What, if any, is the connection between a sentence and the thought intending the fact it represents? (1) is still blurred. Physical facts do not *represent* anything. It is we who may or may not be able to make them represent (stand for) something. (1) can pass only as an abbreviation for (1'): What is there about a sentence that enables us to make it represent a fact? I shall save words by using (1) as an abbreviation for (1'). The question that dominates the *Tractatus* relates most closely to (1). So I shall start and for a long time stay with (1).

The heart of philosophy is ontology. Epistemology is but the ontology of the knowing[6] situation. The linguistic turn merely provides the method. Preoccupation with language as such is fatal to philosophy. (1) merely seems unduly preoccupied with language. If one wants to find out how a sentence manages to represent, he must first find out what there is to be represented. So he must begin with ontology. (Methodologically, we shall see, the order may be reversed.)

I present next my own answer to (1).

To *exist*, to be an existent, to be an entity, to have ontological status is one and the same. To say that something of a certain kind exists is the same as to say that there is something of this kind. This is the commonsensical use of 'exist'. I shall avoid all others.

Let S_1 be a pair of spots; one, red and round; the other, green and square. Green, red, round, square are four entities; S_1 itself is a fifth. Some existents are constituents of others. The two colors and the

---

[5] 'Relation' and 'nexus' I use technically, 'connection' nontechnically and so broadly that a relation as well as a nexus is a connection.

[6] This use of 'knowing' is generic, comprehends the species of perceiving, believing, remembering, doubting, and so on.

two shapes are constituents of S_1. To ask for all the constituents of an entity is to ask for its ontological assay. Two entities are different, i.e., two and not one, if and only if the assay of at least one yields at least one constituent which is not a constituent of the other.

Are the two shapes and the two colors all the constituents of S_1? Let S_2 be another pair of spots; one red and square; one green and round. Red in S_1 and S_2 is one entity, not two. So are green, round, square. Hence, if the assay of S_1, and therefore also that of S_2, yielded only these four entities, S_1 and S_2 would be one and not two. Yet they are different. In S_1 round is "tied" to red, while in S_2 it is tied to green; and so on. That shows the way out of the difficulty. One will so assay S_1 and S_2 that each yields in addition to the four entities called *things* (red, green, round, square) two occurrences of a fifth entity, called a *fundamental tie* (*nexus*), which in S_1 ties red to round, green to square, while in S_2 it ties red to square, green to round. That resolves the difficulty, provided an assay does not list a nexus just once but lists each of its occurrences (in this case, two), together with the entities it ties. (Even if both spots were red, red would be listed only once.) In this sense a thing is and a fundamental tie is not an *independent*₁ entity. That is one ontological difference between things and fundamental ties.

A *complex* is an entity among whose constituents are at least two things. A thing which is not a complex is a *simple*. Simples, to form a complex, must be connected by fundamental ties. (A class of simples is not a complex.) A fundamental tie needs no further tie to tie it to what it ties. (Otherwise we would be faced with an infinite regress à la Bradley.) In this sense things are and fundamental ties are not *independent*₂. That is another ontological difference between things and fundamental ties.

The things we have so far encountered are commonsensical. Common sense calls them (nonrelational) properties (characters). Now let S_3 be one spot, S_4 two spots, such that the three spots agree in all nonrelational properties. S_3 and S_4 are different, of course. Yet, if commonsensical properties were the only simples, they would yield the same assay. There are two ways out of the difficulty. One gives ontological status to bare individuals; the other, to such noncommonsensical properties as being at a certain place or a certain time. Faced with such an alternative, how does one decide? Urgent as the question is, we need not stay for an answer, since both alternatives recognize the ontological status of fundamental ties, which is the crucial issue between Wittgenstein and Stenius on the one hand and myself on the other, while, as it happens, aside from that issue and what it implies, Wittgenstein, Stenius and I have all chosen the first alternative.

As I assay S_1, it yields six simples, four *characters* and two *individuals*, as well as four occurrences of an asymmetrical nexus I call *exemplification*. Nonrelational exemplification connects a character and one individual. Or, as one says, an individual may exemplify a character, a character may be exemplified by an individual. Relational exemplification connects two individuals and a relational character, which latter is not a nexus but a thing. Individuals never exemplify individuals. Characters never exemplify characters.[7]

If we may judge from what is presented to us, every individual exemplifies at least one character, every character is at least once exemplified. Call this the *Principle of Exemplification*. In this respect, individuals and characters are equally *dependent*$_3$. In two others, they differ. (*A*) Individuals exemplify characters, but not conversely. This is of course but another way of stating the asymmetry of exemplification. (*B*) The difference between two characters is of the kind called qualitative. Two individuals differ only in being different, i.e., in being two and not one. That is what is meant by calling them bare.

'Nominalism' and 'realism' have been used in many ways, some not very precise, some not very helpful, some neither. So I propose to use them in a new way, calling a realist$_1$[8] one who holds that (*A*) and (*B*) are the only differences between individuals and characters; or, if you wish, that they are the only differences fundamental enough to be called ontological. All others I call nominalists. That makes for several kinds of nominalism. One kind rejects the Principle of Exemplification, holding that characters but not individuals are

[7] I limit myself to binary relations and the first two types. No harm will be done.

[8] Realism$_2$ is opposed to idealism. See below.

independent$_3$. Its usual name is Platonism. Frege, we shall see, reverses Plato. According to him, only individuals, he calls them things, are independent$_3$; characters, he calls them a kind of function, are not just dependent$_3$ but dependent$_1$.

The ontological ground of the difference between two characters is the characters themselves. Or, with a twist, the differences called qualitative need no ontological ground. The difference between individuals and characters is not qualitative. Nor is being an individual or being a character itself a character (universal); otherwise we would be faced with an infinite regress. What, then, is the ontological ground of the difference? I ground it in two dependent$_1$ entities, call them *individuality* and *universality*.[9] Dependent$_1$ entities being so radically different from all others that it is convenient to have a name for them, I appropriated one from the tradition, call them *subsistents*. The tradition calls a *summum genus* of the ontological inventory a mode. That makes subsistence a mode of existence.

Individuality, universality, and exemplification are three subsistents. The connectives, negation, conjunction, disjunction, and so on, are others.[10] There are still others. But we need not pursue. I shall manage without detailed examination of any but those three: individuality, universality, and exemplification.

Red-or-green is a character. It is also a complex. The nexus that makes it one is disjunction. Characters are things. Some things are thus complex(es). But not every complex is a thing. A complex is either a character or a *fact*. (All individuals are simples.) One individual exemplifying one simple nonrelational character is a fact. So are two individuals exemplifying one simple relational character. These two kinds of fact are called atomic. An atomic fact has no constituent which is itself a fact; hence the name. Notice, for later reference, that facts are independent$_3$.

How does a sentence manage to represent a fact? It will still be

[9] More precisely, nonrelational and relational universality are two entities. So are nonrelational and relational exemplification. When it makes no difference, I permit myself this inaccuracy.

[10] It is clear, I trust, that I use these words not for the marks sometimes so called but for the entities I claim they represent.

possible to join the issues if we limit the question to atomic facts. The "language" I shall examine, following Stenius who in turn follows Wittgenstein, is the familiar fragment of the lower functional calculus.

The fragment contains an indefinite number of marks of three different shapes, lower-case letters ('a', 'b', . . .), upper-case letters ('F', 'G', . . .), Greek letters ('ς', 'σ', . . .). It will save words and do no harm if we assume that each mark is a (geometrical) individual exemplifying one of three simple (geometrical) characters (upper-case, lower-case, Greek). A mark thus is a fact. It occurs in the fragment only if there is a simple which it has been made to represent. The individual in it stands for the thing; the shape in it, for the thing's type; lower-case for individuality, upper-case and Greek for nonrelational and relational universality, respectively. Marks representing in this way are called *names*. Strings such as 'Fa' and '$b\varsigma c$' are made to represent atomic facts by making two kinds of juxtaposition such as 'F' followed by 'a' and 'b' followed by 'ς' followed by 'c' represent the two kinds of exemplification.

In the fragment, facts are thus represented by strings of marks, simples by the individuals in the marks, the subsistents by properties of and relations among these individuals. That illustrates a feature of all systematically constructed languages. Each ontological kind is represented in one and only one way; different kinds in different ways. That makes these languages useful tools for ontological analysis. On the other hand, not every constituent of the representing fact (mark or string) is made to represent something. The shape of a mark, for instance, is tied to the individual in it by exemplification. Yet (this occurrence of) exemplification is not made to represent anything.

The above description of the fragment is of the kind called semantical. A syntactical description, also called formation rules, attends only to the representing facts. In our case it is very simple. First, three kinds of marks are singled out and distinguished by their shapes. Call this the *type distinction*. Then the two familiar kinds of strings are singled out as well formed (sentences).[11] All other strings are ill formed. Call this the *type rule*. If the formation

---

[11] This is of course a proleptic use of 'representing', 'mark', and 'sentence'.

rules of a language were not what they are, it could not represent what it represents. *Our language is what it is because the world is what it is.*

Not every sentence represents a fact. This is of the essence of language. '*Fa*' represents a fact if and only if *a* and *F* are tied by exemplification. Otherwise there is no fact for it to represent. It does not follow that in this case it represents nothing. Since the formation rules are what they are because the world is what it is, the difference between '*Fa*', which is well formed whether or not it represents a fact, on the one hand, and such ill-formed strings as '*FG*', '*aa*', '*aFb*', and so on, on the other, must have an ontological ground. I identify this ground by saying that a sentence represents either a fact or a possible fact and making *possibility* in this sense a mode of existence.[12] Since this is a very special use of 'possible', I mark it by saying that a sentence represents either a fact or a P-fact. If at this point some are shocked, what shocks them is merely the peculiar flavor of the traditional ontological language.

How do '*Fa*' and '*bSc*' manage to represent? To each constituent of the fact represented corresponds one constituent of the representing fact. The nexus connecting two simples, actually or P-wise, is represented by a relational thing connecting the two individuals which represent the simples. Such a correspondence is called an *isomorphism*. The language represents by means of an isomorphism. To understand the language is to know this isomorphism, which is *partial* and *external*. It is partial because, as we saw, not every constituent of the representing fact (sentence) represents something. It is external because the represented and the representing constituents need not and often are not of the same ontological kind. In the fragment all subsistents are represented by characters; characters are represented by individuals. Only individuals are represented by individuals.

Wittgenstein and Stenius make the same fundamental mistake. Neither recognizes that the subsistents exist. Wittgenstein,[13] because of this fundamental mistake, provides no answer to the question how sentences manage to represent facts. Stenius answers it, in spite of

---

[12] As for facts, so for complex characters. 'Centaur' represents a possible character.

[13] Wittgenstein is throughout this study the author of the *Tractatus*.

the fundamental mistake. From where I stand his answer is wrong. But it is not wrong because of the fundamental mistake. Rather, it is wrong because of the nominalism it implies but which Stenius himself does not notice. If the task were merely diagnosis, I would now be ready to conclude. Since the task is also analysis and justification, I have barely begun. It will in fact be best if before turning to Wittgenstein and Stenius I make four further points.

(1) Remember what was said earlier. The heart of the matter is ontology; the linguistic turn merely provides the method. That is why I began with ontology. But the traditional ontological talk is problematic, sometimes even shocking. The thing to do therefore is to make it commonsensical. That is done by reversing the order, beginning with language. We know, commonsensically, that this is red, that green, this to the left of that, and so on. Language represents what we know, otherwise it could not do the job it does. Hence it must represent what must be there if we are to know what in fact we do know, e.g., that S_1 differs from S_2, S_3 from S_4. The method first identifies the representing features of language. Then it explicates the ontological kinds as corresponding to the different ways in which different features represent. If these ways were arbitrary, the method would fail. Thus one must show that in a relevant sense they are not arbitrary. I shall show that, hastily, in one case. Assume that individuality can be represented by a capital letter, say, '*I*'. (If the method works, that amounts to assuming that individuality is a simple character.) Consider now '*Ia*'. This sentence manages to represent what it represents, namely, that *a* is an individual, only because we know already what the shapes of '*a*' and '*I*' and their juxtaposition have been made to represent. In this sense the sentence represents *only with futility*. Or, if you please, the language "shows" what cannot in it without futility be "said." That is the recoverable core of Wittgenstein's famous ineffability thesis. The argument also supports a point made earlier. Systematically constructed languages are useful because they represent the different ontological kinds in different ways. (Natural languages are universal, i.e., in them everything can be said; hence the troubles of philosophy before the linguistic turn.)

(2) The overwhelming majority of modern philosophers failed to recognize that the subsistents exist. Among recent ones the only ex-

ceptions I know of (and admire) are Frege and Husserl. In Frege's world, though, exemplification does not exist. Yet he managed to fill the gap. Since in this study exemplification is the crucial issue and since Frege's influence is clearly visible in the *Tractatus*, we had better understand how he managed. His things are independent₃. His notion of function is taken from mathematics. A function is a "mapping" of entities on entities.[14] That makes it dependent₁ on those entities. Hence it needs no tie to tie it to them. The connectives are one kind of function; characters are another. Characters thus have the same ontological status as the connectives, to which the overwhelming majority of modern philosophers gives no ontological status whatsoever while in my world they "merely" subsist. That makes Frege a nominalist. (It also shows that there is some point in my new way of using that old label.)

Among Frege's things there are two noncommonsensical kinds, propositions and the two things True and False. In my world, a sentence represents either (*a*) a fact or (*b*) a P-fact. In his world there are no facts. Rather, each sentence represents two things, one as its *Sinn*, one as its *Bedeutung*. In case (*a*) it represents a proposition and the thing True; in case (*b*) the same proposition and the thing False. Notice now, first, that the proposition is a thing in either case, e.g., in the paradigm, whether or not exemplification occurs between *a* and *F*.[15] Notice, second, that the occurrence and nonoccurrence of exemplification is "represented" by the two things True and False, respectively. That shows how Frege managed. The price he paid for not recognizing the ontological status of exemplification was the two noncommonsensical kinds of things.

(3) If one says that there are six possible ways of selecting two things out of four, ten to select three out of five, and so on, he uses 'possible' combinatorially. This use needs no explication. Two others do. Both are often marked by the adverb 'logically'. In other words, I claim that 'logically possible' has been used in two different ways, each of which needs explication. As for 'possible', so of course for

---

[14] See "Frege's Hidden Nominalism," *The Philosophical Review*, 67 (1958): 437–59; reprinted in *Meaning and Existence* (Madison: University of Wisconsin Press, 1960).

[15] A P-fact is there (exists in the mode of possibility) if and only if there is no fact for the sentence to represent. That alone shows that a P-fact is not a proposition.

'impossible' and 'necessary'. For the time being I suppress the adverb and distinguish the two uses by subscripts.

'*Fa*' is well formed; '*FG*' is not. It is possible$_1$ for '*Fa*' to represent something; it is impossible$_1$ for '*FG*' to do so. That is the cue. It is possible$_1$ for a well-formed string to represent something, impossible$_1$ for one that is ill formed. Notice also what I did not say, namely, that a well-formed string represents a possible entity. For, whether a sentence represents a fact or a P-fact is an entirely different matter. In other words, the ontological use of 'possible', which was explicated earlier and marked 'P', is a third use.

Replace in a fact all the simples among its constituents so that, first, different ones are replaced by different ones, and, second, each is replaced by one of its own kind, individuals by individuals, and so on. Considering all "possible" replacements, there are two "possibilities." (The two uses of 'possible' in the preceding sentence are combinatorial!) The resulting "complexes" either are all facts or some are P-facts. If and only if they are all facts then all these facts, including the original one, are necessary$_2$, or, synonymously, they are facts of all possible$_2$ worlds. As for facts, so for P-facts. If for a P-fact all possible replacements yield P-facts, then all these P-facts, including the original one, are impossible$_2$, or, synonymously, they are P-facts in all possible$_2$ worlds.[16]

If you doubt whether the two uses are really different, consider a contradiction. Since it is well formed, it is possible$_1$ for it to represent something. Yet what it represents is impossible$_2$. If you are still doubtful, try to use the phrase 'possible world' in connection with possibility$_1$. In this context "all possible worlds" are those corresponding to all possible formation rules. Our world, or, rather, and this is where the difference shows, *all* possible$_2$ worlds are just *one* such "possible world." Or, if you want to say the same thing still differently, possibility$_1$ determines the class of all complexes and P-complexes; necessity$_2$ and impossibility$_2$ single out two subclasses of this class.

While combinatorial possibility enters explicitly into the notion of

[16] More usually one would say that the representing sentences are necessarily$_2$ true (false) or that they are true (false) in all possible$_2$ worlds. But there is some point in avoiding 'true' and 'false' in this study. So I make a point of avoiding them.

possibility$_2$, it does not so enter into that of possibility$_1$. Yet there is a connection. To know all "possible" well-formed strings is the same thing as to know for which strings it is possible$_1$ to represent something. In the fragment that amounts to knowing all "possible" strings of two or three names that are well formed. The two uses of 'possible' in this paragraph that are marked by quotation marks are combinatorial. That shows the connection.

(4) What is the ontological ground of an isomorphism? The answer requires some preparation. "Subsistent characters"[17] are a special kind of subsistent. If there are three chairs in this room, the character chair-in-this-room "exemplifies" the "subsistent property" of being a triple. In a monogamic society the characters husband and wife jointly "exemplify" the "subsistent relation" of equinumerosity. Subsistent characters are not characters, nor are they really exemplified by anything; hence the quotation marks—otherwise the expressions within them may mislead. Individuality and triplicity are both subsistents. Yet there is a difference. That an entity is an individual cannot as we saw (without futility) be said (in a systematically constructed language). That the chairs in this room are a triple can be said. If the statement saying it is appropriately abbreviated by means of definitions then the subsistent appears to be represented by a defined predicate. As for triplicity, so for all subsistent characters; hence the name which may mislead.

There is an isomorphism between *A* and *B* if and only if they jointly exemplify a subsistent relation of a certain kind. That answers the question which opens the last paragraph. Two comments will show its importance. First. Complete philosophical understanding of a statement is inseparable from the identification of its ontological ground. It follows that one cannot fully understand the nature of an isomorphism without realizing that the subsistents exist. Second. We say that we discover an isomorphism, that we establish one, and so on. Discovering and establishing involve mind. We speak of formation and interpretation[18] rules. Again, rules involve mind. That makes it important to grasp firmly that the isomorphism between a

[17] More usually they are called *logical characters*. But it will help the explication of how Wittgenstein uses 'logic' and 'logical' if I avoid using them myself.

[18] To make the individual in a name stand for a certain simple is an instance of an interpretation rule.

sentence and the fact (or P-fact) which by the virtue of this iso-morphism it represents involves nothing mental but merely the sen-tence itself, the fact, and certain subsistents.[19]

I turn to Wittgenstein.

Stenius and I use 'sentence' for the physical fact; Wittgenstein doesn't. I shall continue to use the word as before, marking Wittgen-stein's use by capitalizing its initial (*Sentence*). What matters is not of course how a word is used but, rather, the distinctions which a use helps or hinders.

What is a mind? What is a thought? What is the right assay of the knowing situation? The three questions are but three facets of one. Call it the *problem of mind*. Remember now three other ques-tions. (1) How does a sentence manage to represent a fact? (2) What is the connection between a thought and its intention? (3) What, if any, is the connection between a sentence and the thought intending the fact which it represents? One cannot solve the prob-lem of mind without clearly distinguishing among (1), (2), (3), nor without realizing that the answer to (1) must not involve mind. My answer to (1), we saw, is of that kind. So, we shall see, is Stenius'. His and my use of 'sentence' helps the relevant distinctions. The *Tractatus* is hopelessly blurred on the problem of mind. Call that its fundamental blur. Of this more later.

A Sentence is, *roughly*, a sentence plus the relevant (formation and interpretation) rules. The question which dominates the *Tracta-tus* is not (1) but, rather, (1″): How does a Sentence manage to represent a fact? Now there is of course in this context a way of referring to rules which does not essentially involve mind and which is therefore as harmless as it is often convenient. If the rules in-gredient of a Sentence were harmless in this sense, the difference between (1) and (1″) would be merely verbal. Unhappily this in-gredient is anything but harmless. Thought is essentially involved. The fundamental blur thus spreads to Sentences. The ontological status of their rules ingredient remains hopelessly blurred. I shall mark that blur by once more capitalizing an initial, saying that a Sen-tence is a sentence plus the relevant *Rules*. Nor is that the only rea-son I said "roughly." Some passages may plausibly be taken to imply

---

[19] The fact represented may of course itself be mental. Reread what has been said at the beginning about (1) being merely an abbreviation of (1′).

that a Sentence is something wholly mental. More precisely, they may be taken to imply that the thought of a fact, i.e., a Sentence, and the thought of a sentence representing this fact are one thing and not two. The right answer to (3) is that these are two thoughts and that the connection between them is merely causal.

What is Wittgenstein's answer to (1″)? I limit the task as before. How does an atomic Sentence manage to represent an atomic fact? As before, we cannot answer without answering another question first. According to Wittgenstein, what is there to be represented? A sentence may of course represent a P-fact. But it will be safe to ignore this complication until we come to the only point where it matters.

There is no disagreement about those constituents of atomic facts which are things. The only issue is the three subsistents, individuality, universality, and exemplification. Wittgenstein denies that they exist. That is his fundamental mistake. One cannot understand it accurately without understanding why the way in which he disposes of the first two differs from that in which he disposes of the third. Individuality and universality he calls internal properties, arguing with great care that as such they do not exist. Exemplification he overlooks. Or, at most, he brushes it aside, denying the need for it in one striking passage. The structural reason for this difference is that he attends, again with great care, to something else, he calls it an internal relation, which is not exemplification but which conceivably even though not plausibly may be mistaken for it. Notice that I speak of a structural reason rather than a cause, just as I do not claim that Wittgenstein mistook that internal relation for exemplification, or, even, that he overlooked the need for the latter because of his preoccupation with the former. For I am not in the least interested in biographical conjectures.

The striking passage[20] just mentioned is 2.03:

> Im Sachverhalt hängen die Gegenstände ineinander, wie die Glieder einer Kette.

The image is admirably clear. The links of a chain hang in each other and need no tie to hold them together. There is no need for

---

[20] I approve and therefore follow Stenius' practice of quoting the German original.

exemplification. It is nothing, less than nothing. To be nothing and to have no ontological status are the same. And there is of course no lesser ontological status than none. Thus I spoke metaphorically. Internal characters (properties and relations), we shall see, have no ontological status, are nothing. Exemplification, however, has not even the "status" of an internal relation. That unpacks the metaphor. To say the same thing still differently, even if internal relations existed, it would not follow that exemplification exists.

(a) Individuality and universality are internal characters. (b) Internal characters do not exist. (a) and (b) jointly imply that individuality and universality have no ontological status. Wittgenstein obviously holds (a). The strongest evidence for his also holding (b) is a fragment from 4.123:

> Diese blaue Farbe und jene stehen in der internen Relation von heller und dunkler eo ipso.

Remember what was said earlier. Difference, whether qualitative between two characters or, as one says, merely numerical between two individuals, needs no ontological ground, i.e., no third entity in addition to the two things. But a relation between two things is a third entity. Nor is it just a subsistent, it is a third thing. The strength of the evidence lies partly in the fragment's being so patently wrong. Partly it lies in the "eo ipso," which leaves no doubt that the two colors are the only entities in the case, or, what amounts to the same, that the alleged internal relation has no ontological status whatsoever.

It is possible$_1$[21] for any individual to exemplify any character.[22] Wittgenstein expresses this by saying that an internal relation, call it R, obtains between each individual and each character. R is the connection of which I claimed that it might conceivably be mistaken for exemplification, or, less strongly, that preoccupation with it might cause one to overlook exemplification. The distinction depends on the distinction between possibility$_1$ and the mode of possibility (P). Take a and F. Exemplification either does or does not occur between them. If it does, they jointly form a fact; if it doesn't,

---

[21] As explicated earlier, possibility$_1$ involves marks. But no harm will come from using the term also as above.

[22] The extension of the argument to relational characters, ordered pairs of individuals, and relational exemplification is obvious.

a P-fact. But R obtains between them in either case. Hence R and exemplification are two, not one. That is one way of putting the matter; let me try another. If R and exemplification were one, 'Fa' would merely represent its own being well-formed, which is absurd. What it does represent (by means of juxtaposition!) is either a fact or a P-fact; which of the two we are of course unable to tell by looking merely at 'Fa'. If one is overimpressed by this inability, as I believe Wittgenstein was, and if one does not clearly distinguish between possibility₁ and the mode of possibility (P), the distinction between R and exemplification may become blurred.

The Sentence represents the fact by sharing its "logical form." That is Wittgenstein's answer to (1″). He also calls internal characters structural, or formal, or *logical*. What, then, is his notion of logic? A thread I left dangling will lead to the answer. Possibility₁ and possibility₂ are two, not one. Yet they have both been called "logical possibility." Is there a notion of logic that fits both (undistinguished) uses? Combinatorial possibility, we remember, is an ingredient of both. Mistaking this common ingredient for what it is not, a common core, one arrives at the following notion. "Logic encompasses all possibilities. The nonlogical is the impossible; the logical, the necessary. The necessary, not depending on any one possibility, is common to all possible worlds." This is also Wittgenstein's notion of logic. I shall first connect it with his notion of internal (logical) characters, then show why it is confused.

Let E_1 and E_2 be two sentences. E_2 follows deductively from E_1 if and only if 'If E_1 then E_2' is a tautology. According to Wittgenstein, a Sentence's being a tautology is an internal (logical) property of it; E_2's deductively following from E_1, an internal (logical) relation between the two Sentences. A tautology, we remember, represents a necessary₂ fact. That shows the connection of logical characters with possibility₂. The connection with possibility₁ we know already. 'Fa' is well-formed because the logical relation R obtains between a and F.

Wittgenstein's notion of logic makes both being well-formed (possibility₁) and being a tautology (necessity₂) a "matter of logic."[23] That is the root of the confusion. Its bitter fruit is either

[23] The phrase is vague. But square pegs do not fit round holes. A vague phrase sometimes helps taking apart a confusion. This particular confusion

failure to distinguish between formation rules and tautologies, or, even worse, to mistake the former for a species of the latter. Wittgenstein himself virtually makes that mistake when he asserts in 3.332, 3.333 that the type rule (e.g., that 'ab' and 'FG' are ill formed) follows deductively from the type distinction (e.g., between 'a' and 'F').[24] The mistake is (or may be) facilitated by the equally confused idea that if an internal relation obtains between two entities, then the sentence expressing this fact is a tautology. The internal relation in the case is of course R, which obtains between a and F but not between either a and b or F and G.

The only clear use of 'logic' and 'logical' is the narrow classical one that relates to deductive inference (necessity$_2$). The broader the use, the blunter the tool, the greater therefore the confusion. Wittgenstein's broad use opened the door to even broader ones. His epigones at Oxford rushed through the door. Stenius, even though in most other respects laudably unaffected by Oxford, is also given to a very broad use. This aspect of his book I admire least. That is why I did not select it for examination.

The Sentence and the fact share a *logical form* (logical structure, internal structure). That is how, according to Wittgenstein, the former manages to represent the latter. What, then, is the logical form of an atomic fact? It is a "something" that consists "somehow" of three internal characters, the relation R and the two properties corresponding to individuality and universality. R connects individuals and characters, not individuality and universality; and a structure is not just a class, its constituents must be connected; hence the quotation marks around 'somehow'. But let us waive this objection. Perhaps the blur it spots can be cleared up. Internal characters are nothing, have no ontological status whatsoever. What consists of nothing is itself nothing. Logical form is literally nothing; hence the quotation marks around 'something'. What two entities literally share is itself an entity, has ontological status. If what the Sentence and the fact share has none, then there is nothing they share. This objection is fatal. Wittgenstein's *explicit answer* to ($1''$) is no an-

---

has also been promoted by multiply ambiguous uses of 'formal' and 'linguistic'. These I examined elsewhere; so I ignore them here.

[24] See Allaire's paper on 3.333 cited in n. 3. The mistake is further facilitated by Frege's notion of function.

swer. If we merely wanted to judge, we could stop. Since we also want to understand as accurately as we may, we must continue.

After a fashion, we know what the logical form of the nonrelational atomic fact is. Let us see whether we can find it in the Sentence. The Sentence is the sentence plus the Rules. Let us first look at the sentence, say, '*Fa*'. The three shapes (lower-case, upper-case, Greek) are nowhere mentioned in the *Tractatus;* nor is juxtaposition.[25] A sentence is considered to be a fact; a mark (name), an individual.[26] The logical form of two individuals, or, even, of two individuals in juxtaposition is not that of the nonrelational atomic fact. Yet the latter is supposed to be in the Sentence. Since we haven't found it in the sentence, we must look for it in the Rules. These, I submit, "correspond" to the formation rules. I say "correspond" rather than "are" because, we remember, Rules either are mental, or, at least, essentially involve mind. Even so, we have come upon Wittgenstein's implicit answer to (1″). The sentences (or Sentences) of the fragment manage to represent because there is a one-one correspondence between the members of the class of all possible$_1$ atomic facts and P-facts on the one hand and combinatorially possible well-formed strings (Strings) of the fragment on the other; with the formation rules determining what is combinatorially possible. What is thus really "shared," not to be sure by any pair of corresponding members but, at least, by the two classes themselves is this one-one correspondence. We know that a one-one correspondence is an elementary isomorphism whose ontological status is that of a subsistent relation, which is not "shared" but, rather, jointly exemplified by the two classes; hence the quotation marks around 'shared'.

Is Wittgenstein's implicit answer to (1″) really an answer? If sentences (or Sentences) were names (or Names), it would be one. Since they are not, as he himself so admirably insisted against Frege, and since he overlooked exemplification, he cannot really tell how a string (or String) manages to represent what it represents. Hence not even his implicit answer is really an answer.

---

[25] See, however, what is said below about Stenius' "second group of passages."

[26] Or, if you insist on the type-token distinction, a character. The difference makes no difference for the argument.

Wittgenstein denies that the subsistents exist. That is his fundamental mistake. Since the subsistents are nothing, logical form is nothing. The status of mind in the *Tractatus* is hopelessly blurred. That is its fundamental blur. One can even argue what presently I shall at least assert, that in the *Tractatus* world mind is nothing. On the side of the Sentence, we saw, the logical form, which is nothing, resides in the Rules which, being mental or at least essentially involving mind, are either themselves nothing, or, at best, something whose ontological status remains hopelessly blurred. That shows how the fundamental mistake and the fundamental blur curiously supplement each other, jointly producing the semblance of an answer where there is none.

Why did Wittgenstein overlook exemplification? Intellectual biography is one thing; connections among ideas are another. To explore the *structural* reasons which *may* plausibly have shaped a man's thought is merely one way of exploring connections among ideas. Sometimes it is the most convenient way. I suggest next two further structural reasons why Wittgenstein may have overlooked exemplification.

1. The commonsensical use of 'exist' is also the broadest. (1) To exist is to be an individual. (2) To exist is to be a simple. (3) To exist is to be in space and time. (4) To exist is to be a thing. (5) To exist is to be a fact. (6) To exist is to be an atomic fact. Each of these six sentences is the formula of a narrow use of the kind I call philosophical. (There are still others.) Once a philosopher has adopted such a use he never permits its formula to become false. That may lead him to reject the commonsensical use; or he may fail to distinguish the latter from his own. In either case he will be in trouble.[27] That is indeed one way of diagnosing *the* trouble of classical ontology.

Wittgenstein, with a difference, adopts (2) and (6). I say with a difference because in his world the ontological status of atomic facts (6) is "higher" than that of simples (2). The more "independent" an entity is, the "higher" is its ontological status. That is the idea behind the difference. Its influence throughout the history of phi-

---

[27] If, for instance, wittingly or unwittingly he adopts (1), he may say that characters don't exist without noticing that what he says is patently wrong if 'exists' is taken in its one clear and commonsensical meaning.

losophy is very great indeed. To understand the difference (and un-pack the metaphors between the quotation marks), remember the Principle of Exemplification. Facts (5) are and things (4) are not independent$_3$. Simples (2) are the "simplest" things (4); atomic facts (6), the "simplest" facts (5). The "simpler" an entity is, the "higher" is its ontological status. That is another idea whose influence throughout the history of philosophy was very great. It accounts for the replacement of (5) and (4) by (6) and (2), respectively.

R's being an internal relation expresses the dependence$_3$ of individuals and characters on each other. That is why what follows merely adds a nuance. *Each* individual has *a* character (or some) on which it depends$_3$; each character, an individual (or some). Call this the general dependence of the two kinds on each other. It needs no further ontological ground; that is why R is superfluous and why its being nothing does not hurt. On the other hand, *this* individual depends$_3$ on this character and not on that or that other. This specific dependence does need an ontological ground. Otherwise, what would be the difference between the two pairs of spots with which I began? To put the ontological status of facts "higher" than that of things is to be overimpressed with the general dependence of the latter on each other. If one is so overimpressed, then he may overlook the need for ontologically grounding their specific dependence. That is the nuance.

2. In Frege's world, we saw, there are no facts. There are, instead, the two noncommonsensical kinds of things, propositions and the two things True and False. I say instead because, as we also saw, these two strange kinds enabled Frege to construct an ontology which has no gap at the place which in other ontologies is taken by exemplification. Call this the function of the two strange kinds. Wittgenstein rejected them both. In this I believe he was right. But, then, he cannot have fully understood their function. Otherwise he would not have overlooked exemplification. Call this the negative influence of Frege. Being negative, it does not show in the text. Another one does.

A function, being a mapping and as such dependent$_1$ on the entities mapped and mapped upon, needs no nexus to tie it to these entities. Wittgenstein, partly under Frege's influence, partly because of his preoccupation with combinatorial possibility, thinks of '*Fa*' as a "propositional function" of '*F*' and '*a*'. The sense that makes is obvious and irrelevant; the nonsense, subtle and disastrous. Replace either of the two names by another and you obtain another sentence. That is the sense. Keeping one name unchanged, you may, if you wish, replace the other in all possible₁ ways. That shows the connection with the preoccupation. The nonsense is that a character does not "map" an individual into a fact. Nor of course does an individual so map a character. Rather, an individual and a character, if connected by exemplification, jointly "make" a fact. That shows why one who in thinking about a world in which there are facts thinks about sentences as "propositional functions" may overlook exemplification.

I turn to Stenius.

Unlike Wittgenstein, Stenius, as one must, answers (1), not (1″). His assay of the atomic fact agrees with Wittgenstein's; it yields one or, in the relational case, two individuals, one character and, literally, nothing else. For, like Wittgenstein, he does not recognize the ontological status of the three subsistents. Yet, he does not overlook exemplification.[28] That is why, unlike Wittgenstein, he is able to produce an answer. More precisely, what he says becomes an answer as soon as one recognizes that exemplification exists.

'*Fa*' is for Stenius a fact. Wittgenstein and I agree. '*F*' and '*a*' he takes to be individuals. Wittgenstein agrees, I don't. With the qualification that disagreement implies, all three agree that '*a*' represents the individual in the fact as its *name*. Stenius' innovation concerns '*F*'. This letter for him is not the name of the character in the fact. The linguistic representative of that (nonrelational) character is, rather, the (nonrelational) character standing-to-the-right-of-'*F*' (on paper). The letter itself is merely an ingredient of the representative; he calls it its characteristic, probably because one can by means of it establish the required one-one correspondence between representing and represented entities, where standing to the left of '*F*', of '*G*', of '*H*', and so on, correspond to this, that, and that other character, and so on. Whether one calls these representatives of characters names is a matter of words. How one uses a word, pro-

---

[28] Overlooking exemplification is one thing. Assigning it the "status" of an internal relation is another thing. That should by now be clear.

vided only one knows how one uses it, does not matter. But it will facilitate the exposition if we avoid 'name' and speak instead of *character-representatives*.

To each represented individual corresponds one representing individual, its name, and conversely. To each represented nonrelational character corresponds one character-representative, which is itself a nonrelational character, and conversely. The represented fact or P-fact consists of an individual exemplifying a character, actually or P-wise; the representing fact, the sentence, of the representing individual exemplifying the character-representative. That is an isomorphism. Stenius' answer to (1) is that the sentence represents the fact by virtue of this isomorphism. Notice that each entity corresponds to one of its own kind, individuals to individuals, nonrelational characters to nonrelational characters, (occurrences of) exemplification to (occurrences of) exemplification. In other words, the isomorphism is internal. Notice, too, that *as long as the marks are assayed as individuals* each constituent of the representing fact, *except the mark 'F' itself*, is made to represent something. With these two qualifications, which apparently he did not notice, the isomorphism of Steinus' answer is complete. Thus he thinks of it as both *internal and complete*.

Let us compare the three answers, assaying them ontologically. According to Wittgenstein, the Sentence and the fact "share" something. That is how the former manages to represent the latter. The something "shared" turns out to be nothing. That is why his explicit answer fails. So, we saw, does his implicit answer. According to Stenius the sentence represents the fact by virtue of an isomorphism. If exemplification is given ontological status, that isomorphism is really there. With this obvious qualification, Stenius' answer is really an answer. We know that an isomorphism is a subsistent relation which is not "shared" but, rather, jointly exemplified by the two members of each corresponding pair. This knowledge, though, requires the correct ontological assay of an isomorphism, which in turn requires the insight that the subsistents (not just the three to which I limited the issue) exist. Stenius, who does not have this insight, *seems* to hold that something is "shared." The two individuals, for instance, the represented and the representing one, share individuality. To see how wrong that is, one merely has to remember that individuality, being dependent₁, never occurs as such in an ontological assay. Rather, an assay lists occurrences of individuality. In our case, individuality occurs twice, once in the represented, once in the representing fact. Hence, obviously, neither of the two occurrences is "shared" by the two facts. As for individuality, so for universality and exemplification. I said "seems" when attributing to Stenius the belief that something is "shared" because inevitably at this point he is not as clear as one could wish. Yet no harm is done. He makes his idea perfectly clear nevertheless. Since they "share" something and/or the isomorphism is internal and complete, the sentence and the fact are *similar*. That is the idea. The corresponding entities of an external and partial isomorphism are not similar in this sense. The isomorphism of my answer is external and partial.

If you try to apply Stenius' innovation to the relational atomic fact represented by '$a\zeta b$', you will see that the representative of the relational character must itself be such a character. Hence it can only be standing-to-the-left-and-right-of-'ζ' (on paper), with the letter 'ζ' as its characteristic. Reread now 3.1432:

> Nicht: "Das komplexe Zeichen 'aRb' sagt dass a in der Beziehung R zu b steht," sondern: Dass "a" in einer gewissen Beziehung zu "b" steht, sagt dass aRb.

and you will, if I am not wholly mistaken, for the first time understand the passage. I have been puzzled by it for years. From time to time I brooded over it, to no avail. Others, equally puzzled, remained equally in the dark. Stenius has solved the puzzle. That makes our failure the measure of his ingenuity. But then, one may ask, how does his reading of 3.1432 fit the rest of the text? He himself provides the answer by calling attention to two groups of passages.

One fairly large group, taken in isolation, leaves no doubt that 'a', 'F', 'ζ' are names in exactly the same sense and represent in exactly the same way. That contradicts 3.1432.[29] Since Stenius very carefully points that out himself, I need not quote from that first group.

---

[29] More precisely, it contradicts the first half of 3.1432, up to '*sondern*'. The contradiction does therefore not depend on accepting, as I do, Stenius' reading of the whole passage as the only intelligible one.

I made much of 2.03, the metaphor of the links in the chain, and claimed that it was the only passage that at least implicitly deals with exemplification, if only to brush it aside and dismiss it as superfluous. Given my lack of text-critical enthusiasm in general and the nature of this text in particular, I am not prepared to press the claim. Rather, I agree with Stenius that there is a small group of passages which, taken in isolation, permits, even though it does not require, an interpretation that contradicts my claim. 3.21 is a passage of this second group as characteristic as any:

> Der Konfiguration der einfachen Zeichen im Satzzeichen entspricht die Konfiguration der Gegenstände in der Sachlage.

I incline to the belief that any such passage is merely another tedious reference to that tedious and useless nonentity R. That is why I said "permits even though it does not require." Stenius reads 'verhalten' to stand for exemplification, once of the character by the individual in the fact, once of the character-representative by the name in the sentence. He adds with his usual acuity and candor that with this reading the two groups contradict each other. Then he proposes to disregard the first, *that is his correction*, and bases his interpretation on 3.1432 and the second. But, then, why call interpretation what is really an original idea that may or may not have been suggested by a text which is notoriously contradictory as well as opaque?

Remember the method. Unless secured by the linguistic turn, ontological talk remains problematic. Two entities are of the same ontological kind if and only if in a systematically constructed language they are represented in the same way. Remember next what was said about nominalism and realism$_1$. (A) Individuals exemplify characters but not conversely. (B) The difference between characters is qualitative, that between individuals merely numerical. (A) and (B) are the only differences between characters and individuals. Anyone who either explicitly or implicitly adds another is a nominalist. According to Stenius, individuals are represented by names; characters, by character-representatives. The difference in the way of representation could hardly be more striking. It makes Stenius a nominalist.[30] To me that alone suffices to reject his answer to (1). It

[30] I see another symptom of his (and Wittgenstein's) nominalistic tendencies in their assaying marks as things rather than facts.

is only fair to add that he himself has the good sense to reject nominalism. In fact, he rejects it rather emphatically. But, then, in philosophy it is not enough to reject or deny something. The task is to get rid of all its equivalents and traces in what one asserts. (I have had the good sense to reject phenomenalism long before I knew how to get rid of it completely.)

Recall the task. I promised to present Stenius' central idea and to justify the judgment that it is mistaken. The promise has been fulfilled. But I also undertook to justify the further judgment that Stenius' mistake is extraordinarily illuminating. To this remaining part of the task I now turn. It requires that we face the problem of mind, or, what amounts virtually to the same, the ontological assay of the act,[31] which in turn requires some preparations. Then I shall again confront the three bodies of ideas. This time, though, I shall reverse the order, attend first to Stenius' ideas, then to Wittgenstein's, and only at the end say a few words about my own. For this is of course not the place to expound once more my own philosophy of mind.

You perceive that this tree is green. He knows that two and two are four. She remembers that her lover admires Rilke. I doubt that I shall ever see Vienna again. These are four acts. What one perceives, remembers, and so on, is the act's *intention*. Perceiving, remembering, and so on, are its *species*. My own perceiving something, my having perceived it yesterday, your perceiving it tomorrow are three acts, not one. Acts are *individuated*. Acts (minds) exist. What, then, is the ontological assay of an act, or, what amounts virtually to the same, of the knowing[32] situation? A philosopher's answer depends on his ontological ground plan or schema. The task requires that we attend to the classical (Aristotelian-Thomistic) schema even though, fortunately, we can ignore all its details. So I shall, in presenting it, rather recklessly schematize the schema. But notice first that no assay can be adequate unless it accounts for the three dimensions of each act, i.e., its intention, its species, and its being individuated.

Individuals exist independently; their attributes exist dependently; nothing else exists. That is the classical schema. Its individuals are

---

[31] I.e., in terms of the trio of questions I set up, questions (2) and (3).

[32] Since in this phrase 'knowing' is used generically, the several species are species of "knowing." See n. 6.

substances, not bare. (Substances are continuants, not, as the individuals of my world, momentary.) Their attributes are nonrelational characters (universals). Since substances are not bare and exist independently in a sense in which attributes do not, the nexus between a substance and one of its attributes is not exemplification. The attribute is thought to be *in* the substance. That makes inherence a suitable name for this nexus.

(1) There are two kinds of things:[33] some are physical; some, mental. *Realists*$_2$ hold (1); *idealists* hold that all entities are mental. (2) Minds know physical things; the primary source of such knowledge is perception.[34] (1) without (2) is an empty husk. Realism$_2$ requires an assay of the knowing situation in general and of the perceiving situation in particular that bears out (2). Or, briefly, realism$_2$ stands and falls with a realistic$_2$ account of perception. Such an account must connect a mind with its intentions.

How does the classical schema account for perception? Assume that I perceive a tree. Both I and the tree are substances, one mental, one physical. When perceiving the tree, I abstract the tree's nature and make it temporarily my own. However crudely, that is the gist of the classical abstraction theory. For all we need to know, a nature is a character. Characters being universals, it is possible that while I perceive the tree, one universal, the tree's nature, inheres in two substances, my own and the tree's. Thus, in the perceiving situation the two substances, perceiver and perceived, literally share something. They are connected. The classical abstraction theory of perception is realistic$_2$. It is also compatible with the following formula: (*I*) *A mind knows only what is in it.* For the tree's nature, while a mind perceives it, is an attribute of this mind. Thus it is "in" it. Nor is there in the classical schema any other way to account for knowing. That illustrates how the ontological ground plan determines the account of the knowledge situation. Epistemology so-called is indeed merely the ontology of that situation.

In the late sixteenth and the early seventeenth centuries the abstraction theory fell under the double onslaught of the new science

---

[33] I say "things" rather than "entities" because the subsistents are neither physical nor mental.

[34] We can here safely disregard a mind's knowledge of minds, his own and others'.

and the revived skeptical arguments. Thus a realistic$_2$ account of perception was no longer available. That was a great revolution. Call it, however inaccurately, the Cartesian revolution. But few revolutions, if any, are so thorough that they do not either wittingly or unwittingly preserve some ideas which are compatible only with those they have destroyed. The Cartesian revolution preserved *I*. Yet the only realistic$_2$ account of perception compatible with *I* is the abstraction theory which this very revolution destroyed. This, I submit, is the deepest root of that trend toward idealism which has proved irresistible ever since and which structurally is irresistible as long as wittingly or unwittingly one accepts *I*. That is not to say, however, that the trend has not been resisted. Most resisters took "the way of ideas."

The physical object, so this gambit opens, is indeed not in the perceiver's mind. What is in his mind are ideas. These ideas, though, resemble, are *similar* to, the physical objects of which they are the ideas. That is how through the latter we know the former. The skeptic merely asked two questions. *If all you know is ideas*, how do you know that there are physical objects of which they are the ideas? And, even granted that there is one, how do you know that its idea is similar to it? Those who took the way of ideas had no answer. Upon their gambit, the mind and its intention have fallen apart, are no longer connected. The way of ideas leads to idealism or, for those who can stomach it, materialism. The only way out is to break the stranglehold of *I*.

Historically, it would be foolish indeed to underestimate the impact of the revived skeptical arguments. Structurally, compared with *I*, they are shallow. To see why that is so, or, if you please, to see what I mean by this deliberately strong way of putting the point, return for a moment to the two skeptical objections as they are stated in the last paragraph. The italicized phrase, 'if all you know are ideas,' is only one-half of the shared premise that makes them unanswerable. The other half is *I*: and if all you know is in your mind. That shows what I mean. Structurally *I* is indeed the deepest root of that post-Cartesian trend toward idealism that has still to be stopped.

Speaking of skepticism, I might as well mention another attempted way out. This gambit assays the perceiver and the physical intention as things, perceiving as a relation jointly exemplified by them. Perception is fallible, what it presents as existing does not always exist. (That is the modest sound core of skepticism.) But, then, what does not exist, or exists only in the mode of possibility, cannot exemplify a relation. So the gambit collapses. The only way to keep it alive is to introduce such noncommonsensical things as propositions and construe perceiving as a relation connecting the mind with this sort of thing. For propositions, we remember, exist irrespective of whether or not the corresponding fact does. That is indeed the major structural reason why some philosophers introduced this noncommonsensical sort of thing. Those who do not countenance it cannot take this way out.

I turn to Stenius.

He devotes but a single page (p. 113) to his own thoughts on thought. The page is the key to the book. So I shall venture to state what it barely hints or merely suggests. But let us first agree to call the two members of each of the pairs of an isomorphism *similar* if and only if the isomorphism is internal and complete. Two fields connected by such an isomorphism obviously are similar in a sense in which two fields connected by an ordinary isomorphism, i.e., one which is either external or partial or both, are not similar. The use needs no special justification. Speaking as we ordinarily do, we all might use 'similar' in this way. Such uses, just because they need no special justification, sometimes provide cues to structural connections.

As Stenius and I use the word, (*a*) a *thought* is a mental entity and (*b*) two acts have the same intention if and only if they contain the "same" thought. (*b*) leaves two alternatives. (*b* 1) A thought is a universal. In this case acts with the same intention literally share a constituent (and the quotation marks in [*b*] can be dropped). (*b* 2) A thought is a momentary fact and two such facts are the "same" thought if and only if "they have something in common." In this case the thought individuates the act. Even in this case, though, an act must be more than its thought; otherwise its species could not be accounted for.

According to Stenius, a thought is a mental fact (*b* 2).[35] Also, *a thought and its intention are similar*. The emphasis on their similar-

---

[35] My gambit is (b 1). See n. 41.

ity dominates the book. The answer to the question what two mental facts "have in common" if they are the "same" thought is immediate. Being both similar to their common intention, they are also similar to each other.

Why should a thought and its intention be similar? If thoughts are facts, why won't an ordinary isomorphism do? If I have not been too clumsy, the answer should not come as a surprise. 'Similar' is the cue. *Our ideas are similar to what they are the ideas of.* Stenius' thesis is but the latest variant, and a most up-to-date variant it is, of that old gambit with which those who followed the way of ideas tried to provide a substitute for the connection between minds and their intentions that was lost when the abstraction theory fell. That is why I called that page the key to the book. It is of course also the reason why I find the mistake so extraordinarily illuminating. But, then, this mistake, the innovation or correction, concerns sentences, not thoughts. So we must check how things hang together.

Take perception. There is P, the fact perceived. There is $T(P)$, the thought intending P. There is $N(P)$, a fact caused by P in the body of the perceiver while he perceives P; and there is the sentence 'P'. Stenius clearly distinguishes between these four entities, P, $T(P)$, $N(P)$, 'P'. Nor does he blur the distinction between $T(P)$ and $T('P')$. As things now stand, alas, that alone makes him one of a distinguished minority. On the other hand, he seems to take it for granted[36] that the four entities are all similar among each other. That makes similarity the single idea behind his answers to the three questions with which I started. (1) 'P' can be made to represent P because the two are similar. (2) $T(P)$ and P are similar; that is the connection between a thought and the fact it intends. (3) 'P' can be used to express $T(P)$ because the two are similar. I should like to make two comments.

First. If (1) thoughts are facts and (2) similar to their intentions, then (3) all intentions are facts. I agree emphatically with (3). *Awareness is propositional.* I also believe that the insight is crucial. That makes it important to realize that while (1) follows from (2) and (3), it does not follow from (3) alone.

Second. Consider the following three propositions. (1) Conscious

36 Here I state what Stenius barely hints or merely suggests.

states[37] are mental facts. (2) Bodily and conscious states, e.g., a bodily state containing $N(P)$ and a conscious state containing $T(P)$, so correspond to each other that the "same" bodily state always goes with the "same" mental state. (3) $N(P)$ is similar to P. Or, less strongly, (3') $N(P)$ is isomorphic to P. The point I wish to make is that (1), (2), (3') do not jointly imply that $T(P)$ is a fact. Nor do (1), (2), (3) jointly imply that $T(P)$ is a fact similar to P. Stenius neither makes nor suggests either inference. Even so, the point may be worth making.

I turn to Wittgenstein.

The only passage in the *Tractatus* that deals interestingly and analytically even though most puzzlingly with mind is 5.542. To it I shall presently attend. Certain aphoristic passages toward the end, they have also been called "mystical," I shall not even cite. Some are solipsistic. In others the mind hovers outside the world. In the *Tractatus* world minds either (1) do not exist, or, less strongly, (2) their ontological status remains hopelessly blurred. I am prepared to assert (1). In the light of the philosophical behaviorism (materialism), or nearbehaviorism, or behaviorism with a bad intellectual conscience, if you please, of the *Philosophical Investigations*, (1) is plausible, to say the least. For what really interests me, (2) will do. This weaker assertion needs no defense. Whether (1) or (2), the unresolved tension is unmistakable. The "mysticism" is merely its symptom.[38] The tension is caused by an intellectual impasse. What is this impasse? That is the question which really interests me.

Whether or not Wittgenstein ended as a materialist, with or without the saving grace of a bad intellectual conscience, he did not, I believe, start as one. Rather, *he thought of mind exactly as Stenius does,* in the classical empiricist pattern. If so, that key page of Stenius clears up the fundamental blur. That makes it not, to be sure,

---

[37] I say "conscious states" rather than "acts" because on the one hand some conscious states contain more than just one act while, on the other, the conscious state one is in when sensing something, even though a fact, does not contain an act. Sensing is an act, but this act is not a part of that state.

[38] Some philosophies are analytical; some, mystical. In some analytical philosophers, mysticism so-called is a personality trait which under the strain of unresolved intellectual tensions at certain points appears in their philosophy. This I believe is Wittgenstein's case. If so, then one must not make too much of his so-called mysticism when discussing his philosophy.

a correction, but a clarification as admirable as it is important. But, then, if Wittgenstein had these thoughts, why didn't he express them? If he saw the way, why didn't he take it? I do believe that the author of the *Tractatus* was, however chaotically, a great philosopher. That determines my answer. He at least felt that this way was an impasse. *Similarity, either in the classical style or à la Stenius, does not really connect minds with their intentions.* That is the impasse. Wittgenstein never found the way out. As long as one hasn't found it, the only alternatives are either idealism or materialism or, alas, the agony of unresolved intellectual tension.

Before turning to 5.542 we must recall the linguistic phenomenon of intentionality. Let '*P*', '*Q*', (*a*) '. . . *P* . . .', (*b*) '. . . *Q* . . .' be four sentences. (*a*) contains '*P*'; (*b*) is obtained from (*a*) by replacing at least one occurrence of '*P*' by '*Q*'. The context is *extensional* if and only if, provided (*c*) '*P* if and only if *Q*' represents a fact, (*a*) and (*b*) either both represent facts or both represent P-facts. Let now (*d*) 'the-thought-*P*' and (*e*) 'the-sentence-*P*' represent the thought which intends *P* and the sentence which represents *P*, respectively. In other words, (*f*) 'The-thought-*P* *means* (intends) *P*' and (*g*) 'The-sentence-*P* *means* (represents) *P*' both represent facts. In a systematically constructed language neither (*d*) nor (*e*) would contain '*P*'. We acknowledge that by making '*P*' in (*d*) and (*e*) unavailable for replacement, marking this unavailability by the hyphens. Replace now in (*f*) and (*g*) the single available occurrence of '*P*' by '*Q*'. The result is (*f'*) 'The-thought-*P* means (intends) *Q*' and (*g'*) 'The-sentence-*P* means (represents) *Q*'. There is a commonsensical use of 'means', call it the intentional use, upon which (*f'*) and (*g'*) both represent P-facts, not only if (*c*) represents a fact but even if (*c*) represents a necessary$_2$ fact. It follows that the contexts (*f*) and (*g*) are *intentional* (nonextensional). Notice, too, that if used as in (*f*) and (*g*), 'means' is synonymous with 'intends' and 'represents', respectively.

Es ist aber klar, dass "A glaubt, dass p," "A denkt p," "A sagt p" von der Form " 'p' sagt p" sind: Und hier handelt es sich nicht um eine Zuordnung von einer Tatsache und einem Gegenstand, sondern um die Zuordnung von Tatsachen durch Zuordnung ihrer Gegenstaende.

I shall make four comments. *One*. If it is asserted that '*A* believes *P*', '*A* thinks *P*', and so on, are synonymous with (*h*) ' '*P*' says *P*', then the species has once more been lost. *Two*. 'Says' in (*h*) is vague. Neither a thought nor a sentence literally says anything. The expression preceding 'says' in (*h*) represents either a thought or a Sentence.[39] If it represents a thought, then 'says' stands for 'intends' and (*h*) is (*f*). If it represents a sentence, then 'says' stands for 'represents' and (*h*) is (*g*). If (*h*) is (*g*), then something mental in, say, '*A* believes *P*' has been replaced by something physical. That is, or would be, the decisive step toward materialism.[40] *Three*. A language is extensional if and only if all its contexts are extensional. There is no doubt whatsoever that, according to the *Tractatus*, everything that can be said at all can be said in an extensional language. Both (*f*) and (*g*) are intentional. So therefore is (*h*). It follows that (*h*) cannot really be said. Hence, we cannot really say that *A* believes something, thinks something, and so on. Mind, like logical form, is ineffable. Logical form is nothing. Does it follow that mind is nothing? It is all very confused and confusing. I would not argue that anything follows from anything in that confusion. But it can be argued, I think, that the later materialism or near-materialism has something to do with this very confusion. *Four*. The second sentence of 5.542, after the colon, supports what has been said about Stenius' clarification. Stenius' idea, the classical empiricist idea, is there, implicitly if you insist, yet unmistakably. Thus, if Wittgenstein did not make it more explicit, he probably had his reasons.

In Stenius' world there are thoughts which are unequivocally mental. In his world therefore, as in mine, there are minds. The agreement is basic. In his world a thought is a fact similar to its intention; in mine it is a simple character connected with its intention by a fundamental tie that subsists. The disagreement is hardly less weighty.[41] To argue it out would require another paper as long as this one, which is long enough as it is. All I shall do therefore is

---

[39] If it represents a Sentence, then (*h*) is a blurred mixture of (*f*) and (*g*).

[40] Believing and thinking are acts; saying is not an act. The parallel listing of the three shows that the later materialism is here foreshadowed, to say the least.

[41] See n. 35.

once more identify the issues. That requires two paragraphs about my own philosophy of mind.

I assay an act as an individual exemplifying two simple nonrelational characters. An act thus is a fact. The individual in it, like all others, is momentary and bare. One of the two characters is the act's species; the other, its thought. The fundamental tie connecting the latter with its intention I call the intentional or meaning nexus. In language it is represented by 'means' as used in (f) and (g).[42] The two characters account for the act's species and intention. The sole function of the individual, as of all individuals, is to individuate. Thus the three dimensions of an act are all accounted for. Nor can I think of a simpler way to do the job.

For this to be to the left of that, that must be there. A universal thing (e.g., to-the-left-of) cannot be exemplified by a thing (or fact) that exists only in the mode of possibility. 'P or Q', on the other hand, represents a fact even if one of the complexes represented by 'P' and 'Q' is a P-fact. A fundamental tie (e.g., or) can combine a fact (or thing) and a P-fact into a fact. That is another striking difference between subsistents on the one hand and things or facts on the other. Remember now the modest sound core of skepticism. (f), 'The-thought-P means P', does not imply 'P'. In each case of mistaken belief or memory, or of erroneous perception, the-thought-P exists; (f) represents a fact; 'P', a P-fact. Hence, if there is an entity connecting thoughts with their intentions, it cannot be a thing; it must be a subsistent. But, then, must there be such an entity? Since I merely promised to identify the issues, I shall say no more than that I know no other way of keeping minds and their intentions from falling apart.

Stenius, we saw, has two basic ideas. (S) Sentence and fact are similar; that is how the former manages to represent the latter. (T) Thought and fact are similar; that is how the former manages to mean the latter. I rejected S, yet called it an answer since what I believe to be the right answer can be obtained from it by two "corrections." The three subsistents I call individuality, universality, and exemplification exist. For atomic facts, to which I limited the argu-

---

[42] The use in (f) is primary, the one in (g) secondary, just as 'true' and 'false' apply primarily to thoughts, only secondarily to the sentences representing their intentions as well as to the acts (e.g., beliefs) containing them.

ment, that is the first correction. It removes the intellectual motive for requiring similarity. The second correction replaces this requirement by the weaker one of an ordinary isomorphism.

Is *T* an answer in the sense in which *S* is one? If I am right, one correction is indispensable. The subsistent I call the intentional tie exists. As with *S*, that removes the intellectual motive for requiring similarity rather than merely an ordinary isomorphism. Clearly, this correction and the first correction of *S* have the same root. All subsistents exist. That spots one of the two basic disagreements between Stenius and myself. For exemplification at least, I have here argued my side.

If the intentional tie exists, must thoughts be simple characters rather than facts isomorphic to their intentions? If, as I hold, a thought is a simple, then of course the intentional tie connects it with the fact it intends. But if, as Stenius holds, a thought is a fact, why shouldn't the intentional tie connect each constituent of the fact the thought means with one constituent of the thought itself? That spots the other basic disagreement between Stenius and myself. This one I said I wouldn't argue. So I conclude with a question. If one recognizes that the intentional tie exists, what intellectual motive could he possibly have for insisting on even an ordinary isomorphism between thought and fact?

4

Naming and Saying

WILFRID SELLARS

This chapter adopts the Tractarian view that configurations of objects are expressed by configurations of names. Two alternatives are considered: the objects in atomic facts are (1) without exception *particulars;* (2) one or more particulars plus a *universal* (Gustav Bergmann). On (1), a mode of configuration is always on empirical relation: on (2), it is the logical nexus of 'exemplification'. It is argued that (1) is both Wittgenstein's view in the *Tractatus* and correct. It is also argued that exemplification is a "quasi-semantical" relation, and that it (and universals) are "in the world" only in that broad sense in which the "world" includes linguistic norms and roles viewed (thus in translating) from the standpoint of a fellow participant.

I

THE topics I am about to discuss have their roots in Wittgenstein's *Tractatus.* My point of departure will be Professor Irving Copi's paper on "Objects, Properties and Relations in the *Tractatus*"[1] in which, after a decisive critique of certain misinterpretations of Wittgenstein's so-called picture theory

Reprinted with the kind permission of the author and the editor from *Philosophy of Science*, 29 (1962): 7–26.

[1] *Mind,* 67 (1958).

of meaning with particular reference to relational statements, he proceeds to attribute to Wittgenstein, on the basis of a by no means implausible interpretation of certain texts, a puzzling construction of Wittgenstein's objects as "bare particulars."[2]

I shall not waste time by formulating the misinterpretations in question and summarizing Copi's admirably lucid critique. For my concern is with the theory of relational statements as pictures which, in my opinion, he correctly attributes to Wittgenstein, and, specifically, with the power of this theory to illuminate traditional philosophical puzzles concerning predication generally.

The crucial passage, of course, is 3.1432, "We must not say: 'The complex sign "aRb" says "a stands in the relation R to b"'; but we must say, '*That* "a" stands in a certain relation to "b" says *that* aRb'." Part of Wittgenstein's point is that though names and statements are both complex in their empirical character as instances of sign designs, and hence, from this point of view, are equally *facts*, the fact that a name consists (in various ways) of related parts is not relevant to its character as name in the way in which the division of such a statement as (schematically)

$$aRb$$

into just the parts of 'a', 'R', and 'b' is to its character as making the statement it does. The latter parts are themselves functioning (though not in the same way) as signs, whereas no part of a name is functioning as a sign. But the crucial point that Wittgenstein is making emerges when we ask, "What are the parts of the statement in question the relation of which to one another is essential to its character as statement?" For in spite of the fact that the obvious answer would seem to be "the *three* expressions 'a', 'R', and 'b'," this answer is incorrect. 'R' is, indeed, functioning in a broad sense as a sign and is certainly involved in the statement's saying what it does, but it is involved, according to Wittgenstein, in quite a different way than the signs 'a' and 'b'. To say that 'R' is functioning as a predicate, whereas 'a' and 'b' are functioning as names, is to *locate* the difference but to remain open to perplexity. What Wittgenstein tells us is that while superficially regarded the statement is a con-

2 Ibid., p. 163.

notation of the three parts '*a*', '*R*', and '*b*', viewed more profoundly it is a two-termed fact, with '*R*' coming into the statement as bringing it about that the expressions '*a*' and '*b*' are dyadically related in a certain way, i.e., as bringing it about that the expressions '*a*' and '*b*' are related as having an '*R*' between them. And he is making the point that what is essential to any statement which will say that *aRb* is not that the names '*a*' and '*b*' have a relation word between them (or before them or in any other relation to them), but that these names be related (dyadically) *in some way or other* whether or not this involves the use of a third sign design. Indeed, he is telling us that it is philosophically clarifying to recognize that instead of expressing the proposition that *a* is next to *b* by writing 'is next to' between '*a*' *and* '*b*', we could write '*a*' in some relation to '*b*' using only these signs. In a perspicuous language this is what we would do. Suppose that the Jumblies have such a language. It contains no relation words but has the same name expressions as our tidied-up English. Then we could translate Jumblese into English by making such statements as

$$\begin{matrix} \text{`a'} \\ \text{b} \end{matrix} \text{ (in Jumblese) means } a \text{ is next to } b$$

and be on our way to philosophical clarification. Of particular interest in this connection would be the Jumblese translation of *Appearance and Reality*.

It will be noticed that I have correlated the fact that in '*aRb*' the '*R*' plays the predicate role with the fact that in Jumblese the proposition expressed by '*aRb*' would be expressed by relating the two names without the use of a predicate expression. Now in Frege's system, '*R*' would be said to stand for (*bedeuten*) a concept, whereas '*a*' and '*b*' stand for objects. Thus what Wittgenstein puts by saying that configurations of objects are represented by configurations of names (3.21)—so that Jumblese $\begin{smallmatrix} \text{a} \\ \text{b} \end{smallmatrix}$ and PMese '*aRb*' are equally configurations of two names, though the latter is not perspicuously so —could also be put by saying that to represent that certain objects satisfy an *n*-adic concept, one makes their names satisfy an *n*-adic concept.[3] Roughly, Wittgenstein's configurations are the counter-

---

[3] *Which n*-adic concept the names are made to satisfy is, of course, as philosophers use the term, a matter of convention.

parts of a subset of Frege's concepts, and Wittgenstein is taking issue with Frege by insisting that perspicuous language would contain no concept words functioning predicatively, that is to say, as '*R*' functions when we say that *aRb*. How a perspicuous language would do the job done by concept words in their nonpredicative use is something on which Wittgenstein throws less light, though his sketchy treatment of the parallel problem of how a perspicuous language would handle belief statements in which, according to Frege, the *Bedeutung* of the subordinate clause is what would ordinarily be its sense, gives some clue to the answer.

Now the above remarks adumbrate many topics of importance for ontology and the philosophy of logic. Some of them I shall pick up at a later stage in the argument. For the moment, however, I shall concentrate on the question, "What sort of thing are Wittgenstein's objects?" And the first thing I shall say is that in my opinion Copi is undoubtedly right in insisting that Wittgenstein's objects are particulars. To put the same point in a somewhat different way, Wittgenstein's names are names of particulars. This is not to say, of course, that expressions which function in unperspicuous languages in a superficially name-like way, but do not name particulars, are meaningless. It is simply to say that they would not translate into the names of a perspicuous language. Roughly, unperspicuous name-like expressions fall into two categories for Wittgenstein: (1) those which would translate into a perspicuous language as, on Russell's theory of descriptions, statements involving descriptive phrases translate into unique existentials (compare Wittgenstein's treatment of complexes in 3.24); (2)—which is more interesting—those which would not translate at all into that part of a perspicuous language which is used to make statements about what is or is not the case in the world. It is the latter which are in a special sense without meaning, though not in any ordinary sense meaningless. The "objects" or "individuals" or "logical subjects" they mention are pseudo-objects in that to "mention them" is to call attention to those features of discourse about what is or is not the case in the world which "show themselves," i.e., are present in a perspicuous language not as words, but in the manner in which words are combined.[4] Thus it is per-

---

[4] One is reminded of the peculiar objects which, according to Frege, one talks about when one attempts to talk about concepts.

fectly legitimate to say that there are "objects" other than particulars, and to make statements about them. These objects (complexes aside) are not in the world, however, nor do statements about them tell us how things stand in the world. In Wittgenstein's terminology no statements about such objects are "pictures," and, therefore, in the sense in which pictures have sense they are without sense.

Now one can conceive of a philosopher who agrees with Wittgenstein that in a perspicuous language the fact that two objects stand in a dyadic relation would be represented by making their names stand in a dyadic relation, but who rejects the idea that the only objects or individuals *in the world* are particulars. Such a philosopher might distinguish, for example, within the fact that a certain sense-datum (supposing there to be such entities) is green, between two objects, a *particular* of which the name might be '*a*', and an item which, though equally an *object* or *individual*, is not a *particular*. Let us suppose that the name of this object is 'green'.[5] Let us say that green is a universal rather than a particular, and that among universals it is a quality rather than a relation. According to this philosopher,[6] the perspicuous way of saying that *a* is green (abstracting from problems pertaining to temporal reference) is by putting the two names '*a*' and 'green' in some relation, the same relation in which we would put '*b*' and 'red' if we wished to say that *b* is red. Let us suppose that we write 'Green *a*.'

Our previous discussion suggests the question: What would be the *unperspicuous* way of saying what is said by 'Green *a*', i.e., which would stand to 'Green *a*' as, on Wittgenstein's view '*aRb*' stands to, say, '$_b^a$'? The philosopher I have in mind proposes the following answer:

a exemplifies green.

And this is not unexpected, for where, as in this case, two objects are involved, what is needed for the purpose of *un*perspicuity is a two-place predicate which is appropriately concatinated with the

---

[5] I shall subsequently discuss the dangers involved in the use of color examples with particular reference to the interpretation of color words as names.

[6] The philosopher I have in mind is Professor Gustav Bergmann, and the views I am discussing are those to be found, I believe, in certain passages of his interesting paper on "Ineffability, Ontology and Method" which appeared in the January, 1960, number of the *Philosophical Review* and is reprinted in this volume.

name of a particular on one side and the name of a universal on the other, and this is one of the jobs we philosophers pay 'exemplifies' to do. Thus this philosopher would be saying that as on Wittgenstein's view the perspicuous way of saying that *a* is next to *b* is by writing '*a*' in some relation to '*b*', so the perspicuous way of saying that *a* exemplifies green is by writing '*a*' in some relation to 'green'. Having thus made use of Wittgenstein's ladder, he would climb off onto his own pinnacle. For he must claim that Wittgenstein made a profound point with the wrong examples. He must, in short, deny that the perspicuous way of saying that *a* is next to *b* is by writing '*a*' in some relation to '*b*'. That this is so is readily seen from the following considerations.

Exemplification is not the sort of thing that philosophers would ordinarily call an empirical relation. This title is usually reserved for such relations as spatial juxtaposition and temporal succession. Yet exemplification might well be an—or perhaps *the*—empirical relation[7] in a more profound sense than is usually recognized, as would be the case if the simplest atomic facts in the world were of the kind *perspicuously* represented by 'Green *a*' and *unperspicuously* represented by '*a* exemplifies green'.

For let us see what happens to what we ordinarily refer to as empirical relations if relational statements are approached in a manner consistent with the above treatment of '*a* is green'. According to the latter, the fact that *a* is green is perspicuously represented by the juxtaposition of two names, '*a*' and 'green', and unperspicuously represented by a sentence which contains three expressions, two of which are names, while the third, which might be taken by unperceptive philosophers to be a third *name*, actually serves the purpose of bringing it about that a distinctive dyadic relation obtains between the names. It is clear, then, that the parallel treatment of '*a* is below *b*' would claim that it is perspicuously represented by a suitable juxtaposition of *three* names, '*a*', '*b*', and 'below', thus,

Below *a b*

and unperspicuously represented by a sentence which uses *four* expressions, thus, perhaps

[7] Ibid., p. 23, n. 2.

Exempl[8] *a b* below.

I will comment later on the interpretation of 'below' as a name, and on the fact that it is prima facie less plausible than the similar move with respect to 'green'. I should, however, preface the following remarks by saying that I share with Professor Bergmann the sentiment which might be expressed by saying that ordinary grammar is the paper money of wise men but the gold of fools. For my immediate purpose is to contrast the Tractarian theory of predication with that of Professor Bergmann, who, though he decidedly prefers Saul to Paul, is by no means an orthodox exponent of the Old Testament; and I regard the point as of great philosophical significance.

According to the *Tractatus*, then, the fact that *a* is below *b* is *perspicuously* represented by an expression consisting of *two* names dyadically related, and *unperspicuously* represented by an expression containing, in addition to these two names, a two-place predicate expression. According to Professor Bergmann, if I understand him correctly, such facts as that *a* is below *b* are perspicuously represented by expressions consisting of *three* names triadically related, and unperspicuously represented by an expression containing, in addition to these three names (suitably punctuated), an expression having the force of 'exemplifies'. What exactly does this difference amount to? And which view is closer to the truth?

To take up the first question first, the difference can be reformulated in such a way as to bring out its kinship with the old issue between realists and nominalists. Wittgenstein is telling us that the only objects in the world are particulars; Bergmann is telling us that the world includes as objects both particulars and universals. Bergmann, of course, has his own razor and in his own way gives the world a close shave, but not quite as close as does Wittgenstein. Another way of putting the difference is by saying that whereas for Wittgenstein (Saul) it is *empirical* relations in the world that are perspicuously expressed by relating the names of their relata, for Bergmann empirical relations appear in discourse about the world as

---

[8] I use this way of putting the matter to make the point with minimum fuss and feathers. It is worth reflecting, however, that the grammatical parallel to '*a* exemplifies green' would be either '*a* exemplifies being below *b*' or '*a* and *b* jointly exemplify below-ness (the relation of one thing being below another)'.

nominata, and it is *exemplification* and *only* exemplification which is perspicuously expressed by relating the names of its relata.

To clarify the latter way of putting the matter, some terminological remarks are in order. If we so use the term 'relation' that to say of something that it is a relation is to say that it is perspicuously represented in discourse by a configuration of expressions rather than by the use of a separate expression, then for Bergmann there is, refinements aside, only *one* relation, i.e., exemplification,[9] and what are ordinarily said to be relations, for example *below,* would occur in the world as *relata.* Thus if we were to continue to use the term 'relation' in such a way that *below* would be a relation, then exemplification, as construed by Bergmann, would not be a relation. For although, as he sees it, both *below* and exemplification are in the world, the former appears in discourse as a nominatum, whereas exemplification does not, indeed *can* not.

To keep matters straight, it will be useful to introduce the term 'nexus' in such a way that to say of something that it is a nexus is to say that it is perspicuously represented in discourse by a configuration of expressions rather than by a separate expression. If we do this, we can contrast Bergmann and Wittgenstein as follows:

> *Wittgenstein:* There are many *nexūs* in the world. Simple relations of matter of fact are nexus. All objects or individuals which form a nexus are particulars, i.e., individuals of type O. There is no relation or nexus of exemplification in the world.
>
> *Bergmann:* There is only one[10] nexus, exemplification. Every atomic state of affairs contains at least one (and, if the thesis of elementarism be true, at most one) individual which is not a particular.

If one so uses the term 'ineffable' that to eff something is to signify it by using a name, then Wittgenstein's view would be that what are ordinarily called relations are ineffable, for they are nexus and are expressed (whether perspicuously or not) by configurations of names. For Bergmann, on the other hand, what are ordinarily called relations are effed; it is exemplification which is ineffable.

---

[9] Strictly speaking, there would be a relation of exemplification for each order of fact, and, on nonelementaristic views, a family of such relations for each type.

[10] See n. 9.

Before attempting to evaluate these contrasting positions, let us beat about the neighboring bushes. And for a start, let us notice that Wittgenstein tells us that atomic facts are configurations of objects, thus

2.0272 The configuration of the objects forms the atomic fact.

The question I wish to raise is how strictly we are to interpret the plural of the word 'object' in this context. Specifically, could there be a configuration of one object? It must be granted that an affirmative answer would sound odd. But, then, it sounds odd to speak of drawing a conclusion from a null class of premises. Philosophers of a "reconstructionist" bent have often found it clarifying to treat one thing as a "limiting case" of another; and if Russell, for one, was willing to speak of a quality as a monadic relation, there is no great initial improbability to the idea that Wittgenstein might be willing to speak of a monadic configuration.

Would he be willing to do so? The question is an important one and calls for a careful examination of the text. I do not think that 2.0272, taken by itself, throws much light on the matter. Yet when it is taken together with such passages as

2.031 In the atomic fact the objects are combined in a definite way.
2.03   In the atomic fact objects hang in one another like the members of a chain.

which are accompanied by no hint that there might be monadic "combinations" or, so to speak, chains with a single link, the cumulative effect is to buttress the thesis that there is no provision in the *Tractatus* for monadic atomic facts.

Yet at first sight, at least, this would not seem to be inevitable. After all, one who says that the fact that *a* is below *b* would be perspicuously represented by an expression in which the name '*a*' stands in a dyadic relation (to '*b*') might be expected to say that the fact that *a* is green would be perspicuously represented by an expression in which the name '*a*' stands in a monadic relation, i.e., in a more usual way of speaking, is of a certain quality. Thus one can imagine a philosopher who says that in a perspicuous language, monadic atomic facts would be represented by writing the name of the single object they contain in various colors or in various styles of type. The idea is a familiar one. Is there any reason to suppose that it was not available to Wittgenstein?

One line of thought might be that in such a symbolism we could not distinguish between a name and a statement. After all, a name has to be written in some style or other, and, if so, would not every occurrence of a name, in this hypothetical symbolism, have by virtue of its style the force of a statement, and therefore not be a name at all? This objection, however, overestimates the extent to which empirical similarities between expressions imply similarity of linguistic role. Obviously, writing '*a*' alongside '*b*' might be saying that *a* temporally precedes *b*, whereas an '*a*' below a '*b*' might have no meaning at all. Thus, to write '*a*' in boldface might be to say that *a* is green, whereas an '*a*' in ordinary type might function merely as a name. How this might be so will be discussed later on. My present point is simply that to understand expressions is to know which of the many facts about them (shape, size, color, etc.) are relevant (and in what way) to their meaning. It could surely be the case that in a perspicuous language the fact that a heap of ink was a token of a certain name was a matter of its being an instance of a certain letter of the alphabet written in one or another of a certain number of manners. But one or more of these manners might be, so to speak, "neutral" in that to write the name in such a manner would not be to make an assertion, but simply to write the name, whereas to write the name in other manners would be to make various assertions. Only, then, in the case of the non-"neutral" manners would the writing of the name be the assertion of a monadic fact.

Another line of thought would be to the effect that in a language in which monadic atomic facts (if such there be) were expressed by writing single names in various manners, there would be a difficulty about variables—not about variables ranging over particulars, for here the device of having special letters for variables could be used, but about variables such as would be the counterparts of the monadic predicate variables of *Principia* notation. Thus we could represent the sentential function '*x* is green' by using the variable '*x*' and writing it in boldface, thus

But how would one say of *a* that it was of some quality or other? What would correspond to '*a* is *f*' and '(E*f*) *a* is *f*' as '**x**' to '*x* is green' and '(E*x*) **x**' to (E*x*) *x* is green'? Would we not have to introduce an expression to be the variable—after all, one cannot write a manner by itself—and if one has separate variables to make possible the expression of what would be expressed in PMese by

$$(Ef)\ fa,\ (g)\ gb, \text{etc.}$$

i.e., variables other than those which range over *particulars*, would this not be, in effect, to treat the atomic propositions which are supposedly represented by, for example,

a

as involving two *constants*, and hence two *names?* Must not its truly perspicious representation be rather

Green *a*

as Bergmann claims?

Consider the following schema for translation from PMese into Jumblese:

PMese	*Jumblese*
I. *Names of particulars*	
a, b, c, . . .	The same letters written in a variety of neutral styles, the variety being a matter of height, the neutrality a matter of the use of the ordinary font: a, b, c, . . . ; a, b, c, . . . ; a, b, c, . . .

II. *Statements* (not including relational statements, which will be discussed shortly)

Green *a*, red *a*, . . .	a, *a*, . . .

III. *Statement functions*
 (1) *Predicate constant, individual variable;*

Green *x*, red *y*, . . .	x, *y*, . . .

(2) *Predicate variable, individual constant;*

fa, gb, . . .   Names in neutral styles (see I):

a, . . . ; a, . . . ; a, . . .

(3) *Predicate variable, individual variable;*

fx, gy, . . .   Name variables in neutral styles:

x, y, z, . . . ; x, y, z, . . . ; x, y, z, . . .

IV. *Quantification*

(E*x*) green *x*   (E*x*) x
(E*f*) *fa*, (E*g*) *ga*, . . .   (E⟨⟩) a, (E⟨⟩) a, . . .
(E*f*) (E*x*) *fx*, (E*g*) (E*x*) *gx*, . . . (E⟨⟩) (E*x*) x, (E⟨⟩) (E*x*) x, . . .

Notice that in the final samples of Jumblese, the ⟨-shaped symbols serve to represent a neutral style; *which* depends on its size.

It is to be noted that in this form of Jumblese, the neutral styles by virtue of which an expression functions as a name without making a statement is also the neutral style which is illustrated by the expressions serving as the counterparts of the predicate variables of PMese. It is therefore an interesting feature of this form of Jumblese that expressions which function as names but not as statements *have the form of a statement.* It is often said with reference to PMese that the form of a predicate is, for example,

Red *x*.

It is less frequently said that the form of a name is, for example,

fa.

In the variety of Jumblese sketched above, the latter would be as true as the former. (Cf. *Tractatus* 3.311.) This point clearly should be expanded to take account of the forms of relational statements, but I shall not attempt to do this, save by implication, on the present occasion.

Now the difficulty, if there is one, pertaining to predicate variables is not limited to predicate variables pertaining to these putative monadic atomic statements. If there were a point to be made along the above line, it would pertain as well to dyadic and polyadic statements as Wittgenstein interprets them. Thus, to continue with our translation schema, we have

PMese	*Jumblese*
Larger (ab), Redder (ab)	$^a_{\ b}$, $^a_{\ b}$
$R(ab)$, $S(ab)$, $T(ab)$, . . .	ab, a b, a b, . . .
Larger (xy), Redder (xy), . . .	$^x_{\ y}$, $^x_{\ y}$, . . .
$R(xy)$, $S(xy)$, . . .	xy, x y, x y, . . .
(Ex) (Ey) Larger (xy)	(Ex) (Ey) $^x_{\ y}$
(ER) $R(ab)$, (ES) $S(ab)$, . . .	$(E..)$ ab, $(E..)$ a b, . . .
(ER) (Ex) (Ey) $R(xy)$	$(E..)$ (Ex) (Ey) xy

Here again we find the introduction of symbols to be counterparts of the relation variables of PMese, i.e., symbols to illustrate the neutral manners which in

ab, a b, a b, a b, etc.

express what is expressed in PMese by the statement functions

$R(ab)$, $S(ab)$, $T(ab)$, etc.

Thus, in addition to the variables '(', '(', '(', . . . which correspond to the one-place predicate variables of *Principia*, we have the variables '..', '. .', '. .', . . . to correspond to the dyadic predicate variables of *Principia*.

The topic of perspicuousness with respect to variables and quantification is an interesting and important one in its own right, and the above remarks have barely scratched the surface. The only point I have wanted to make is that if considerations pertaining to quantification or to distinguishing between names and statements support the idea that the atomic statements of a perspicuous language must contain at least two names, these considerations would do so *not* by supporting the idea that a minimal atomic statement would contain the names of two *particulars*, but by supporting the idea that it would contain the name of a universal. In other words, they would point to Bergmann's form of logical atomism as contrasted with that of Wittgenstein.

Now I side with Wittgenstein on this matter, that is to say I would argue that the atomic descriptive statements of an ideal language would contain names of particulars only. As I see it, therefore, it is of crucial importance to ontology not to confuse the contrast between *constant* and *variable* with that between *name* and *variable*. For to confuse these two contrasts is to move from the correct idea that

$$\text{Green } a$$

can be viewed against the doubly quantified statement

$$(Ef) \ (Ex) \ fx$$

to the incorrect idea that

$$\text{Green } a$$

is the juxtaposition of two *names*, and says perspicuously what would be unperspicuously said by

$$a \text{ exemplifies green.}$$

To view the Jumblese statement

$$\mathbf{a}$$

against the doubly quantified statement

$$(E() \ (x) \ x$$

is, indeed, to highlight two facts about the expression 'a', the fact by virtue of which it is a writing in some style or other of a certain name, and the fact by virtue of which, to speak metaphorically, green comes into the picture. But I see no reason to infer that because the expression's being a case of a certain name, and the expression's pertaining to green are each bound up with a monadic (though not, of course, atomic) fact about the expression, that both its being about *a* and its being about green come into the picture in the same way, i.e., that they are both *named*.[11]

For the being about *a* and the being about green could each be

---

[11] For an earlier exploration of this point see my contribution to a symposium with P. F. Strawson on "Logical Subjects and Physical Objects" in *Philosophy and Phenomenological Research*, 17 (1957).

true of the expression by virtue of monadic facts about it and still not pertain to its meaning *in the same way* in any more important sense. The crucial thing about an expression is the role it plays in the language, and the fact that a certain expression is an '*a*' in some style or other and the fact that it is in boldface may both be monadic facts and yet play different roles in the language. In which connection it is relevant to note that the monadic fact about the expression by virtue of which it pertains to green is not the monadic fact that it is thick, but the monadic fact that it is a thick instance of a name or name variable.

II

Before continuing with the substantive argument of this paper, I shall say something more to the historical question as to whether Wittgenstein himself "countenanced" monadic atomic facts. I have argued that the passages in which he speaks of atomic facts as configurations of objects (in the plural) are not decisive, by pointing out that Russell might have spoken of atomic facts as related objects, but I have so used the term 'relation' that one could speak of monadic relations. It seems to me that similar considerations prevent such passages as

2.15 That the elements of the picture are combined with one another in a definite way represents that the things are so combined with one another.

3.21 To the configuration of the single signs in the propositional sign corresponds the configuration of the objects in the state of affairs.

from deciding the issue against the idea that an atomic proposition might contain only one name.

On one occasion Wittgenstein seems to me to come as close to saying that there are monadic atomic propositions as he could have come without saying it in so many words. Thus consider

4.24 The names are the simple symbols. I indicate them by single letters ('*x*', '*y*', '*z*').

The elementary proposition I write as function of the names, in the form 'fx', '$\phi(x,y)$', etc.

This passage is the more striking in that it occurs very shortly after

4.22 The elementary proposition consists of names. It is a connection, a concatenation of names.

Now to interpret 4.24 it is important to note that although Wittgenstein tells us that atomic facts to the effect that two objects are dyadically related would be perspicuously represented by placing the names of these objects in dyadic relation without the use of any relation word, the *Tractatus* contains no *use* but only *mentions* (and indirect ones at that) of such perspicuous representations. Thus Wittgenstein does not *use* Jumblese, but always PMese, in illustrating the form of atomic propositions, thus always 'aRb' (cf. the '$\phi(x,y)$' of 4.24). What he does do is to tell us that the symbol 'R' serves not as a name, but as a means of bringing it about that the names 'a' and 'b' are dyadically related.

This being so, Wittgenstein is telling us in 4.24 that when he uses an expression of the form 'fx' to write an elementary proposition, the function *word* represented by the 'f' is occurring not as a name, but as bringing it about that the name represented by 'x' occurs in a certain manner, i.e., that the name as occurring in a certain monadic configuration is a proposition.

Now if a philosopher combines the two theses, (1) there are no atomic facts involving only one particular and (2) all objects are particulars, it would be reasonable to say that he is committed to a doctrine of bare particulars. For, speaking informally, he holds that though objects stand in empirical relations, they have no qualities. Notice that this would not be true of Bergmann's position, for while he holds that there are no atomic facts containing only one *object*, he insists that there are atomic facts which contain only one *particular*. Thus he can deny that there are bare particulars by insisting that every object exemplifies a quality.

Now in my opinion Copi is correct in attributing to Wittgenstein the second of the above two theses (all objects are particulars). If, therefore, he were correct in attributing to Wittgenstein the first thesis, his claim that Wittgenstein is committed to a doctrine of bare particulars would be sound. Conversely, if Wittgenstein did hold a doctrine of bare particulars, then he was committed to the thesis that there are no monadic atomic facts. It is not surprising, therefore, to find Copi arguing that his contention that Wittgenstein rejects monadic atomic facts is supported by what he (somewhat reluctantly) takes to be an affirmation of the doctrine of bare particulars. Thus after confessing that "It must be admitted that several of Wittgenstein's remarks suggest that objects have 'external' properties as well as 'internal' ones (2.01231, 2.0233, 4.023)," he writes (p. 163):

> Despite the difficulty of dealing with such passages, there seems to me to be overwhelming evidence that he regarded objects as bare particulars, having no material properties whatever.
>
> In the first place, Wittgenstein explicitly denies that objects can have properties. His assertion that 'objects are colourless' (2.0232) must be understood as synechdochical, for the context makes it clear that he is not interested in denying colour qualities only, but all qualities of 'material properties' (the term first appears in the immediately preceding paragraph (2.0232).

Now I think that this is simply a misunderstanding. The correct interpretation of the passage in question requires only a careful reading of the context. What Wittgenstein says is, "Roughly speaking (*Beilauefig gesprochen*): objects are colourless," and this remark occurs as a comment on

2.0231 The substance of the world *can* only determine a form and not any material properties. For these are first presented by the propositions—first formed by the configuration of the objects.

What Wittgenstein is telling us here is that *objects* do not determine *facts:* thus even if *a* is green, the fact that *a* is green is not determined by *a*. It is interesting, in this connection, to reflect on

2.014 Objects contain the possibility of all states of affairs.

Thus, while *a* does not determine the fact that it is green, it does determine the range of possible facts of which the fact that it is green is but one.

Names exist in a logical space which includes the predicates which combine with it to make statements. (*In a perspicuous language—Jumblese—the predicate words, as has been pointed out, would appear as manners of being names, as, in a literal sense, internal features of the names.*) And no atomic statement is analytic, hence,

2.0132 In order to know an object, I must know not its external but its internal properties.

When Wittgenstein says that

2.0123 If I know an object, then I also know all the possibilities of its occurrence in atomic facts,

this is as much as to say that if I understand a name, then I also know all the possibilities of its occurrence in atomic statements. When he says

2.013 Everything is, as it were, in a space of possible atomic facts,

this is as much as to say that every name is, as it were, in a space of possible atomic statements.[12] And when he says

2.0131 . . . A speck in a visual field need not be red, but it must have a colour,

he is making the point that objects are internally related to sets of "external" properties, but not to any *one* "external" property, i.e., that names are internally related to sets of primitive predicates[13] (configurations; cf. Jumblese).

Thus it is not surprising to us (though disturbing to Copi) to find Wittgenstein saying in the passage following that in which he says that (roughly speaking) objects are colorless,

2.0233 Two objects of the same logical form are—apart from their external properties—only differentiated from one another in that they are different.

---

[12] When he adds that "I can think of this space as empty, but not of the thing without the space," he suggests the intriguing possibility that we can make sense of the idea that the language we use might have had no application.

[13] Whether these sets constitute embracing sets of primitive predicates of different orders or whether they fall into subsets (families of determinates) is a topic for separate investigation.

For this means *not*, as it might seem, that objects are *bare*, but simply that two objects of the same logical form[14] determine the same range of possible facts, i.e., two names of the same logical form belong to the same range of configurations.

As far as I can see, Copi's second argument to show that Wittgenstein's objects are bare particulars is also a misunderstanding. He begins by correctly pointing out that according to Wittgenstein objects are named, whereas states of affairs are "described"—the word is Wittgenstein's. He then writes (p. 164):

> . . . if an object *had* a property, that would be a fact whose assertion would constitute a *description* of that object. But objects can not be so described, whence it follows that objects have no properties.

This argument overlooks the fact that Wittgenstein, under the influence of logistical jargon, uses the term 'describe' where one would expect 'assert' (cf. 3.221). Thus he is simply telling us that objects cannot be "described," i.e., *asserted;* from which it by no means follows that they cannot be described in the ordinary sense. Indeed, in 4.023, Wittgenstein writes, "As the description of an object describes it by its external properties, so propositions describe reality by its internal properties."

The third argument has the form ". . . if an object had a material property, *that* it had the property would be a fact involving only one particular, hence no object can have any material property, and all particulars are bare" (p. 164). The hypothetical is sound. The evidence adduced for denying the consequent is 4.032 which is interpreted as saying that all propositional signs are composite, and must consequently contain at least two elements, that is, at least two names. But 4.032 does not say that all propositional signs are *composite,* but that they are all "logically articulate," and I have attempted to explain how a propositional sign can consist of *one logically articulated name.* I grant that in a parenthetical remark which immediately follows Wittgenstein writes, "(Even the proposition 'ambulo' is composite for its stem gives a different sense with

[14] I find here the implication that primitive one-place predicates (configurations)—if not all primitive predicates—come in families (determinates) and that objects are of different logical form if, for example, one exists in the logical space of color, the other in the logical space of sound.

another termination, or its termination with another stem)," but I do not believe that this remark, which correctly points out that ordinary Latin is not perspicuous with respect to logical articulation, is decisive. (I am happy to acknowledge that my interpretation, like Copi's, has its difficulties.)

Copi's concluding argument is to the effect that Wittgenstein tells us in the *Investigations* that the objects of the *Tractatus* were primary elements like those described in the *Theaetetus* (21e). This would be cogent if we were given a reason for supposing either that the elements of *Theaetetus* (21e) were bare particulars, or that Wittgenstein thought they were. I see no reason to think that either is the case.

The most telling argument in Copi's paper against the idea that the *Tractatus* countenanced monadic atomic facts is not used by Copi directly to this end, but as part of his brief for the sound thesis that Wittgenstein's objects are not properties. Slightly redirected, it is to the effect that if there are any monadic atomic facts, surely they include such facts as that a certain point in a visual field is red. But, the argument proceeds, if '*a* is red' is an elementary proposition, then '*a* is blue' cannot contradict it. But, as is well known, Wittgenstein tells us (6.3751) that "for two colours, e.g., to be at one place in the visual field, is impossible, logically impossible, for it is excluded by the logical structure of colour. . . . (It is clear that the logical product of two elementary propositions can neither be a tautology nor a contradiction.)" Copi draws the conclusion (p. 162) that "colour predications are *not* elementary predications."

Now, two points require to be made in this connection. The first is that one might be convinced that there *could* be monadic atomic facts (in that peculiar sense in which, for any *n* there could be *n*-adic atomic facts) without being able to give any examples. It is worth noting, in this connection, that in *Some Main Problems of Philosophy*, Moore, in effect, wonders whether there are any qualities (as opposed to relational properties), and specifically explores the logical space of colors to see if it provides us with examples of qualities. Moore was prepared to find that there are no qualities, i.e., that the simplest facts are already relational. True, Moore's qualitative facts would be Bergmannian rather than Wittgensteinian, that is, would each be a nexus of a particular *and a universal*, but the fact that Moore was prepared to suspend judgment with respect to the question "Are there qualities?" combined with the fact that he found the logical structure of color to be very complex indeed, suggests that Wittgenstein might well have taken a similar attitude. After all, as Anscombe points out, Wittgenstein regards it as in some sense a matter of fact that the most complex *atomic* fact is n-adic rather than m-adic $(m>n)$—cf. 4.2211. Could it not be in the same sense a matter of fact that the least complex is, say, dyadic rather than monadic?

Thus, *perhaps* the correct answer to the historical question is that Wittgenstein would have regarded the question "Are particulars bare?" as, in a deep sense, a factual one, a question to which he did not claim to have the answer, and to which, as logician, he was not required to have the answer. I regard this as most unlikely.

The second remark is that Wittgenstein may well have thought that there are monadic atomic facts, indeed that their existence is obvious, but that no statement in ordinary usage represented such a fact, so that no example could be given in the sense of written down. Although he thought that ordinary language contained elementary propositions, he emphasizes that they are contained in a way which is not perspicuous. There is no presupposition that any ordinary sentence as ordinarily used in the context of everyday life ever expresses an atomic proposition. Indeed, the presupposition is to the contrary.

III

It has been said by Broad, among others, that philosophers have been led into error in perception theory by concentrating their attention on visual examples. In my opinion they have been at least as frequently led into error in logical theory by a similar concentration on color. The danger arises from the fact that such a word as 'red', for example, is really three words, an adjective, a common noun, and a proper name, rolled into one. Thus we can say, with equal propriety,

> The book is red
> Scarlet is a color
> Red is a color.

A moment ago I urged the importance of the distinction between descriptive *constants* and *names*. I suggested that while it would be correct to say that the statement

Green a

consists of two *constants*, as is brought out by viewing it against the three quantified statements,

$$(\mathbf{E}x) \text{ Green } x$$
$$(\mathbf{E}f) \ fa$$
$$(\mathbf{E}f) \ (\mathbf{E}x) \ fx$$

it is most misleading to say that it consists of two names. And the reason, by now, should be clear. For if one does view the sentence 'Green *a*' as a juxtaposition of *names*, one will be bound, particularly if one has read the *Tractatus*, to think that by juxtaposing the names 'Green' and '*a*' it affirms that the two objects or individuals or logical subjects *green* and *a* are "united" or "hang in each other" or are bound together by a "characterizing tie" or whatever.

Now what makes this move all the more plausible is that there *is* an "object" *green* and that there *is* a "relation" which is often called exemplification such that if *a* is green *then it is also true that a exemplifies green*. Thus it is tempting indeed to say that

a exemplifies green

is simply an unperspicuous way of saying what is said perspicuously by

Green a.

And the fascinating thing about it is that this claim would be absolutely correct *provided that 'green a' was not taken to say what is ordinarily said by 'a is green'*.

The point stands out like a sore thumb if one leaves colors aside and uses a geometrical example. Thus consider the statement

a is triangular

or, for our purposes,

Triangular *a*.

It would clearly be odd to say

a exemplifies triangular

although it is not odd to say

a exemplifies green.

The reason is that 'triangular', unlike 'green', does not function in ordinary usage as both an adjective and a singular term. What we must say is

a exemplifies triangularity.

Now in a perspicuous language, i.e., a language which had a built-in protection against Bradley's puzzle, we might say *that a exemplifies triangularity* by concatenating '*a*' and 'triangularity' or *that Socrates exemplifies Wisdom* by writing

Socrates: Wisdom.

Our language is not such a perspicuous one, and to bring this out in this connection, we might write,

We must not say, "The complex sign '*a* exemplifies triangularity' says '*a* stands in the exemplification relation to triangularity'," but we must say "*that* '*a*' stands in a certain relation to 'triangularity' says that *a* exemplifies triangularity."

Thus it is correct to say that

Green *a*

says perspicuously what is said by

a exemplifies green

only if 'green' is used in the sense of the singular term 'greenness'. And when it is used in this sense, the statement

Green *a*

does not have the sense of the ordinary statement

a is green,

though it is logically equivalent to it.

Professor Bergmann thinks that

Green *a*

consists of two names, '*a*', the name of a particular, and 'green', the name of a universal, and, by being their juxtaposition, asserts that the one exemplifies the other. On his view, philosophers who insist that '*a* is green' says that *a* exemplifies green but do not realize that '*a* exemplifies green' is simply an unperspicuous way of juxtaposing '*a*' with 'green' are attempting to eff the ineffable. He thinks, to use the terminology I proposed earlier, that exemplification is the nexus, the mode of configuration of objects which can only be expressed by a configuration of names. Professor Bergmann sees configurations of particulars and universals where Wittgenstein saw only configurations of particulars.

But what does

a exemplifies triangularity

say if it is not an unperspicuous way of saying

Triangular *a*.

Instead of giving an answer (as I have attempted to do on other occasions) I shall attempt an analogy, and then claim that it is more than a mere analogy. It seems to me that the necessary equivalence but nonsynonymy of

a exemplifies triangularity

with

a is triangular

is analogous to the necessary equivalence but nonsynonymy of

That *a* is triangular is true

with

a is triangular.

That the analogy is more than a mere analogy is suggested by the fact that instead of saying that *a* exemplifies triangularity, we might with equality say that triangularity is true of *a*, or holds of *a*.

Now if

> *a* exemplifies triangularity
> triangularity is true of *a*
> triangularity holds of *a*

are to be elucidated in terms of

> That *a* is triangular is true

then exemplification is no more present in the world of fact in that narrow sense which tractarians like Professor Bergmann and myself find illuminating, than is meaning, or truth, *and for the same reason*.

The crucial ineffability in the *Tractatus* concerns the relation between statements and facts. Is there such a relation? And is it ineffable? The answer seems to me to be the following. There is a meaning relation between statements and *facts*, but both terms are in the linguistic order. To say that a statement means a fact is to say, for example,

'Gruen a' (in German) means *Green a*, and it is a fact that Green *a*.

The first conjunct appears to assert a relation between a linguistic and a nonlinguistic item, between a statement and an item in the real order. And the second conjunct to say of this item that it is a fact. As I see it, the first conjunct does assert a relation, but the relation obtains between a German expression and an English expression *as being an expression in our language*. It has the force of

'Gruen a' (in German) corresponds to 'Green *a*' in our language.

We could also put this by saying

> 'Gruen a' (in German) means *that green a*

for to put 'that' before a sentence has the force of quoting it with the implication that the sentence is in our language, and is being considered as such.[15] The reason why we find it counterintuitive to

---

[15] It is to form the name of the sense expressed in our langauge by the design which follows it.

put it in this way is that since 'means' is the translation rubric, this would conflict with the usage according to which we say

'Dass gruen a' (in German) means *that green a.*

Suppose it is granted that meaning is the translatability relation between an expression which may or may not be in our language and one which is, and is being considered as such. What, then, does it mean to say

That green *a* is a fact.

Clearly this is equivalent to saying

That green *a* is true

which calls to mind the equivalence

That green *a* is true = green *a*.

This, however, is not the most perspicuous way to represent matters, for while the equivalence obtains, indeed necessarily obtains, its truth depends on the principle of inference—and this is the crux—

From 'that green *a* is true' (in our language) to infer 'green *a*' (in our language).

And it is by virtue of the fact that we *draw* such inferences that meaning and truth talk gets its connection with the world. In this sense, the connection is *done* rather than *talked about.*

Viewed from this perspective, Wittgenstein's later conception of a language as a form of life is already foreshadowed by the ineffability thesis of the *Tractatus.* But to see this is to see that *no* ineffability is involved. For while to infer is neither to refer to that which can be referred to, nor to assert that which can be asserted, this does not mean that it is to fail to eff something which is, therefore, ineffable.

5

The Ontology of Wittgenstein's Tractatus

E. D. KLEMKE

THE *Tractatus logico-philosophi-cus* is one of the great wor..s in ontology and the philosophy of logic. Its aphoristic style makes it a difficult work to interpret, and as a result it has, I think, been grossly misinterpreted by some. For example, it has been construed as being primarily a treatise about language, a version of a phenomenalist sense-data philosophy, or a work concerned with finding a verifiability criterion of meaningfulness. Such interpretations are, I think, either erroneous or misleading. I do not deny that a substantial part of the book deals with language. But almost all of these passages are concerned with language in relation to the *world*. And in spite of certain passages toward the end, it seems clear that it is the world with which Wittgenstein is primarily concerned. Because of this, I wonder how anyone can fail to see that the *Tractatus* is chiefly a treatise of *metaphysics* and, in many ways, a work which falls within the great tradition of metaphysics throughout the history of philosophy.

Someone might object that Wittgenstein's own remarks at the end of the *Tractatus* refute a view such as I wish to maintain. I refer to the well-known passage in which he says that anyone who understands him must recognize the propositions of his book as being nonsensical. But one who interprets this passage with such intent fails to take into account all that Wittgenstein says in that passage. He says that his propositions are *elucidations* and that anyone who understands him must eventually recognize them as nonsensical "when he has used them—as steps—to climb up beyond them." And he adds: "He must transcend these propositions, and then he will *see the world aright*"[1] (6.54, my italics). Further evidence for my thesis may be found in two other works by Wittgenstein which were written shortly before the *Tractatus*. In *Notebooks, 1914–1916*, he says, "The great problem round which everything I write turns is: Is there an order in the world a priori, and if so what does it consist in?"[2] To be sure this is not a quotation directly from the *Tractatus*, but it does state the chief problem of the *Tractatus*. Again, in the *Notebooks*, he writes, "My work has stretched out from the foundations of logic to the essence of the world."[3] Finally in the "Notes on Logic," Wittgenstein says that philosophy "consists of logic and metaphysics, the former its basis."[4]

Within the *Tractatus*, the opening pages (1–2.063) are as explicitly ontological as anything can be. It seems to me that these sections cannot be considered as an intrusion or appendage, for the rest of the work is intimately connected with these passages. One must interpret the rest of the book in the light of these opening sections.

Wittgenstein begins by saying: "The world is all that is the case" (1). I agree with those who maintain that this must be intended as a universal statement regarding *any* world and not merely as an assertion about *this* world. If, as Wittgenstein said, his chief problem is whether or not there is an order in the world a priori, then this statement must be interpreted in the former way, for if it were one which pertained merely to this world, then it could conceivably be only a contingent statement about how, as a matter of fact, this world stands, and that it could be otherwise. Wittgenstein then adds, "The world is the totality of facts, not of things" (1.1). In 2 we are told that "what is the case—a fact—is the existing of states of affairs" (or atomic facts), and in 2.01 that "a state of affairs . . . is

---

[1] Ludwig Wittgenstein, *Tractatus logico-philosophicus*, trans. D. F. Pears and B. F. McGuinniss (London: Routledge & Kegan Paul, 1961). All numbers in parentheses refer to the section numbers of this book. Most quotations are from this translation, although I shall in my discussion sometimes use alternate translations of certain terms.

[2] Ludwig Wittgenstein, *Notebooks, 1914–1916*, ed. G. H. von Wright and G. E. M. Anscombe, trans. G. E. M. Anscombe (Oxford: Basil Blackwell, 1961), p. 53.

[3] Ibid., p. 79.

[4] Ludwig Wittgenstein, "Notes on Logic," in *Notebooks, 1914–1916*, p. 93.

a combination of objects" (or a "configuration" of objects [2.0231]).
Hence we may construe 1.1 as saying that the world (any world)
consists in or is composed of, not the totality of objects, but the
totality of configurations of objects. Wittgenstein adds, "The world
is determined by the facts, and by their being all the facts" (1.11).
I take Wittgenstein to mean that it is only when the *facts* have been
specified that the world is fully determined. That is, it cannot be so
determined by merely listing all the objects. We must also be given
information as to all of the *configurations* of objects which actually
obtain. Once this has been done, we determine not only what is the
case but also whatever is *not* the case (1.12).

Thus far we have been told that the world is composed of the
totality of facts, not of things. Wittgenstein goes on to say, "The
facts in logical space are the world" (1.13). Does this mean that
the world after all does not really consist in just facts, but in facts
plus something else, logical space? And if so, what is logical space?
Let me for a moment defer answering these questions and first
examine what Wittgenstein says about objects and states of affairs
(or atomic facts), especially with regard to their dependence or
independence. First, states of affairs: "Each item [fact] can be the
case or not while everything else remains the same" (1.21). That is,
each atomic fact exists independently of all others (2.061). "From
the existence or non-existence of one state of affairs it is impossible
to infer the existence or non-existence of others" (2.062). Nevertheless, there is a kind of dependence of states of affairs, in this sense:
"For the totality of facts determines what is the case, and also whatever is not the case" (1.12; cf. 2.05). That is, if we determine all of
the actual configurations into which objects enter, then we necessarily determine that they do not have some other configuration. For
example, suppose that there were a universe of only four objects, with
a configured with *b* and *c* with *d*. Then merely from the fact that *a* is
configured with *b*, we could not deduce that *c* is configured with *d*.
But if we know that *a* is configured with *b* and *c* with *d* and that
these are *all* the facts (1.11), then we may deduce that, say, *b* is not
configured with *c*. There is a similar duality of dependence and independence, or necessity and contingency, with regard to objects
(things). "It is essential to things that they should be possible constituents of states of affairs" (2.011). "If a thing *can* occur in a

state of affairs, the possibility of the state of affairs must be written into the thing itself" (2.012). This is an essential characteristic of objects. Not only may they occur in states of affairs, but they cannot *not* occur in any, in the sense that there cannot be objects which are incapable of being combined into configurations with other objects in atomic facts. Thus Wittgenstein says: "Things are independent insofar as they can occur in all *possible* situations, but this form of independence is a form of connexion with states of affairs, a form of dependence" (2.0122). That is, any given object (say, *a*) need not occur in some particular atomic fact (say, *ac*) and in that sense it is independent. But it must be *possible* for any such object to occur in some atomic facts, and in that sense it may be called dependent. This possibility is "part of the nature of the object" (2.0123). It is simply a matter of logic, and "in logic nothing is accidental" (2.012). That is, even though objects are such that it is logically possible for them to occur in any state of affairs, nevertheless logical possibility also involves a logical necessity in that the possibility of objects so occurring must be "in" objects "from the beginning" (2.0121). Thus "nothing in logic can be merely possible. Logic deals with every possibility and all possibilities are its facts" (2.0121). Since this possibility of being constituents of states of affairs is the essential nature of objects, it follows that, in order to know objects, we need only know all their possible occurrences in states of affairs (2.0123). We need not know whatever other characteristics they possess. Hence Wittgenstein says, "If I am to know an object, though I need not know its external properties, I must know all its internal properties" (2.01231), i.e., its possibilities of occurring in configurations or states of affairs. (I will return to this distinction between "external" and "internal" later.)

Let us now return to Wittgenstein's notion of logical space. He first says, "If all objects are given, then at the same time all *possible* states of affairs are also given" (2.0124). That is, if one could name every object in the universe, one could also express every possible configuration of all such objects. He continues: "Each thing is, as it were, in a space of possible states of affairs. This space I can imagine empty, but I cannot imagine the thing without the space" (2.013). This is, of course, stated abstractly without any indication thus far as to what objects (and states of affairs) are. In the next section, Wittgenstein presents what might be considered as examples. "A spatial object must be situated in infinite space. . . . A speck in the visual field, though it need not be red, must have some colour: it is, so to speak, surrounded by colour space. Tones must have *some* pitch, objects of the sense of touch *some* degree of hardness, and so on" (2.0131). These statements are very misleading. They make it appear that some objects are capable of having spatial properties, that some are colored, that others have pitch, etc. But it is clear from the sections beginning with 2.02 that Wittgensteinian objects cannot have any of these properties, as we shall see shortly. Hence the illustrations presented in 2.0131 cannot strictly be illustrations in the sense of examples; they can only be considered as analogies. To say that an object or fact occurs in logical space is something like saying that a visual patch must have some color. And so on for any other analogy.

In his able commentary on the *Tractatus*, Max Black has attempted to unpack the metaphor of logical space as follows:

> Objects are like the co-ordinates of empty positions in physical space, atomic facts are like the material points that sometimes occupy such positions. But just as talk about 'physical space' is a compendious way of referring to possibilities of spatial relation, so talk about 'logical space' proves to be a picturesque way of talking about the logical relations between objects and atomic facts.[5]

But it is difficult to consistently employ such analogies, and many problems arise in connection with them. Perhaps we can try to explicate the notion of logical space without them. Let us assume that the world contains only four objects, *a*, *b*, *c*, and *d*. Then there are various possible configurations which could obtain. If we express the configuration of one object with another by writing the name of the one following by the name of the other, then (assuming that a configuration must consist in at least two different objects) we may express these as: '*ab*', '*ac*', '*abc*', '*abcd*', etc. (I ignore the question as to whether the configuring relationship is asymmetrical.) And upon this basis, we have several possible worlds: one in which

[5] Max Black, *A Companion to Wittgenstein's "Tractatus"* (Ithaca: Cornell University Press, 1964), pp. 9–10. I am much indebted to certain sections of this work.

only *a* is configured with *b*, another in which *a* is configured with *b*, and *b* with *c*, and so on. To say then that an object exists in logical space or in a space of possible states of affairs is to say that all of these configurations of one object with another are logical possibilities and that any one of these single configurations or any set of them constitutes a logical possibility. The notion of things in logical space, then, simply comes down to this: *If* we had a language which contained names for all objects, then we would *not* be able to know a priori and state which objects are configured with others—that would be a contingent matter depending upon what the world actually consisted in, that is, which states of affairs, as a matter of fact, obtained. But we *would* be able to know a priori and express all *possible* configurations of objects, both those which do obtain and those which do not. Knowing which obtain would be a matter of extra-logical knowledge—if such were possible at all. But knowing all the possibilities for configurations is a matter of logic.

Let us return now to the question which I asked earlier. In 1.1, Wittgenstein says that the world is the totality of facts and not of things. In 1.13, he says that the (atomic) facts in logical space are the world. Do we have here two different conceptions of the world, the first where the world consists only of facts and the second where it consists of facts plus logical space? Let us return to our model universe, consisting of objects *a*, *b*, *c*, and *d*, and let us assume that the only atomic fact is *a* configured with *b*. Then if the world is all that is the case, the totality of facts (1–1.1), and if what is the case, a fact, is the *existence* of states of affairs (2), then the world consists in *a*'s being configured with *b*, and that alone. But the totality of facts determines not only what is the case, but also what is not the case (1.12). However, this determination would not be possible solely on the basis of determining which states of affairs obtain. Knowing only that *ab* obtains would not enable us to know whether *cd* obtains. The only way by which we could know this is by knowing (or having "given") all objects. Then we could determine not only which atomic facts hold but all possible states of affairs. Hence, in one sense, the world consists only in all those atomic facts which obtain. But in another sense, it consists in the totality of objects in logical space. In this latter sense, the world includes not only existent states of affairs, but also those which do not exist. Hence, Wittgenstein later says "the totality of existing states of affairs in the world" (2.04). But "the totality of existing states of affairs also determines which states of affairs do not exist" (2.05). Wittgenstein calls the former "positive facts" and the latter "negative facts" (2.06). Hence we may say that "the existence and nonexistence of states of affairs is reality" (2.06).

Now this may *appear* to solve our problem. One might argue that the world consists only in positive facts, the totality of existing states of affairs, whereas reality consists in both positive and negative facts, the totality of existing and nonexisting states of affairs. The only difficulty with this view is how to reconcile it with two of Wittgenstein's other claims. First: "The facts in logical space are the world" (1.13)—not reality. And second: "The sum-total of reality is the world" (2.063). If this latter assertion is accepted, then there cannot be two different conceptions—one, the world; the other, reality.

One way of attempting to avoid this problem is to claim that Wittgenstein does not really *mean* that there are any negative facts, i.e., any nonexistent states of affairs. In this view, when Wittgenstein speaks of negative facts, he merely means that when we have the totality of existing states of affairs determined, we also have determined which do not exist (2.05). That is, Wittgenstein holds that, literally, there are no negative facts. But once you have the set of all positive facts given, you also know which do not exist. We may *call* the latter "negative facts" (in quotation marks), but this is not to be taken literally. To say 'There are negative facts' is then to speak metaphorically, like saying 'It was raining cats and dogs'. The major difficulty with this view is that it conflicts with what Wittgenstein says in 2.06. It seems clear that he really does hold that there are negative facts, i.e., nonexistent atomic facts, and that these along with existent atomic facts are part of reality or the world.

However, even if we must recognize that Wittgenstein *claimed* that there are negative facts, one might nevertheless argue that he was *wrong* in so claiming. Let us go back to our model universe consisting in objects *a*, *b*, *c*, and *d*. And let us suppose that only one configuration of objects obtains, *a* configured with *b*. Then in Tractese talk, we may say that there is one positive fact, *ab*, and several negative facts, *ac*, *ad*, *bc*, *bc*, *cd*. By 2.06, this would mean that state of affairs *ab* exists, but *bc*, *cd*, etc., do not exist. But does this not mean that there is an atomic fact *ab*, but that there is *no* atomic fact *bc*, and *no* atomic fact *cd*, etc.? If so, this is indistinguishable from an alternative way of talking—call it Moorese[6]—according to which there are facts and nonfacts, rather than positive and negative facts. In Moorese we would say that *ab* is a fact, whereas *bc*, *cd*, etc., are *not* facts at all. That is, there is an atomic fact, *ab*, but *no* atomic facts *bc*, *cd*, etc. Thus both views end up the same. We may see this even more clearly if we transcribe these assertions about facts into assertions about the truth-values of atomic sentences. In Tractese, '*ab* is a positive fact' transcribes into ' '*ab*' is true'; and '*bc* is a negative fact' transcribes into ' '*bc*' is not true', etc. But in Moorese, '*ab* is a fact' also transcribes into ' '*ab*' is true'; and '*bc* is *not* a fact' transcribes into ' '*bc*' is not true'. Hence these two theories seem to be equivalent, in that Tractese talk is reducible to Moorese talk. But if there are no negative facts in the latter, then there cannot be any in the former either. Whether this view is ultimately tenable, we must determine later on.

Let us now turn to the question: What are states of affairs, or atomic facts? All that we have been told in the passages thus far is that (1) they are what the world consists in (1–1.2); (2) they "lie" in a network of logical space, that is, a range of logical possibilities over and beyond those existing facts; and (3) they are combinations (or configurations) of objects (2.01). I have attempted to explicate (1) and (2). Let us now turn to a preliminary consideration of (3). What does it mean to say that an atomic fact is a combination or configuration (2.0231) of objects? Let us defer, for a moment, the question "What *are* objects?" and let us see what can be said apart from the answer to that question. First, it would seem that, if states of affairs *are* configurations or combinations of objects, then they must consist in objects and only objects, whatever objects are. Let us assume a configuration of two objects, *a* and *b*. Then the atomic fact *ab* must consist in *a* and *b* and in nothing else, no third thing. Further support for this will come up in 2.03. Second, Wittgenstein says, "There is *no* object that we can imagine [or think of]

---

[6] Named after my friend, Mr. G. Moor, with whom I have spent many profitable hours discussing Wittgenstein.

excluded from the possibility of combining with others" (2.0121).
Does Wittgenstein mean that we cannot think of any objects which
are incapable of combining with *some* others, or that we cannot
think of objects which are incapable of combining with *any* others?
If the former is correct, then presumably there could be several
types of objects, but if the latter is true, then there can be only one
type. And this, in turn, could be taken to mean that, in the former
view, there can be many types of atomic facts, whereas in the latter
view, there can be only one type of atomic facts. Again, in the sections which have been considered thus far, we do not know enough
to answer these questions; hence let us move on to a consideration
of objects and then return to a discussion of atomic facts.

As we have seen, the determination of what is *not* the case cannot
be achieved merely by the determining of what *is* the case, for in
knowing what is the case we only know those configurations of
objects which actually obtain (2.061). Such determination of what
is *not* the case is possible only by virtue of all *objects* being "given"
(2.0124), objects which "contain the possibility of all situations" or
atomic facts (2.014). This suggests that, in spite of the references in
1–1.21 to the world consisting of *facts* and not of things, nevertheless in another and perhaps even more basic sense, the world, or perhaps reality, consists of *objects*. And, indeed, I think that this is so,
as can be seen from sections 2.02–2.03. This brings us to two most
important difficult questions: (1) What are (Wittgensteinian) objects? (2) How are objects related to states of affairs?

We already know something about objects—first, that they are
constituents of states of affairs (but that doesn't tell us very much);
second, that they are independent insofar as they can occur in all
possible atomic facts and dependent in the sense that this possibility
is essential to them, in that they cannot be excluded from the possibility of combinations with others into states of affairs (2.0121).
Since any given object need not occur in some specific atomic fact,
it is independent; but since it *must* be *possible* for it to occur in
atomic facts, it is in that sense dependent (2.0122). This possibility
of an object's occurring in states of affairs Wittgenstein calls the
form of an object (2.0141).

What else may be said about objects? First, they are *simple*
(2.02). That is, whereas an atomic fact is complex in the sense that

it is made up of at least two constituents in a combination, an object has no such complexity. Facts are composite, but objects are not. Why not? Because, says Wittgenstein, "Objects make up the substance of the world" (2.021). "If the world had no substance, then whether a proposition had sense would depend on whether another proposition was true" (2.0211). "In that case we could not sketch out any picture of the world, true or false" (2.0212). I agree with those who take this to be an incomplete argument, the rest of which runs as follows: Since we can produce pictures of the world (2.1ff.), then whether a proposition has sense does not depend on whether some other proposition is true; and since the latter is the case, the world must have a substance. That is, the entities which make up atomic facts must be noncomposites. Otherwise one could go on indefinitely and never obtain true propositions which correspond to the facts of the world.

Second, objects constitute the "unalterable form" of the world (2.023)—this form being that which any imagined or thought-about world must have in common with the actual world. Consider again our model universe with four objects, a, b, c, and d. And let us again suppose that the actual world has only one atomic fact, a configured with b. Now we can conceive of alternative worlds: one in which there exists only the configuration of c with d, another in which there exist both configurations, etc. Although all these worlds are different from the standpoint of *which* states of affairs actually obtain in each, nevertheless they all share something in common, a form. And what else can this form be but the objects a, b, c, and d, whose logically possible configurations remain the same, no matter which actual configurations obtain (hence an unalterable form)?

Among the sections on objects as constituting the form of the world, there occurs a section which has provided much puzzlement. Wittgenstein says: "The substance of the world *can* only determine a form, and not any material properties. For it is only by means of propositions that material objects are represented—only by the configuration of objects that they are produced" (2.0231). It is clear, I think, that material properties are to be contrasted with formal properties. The property of being an object might be called a formal property. But the properties circular, red, two inches in diameter, etc., are material properties. Thus material properties are factual or empirical properties. Now Wittgenstein says that material properties can be represented only by means of *propositions*. That is, they cannot be represented or referred to by parts of propositions, i.e., names. Furthermore, material properties can be produced only by or constituted only of configurations of objects. That is, if the world contained only objects and no configurations of objects, then the world would contain no material properties whatever, although it would still contain formal properties, since objects constitute the world's form.

I shall illustrate this by an analogy. Let us think of objects as points on a plane, and let us label some of these as follows:

$$\begin{array}{cccc}
\cdot & \cdot & \cdot & \cdot \\
\\
\cdot & \cdot & \cdot & \cdot \\
e & f & g & h \\
\\
\cdot & \cdot & \cdot & \cdot \\
a & b & c & d
\end{array}$$

The totality of all of these objects determines all spatial configurations of them into various geometrical shapes—square, triangular, etc. Hence they may be thought of as constituting the form of this spatial world. Now none of these objects itself has any material (spatial) property. None is itself square, triangular, etc. However, when various of these objects are brought into relations, when they are *configured*, then we get material properties such as square, etc. For example, the configuration of *a b f e* produces the material property square. The configuration of *c d h* produces the material property triangular, etc. The same holds for Wittgenstein's objects. They have no shape or size or any other material properties, since these and all other material properties result only when there are configurations of objects. Griffin has stated the matter nicely: Objects are not what *bear* properties but what *make* properties.[7] Thus Wittgenstein goes on to say: "In a manner of speaking, objects are

---

[7] James Griffin, *Wittgenstein's Logical Atomism* (Oxford: Clarendon Press, 1964), p. 71.

colorless." Indeed they are colorless, nonspatial, etc.; they have no material properties whatever.

It may be recalled that earlier (in 2.01231) Wittgenstein spoke of an object's external and internal properties. May we identify the dichotomy material-formal with that of external-internal? I think not. Objects have both external and internal properties, whereas, as we have seen, they do not have material properties. What then are the external properties of objects? I think that there can be only one answer. Consider again our model universe of four objects, *a*, *b*, *c*, and *d*, and one configuration *ab*. The property of standing in a certain relation or configuration to *b* is a material property of *a*. But the possibility of *a* occurring in other atomic facts (*ac*, etc.) is an internal property of *a*. It would seem then that internal properties are also formal properties. But not all formal properties are internal properties. For the property of *being an object* is also a formal property, but not an internal one.

Since objects constitute the world's form, and since this form is not merely the form of the actual world but the form of any possible world, Wittgenstein goes on to say, third, that objects are "unalterable and subsistent" (2.071). They subsist independently of what actually is the case (2.024). To say that they are unalterable is to say that they are unchanging. To say that they subsist independently of what is the case is to say that, no matter what the facts are (which is a contingent matter), and perhaps, indeed, even if there were no facts at all, there would still be objects. It ought to be apparent that those who have taken Wittgenstein's objects to be phenomenal individuals (sense-data) have radically missed the mark. Similarly those who have taken them to be physical particulars must be wrong. For neither phenomenal nor physical objects are unalterable and subsistent. What then are they? I shall return to this question shortly.

In 2.025, Wittgenstein says that substance is "form and content." What does this mean? We know that objects make up the substance of the world (2.021). Hence 2.025 says that objects constitute both the world's form and its content. I have already dealt with the matter of objects constituting the world's form. But how can objects also constitute its content? Let us return once more to our model universe consisting of objects *a*, *b*, *c*, and *d*, with the single atomic fact *ab*. As we have seen, objects constitute not only the form of this world, but any other world, for example, the world in which *a* and *c* are configured. But besides playing this role, objects also constitute the "materials" or substance of which facts are made. The atomic fact *ab* consists of two objects in configuration. Hence objects constitute the *content* of the world, too. They do not merely provide a form common to this actual world and any other. They also constitute the facts which actually obtain and which could be recorded in atomic propositions which express what the world is like, what its actual content is.

We now come to a puzzling passage: "Space, time, and colour (being coloured) are forms of objects" (2.0251). Presumably this means that they are forms and *not properties* of objects. Now the form of an object, we have seen, is the possibility of its occurring in states of affairs (2.0141). Hence space, time, and color are not properties of objects but possibilities of configurations of objects. Again consider an array of geometrical points on a two-dimensional plane. None of these objects has, say, space as a property. You can't say, for instance, that *a* is spatial. What you mean by space is: the possibility of *a* configured with *b;* the possibility of *b* configured with *c;* and so on.

We may now return to the subject of facts and the relation of objects to facts. Again, atomic facts are configurations of objects (2.0272). Whereas objects are unalterable and subsistent, their configurations are "changing and unstable" (2.0271). But exactly how are objects configured with others so as to constitute atomic facts? Wittgenstein says, "In a state of affairs objects fit into one another like the links of a chain" (2.03). Now of course this must be a metaphor. Since objects are not spacial entities, they cannot literally *fit* into one another like the links of a chain. Wittgenstein's further comments here do not help very much. He merely says that "in a state of affairs objects stand in a determinate relation to one another" (2.031). That is, they combine in a definite way and are not just jumbled haphazardly.

Wittgenstein then defines the *structure* of a state of affairs as the determinate way in which objects are connected in the state of affairs (2.032). And he defines the *form* of a state of affairs as the possibility of its structure (2.033). Let us adopt a PMese way of speaking about the configuration of two objects *a* and *b*. Let 'C' represent the configuration. Then the structure of the fact *a* configured with *b* could be represented by '*aCb*', and the form of the fact by '*xRy*'. (And of course the form of the objects by the '*x*' or '*y*' of '*xRy*'.)

Let us now return to our question: What exactly are (Wittgensteinian) objects? I have said (above) that they cannot be either phenomenal objects (sense-data) or material objects. First, neither sense-data particulars nor physical objects are unalterable, subsistent, etc., whereas Wittgensteinian objects are both. Furthermore, both phenomenal material objects (individuals) have properties—color, size, shape, etc., whereas Wittgensteinian objects are propertyless (except for formal properties). One might argue that, although we cannot identify Wittgenstein's objects with physical objects, we can identify Wittgenstein's atomic facts with material objects. In this view, an ordinary physical object consists in two or more Wittgensteinian objects *in configuration*. There is little or no evidence for this view, and there is a major objection to it. For if this were a true account of what Wittgenstein intended, then it would mean that what Wittgenstein is presenting in the opening pages of the *Tractatus* is a theory of *physics*, and not a *metaphysical* position; or it would mean that he is presenting a theory which may be called physics *or* metaphysics, since there is no distinction between the two. From the passages which I quoted at the beginning of this chapter and upon the basis of many others in the *Tractatus* (e.g., 6.341ff.), it seems clear that Wittgenstein did distinguish metaphysics from physics. Furthermore, Wittgenstein maintains that philosophy is different from science (4.111ff.). For these reasons, it seems to me that this position which I have been entertaining cannot be accepted.

What, then, are (Wittgensteinian) objects? What is their ontological status? What is left to say but that they are peculiar *metaphysical* objects—objects which can never be apprehended by any experience, but which nevertheless are real and which form the substance of the world. We can only more or less repeat what Wittgenstein has said—they are unalterable, subsistent, etc. And they *must* exist.

But why must they? I have already dealt with Wittgenstein's brief argument for their existence in 2.021–2.0212. Let us enlarge the question: Why must the world be what it is characterized as being in this ontology? Why must there be objects, in logical space, and atomic facts which consist in configurations of objects, etc.? If there is no way by which to test such an extraordinary view, had we not better recognize it as nonsense to begin with? And in that case, why does it occur in the most prominent place in Wittgenstein's book? I can only argue in reverse order. The fact that it *does* occur indicates that we are to take it seriously and that therefore it is not sheer nonsense after all. So we are back with the question: Why does Wittgenstein hold that the world *must* be as he characterizes it to be? The answer to this question is, I think, that it must be thus in order to answer *another* question. Let me elaborate.

Almost every ontological position is not only an answer to the ontological question 'What is there?' or 'What is real?' It is also an answer to some other question. The relation between the two is this: In order to be able to give an adequate answer to this first question, we must give a certain answer to the second. For example, I doubt if Plato ever came upon his metaphysics by asking "What is there?" or "What is real?" etc., and then answering "Forms." Rather he seems to have been concerned with answering other questions, namely, 'How is genuine knowledge possible?' and 'What must be the conditions for genuine knowledge?' And, of course, in Kant this is explicit in his concern with the question 'What must be the conditions which make synthetic a priori knowledge possible?' The *Tractatus* is not an epistemological work. Hence, Wittgenstein's "second" question is not one about our knowledge of anything. Rather, his second question is a logical one —some might call it a semantic or linguistic question. I do not want to quibble about labels. The question is: 'What must be the necessary conditions in order for language to be used in its assertive function to state true propositions about the world?' Note, first, that this is not an epistemological question. It is not the question 'What must be the case in order for us to *know* truths about the world?' It is the question 'What must be the case for discourse to be used to *express* truths about the world?' Note, second, that it is not a linguistic question in the sense of being merely about language. It asks about how language relates to the *world* in its assertive function and as a condition for language being so used, it requires (as the necessary condition) a metaphysical world view. Once again, the answer to the question 'What must hold in order for discourse to be used to state truths about the world?' is this: There are unalterable and subsistent objects, in a network of logical space, which are capable of forming configurations with others, and some of which do. It is a beautiful answer. But *is it true?*

6

Material Properties in the Tractatus

HERBERT HOCHBERG

COMMENTATORS on the *Tractatus* have tended to treat the phrases 'material property' and 'external property' as synonymous expressions.[1] Thus

> 2.0231 The substance of the world *can* only determine a form, and not any material properties. For it is only by means of propositions that material properties are represented—only by the configuration of objects that they are produced.[2]

is taken to assert that external properties are produced by configurations of objects and represented by propositions. Taken together with other statements in the *Tractatus* about external properties, this interpretation can lead one to hold that a color property, being external, is a material property and, hence, is produced by a configuration of objects. Being produced by a configuration of objects, a color property cannot then be an object itself. One thus arrives at the view that Wittgenstein does not intend to include properties among the objects in the world. 2.0231 is thus a crucial passage for the rejection of properties like red, yellow, etc., as objects. But the interpretation of 2.0231, which is presupposed by the above line of reasoning rejecting properties as objects, is misguided. 'Material

---

[1] For example, Max Black, *A Companion to Wittgenstein's "Tractatus"* (Ithaca: Cornell University Press, 1964), p. 64.

[2] Ludwig Wittgenstein, *Tractatus logico-philosophicus*, trans. D. F. Pears and B. F. McGuinness (London: Routledge & Kegan Paul, 1961), p. 11. 'Produced' renders the German 'gebildet'.

property' and 'external property' mean quite different things in the *Tractatus*.

An external property may well be a property like the color red as opposed to an internal or formal property like being a color spot or, perhaps, being an object. In any case, it is clear that objects, as well as states of affairs and facts, are characterized as having internal and external properties and relations.[3] A material property, however, is not contrasted with an internal property but with the "substance of the world." This latter determines a form and "not any material properties." In short, a material property is a property of the world as opposed to the form of the world, which is determined by the substance of the world. What Wittgenstein seems to have in mind is that a material property of the world tells us how the world in fact is as opposed to how it possibly is. Thus, *that* an object is red would be a material property of the world if the object were in fact that color. It would be an internal or formal property of *the object* that it could be red. Red would be an external property of *the object*, but not a material property of it. Rather, to repeat, *that the object is red* is a material property of the world. An object can have external or internal properties; the world has material and formal properties. Unfortunately, Wittgenstein uses the term 'formal' in contrast to both 'external' and 'material', which, of course, leads one to take these latter as synonyms. But, if I am correct, while both the world and the objects in it have *form*, only the world has material properties, while only objects have external properties like red. On this interpretation, it is natural for Wittgenstein to say that material properties are represented by *propositions* and to speak of them exactly as he speaks of states of affairs and facts—as configurations or combinations represented by propositions and not by names.

It is relevant to recall that, in the opening sentences of the *Tractatus*, Wittgenstein speaks of the world as dividing into facts, and he contrasts possibilities, matters of form, with what is the case, matters of fact. This is the same contrast that occurs in 2.0231 between the substance of the world as determining a form and material properties. The world is characterized or determined by facts and is thus describable by means of propositions. To partially an-

[3] Ibid., 2.01231, 4.122.

swer the question 'What is the world like?' requires uttering propositions like 'a_1 is red', where 'a_1' is the name of an object. That a_1 is red serves to differentiate one possible world from another, one in which a_1 is not red. Thus, the fact that a_1 is red is a characteristic, or property, of the world. (That a_1 could be red would be a formal property of the world.)

The advantage of the present interpretation is not merely that it jibes with the opening statements of the *Tractatus* but that it allows for a simple and straightforward reading of 2.0231. One is no longer forced to attribute to Wittgenstein the esoteric doctrine that properties, like color properties, are "configurations of objects." Moreover, looked at in this way, 2.0231 cannot be taken to support the claim that Wittgenstein does not consider properties to be objects. It is perfectly possible for *external* properties to be objects, though of a different form than individual objects, and *not configurations of objects*.[4] Only material properties are explicitly held to be configurations, or facts, in the *Tractatus*.

---

[4] That is, 2.0231 does not preclude the possibility. That there are other considerations that may weigh against taking properties as objects is not relevant here.

7

Wittgenstein's Pantheism
A New Light on the Ontology of the Tractatus

NEWTON GARVER

W ITTGENSTEIN says in his 1913 "Notes on Logic" that philosophy "consists of logic and metaphysics, the former its basis."[1] The *Tractatus* reflects this attitude, its core being given over to the problems of meaning and inference as they pertain to the different aspects of scientific discourse. In reading the *Tractatus*, one gets the impression that Wittgenstein, having resolved to his satisfaction the problems about language, logic, science, and mathematics, sets these painstakingly articulated findings in a disproportionately skimpy setting. There is a perfunctory ontology at the beginning, which is highly original as well as austere and perplexing; and at the end he hurries even more than usual through ethics, aesthetics, and religion—as if the silence was already coming upon him, prematurely. The *Notebooks, 1914–1916* help a good deal in understanding this skimpy setting. They give little direct indication of the ontological overture, apart from their frequent reiteration that there must be simples of some sort if the sense of expressions is to be determinate, but they give a fuller treatment to the other topics. This is particularly true of the latter half of 1916, when this parcel of topics seems to have become uppermost in Wittgenstein's mind. Though it is exceedingly difficult to know what to make of what are in effect discarded notes, some of the entries are just too interesting to ignore. I wish to consider what

[1] Ludwig Wittgenstein, *Notebooks, 1914–1916* (Oxford: Basil Blackwell, 1961), p. 93.

light they throw on his thought at roughly the *Tractatus* period, and in particular on the ontology that apparently springs up full-grown at the beginning of the *Tractatus*.

Two of the three sentences entered on the first day of August, 1916, read as follows:

> Wie sich alles verhält, ist Gott.
> Gott ist, wie sich alles verhält.

They express what God is in terms very like those used in the *Tractatus* to say what the world is or what a fact is, and therefore they suggest either a pantheism of sorts or else a change of mind in the intervening two years. The second alternative has a superficial plausibility, but in the absence of other evidence of a change of mind it must be wrong. In a way, these sentences are typical of what Wittgenstein suppressed when he extracted material for the *Tractatus* from the *Notebooks*, just because of their concern for what God is. Over a two-month period the word 'God' occurs twelve times,[2] each time in an attempt to say what God is. The whole attempt is given up in the published work, the only remnant of it being the guarded remark in 6.432—"God does not reveal himself *in* the world"—which might reasonably be said to presuppose some notion of what God is but which can hardly be counted as an attempt to *say* what God is. Since there is a whole interconnected set of remarks in the *Notebooks* that are nowhere repudiated, other than by being omitted from the published work, it is at least reasonable to hold that Wittgenstein simply opted for the wisdom of silence on this matter. Such a view fits well with Wittgenstein's known piety, and I think it can be supported by consideration of relevant texts.

At first glance it might seem from some of the published text that the opposite is true, that Wittgenstein had changed his mind, at least with respect to the entries quoted above. The full text of *Tractatus* 6.432 is:

> *How* things stand in the world is a matter of complete indifference for what is higher. God does not reveal himself *in* the world.

---

[2] In the entries for 11.6.16, 8.7.16, and 1.8.16. Concern for some of the matters involved when 'God' is mentioned continues throughout the rest of these notebooks, which terminate in January, 1917.

Taken as a whole, this section could appear to be a repudiation of the entries of 1.8.16, especially as the latter are translated by Miss Anscombe:

> How things stand, is God.
> God is, how things stand.

But closer inspection shows that the German expressions are not so similar as the translators make them appear. In particular the *Notebooks* entries refer to a totality, signified in the German word *alles*, that Miss Anscombe has omitted to translate, and they might better be rendered:

> How everything hangs together, is God.
> God is, how everything hangs together.

In the passage from the *Tractatus*, on the other hand, the German clause "*Wie* die Welt ist" could equally well be rendered as "*How* the world is," rather than "*How* things stand." But it is not the wording so much as the primary reference of the two passages that confirms that they do not conflict. In the *Notebooks* the reference is to a totality, God being identified not with how this stands and how that stands but rather with how *everything* stands (or hangs together). In *Tractatus* 6.432, on the other hand, the reference is not to a totality or a hanging-together-of-everything, but to the details of the arrangement, that is, to how this stands and how that stands.

Besides the fact that he did not repudiate these notions expressed in the *Notebooks* in other passages that I know of, there are two considerations that count for the view that Wittgenstein, when he wrote the *Tractatus*, still held to what he expressed on 1.8.16. One is the special respect he has for totality in the *Tractatus*, regarding generality as a "logical prototype" rather than as an indefinite conjunction or disjunction. The world, too, is a totality, as he says in the very first proposition, and conceived as a totality it surpasses rational comprehension:

6.44 Nicht *wie* die Welt ist, ist das Mystische, sondern *dass* sie ist.

Though there may possibly be other explanations for this remark, it seems to express a sort of pantheism in that the attitude expressed toward the world conceived as a totality—that is, when one regards it as a limited whole rather than focusing on details of it—is an attitude that is paradigmatically appropriate toward God; furthermore, the remark of 6.44 is the sort of thing that Wittgenstein would reasonably have been led to say if he still had in mind the ideas set down on 1.8.16. The other consideration is similar: there is a conception of God presupposed by *Tractatus* 6.432, such that God cannot reveal himself *in* the world, and one of the simplest conceptions that might be so presupposed is that God is the whole of the world; for it seems obvious that God cannot both *be* the world and also be *in* the world.[3] These two considerations are, of course, not definitive. They are only sufficient to allow us to put aside the all-too-easy comment that Wittgenstein must have changed his mind, and to explore a little further the nature of Wittgenstein's pantheism and what the consequences are of supposing that these remarks in the *Notebooks* express Wittgenstein's views through the *Tractatus* period.

There is an ambiguity about the entries of 1.8.16 that is not important in itself but that deserves to be mentioned both because it might cause confusion and because it is connected with one of the distinctive features of Wittgenstein's pantheism. What is identified with God in the entries quoted might be either a collection of all the facts there happen to be, or a single fact—a kind of world fact, so to speak—comprising how everything hangs together with everything else. These different ways of explicating Wittgenstein's words conjure up different pictures, but I do not think that they signify genuine alternatives in the context of the *Tractatus*, since the propositions that express the facts in question will by their very nature show how all the objects involved are related to one another. What makes a difference for Wittgenstein is not how the totality is conceived, given that it is a totality that includes all facts, but rather that it is such a totality. One important feature of Wittgenstein's pantheism depends on the critical significance of such a totality: namely, the distinction between what is in the world and what is higher, such that a fact of the world is always one fact among many,

---

[3] This point was first suggested to me by Professor Richard G. Henson of Rutgers University, when I read an early version of this paper there in March, 1970.

whereas what is higher, or divine, leaves nothing out of account pertaining to the all-inclusive totality, the world as a limited whole.

The distinction between what is in the world and what is higher seems at first incompatible with the view that it is the world that is divine, but Wittgenstein held both these views in both the *Notebooks* and the *Tractatus*. In the *Notebooks* the view that the world of fact is divine is clear from the entries already quoted. The view that what is higher is distinct from the facts of the world is clear in the entries of 5.7.16, particularly the ones that are a preliminary version of *Tractatus* 6.43, and in the following entry:

> 8.7.16 To believe in a God means to see that the facts of the world are not the end of the matter.

In the *Tractatus*, Wittgenstein's view that what is higher is not to be found *in* the world is clear from 6.432, quoted above, but it is equally clear that what is higher does have to do with the world rather than with anything otherworldly:

> 6.43 If the good or bad exercise of the will does alter the world, it can only alter the limits of the world, not the facts. . . . In short the effect must be that it becomes an altogether different world. It must, so to speak, wax and wane as a whole.

> 6.45 Feeling the world as a limited whole—it is this that is mystical.

Wittgenstein's pantheism, therefore, differs from some others in that the divinity of the whole is not inherited by component parts of that whole; this is certainly one of the most distinctive aspects of Wittgenstein's view, and one that makes it difficult to follow him, as will be seen below.

Needless to say, Wittgenstein's pantheistic conception of God is difficult to reconcile with the dominant features of a personal God. Nevertheless he says in the *Notebooks* (11.6.16) that we can call God the meaning of life or the world (he identifies the two) and connect this with the comparison of God to a father. Later (17.10.16) he also speaks of "a will that is common to the whole world," which could, I suppose, be thought of as God's will. I shall have no more to say about these matters.

Pantheism recalls Spinoza to mind. Once recalled to mind, Spinoza's *Ethics* presents striking parallels to Wittgenstein's *Tractatus* —or, more accurately, to what is presented jointly in the *Tractatus* and *Notebooks* for the latter half of 1916, if Wittgenstein is taken to be a pantheist. There are, to begin with, certain obvious and apparently superficial similiarities in structure, in particular that the works consist of a few main chapters that are broken down into numbered propositions. I do not think there is anything philosophically profound in this style. It is rather a style which they shared and which each may well have adopted for the same reason, namely out of a determination (no doubt morally admirable) not to allow his passion to find the truth about important matters to be corrupted by the flowing rhetoric that so easily comes to dominate long paragraphs. It is an austere style, reminiscent of Socrates in ways, and may be connected with the fact that Spinoza and Wittgenstein both chose to live more simply and more austerely than they need have lived, and that both were fearful of the danger of corruption involved in professional philosophy and in what was (is?) usually expected in connection with a university appointment.

It is far more significant and more useful for understanding Wittgenstein's ontology that the line of thought proceeds in the same manner in the *Ethics* and in the *Tractatus*. Both begin with a characterization of *deus-sive-natura*, or of that which is at the same time contingent creation considered as a whole (*natura naturata* / the totality of facts) and also the appropriate object of unqualified reverence (*natura naturans* / the mystical and inexpressible). Both also characterize the world (or God) in such a way as to make clear what the component parts are (finite modes / facts), and therefore how the world breaks down, so to speak, while still always remaining a unity or totality. It is worth noting that Spinoza and Wittgenstein, by proceeding in this manner, share a view of the relation of parts to wholes that is more characteristic of rationalism than of empiricism and of idealism than of materialism, and that is very different from the view of the relation of atomic propositions to complex propositions that is developed in the *Tractatus*. No doubt this view of the relation of parts to wholes, which is also evident in the relation of simples to facts and of names to propositions, is one thing that can lead commentators to characterize Wittgenstein as a rationalist or an idealist of sorts.[4]

Having characterized *deus-sive-natura* and its components, both Spinoza and Wittgenstein proceed to show how it is possible to come to comprehend the whole through knowing about or being able to speak about the components—though the comprehension of the whole is a different kind of knowledge and there is no guarantee that it will be achieved even through the best scientific knowledge of limited aspects of it. In both cases there are three sorts of knowledge, the first two comprising scientific knowledge. For Spinoza this involves distinguishing finite from infinite modes (roughly, things and events, or phenomena, from general laws and overriding features of the world like motion-and-rest) and then distinguishing the lowest sort of knowledge, empirical knowledge, as a simple awareness of finite modes, and rational or scientific knowledge as an understanding of the infinite modes and how the finite modes are related to and dependent on them. For Wittgenstein it involves distinctions among kinds of propositions: atomic and (contingent) molecular propositions can be directly compared with facts and hence are empirical; whereas science, although it comprises all true propositions, involves tautologies and generalizations[5] which cannot be

---

[4] See, for example, E. Stenius' account of Wittgenstein as a Kantian philosopher, in *Wittgenstein's "Tractatus"* (Oxford: Basil Blackwell, 1960); and Max Black's account of Wittgenstein's "organic" view of the world's essence, in *A Companion to Wittgenstein's "Tractatus"* (Ithaca: Cornell University Press, 1964), p. 10.

[5] The status of scientific laws and theories, vis à vis propositions and tautologies, is one of the very hard questions about the *Tractatus*. See Black, pp. 344ff.; and G. L. Proctor, "Scientific Laws and Scientific Objects in the *Tractatus*," *British Journal for Philosophy of Science* 10 (1959):177-93. The status of the infinite (or eternal) modes is equally obscure in the metaphysics of Spinoza, as has recently been brought to our attention again by E. M. Curley in his essay, *Spinoza's Metaphysics* (Cambridge: Harvard University Press, 1969). Throughout his work, Curley uses logical atomism as a kind of baseline from which to approach Spinoza, and in the second chapter he presents, in terms very different from mine, a comparison of the metaphysics of Spinoza with that of the *Tractatus*. Particularly relevant to the present point is his identification of the infinite modes with "nomological facts."

compared directly with facts. There are, of course, many details and complications that sketching with such broad strokes leaves out of account, but the structure becomes clearer and we can see better that both the *Ethics* and the *Tractatus* end with a vision of salvation that depends on a third kind of knowledge that transcends empirical and rational knowledge, a kind of cognition that does not, so to speak, add any new information to what is already known, but serves instead to bring everything already known into a single perspective. For Spinoza this sort of apprehension is *"scientia intuitiva"* and results in an "intellectual love of God." For Wittgenstein it is "feeling the world as a limited whole" and results in clarification of the meaning (*Sinn*) of life, or of the world. Thus Wittgenstein writes in the *Notebooks* entries of 8.7.16: "To believe in a God means to see that the facts of the world are not the end of the matter. To believe in God means to see that life has a meaning."

For both Spinoza and Wittgenstein, happiness, or the highest good, consists in a sort of identification with God or the universe, which is to be achieved intellectually. In both cases, too, it is easier to see that this is the goal set out in the work prepared for publication by examining preliminary studies. Thus it is at the beginning of *On the Improvement of the Understanding*[6] that Spinoza explains the nature of the highest good ("that it is the knowledge of the union existing between the mind and the whole of nature") and indicates how learning is directed toward that end. In the case of Wittgenstein we are even more dependent on the preliminary studies to see the goal of the published work; it becomes clear in the following passages from the *Notebooks*, which are neither repudiated nor recapitulated in the *Tractatus*:

> In order to live happily I must be in agreement with the world. And that is what "being happy" *means*.
>
> I am then, so to speak, in agreement with that alien will on which I appear dependent. That is to say: 'I am doing the will of God'. [8.7.16]
>
> I cannot bend the happenings of the world to my will: I am completely powerless.

[6] B. Spinoza, *Chief Works*, trans. R. H. M. Elwes, vol. 2 (New York: Dover, 1951), p. 6ff.

I can only make myself independent of the world—and so in a certain sense master it—by renouncing any influence on happenings. [11.6.16]

How can man be happy, since he cannot ward off misery of this world?

Through the life of knowledge. [13.8.16]

As in Spinoza's work, the goal is salvation through acquiescence, to be achieved intellectually by knowing the world well enough to put oneself in agreement with it. The problem is to see how this goal, and the pantheism in which it is embedded, may have influenced the ontology of the *Tractatus*.

I I I

"It would be quite wrong," says Max Black, in his *A Companion to Wittgenstein's "Tractatus,"* "to treat the metaphysics as a mere appendage: indeed it would be plausible to read the book as being primarily concerned with metaphysics."[7] And yet the metaphysics remains obscure, and the parts of it that we can understand seem to lead to difficulties at a deeper level. Black says that the ontology presented in the early installments was probably the last part of the book to be written.[8] One bit of evidence for this, as well as one ground for the continuing obscurity of the passages, is that the metaphysical scheme of the *Tractatus* is largely absent from the *Notebooks*. It is true that the *Notebooks* contain many entries about simples and objects, but they do not clear up the metaphysical difficulties. For one thing these remarks mostly have to do with the necessity that there be simples rather than with what simples are; and although a few of the entries are along the latter line,[9] Wittgenstein seems to have decided by the time he prepared the *Tractatus* for publication that all the problems of logic could be resolved without determining the nature of the simple objects that there must

---

[7] Black, p. 8.

[8] Ibid., p. 27.

[9] E.g., "As examples of the simple I always think of points of the visual field" (6.5.15). "Relations and properties, etc. are *objects* too" (16.6.15).

be.[10] It therefore remains unclear, though not uninteresting, whether the metaphysics of the *Tractatus* is realistic or nominalistic;[11] but I shall have nothing to say about this difficulty, for I cannot see that Wittgenstein's being a pantheist throws any light on the problem.

The other reason why the numerous remarks about simples do not ultimately help to understand the metaphysics of the *Tractatus* is that the ontology of simples is only one aspect of that metaphysics— very likely a secondary aspect at that. Wittgenstein gives primacy —the primacy of place at the very least—to facts rather than objects. This, as Black has noted,[12] is Wittgenstein's great innovation in metaphysics. It is a brilliant and awesome stroke that cannot fail to catch the attention of readers of the *Tractatus*. But it is puzzling because of the intrinsic difficulty of understanding what exactly an ontology of facts is, and also because of the uncertain metaphysical status the objects have if they must be thought of in relation to facts. It does not seem that objects and facts can be independent of one another, in separate realms, so to speak; for facts are concatenations or configurations of objects. But how are the two ontologies related to one another in the metaphysics of the *Tractatus?* On this question the *Notebooks* seem to give no help at all, because they contain no trace of the ontology of facts.

One might try to get some light on this metaphysical question by considering why there should be two ontologies at all. It seems reasonable to say that the dual metaphysics grew out of the problems about language that Wittgenstein was coping with. His account of language had to meet three requirements: there must be a way to determine the meaning of propositions; there must be a way

[10] In line, perhaps, with his dictum, "If logic can be completed without answering certain questions, then it *must* be completed without answering them" (4.9.14).

[11] See E. Allaire, "The *Tractatus*: Nominalistic or Realistic," reprinted in I. M. Copi and R. W. Beard, eds., *Essays on Wittgenstein's "Tractatus"* (New York: Macmillan, 1966). Allaire argues for a realistic interpretation and cites Copi and Anscombe as his principal antagonists. Black (p. 11) thinks the controversy irresolvable.

[12] Ibid., p. 27. Curley, in *Spinoza's Metaphysics*, presents Spinoza's metaphysics as a metaphysics of facts rather than of things or events; but since Spinoza did not present it that way, and since Curley uses Wittgenstein's *Tractatus* as a model for understanding Spinoza, Curley's remarks can hardly be used to rebut Black's claim.

to determine the truth or falsity of propositions; and the criterion of meaning must be independent of the criterion of truth. So when Wittgenstein finally decided that language must be metaphysically grounded, it was clear that he would have to have two ontologies, one to provide determinateness of meaning and the other to provide the determination of truth and falsity. Unfortunately this line of thought, having got this far, runs afoul of our original question about the metaphysical priority of the two ontologies. Since knowing what a proposition means is prior, necessarily, to knowing whether it is true, one might expect that the metaphysical ground of meaning should have an analogous priority over the metaphysical ground for truth. But Wittgenstein seems to put things in just the opposite order at the beginning of the *Tractatus*. So this line of thought only deepens the mystery.

A second attempt to explain the primacy Wittgenstein gives to facts might begin by focusing on the famous dictum he adopted from Frege: "Only in the nexus of a proposition does a name have meaning."[13] One consequence of this dictum is that propositions are prior to names at the level of semantics. Sentences are, to be sure, composed of names; therefore, in a certain sense, there could not be sentences if there were not names. But when we come to consider how it is that these two sorts of linguistic expressions are understood, then, according to Wittgenstein, propositions are the primary units into which language breaks down, names being intelligible (having meaning, or reference) only if the sentences in which they occur are intelligible (have sense). This line of thought proves, then, to be more rewarding than the first, for it seems only fitting, in view of the semantic priority of propositions over names, that the metaphysical correlates of propositions should have analogous priority over the metaphysical correlates of names. This is helpful. But there remain two problems. One is that this position is difficult to recon-

---

[13] *Tractatus* 3.3. The complete section reads: "Nur der Satz hat Sinn; nur im Zusammenhange des Satzes hat ein Name Bedeutung." Here we also see Wittgenstein's use of Frege's sharp distinction between *Sinn* and *Bedeutung*, where *Sinn* is accorded a semantic priority that corresponds to the metaphysical priority of facts. We see further in the semantic priority of propositions over names, however difficult it is to reconcile with the metaphysical grounding of meaning in *objects*, a harbinger of the later slogan that "the meaning of a word is its use in the language."

cile with the familiar fact that we understand "new" sentences on
the basis of the meaning of familiar component words (= names?),
and with Wittgenstein's view that the sense of propositions, as distinct from their truth value, is ultimately determined by the correlation of names with objects. I can make no comment on this
dilemma here. But even if it could be resolved, there would remain
the question why metaphysical priority should be determined by the
semantic priority of propositions over names, rather than by the
epistemological priority of meaning over truth. Wittgenstein's ontology of facts is, after all, unconventional and at least initially implausible, and it is difficult to see why he should adopt it if he had
an equally good reason, or perhaps even a better one, for having
the world break down, more plausibly, into simple objects.

Wittgenstein's pantheism supplies the explanation that these other
lines of thought cannot provide. If God is identified with the world,
and if the idea of God is to continue to play the role it does for
Wittgenstein in the *Notebooks*, then the world must be composed of
facts rather than of objects. The reason for this is that facts are the
hard, unalterable data we must accept and come to terms with in our
lives. It is true that objects are, in a certain sense, unalterable.[14] But
what is unalterable about objects is their form, the possibilities they
comprise; whereas the hard data we have to accept and cope with are
never mere possibilities but actualities. Since the actualities, reality,
must be determined by what facts there are rather than by what
objects there are,[15] the world must be composed of facts rather than
of objects,[16] if the *Tractatus* is to be compatible with the pantheism
of the *Notebooks* and with the ethical insights on which the pantheism is founded.

Among the entries for 11.6.16, Wittgenstein speaks of God as the
meaning of the world. Here is one powerful religious idea which
must be preserved in the metaphysics of the *Tractatus*, if the pantheism and piety of 1916 carry over into the book. Could God be
thought of as the meaning of the world if the world were an aggregate of objects? Only by making a mockery of the idea and robbing
it of the religious depth expressed in Wittgenstein's *Notebooks*.

[14] See *Tractatus* 2.012–2.0123, 2.023.
[15] Ibid., 2.06.
[16] Wittgenstein spells this out in *Tractatus* 2.03–2.063.

"Objects contain the possibility of *all* situations,"[17] and hence they cannot convey to us the why and the wherefore of our *actual* situation. Objects constitute a form which our world must have in common with any other imaginable world,[18] so the totality of objects cannot help us to understand the meaning of this particular world—which is what we need to know, since it is with this particular world rather than with other possible ones that we must, through our apprehension of God, reconcile ourselves. To say in response that we must also reconcile ourselves to what possibilities there are would perhaps be true, but it would betray a failure to comprehend the existential situation in which it is important to see God as the meaning of the world. For it is the world with its actual miseries, not the world with its possible glories, that we must come to understand and to reconcile ourselves with. It is the world of facts, not objects.

Another theme of Wittgenstein's pantheism is the ethic of acquiescence. Consider how the following passage from the *Notebook* entries for 8.7.16 shows a line of thought that leads to the identification of God and the world:

> The world is *given* me, i.e., my will enters into the world completely from outside as into something that is already there.
>
> That is why we have the feeling of being dependent on an alien will.
>
> *However this may be*, at any rate we *are* in a certain sense dependent, and what we are dependent on we call God.
>
> In this sense God would simply be fate, or, what is the same thing: the world—which is independent of our will.
>
> I can make myself independent of fate.
>
> There are two godheads: the world and my independent I [*mein unabhängiges Ich*].
>
> In order to live happily I must be in agreement with the world. And that is what 'being happy' *means*.
>
> I am then, so to speak, in agreement with the alien will on which I appear dependent. That is to say: 'I am doing the will of God'.

This passage has its difficulties. Perhaps the greatest difficulty is that individual happenings in the world, or facts, seem at least as fateful

17 Ibid., 2.012. My italics.
18 Ibid., 2.022–2.023.

as the world as a whole; so that if God is fate, it would seem that God would be revealed *in* the world, contrary to *Tractatus* 6.432.[19] There are also certain ambiguities, so that some lines of the passage would be compatible with the world being composed of objects rather than of facts. Both possibilities and facts, for example, are already there, given to me, and are independent of my will. But the main line of thought in the passage resolves these ambiguities decisively through its reference to fate. Fate cannot be understood just in terms of possibilities, just in terms of the form of the world. It has to do instead with what actually happens, with which of the possibilities happened to be actualized. What one has to learn to be in agreement with, according to the highly Spinozistic lines at the end of the passage, is not what possibilities there are, for one could hardly fail to be in agreement with that. It is the world as it actually is that one must strive religiously to be in agreement with. In spite of difficulties in the above passage, therefore, it is clear that the main thrust of it requires that the world have facts rather than objects as component parts.

That the pantheism of the *Notebooks* succeeds in providing an explanation for one of the prominent puzzles about the metaphysics of the *Tractatus* is a powerful consideration, in the absence of contrary evidence, in support of the view that Wittgenstein, although unwilling to allow it in print, continued to hold to that pantheism and to the ethical views associated with it. Such a view is attractive on other grounds. Certainly the setting in which the logical doctrines are set proves to be far less skimpy than it appeared if it is a full-blown Spinozistic ethic. Ultimately the *Tractatus* may well be unacceptable because of its commitment to the ontology of simples and its rejection of intentional contexts; but it would nonetheless be extremely interesting to work from the other direction, from the problem of reconciling Spinoza's noble ethic with the indeterminacy

---

[19] Perhaps an answer to this difficulty might be that whereas a fact can be a fact independent of everything else, it cannot be understood as fate, or as an aspect of fate, unless it is seen to be part of a whole universe of fate. I cannot pursue this interesting thought here.

A second difficulty resides in the dualism between oneself and the world, for the sharp dichotomy seems to require either denying that one's body is in the world or (Wittgenstein's apparent choice) denying responsibility for one's body.

of modern physics, to see whether Wittgenstein's identification of God with fate, and his further identification of both with the universe conceived as an aggregate of facts, might provide a way of bringing Spinoza's ethico-religious philosophy into harmony with twentieth-century views about science and nature. For the present, however, it is enough simply to see how the recognition of Wittgenstein's pantheism helps to see the coherence of the *Tractatus*.

8

Science and Metaphysics:
A Wittgensteinian Interpretation

HUGH G. PETRIE

Iᴛ is not an uncommon occurrence
for teachers of philosophy to be asked at some point in introductory
courses what metaphysics is. Nor is it uncommon, I think, for such
teachers of philosophy to respond with a paraphrase of the Aristotelian answer to this question. "Metaphysics," the eager student is
told, "is the science of Being as such."[1]

But now, if the student is not wholly silenced, and especially if
he is at all scientifically sophisticated, he may have a further query.
How, then, is metaphysics different from physics? For surely physi-
cists study the fundamental building blocks of nature, and is this
not the same as the study of Being as such? As late as 1965, one
answer to this further query consisted in pointing out to the student
that metaphysics is broader than physics.[2] The student was told that
although physics is perfectly general with respect to its domain, if
we wanted to find out, for example, about biological features of
being, we would have to turn to biologists.

Of course, this answer, as the skeptical student of today quickly
perceives, will not do. In the first place it does not take into account

[1] Aristotle, *Metaphysics*, B. 4, Ch. 1, 1003ª–18ff.
[2] D. F. Pears, ed., *The Nature of Metaphysics* (New York: St. Martin's
Press, 1965), pp. 4–5.

the incredible advances in molecular biology which have occurred in the last few years. It seems today, as never before, that in some clear sense physics *will* be able to achieve the generality apparently required. And, of even more importance, even if all of science cannot somehow be unified, this result would allow the distinction between science and metaphysics to degenerate into a merely accidental feature rather than the essential distinction being sought.

No, if the philosopher is going to distinguish metaphysics conceived as the study of Being as such from contemporary science, he is going to have to bring up his big guns. And at least three of these big guns usually have to do with the following points. *One.* The objects and, hence, the methodologies of science and metaphysics are fundamentally different. As a paradigm example, the former deals with empirical truth while the latter deals with conceptual truth. *Two.* Even granted a completely unified science, philosophy is a completely different order subject, dealing as it does with problems and conflicts which arise within and between science and common sense.[3] *Three.* In any event, the tradition of separating science and metaphysics places the burden of proof on those who would assert their continuity. In other words, an argument, and a philosophical one at that, must be offered asserting the continuity of science and metaphysics.

After these points, suitably embellished, are made, the philosophy teacher can be confident of having silenced, if not convinced, all but the most obstreperous student. And yet the doubt lingers on. Can metaphysics *really* be distinguished from science? Many students

[3] I realize that some philosophers, e.g. Gilbert Ryle, believe that a sharp distinction needs to be drawn between science and common sense. This conception seems nothing less than incredible to me. Surely nothing could be more obvious than that science, broadly conceived, is nothing more than a sophisticated extension of common-sense investigation. However, to argue this point in detail here would take me too far afield. I can only hope that it will be apparent that nothing I shall say in the sequel hangs on my ability to show the continuity of scientific and common-sense investigation. The reason for this is that those who would draw the line between science and common sense do so in order to attach philosophy (and especially metaphysics) to the problems arising from conflicts in common sense. But it must be obvious that even if such a move is legitimate, it does not suffice to distingiush science from metaphysics. Both would be separate from common sense, but not necessarily separate from each other.

(along with some unregenerate philosophers) continue to wonder. It will be the purpose of what follows to suggest that the scientifically minded metaphysician can find arguments in Wittgenstein's *Philosophical Investigations* which, if they are indeed sound, would serve to rebut the three major points advanced above.

Let me quickly enter some caveats to such an "unphilosophical" assumption. First, I am not claiming that the above three points constitute the sole means of drawing a distinction between science and metaphysics. Thus, even if I am wholly successful, I will not have shown that science *is* identical or continuous with metaphysics. Nevertheless, these three points are quite crucial to all the attempts to draw the distinction which I have seen. So, if I can cast some doubt on them, I think a great deal will have been accomplished.

Second, I do *not* claim that Wittgenstein himself (nor especially any of his disciples) ever used the arguments of the *Philosophical Investigations* to draw the kinds of conclusions I am trying to draw. However, in the next section I will outline a strategy of attack on the three above-mentioned principles. In the following three sections, I will argue that Wittgenstein does hold the positions outlined in the strategy.

Third, I grant that Wittgenstein argued explicitly against the kind of scientific metaphysics I am here defending. In the last section I shall examine this argument and try to show that it is neither convincing nor central to his position. I will also argue that the central Wittgensteinian features which *do* support my claim help explain why Wittgenstein and his followers have never taken the final step I am urging be taken.

Finally, I will not have the space actually to defend in detail the Wittgensteinian arguments which I am claiming support scientific metaphysics. However, I believe that these arguments are among those most widely accepted and most influential in contemporary philosophy. Hence if I am successful, I will at least have presented the following dilemma: If philosophers accept Wittgenstein's arguments, they ought to be more patient with the student who cannot easily disentangle science and metaphysics; on the other hand, if they believe such a distinction is obvious, they should relook at the Wittgensteinian arguments they all seem to accept.

II

I turn first to the strategy of attack. The first point was that empirical and conceptual truths must be distinguished—assigning science to the study of the former and metaphysics to the study of the latter. This point will be attacked in two parts. First, I will deny that conceptual truths, whatever their analysis, are absolute and eternal and to be known only through some specialized philosophical method, i.e., metaphysics. This would move philosophy toward science and will be explored in the next section.

Second, I will deny the applicability of the popular caricature of an empirical question's being decidable one way or the other by appeal to neutral experience (or a neutral observation language). I will argue that there is no fundamentally clear distinction between theory and observation and hence no univocal way of deciding empirical questions by appeal to experience, i.e., the observable. This would cast doubt on the scientific method as something which could be clearly and distinctively specified. The particular way in which theory conditions observation is more nearly like the way philosophical method is often described, i.e., as providing a new way of looking at things. This will be discussed in Section IV.

As regards the claim that metaphysics is a different order subject than science or common sense, I challenge this by admitting hierarchical levels of investigation but denying that anything peculiarly metaphysical results from this hierarchy. In other words I will deny that any other levels than appear in science need be invoked to explain commonsensical and scientific conflicts. An investigation of this point will be undertaken in Section V.

Finally, the above investigation would constitute a "philosophical" argument in favor of the scientific metaphysics position—albeit, not a conclusive one. For if one can show that it is highly unlikely that we can clearly separate the empirical from the conceptual, ipso facto, we will be unable clearly to separate the scientific from the metaphysical. If one can show that the conflicts encountered in science and common sense need no more of an explanation or account than what is given by science and common sense, then a different order of metaphysical explanations will not appear necessary—and, of course, the need for such metaphysical explanations has seldom been "obvious."

III

What then is a "conceptual" truth? It is presumably a truth concerning the relations of concepts, but this is rather vague. It is vague in two senses. First of all, it is very unclear just what a concept is, and a fortiori unclear as to just what sorts of relations these entities can enter in. But, second, it is also unclear whether the entity called a conceptual truth is true because it is *about* concepts and their relations or whether it is true in virtue of the concepts involved, where this "in virtue of" relation is different from an ordinary Tarski-like satisfaction relation.

To put the point in another way, a conceptual truth is a necessary truth and, at least prima facie, necessary truths have two separate aspects of philosophical interest—their truth and their necessity. I am not denying that some theories of necessary truth may actually fuse these two aspects. However, if such is the case, such a fusion must be made explicit. For it seems to me that all too many discussions of necessary truth are completely vitiated by not keeping these two aspects distinct.

Consider, for example, a standard conventionalist account of necessary truth. Although there are many variations, such an account essentially ties necessary truth to conventions to use language in certain ways. Thus necessary truths are truths concerning proper linguistic usage. But most philosophers who accept a conventionalist account of necessary truth also seem to accept some version or other of Tarski's truth criterion, the particular one depending on their view of the appropriate truth-bearer—sentence, utterance, etc. What happens when acceptance of a Tarski-like criterion is combined with a conventionalist account of necessary truth is that a basic confusion results. That this is so has been argued in several places.[4]

---

[4] Henry Veatch, *Two Logics* (Evanston: Northwestern University, 1969), Ch. 5. Roderick Chisholm, *Theory of Knowledge* (Englewood Cliffs, N.J.: Prentice-Hall, 1966), pp. 82–84.

Basically the argument is this: According to Tarski, 'Copper is copper' is true if and only if copper is copper. Thus the truth condition is given by the words to the right of 'if and only if'. But to assert that this condition is some sort of convention to use words in a certain way is simply to confuse use with mention. For 'copper is copper' is *used*, not *mentioned*, in its occurrence to the right of the 'if and only if' in Tarski's criterion. As such these words are *about* copper in the world. Furthermore the sentence 'Copper is copper' will not be true if the condition is not satisfied, that is, if copper is not copper. Such a commitment to the Tarski criterion renders irrelevant the remark that it is conventional that we use the sign-design, 'copper', as we do. Of course that is conventional, but it does not touch the point that whatever the sign-design, it is *used*, not *mentioned*, in its occurrence to the right of the 'if and only if'.[5] Notice finally that to say, "Yes, but 'Copper is copper' will be true no matter what," is not to object to the above argument. It is at best to call attention to the necessity feature of necessary truths.

The point that emerges here is that prima facie one account might be offered of the *truth* of necessary truths and a quite different account offered of the *necessity* of necessary truths. Thus someone who believes that necessary truths are about the world is not thereby committed to locating the source of necessity in the world in some kind of necessary property or relation. He could, for all that has been said so far, locate the necessity in some sort of linguistic conventions. On the other hand, one who wishes to locate necessity in conventions is not thereby committed to the view that necessary truths are not about the world and are hence uninformative.

It is my belief that Wittgenstein proposes a view of conceptual truth which neatly exploits the prima facie separability of the truth and necessity aspects of conceptual truths in a way which avoids

Gilbert Harman, "Quine on Meaning and Existence, I," *Review of Metaphysics*, 21 (1967): 130–31, summarizes Quinean arguments against a conventionalist theory of truth. These arguments depend implicitly on accepting a Tarski-like criterion.

[5] I have, for simplicity's sake, ignored the necessary relativization of the truth-predicate to a language. Nothing in the above argument hangs on this relativization.

the standard criticisms. Thus I believe he holds a modified conventionalist account of necessity which meets the standard objections to conventionalism by showing that these objections are directed at the truth aspect instead of the necessity aspect of conceptual truths. In other words, the standard objections to conventionalism are valid only against a conventionalist account of necessary truth as a fused concept; they are not necessarily valid against a conventionalist account of the necessity aspect of conceptual truth. Contrariwise, I believe Wittgenstein admits that conceptual truths are about the world, but he can turn aside objections to realist accounts of necessary truths by noting they are objections to the fused concept of necessary truth and not to the truth aspect of conceptual truth. In doing this, I believe he shows that the empirical-conceptual distinction cannot be drawn absolutely, once and for all, but is rather relative to a set of language games which themselves are not absolute, being in turn dependent on a form of life.

Wittgenstein's rejection of the realist position on necessity is well known. I will mention just two indications of this rejection. The first is textual. In the famous Section 66 of the *Philosophical Investigations* in which he introduces the notion of family resemblances in criticizing the search for the "essence" of games, he says, ". . . *look and see* whether there is anything common to all."[6] And of course there is not. In fact, the admonition to look and see is applied throughout the work to 'meaning', 'understanding', etc., and in *no* case is an essence to be found. But if anything is a conceptual truth, it is an essential predication, and Wittgenstein, having looked, found nothing in the world to justify this necessity, no real necessary connections.

This also indicates the philosophical reason for Wittgenstein's rejection of the realist account of necessity. If we accept his "meaning is use" doctrine and the claim that "*essence* is expressed by grammar" (371), we can see that Wittgenstein will apparently have to locate the source of necessity in language.

---

[6] Ludwig Wittgenstein, *Philosophical Investigations*, 3rd ed. (Oxford: Basil Blackwell, 1967). In the following I shall use the by now standard practice of referring to the *Philosophical Investigations* by a number simpliciter to indicate the section number in Part I and by a page number for references in Part II.

Considerations such as the above have led many philosophers to attribute a conventionalist account of necessity to Wittgenstein. And indeed there are many places where he gives just such an impression (e.g., 116, 199, 492, p. 185). What traditionally looks like a conceptual truth, Wittgenstein often claims is a remark on the "grammar" of the concept involved. In short it looks as if Wittgenstein is claiming that to accept a statement as necessarily true is to note the grammar of its employment in language which in turn is to recognize that "this language like any other is founded on convention" (355).

Despite this evidence, several writers have recently denied that Wittgenstein does in fact hold such a standard conventionalism.[7] He says, "When I obey a rule, I do not choose, I obey the rule blindly" (219). And in response to his interlocuter's asking if he is a conventionalist, he says, ". . . they [human beings] agree in the *language* they use. That is not agreement in opinions but in form of life" (241).

But of even more importance than these textual indications, which can perhaps be given alternative interpretations, is a philosophical reason. If Wittgenstein were a standard conventionalist, that is, if for him necessity were grounded in our agreement to use language in a certain way, then the following triad (185) should be inconsistent: (*A*) A person understands some linguistic formula, i.e., he has adopted and assented to the conventionally formulated or formulable semantical rules governing the meaning of that formula. (*B*) He performs an action which we would ordinarily say constituted a mistake in applying the rule, e.g., he writes down . . . 998, 1000, 1004, 1008 . . . at the order "+2." (*C*) He does *not* acknowledge

---

[7] Michael Dummett, "Wittgenstein's Philosophy of Mathematics," *The Philosophical Review*, 63 (1959):324–48; and Barry Stroud, "Wittgenstein and Logical Necessity," *The Philosophical Review*, 74 (1965):504–18. Indeed it will be obvious in what follows that I am heavily indebted to Stroud's treatment of this point. However, I think I can advance additional arguments for the conclusion that Wittgenstein accepts a compromise between realism and conventionalism as well as put this conclusion to a use which Stroud perhaps did not foresee (and would perhaps reject). Both Dummett and Stroud base most of their arguments on passages in the *Remarks on the Foundations of Mathematics*. I think the point that Wittgenstein rejects standard conventionalism can also be made with reference to the *Philosophical Investigations*.

that he has made a mistake, i.e., he says that's what he thought the linguistic formula meant. He believes he has acted perfectly rationally.

The reason this triad should be inconsistent on the conventionalist view is that it is part of the rules of use of 'understand' that B or C or both fail to hold. It might even be urged that the man could not really have "adopted and assented to the conventionally formulated semantical rules" and yet fail to acknowledge his mistake. For "adopted and assented" just *means* that he must acknowledge such a mistake. And yet it seems obvious that this reply is nothing but a piece of linguistic legislation. The beauty of Wittgenstein's description of the case lies in its pointing out that however odd the situation is, it is not obviously a *linguistic* oddity. It is rather more like the "one in which a person naturally reacted to the gesture of pointing with the hand by looking in the direction of the line from finger-tip to wrist, not from wrist to finger-tip" (185).

That Wittgenstein meant to assert the consistency and comprehensibility of the above triad can be brought out in yet another way. Suppose we think of the formula '$+2$' as a syntactic string in an uninterpreted calculus. Then the meaning of this sign-design is conventionally fixed by the interpretation we give to this sign-design. A man will "understand" '$+2$' just in case he gives it this conventional interpretation. Looked at in this way, the conventionalist position seems almost inevitable. Once the interpretation has been made, i.e., the conventions established, the triad must be inconsistent. How can Wittgenstein believe that it is consistent?

The answer lies, I believe, in Wittgenstein's doctrine that rules (conventions) can always be variously interpreted (85).[8] Notice that this cuts much deeper than the somewhat trivial observation that the sign-design '$+2$' can be given different interpretations. It rather means that the sense of '$+2$' depends not only on the interpretation, but also on the way the interpretation is given.[9] Indeed if one is to take seriously Wittgenstein's remarks concerning the role

[8] See Wilfrid Sellars, *Science, Perception and Reality* (New York: Humanities Press, 1963) Ch. 11, for a similar discussion of the crucial notion of the variability of rule interpretation.

[9] See Benson Mates, *Elementary Logic* (New York: Oxford University Press, 1965), Ch. 5, for a discussion of the difficulty of giving a canonical form for interpretations of a formal calculus.

of what seems "natural" in the situation described by the triad, we must go even further. We must assert, in effect, that the background natural language, which is and must be assumed even to state the notions of calculus and interpretation, is *itself* a set of rules which can be variously interpreted. Thus the seeming inconsistency in the triad arises from a too-narrow conventionalist view of language. As long as we are assuming that we can assign a canonical role to some language (ideal or ordinary) in the sense that what the rules of that language *say* is "natural," then the triad will appear inconsistent. But if we see that the canonical nature of any language is relative to what the users of that language find it natural to *do*, we can see that the triad is consistent for the man who finds it natural to go on in that way.

The conventionalist appeal to rules for the correct use of terms is thus not ultimately explanatory, for we want to know, of two people who react in different ways to an order, which one is right? Which one *is* following the rule, the convention (206)? But if rules can be *variously* interpreted, then the standard conventionalist appeal to rules as the source of necessity fails. For the rules, even if they are rules of the meta-language, do not carry their own interpretation on their face (86).

Faced with this apparent rejection of the standard conventionalist position by Wittgenstein, Dummett attributes to him a *radical* conventionalism.[10] This radical conventionalism is such that it must constantly and at each instance be renewed. In other words, even in a mathematical proof, the necessity of each step consists in our deciding at that particular time to treat that very statement as unassailable. If rules can always be variously interpreted, then in any particular case they must be given an application then and there.[11]

Although such a move would serve to block the problem raised for standard conventionalism by the ever-present possibility that rules may be variously interpreted, it is quite clearly *not* the route

[10] Dummett, "Wittgenstein's Philosophy of Mathematics."

[11] It also seems to me that Chihara interprets Wittgenstein in a similar way. His idea that, for Wittgenstein, different people may have different concepts of the "same" notion (same formula) seems to me comparable to the requirement of constantly interpreting the formula in each individual case. See Charles S. Chihara, "Mathematical Discovery and Concept Formation," *The Philosophical Review*, 72 (1963): 17–34.

that Wittgenstein takes. For in discussing the language game of 185 mentioned above, he says, "It would *almost* be more correct to say, not that an intuition was needed at every stage, but that a new decision was needed at every stage" (186, my italics).

But if Wittgenstein rejects the interpretation Dummett wishes to foist on him, what is his answer to the constantly present possibility of variable interpretation of rules? I think Stroud's notion that the key is to be found in Wittgenstein's appeal to forms of life and natural history is the answer.[12] Let me begin by quoting Wittgenstein at some length.

> This was our paradox: no course of action could be determined by a rule, because every course of action can be made out to accord with the rule. The answer was: if everything can be made out to accord with the rule, then it can also be made out to conflict with it. And so there would be neither accord nor conflict here.
>
> It can be seen that there is a misunderstanding here from the mere fact that in the course of our argument we give one interpretation after another; as if each one contented us at least for a moment, until we thought of yet another standing behind it. What this shows is that there is a way of grasping a rule which is *not* an *interpretation*, but which is exhibited in what we call obeying the rule and going against it in actual cases [201].

I take it that Dummett's proposal to substitute a constantly recurring decision as to application in the place of an appeal to a standard—in the place of being in accord or in conflict—is the position of the first paragraph. This is clearly rejected by Wittgenstein. In its place, he suggests that there is a way of grasping the rule which is not an interpretation but which is exhibited in actual cases.

But what is this way in which Wittgenstein hopes to block the infinite regress of rule, interpretation, rule, etc.? He says, "The common behavior of mankind is the system of reference by means of which we interpret an unknown language" (206). "What has to be accepted, the given, is—so one could say—forms of life" (p. 226). But what is a "form of life"? And in what sense is it basic? Wittgenstein gives us the answer in 208 and amplifies and defends it in the following sections through 241.

---

12 Stroud, "Wittgenstein and Logical Necessity."

To see what a "form of life" is, one needs first to distinguish it rather sharply from one sense of language game.[13] The distinction I wish to draw is the one hinted at by Wittgenstein in 23. There he contrasts the multiplicity of language games with the larger activity or form of life. The *speaking* or *using* of language, the *playing* of the language games is part of the form of life. It is this contrast between the total activity and behavior of a human organism on the one hand, and certain games, language games, with end points, sets of rules, etc., on the other to which I wish to draw attention.

Put in terms more familiar to logicians, a form of life could be a meta-language *in use*, while a language game ranges from an uninterpreted formal calculus through an explicitly formulated and interpreted calculus as an object of study to a part of the meta-language itself *either* conceived as an object *or* as a part of the meta-language in use.[14] It is the distinction between the active use of the meta-language as a form of life on the one hand and any part of that language considered in a nonactive way as an object of study on the other that is here crucial.

But this way of stating the problem is misleading. For when we think as logicians, we constantly feel that we can equally make the meta-language an object of study. We can make its implicit rules explicit by giving *them* an interpretation in the same old way. What Wittgenstein does for us here is to point out that such a procedure

---

[13] For a detailed defense of this, see the excellent article by J. F. M. Hunter, "'Forms of Life' in Wittgenstein's *Philosophical Investigations*," *American Philosophical Quarterly*, 5 (1968):233–43. I also believe that the adumbrated account of 'form of life' which *I* offer above is similar to Hunter's own "organic account." "The sense I am suggesting for it [form of life] is more like 'something typical of a living being': typical in the sense of being very broadly in the same class as the growth or nutrition of living organisms, or as the organic complexity which enables them to propel themselves about, or to react in complicated ways to their environment" (p. 235).

[14] When I speak here of a "meta-language in use," I do not mean to imply that a form of life *must* be linguistic in nature, although, of course, it could be and often is, at least partially. Rather, I mean to say that it is a system of human activities with point, purpose, and regularity. Such activities are most easily *represented* in linguistic terms because they are rule-governed and intentional. I use the meta-language in use simile because for logicians I wish to draw attention not to the interpretation of a formal calculus which some might compare to the relation a form of life stands in to a language game, but rather to the language in use which allows us to understand the notion of giving any particular interpretation in the first place.

is not ultimately explanatory. To avoid an infinite regress of the interpretation of the rules of a language we must, as noted above (201), stop the regress by an exhibition of actual performance. It is this function that a form of life performs. Wittgenstein has simply pointed out to us that we need something like the notion of a meta-language *in use* to make sense of the results we can obtain using the meta-language–object-language distinction. For any investigation, there is an assumed, noninvestigable, language in use or set of accepted human activities which enables us to frame our investigations. But now how can this form of life, this meta-language in use, serve as an explanation of the grasping of rules which is not an interpretation but which is exhibited in the actual cases?

The answer is really quite simple. It consists of two parts. In the first case, if we already know a language, then we can appeal to that language and our understanding of it to explain how a particular rule is to be followed. In other words, *within* an established language game as played, as a part of a form of life, we can always use the already established rules and conventions in use to explain a new rule or convention. It is this possibility which Wittgenstein believes misleads those who would base their theory of language on ostensive definitions. "And now, I think, we can say: Augustine describes the learning of human language as if the child came into a strange country and did not understand the language of the country; that is, as if it already had a language, only not this one. Or again: as if the child could already *think*, only not yet speak. And 'think' would here mean something like 'talk to itself' " (pp. 15–16). Their mistake is in believing that what one can do assuming a language game as played, a part of a form of life, one can also do in general, without such an assumption.

But in the absence of a form of life, we do *not* use ostensive definition, we do *not* explain a formula by another formula. Rather we *train* people into our form of life, into the general behavior of mankind (86, 143). "If a person has not yet got the concepts, I shall teach him to use the words by means of examples and by *practice*— and when I do this I do not communicate less to him than I know myself" (208). The qualification is *crucial*. There is nothing over and above the practice and examples; nothing in the situation, nothing in me. I *train* the student into my (our) form of life. And "our pupil's capacity to learn may come to an end" (143). He may be *un*trainable in certain areas.

But what is the force of this possibility?

> I am not saying: if such-and-such facts of nature were different people would have different concepts (in the sense of a hypothesis). But: if anyone believes that certain concepts are absolutely the correct ones, and that having different ones would mean not realizing something that we realize—then let him imagine certain very general facts of nature to be different from what we are used to, and the formation of concepts different from the usual ones will become intelligible to him [p. 230].

To understand this passage, one needs, I think, to pay attention to yet another distinction in Wittgenstein's use of language games. The distinction is between an interpreted language game which it is physically possible to play and one which it is *not* physically possible to play. We cannot train our pupil into the latter, either because of some fact about him or some general facts of nature which render that interpreted language game unplayable. The above passage is hinting at the contingent conditioning of our concepts and the very general empirical grounding of these concepts. People may be untrainable in just the sense that they may be organisms which it is impossible to train. And this "impossibility" is not easily classifiable as either contingent or conceptual, despite its ultimate dependence on the very general facts of nature.

But now let me return to the question of the status of necessity in Wittgenstein. His proposal is really twofold. Assuming a form of life as given, we can make sense of the necessity of a proposed conceptual truth by an appeal to the conventions and rules governing the way the language games which are a part of this form of life are actually played. Most modern ordinary language analysts are thus right in looking at "what we would say if."[15] And, of course, it is not an accident that, almost one and all, these philosophers hold some sort of linguistic or conventionalist view of necessity. A person has the "right" concept or is following a rule "correctly" if he is behaving in accordance with the form of life into which he has

---

[15] E.g., Stanley Cavell, "Must We Mean What We Say?" in V. C. Chappell, ed., *Ordinary Language* (Englewood Cliffs, N.J.: Prentice-Hall, 1964).

been trained. Further, since most of us have been trained into that form of life, we can, in a certain sense, perceive its rules without undertaking an empirical investigation. In particular we can do this for the very general rules which, ex hypothesi, would be assumed as part of the form of life which gives structure to the empirical investigation. Thus in a certain sense the conceptual-empirical distinction *can* be drawn *within* an actually played language game. The necessary truths are those which are treated as necessary within this actually played game.

However, as critics of conventionalism and ordinary language analysis have pointed out, there is the danger of taking these parochial (to an actually played game) results as somehow the "absolutely correct ones."[16] It is at this point that Wittgenstein's admonition to consider the very general facts of nature as being slightly different comes into play. When we cannot assume a given form of life or language game as played, then the search for necessity is meaningless *except* in the sense that these most general features of the world almost assuredly have conditioned the range of language games which it is physically possible for us to play. After all, evolution assures us that those pupils whose capacity to learn (to be trained into a form of life) fairly quickly and fairly often comes to an end are not likely to survive. Thus the realist, too, is right in his contention that it is the features of the world which are responsible for the necessity of necessary truths. These features need not themselves be necessary. Rather it is through the screening function that these features play with respect to the physical possibility that certain forms of life will survive that they are responsible for necessity.

Furthermore, it is, I think, an open question as to whether or not there are any identity criteria for forms of life. Thus I think it is simply undecidable at present whether the general features of the world have already so limited the language games we can successfully play that we can justifiably say there is only one form of life or not. At any rate, there is a serious epistemological question concerning the supposition of more than one possible form of life. For

---

[16] See, for example, Benson Mates, "On the Verification of Statements about Ordinary Language," in Chappell, *Ordinary Language*.

if I am correct, it is a *given* form of life which would allow us to understand this possibility in the first place by providing the background against which we would test our concepts concerning an alternative form of life. Thus in the largest sense, we are, epistemologically, locked into the form of life we have. However, it may be very useful not to construe 'form of life' quite so broadly. If we take a narrower view, we may be able to understand as actually misguided some of the current controversies surrounding scientism and humanism. These two movements might be different forms of life and hence irreconcilable by anything but an evolutionary process.

Interestingly, this account points up the traditional strengths and weaknesses of conventionalist and realist accounts of conceptual truths. A conventionalist account has always been strongest in accounting for conceptual change and the mistakes that have historically been made in certifying something as conceptually true. If necessity depends on the rules of use of evolutionarily selected language games, then both mistake and change are easily seen to be compatible with Wittgenstein's account. On the other hand, the traditional weakness of a conventionalist account has always been its inability to explain the nonarbitrary element in conceptual truths. In other words, one simply cannot alter the conventions, and hence the necessity, at will. On the foregoing account this is explained first by noting that even conceptual truths are *about* the world and hence nonarbitrary in that sense. But even more important is the fact that conceptual truths reflect the most general features of the world which are, in turn, the structural elements in the language games which have been selected through evolution and which constitute a part of our form of life. But now the typical criterion of a conceptual truth, the inconceivability of the denial, finds its grounding ultimately in the notion of a form of life. (Recall that in order to stop the regress of the rule, interpretation, rule, etc., we had to appeal to a form of life in which obeying the rule was exhibited, shown, in actual cases.) Now our present form of life may be the only one which can exist for evolving organisms like us in an environment like ours. If so, we will be unable to "conceive" of an alternative and hence the conceptual truths will be even more strongly nonarbitrary than ordinary empirical truths. Even if there are other possible forms of life, we can only contemplate them from within the one that is ours; thus here, too, a strong nonarbitrary character to conceptual truths emerges. Yet there is a larger sense in which alternative forms of life are possible.

Turning to the realist account—traditionally its strength has been that conceptual truths do seem to be about the world and not about language. It also seems that even the necessity is somehow grounded in the world. On this account, all these features are retained because the most general and pervasive features of the world are responsible for the conceptual truths reflected in the evolutionarily selected language games we can play. The change is that generality reinforced by evolutionary selection replaces necessary connections in the classical sense as the locus in the world of the necessity of conceptual truths. The major weakness of a realist account has always been that no special "necessary" connection in the real world seems discoverable over and above the connections which ground ordinary empirical truths. This fact is the basis of Hume's critique of necessity. On Wittgenstein's account, no such special connection is presupposed. Necessary connections turn out to be just very general and pervasive ordinary connections. The difference between conceptual and empirical can be drawn but it is one of degree, not of kind.

To summarize this section, Wittgenstein has a theory of conceptual truth which renders the conceptual-empirical distinction relative to a presupposed language game actually being played. In this respect we can distinguish within the form of life into which we have all been trained between science and metaphysics. Within the game of philosophy and science as now played, there are clear conceptual parts and clear empirical parts and a continuum in between. But a line between the two, while it can be drawn for particular purposes within a language game, *cannot* be drawn absolutely. In this latter respect—the respect in which science and philosophy are both instruments for coping with the world—there will be no hard and fast line between them. I conclude, then, that insofar as a clear distinction between empirical and conceptual truths is presupposed by the attempt to separate metaphysics from science, this attempt can in a sense succeed, but in a larger sense will fail.

IV

It has been a popular view of science that its job is to apply varying theories, uninterpreted calculi, to the neutral unproblematic data of observation. The true theory would then be the one which best "fit" this neutral data. (Specifying just what constitutes this "fit" turns out to be rather technically complex, but this is irrelevant here.) Perception then would be primarily concerned with establishing what is the case, with assembling the data preparatory to theorizing. Whatever perceptual errors we might make would be explained with reference to some kind of "correct" and theoretically neutral perception.

But if, as I have argued in the preceding section, Wittgenstein rejects the possibility of drawing a line between the conceptual and the empirical, then this indeterminacy should be reflected in perception as well. Notice, too, that the rejection of the distinction between conceptual and empirical is a radical rejection. There is *no* line to be drawn. It is not just that the line is somehow hazy. The latter, weaker, position would be compatible with the standard view of perception sketched above. Thus phenomena such as "seeing things that aren't there," or "reading something into the situation," or "failing to notice that aspect" are, on the standard view, all to be explained as failures or errors of *perception*. On the more radical view, there remains room for some of these "perceptual" errors to be explained as "conceptual" errors.

The radical rejection of the empirical-conceptual distinction involves, I think, the realization that there are unmistakably cognitive elements in perception (as well as perceptual elements in cognition). One would, therefore, be led to expect Wittgenstein to reject the standard view of perception. One would also expect him to urge that there is something cognitive in all perception. Yet because of the empirical limits imposed by our being trainable into only a few forms of life and probably trained into only one, one would also expect Wittgenstein to set some limits to the cognitive interpretations which can be imposed on perception. I think that these predictions are precisely borne out in his discussion of 'seeing' and 'seeing as'.

Wittgenstein introduces his discussion of 'seeing' and 'seeing as' with reference to a typical schematic box-figure (p. 193).[17] He asks us to consider the contrast between some simple, bare-bones kind of seeing of the illustration on the one hand and what we see the illustration *as* in the context of its appearance. Now we see the illustration as a box, now as a wire frame, now as a solid angle made of boards. The question then is, just what is this phenomenon of "seeing as" and how is it related to just plain ordinary seeing?

The suggestion which perhaps most naturally appears is that 'seeing as' is to be analyzed as seeing with an interpretation. Such a view would accord nicely with the standard scientific view of observation. Wittgenstein, however, rejects this view for a very interesting reason. If such an analysis were correct, one ought to be able to specify the seeing simpliciter which forms the basis for the then-added interpretation (p. 194). But this is just what we *cannot* do. We cannot describe the perceptual content of seeing in any ultimate noninterpretative terms. The failure of the phenomenalists' search for a neutral sense-datum language underscores this point.

But what then *is* the proper analysis of 'seeing as'? And what is its relation to seeing? We must, Wittgenstein tells us, "distinguish between the 'continuous seeing' of an aspect and the 'dawning' of an aspect" (p. 194). 'Seeing as' will refer only to the latter (pp. 195, 206). Once the distinction is drawn, we can see that "the flashing of an aspect on us seems half visual experience, half thought . . . an amalgam of the two, as I should almost like to say. The question is: *why* does one want to say this?" (p. 197).

This is indeed the question: Why is seeing as an amalgam of seeing and thinking? It is not seeing some object and then adding an interpretation. Wittgenstein has already rejected that possibility. (See also p. 200.) I seem to see something different each time, for "to interpret is to think, to do something; seeing is a state" (p. 212).

---

[17] I do not consider Wittgenstein's more famous example of a duck-rabbit (an ambiguous picture); for, although I think the particular example is immaterial, someone might easily accuse me of picking a special case. It is for this reason I have chosen the box-figure. Actually I think any object whatsoever will do, e.g., the cathode ray tube used by N. R. Hanson, *Patterns of Discovery* (Cambridge: Cambridge University Press, 1965), p. 15.

But what kind of state? "What I perceive in the dawning of an aspect is not a property of the object, but an internal relation between it and other objects" (p. 212).

An internal relation between it and other objects! But now we are back on familiar ground. For "internal relations" are conceptual truths concerning the categorization of various objects. They are generic identity criteria. And if what I have urged in the preceding section is correct, these conceptual truths are such as a result of our having been trained into a language game for which they provide the structure. The question there was how one could tell that someone had a concept "right." In order to stop a possible infinite regress of rules and interpretations as an explanation of the correctness of application of a concept, Wittgenstein urged that a form of life be taken as the given, as a way of grasping a rule which was exhibited in actual practice. In turn, the form of life is often a set of very general language games *as played*. But, of course, a good part of a language game as played will be connected with actual perceptual experiences—at least with the perceptual parts of the language. Thus getting a perceptual concept, X, "right" and perceiving X's are all wrapped up with each other.

But now we must recall the two *different* ways in which a concept can be gotten "right." It can be interpreted in terms of an already given language game as played, or else we can simply be trained into its use. Seeing as, when contrasted with seeing simpliciter, fits the former characterization. When we see X as Y, we place the perceived object originally categorized as an X into the language game which is the necessary condition for its being categorized as a Y. Seeing as marks the transition from one perceptual language game to another. It marks the taking of an object associated with one set of internal relations and placing it in the context of another set. But of even more importance, this view tells us what it is to be an object in a set of internal relations in the first place. It involves at its most basic level, having been trained into a language game.

But as there are empirical limits to the language games which can be played, so there are limits on the ways in which any object can be seen as something else. We can only see something as something else if we can put it into different patterns of behavior—if we can put the duck-rabbit into a picture with ducks *or* a picture with rabbits. It makes no sense, Wittgenstein says, to say we see a knife *as* a knife simply because knives function almost exclusively in *one* language game (p. 195). Yet even here one could, no doubt, invent a language game in which it would make sense to say of someone that he is seeing a knife *as* a knife. (Perhaps a culture which used knives in a way which *we* describe as phallic symbols would serve as an example. For this culture they would not be *symbols*. One can also note the psychological experiments designed so that the subjects are required to use [see] objects, e.g., hammers, in new ways, e.g., as plumb bobs.)

This limitation on seeing as, e.g., our inability to see a knife as a knife, does not show that seeing as is seeing plus an interpretation—as, I think, has been wrongly supposed by many. Seeing is just as much an "interpretation" as is seeing as. More precisely, neither is an interpretation. Rather, seeing X is part of an actually played language game with X's into which one has been trained and which is largely independent of other language games. 'Seeing as' is the ability (propensity might be better) to play more than one game with the object. This is why an ambiguous figure like the duck-rabbit illustrates 'seeing as' so beautifully. It precisely straddles two language games.

These remarks also illustrate why "The substratum of this experience [seeing as] is the mastery of a technique" (p. 208). One must have been trained into the alternate language game, must have mastered its techniques, in order to see some object as having the internal relations of that game. *Within* a given language game we can, perhaps, dismiss as nonsensical the claim that someone can see the schematic cube as a paper box or a tin box (p. 208).

So far, I have only discussed the limits on 'seeing as' which are connected with whether or not someone has in fact been trained into the appropriate language game. There are also the limits imposed by the very general facts of nature on what language games can be played. In fact if one reflects on the evolution of language games, and one thinks about the many language games we do not play because it is not physically possible to train human organisms into them, we can get a sense of how to analyze seeing simpliciter.

If we figuratively take the intersection of all the actually played language games to get the most general features (this result would be very like a form of life), then the very general perceptive categories which result could serve as the categories of seeing simpliciter.

I would have no objection to this as long as it is realized that even here we have only the very general empirical conditions on training together with the internal relations of these general language games into which we have been trained. That is, even seeing simpliciter partakes of the central features of seeing as, viz. the training into and accepting and using of a set of conceptual connections. When we reach a set of language games general enough to constitute a form of life—when, that is, we are no longer within a language game (or games)—then we must simply fall back on evolution and natural history for an account of the "correct" use of a concept. If we have been trained into the mastery of a technique, we see X's where X's are categorized by their internal relations to other objects and events, in this game. We are accustomed to treating X's as they are treated in this game (p. 198). This disposition can often be a very complex one. When X's also are categorized as Y's in another game, then we can see X's as Y's, provided we have been trained in the alternate game as well. Once more the crucial distinctions are relative to an empirically conditioned form of life. But one can also see that perceptual experience, scientific data in the standard sense, is itself relative to a language game as played. Thus at least a part of the justification of scientific theories rests on the way in which they help us see the world. A part of the justification depends on the conceptual adequacy of the observational categories used. And a determination of this conceptual adequacy has traditionally been a part of philosophy. The preceding section stressed how empirical conditions are relevant to deciding on necessary truths. This section has stressed how conceptual conditions are relevant to the empirical data. In short, there is a continuum between science and philosophy. Distinctions relative to an actually played language game can be made, but, unfortunately, these distinctions are usually taken as absolute—absolute in the sense that misses the important fact that the language games from which both science and philosophy arise are empirically conditioned and the product of evolutionary selection. Science and philosophy can be distinguished only as to the relative positions of concentration each adopts on the continuum of human inquiry into the world.

v

But now it will be urged by some that I have completely missed the force of Wittgenstein's philosophy in the foregoing. What I have done, it will be said, is to foist off on Wittgenstein a theory of conceptual truth, when in actuality his greatest contribution has been to point out that conceptual matters are grammatical and grammatical remarks are not really assessable on the dimension of truth and falsity at all. Philosophy differs from science not in the kinds of truth with which each deals but rather in that science deals with statements which can be true or false while philosophy deals with grammatical remarks which are neither true nor false. In short, philosophy is a different "order" enterprise from science.

Of course, this claim cannot mean merely that philosophy is more general in the sense that it is a meta-language and science and common sense are its object-languages. This may indeed be true, but a meta-language–object-language distinction is necessary in any number of "empirical" disciplines—lexicography, linguistics, grammar—to name just a few. For that matter, Wittgenstein claims that just because philosophy deals with 'philosophy' it does not follow that there must be a second order philosophy (121). I take this to be a textual reason for denying that Wittgenstein believes the object-language–meta-language distinction to be sufficient to distinguish philosophy from science. But even more important, the meta-language–object-language distinction does not square with the supposed absence of the true-false dimension in philosophy.

No, we must look elsewhere. It seems to me that Wittgenstein himself can easily be interpreted as suggesting a clear distinction in kind between philosophy and science. This distinction is the distinction between description and explanation. The philosopher can only describe; the scientist explains. "Philosophy simply puts everything before us, and neither explains nor deduces anything. —Since everything lies open to view there is nothing to explain" (126). "Philosophy may in no way interfere with the actual use of language; it can in the end only describe it" (124).[18] "We must do away with all explanation and description alone must take its place" (109). "The problems are solved, not by giving new information, but by arranging what we have always known" (109). It is important to notice here that on the present interpretation of Wittgenstein these descriptions are not to be taken as assessable in the true-false dimension. Of course they could be so taken, and if they are, the arguments of the preceding sections came into play. But what I am primarily concerned with here is to take the notion of 'description' as more closely allied with "assembling reminders for a particular purpose" (127), where the reminders are not so much true or false as they are suggestions to look at the matter in a different way.

It is also important to note here that even if we take 'descriptive' in a way which avoids the true-false dimension, this does not mean that we thereby avoid rational criticism. Surely it is contrary to the present way of interpreting Wittgenstein to suppose that we cannot say that one way of looking at things is somehow "better" than another way. And surely which is "better" is open to rational discussion and criticism. Thus in the sequel if I appear to be lapsing into treating descriptions as true or false, I mean merely to be appealing to this rationally criticizable dimension of description.

But now, even if we wholly accept such a descriptive role for philosophy, that will not by itself be sufficient to distinguish science from metaphysics. The reason for this is that if the preceding view of science is correct, there will be a similarly descriptive part to science as well. It will consist of clearing up conceptual confusions in the "foundations" of science. Given the continuum picture of science I have presented, such a descriptive investigation into the foundations of any science will be separable from that science itself only relative to a particular language game as played. It will not be separable from science in the larger sense of the form of life which has evolved. Wittgenstein, I think, makes precisely this point (p. 232).

Let us see, however, whether philosophy really can eschew explanation in the sense of proposing accounts which can be either

---

[18] I shall grant for the sequel that scientific explanations do disturb the use of language. However, I do not think that this is actually true in any important respect.

true or false. Paul Feyerabend had taken this insistence on the solely descriptive role of philosophy and combined it with the characteristically Wittgensteinian "meaning is use" doctrine in a most illuminating way.[19] Feyerabend argues that from these two doctrines—"meaning is use" and "philosophy is description"—it follows that it should be *meaningless*, not just false, to assert that there are any philosophical theories in the sense in which these might be explanatory. And indeed this seems to fit well into the general gestalt of Wittgenstein's works.

However, there are two problems with this view, both of which Feyerabend recognizes. The first is textual. Wittgenstein says, "If one tried to advance *theses* in philosophy, it would never be possible to debate them, because every one would agree to them" (128). But if Feyerabend's interpretation were correct, Wittgenstein ought not have allowed the theses to be true, even though trivial. Rather, he should have condemned them as meaningless. Feyerabend simply notes this inconsistency and lets it pass.

Closely allied with this point is a philosophical one. If meaning is use and philosophy is description, then Wittgenstein's celebrated attack on "essentialism" must be wholly out of place. It would be consistent for Wittgenstein to condemn essentialists for having *believed* they were explaining. That would have resulted from their misconception of the role of philosophy. But once that misconception is removed and the obvious fact of the traditional use of that kind of philosophical language is noted, an inconsistency arises. On Feyerabend's interpretation, Wittgenstein could not argue that this language is wrong; he should rather claim it to be meaningless. Yet quite clearly Wittgenstein's criticisms of essentialism go beyond what Feyerabend's interpretation allows him. Feyerabend here simply suggests Wittgenstein is wrong and is actually in the philosophical tradition of explaining after all.

But now one faces a dilemma. If one agrees with Feyerabend that philosophy does explain, we seem to be driven back to the distinction between science and philosophy as resting on the types

---

[19] Paul Feyerabend, "Wittgenstein's *Philosophical Investigations*," *The Philosophical Review*, 64 (1955):449. D. Gruender, "Wittgenstein on Explanation and Description," *Journal of Philosophy*, 59 (1962):523, maintains a view almost identical to Feyerabend's.

of truths, empirical or conceptual, with which each deals in its own characteristic way. On the other hand we can allow that these traditional philosophical pronouncements and criticisms are indeed meaningless, yet somehow indispensable for leading us to "higher" truths. I have argued in the preceding sections that the former horn is incapable of distinguishing science and metaphysics. Similarly, the second horn, in addition to its somewhat mystical unpalatability, simply begs the question as to a differentiation between science and metaphysics. The "higher truths" will be "higher," i.e., metaphysical, only if they are independently separable from scientific truths.

But I think there is another way out which can avoid this dilemma altogether and will furthermore render Wittgenstein's position (as so far presented) totally consistent. Let me return to the epigrammatic 128. "If one tried to advance theses in philosophy, it would never be possible to debate them, because everyone would agree to them." How are we to interpret this? Consider the following salient points. *One*. Wittgenstein criticizes any theory of meaning which relies upon the word's being constantly accompanied by any object or event—mental or physical. *Two*. Wittgenstein rejects the search for hidden essences as explanatory principles. Everything must be open to view. *Three*. Meaning is due to roles in language games as played which, in turn, are manifestations of parts of a form of life which, in turn, must be accepted. We can only be trained into a form of life. *Four*. The mistakes of other philosophers are not stupid (340). These points suggest very strongly to me the following interpretation of the crucial passage: The philosopher is never to advance theses in philosophy in the sense of postulating *ontological* entities, like particularity, in order to explain any problems. The reason for this is that when we look at our ordinary language games, we find no use for such a notion. It is not ordinarily used; it would have to be hidden if it is there at all; and when we look and see, we do not find it. Nevertheless generations of philosophers and reflective people who have read philosophers no doubt do constitute a traditional language game into which a number of people have been trained. So the mistakes made are not stupid and 'particularity' must have *some* meaning since it is used in this actually played game. Only its meaning does not point to a different order enterprise from that of common sense or refined common sense—science. If someone claimed, as a thesis, that there are particulars or that every accident is the accident of some substance, the thesis would be trivial. Who could deny it? These are just remarks which lay open to us a clear view of how we use our language. They are to be interpreted as saying this is how the game is played. But in such a role they *explain* nothing. They serve to refocus our concern, for example, on what kinds of things are particulars. But that concern, of course, is shared by atomic physics. The philosopher errs only in believing something special is needed to explain or ground these "grammatical reminders." We only need to get a clear view of the actual working of our language in order to see that most of our problems disappear. We can stop doing philosophy. And those problems which do not disappear can, perhaps, be theoretically handled, but in a way not different in kind from that of scientific problems.

If some such view as this is adopted, the inconsistencies noted by Feyerabend vanish, and it is possible to see how Wittgenstein can legitimately criticize other philosophers for being actually wrong rather than for speaking nonsense. There is a meaning to their words within the language games as philosophers play them. But these meanings are not hidden or pretentious. They are not independent of any language game into which we might be trained. Just as the duck in the duck-rabbit is not hidden and is not independent of our having been trained to recognize ducks, we must simply rearrange materials that have always been there. And it is important to note that these materials are simply the way the world contingently happens to be in its most general features.

> What we are supplying are really remarks on the natural history of human beings; we are not contributing curiosities however, but observations which no one has doubted, but which have escaped remark only because they are always before our eyes [415].

Natural history which is always before our eyes! From this we can surely get generality as a mark of philosophy, but a unified science also possesses the same generality. From this we can surely get a concern by philosophy with the highest levels of theorizing, with the rearranging of materials already present. But my remarks on seeing and seeing as were meant precisely to push at least a part of science in that direction as well. In short, I do not think that any of the ways of distinguishing science from philosophy which seem to depend on a different "order" of inquiry succeed. Description in the sense of assembling reminders seems no different from high-level theorizing in science. (The one exception, noted at the beginning of this section, is the meta-language–object-language distinction. I am perfectly willing to grant a meta-status to philosophy. But I deny that this secures a special place for philosophy as opposed to unified science.)

V I

And yet, scholars of Wittgenstein will have become more and more outraged with my treatment of him. Such a misuse (I did not claim it to be a totally faithful interpretation) of Wittgenstein's position is absurd. Let Wittgenstein himself retort.

If the formation of concepts can be explained by facts of nature, should we not be interested, not in grammar, but rather in that in nature which is the basis of grammar?—Our interest certainly includes the correspondence between concepts and very general facts of nature. (Such facts as mostly do not strike us because of their generality.) But our interest does not fall back upon these possible causes of the formation of concepts; we are not doing natural science; nor yet natural history—since we can also invent fictitious natural history for our purposes [p. 230].

Surely in the end (the literal end of the book) there can be no more decisive rejection of the view I have tried to sketch. We can *invent* natural history for our purposes (cf. Husserl's use of free variation).[20] So how could the actual course of events make any difference?

The answer is, I think, implicit in what I have already said. There is a most crucial ambiguity in 'natural history' as previously used in 415. It is this: When Wittgenstein denies philosophy is doing natural history, he means natural history as conceived within a language game as played. I have already conceded that a distinction be-

---

[20] Edmund Husserl, *Ideas*, trans. W. R. Boyce Gibson (New York: Collier, 1962).

tween science and metaphysics can be drawn *relative* to a given language game. On the other hand, in 415 'natural history' is being used in its supra-language game sense; that is, in the sense in which the most general features of experience condition our form of life and the language games we can play. Yet despite the contingency of these features, they are so general and so obvious that they both enable us to speak of conceptual truths relative to a language game while at the same time freeing us from having to carry out an empirical investigation as that is popularly caricatured. (It has been a major purpose of Section IV to attempt to remove just that caricature.) But if it is now asked how *invented* natural history would do as well as *real*, I can reply that the invented language games serve their purpose precisely in pointing up what these most general features of actually played language games are. "The work of the philosopher consists in assembling reminders for a particular purpose" (127).

It should also be recalled in this connection that invented language games will serve their purpose and remind us of the pervasive features of our experience only if they do not differ too much from the language games which express our present form of life. For the form of life determines intelligibility generally, and, a fortiori, determines the intelligibility of the invented history (cf. Section III). But now one can see why Wittgenstein and his followers did *not* see the implication of his work.

It is far too easy to slip unnoticed from questions concerning the correct interpretation of a rule *within* a language game as played, wherein we simply assume the larger form of life which provides the background, to questions concerning the background assumptions themselves. The *formal* distinction between the logical *role* played by the background assumptions versus the logical role played by particular analyses *within* the scope of these assumptions gives the illusion of being able to determine in some absolute sense the material content of this distinction. As long as the inquiry stays fairly close to the most general features of the language game as played, the analyses will, in fact, have fairly clear referential implications. We *will* be able to say something about the most general features of the world. But the reason for this is precisely that the world is, through evolution, empirically responsible for the fact that these games are played in the first place. On the other hand, it is a parochially contingent fact that philosophers are trained into the particular language games they play. Further, philosophers are generally *not* trained into modern scientific language games. Hence it would be all too easy for a philosopher with the usual philosophical training, but lacking, e.g., scientific training, to take a general feature of his set of language games as somehow much more pervasive than it is.

In fact, one may well wonder why philosophers make as few mistakes as they do. I suspect the reason is that throughout history there has been a close enough connection between science and philosophy so that philosophy does in fact incorporate into its language games a good deal of science. On the other hand, scientists have tended to hold down their mistakes by actually doing philosophy (as is, I think, the case in the foundations of the natural sciences), or else by borrowing heavily from philosophers of science (as is, I think, the case in the social sciences, where an austere positivism is still painfully evident). Because of this interaction, most results of science, of natural history, will not be relevant to our philosophizing. But *some* will, and some of our philosophizing will be relevant to science.

In addition, I think that this view gives me a handle for diagnosing why so many arguments in contemporary analytic philosophy seem just to pass each other by. A will claim X to be a conceptual truth because he cannot conceive $-X$. (Translation: A is working within a particular language game and has at least thus far been unable to train himself or be trained into another. Possibly the contingent facts in his case preclude his so being trained. In A's game, X is a conceptual truth.) B claims X is not a conceptual truth (and possibly even false); for here is a counter-example in which $-X$ is perfectly intelligible. (Translation: B is inviting A to consider a new language game which allows the conceivability of $-X$. This may or may not be a language game which is precluded by natural history.) We may not know who to believe. But quite clearly science—natural history—may be, and often is, relevant. We may need only to point out to A (or B) what most people have known a long time. We may have to train A (or B) into a current scientific language game of which they were unaware and which reflects the requisite natural history clearly enough to settle the dispute. Or we may even have to await the development of science to see if *A*'s (or *B*'s) presupposed language games actually are ones we can successfully play. What is one man's conceptual truth is another's empirical falsehood, and the only way to settle the issue is by considering *all* the language games humans play and can play. The charge of parochialism leveled at the more extreme advocates of ordinary language analysis is often justified.

On the other hand, the various competing theories in science serve the same function as invented language games. We can "invent" theories and models (of subatomic physics?) as long as these models are somewhat constrained by our actual experience. Their primary justification for acceptance is not their one-one correlation with observation but their fruitfulness in making our original problems clear. We can now see things differently.[21]

There is another way of viewing the activities of analytically minded philosophers, both contemporary and traditional. They are attempting to formulate identity conditions for language games and forms of life. I have already urged that all concepts, including perceptual ones (Section IV), are inextricably entwined with the very general features of how one behaves in the world, so conceptual analysis will include the actual "use" of language games. This is the kernel of truth in Wittgenstein's "meaning is use" doctrine. This doctrine has been sadly perverted into the "what one would say if" doctrine. At any rate, the results of such conceptual investigations should be looked on as normative recommendations as to how most fruitfully one should organize language games to cope with reality. But these normative recommendations are constrained by exactly the same kinds of empirical conditions as are foundational scientific theories. The justification for their acceptance is likewise the same in principle as for scientific theories. We do not look for a one-one correspondence with "philosophical" facts or intuitions, but rather we ask how well the philosophical analysis enables us to see our problems more clearly and how fruitful it is for further *human* inquiry.

---

[21] I do not here have the space to develop in detail this view of science. However, it is a more and more common view and it is expressed with great power by N. R. Hanson, *Patterns of Discovery* (Cambridge: Cambridge University Press, 1958).

Wittgenstein's mistake was then a simple one. It was one which he himself diagnosed as incredibly easy to fall into. It was the mistake of being held captive by a picture generated by a language game into which one had been trained. In Wittgenstein's case it was the picture of science concerning itself with detailed laboratory experiments. It was the picture of science as clearly empirical, as opposed to conceptual.[22] And the pernicious thing about this picture is that a sense within a language game as played can be given to it. Yet in the larger sense, science in its conceptual aspects seems not separable from philosophy after all. "Philosophical Investigations: conceptual investigations. The essential thing about metaphysics: it obliterates the distinction between factual and conceptual investigations."[23]

[22] If one looks at all the places Wittgenstein draws the distinction between science and philosophy—e.g., 37, 81, 89, 109, 124, 203, 392; p. 212, p. 230—one can see, I think, just this picture operating.

[23] Ludwig Wittgenstein, *Zettel* (Berkeley: University of California Press, 1967), p. 82e, §458.

PART TWO

Epistemology and Philosophy of Language

9

Wittgenstein on Private Languages

CLYDE LAURENCE HARDIN

*1. Wittgenstein's Criticisms of the Concept
of a Private Language*

In his *Philosophical Investigations*,
Wittgenstein devotes several pages to the idea that one could have
a language the sense of whose words could be known only to its
user. These expressions would have, as their primary reference, the
sights and sounds and smells and pains sensed by each individual
observer. The language would be essentially private, for each person
can know, in a certain intimate way Russell has called "knowledge
by acquaintance," only his own pain, or visual or auditory or
gustatory experiences, though he may be able to *infer*, by an argument from analogy, that other individuals have them too. The sensation words in our language have, it is claimed, two senses, one
known only to me by my inner feelings, the other known to everyone by the behavior which occurs in certain circumstances.

What Wittgenstein wants to argue is not only that our language
does not have a double use, but that it is impossible that it should
be employed in a private use or even that some expressions could
be so employed. I shall briefly summarize certain of his arguments,
sometimes quoting his own words, sometimes employing expressions

Reprinted with the kind permission of the author and the editor from
The Journal of Philosophy, 56 (1959):517–28.

of my own. For the full text, the reader is referred to Sections 243–315 of the *Philosophical Investigations*.

Essential to the whole argument is the concept of language as a system of habits of verbal usage which can be acquired and taught by human beings and which is governed by a set of rules by reference to which the linguistic efforts of any user are subject to correction. A "private language" is supposed by its advocates to "refer to sensations" in some way. How is this to be done? One way to establish the necessary connection is to substitute words for the natural expression of sensations, e.g., to substitute "I am in pain" for crying. But if sensation words are tied up in this way with the natural expression of sensation, the resultant language can no longer be said to be private, since the proper use of the words is governed by the occurrence of publicly observable pain-producing situations. Another way to refer to the sensation is to denote it by a sort of inner nod or private baptism. But these rituals in themselves mean nothing, for nothing counts as naming unless it is part of a language game in which the use of names is already understood as is the method by which they are to be bestowed. So one must inwardly undertake to use the word in a particular way. But to "inwardly undertake" must here mean at least to establish a rule of use and act in accordance with it. But how can I decide if I am following my rule properly? By memory? But what test do I now have that my memory does not deceive me (we are not here entitled to use physical—public—criteria for the veracity of our remembering)? Do I look up the rule in an imagined rule book? "(As if someone were to buy several copies of the morning paper to assure himself that what it said was true.)" To think that one is using a language correctly is not the same thing as to use it correctly. In private language there is no criterion of correctness for one's ostensible memories of which name designates which sensation.

Furthermore, 'sensation' is a word in the public language. What is our justification for using this word here? And what other word could we use? We have learned the use of expressions for sensations (such as 'pain') by means of public situations and public behavior. Outside of accepted contexts, they have no use. Compare the sense of: 'the stone feels pain', 'the corpse feels pain', and 'the fly feels pain'. While the first two do not make sense, the last does: this shows that by 'pain' we mean something which can be publicly manifested. A private sensation is like a beetle in a box; everyone might have a different beetle or no beetle at all; the language game goes on just the same, for the beetle plays no part in it. When we attempt a "private" use, saying, "*This* is what we mean!" and "nod" to our felt pain, we give no information at all.

2. Two Aspects of Wittgenstein's Argument

Wittgenstein's argument breaks down into two main parts. The first part consists of concrete arguments against the possibility of a "private," i.e., purely phenomenal, language. These arguments are two, though closely related. (*a*) Language is a social function which depends upon the possibility of correction by another person; without this social context there is no distinction between following a rule and thinking that one is following a rule, so that a private language becomes a meaningless babble. (*b*) There is no objective check upon memory mistakes in a purely phenomenal language, so that one can never know whether today's rules are the same as those of yesterday.

The second part is an attempt to show that the sensation words of ordinary language have public criteria for their use, so there is no need of constructing private languages to show how they are meaningful. I shall not argue this question here, for it would lead us too far from the present topic. We may, in this context I think, ascribe to Wittgenstein the doctrine of *physicalism*, i.e., the thesis that the criteria of application of a descriptive expression can be given by reference to material things and their properties. It may be the case that this thesis can in fact be established, or even that the descriptive expressions of ordinary language are physicalistically founded. I do not now wish to dispute either of these possibilities. What I want to argue here is that if physicalism does obtain, its obtaining is a contingent fact about our universe and not a necessary truth. I wish to argue that a nonphysicalistic use could be given to phenomenal predicates like 'headachiness', 'red', 'smooth', etc., and that there are circumstances which would strongly impel one to differentiate clearly two uses of these predicates, or even abandon the physicalistic use altogether. I therefore do not here claim (though neither do I deny) that the two uses are *distinguished* in everyday use; I maintain only that they are *distinguishable* and hence two rather than one.

It should first be made clear that in defending the possibility of a private "sensation language" one is not committed to the position that it is possible for a person who knows no language at all to devise a private language. It needs only to be shown that such a language is possible for at least some people who, like us, are already masters of a language. Thus we may suppose that we are already in possession of sensation words and observable predicates and schooled in their public use.

But are we entitled to use words such as 'red', 'soft', 'acrid', etc., as the nonlogical terms in a private language? It may be argued that the experiences supposedly referred to in a truly private language must be those to which no analogies may be drawn in terms of the experiences which others might have. Thus, one might say, if you use 'red', to refer to the sort of visual experience you commonly have when you see a fire truck or a Soviet flag, your auditor knows what it would be like to have the sort of experience you claim to be having now. I take it, however, that supporters of the notion of phenomenal languages have not intended to deny the considerable degree of structural similarity that holds between the experiences of different observers, but have rather wished to emphasize the so-called "incommunicability of content." I therefore propose that we are to regard the sense of a word as known only by a single individual if there are situations in which only he can decide whether or not the word can properly be applied. In any case, this criterion of private use will suffice for the examination of Wittgenstein's remarks, since the chief point of these is that it is not proper to talk of a language at all when there is no public check upon the correctness of the use of its expressions. Furthermore, it is not necessary to require that the syntax of a private language be incommunicable, nor that the language be complete, i.e., adequate for the description of all phenomenal experience.

3. Explicit Recollection and the Correctness of Linguistic Usage

Let us become clear as to exactly what Wittgenstein wants to assert. He surely does not mean to deny that a man like Robinson Crusoe,[1] who is as a matter of fact isolated from the human race for a long period of time, is rendered incapable of using a language correctly, even though nobody is present to correct possible language mistakes. Crusoe's only guide to correctness of speech is what he thinks correct speech to be. Yet if he stays sane during his long isolation, one would doubt that his language skills would be seriously affected. How is Crusoe's case different from that of one who undertakes to use a private language?

One important difference lies in Crusoe's background and previous training. From earliest childhood he underwent a continuous process of learning and practicing his language and being corrected whenever he made a mistake. The language behavior of the community became part of his own behavior as he acquired habits of correct use. It is no longer necessary for him explicitly to consult a physical or a remembered dictionary to be quite justifiably assured of the propriety of the great bulk of his verbal usage. He must rely on memory, but it is disposition or habit memory rather than explicit or recollection memory.

Most of us are not habitual users of a phenomenalist language. If we should wish to use one at all, we must decide upon rules for its use and be able to recall our decisions. We must be in the "dictionary stage" in which the rules must in some way be kept before us. It is here that we are subject to mistakes of memory, and it is in a private language that mistakes of memory can prove to be disastrous. How can a mistake in remembering the rules be corrected? By other memories? But how do we know that the other (ostensible) memories are in fact veridical? By other memories still? Perhaps one could keep a written rule book or private diary to

---

[1] The use of Crusoe as an illustration is found in an article by Helen Hervey in *Philosophical Quarterly* 7, no. 26 (1957). This article and those by Ayer and Rhees to which Miss Hervey refers are interesting discussions of Wittgenstein on private languages from which I have benefited. However, my own considerations are, in large degree, different from theirs.

which he could refer whenever in doubt. But this would not help. He cannot retain the sense impression to which his word refers as one might keep a piece of fabric to guide him in matching his previous upholstery. The rule book and the diary must themselves depend upon the veracity of memory. It is in this that the difficulty of a private language supposedly lies. It is here logically impossible, as it is not in Crusoe's case, that there should be any other methods of discovering one's mistakes. It is this difference in logical character between the two situations that, according to Wittgenstein, makes one a language and the other a series of verbalisms.

I do not find this argument at all convincing. It is at its most persuasive against views like those of Russell and the early Wittgenstein,[2] according to which the mastery of a private language is logically prior to the learning of a public one. When applied to one who already knows a public language, it loses much force. Suppose, for example, that I wish to report my visual states in terms of color patches in my visual field. These states might not be produced by observation of physical objects, but rather by drugs or electrical stimulation of the cortex. Clearly, I might simply use the color words previously employed to indicate qualities of physical objects. There is, in this case, no more question of a memory mistake than with our isolated islander. The language would be private in the sense that it is not at present known how to reproduce closely similar subjective states by means of cortical stimulation, etc. One might indirectly maintain a control over the proper use of color words in such cases by periodically subjecting the participants in the experiments to tests by means of color charts. It would not be difficult, however, to remove the effectiveness of this test as well. We might suppose that the subject was permanently blinded during the course of the experiment by the destruction of retinal tissues. Color impressions could be evoked centrally, though not peripherally, although the subject still could use color words correctly in public situations by employing various scientific instruments.

One might, of course, still hold that the user of the phenomenalist color expressions is in theory subject to correction, since we may find the particular patterns of neuron firing which correspond to the

---

[2] The view that "atomic facts" are to be understood as the occurrences of sense-data has been upheld by Urmson in his *Philosophical Analysis*, Ch. 5.

having of certain color impressions. I should not at all like to deny that this is possible and even probable. But that this should come about is by no means entirely a matter of the logic of the use of color words, but rather a question of what contingencies obtain. Physicalism should be regarded as a program and a belief in the success of that program. It has not been shown to be either an accomplished fact or a guarantee that certain facts will obtain.

4. Schlick's Illustration of the Contingency of Physicalism

Schlick made the contingency of the fulfillment of the physicalist thesis very clear, illustrating his point by asking his readers to imagine a world in which the visual coincidences[3] of our world should occur, but be "accompanied by entirely different perceptual contents from those to which we are accustomed, and, indeed, in a fully irregular way . . . while I could always order the colors in classes and assign them symbols, these symbols would not belong to an objective language; they would have only a private use."[4] I shall quote Schlick's examples in full, not only to illustrate the contingency of the physicalistic thesis, but also to supply the basis for an answer to another of Wittgenstein's criticisms:

1. At every moment, the entire visual field has only one color—with different intensity at different places—but undergoes a temporal variation such that the various colors appear in their spectral order: red, yellow, green, blue, etc.
2. We see the world as red when we are in a cheerful mood; as blue, on the other hand, when we are in an unpleasant mood. These feel-

[3] "Every measurement springs from a counting, and can in the last analysis always be traced to a number of 'coincidences,' where by a coincidence is to be understood the spatial coming together of two previously separated singularities of the visual or tactual fields (marks, pointers, etc.). This characteristic of measurement whereby spatial extension is, as it were, mastered by division into discrete parts has often been pointed out. It is this way of determining the spatial which is the physical. . . . The meaning of all physical propositions thus consists in the fact that they formulate either coincidences or laws relating to coincidences; and these are spatial-temporal determinations." (Moritz Schlick, "On the Relation between Psychological and Physical Concepts," reprinted in Feigl and Sellars, *Readings in Philosophical Analysis*, pp. 397–98.)
[4] Ibid., pp. 405–6.

ings—in accordance with our assumptions—must be in no way bound up with bodily events.

3. I have the ability to bring about "arbitrary" changes of quality; I can act in this domain. This, however, can only be allowed on the assumption that the motive for such activity always lies in the qualities themselves, and never in the coincidences. These would not, if I may so express myself, influence my will in so far as it was concerned with qualities; nor, on the other hand, could my will be influenced (if we are to be consistent with our assumptions) by the qualities in so far as it was concerned with coincidences (actions in the external world).

4. If I feel warm, the color qualities change in one direction of the spectrum, if I feel cold, in the other—here as well, needless to say, warmth and coldness must be independent of coincidences,—etc., etc.[5]

One can imagine a man who wakes up one morning to discover that he inhabits such a Schlickian world. Could such a man describe his experiences? Would his descriptions constitute a language? I can see no reason why the answers to both questions should not be "yes." Would such a language be private? I should think so, for the subject would not be able—without the benefit of scientific instruments—to use our color words in all the situations in which we could use them. If he also became insensible of physical coincidences, he would not be able to use our language at all. We could not use his language either, although we might learn the form of his laws from his verbal reports, and know that when he uttered 'red' he would then be disposed to utter 'yellow'. Furthermore, he would have no way of telling whether or not he was misusing his words systematically.

5. Phenomenal Laws and Memory Errors

These considerations naturally introduce another. In criticizing the notion that we can formulate a private language by "baptizing" our sensations with an "inward nod," Wittgenstein at one point asks, "What's the ceremony for?" One names in order to go on to assert. In a truly private language, what is there to assert? What is the

[5] Ibid., p. 406.

function of this particular language game? Schlick's examples provide us with an answer: "To formulate and confirm phenomenal laws." One might well find regularities in the occurrences in his sensory fields, or be able to construct regularities by suitable postulations (e.g., formulating Price's "gap-indifferent series").[6] Language would be very important in gaining the explicit concept of such regularities, since the regularity is not "given" in the way that impressions of sense may be said to be. (The success of a phenomenalistic construction of material-object concepts depends upon the formulability of such regularities within experience.)

This law-stating function of a phenomenalist language game brings to light certain interesting characteristics. First, it preserves the framework of the language from certain types of systematic memory errors. Let us illustrate this point by formulating a simple law in the hypothetical language of Egosensa.

Egosensa law (*a*): If red and green occur together, shrill whistle follows.

Suppose that my systematic memory error consists in confusing red, green, and shrill whistle with yellow, blue, and dull thud, respectively. When red and green next occur, I call them 'yellow' and 'blue'. But this does not affect my expectations or the confirmation of my law, since I now remember *Egosensa law* (*a*) as

Egosensa law (*a'*): If yellow and blue occur together, dull thud follows.

The integrity of my system of laws thus remains secure.

If my memory failures are less systematic, I may use my system of laws to decide that I have made a memory mistake, and withdraw a previously accepted statement, just as Robinson Crusoe might correct an error in his diary by discovering it to be out of line with several other observations or regularities. This is what Goodman[7] probably has in mind when he recommends that a phenomenalist language be based in part upon a system of "decrees," which are attributions of phenomenal qualities ("qualia"), any of which may be withdrawn if its consequences conflict with the rest of the sys-

---

[6] Cf. H. H. Price, *Hume's Theory of the External World*, p. 60ff.
[7] Nelson Goodman, *The Structure of Appearance*, p. 99ff.

tem. Obviously, this also has bearing upon the incorrigibility question. I would suggest that the reason Wittgenstein found the possibility of memory mistakes so damaging is that he went on the assumption that since no phenomenal event is repeatable and thus available for inspection at some later time, all statements about "immediate experience" must be taken as incorrigible. It then follows that there can be no verification, no correction, and anything that the subject thinks to be correct is, within the frame of the system, correct. Since the system itself is free from external criticism (this is a "private" language), there is *no* objective standard of correctness, and the private language cannot be said to be a language at all. If we reject incorrigibility[8] and govern the use of our language by the concepts of law and decree, we escape, I think, from the force of Wittgenstein's criticisms.

6. The Interdependence of Memories

There are two ways of interpreting Wittgenstein's argument against the validity of remembered rules in a private language. Memory judgments which cannot be confirmed by reference to material objects, he may be saying, are either (1) untestable and therefore worthless, or (2) unreliable. He cannot consistently argue for both since, as Goodman has pointed out,

> . . . no type of judgment can be *both* unreliable and untestable; for an unreliable judgment, after all, is one that is frequently found to be false *when tested*.[9]

Since we are not at all used to making judgments about phenomena, we are likely to be unsure about whether one sense presentation is like another in some phenomenal quality, and we are apt to change our minds easily. We are better able to remember what a thing had at a given time than what properties it seemed to have. It does not, however, seem to be in this sense that Wittgenstein wishes to attack the legitimacy of designative rules which depend upon memory

---

[8] I shall not discuss this question here. The case against incorrigibility has been made by J. L. Austin in his "Other Minds" (reprinted in A. G. N. Flew, *Logic and Language*, 2nd series), and by A. J. Ayer, *The Problem of Knowledge*, p. 52ff., among others.

[9] Goodman, *The Structure of Appearance*, p. 98.

alone. In the following passage, it is the untestability that is attacked:

> "But surely I can appeal from one memory to another. For example, I don't know if I have remembered the time of departure of a train right and to check it I call to mind how a page of the time-table looked. Isn't it the same here?"—No; for this process has got to produce a memory which is actually *correct*. If the mental image of the time-table could not itself be *tested* for correctness, how could it confirm the correctness of the first memory? (As if someone were to buy several copies of the morning paper to assure himself that what it said was true.)[10]

One may now ask what the method is by which Wittgenstein would have us test our memories. The answer would undoubtedly be that we should employ the techniques we do in fact employ in everyday life. Thus we might test the correctness of our mental image of the timetable by looking at the timetable, or asking at train information, or observing the train with a stopwatch in hand. The recommended way would seem to consist in an appeal to various experiences of material objects and a number of beliefs concerning them. If certain general and lawlike statements about the properties of material objects and certain specific statements about the circumstances which occur in this particular situation are true, then we are justified in asserting that our mental image was veridical.

Now notice the difficulty that a defender of Wittgenstein is in. Our beliefs about material objects are dependent upon memory and the character of our present experience. For example, our belief that the print on timetables does not change spontaneously can ultimately be justified only by an inductive inference, the evidence for which is neither remembered or in some way recorded. The integrity of various methods of recording must be justified by a similar inductive argument. It is indisputably clear that our knowledge of the past must ultimately come down to our ability to remember and interpret physical signs on the basis of what we can remember (by habit as well as by explicit memory). It is logically possible that, to use a well-known example of Russell's, the world might have come into existence less than five minutes ago, with all of the physical

---

[10] Ludwig Wittgenstein, *Philosophical Investigations* (Oxford: Basil Blackwell, 1967), pp. 93–94.

evidence and the memories of organisms just as they would have been if the world had existed for billions of years.

I do not wish to press the skeptical doubt any further. It does not impress us as being conclusive just because it is set up in such a way as to preclude an answer. But it does serve, as many skeptical doubts do, to remind us of the justificatory foundations of knowledge. In this particular case, the skeptic makes us see that the validity of memory cannot be justified in general, but that any given memory may be justified by its place in the corpus of remembered propositions, images, laws, implicit postulations, and all of the dispositions that depend upon past learning. A memory may thus be justified pragmatically, but not absolutely. Any confirmation must involve some sort of prediction. The ostensible memory of a past occurrence or fact may always be taken to be veridical if we are willing to replace a sufficient number of propositions which we must now accept by propositions we would now regard as false. This is the holistic fact of life, and I trust that it is by now sufficiently well-known to require no further argument. It is important to see that no memory may be justified by simply comparing it with some experienced object. The confrontation cannot—and this is a logical 'cannot'—be direct, since the memory is of something past, while the object is present. The confrontation thus depends upon a large number of propositions which can themselves only be confirmed by virtue of their conformity to one another and to future experience. The difference between a Wittgensteinian test for correctness and the standards for a successful Goodman decree is, as far as I can see, a difference only of degree.

There is a less general way of showing that there is a certain legitimacy in the phenomenalist coherence theory of memory. This is by examining the way in which we make decisions as to the validity of ostensible memories in the absence of appropriate physical evidence. We savor the feeling of "rightness" that accompanies the belief; we perhaps examine our own motives to see whether or not we might have made it all up; we ask whether the consequences of the proposition we entertain are in conflict with propositions to which we already strongly adhere. It is quite true that a piece of relevant physical information will in the majority of cases carry more weight than many of these considerations. Such information can surely confirm our memory findings reached by the more "internal" criteria, but it cannot serve as an absolute and final *verification* of them. The point here is that we do make decisions without such material evidence and do not always later confirm these decisions with it. We recognize these techniques as having a certain validity and can from time to time check the conformity of their results with the results obtained by more Wittgensteinian methods. Why may we not apply the same type of criteria in situations which lack the opportunity for such checks, especially when the circumstances seem favorable, as they would be in employing color words phenomenally (i.e., as designating qualia rather than qualities)?

In a Schlickian world, one would not be able to confirm quale judgments by physical tests. It has been my contention that a phenomenal language would be possible in even such circumstances as these. But in our present world, we need not be so austere. If the phenomenalist is right, we have pre-analytically grouped qualia into a schema to which we refer as material objects. Some qualia of the schema are reliable indicators of the presence of others, and the entire schema serves as a construct by means of which various qualia can be interrelated by laws. According to this picture of the world, physical objects may be appealed to as constructs in a theory which enables us to facilitate the passage of judgment from one quale to another. Thus the test of memory by a physical object is but a particular case of decision by law and decree. It may, says the phenomenalist, be hard for us to see this picture other than as highly artificial and post-analytic, but this is because the most important of the laws were established pre-verbally as patterns of expectation and behavior which have become so dominant in our later life as to render isolated quale judgments very difficult.

7. *Summary*

I do not think that Wittgenstein would wish to deny that there are, in some sense, "inner processes"[11] that we can, in certain circumstances, justifiably ascribe pains or after-images to ourselves

[11] Cf. p. 102 of the *Philosophical Investigations*.

even though nobody around us happens to have any evidence other than our reports that we are indeed in pain or sensing an after-image. What he does wish to deny is that such experiences can be used as the designata of expressions in a private language. His grounds for this are that nothing counts as naming unless the putative names may be used for some further purpose, e.g., in making assertions. But the assertions of a private phenomenalist language serve no function; in particular, they are not informative even for the sole user of the language, since such an assertion could not be wrong if made in good faith at the time of the experience and could not be confirmed if made at any other time. Furthermore, because certain common techniques of checking one's memory mistakes are not available to us here, the distinction between being right and thinking that one is right disappears. In such a case we cannot be said to be speaking a language at all.

I have tried to argue that if we are willing to give up an ironclad principle of incorrigibility and admit degrees, it is at least conceivable that a phenomenalist language could be used to formulate purely phenomenal laws. If such a use were made, a coherence criterion would be provided for the confirmation of memory judgments. Admittedly, arguments could be found which could call this criterion into question, but they would equally serve to cast doubt upon our ordinary criteria. I therefore claim that Wittgenstein has at least failed to show the *logical* impossibility of a purely phenomenalist language. I have not attempted to maintain that ordinary language is based upon or contains instances of phenomenalistic usage, though I believe that this is still arguable.

IO

Wittgenstein on Private Language

NEWTON GARVER

WITTGENSTEIN poses a problem by asking: "Could we also imagine a language in which a person could write down or give vocal expression to his inner experiences—his feelings, moods, and the rest—for his private use?"[1] The doctrine contained in the following sections is one of the central results of Wittgenstein's later work, and our aim in this paper will be to set it out in clear form.

It is crucial for understanding what follows not to confuse this problem about the possibility of private language with either (a) the question whether I can, for my private use, keep a diary in ordinary English to record my pains, moods, and so on; or (b) the question whether there could be a language in fact used by only one person but capable of being understood by any explorer clever enough to see the connection between certain sounds (or marks) and certain circumstances. The answer to question (a) is clearly affirmative, and no one will mistake it for the question Wittgenstein raises. But a discussion between Professor A. J. Ayer and Mr. R. Rhees[2] indicates that question (b) is more difficult and that it may

Reprinted with the kind permission of the author and the editor from *Philosophy and Phenomenological Research*, 20 (1960):389–96.

[1] Ludwig Wittgenstein, *Philosophical Investigations*, 3rd ed. (Oxford: Basil Blackwell, 1968), 243. (References are to sections in Part I rather than to pages).

[2] Symposium on Private Languages, *Proceedings of the Aristotelian Society*, Suppl. Vol. 28 (1954):63–94.

become confused with Wittgenstein's problem. Both Ayer and Rhees show a correct verbal understanding of the problem: Ayer formulates the thesis he is attacking as "that for a person to be able to attach meaning to a sign it is necessary that other people should be capable of understanding it too";[3] and Rhees says that the main question "is a question of whether I can have a private understanding; whether I can understand something which *could* not be said in a language which anyone else could understand."[4] Appearances notwithstanding, however, the point of contention between them is question (*b*). Ayer's argument shows that there might be a Robinson Crusoe with a language which no one else understands, but which could be understood by another person (say by a Man Friday). Rhees' main concern is to reject this argument, on the grounds that a language must consist of rules, and there could be nothing to show that a Crusoe was following rules rather than simply behaving (as ants do) with regularity. It appears to me that Rhees is wrong in this contention against Ayer; but at any rate this controversy should be distinguished from the question they formulated—sc. the question raised by Wittgenstein about private language.

Wittgenstein's direct discussion of the problem he has posed continues through section 280; it forms the initial part of an investigation of the grammar of "pain" and other sensation-words, which extends through section 317. The two sections of this paper will be devoted to an exegesis of the first two steps in this presentation: (*a*) the exposé of certain considerations which lend plausibility to the notion of a private language (244–54), and (*b*) a *reductio ad absurdum* of the notion of private language or private understanding[5] (256–70).

I

Sections 244–54 can best be understood against the background of the following argument (*P*):

[3] Ibid., pp. 69–70.
[4] Ibid., p. 83.
[5] In the sense of something which could not conceivably be grasped by another person, and not just in the Crusoe sense.

(1) Sensations are private; no one else can have my pains.

(2) I commonly use words to refer to my sensations.

(3) In any category the meaning of at least some of the words I use to refer to things are the things to which these words refer.

Therefore,

(4) the meanings which I have for the words which I use to refer to my sensations *cannot* be grasped by another person; I have a private understanding of these words, and so (by analogy) does every other person when he uses such words.

Each of the steps in *P* has a great deal of plausibility, and the argument itself, although not strictly deductive, has a great deal of force. Even without (3), which is the only premise that can be flatly rejected,[6] one is strongly tempted to agree to the conclusion on the basis of (1) and (2). And yet the conclusion is unacceptable, because all the evidence (apart from this philosophical argument) supports the proposition that other people *do* understand me when I refer to my pains, itches, etc. The first problem for Wittgenstein is to remove this puzzle by bringing out the real import of (1) and (2).

When Wittgenstein asks the question at the beginning of 244, "How do words *refer* to sensations?" he is not asking a question about private language but about our ordinary everyday language. And of course there is no problem about that; we all know how to use words to refer to and talk about our sensations. If we then ask how the connection between the name and the thing named (the sensation) is established, what kind of answer do we expect? Wittgenstein reminds us that the only way to answer such a question is to see how a human being learns the meaning of names of sensations—of the word 'pain', for example. A child might be taught verbal expressions of pain (exclamations or sentences) in circumstances when adults see from his behavior, from his natural expressions of pain, that he is hurt. A foreigner might learn by our prick-

---

[6] Wittgenstein emphatically rejects this echo of his philosophical past for the view that "the meaning of a word is its use in the language" (43), where by 'use' he means the usual practice of speakers of the language with the word. We cannot pursue this matter further in the present paper. Wittgenstein's elaboration and defense of his new position is to be found in 137–242; he makes clear in 257 that the formula 'the meaning is the use' applies to names of sensations.

ing him with a pin and saying, "See, that's pain!" or by our pretending to be in pain. What is common to these and other learning
situations is certain circumstances, which always include a particular sort of action or expression on the part of some living being (sc.,
pain-behavior); and what is learned is the regular connection between the word 'pain' and such circumstances. Therefore the meaning of 'pain' is logically dependent upon there being natural
expressions of pain. Wittgenstein generalizes this point in 281: "It
comes to this: only of a living human being and what resembles
(behaves like) a living human being can one say: it has sensations;
it sees; is blind; hears; is deaf; is conscious or unconscious."

The point of these remarks is to show that our use of words for
sensations is tied up with the natural expressions of sensation (which
are publicly observable): 'pain' depends upon pain-behavior rather
than on any inner private experience for its meaning. Hence when
we explain how it is that words refer to sensations we do not have
to fall back on mysterious private experiences. If we understand this
much about premise (2) of *P*, we shall be less tempted to use it as a
justification for asserting (4).

The examination of premise (1) extends through paragraphs 246–
54. Wittgenstein's main point is that both parts of (1) are grammatical statements; that is to say, they might be used to teach a person how to use the words 'pain' or 'sensation', but could not be used
for ordinary communication between persons already fully conversant with the language. In this respect these propositions differ
sharply (in spite of a resemblance in the pattern of words) from
'My headaches are severe' and 'No one else can look at my diary'.
They are—like 'You play solitare by yourself' (248) and 'Every rod
has a length' (251)—propositions which are misleading because their
form makes them look empirical, whereas they are really grammatical.

Three points should be noted about the logic of grammatical
propositions. *One.* The absurdity which results from the denial of a
grammatical proposition is not a formal contradiction,[7] and in this
respect a grammatical proposition differs from what has ordinarily

---

[7] Several debater's points which Ayer makes against Wittgenstein are a result
of his failure to appreciate this point. (See Ayer, *Proceedings*, p. 69ff.)

been called an analytic one.[8] *Two.* There is no sharp boundary between grammatical and empirical propositions. Wittgenstein is aware of this when he takes note of "the fluctuation of scientific definitions: what today counts as an observed concomitant of a phenomenon will tomorrow be used to define it" (79). *Three.* Some propositions may be used as either grammatical or empirical—e.g., "Pure water freezes at 0° centigrade" may either be used to teach someone what we mean by '0° centigrade' or to teach him a physical fact.

The fact that the propositions in (1) are grammatical bears on the issue in hand in two ways. First, the natural employment for a grammatical proposition is to teach someone about the use of a word, and *not* to support a metaphysical thesis. This fact gives us a good reason for maintaining that (1) is misused in *P.* In particular, 'No one else can have my pains' cannot be used to support the contention that your pains must be different from mine; for if there is no criterion for my pain being identical with yours, it makes no sense to say that our pains are different ones. Second, to say that a proposition is grammatical is to say that it expresses some feature of the language—in the case of 'No one else can have my pains' that it ordinarily *makes no sense* to say of two people that they both have one and the same pain. This tells us something about the *use* of 'pain', about the common practice with the word. If there were no common practice with the word, there could be no grammatical propositions about it. If, therefore, the warrant for saying 'No one else can have my pains' is the grammar of the word 'pain' (and it is), 'pain' must have a use, must have an ordinary meaning rather than a private and incommunicable one. Understood in this way (1) not only does not support (4) but is incompatible with it.

---

[8] I take Frege's explanation of what an analytic proposition is as clear and adequate, provided we follow Frege in accepting only arbitrary or stipulative definitions and only strictly formal logical laws: "The problem becomes that of finding the proof of the proposition, and of following it up right back to primitive truths. If, in carrying out this process, we come only on general logical laws and definitions, then the truth is an analytic one." *Foundations of Arithmetic,* trans. J. L. Austin (London: Basil Blackwell, 1950), p. 4. Kant's conception of analyticity is more complicated. See Garver, "Analyticity and Grammar," in L. W. Beck, ed., *Kant Today* (LaSalle, Ill.: Open Court, 1969).

II

P is only one of a number of arguments which have led people to accept (4) or some similar doctrine. Probably the most influential of the views which lead to an acceptance of such a doctrine is Cartesian dualism, which maintains that Mind has nothing to do with Matter—i.e., that there can be no casual or conceptual connections between "mental phenomena" (such as sensations) and material or physical phenomena (such as bodily movements or other behavior). An obvious consequence of this view is that the meaning of 'pain' and other sensation words *cannot* be tied up with natural expressions of pain and certain physical circumstances. It would seem that on this view we must be able to learn these words only by associating them (each one of us privately) with appropriate sensations.

In 256, Wittgenstein proposes a thoroughly Cartesian account of the matter: "But suppose I didn't have my natural expression of sensation, but had only the sensation? And now I simply *associate* names with sensations and use these names in descriptions." In the following section, speaking for himself now, he makes two observations on this account: first, a person could not make himself understood when he used these words, since no one else could know with what he associated them; second, we cannot say that these words are names of sensations, since to name sensations presupposes the *grammar* of sensation words, and this grammar, as we have seen, depends on the natural expression of sensations which is by hypothesis ruled out.

These comments are apparently accepted by Wittgenstein's Cartesian interlocutor, and the problem that then remains is the one which Rhees rightly regards as central:[9] can't there be a *private* understanding of such words, even though they could not be understood by other people? In order to proceed with his *reductio ad absurdum* argument against this proposal, Wittgenstein allows his interlocutor to propose the following case for consideration at the beginning of 258: "Let us imagine the following case. I want to keep a diary about the recurrence of a certain sensation. To this end I associate the sign 'S' and write this sign in a calendar for every

[9] Rhees, *Proceedings*, p. 83.

day on which I have the sensation." Wittgenstein's examination of this case and its absurdity extends through paragraph 270.

In order to understand the case which is being examined it is important to realize that it is being proposed by the Cartesian interlocutor and not by either Wittgenstein or an ordinary man. It could not be seriously put forward by Wittgenstein because on his view the case is unintelligible (though not logically self-contradictory); for to say that 'S' is used to record the recurrence of some sensation implies that 'S' is in some sense a sign for a sensation, and this in turn presupposes that 'S' shares the ordinary grammar of sensation words, which is precisely what the proposed case attempts to rule out. It also could not be an ordinary man who proposes the case; for I can write 'S' in a diary to keep track of the recurrence of a certain sensation (say an ache in my left shoulder) and, because the grammar of the sensation words is presupposed, many of the difficulties which Wittgenstein urges against the proposed case will not arise. It is only when the case is proposed by a Cartesian, who rules out any conceptual connection between sensation words and natural expressions of pain, that the case is philosophically interesting.

The only avenue open to the Cartesian is to suggest that the connection is established by a kind of ostensive definition—not the ordinary sort, to be sure, since no one can point to a sensation, but a *private* ostensive definition: I concentrate inwardly on the sensation when I write the sign down. The whole idea of giving oneself a private definition is suspect from the start, because it is pointless; like my right hand's giving money to my left hand, no one would be any the richer for it (268). But pointless or not, let us see if the idea might work. Wittgenstein presents three telling objections which show that it cannot.

1. If this private ostensive definition is to achieve anything it must enable you to get the connection *right* each time, but in the present case there is no criterion of correctness: because there could be no distinction between thinking you were right and being right, we cannot speak of rightness here at all (258). You cannot even *believe* you get the connection right (that that sensation is the same one again); for you can only believe what can be true or false, and that that sensation is the same one again could not be determined to be true or false; at best you may believe that you believe it (260).

Since there is no criterion for saying that a sensation is that certain one again, you could not promise yourself, or privately undertake, always to use '*S*' for that certain sensation; the undertaking would be empty because you could never know whether you had fulfilled it or not (263). In all of these ways, Wittgenstein shows us that the lack of any criterion of identity for the sensation makes a "private" definition impossible. Therefore there is no possible way, on the Cartesian view, that a connection could be established between a word and a sensation, and the mere fact that we do use words to refer to sensations is a refutation of dualism.

2. We naturally assume that when you write down '*S*' in your diary you must be making a note of something, but Wittgenstein reminds us that the assumption is unjustified (270). '*S*' is an idle mark; it has no use, no function, no connection with anything. How *could* we make a record of anything with such an idle mark?[10]

3. Even assuming, *per impossibile*, that a connection between '*S*' and a certain sensation were to be established by means of a private ostensive definition, where would that get us? There would be a certain sign '*S*' which you privately understand. Could we call it the name of a sensation? We would have no justification for doing so, for by calling some mark the name of a sensation we make it intelligible in the common language (or perhaps better: in calling it the name of a sensation we presuppose it to be intelligible in the common language), whereas '*S*' is intelligible to you alone (261). Names of sensations have a certain grammar, and '*S*' as yet has none.

These points constitute an effective *reductio ad absurdum* of the Cartesian's proposal: writing '*S*' in the diary is a pointless act, a record of nothing whatever; '*S*' itself is a meaningless mark, having no established connection with anything and no possible use.

We have now left to consider only the perplexing section in which Wittgenstein appears to make an about-face (270). He says:

[10] Wittgenstein's remark in 260 is on the grammar of making notes, not on the grammar of sensation. Ayer apparently overlooked this section, or he missed the point of it. He says: "It is all very well for Wittgenstein to say that writing down the sign '*S*', at the same time as I attend to the sensation, is an idle ceremony. How is it any more idle than writing down a sign, whether it be the conventionally correct sign or not, at the same time as I observe some 'public' object?" (p. 68). The answer, of course, is that it is not, but Ayer's suggestion that Wittgenstein would make a different answer is absurd. The object of 260 is to bring out just this point.

"Let us now imagine a use for the entry of the sign '*S*' in my diary. I discover that whenever I have a particular sensation a manometer shows that my blood-pressure rises. So I shall be able to say that my blood-pressure is rising without using any apparatus. This is a useful result." After what Wittgenstein has said about '*S*', this turn strikes us a bit surprising. A moment ago the entry of '*S*' in the diary was "a note of nothing whatever," and now it leads to a useful result! There is a weird twist here; all of a sudden the whole case changes.

Note first that we can give a sort of definition of '*S*' now: '*S*' is the sign for the sensation you have when your blood pressure rises.[11] From this it follows (*a*) that when you write '*S*' in your diary, you are really making a note of something, viz. of a sensation, and (*b*) that the sign '*S*' can be explained to other people; it is no longer intelligible only to you. '*S*' is presented to us in 270 as a sign for a sensation, and since it is no longer supposed that the whole significance of the sign comes from being "associated" with "something about which nothing can be said" (304), we no longer have any ground for doubting that it really is just what it is presented as; and we have a further justification in calling '*S*' the name of a sensation in the fact that '*S*' has the grammar of a sensation word: only you can know when to write down '*S*', and so on. Note second that the problem about the identity of the sensation which you record by the entry of '*S*' in your diary has completely disappeared. If your blood pressure has risen, it makes no difference at all whether, in the sense required by the Cartesian, the sensation was "really" the same or not. As Wittgenstein says: "Now it seems quite indifferent whether I have recognized the sensation *right* or not. Let us suppose that I regularly identify it wrong, it does not matter in the least. And that alone shows that the hypothesis that I made a mistake is mere show."[12]

Thus we see that in 270 the entry of '*S*' in your diary can no longer be supposed to get its significance in the Cartesian manner outlined in 256; in order to give it a use we have to jettison all of the restrictions of the Cartesian proposal. In 256–69 Wittgenstein's

---

[11] Such a definition could be used to explain the use of '*S*' to other people, but not to *you*. There can never be an occasion for defining for you words which you use to refer to your own sensations.

[12] 270; see also 271, 293.

purpose is to show that a sign which is supposed to be simply "associated" with a sensation cannot have a use; in 270 he wants to show the converse, viz. that any sign which has a use cannot be supposed to be simply "associated" with a sensation. The utility of a sign and its intelligibility in the common language go hand in hand, and it is this point which Wittgenstein brings out in 270—another nail, as it were, in the coffin of the idea that there might be a private language.

II

Wittgenstein and Private Languages

WILLIAM TODD

Iɴ discussions of the private language question two different issues are often confused. One of the questions deals with the possibility of what I will call a personal sensation language. By this I mean simply a language invented by someone in order to talk about his sense experiences, provided that this language is not derived from any other language. It must be independent of other languages in that all of its terms must be meaningful to its originator without his having to define them in terms of another language. The syntax of the language may be similar to the syntax of a natural language; it may have in it words that have the functions that 'and', 'if', 'but', etc., do in our language, again as long as they can be understood without going beyond the personal language. It should be noted that if such a language as this is possible, a somewhat stronger sense of 'personal sensation language' will also be theoretically possible. This would be a similar language which was evolved by someone who had never been in contact with any other language. We can see that if a personal sensation language is possible in the weak sense, it will be in the strong sense as well, since it is always possible that someone might be ingenious enough to develop the mechanics of language all by himself; at least there is no con-

Reprinted (with minor corrections) with the kind permission of the author and the editor from *The Philosophical Quarterly*, 12 (1962): 3–14.

tradiction in the concept of his doing it. Hence we will always be able to use the term in the weak sense. This is basically the sort of language Wittgenstein had in mind in the *Philosophical Investigations*[1]; it is also that which most writers have described as a private language.

However, the question as to the possibility of such a language is separate from the question as to whether it would be logically possible for anyone else to understand it if it did exist. A language is usually called "private" if and only if the second condition is not fulfilled. It is true that the objects being talked about are private in the sense that a sensation belonging to one man cannot be identified with a sensation belonging to some other person. I will take it that two entities are logically distinct if there are *any* differences between them, even relational ones. In this case my sensation is distinct from anyone else's on the grounds that I come to be aware of it in a different way: by having it as opposed to observing behavior. Further, its nonexistence would have had different causal effects. Thus there is a sense in which the personal language is limited to talking about private objects. Despite the fact that the personal sensation language may be about private objects in this sense, we do not yet want to say that it is logically impossible for anyone else to understand the language.

We will now make a number of comparisons between personal sensation languages and ordinary natural languages. Let us suppose that someone originates a language of the former sort and keeps a diary of sensations which have occurred, and perhaps includes predictions of others which he expects to occur from time to time. This diary might be deciphered by someone who came across it and who was closely acquainted with the life of the diarist. He might realize that the manuscript was a diary and be able to correlate sentences in it with events which he knew to have taken place in the life of the diarist. He would also, of course, misinterpret every sentence in the diary and construe it as a statement in a different public language. He would naturally suppose that the terms refer to objects or kinds of object, whereas in fact they have been introduced as the names of sensations or kinds of sensation. Hence one might say that the

---

[1] Ludwig Wittgenstein, *Philosophical Investigations* (Oxford: Basil Blackwell, 1967), p. 92.

diarist and the reader are talking about systematically different sets of entities. We might compare this situation with the ordinary one where two people are using the same public language to converse about the same objects; there are certain similarities between the two cases. Even in the public case a man would be willing to make such statements as "There is a chair over there" only after having had certain sensations which are not identical with any sensations another man may have; similarly, he will alter or take back his statement if he has certain other sensations. Further, the way he describes the objects that he sees will depend not on what sorts of objects are there, but rather on the kinds of experiences that he has; if he is subject to a sensory illusion the description may be false, or, if he is having a hallucination, there may not be anything there at all. Hence the statements made by two men talking about the same objects in a public language will be prompted by, and corrigible with respect to, events which are private each to each. This is explicitly true for the diarist and his personal language, since he claims to be doing nothing more than reporting and predicting his sensations.

There are also differences between the personal and the public languages. Most important, the reader of the diary would say that the statements he is reading are about objects in the world whereas the diarist would say that they are about sensations. We might at this point say that within his language the reader makes the distinction between talking about sensations and talking about objects, but that the diarist does not. However, it would be possible for the diarist to make a distinction of this sort, although it might not be the same one. He might, for instance, incorporate within his language logical constructions and the other paraphernalia of phenomenalists; he could do this without ever leaving his language and without in any way introducing a term with reference to material objects. He could have within his language ways of saying 'and' and 'if . . . then', and he could then build up sets of statements which amounted to the phenomenalist's logical constructions, which are supposed to be equivalent to material object statements. He could then introduce other terms which would serve as abbreviations for the logical constructions and would thus be defined into the personal language and in no way go beyond it. Hence the diarist would

now be in a position to make a distinction between sensation statements and object statements within his language; the latter would
simply be more complex patterns of sensation statements. The question that now remains is whether there is any difference between
the language of the diarist and that of his reader. According to the
diarist, the difference between talking about sensations and objects
will be that in the latter case his statements will be more complex in
various ways. If the distinction is the same for the reader there will
be no important difference in the two languages; if the distinction is
different for the reader and he means something more by "talking
about objects" than just making more complex statements about
sensations, then there will be an important difference in the two languages, which might be grounds for saying that the reader misunderstands the diarist and that the latter has a private language.
But the important issue here, the analysis of what it means to talk
about material objects as opposed to sensations, is just the issue of
the truth or falsity of phenomenalism. That is, the question is not
about the personal sensation language, but of the proper analysis of
material object statements in the public language. Assuming that it is
possible for personal sensation languages to arise at all, their nature
seems to be fairly clear, and it is the status of part of the public
language which is controversial.

The diarist might even have in his language logical constructions
similar to the phenomenalist behaviorist's analysis of statements
about other minds. Again in asserting the logical construction, or
the sentence which abbreviates it, he will only be making predictions about his own future sensations and will be entirely within his
personal sensation language. The reader might construe the diarist's
sentence abbreviating a logical construction as a statement about
another mind; again the controversial question is not the analysis of
what the diarist means by the sentence, but the analysis of what the
reader means by it. If we say that the reader misunderstands the
diarist, or that any reader other than himself must misunderstand
him, it will be because we reject this sort of behaviorism as an analysis of statements in the public language.

For the phenomenalist, then, there will be no important differences between personal sensation languages and public languages,
since he does not suppose that we ordinarily talk "about" objects in

any way that the diarist cannot. The fact that statements in the ordinary language are usually intended to cause their hearers to act in certain ways does not distinguish them from the statements of the personal diarist in any basic way. It is, of course, possible to keep a secret diary that is not supposed to affect anyone in the ordinary public language. On the other hand it is possible for the diarist in the personal sensation language to write with the intention of influencing readers; all that is required is that the terms of his language be introduced by associating them with sensations or by defining them within the language so begun without reference to any other language. He might still be aware of the possibility that someone could decipher his language, even though that person might misinterpret it.

If, on the other hand, we reject this sort of analysis of statements about material objects and other minds, there will then be a basic difference between the statements of the diarist in the sensation language and corresponding statements of the ordinary language. Just what this difference is will depend on what analysis of these statements, if any, we do accept. The analysis of statements about material objects and other minds is far beyond the scope of this paper, and we will point out only that if these statements of the ordinary language are held to be irreducible to any other kinds of statements, the difference between the statements of the diarist and those of ordinary language will also be unanalyzable; we would be able to say only that there is a difference. The question now is whether this difference is sufficient to justify us in saying that it is logically impossible that anyone else should understand the statements of our diarist. It is clear that the reader does not fail to understand the speaker in the way that an Englishman who does not understand German fails to understand a German. It would be more a case of misunderstanding than a case of lack of understanding, but it would also differ from the usual sort of misunderstanding. In the latter case the misunderstanding can always have practical consequences; if a man misunderstands a command he may perform the wrong action, or if he misunderstands an indicative statement, he may be led to expect some state of affairs which the speaker did not intend. In our case, however, the misunderstanding would not have consequences of this sort; the statements of the diarist, if they are believed, would lead the speaker to always have the same sorts of expectation that the diarist himself had when he wrote them; hence if the diarist asserted that he kept a dog, meaning thereby a long conjunction of statements about sensations, the reader might interpret the statement as meaning something slightly different, but this difference would not come to light in ordinary practice. Whether it could make an empirical difference even in theory depends on our analysis of statements of the ordinary language. Thus the misunderstanding would be at most very slight in any particular case, but it would also be very general, as it would occur in the case of every such statement made by the diarist. We might then suppose that the reader was informed in some way that the diary was written in a personal sensation language (this might happen if the diarist could speak the public language as well as his own language). The misunderstanding would then disappear in that the reader would then realize that the diarist is talking about his own sensations rather than about objects. He could still draw information from the diary because a correlation would exist between certain terms in the diary describing kinds of sensation and certain kinds of objects which the diarist had been known to have encountered. Given our assumption that the diarist was in the main talking about events in his life in chronological order, and this assumption would turn out to have great explanatory power, we would then be able to match sensation words with the objects which caused the sensations to occur. Thus the reader would, in effect, be treating the statements of the diarist as signs accompanying events. Thus there would be no misunderstanding left, but it could be argued that the reader understands the diarist only in the sense that he understands black clouds to be the signs of a storm, and not in the way in which he usually understands what someone is saying. The argument here would presumably be that the reader has no idea what the sensations of the diarist are like, and hence does not know what the diarist is talking about. For all the reader knows the diarist may be conscious of a red apple in the way he is conscious of a green apple. This is the sort of situation that arises all the time in the view of the phenomenalist, but he has a weaker criterion for mutual understanding. He admits that the same object may consistently cause different people to have different sorts of sensation, but holds that they can understand each other if they use the same words, not to describe the same sorts of sensation, but to describe sensations which occur in similar circumstances; and this is what people are taught to do in childhood. Even if we reject phenomenalism, we could still adopt this criterion of understanding, which would entail in this case that the reader understands the diarist even though he is not acquainted with his sensations. Thus the question whether it is possible for anyone else to understand the diarist depends on the sort of criterion we adopt for understanding.

Further, it seems clear that this question cannot be settled by looking at the ordinary use of the term 'understanding', since this is a very extraordinary kind of case and there is no ordinary way of talking about it. Thus whether we say that it is logically possible for someone else to understand the statements of the diarist or not, we are adding to the concept of understanding; there is, of course, no reason why we should not do this, but if we do so we should be aware of it. The important point here is to notice the similarities and differences between cases of this sort and cases of the usual sort; having done this, it is not particularly important whether we call the personal sensation language a private language on account of the differences, or a public language on account of the similarities.

The important question now is the possibility of a personal sensation language. Many of the objections to private languages are not logically dependent on the classification of personal languages as private languages but are based on the nature of a personal sensation language itself. Thus I will adopt the conventional terminology and speak only of "private languages" in the future.

There are two main types of objection. First, there are those which seek to establish that a private language can never get started, in that an individual can never succeed in attaching meaning to terms which refer only to his own sensations independently of a public language. Second, there are those who argue that even if a private language could get started, there would be no criteria for correct use of the language, hence no rules for its use; the conclusion is then that it would not be a language at all.

As an example of the first type of argument we will take some of the objections Professor Malcolm uses in his review of Wittgenstein's *Philosophical Investigations.*[2] Some of these arguments come from Wittgenstein directly, while others represent Malcolm's interpretation of the former's views; since Wittgenstein and Malcolm seem to agree on this question, I will not attempt to distinguish their arguments. First, Malcolm considers the case where a user of a private language resolves to use the same words for the same kinds of sensation. However, we cannot suppose that the word 'same' means what it does in the public language; the word could be applied in various ways to sets of things which would not usually be called the same.

> The point to be made here is that when one has given oneself the private rule "I will call this same thing 'pain' whenever it occurs," one is then free to do anything or nothing. That "rule" does not point in any direction. On the private-language hypothesis, no one can teach me what the correct use of 'same' is. I shall be the sole arbiter of whether this is the *same* as that. What I choose to call the "same" will *be* the same. No restriction whatever will be imposed upon my application of the word. But a sound that I can use *as I please* is not a word.[3]

Part of Malcolm's argument seems to be that there is no way of discovering whether the rule has been obeyed, and we will deal with that later. His main point here is that since the usual meaning of 'same' cannot be taught to someone who knows only a private language, his resolution to call the same sensations by the same name is an empty one. The supposition here seems to be that one must be able to say the rule to oneself in the language before one can follow the rule. This would, of course, make it impossible to learn any language; if one had to be able to state the rules for the use of *'Buch'* correctly in German before one could learn the word and use it correctly, one could never learn the word. The complex notions such as 'same' which are used in stating such rules are never the first parts of a language to be learned. The user of the private language need not say to himself "I will always use this word to refer to the

---

[2] Norman Malcolm, "Wittgenstein's *Philosophical Investigations,*" *Philosophical Review,* 63 (1954):530–59.

[3] Ibid., p. 536.

same kind of sensation" in order, in fact, to use the word for the same sensations. We might say *of* a language in some other language that if it is used consistently the same words will be used for the same sorts of entities; this admits of some ambiguity (how similar things must be to have the same name, etc.), but in practice we have no difficulty in understanding such statements. In general it is not necessary that people using the language *consciously* follow this rule or that they have ever even thought about it. The case usually is that they just develop habits of speech which this rule describes; thus a man could in fact use the same words for the same things even if he did not know the meaning of 'same' or any similar word. Thus when we say that if the private diarist speaks consistently he uses the same words for the same sorts of sensations, we are making a statement about his language in the public language; if there is a problem about the word 'same', it is a problem for the user of the public language, but not yet a problem for the private diarist. It is true that the private diarist must have the ability to follow a habit that has once been initiated; he must in fact use the same words for the same sensations even though he will not, in the beginning anyway, be able to say that he does this in the language. This ability need not be dependent on knowing another language, although we do not require that the private diarist be totally ignorant of public language; neither is this entailed by Malcolm's definition of "private language." A cave man who had no language whatever might discover by trial and error what is the best size stone for throwing, and establish a habit of picking out a certain size of stone for this purpose. He would then presumably be able to abide by this habit, and this would involve picking out the right size of stone from among the many possibilities. This ability seems to be very similar to the ability to pick out a certain word in accordance with habit. The criteria for whether this has been done correctly are another matter which we will consider later.

Malcolm also argues that if we learn a term like 'pain' privately as the name of a sensation, it will be contradictory to suppose that someone else is in pain when the user of the private language is not; part of its meaning is that it exists only when it is felt.[4] This conclusion seems to be drawn from the fact that in order to associate a

---

[4] Ibid., p. 538.

word with a sensation, it is necessary that the sensation be present. In the public language, on the other hand, we can often explain to someone the meaning of a material object word when no object of the sort referred to is present. However, this happens only when we can define the new word in terms of other words which are already understood. In the case of a child or someone who knows very few other words, we usually have to introduce the names of things when the objects named are present. In this way a child may learn the word 'table' from hearing it talked about, and a table may always be present; he does not on this account conclude that there is a contradiction in the notion of a table's existing when it is not being perceived. In Malcolm's argument it is implicit that in an ostensive definition all the circumstances which obtain at the time it is given become involved in the meaning of the term and have to be re-enacted in order for the term to be correctly applied. It is conceivable that someone might interpret such a definition in this way, but it is not necessary that he do so. It is a psychological fact that when people learn the meaning of a noun they usually do not even interpret it as a singular term, much less as being properly applicable to something which must have a particular location in space and time, or which must be in a certain relationship to the speaker, such as being present or being perceived. In the private language the situation is somewhat different, since the primitive terms of the language, at least, are names of kinds of entities which are not supposed to exist when they are not present to consciousness. The user of the private language might teach himself these terms by making up sounds, or words, and associating them with certain sensations which he is having, or perhaps with corresponding images. This process would then be the counterpart of ostensive definition in the public language; however, the nature of this process does not entail that part of the meaning of the term introduced is that the sensation referred to must be present to the speaker in order to exist. There is nothing about the private language which prevents the user from supposing, as Russell once did, that his sensations continue to exist when they are not present to him, or from supposing that other people sometimes have the same kinds of sensations. It is true, of course, that the private language was intentionally limited in certain ways. The private diarist cannot ascribe sensations to other people within his language using the same words and sensations as he uses to report his own sensations. This is a direct consequence of his practice of always using the basic terms of his language to refer only to his own sensations, and it cannot be objected against the private language that it does not accomplish more than it was intended to accomplish. But it does not follow from this that the private diarist believes that only he has sensations, or that no one else can be in pain. If he were to learn a richer language he could state his beliefs to the effect that other people suffer pain, etc.; further, to the extent that we can have beliefs without being able to express them linguistically, he might have had these beliefs all along. Thus there is nothing about ostensive definition or its counterpart in the private language that prevents us from associating a word with certain features of the context in which it is introduced and dissociating it from other features. Whatever the user of the private language, or anyone else, may mean by another's being in pain, the fact that he has learned the term with reference to his own pain need not prevent him from thinking about other people's pain without falling into contradiction.

Another sort of objection used by Malcolm and others centers on the kind of private ostensive definition used in the private language. Here one would consider a sensation (which is either occurring at the moment, is remembered, or is imagined) and associate a word with its qualities; we have already seen that if this association is to be useful it must not be between the word and *all* aspects of the sensation, such as its occurring, being remembered, or being imagined; the association must be strong enough so that we do not apply the word to totally different kinds of sensations, yet loose enough so that the word can be applied to sensations which are closely similar to the example, but not exactly similar. In fact we do seem to be able to direct our attention to certain aspects of a situation or sensation when receiving an ostensive definition in the public language, and there is even more reason to think that we can do this when giving ourselves an ostensive definition (associating a word with certain aspects of our consciousness at a given time). In this case there is no room for the sort of misunderstanding that can take place in the public case. It is still presupposed that we have the basic ability to focus our attention on certain aspects of consciousness while ignoring others, and this assumption is certainly borne out by our ordinary experience in dealing with public languages. Whether we are born with this ability or acquire it does not matter for our purpose; it is clear, however, that we do not learn this skill from other people via a public language, or no language could ever have begun.

The objection is that a word in the public language is not learned by hearing it uttered in the presence of the object because the sound could refer to anything or nothing. In other words, the intended ostensive definition might be misunderstood or not understood at all. Rather Malcolm thinks that to be learned it must play a part in such activities as calling, fetching, distinguishing the object from other objects, distinguishing pictures, etc.[5] The point would then be that these cannot be duplicated in the private case. There are two advantages that such a process as telling a child to bring an x and pointing to it might have over just pointing to the object and uttering 'x'. First, one can tell by his behavior whether he has understood, and praise or blame him accordingly. Secondly, he may bring the wrong thing, in which case one can cause him to dissociate the word 'x' from things which are not x by expressing displeasure. However, there is no difference in kind between these activities and ostensive definition, but only a difference in degree. The possibility of misunderstanding or not understanding at all is still present. When the child is asked to bring an apple he might not understand that he is being asked to bring something at all, and perhaps thinking that his father is angry, bring him a nearby apple to appease him, without having any idea that 'apple' is the name of that kind of object. The father would then assume that the child understood and let the matter drop for the time being. Of course, the more this sort of thing is repeated, the less chance there is of misunderstanding; but this is also true of repeated ostensive definitions where the nonessential parts of the environment are varied. In any case there is no possibility of this sort of misunderstanding in the private case anyway, so it is no objection that in the private language we cannot ask ourselves to fetch things in the same way. On the second point, it is as important that we dissociate a word from the things that it does not refer to as it is that we associate it with the things that it

[5] Ibid., p. 553.

does refer to. Pedagogically there may be some advantage in using the processes Malcolm mentions, but again it is a difference of degree rather than kind; this sort of dissociation occurs whenever an ostensive definition has any effect, even when it is misunderstood. And, as we have seen, it is reasonable to suppose that an association can be set up between the word and that part of the situation on which we focus our attention, and not with the rest of the situation.[6] Further, as we have also seen, if such processes as calling for things and telling someone to fetch things were essential to the learning of language, there would always have to be someone skilled in language for anyone else to learn language; from this it would follow that language had no beginning. While we do not wish to speculate about the origins of language, we do not wish to assume that language either had no beginning on our planet or that it was brought here by a teacher from another planet, and so on, ad infinitum.

Throughout his arguments Malcolm seems to have a more restricted idea of a private language than that of the writer. We have seen, however, that there are some grounds for calling the personal sensation language a private language. If it is not, private languages will be impossible, not for the reasons he has given, but because there would be no subject matter for a private language to talk about.

Assuming that it would be possible for the originator of a private language to attach names to sensations, we come now to the question whether there is any criterion for the correct use of these words. Wittgenstein here argues in the following way. Suppose that someone is keeping a private diary about the recurrence of a certain sensation. For this purpose he associates the sign 'S' with the sensation, perhaps by concentrating his attention on the sensation and repeating the sign. If this process establishes the meaning of the sign it must bring it about that the connection is remembered *right* in the future. However, there is no criterion for whether 'S' has been used correctly except memory. Thus whatever seems right will be right and this means that we cannot talk about "right" here. Thus when the private diarist says that a sensation is an *S*, his sole

[6] For a more complete discussion of this matter, see William Todd, *Analytical Solipsism* (The Hague: Martinus Nijhoff and Co., 1969), pp. 27-31.

grounds for saying this will be his recognition of the sensation, and there is seemingly no independent check for this. As against Wittgenstein, A. J. Ayer tries to draw a parallel between the private language and the public language on this point.[7] First, he argues that it is sometimes possible to check one memory against another, so that the private diarist is not always totally without any criterion for detecting false recognitions of a sensation. More important, he points out that even in verifying a public statement about a material object, one's ultimate appeal must always be to one's own sensations. Thus if we want to verify the fact that there is a table in the next room, our last appeal must always be to the fact that we see it there when we look, etc. It is always conceivable in such a case that we fail to describe and identify our own sensations correctly. When I look into the next room I might in fact have the sensations I usually have when observing a chair, but mistakenly classify them as table sensations. Of course, other people then point out my error, but in order for me to understand and take account of what they say, I must recognize and classify correctly the auditory sensations of their words. Hence Ayer's conclusion is that even where the recognition of a public material object is involved we must always depend on being able to recognize sensations correctly, and there is no independent check for this, beyond memory, any more than in the case of the private language. Despite this there seems to me to be still an important difference between the criteria for the correct use of the two kinds of language. In the private language, even in the few cases where we can check one memory against another, our attempt to determine whether we are using a word consistently for the same kind of sensation must come to an end very quickly. Having called up all the memories one can, and having seen whether or not they are consistent, there seems to be nothing else to do and our investigation comes to a dead end. The situation is different in the case of the public object. Here we can keep on investigating the question whether the object was correctly recognized as long as we like without ever going over the same ground twice. While we must always recognize sensations in the end, we can go about verifying the truth of a statement about a material object in an in-

[7] A. J. Ayer, Symposium on Private Languages, *Proceedings of the Aristotelian Society*, Suppl. Vol. 28 (1954):63–76.

definite number of ways and keep on adding to the probability of the statement. The sensations which have to be recognized in each investigation will be different ones, and we may never reach a point where investigation is senseless. As the matter now stands we would be justified in saying that the criteria for the truth of statements in the public language are very much stronger than for statements in the private language, and we might make this the basis for saying that a private language is not a language in the same sense that a public language is.

We will now see if it is possible to conceive of a situation where a private diarist could have evidence independent of memory as to whether or not he is using a word consistently for the same kinds of sensation. Let us suppose, then, that the subject is marooned alone on an island and that he has developed a private language with a primitive set of words, which are the letters of the alphabet. He has kept a private diary since he has been on the island of the sensations he has had during certain periods of the day. This diary does not mention images that he has, but only sensations. In looking over his diary he finds the word 'S' entered for fifteen years before. At the moment he would put down 'S' only if he had a sensation characteristic of smelling an elephant. In fact he remembers giving that name to that sort of sensation (perhaps with the help of a memory image) since he had always lived among elephants before being marooned, and this was a familiar sort of sensation. But now on reading his diary he thinks that he very likely made a mistake in putting down 'S', or at least that its meaning has changed; he is quite certain that there are no elephants on his island, and he knows of nothing else that would produce the same peculiar odor. He could, of course, have been suffering from a hallucination, but this is very unlikely, since he has never been subject to that sort of phenomenon. Thus he has good inductive evidence for thinking that he has violated a rule of his language. There can also be further evidence in either direction, just as in the case of statements in the public language. Suppose that he goes for a walk that afternoon and happens upon a cave that he has not gone into for fifteen years. He decides to go in and, immediately upon entering, becomes aware of a strong smell S (the elephant-smell); he then traces it to a certain moss which does not grow elsewhere on the island. Now everything is explained; he concludes that when he went into that cave fifteen years before he had experienced the same smell and noted the fact in his diary. In the meantime he had forgotten this rather unimportant incident and naturally supposed that there was nothing on the island capable of producing that smell. Hence he now concludes that he has used '*S*' correctly all along; the interplay of evidence is the same as it is in the public language. Hence there are at least some cases where there are independent criteria for discovering whether the rules of a private language have been obeyed.

Wittgenstein's example of a manometer[8] suggests that he would here argue that the private diarist is no longer talking about his sensations, but is now using a public language to talk about the existence of a certain smell in the cave, and that the sensation is no longer important. We have already argued that the occurrence of sensations is crucial for the recognition of objects, but, apart from this point, there seems to be no reason to say that the private diarist all along must have meant to make a statement about a public object when he supposed that he was making a statement about a sensation. When he made the statement '*S*' he may have had no idea that there would be any way of verifying it in the future, as we usually suppose that smells in the air are transitory and not permanent. When he reconsidered the truth of the statement fifteen years later, the later evidence indicated that he still attached the same meaning to it, but he would never have guessed the manner in which it was to be at least primarily verified. Hence it is not plausible to suggest that by '*S*' he ever meant to talk about the existence of a smell in the sense of a material object as opposed to a sensation.

In fact there is a general method which any private diarist could use for checking the inconsistency of his terminology. If he did not already know a public language, he could learn one in the usual way and then compile a notebook in which, opposite each sentence in the private language, there would be its correlate in the public language. Thus opposite some such statement in the private language as 'chair-like sensations occurred when I had sensations characteristic of looking in that direction' might be 'there is a chair' in the public language. Whenever the private diarist wanted to check a

8 *Philosophical Investigations*, p. 95.

statement in the private language, he could then utter the corresponding statement in the public language and verify the latter in the usual way by asking other people, etc. As we have seen, the two statements may have different meanings even if the statement in the private language were much more complex, but there will still be a strong inductive correlation between the truth of the two statements. In the great majority of cases one has these sorts of sensations if and only if there is a chair nearby; the private diarist would be able to infer with a high degree of probability that the statement in the private language is true if the statement in the public language has been confirmed. Since there is no possibility of his being mistaken about the sort of sensation he is having, as opposed to the proper description of it, he can infer that he is using the terms of his private language in the same way that he did when he compiled his notebook, and that he is following the rules of the private language. Our conclusion, then, is that Wittgenstein and Malcolm are mistaken, and that a private language, in the sense of a personal sensation language, constitutes a logical possibility.

12

*The Private-Language Argument**

HECTOR-NERI CASTAÑEDA

Preface

THE ensuing essay is one part of the author's studies on Wittgenstein's reflections on private language, and these studies, in turn, are steps in the development of the author's views on the connection between consciousness and behavior. The private language issue is at bottom the question of whether or not a language that is a means of thinking *must* also be a language that is a means of communication. The negative answer to this question is tantamount to the thesis that private languages are impossible. This is the answer given by Wittgenstein and his followers. The ensuing essay examines in some detail several rounds of argumentation in favor of that answer. All those rounds hinge on the claim that the speaker of a private language either

Reprinted from *Knowledge and Experience*, ed. C. D. Rollins, by the kind permission of the University of Pittsburgh Press.

* *Editor's note:* In this symposium, many references are made to Ludwig Wittgenstein's *Philosophical Investigations* (Oxford: Basil Blackwell, 1953, 1958) and for simplicity most of these references are placed within the texts of the symposium papers. But whether within the texts, or in the footnotes, references to numbered sections of Part I of this work are given in the form, e.g., '217'; references to pages in Part II are given in the form, e.g., 'p. 207'.

In Mr. Castañeda's references one other abbreviation occurs: '*Disc.*' referring to Norman Malcolm's discussion, "Wittgenstein's *Philosophical Investigations*," in *The Philosophical Review*, 63 (1954):530–59.

cannot violate the rules of his language, or cannot correct his violations of them, or cannot have the very conception of what is a violation of those rules. The arguments depend very intimately on some general assumptions, such as: (1) thinking is impossible without language; (2) to use language is to comply with rules; and (3) no rule can be obeyed by merely thinking that one is obeying it. The first assumption has been given a tentative negative answer in the author's "Lenguaje, pensamiento y realidad," *Humanitas* (yearly publication of the University of Nuevo León, [Mexico]). The second and third assumptions are discussed in "Private Language Problem," in Paul Edwards, ed., *The Encyclopedia of Philosophy*, Vol. 6 (New York: Macmillan, 1967).

But Wittgenstein adduced another line of argumentation, one that Malcolm has called "Wittgenstein's external attack upon private language." This line of argumentation is examined in two complementary discussions, contained in the author's "Knowledge and Certainty," *The Review of Metaphysics*, 18 (1965): 529–37, and "Consciousness and Behavior: Their Basic Connections," in H.-N. Castañeda, ed., *Intentionality, Minds, and Perception* (Detroit: Wayne State University, 1967, 1969), pp. 138–45.

Part 3 of the last-mentioned essay defends and develops the non-Wittgensteinian view that ordinary mental concepts are complex and recursive in character. For instance, the concept of pain is an amalgam of: (1) a first-person concept, which is observation-like; (2) a third-person theoretical concept, and (3) a second- and third-person concept which is part of a causal psycho-physical "theory" and presupposes a framework of thoughts. Here an important part of the philosophical task consists in sorting out the different logical and ontological presuppositions undergirding ordinary mental concepts.

Prominent among the logical presuppositions underlying our concept of pain are the debated properties of privacy and incorrigibility. The author's first attempt at clarifying them appears below in part 2 as the pain postulates. But these raise a serious problem of formulation. They contain the difficult words 'he' and 'then' in *oratio obliqua*, which require special logical machinery. Consider 'The Editor of *Soul* knew at 3 p.m. that he(*himself*) was in pain *then*.' The words 'he' and 'then' have antecedents, but cannot be replaced with their antecedents *salva propositione*. They are what the author has called *quasi-indicators* and studied in several essays, particularly in "Indicators and Quasi-indicators [A study of the structure of the language about mind]," *American Philosophical Quarterly*, 4 (1967); "On the Logic of Attributions of Self-Knowledge to Others," *The Journal of Philosophy*, 65 (1968); and "On the Phenomeno-logic of the I," *Proceedings of the 14th International Congress of Philosophy*, Vol. 3 (Vienna: 1968).

In short, the examination of the private language argument led to the formulation of the pain postulates, and the latter led to the discovery of quasi-indicators and their central place in the conception of other minds.

Introduction

In the great revolution in philosophy brought about by Ludwig Wittgenstein, a central place is occupied by a cluster of ideas and arguments to the effect that a private language is impossible.

In sections 250–70 of his *Philosophical Investigations*, Wittgenstein does seem to be presenting *one* argument against private language in the form of a *reductio ad absurdum*. He writes:

> Let us imagine the following case. I want to keep a diary about the recurrence of a certain sensation. To this end I associate it with the sign 'E' and write this sign in a calendar for every day on which I have the sensation . . . [258].

He argues that the sign '*E*' as described, as a symbol of a private language, has no meaning at all.

Similarly, Malcolm writes at the end of his now classic discussion of those sections:

> The argument that I have been outlining has the form of a *reductio ad absurdum:* Postulate a "private" language; then deduce that it is not a *language* [*Disc.*, p. 537].

1. The Private-Language Thesis

The assumption for the reductio ad absurdum. Wittgenstein's thesis is that a private language is logically impossible. He seems to define a private language by saying: *"The individual words of this language are to refer to what can only be known to the person speaking; to his immediate sensations. So another person cannot understand the language"* (243, my italics). He means to include not only sensations, but everything that has been called a "mental act." He presents himself as attacking the picture of all of them as objects, i.e., as private objects (207, 222, 293, 304, etc.).

Both Wittgenstein (243, just quoted) and Malcolm (*Disc.*, p. 530ff.) infer from their definition of private language that only the speaker can understand it.

Language. It is nowadays a commonplace (thanks especially to Wittgenstein's own teaching) to say that a language is a system or aggregate of rules, a system or aggregate of linguistic activities. Thus naming, describing, identifying, commanding, questioning, etc., all support one another, in different degrees and ranges, to be sure; but, e.g., *there is no naming in isolation from the rest of a language*, existing as it were in a linguistic vacuum. As Wittgenstein so beautifully puts it:

> . . . a great deal of stagesetting in the language is presupposed if the mere act of naming is to make sense. And when we speak of someone's having given a name to pain, what is presupposed is the existence of the grammar of the word 'pain,' which shows the post where the new word is stationed [257].

Consequently, the assumption for the private-language argument cannot be that a man is trying to keep a diary with *only* the sign 'E'. We must assume that he has at his disposal a set of signs interrelated by means of a network of merely linguistic rules and a good deal more, since what Wittgenstein calls "grammar" includes a lot more than the mere tautologies of a language.

It is not clear that Wittgenstein's is the issue between a public and an *absolutely* private language. Very naturally, one would expect to find many cases of private language all linked up by a series of family resemblances, ranging off from a language *all* of whose individual words refer only to private objects. It is also worth noting that the issue private vs. public language, as raised, has nothing to do with the extremely difficult problem concerning the *origin* of language. Even if it is a psycho-sociological law that language can be developed by groups only, that law is irrelevant to the present issue. For as Malcolm (with characteristic penetration) says: "It is logically possible that someone should have been born with a knowledge of the use of an expression or that it should have been produced in him by a drug" (*Disc.*, p. 544).

Private objects. Wittgenstein's definition makes the privacy of the language depend *solely* on the privacy of the objects the language is used to think about. From that definition, however, it does not follow that, e.g., a private language cannot have a single word in common with a public language. Yet, Wittgenstein himself argues:

> What reason have we for calling 'E' the sign of a sensation? For *'sensation' is a word of our common language*, not one intelligible to me alone. . . . And it would not help either to say that . . . when he writes 'E', he has something. . . . *'Has' and 'something' also belong to our common language* [261, his italics in 'sensation' and 'something' only].

And Malcolm challenges:

> If I recognize that my mental image is the "same" as one that I had previously, how am I to know that *this public word 'same'* describes what I recognize? (*Disc.*, p. 537, my italics).

If Wittgenstein's definition of a private language in 243 is taken as an honest effort at giving the idea of a private language a full run, it must *not* be understood to deny a private language all logical terms: (*a*) connectives, (*b*) inferential terms, (*c*) copulas, (*d*) quantifiers, (*e*) numerals, etc. Since the meanings of all these expressions have nothing to do with whether the objects talked about are private or public, it is not at all clear why a language about private objects should by that reason alone be prevented from including any of them.

Similarly, to consider a private language as having no propositions in common with any other language is also to deny it all logical signs. If a language has logical terms, then tautological propositions are expressible in sentences of it that are translatable into other languages. Thus a private language is one which has *some* words descriptive or designative of private objects.

Now, there are several senses of 'private object':

(1) one which the speaker alone can (i.e., logically can) have experience of, or be acquainted with;

(2) object whose existence is (logically) determinable by the speaker alone:

   (2a) nobody else but the speaker can think (or say) with original certainty that the object exists;

   (2b) it is logically necessary that if the object exists, the speaker knows that it exists (others may know of the existence of the object, but their knowledge is not a logical consequence of the object's existence);

   (2c) the object's existence is entailed by the speaker's belief that it exists (others' belief that the object exists may be never mistaken, but it does not entail the objects' existence);

(3) objects whose possession of some characteristic A is (logically) determinable by the speaker alone:

   (3a) nobody else but the speaker can think (or say) with original certainty that the object is A;

   (3b) it is logically necessary for the speaker, and only for him, that if the object is A, he knows that it is A;

   (3c) the object's being A is entailed by the speaker's, and only by the speaker's, belief that it is A;

(4) objects about which the speaker alone can determine for any first-order statement whether it is true or false of them;

(5) objects about which the speaker alone can make first-order statements, i.e., objects which only first-order predicates which the speaker alone can use, apply to;

(6) objects about which the speaker alone can make any statement at all.

In each alternative, 'can' is a logical, or (more strictly) a conceptual, 'can'.

The difference between (5) and (6) is that the former does, whereas the latter does not, allow other persons to refer to my private objects indirectly or vicariously, via my statements about them. (6) is a very extreme, empty conception of a private object, not worth discussing.

(1)–(4) do not require fully private predicates; for them it suffices that the predicates in question have only private applications, e.g., after-images and physical surfaces can have the same (or very similar) characteristics of color and shape. Thus (1)–(4) can hold in purely private as well as in mixed languages.

What did Wittgenstein have in mind when he attacked private language in order to explode the idea of a private object? Wittgenstein attacks the fundamental idea of a private object ("if we construe the grammar of the expression of sensation on the model of 'object and name' the object drops out of consideration as irrelevant," 293; v. also 304, pp. 207, 222, etc.). Thus it is fair to see him as attacking all types of language which involve the idea of a private object in any of the senses (1) to (6). He particularly attacks mixed languages:

> Or is it like this: the word 'red' means something known to everyone; and in addition, for each person, it means something known only to him? (Or perhaps rather: it *refers* to something known only to him) [273].

Final statement of the assumption for the reductio. We are then to assume that a certain person (to be called *Augustine Privatus*) speaks and writes a language (hereafter called *Privatish*) which is private. *Privatish contains several logical signs, which we shall assume to be identical with those of ordinary English.* In some cases we shall assume that Privatish includes *a public sub-language* of the relevant kind, whose purely public words will be supposed to be identical with their English counterparts.

2. Some Counter-Examples

Privately experienceable objects. If Wittgenstein conceived of private objects in sense (1), his thesis seems to admit of an obvious counter-example. Many philosophers and nonphilosophers alike have held that one cannot (logically cannot) be acquainted with, or have experience of, someone else's sensations or after-images. These are all regarded as private in sense (1).

Privately ascertainable objects: pains. If Wittgenstein and his followers have senses (2) and (3) of 'private object' in mind, then the private-language thesis is amenable to refutation by existing counter-examples. Ordinary pains and after-images are private in those senses.

The ordinary language of pains which I employ is such that the following propositions are all logically true (or true *ex vi termino-rum*):

Meaning Postulates of Pain:

A. (*Postulate of Subjectivity.*) If X has a pain Y at time t and is not distracted from it, he feels Y at t.

B. (*Postulate of Subjective Ownership.*) If X feels a pain Y at t, X has Y at t.

C. (*Postulate of Direct Access.*) If X feels a pain Y at t, and at t he is capable of thinking that he has a pain at t, and is attending to his feelings (or his mental goings-on), then at t X knows that he has Y.

D. (*Postulate of Incorrigibility.*) If X thinks attentively at t that he has a pain Y at t, then X knows at t that he feels Y then.

E. (*Postulate of Subjective Thought.*) X thinks at t that he has a pain Y if and only if at t he thinks that he feels Y.

F. (*Postulate of Corrigible Access to Others.*) It is logically possible that everyone else thinks attentively at t that X has (had or will have) a pain Y at t_1 without X having Y at t_1.

G. (*Postulate of Indirect Access to Others.*) It is logically possible that X has a pain Y at t without anybody else knowing at any time that X has Y at t.

The following propositions can be derived from the postulates:

J*. (*Theorem of Limited Private Access.*) There are some kinds (or predicates) ϕ such that if X has a pain Y of kind ϕ at t, nobody else knows that X has Y at t.

Jᵃ. (*Theorem of Qualified Private Access.*) If X has a pain Y at t, nobody else knows, whatever the time, that X has Y at t, *in the same way* that X knows that he has Y at t.

Proposition J* makes of the ordinary language of pains (as I understand it) a private language. According to it, the speaker alone can determine whether a pain of kind ϕ exists or not and, of course, whether the pain (in case it exists) is ϕ or not. Thus, pains are private in senses (2a) and (3a).

Postulates C (of Direct Access to One's Own Pains) and G (of Indirect Access to Others' Pains) entail that ordinary pains are private in sense (2b). One knows, according to them, of his own pains by merely having them. That is, one knows of them privately. Likewise, postulates D (of Incorrigibility Concerning One's Own Pains) and F (of Corrigibility Concerning Others' Pains) entail that pains are private objects in sense (2c). Therefore, the ordinary language of pains is a counter-example to Wittgenstein's thesis, if interpreted as the claim that a language employed to think about private objects is of type (2).

Finally, the same postulates C and G, or D and F entail that the speaker is, of logical necessity, in a privileged position to determine whether or not a certain predicate applies to a pain he feels. Pains are, then, private objects in both senses (3b) and (3c).

3. Some Wittgensteinian Arguments

Wittgensteinians hold the view, W, that 'I know that I am in pain' is either senseless or a verbose synonym of 'I am in pain'. W suggests a reply to my claim that pains are private objects in senses (2) and (3). A Wittgensteinian may say that since it is senseless to say 'I know that I am in pain', it is senseless to say that one's own pains are objects which one alone can *know* in either sense (2) or (3); hence, it is senseless to say that one's language about one's own pains is private. Wittgensteinians have offered four arguments in support of W. The ensuing discussion of these arguments should be understood as making its points cumulatively.

1. The first argument runs: If a proposition is contingent, it is logically possible to believe falsely that it is true. If 'I am in pain' expressed the contingent proposition we normally take it to express, one could believe that one is in pain without being in pain. This is impossible, hence there is no such proposition that one can believe or know.

This is a howler. From 'It is impossible to believe falsely that one is in pain' it follows that it is necessary that if one believes oneself to be in pain, one's belief is true. Since 'I am in pain' cannot but be contingent, the major premise of the argument is false.

Probably Wittgensteinians mean to argue: A contingent proposition can be believed falsely to be true; if 'I am in pain' expressed a contingent proposition as we normally take it to do, the sentence 'I believed falsely at time t that I was in pain at t' would be meaningful. It is not; hence there is no such proposition.

But obviously 'I believed falsely at t that I was in pain at t' is meaningful; indeed it is meaningful even in the disputed sense that it can express a false proposition for pain postulate D leaves it open to believe falsely, when inattentive, that one is in pain. In any case, the conclusion of the argument is false. 'I am in pain' asserted by me has the same truth value as 'Castañeda is in pain' uttered by you, which expresses (or is) a proposition. Furthermore, 'I am in pain' expresses something which is true or false, which can be contradicted, that has entailments, and appears as a premise in arguments. These five features together are sufficient to make the utterances of 'I am in pain' the expressions of propositions.

2. The second argument for W runs: It is odd and out of order in ordinary language to say that one believes or thinks that one is in pain. 'I believe that p' is used to make weak assertions that p, i.e., to suggest the possibility of a mistaken belief or a doubt. There is no room for doubt or mistaken belief about one's own pains. Hence, 'I believe that I am in pain' is senseless, and so is 'I know that I am in pain'.

This argument is invalid, unless 'senseless' means 'out of order or odd'. Once again, from 'there is no room for a mistaken belief' it follows that if one believes that one is in pain, one's belief is true. And this explains fully why it is odd to say merely 'I believe that I am in pain', given that this assertion suggests the possibility of a mistake.

3. The third argument for W: In ordinary language it is odd and out of order to ask a person who has declared that he is in pain 'How do you know?' Hence, it is senseless to say, 'I know that I am in pain', unless this just means 'I am in pain'.

This is an inconclusive argument, even if 'senseless' means 'odd or out of order'. Given the fact that when attentive to one's mental goings-on one cannot be mistaken about one's pains, the senselessness of the question amounts to the pointlessness of asking a person for an answer which the person knows that one already knows. The only answer to 'How do you know?' is here: 'By having the pain' or 'By attending to my feelings'. Since both persons know that they know the meanings of 'pain', 'know', etc., the question is quite pointless.

Nothing in the argument shows that it is even pointless—let alone nonsensical—to speak of knowing one's own pains. In making an inventory of the ways of knowing, one lists physical objects as known by perception, pains as known by feeling, or introspection, mathematical theorems as known by deduction, etc. This also refutes the fourth argument for *W*, which is:

4. It is correct to speak of knowledge only when there is a question of finding out, of checking and testing. But it is absurd to suppose that one can make tests for finding out whether one is in pain or not.

Since it is correct to speak of knowing one's own pains, the major premise is false.

In sum, it is odd, because pointless, to inform another person that one believes or thinks that one is in pain, or to insist that one knows that one is in pain. But this fact about ordinary *reporting* in no way shows that there are no facts that would not be reported if one were to make pointless assertions. The pointlessness of the assertions is not only compatible with their intelligibility, but even presupposes it. I conclude, therefore, that the ordinary language of pains is still a mixed private language in several senses and remains, therefore, a counter-example against some interpretations of Wittgenstein's thesis.

4. *The Private-Language Argument*

The charge: possibility of mistakes. From the assumption formulated above we are, according to Malcolm, to deduce that Privatish is *not* a language. Since a language is an aggregate of rules, it would suffice to show that in using Privatish, Privatus cannot be following rules.

Wittgenstein's argument is very compact, but the following un-packing seems to be true to what he had in mind. A rule is essen-tially the sort of thing that can be followed (obeyed or satisfied) or not, and also the sort of thing that can be misapplied; a person trying to follow a rule can make a mistake and end up by not following it. Thus the possibility of not acting in accordance with a rule is of the essence and substance of a rule. Hence it must be possible for Privatus to make mistakes in the exercise of the rules constituting Privatish. If there is no way in which Privatus can mis-apply the signs belonging to Privatish, then this is not made up of rules and is, therefore, not a language. Naturally, Wittgenstein does claim that it is impossible for Privatus to make mistakes in using the (so-called) signs belonging to Privatish. This claim has been rounded out by Malcolm as follows:

1. Now how is it to be decided whether I have used the word consistently [i.e., correctly]?
2. What will be the difference between my having used it con-sistently and its *seeming* to me that I have?
3. Or has this distinction vanished?
4. "Whatever is going to seem right to me is right" (258).
5. "And that only means that here we can't talk about 'right'" (Ibid.).
6. If the distinction between 'correct' and 'seems correct' has disappeared, then so has the concept *correct*.
7. It follows that the "rules" of my private language are only *impressions* of rules (259).
8. My impression that I follow a rule does not confirm that I follow a rule, unless there can be something that will prove my impression correct.
9. And the something cannot be another impression—for:
10. This would be "as if someone were to buy several copies of the morning paper to assure himself that what it said was true" (165).
11. The proof that I am following a rule must appeal to some-thing *independent* of my impression that I am.

12. If in the nature of the case there cannot be such an appeal, then my private language does not have *rules*.

These are Malcolm's sentences and quotations, in sequence (*Disc.*, p. 532), but the numbering is mine.

The first remark to be made is that Wittgenstein's and Malcolm's discussions relate to the assumption that Privatus wrote the isolated symbol '*E*' on a calendar, while he is not given the privilege of using the rest of Privatish. As we said this is an unfair *reductio ad absurdum*.

The second remark is that the quotation from Malcolm does *not* prove that in a private language the distinction between 'correct' and 'seems correct' is missing—except in as much as this follows from sentences 8 and 9 or 11 and 12. The first three sentences are questions, *not* reasons, which simply formulate the issue in slightly different ways. Sentence 4 formulates, precisely, the *conclusion* to be established ("Whatever is going to seem right to me [or Privatus] is right"). Sentence 5 is a consequence of the fourth one—but it cannot be asserted unless the fourth is established. The next assertion, in sentence 6, follows from the preceding one, and so depends on the thesis formulated in the sentence 4, which *still* is to be proven. Sentence 7, I think, is a logical truth ("It follows that . . ."), viz., that something follows from sentence 6; but what comes after the word 'follows' is still hanging in mid-air, and will be there, until what the fourth sentence asserts is shown to be true. The next two assertions, in sentences 8 and 9, can be taken to constitute the premises of an argument. The tenth sentence gives, as a reason for the ninth, an analogy, which by itself proves nothing. Sentences 11 and 12 look like a repetition of sentences 8 and 9. But there is a difference.

Thus, to examine Malcolm's and Wittgenstein's argument in their *reductio ad absurdum*, we must first focus our logical microscopes on 8 and 9:

8. My impression that I follow a rule does not confirm that I follow a rule, unless there can be something that will prove my impression correct.
9. And the something cannot be another impression.

Clearly, these two assertions by themselves do not entail that a private rule, or a private language, is impossible. To prove this we need a minor premise.

9A. The user of a private language can avail himself of impressions only.

Unfortunately, 9A is far from being obviously true. It might be thought that all private objects are impressions. But even if this were to be granted, 9A would still be true only of the purely private languages. With the equation of private object and impression, propositions 8 and 9 would then amount to the statement that the user of a purely private language cannot resort to his private objects to check whether he is following a rule of his language. But neither this proposition nor the equation of impression and private object is self-evident. It is not even clear how one should attempt to prove them. At any rate, the argument so produced would not exclude the possibility of a mixed language.

Let us turn now to the alternative premises:

11. The proof that I am following a rule must appeal to something *independent* of my impression that I am.
12. If in the nature of the case there cannot be such an appeal, then my private language does not have *rules*.

Sentence 12 seems to be saying essentially the same as 8, but the meaning of 12 is clarified by 11, which differs from 9, which supplements the meaning of 8. Sentences 11–12 do not forbid Privatus to check whether he is following a rule of Privatish by means of other impressions of his; they only require that he make use of impressions which are independent of his impression that he is following the rule (correctly). They do not beg the question against a purely private language. In short, 11 and 12 are very reasonable; the only restriction one should impose on them is *that they must also hold for public languages* if the alleged *reductio* is to be genuine, not an ad hoc gerrymandered argument against private languages.

No doubt, from 11 and 12 it does follow that Privatish is not a language—provided that we can establish the antecedent of 12:

12A. In the nature of the case there cannot be an appeal to something independent of Privatus' impression that he is using a rule of Privatish correctly, to check whether his use is in fact correct or not.

But this proposition must be established. Indeed, given the direction of the argument, it is precisely the substance of Wittgenstein's thesis.

The charge reformulated: self-correction. Can Privatus avail himself of something independent of his impression that he is following a rule of Privatish to check whether he is in fact following it? If there is something which meets the requirements, then the argument of Wittgenstein and Malcolm cannot succeed, unless it follows some line different from the one now being discussed.

Before proceeding any further, it should be noticed that the above formulation of the issue is misleading and biased. It presents Privatus as deciding whether a certain utterance of his accords with a certain rule. The contention is that the utterance is arbitrarily chosen so that it is legitimate to generalize to all utterances in Privatish. But the initial setup is distorted. We cannot require Privatus to know the formulation of the rule in question and deliberately *obey* it.

There is an insight in saying that language is a set of rules; but it is misleading to say that to use language is to *obey* or *follow* rules. For the most part one's actions exhibit certain regularities, which one would describe in accordance with certain rules. But one is not obeying or trying to follow a rule. If an action is successful, i.e., if there are no unexpected obstacles, there is no question about having followed a rule correctly. Inasmuch as it makes sense to say that when a person speaks or writes he applies the rules governing the use of expressions he employs, *linguistic rules have to be precisely rules which are much more often than not applied correctly without their correct application being an issue at all,* as Wittgenstein well knew (cf. 207). If every sound or word were uttered from the conception of its rule, we would have to be aware of the rules in question in a language or in words (including the logical words), altogether different from the language or words we are to use in following those rules. But we would need another language to formulate and try to obey those rules, if every use of language is a case of obeying rules, and so on ad infinitum. This is a platitude, but it is worth emphasizing, for it would be bad logic to suppose that Privatus must decide for each rule he abides by in making a Privatish utterance, that he is following it. He should be supposed, *like any speaker of a public language,* both:

(*a*) to be using Privatish words (correctly or incorrectly) without having to *think,* let alone decide, that each one is used correctly, and
(*b*) to be using most of them correctly as a matter of course.

As Wittgenstein has greatly emphasized, a language (and, naturally, he is speaking of a public language) has to have "enough regularity" (207), i.e., people cannot always be mistaken in their use of words; for the most part they must get to use them rightly (see also 222–224, 245). Indeed, as he goes on to stress:

> If language is to be a means of communication there must be agreement not only in definitions but also (queer as this may sound) in judgments . . . what we call 'measuring' is partly determined by a certain constancy in results of measurement [242].

Thus, in the case of Privatus and Privatish it is fair to assume, insofar as for the purpose of our *reductio ad absurdum* we are assuming that Privatish is a language, that Privatus is for the most part consistent in his use of Privatish, that his use of signs possesses "enough regularity," and also that he holds certain true beliefs about his private objects, which beliefs are the counterparts of the judgments agreed on in the case of a public language.

Wittgenstein or Malcolm cannot imply that Privatus must decide whether each word is used correctly or not. All that they may argue is: (1) that it must be *possible* for Privatus to misapply the rules of Privatish, (2) that it must be *possible* for Privatus to know that he has made a mistake, and (3) that he must know how to correct some of his mistakes.

Examination of the charge. Now Privatish is not a language, if Wittgenstein's and Malcolm's contention is true that Privatus cannot appeal to something independent of his impression that he is following a rule to check whether he is in fact following it or not. But is this contention true?

It is false. Privatus can resort to practically all the "things" to which the speakers of public, or of ordinary, languages have recourse—he can do this even in the case in which Privatish is a *purely* private language. In general, to determine whether or not a word has been correctly used, we resort to the objects of our experience, the noises or marks which constitute our language, the memories of past utterances, the entailments among our concepts, and the generalizations which relate different kinds of objects. In the case of a public language, we can ask a fellow speaker, or we can receive his unsolicited corrections. This is, of course, not open to Privatus. Yet that circumstance cannot be at this juncture an objection against Privatish being a language. The very issue is, in part, whether that circumstance *is* a necessary condition for a language.

One thing, however, is definitely clear, namely, *that a person possesses a language only inasmuch as he is capable of self-correction.* A person has not learned color words or English, unless he is able to use his symbols independently of another's approval; but then he will know how to correct his occasional mistakes.

Privatus *qua* speaker of Privatish has his experiences and the objects, private or public, which he apprehends in them, his memories of previous utterances, the words of Privatish, the logical connections among these, and the generalizations which link some objects to others. Clearly, most of them are independent of his impression that he is using a certain word correctly. Even his memory images that on, say, five occasions in the past he described a private object as *A* may be wholly independent of his present impression that '*A*' applies to the same or some similar object.

Privatus can correct his mistaken uses of words in essentially the same way in which we normally correct our linguistic errors. For instance, an English speaker can correct his misapplication of a word simply by noting that the object is not what he called it; he may say: "That red, . . . I mean, brown chair. . . ." Here we have a linguistic self-correction. If a rule of language was not followed (I suppose, the one governing the use of the expression 'red' or 'brown') and a correction was made, then Privatus may be correcting his having not followed a linguistic rule of Privatish in a case in which he says: "This *A*, that is, this *B* . . . ," where '*A*' and '*B*' may very well be private predicates. Often, in the English example, the speaker knows of his slip on hearing his utterance of the word 'red', and clearly, both his hearing of it and the noise he hears are independent of his impression that he was using the correct word. Exactly the same can be said of Privatus and his Privatish expressions '*A*' and '*B*'. The possibility of such a case provides a counter-example to Wittgenstein's and Malcolm's contention.[1]

It may be argued that the English speaker can correct himself without having anything at all independent of his impression that he used the word 'red' correctly, that he can correct his slip without hearing his words, etc. Then it is argued that in the case of an ordinary language, which is assumed to be public throughout, since private languages are claimed to be impossible, a person can correct himself without the aid of anything independent of his impression that he has used a word correctly. *But then it is bad logic to require a private language qua language to meet a condition which is not regarded as necessary for language.* It may be replied that in the English case, others can in principle correct the speakers. This is certainly true. But it cannot be adduced as a reason by itself, for the argument is precisely intended to prove that *because* of the fact that others cannot correct him Privatus cannot correct himself. The fact in question has been assumed from the very beginning; the issue is the *because*.

To belabor the point, let us consider another situation. A person can become aware of, and correct, a slip thanks to his wanting to make a certain inference and finding himself using the right generalization. For instance, one may say "This is an elephant; since every rhinoceros has a horn on its nose, this, I mean, this rhinoceros, not this elephant, will have a horn on its nose." Here the items independent of the impression attached to the first use of the word 'elephant' that it is a corrrect use are (or may very well be): the desire to make the valid reasoning in question (which requires the premise 'This is a rhinoceros'), the awareness of uttering or thinking that every rhinoceros has a horn on its nose, the utterance, the uttered premise 'This is an elephant' (whose lingering presence to

---

[1] The point I was making here is twofold: (*a*) there are no criteria for the use of color words which are to be used to "*prove*" that a given use of 'red' is correct; (*b*) a speaker of English simply must be able to recognize the colors he calls "red" if he is to be what he must be, namely, a self-correcter. But then it is incorrect to require Privatus to have a criterion of correctness for each of his words.

the mind is necessary as part of the inference), the awareness (or "feeling" or impression) that the validity of the inference requires the two premises to have a common term at those places, etc. These are not all impressions (in any normal sense of the word), but even if impressions, they are independent of the impression that the word 'elephant' was used correctly. There is nothing in the case which requires that other persons can correct the speaker, even if merely in principle. Privatus may do exactly the same while using Privatish.

Furthermore, on the assumption, as presented in the final statement of the assumption for the *reductio*, that Privatish is a private language, Privatus is automatically allowed to avail himself of other items which are independent of his impression that he has used a certain term correctly. He may write one afternoon, under our telescopes:

(a) This is an *E*. Since all *A*'s are followed by *B*'s, this *A* will be followed by a *B*.
There is a *B*.

Suppose, in accordance with the assumption *to be shown* to be self-contradictory, that '*A*', '*E*', and '*B*' are purely private predicates. Clearly, Privatus can a few minutes later (as measured by our clocks) read the entry (a) in his diary. He reads it aloud, stops at the symbol '*A*', scratches it off and writes just above it the symbol '*E*'. Here, in addition to the items mentioned above, he has the written text and his visual perceptions, which are certainly independent of his impression that he used the word '*A*' correctly.

I conclude, then, that if for the purpose of a *reductio ad absurdum* it is fully assumed that Privatus possesses a private language, i.e., a whole system of symbols whose use is interrelated, habits of using such symbols, and enough private objects which manifest sufficient regularities, then Privatus has everything necessary for linguistic self-correction, which after all is really the necessary condition at issue for the possession of a language. The symbols of the language, the private objects themselves, the logical or grammatical interrelations among the former, the empirical generalizations linking the latter, the memories of previous uses of language, are all available to the speaker of a private language. Hence, the important premises 9A and 12A quoted above (under *The charge: possibility of mis-*

takes), necessary for the success of the Wittgenstein-Malcolm argument under discussion, cannot be established.

First rejoinder: infinity of doubts. It is sometimes argued that the speaker of a private language can never be sure that he is using a (private) sign correctly, even if he has something with which to test his use of the sign for correctness. Suppose Privatus has something, say *B*, against which he can test his present use of the sign '*A*'; surely, he can misinterpret *B;* so he can be in doubt as to whether he is using *B* correctly; thus he would have to appeal to something else, say *C*, to test the correctness of his application of *B;* but again, he can misinterpret or misapply *C*, and so on ad infinitum.

The argument is a telling one. It shows that there can be no *logical* certainty that a descriptive word has been used consistently throughout. *But this is also true of public languages.* If I say "this is red," and you tell me that it is blue, to be sure that my use of 'red' is incorrect I must be sure that your use of 'blue' is correct. But to be sure of that I must be sure that it is true that you have in fact said "No, it is blue," and for this I must be sure that you are there, are not deaf-mute, were talking to me, etc. And each of these *can* also be subjected to a doubt. So, if to be certain that a word has been used correctly (or incorrectly) I must reach a point where no doubt is possible, then public languages also fall under the axe of the present argument. This is a *reductio ad absurdum* of the rejoinder.

Second rejoinder: "Mistakes, not slips." Often a defender of Wittgenstein's thesis argues that the issue whether or not Privatus can misapply the rules of Privatish and correct himself has not been touched by such discussion. He might insist that a relevant mistake and a relevant correction are a mistaken belief of Privatus and his correction of such a belief about his private objects or about the rules of Privatish. The Wittgensteinian would argue that whatever Privatus believes to be *A* will have to be *A*, for it is so for him and he has nothing independent against which to check his *belief.*

A verbal slip is as good as any other case of not doing what the rule prescribes. The essential feature of rules, which distinguishes them from descriptions of action, is that they can hold (be true or valid) regardless of what the agent (for whom they prescribe some action) performs, while at the same time they differ from grammatical or analytic statements in that they can be fulfilled (satisfied) or not. Whether it is because of a slip or a misinterpretation or something else that an agent does not satisfy the rule is completely immaterial.

Is it not true that if Privatus follows the rules of Privatish, he calls every case of A 'A'? Then, since in the case of a slip he calls an instance of A 'E' and not 'A', he did not follow, or write in accordance with, all the rules of the Privatish language.

Let us accept then that the possibility of verbal slips is not enough to show that Privatish conceived as having objects of type (6) or type (5)—as we listed them at the outset—is a language; let us take it as established that Privatish must allow Privatus the possibility of holding some false belief. As in the case of mistakes in doing something in accordance with a rule, we must concede: (1) that Privatus must be in a position to have some false beliefs, even if in fact he never does; (2) that Privatus must be in principle capable of knowing of some of his false beliefs that they are false; and (3) that Privatus must be able to correct some of his mistakes in belief.

It is quite apparent that Privatus can make predictions about his private objects, and those predictions can turn out to be false. Hence, Privatish does not prevent Privatus from entertaining false beliefs.

Suppose that Privatus calls an object a 'B' if it is M and becomes P while remaining M. Then he can be mistaken and find out that he is mistaken when he says that a certain object is a B on the evidence that it is M. However, it may be replied that Privatus cannot be mistaken about something being M, provided that he is using the term 'M' correctly.

Suppose that Privatus cannot have a false belief about his present directly experienceable private objects or pains, unless he has forgotten the meaning of the relevant terms. But even this is not so simple as it looks. The application of every predicate involves an implicit comparison with both previous and later applications, as well as an implicit connection between the predicate in question and other predicates. Thus one can be mistaken about those implicit features which constitute the grammar of the predicate. Privatus can have a doubt as to whether something he is experiencing is an M or not only because he has forgotten the meaning of 'M', without this entailing the absurdity that he lacks even the faintest idea of what an *M* is like while he can formulate his doubt about the object being *M* or not. Forgetting the meaning of '*M*' is not a black-or-white situation. One may have forgotten the meaning of 'orange' *enough* so as not to be able to tell whether a given object is orange or not; but one can have the doubt because one knows that orange is a color and knows that it keeps certain similarities to red, for instance. One can even resolve one's doubt by testing for the appearance of the color of the object in question by mixing red and yellow pigments, if one remembers that orange is thus producible. And this need not involve the claim that orange is defined as the color obtained by mixing red and yellow pigments. All that one needs is to hold fast to the generalization that orange is as a matter of empirical fact so produced. *It is an essential part of the meaning of a word that it must enter into well-grounded generalizations.* Likewise, one may even decide whether a certain sensation is of pain or not by cutting oneself and experiencing a typical case of pain. Again, here it is only necessary that the empirical link between pains and wounds of the relevant sort be well established.

Once again, we find that if Privatus is allowed to support a given application of an expression of Privatish with the rest of the Privatish language, he can avail himself of the objects of his experience, the other expressions, the entailment relationships, and the empirical generalizations, and thus he can check whether *some* of his beliefs are true or false.

The rejoinder, then, is met. Privatish allows Privatus to have some false beliefs, to experience some doubts about certain facts (or propositions) formulable in the purely private part of Privatish, and to resolve some of those doubts.

Further rejoinder: other persons' corrections. We have encountered the suggestion that other persons' corrections are (in principle) necessary for the acquisition of the concept of *correct*. At some place Malcolm, for instance, alleges that "on the private-language hypothesis, no one can teach me what the correct use of 'same' is" (*Disc.*, p. 536). Wittgenstein expresses himself in the same vein:

> "Before I judge that two images which I have are the same, I must recognize them as the same." And when that has happened, how am

I to know that the word 'same' describes what I recognize? Only if I
can express my recognition in some other way, and *if it is possible
for someone else to teach me that 'same' is the correct word here*
[378, my italics].

Here the argument is not that Privatus *has* not learned from others the correct use of a word, but that he *could* not have learned it
from others.

It is true that in the case of a purely private language nobody else
can teach the speaker how to use a private predicate. This is a trivial
consequence of the definition of private language. But the major
premise of the argument is not obvious at all: that if nobody else
can teach Privatus the use of some word he does not know how to
use it. Indeed, the argument along the present lines just reduces to
the proof of that conditional. We have a right to expect an argument to show that if other persons' corrections are not available the
whole idea of *correct* is not available, either.

The need for others' corrections. Even though neither Malcolm
nor Wittgenstein has proved that Privatus' concept of correct use
must come from outside Privatish, may this not be so? Our discussion (in *The charge reformulated: self-correction,* and later) seems
already to show that it need not be so. Nevertheless, somebody may
stress that if it is *logically* impossible for another person to correct
Privatus' use of language, then he cannot tell whether his use is correct or not. But 'Nobody else can correct Privatus' does *not* entail
'Privatus cannot correct himself', regardless of whether 'can' expresses here a logical modality or not.

It seems strange that a *mere* logical possibility of being corrected
by somebody else could serve as an antidote against Privatus' mistakes. To know that he has made a mistake and to know how to
correct it require a good deal more than the purely abstract possibility that if somebody were to speak Privatus' language such a person could tell him what he did wrong and why. If nobody is *in fact*
around to correct Privatus' mistakes, or if nobody can correct his
mistakes simply because nobody around him speaks his public language, then he will be in just as bad a predicament as if his language were private (in the sense characterized in 243). He would
be left entirely to himself and his mistakes, without any help which

could in fact enable him to distinguish the correct from the incorrect. As I see it, if it were legitimate to require seriously the possibility of other persons' corrections, it would be impossible to have the case of a single person speaking a public language, e.g., Dalmatian or ordinary English. Yet at the end of the nineteenth century there was just Antonio Udina who spoke Dalmatian, and it makes sense to suppose that World War III may leave on earth exactly one English speaker with no knowledge of any other language. Obviously, whatever the last speaker of English were to say would be right—insofar as nobody else could correct him. It would be of no avail to say, "Well, if there were another English speaker near him, such a speaker *could* correct him." The issue is not whether he *could* have a language, but whether he *has* one. The point is that he would in fact be uttering sounds under no checks whatever—except what he remembered and what he experienced.

Indeed, it is not even clear that a person who spends some time in isolation would be actually using rules—if we are to require that other persons' checks be necessary. Clearly, the longer he remains alone the greater are his chances of making mistakes, and, once again, the *mere* abstract logical possibility of another person's corrections is too tenuous to be of real help. It is very difficult to see how the mere fact that *if* another person were beside the isolated speaker he could correct him, provides that speaker with checks and criteria and the conception of *correct* and the conception of *true*, even though *in fact* there is nobody beside him and he hears no voices approving of his use of language or confirming his beliefs! The only positive way in which the isolated speaker can detect and correct his mistakes is by actually checking his assertions or beliefs against the objects as they appear to him or as he remembers them —exactly as Privatus has been doing all along while using Privatish.

It may be adduced that there is a difference between Privatus on the one hand, and on the other Antonio Udina (when he became the last speaker of Dalmatian), Robinson Crusoe, and an isolated speaker of, say, Spanish. These persons have all *acquired the concept* of correctness from their elders, whereas Privatus did not; and it may be alleged that the issue is not whether a person's uses of words are corrected or not, but whether the person has come into possession of the concept of correctness. Thus, according to this allegation,

Antonio Udina's knowledge of Dalmatian may deteriorate if nobody can in practice correct him, but since he has acquired the concept of correct use he can go on speaking Dalmatian indefinitely. This is an exciting line of argument, but it is irrelevant to the private language issue. As noticed at the beginning, the mode of acquisition of the use of words, i.e., of a concept, is not a characteristic feature of language: "It is logically possible that someone [why not either Privatus or Antonio Udina indifferently?] should have been born with a knowledge of the use of an expression or that it should have been produced in him by a drug" (*Disc.*, p. 544).

5. Conclusion

Wittgenstein characterizes a private language as one whose individual words "refer to what can be known only to the person speaking" (243). Thus many types of private language are open: with just one symbol or with many, with or without logical vocabulary, etc. The Wittgensteinian dialectic around both the concept of violating a rule of language and the possibility of a correction of such a violation does establish that certain private or *public* languages are impossible, in particular: languages with no logical words, languages with just one rule, and languages with just one symbol 'E' for sensations. But none of the examined moves is capable of showing that a purely private or a mixed language with logical structure is conceptually impossible. If, as Wittgenstein suggested, some contingent generalizations are noninductive and must be built into the language, then a private language must be given the benefit of this suggested necessary condition for a language. Then it is even harder to show that private languages are impossible.

The Wittgensteinian attack upon private language is actually weaker than the preceding examination of it shows. That attack is predicated on three crucial premises: that it is impossible to think without using or possessing a language, that languages are systems of rules, and that one cannot obey a rule merely by thinking that one is obeying it. These are questionable assumptions. Our examination establishes that *in spite of* all three of these sweeping assumptions the argument against private language fails to reach its target.

Appendix

It is my conviction that in spite of what Malcolm says about Wittgenstein's attack on private language, Wittgenstein did recognize that both private and public language lack criteria of correct use of words, i.e., criteria which *prove* that a given use is, or is not, correct. This recognition together with an assumption of strong nominalism led him to find in social practices what constitutes correctness. For a brief discussion of this the reader is referred to "Private Language Problem," in Paul Edwards, ed., *Encyclopedia of Philosophy*, Vol. 6 (New York: Macmillan, 1967).

13

Wittgenstein on Privacy

JOHN W. COOK

Recent discussions of Wittgenstein's treatment of the idea of a private language have made it clear that the point of what Wittgenstein is doing has been widely misunderstood. I should here like to take one step toward remedying that situation. A chief complaint against Wittgenstein is that he does not make it sufficiently clear what the idea of a private language includes—what is meant by "a private language."[1] It is this complaint that I mean to examine, and I will argue that there can be no such genuine complaint even though it is true that Wittgenstein does not say clearly what is meant by "a private language." He does not try to make this clear because the idea under investigation turns out to be irremediably confused and hence can be only suggested, not clearly explained. Moreover, the philosophical idea of a private language is confused not merely in that it supposes a mistaken notion

Reprinted with the kind permission of the author and the editor from *The Philosophical Review*, 74 (1965):281–314.

[1] See, e.g., the papers by H.-N. Castañeda and J. F. Thomson in *Knowledge and Experience* (Pittsburgh, 1964), ed. C. D. Rollins. Thomson (pp. 121–23) asks, "What kind of language is here being envisaged?" and concludes that Wittgenstein's account is "obscure." The controversy over whether there can be a private language rages, he thinks, over "some unexplained sense of 'private language,'" and so "the claim that Wittgenstein answered it [must be] obscure." Castañeda (p. 129) says that "the idea of a private language is so obscure that there are many senses of 'privacy'," and he implies that "Wittgenstein's definition of a private language" is not "an honest effort at giving the idea of a private language a full run" (p. 90).

of language (or meaning) but in its very notion of the privacy of sensations. It is this last point which is generally missed and which I mean here to insist on.

I

The philosophical idea of a private language is a consequence of the following argument (hereafter called A):

No one can know that another person is in pain or is dizzy or has any other sensation, for sensations are private in the sense that no one can feel (experience, be acquainted with) another person's sensations.

The conclusion of argument A leads, in turn, to the further conclusion that no one can be taught the names of sensations; each of us must give these words their meanings independently of other people and of other people's use of sensation words. (The missing premise here is that in order to teach another person the name of a sensation, it would be necessary to check his use of the word, and this would require knowing from time to time what sensation the learner is having.) The result is the idea that anyone who says anything about his sensations is saying something which he alone can understand. Names of sensations, the word 'sensation' itself, and the expression 'same sensation' will have no genuine public use, only a private use.

It is this consequence of A that Wittgenstein refers to in Section 243 of the *Philosophical Investigations*[2] when he asks whether we could imagine a language whose words "refer to what can only be known to the person speaking; to his immediate private sensations. So another person cannot understand the language." But having raised this question, he almost immediately (246–54) launches attacks against both the premise and the conclusion of A. That is, he undertakes to show that the very notion of privacy on which the description of this language depends is a tangle of confusions. Hence, when he returns in 256 to the consideration of "the lan-

[2] Ludwig Wittgenstein, *Philosophical Investigations* (Oxford: Basil Blackwell, 1953). Unless otherwise indicated, numbered references will refer to sections of Part I; page numbers will refer to sections of Part II.

guage which describes my inner experiences and which only I myself can understand," he points out that (contrary to argument *A*)
our ordinary use of sensation words is not such a language. Thus,
the temptation behind the idea of a private language has already
been disposed of. What Wittgenstein goes on to do, then, in the
ensuing discussion of this "language which only I myself can understand" is to "assume the abrogation of the normal language-game,"
that is, to consider what the result would be "if we cut out human
behavior, which is the expression of sensation" (288). He introduces
the discussion as follows: "But suppose I didn't have my natural
expression of sensation, but only had the sensation? And now I simply *associate* names with sensations and use these names in descriptions" (256). Here we have what might be an allusion to Descartes,
who assumes that even if his philosophical doubts be justified, so
that he has "no hands, no eyes, no flesh, no blood, nor any senses,"
still he can privately understand and inwardly speak a language. It
is this picture of language as a phenomenon made possible by "some
remarkable act of mind" (38) that Wittgenstein means to investigate. In rejecting this idea of a private language, then, what he
rejects is not our normal language game but a philosophically trun-
cated version of it. Defenders of argument *A*, however, because
they must regard sensations as only privately namable, must regard
Wittgenstein's rejection of this either as a rejection of our normal
language game or as committing him to an extremely odd account
of our normal language game. Thus, on the one hand, Wittgenstein
has been "refuted" on the grounds that since sensations are private,
and since each of us does have names of sensations in his vocabulary,
there could not be any real difficulty in the idea of a private language: "the ordinary language of pains is . . . a counter-example
against Wittgenstein's thesis."[3] On the other hand, it has been argued that since sensations are private, and since Wittgenstein denies
the possibility of naming private objects, he must be denying that
ordinary language contains any genuine names of sensations: on
Wittgenstein's view "private sensations do not enter into pain language games."[4]

[3] Castañeda, p. 94.
[4] George Pitcher, *The Philosophy of Wittgenstein* (Englewood Cliffs, 1964),
p. 299.

In order to expose the errors of these two views, it is necessary to bring out the force of Wittgenstein's attack on argument *A*. I have given the argument in a form commonly found, but as it stands certain of its premises are suppressed. The premise

(P_1) No one can feel (experience, be acquainted with) another person's sensations

does not entail the conclusion

(*C*) No one can know what sensations another person is having.

Argument *A*, as it stands, is really no better than (and I will show that it cannot be made to be better than) the following argument: "No one can have another person's shadow, and therefore no one can know anything about another person's shadow." This argument is unsatisfactory for the obvious reason that the premise has no bearing on how one gets to know something about another person's shadow. In the same way, the premise of *A* has no bearing on how one gets to know about another person's sensations. And yet it is just this bearing that P_1 is thought to have by those who advance argument *A*. What, then, are their suppressed premises? One of them must be this:

(P_2) The proper and necessary means of coming to know what sensation another person is having is to feel that person's sensation.

With this premise added, argument *A* purports to be denying that anyone can avail himself of the sole proper means of ascertaining what sensations another person is having. Hence, what the argument must also show, if it is to be at all plausible, is that the sole proper means of ascertaining whether another person is in pain, for example, is to feel his pain. This is usually thought to be shown as follows:

(P_3) Anyone who has a sensation *knows* that he has it because he feels it, and whatever can be known to exist by being felt cannot be known (in the same sense of 'known') to exist in any other way.

With these two premises added, is argument *A* complete? In recent defenses of the argument it has been common to add to P_1 the qualification that the impossibility of experiencing another person's sensations is a *logical* impossibility. What bearing this qualification has on the form of the argument will depend on which of the several current interpretations is placed on 'logical impossibility'. I will examine these interpretations in Sections II and III and will show that they fail to make sense of the claim that no one can feel another person's sensations. Therefore, I will give no further attention here to the qualification that P_1 expresses a logical impossibility. In the remainder of this section I will try to bring out the force of Wittgenstein's attack on the premises P_2 and P_3, which purport to state a necessary condition for knowing what sensation another person is having.

What these premises say is that I can *know* that I am in pain because I *feel* my pain and that if anyone else is to know that I am in pain, he too will have to feel my pain. What the argument presupposes, then, is that there is a genuine use of the verb 'to know' as an expression of certainty with first-person present-tense sensation statements. This is essential to the argument, for what the conclusion (C) states is that no one can know, in this sense of 'to know' appropriate to first-person sensation statements, what sensations another person is having. Hence, if this presupposition of the argument should turn out to be indefensible, we must reject not only P_2 and P_3 but also the conclusion. For if the alleged use of 'to know' is spurious, then all three are infected by the confusion.

Does it make sense, then, to say 'I know that I am in pain'? Consider the following. A man has been complaining for several days that his stomach hurts dreadfully, though he has sought no relief for it. His wife has nagged him repeatedly, 'You're in pain, so go to a doctor!' Might he not at last exclaim in exasperation, 'I *know* I'm in pain, but we can't *afford* a doctor'? No one would want to maintain that this expression of exasperation was unintelligible. What argument *A* presupposes, however, is not that 'I know I am in pain' be intelligible as an expression of exasperation but that it be intelligible as expression of certainty. What, then, would be necessary for it to be an expression of certainty? Consider the following case. Someone asks you whether it is raining; you tell him that it is, and then he asks, 'Are you certain?' Here one might reply, 'Yes, I know it's raining; I'm looking out the window'. (This might be a telephone conversation, for example.) Now, what is the function of 'I know' here? To put it roughly and briefly, the function of these words is to indicate that in answering the question one is not merely guessing or taking someone's word for it or judging from what one saw ten minutes before or something else of the sort. Their function is to indicate that one is in as good a position as one could want for answering the question 'Is it raining'? What makes it possible to use 'I know' here as an expression of certainty is that it would be intelligible for someone to suppose that the speaker is not, in the particular instance, in as good a position as one could want for correctly answering a certain question or making a certain statement. More generally, for 'I know that . . .' to be an expression of certainty, it is at least necessary that the sense of the sentence filling the blank allow the speaker to be ignorant in some circumstances of the truth value of statements made by means of the sentence (or equivalents thereof). But now, it is just this, as Wittgenstein points out (246 and pp. 221–22), that does *not* hold for 'I am in pain'.

It should be noticed that Wittgenstein is not saying that the addition of the words 'I know' to 'I am in pain' would be *pointless* and therefore senseless. That might be said of the following case. The two of us are seated in such a way that you cannot see out the window, although I can. As you notice that it is time for you to leave, you ask me whether it is still raining. I peer out the window, straining to see in the failing light, and then go to the window, open it, and put my hand out. As I close the window, wiping the drops from my hand, I say, 'Yes, it is raining rather hard'. Because you have watched me take the necessary pains to answer your question, you would have nothing to gain by asking, 'Are you certain?' or 'Do you *know* that it is?' For the same reason, I would not be telling you anything by adding to my answer the words 'I know. . . .' If I were to add them, you might cast about for an explanation. Did he think I didn't see him put his hand out? Or is adding those words some eccentricity of his, like the character in one of Dostoevsky's novels who is always adding "No, sir, you won't lead me by the nose"? If no explanation is found (and it would not be an explanation to say that I added those words because they were *true*), my utterance of them would have to be judged senseless. But for all that, in the situation we began by describing, if someone in the street had seen me put my hand out, he might have said of me, 'He knows it's raining'. Or had my wife called from the next room to ask whether I knew it was raining, I could have answered that I do know.

Now the point that Wittgenstein is making about 'I am in pain' can be made clear by the contrast with 'It is raining'. The sense of the latter sentence is such that, although in a given situation my *saying* to a particular person 'I *know* it is raining' may be senseless, still in that same situation I could be said by some other person to know that it is raining. In that same situation I may be asked by someone whether I know it is raining and may sensibly answer the question. By contrast, the sense of 'I am in pain' (or of any other first-person present-tense sensation statement) does not provide for *any* situation such that the addition of the words 'I know' would be an expression of certainty. It would not be merely pointless to utter the sentence 'I know I am in pain' (indeed, we have seen how its utterance might express exasperation); it is rather that no utterance of it could be sensibly taken to be an expression of certainty.[5]

Wittgenstein's point here is often missed because, instead of considering what function the words 'I know' could have in 'I know I'm in pain', one wants to say something like this: "Surely a man who is in pain could not be like the man who has a stone in his shoe but does not know it because he does not feel the stone. A man who has a pain *feels* it, and if he feels it, he must *know* he's in pain." But this is making a wrong assimilation of 'I feel a pain in my knee' to 'I feel a stone in my shoe', which will be discussed below. At any rate, what we are inclined to contrast is the case of a man

---

[5] This point has been widely missed. Castañeda, for example, argues "it is odd, because pointless, to inform another person that one believes or thinks that one is in pain, or to insist that one knows that one is in pain. But this fact about ordinary *reporting* in no way shows that there are no facts that would be reported if one were to make pointless assertions. The pointlessness of the assertions is not only compatible with their intelligibility, but even presupposes it" (p. 94). I do not know what could be meant here by "pointless assertions," i.e., what would make them *assertions*. But it should be clear that Wittgenstein's point about 'I know I'm in pain' is quite different from the point I have made about the sometimes senseless addition of 'I know' to 'It is raining', and this is the difference Castañeda has missed. The same mistake is made (in almost the same words) in Ayer's criticism of Wittgenstein in "Privacy," *Proceedings of the British Academy* (1959), p. 48.

in pain with the case of a man with a (possibly unnoticed) stone in his shoe, and we want to mark the contrast by saying that, invariably, the man in pain *knows* that he is in pain. But this is a wrong way of marking the contrast. The right way is to say that whereas it makes sense to speak of ignorance and knowledge, doubt and certainty, in the case of the stone in the shoe, it does not make sense to speak this way in the case of the man in pain. Or, as I would prefer to put it (see Section III below), the moves that are part of the one language game are not part of the other.

I have not here argued for Wittgenstein's point; I have merely tried to clarify it. To argue for it, I should have to go some way toward showing the "incorrigibility" of first-person sensation statements. It is not clear to me, however, what "showing this" would involve. The most one could do, I should think, is to provide reminders as to how the names of sensations are taught, for example, that such teaching contains no counterpart of teaching a child to put a color sample under a better light or to move in closer for a better look. Also, one might show a person that where he thinks we can (or do) doubt or make mistakes about our sensations, he has merely oddly described something else. For instance, I have heard it objected against Wittgenstein that we sometimes exclaim 'Ouch!' in anticipation of a pain which never comes, but it would be misleading, at best, to call this "a mistake about *being* in pain." There is also the fact that such words as 'stomach-ache', 'headache', and 'dizziness' are partly diagnostic. Thus, a doctor might correct someone by saying, 'It's not stomach-ache you have; it's appendicitis!' Or a man might correct himself by saying, 'Never mind the aspirin; I didn't have a headache, after all. It was just this tight hat I've been wearing'. These are corrections of mistaken diagnoses. Another objection that is raised is that victims of accidents sometimes hysterically scream that they are in dreadful pain, although they are scarcely injured. But it should be clear that the screamings of hysterical people are no more to be counted genuine uses of language than are the ravings of delirious people or the mumblings of sleep-walkers. It is not my intention here to answer all such objections; I have no idea how many an ingenious person might propose or how far he would go to defend them.

The preceding discussion has shown, insofar as showing this is possible, that the alleged use of 'to know' presupposed by argument *A* is not a use at all but a confusion. Thus an essential presupposition of argument *A* has been defeated, and the argument will have to be abandoned. The possible criticisms of *A*, however, are by no means exhausted. In the remainder of this section I will deal with several points related to those already made. Sections II and III will present Wittgenstein's criticisms of P_1 and the claim that it states a logical impossibility.

There is a use of the verb 'to feel' (as in 'I feel a stone in my shoe') that is related to the verb 'to know' in the following way. If I am asked how I know that there is a stone in my shoe or that the grass is wet or that a certain man has a pulse beat, there will be cases in which it will be correct to answer, "I know because I feel it." I will call this the *perceptual sense* of 'to feel'. Now it is clear that argument *A* presupposes that it makes sense to speak of feeling (in the perceptual sense) a pain or an itch or dizziness. P_3 says that I can *know* that I am in pain because I *feel* my pain. It no doubt contributes to the plausibility of this that we commonly say such things as "I feel a slight pain in my knee when I bend it." That this is not the perceptual sense of 'to feel' should be clear from the fact that in all such sentences the words 'I feel' may be replaced by either 'I have' or 'there is' without altering the sense of the sentence (cf. 246). Thus, 'I feel a slight pain in my knee' comes to the same as 'There is a slight pain in my knee'. Such substitutions are not possible when 'to feel' is used in the perceptual sense. 'I feel a stone in my shoe' implies, but does not mean the same as, 'There is a stone in my shoe'. It will make sense to say, 'There was a stone in my shoe, but I didn't feel it', whereas it will not make sense to say, as an admission of ignorance, 'There was a pain in my knee, but I didn't feel it'. Sensation words cannot be the objects of verbs of perception in first-person sentences. And once this is seen, the plausibility of argument *A* altogether disappears. For when it is recognized that it does not make sense to say, 'I know that I am in pain because I feel it', it will no longer be tempting to say, 'Another person can know that I am in pain only if he feels it'.

There remain difficulties with argument *A* which have gone generally unnoticed. P_2 purports to state the proper and necessary means of ascertaining what sensations another person is having, and what it says is that one must feel his sensation. But even within the presuppositions of the argument, this is inadequate; it ought to require not only that one feel the other person's sensation, but also that one correctly identify it as being *his*. The plausibility of *A* depends on its seeming to be analogous to something like this: to ascertain whether my neighbor's crocuses are in bloom, as opposed to merely taking his word for it, I must see his crocuses. But I must also know which are his and which are mine, and I know this by knowing where the line runs between our gardens. I identify our respective crocuses by identifying our gardens, and this is presupposed in the sense of 'I saw his crocuses' and 'He saw my crocuses'. But how am I supposed to distinguish between the case in which I am in pain (whether he is or not) and the case in which he is in pain and I feel it? How do I know whose pain I feel? I will postpone the discussion of this question until the next section, but it is worth noticing how far the analogy with seeing my neighbor's crocuses has been carried. Thus Russell says that "we cannot *enter into the minds of others* to observe the thoughts and emotions which we infer from their behavior."[6] The italicized phrase seems to provide a criterion of identity of the same kind as in the case of the crocuses, but of course it does not. It merely raises the further question of how one is to identify whose mind one has "entered into." What that question should show is that one is being led on by an analogy that has no application. Why, in the first place, is one tempted to speak of "feeling another's sensations"? A part of the answer is that one thinks that just as such a sentence as 'My neighbor's crocuses are in bloom' has a place in its grammar for both 'I know because I *saw* them' and 'I didn't see them but took his word for it', so the sentence 'He is in pain' should have a place in its grammar for both 'I know because I *felt* his pain' and 'I didn't feel his pain but took his word for it'. And now if we somehow exclude 'I felt his pain', it will seem that we are left with 'I only took his word for it'. If, instead of seeing for myself, I ask my neighbor whether certain of his flowers are in bloom, this may be owing to a garden wall. It may seem that some comparable circumstance must account for the fact that we ask people what they feel. "Other peo-

---

[6] Bertrand Russell, *Human Knowledge* (New York, 1948), p. 193 (my italics).

ple can tell us what they feel," says Russell, "but we cannot directly observe their feelings."[7] Thus is argument *A* born. It makes out the difference between first- and third-person sensation statements to rest on a matter of circumstance (like being unable to see my neighbor's crocuses), whereas Wittgenstein has made us realize that the difference resides in the language game itself. The difference does not rest on some circumstance, and therefore argument *A*, which purports to name such a circumstance with the words 'being unable to feel another's sensations', is inherently confused.

There remains a difficulty with premise P_3 related to the above. P_3 states that I can know what sensations I am having because I feel them. Now if someone wants to defend argument *A*, he will have to show how it is supposed to account not only for what we have here called "sensation statements" but also for their negations, 'I am not in pain' and 'He is not in pain'. This may not seem to pose a difficulty if one thinks he understands Russell's phrase about entering into the minds of others to observe their thoughts and emotions. For if one enters a room to observe what is there, one may also observe that nothing is there or that certain things are not there. But if one does not pretend to understand Russell's phrase, how (on the presuppositions of argument *A*) is one supposed to understand either 'I am not in pain' or 'He is not in pain'? The same difficulty may be raised about negative statements containing 'dream' or 'image' instead of 'pain' (see 448). But if we stick to the case of bodily sensations, one might be tempted to substitute for the word 'mind' in Russell's phrase the word 'body'. One would then suppose that if someone says, "I didn't feel any pain in my knee that time," he is reporting an observation: I felt around in my knee for a pain and found none. But what is the feeling in this case? Is it the same feeling as when feeling pain? But if not that, then what? There *is* such a thing as making oneself receptive to pain—and even to pain in a particular place. (Perhaps a doctor wants to know whether your injured knee still hurts when it is bent in a certain way.) One relaxes, stops moving and talking, and then one feels pain—or one does not. But although there is no difficulty with the idea of being receptive to pain when there is no pain, it is not even prima facie

[7] Bertrand Russell, *The Analysis of Mind* (London, 1951), p. 118.

plausible to speak of a feeling which might have disclosed a pain but did not. How, for instance, could one make out the difference between not feeling for pain and feeling for a pain but finding none? Here all talk about a kind of observation appropriate to sensations becomes obvious nonsense. On the presuppositions of argument *A*, then, no account of negative sensation statements can be even suggested. It was tempting to say, "I can know that I am in pain because I *feel* my pain, and that is what I cannot do in the case of another person." But the plausibility of this is lost if one says, "I can know that I am not in pain because I can *feel* the absence of pain in myself, and that is what I cannot feel in the case of another person." One would want to reply: perhaps you are feeling the absence of it right now!

II

The one premise of argument *A* which we have so far neglected is in some respects the most pertinacious: "No one can feel (have) another person's sensations." I remarked in Section I that it is now commonplace to say that this premise expresses a "logical impossibility." This is intended, no doubt, as an improvement over older ways of talking. Russell once said of our sensations and images that they "cannot, even theoretically, be observed by anyone else."[8] But substituting 'not even logically possible' for 'not even theoretically possible' has proved to be an empty gesture, for the meaning of 'logically impossible' has at best remained dubious. Two interpretations are current. (1) Some philosophers have held that to say that it is logically (or conceptually) impossible that *p* is to say no more and no less than that the sentence '*p*' is senseless. In the present case, this would amount to saying that such sentences as 'I felt his pain' and 'He feels my dizziness' are senseless.[9] (2) Others seem to hold

[8] Ibid., p. 117.
[9] "The barriers that prevent us from enjoying one another's experiences are not natural but logical. . . . It is not conceivable that there should be people who were capable of having one another's pains, or feeling one another's emotions. And the reason why this is inconceivable is *simply that we attach no meaning to such expressions* as 'I am experiencing your headache', 'She is feeling

that to say that it is logically (or conceptually) impossible that p is to say, not that 'p' is senseless, but that the negation of 'p' is a necessary truth. In the present case, this would amount to saying that a sentence such as 'I did not feel his pain' (or perhaps 'Any pain I feel is my own pain') expresses a necessary truth.[10] Both versions speak of sentences—one saying that certain sentences are senseless, the other saying that the negations of those sentences express necessary truths. This presents a difficulty.

Any sentence may, so far as logic can foresee, find its way into some nonphilosophical context. Thus, in the last section a context was imagined in which the sentence 'I know I'm in pain' was uttered as an expression of exasperation. No one would want to say that in that context the person who exclaimed, 'I know I'm in pain!' was uttering either nonsense or a necessary truth—any more than they would want to say this of 'Business is business'. Now there are, no doubt, a great many philosophical propositions for which it would be extremely difficult, if not impossible, to provide a nonphilosophical context. But it should be clear that to specify merely a sentence is not to specify what (according to which view you take) is said to be senseless or to express a necessary truth. At this point it is tempting to say that, in the context I imagined for it, the sentence 'I know I'm in pain' was not meant literally. Similarly, someone might insist that if we were ever to say, 'I feel your pain', this could not, at any rate, be *literally* true. Thus, Ayer says that "it is logically impossible that one person should *literally* feel another's pain."[11] What is said to be logically impossible, then, is what is expressed by 'I feel his pain' in its literal sense. But can we now

---

his remorse', 'Your state of anger is numerically the same as mine'." A. J. Ayer, *The Foundations of Empirical Knowledge* (London, 1953), pp. 138–39 (my italics).

[10] For example, Castañeda, who regards it as a logical impossibility to experience another's sensations (p. 90), seems to take this view of "logical impossibilities." In his discussion of the sentence 'I believe falsely at time t that I was in pain at t' (which he says would be regarded as meaningless by Wittgensteinians), he gives his own position as follows: "But obviously 'I believed falsely at t that I was in pain at t' is meaningful; it expresses a conceptual contradiction; its negation is a necessary truth" (p. 93).

[11] A. J. Ayer, *The Problem of Knowledge* (Edinburgh, 1956), p. 202 (my italics).

apply either of the aforementioned versions of logical impossibility? Those who adopt version (1) would find themselves in the odd position of saying that it is the literal *sense* of a sentence which is senseless. (This is what Wittgenstein warns against in saying that "it is not the sense as it were that is senseless" [500].) Those who adopt either (1) or (2) will somehow have to specify, for the particular sentence, what its alleged literal sense is. One way of attempting this is by presenting the parts of the sentence (either words or expressions) in some familiar context in which *they* have the desired meaning and then specifying that it is when the sentence in question combines the words or expressions as used in *these* contexts that it has its literal sense. But what could it mean to speak of transferring a word or expression *and its meaning* from a context in which it has a particular use to a sentence in which it has no use at all (except as a part of speech)—and certainly not the use it had in the context from which it was allegedly transferred? The most that would seem to be possible here is that one might be under the *impression* that he had combined the original meanings into the sentence. This, I think, is exactly the case with philosophers who declare either that certain sentences are senseless or that their negations are necessary truths.

To illustrate this point, I want to consider a fictitious philosophical argument designed both for its transparency and for its similarity to the case of someone's saying that no one can have another person's sensations. Here, then, is the argument of an imaginary philosopher:

> We commonly speak of a child as having his father's build, but this is really absurd when you come to think of it. How *could* someone have another person's build? I know what it is for someone to have his father's watch or for someone to have another man's coat, but no one could literally have another person's build. A build is not something which, like a coat, can be removed and passed around from person to person. That is not even conceivable. And this is why no one can have another person's build. So when, ordinarily, we say of someone that he has another person's build, or when we say that two people have the *same* build, we are using these words, not in their literal sense, but in a sense that

is arbitrary and does not fit the meaning of the words at all. We are saying only that the one person has a build that is *like* the other person's, not that he has the other person's build itself. It is the same when we say that a child has her mother's eyes. We don't mean this literally—that her mother's eyes have been transplanted into her head. Of course, this could theoretically be done. But having another's build, in the literal sense, is not even theoretically possible. No amount of surgical skill will enable doctors to transfer a build from one person to another. They may graft skin and bone, but each person will still have a build all his own, not someone else's. Builds, one might say, are among the most inviolable forms of private property.

Now what has happened in this argument? Our imaginary philosopher purports to have identified the "literal sense" of such sentences as 'He has your build' and 'You have your father's build' and to have discovered that these sentences, in their literal sense, mean something impossible. But what is being referred to here as the literal sense of 'He has your build'? What I should like to suggest is that though this is no sense at all, what may strike one as being the literal sense—the real meaning—of 'He has your build' is this sentence construed on analogy with such a sentence as 'He has your coat'. The temptation so to construe it lies, of course, in the surface similarity of the two sentences. Moreover, quite apart from these sentences, there is our familiar use of possessives in 'my build', 'your build', and so forth, and one may be tempted to construe this use of possessives on analogy with possessives of ownership. That this is a false analogy can be shown as follows. In order to use a possessive of ownership (as in 'his coat') to make a true statement, we must correctly identify the owner of the article. It is this identification that makes the difference between saying, '*His* coat is too large for him', and saying merely, '*That* coat is too large for him'. If I should say, '*His* coat is too large for him', without having made the correct identification, I can be corrected by being told, for example, 'That's not *his* coat; it's his father's'. Now contrast this case with one in which I notice a child's build and comment, 'His build is rather angular'. Here the step of identifying an owner plays no part: I need only observe the child. And so my statement could not be challenged by someone saying, 'The build *is* rather angular, but are you sure that it's *his?*' This question would be senseless because, intended as a particular kind of challenge to my statement, it wrongly presupposes that in the language game played with 'his build' there is a move of the same kind as in the language game played with 'his coat', that is, the identification of an owner. But now it is just this question that would have to make sense if the so-called "literal sense" of 'He has his father's build' were to *be* a sense. Hence, the "literal sense" was no sense at all.

To put the matter in another way, what would not make sense would be to ask, as though requesting an identification, 'Whose build does he have: his own or his father's?' But in its so-called "literal sense" the sentence 'He has his father's build' was supposed to be a sentence of the kind used in answering that supposedly genuine identification question. So again, the "literal sense" was no sense at all. Here it is important to notice that in thus rejecting the "literal sense" of 'He has his father's build' we must also reject its correlatives, 'I have my own build' and 'Everyone has his own build'. For these sentences, too, in the context of the above argument, are supposed to be of the kind used in answering that supposedly genuine identification question. But as we have seen, there is no such genuine question, and so there are no answers either. The question and the answers we were made to believe in by the analogy with 'He has his father's coat' are not moves in the language game played with the word 'build'. Hence, what we were to understand as involving some kind of impossibility—namely, 'literally having another's build'—and also what we were to take as being necessarily true—namely, 'I have my own build'—turn out to be illusions. Therefore the statement 'Builds are private' must be given up.

The points I have made here apply, *mutatis mutandis*, to the philosophical assertion 'Sensations are private', where this is meant as 'No one can have another person's sensations'. I will not rehearse the arguments again. It is enough to say that in order to be in a position to use correctly the expression 'his pain' (as in 'His pain is worse, so you had better give him a hypo'), it is sufficient to know *who* is in pain. There is no further step required here comparable to that of identifying an owner as in the use of 'his coat'. (Hence in the first-person case, where there is no question of *who* is in pain [404–8], there is no identification of any kind.) Or to put the point in still another way, when we say of someone, 'His pain is quite severe', the word 'his' is performing the same function (apart from surface grammar) as the word 'he' in 'He is in severe pain'. It was this that Wittgenstein meant to bring out when, in reply to "Another person can't have my pains," he asked: "Which pains are my pains?" (253). He did not intend that one should *answer* that question, saying something like "All the pains I have are mine." He intended, rather, that that "answer" and the "question" that prompts it should be recognized as spurious, as not belonging to the language game.[12] Hence, for the reasons adduced in the previous case, when it is said that no one can, literally, have another person's pain, the supposed literal sense is no sense at all.

Before leaving the topic of possessives, it will be well to notice a source of frequent confusion. It was briefly mentioned in Section I that such words as 'stomach-ache' and 'headache' are partly diagnostic. Thus, a man might say, "Never mind the aspirin; I didn't have a headache after all. It was only this tight hat I've been wearing." Now it is easy to imagine a use of possessives related to this in the following way. Philosophers have imagined wireless connections of some sort being set up between people such that when one of them is in pain the other is, too. In such cases, it is suggested, the question 'Whose headache do I have?' would come to have the following use. It will be correct to answer that I have my own headache when, or detaching the wireless device, the pain continues unaffected, but if instead the pain immediately stops, it will be correct to say that I did not have my own headache, that I had Smith's headache, and so forth. Now granting all this, it is still important to be clear about two points. First, the sentence 'I did not have my own headache' will not mean the same as 'I was not in pain'. The man who asks, 'Whose headache do I have?' will be one of whom it will be true to say, 'He is in pain' or even 'He is in severe pain'. Secondly, when we say of a person, 'He is in severe pain',

---

[12] In another passage (411) Wittgenstein asks us to consider a "practical (non-philosophical)" application for the question 'Is this sensation *my* sensation?' Perhaps he was thinking that this form of words might be used in place of 'Am I the *only* one having this sensation?' which would be like asking, 'Am I the *only* one who is dizzy?'

we also say indifferently, 'His pain is severe'. (As noted above, the words 'he' and 'his' in these two sentences perform the same function.) So the statement 'His pain was severe' will be true even though it is also true that he did not have his own headache. Because 'his pain' in the former statement is not an answer to an identification question, it does not compete with the new idiom. Moreover, this would remain true even if we should lapse into using the word 'pain' in the same kind of way we have here imagined the word 'headache' to be used. That is, even if we should superimpose on our present use of 'pain' the question 'Whose pain do I have?' with the possible answer 'I have Smith's pain', it will still be possible to say of me 'His pain is severe' in case I am in severe pain. It is thus as a comment on this use of possessives that one can say: any pain I feel will be mine. The mistakes one is inclined to make here are, first, to suppose that this is a truth about the nature of pains or of human beings, and second, to suppose that the word 'mine' here is a possessive of ownership. Those who have sought to avoid the first mistake by resorting to talk about "logical impossibility" have nevertheless persisted in the second mistake, and thus they have reinforced the fundamental confusion by serving it up in a terminology that commands great respect. We can see more clearly what this amounts to if we return to the argument of our imaginary philosopher. Having concluded that no one can have another person's build, he might go on to argue that therefore we need never worry that the build someone has will not last out his lifetime owing to its previous hard use by another person. Now if a more up-to-date philosopher were to offer further relief from this worry by maintaining that it is not even *logically* possible to have another's build, this would be merely a perpetuation of the original confusion. This is what happens when philosophers seek to strengthen argument *A* by adding that it is a *logical* impossibility to feel another's sensations.

If we can make any sense of the insistence that pains are private—that is, that any pain I feel is my own—this amounts to no more than a comment on the kind of possessive commonly used with the word 'pain'. Of course, this is not what philosophers have supposed they were saying with the premise 'No one can feel another's pain', but since nothing but this can be intelligibly made of that premise, it can hardly do the job that philosophers have given it. There would not be even the semblance of plausibility in an argument running: no one can know what sensations another person has, because the possessives commonly used with names of sensations are not possessives of ownership.

III

The preceding section began with two criticisms of the view that 'No one can have another's pain' expresses a logical impossibility. The criticisms were these: (*a*) when something is said to be logically impossible it is necessary to specify more than a sentence, but what must be specified cannot be the sense of a sentence, for it is absurd to speak of the sense as being senseless; and (*b*) attempts at specifying such a sense must come to grief in requiring the parts of the sentence (either words or expressions) to retain their meaning though shorn of their use. Have my own arguments of the preceding section avoided these criticisms?

The chief difficulty with the views against which these criticisms were directed is that they propose to deal with sentences, and then in order to specify what is said to be logically impossible, they find themselves resorting to talk about the literal sense of a sentence. This is what Wittgenstein meant to oppose when he wrote, "When a sentence is called senseless, it is not as it were its sense that is senseless. But a combination of words is being excluded from the language, withdrawn from circulation" (500). But what does it mean to speak of "a combination of words being excluded from the language"? *What* is being excluded from *what?* When Wittgenstein says, for example, that "it can't be said of me at all (except perhaps as a joke) that I *know* I am in pain" (246), he does not mean to exclude the joke. In fact, one can think of a variety of contexts for the sentence 'Now he *knows* he's in pain'. (Think of how a torturer might say it.) So again I ask: what is being excluded from what? The answer to this can be seen from the following segment of argument from Section II:

> If I should say, "His coat is too large for him," without having made the correct identification, I can be corrected by being told, for

example, "That's not *his* coat; it's his father's." Now contrast this case with one in which I notice a child's build and comment, "His build is rather angular." Here the step of identifying an owner plays no part: I need only observe the child. And so my statement could not be challenged by someone saying, "The build *is* rather angular, but are you sure it's *his?*" This question would be senseless because, *intended as a particular kind of challenge to my statement*, it wrongly presupposes that in the language game played with 'his build' there is a move of the same kind as in the language game played with 'his coat', that is, the identification of an owner.

What is appealed to here is the reader's familiarity with a pair of language games. What is said to be senseless is not merely a combination of words but rather an attempt, by means of a combination of words, to make in one language game a move that belongs only to the other language game. In other words, by showing that the apparent analogy between the language games is in fact a false one, the argument shows that if one tried making the moves suggested by the analogy, one would not be *saying* anything but would be merely under the impression that he was. It is this mistaken *impression* of saying something that the argument condemns as senseless, and therefore (to answer our original question) the argument cannot be accused of saying that the *sense* of some sentence is senseless. It should be evident, however, that an argument of this kind, unless it is carefully formulated, is peculiarly open to misunderstanding. For in order to specify what it is that one is condemning as nonsense, one must repeat that nonsense in *some* form, and if a reader insists on taking one's words "straight" at this point and thus looks for or imagines a sense where none was intended, then one's argument will have the paradoxical air of trying to prove that the sense of something is senseless.

Since the point I have been making here is important to Wittgenstein's thought, it is worth noticing the following pair of passages. The first is from Moore's report of Wittgenstein's 1930–33 lectures:

[Wittgenstein] then implied that where we say "This makes no sense" we always mean "This makes nonsense *in this particular game*"; and in answer to the question "Why do we call it 'nonsense'? What does it mean to call it so?" said that when we call a sentence "nonsense," it is "because of some similarity to sentences which have sense," and that "nonsense always arises from forming symbols analogous to certain uses, where they have no use."[13]

The second passage is from *The Blue Book:*

> It is possible that, say in an accident, I should . . . see a broken arm at my side, and think it is mine when really it is my neighbor's. . . . On the other hand, there is no question of recognizing a person when I say I have a toothache. To ask "are you sure that it's *you* who have pains?" would be nonsensical. Now, when in this case no error is possible, it is because the move which we might be inclined to think of as an error, a "bad move," *is no move of the game at all.* (We distinguish in chess between good and bad moves, and we call it a mistake if we expose the queen to a bishop. But it is no mistake to promote a pawn to a king.)[14]

It is clear that Wittgenstein came to think that there is more than one kind of senselessness, but the description of the kind mentioned here is the description of 'No one can feel another person's pain'.[15]

Going back now, briefly, we can say one thing more about the so-called "literal sense" of 'He has his father's build' or 'I feel your pain'. Seeming to see in such sentences a sense that is somehow impossible is a queer sort of illusion, produced by seeing one pattern of grammar on analogy with another and quite different pattern of grammar. This sort of illusion is not altogether peculiar to philosophy, however. Seeming to see in a sentence a meaning that is somehow impossible is the stuff of which grammatical jokes are made (cf. 111). Consider, for example, a cartoon by S. J. Perelman. It shows a distraught gentleman rushing into a doctor's office clutching a friend by the wrist and whimpering: "I've got Bright's disease, and he has mine." This is more than a play on the name 'Bright's disease'. The surface grammar reminds one of such a sentence as 'I've got his hat, and he has mine', as used to report a mix-up in the coatroom. So the caption gives the illusion of making sense—of reporting an extraordinary mix-up, which the doctor is

---

[13] G. E. Moore, *Philosophical Papers* (London, 1959), pp. 273–74.

[14] Ludwig Wittgenstein, *The Blue and Brown Books* (Oxford, 1958), p. 67 (the last italics are mine).

[15] Another kind of senselessness is that illustrated in Section I by the sometimes senseless addition of the words 'I know' to 'It is raining'. Other examples are noticed in 117, 349, 514, 670, p. 221, and elsewhere.

supposed to set straight. And yet "getting the joke" consists in feeling its senselessness. So there seems to be a sense that is somehow senseless. But what we understand here is not a *sense* but rather the two language games that have been (humorously) assimilated. When this is intentional and fairly obvious, it produces a laugh; when it is unintentional and unrecognized, it may seem to provide an original and penetrating insight into the nature of things. Thus, in the case of my imaginary philosopher, once he is captivated by the grammatical analogy suggested by 'He has his father's build', he is led to treat the word 'build' at every turn on analogy with the word 'coat'. The whole complex grammar of words for physical objects opens out before him as a new field for the word 'build' to run in. A new range of sentences is thus opened up, suggesting what appear to be new "speculative possibilities"—builds being removed like coats, being passed around from person to person, becoming more worn and shabby with the years, and so forth. When we are captivated by such an analogy, we may succumb to temptation and play in these new fields. But we may also feel considerable resistance here, for the grammatical analogy behind it is a false one, and the signs of this may be too clear to be missed altogether. My imaginary philosopher expresses this felt resistance by insisting that "no one can literally have another's build." This, of course, does not reject the analogy; it merely denies that the supposed "speculative possibilities" can ever be realized. Nor would it improve matters to say that the impossibility involved is a *logical* one. This would be merely a new jargon for calling a halt to the analogy in midcourse. One finds the same thing when David Pole, in his commentary on the *Investigations*, writes: "In some sense experience is clearly private; one person cannot be said literally to feel another's feelings," and this cannot be said, he thinks, because grammar "forbids us" to say it.[16] This talk of grammar "forbidding us" to say something is nothing but the most recent jargon for calling a halt to an analogy whose oddness has begun to dawn on one. Because Pole is still in the clutches of the analogy, he is under the impression that there is some "literal sense" of the phrase 'feeling another's feelings' which grammar somehow forbids. Because in general he

[16] David Pole, *The Later Philosophy of Wittgenstein* (London, 1958), pp. 68–69.

thinks that grammar forbids us at many points to express a sense that we fully understand, he vehemently opposes Wittgenstein's expressed intention to "bring words back from their metaphysical to their everyday use" (116). Thus, he speaks of Wittgenstein's "characteristic anxiety to pin language down within the limits of its origins" and of Wittgenstein's insistence that "existing usage is to be accepted as we find it and never tampered with."[17] The result of this, Pole warns, is that "the advance of speculation may well be halted; thought may well be 'contained' within its existing frontiers."[18] What Pole fails to recognize is that the "metaphysical use" from which Wittgenstein wants to "bring words back" is not a *use* but the illusion of a use. Wittgenstein himself says that to reform language "for particular practical purposes . . . is perfectly possible. But these are not the cases we have to do with" (132).

IV

There is another expression for the idea that sensations are private. It is said that no two people can have (feel) the *same* sensation. This has an analogue in the case of our imaginary philosopher, who argues that when we say of someone that he has his father's build or that they have the same build, "we only mean that the one person has a build that is *like* the other's, not that he has the other person's build itself." He means to say that, however alike they may be, there are two builds here, not one. This, of course, is a mistake as to how builds are counted, but it goes with his prior mistake of taking possessives as used with 'build' to be possessives of ownership. He reasoned that if we say, 'His build is rather angular, and so is mine', there must be two builds: his and mine. But this is wrong. If one wanted to count builds, one would proceed differently—as one would proceed to count diseases or habits or the gaits of horses. One counts in such cases in accordance with more or less detailed descriptions. A five-gaited horse is one that can ambulate in accordance with five descriptions of foot movements, and two horses are performing the same gait if their foot movements fit the same rele-

[17] Ibid., pp. 91 and 94.
[18] Ibid., p. 95.

vant description. What would not make sense (if one meant to be using 'gait' in its present sense) would be to say, 'They are performing different gaits which are exactly alike'. To say that this makes no sense is to say that the identity of a gait is just given by a description of it. To count two gaits among those being performed, one must make out some difference in foot movement that would be relevant in describing (identifying) gaits. In the same way, a person has the same build he had before if he still fits the same (relevant) description; and if ten people fit that description, then all ten have the same build. Our imaginary philosopher's error lay in this: having confused the use of 'his build' with that of 'his coat', he inevitably repeated the mistake with the 'same build' and 'same coat'. Of course it does make sense to speak of two coats being exactly alike, for one may identify coats independently of descriptions of them. Now, no doubt we do say such things as 'His build is exactly like mine', but this is not used in opposition to 'He and I have the same build'. It is rather that 'same' and 'exactly like' are used interchangeably here, as in the case of color we might say indifferently either 'The color here is exactly like the color over there' or 'This is the same color here as over there'. Whichever we say, there is but one color—red, for example—and it would be a mistake to say: there cannot be only *one* color, for there is *this* color *here* and also *that* color *there*.

The point is that there is no such thing as being just the *same*—no such thing as identity pure and simple. It would be a mistake to think that the same is the same whether we are speaking of builds or coats or gaits or sensations. 'Same' must always be understood together with some general term, such as 'build' or 'coat', and the criterion of identity in any particular case is determined by the general term involved. Or when we use the phrase 'the same one', it is determined by the general term that is understood in the context to have been replaced by 'one'. Similarly, there is no such thing as being an individual pure and simple. It is always a matter of being one build or one coat, and the criterion for counting will vary with the general term. Now one consequence of failing to be clear on this point is that we may unwittingly take the criterion of identity determined by one kind of general term as showing us the meaning of 'same' by itself, with the result that we construe the use of 'same'

with all general terms on this one model. Thus, my imaginary philosopher supposed that if someone were to have the *same* build as
his father, he would be getting an already well-worn article. He was
clearly taking as his paradigm the use of 'same' with words for
physical objects and supposing that *that* is what 'same build' must
mean. The same mistake is made by Ayer when he writes:

> The question whether an object is public or private is fundamentally
> a question of . . . the conventions which we follow in making
> judgements of identity. Thus physical objects are public because
> it makes sense to say of different people that they are perceiving the
> same physical object; mental images are private because it does
> not make sense to say of different people that they are having the
> same mental image; they can be imagining the same thing, but it is
> impossible that their respective mental images should be literally the
> same.[19]

When Ayer speaks of "judgements of identity" and "being literally
the same," he is taking the use of 'same' with words for physical
objects as his paradigm for all uses of 'same'. So he thinks that if two
people were to see the same mental image, they would be in a position to add to, correct, and corroborate one another's descriptions
in the same kind of way as we do when two of us have seen the
same house.

But we do, of course, constantly speak of two people having the
same image or the same sensation. The identity of an image is given
by the description of that of which it is an image (cf. 367), and thus
we say, 'There is one image that keeps coming back to me: that
little boy standing there . . . ', and someone else may remark, 'I
have that same image'. Again, someone descending in an elevator for
the first time may complain of the feeling in his stomach, and someone else tells him, 'I get the same sensation; it will go away when
the elevator stops'. Nor would it be odd for someone to say, 'We
always get the same pain whenever it rains: an intense aching in the
joints'. Now we may also say, 'He gets a pain exactly like mine',
but nothing turns on the choice of idiom. We say indifferently
either 'Now I have the same pain in both knees' or 'Now there is
a pain in my left knee exactly like the one in my right knee'. As

---

[19] A. J. Ayer, *The Problem of Knowledge*, p. 200.

Wittgenstein remarks: "In so far as it makes sense to say that my pain is the same as his, it is also possible for us both to have the same pain" (253). His point is that where it is correct to say, 'His pain is the same as mine', it is also correct to say, 'We have the same pain'. It would be a mistake to think that 'same pain' here really means 'two pains exactly alike'. Ayer, for example, has said that though we speak of two people having the same pain or the same thought, 'same' here does not have the meaning of 'numerical identity'.[20] Apparently he thinks that in all such cases we are comparing two pains or thoughts or images. But Ayer gives no defense of this, except by invoking the very doctrine he is trying to defend: that sensations and thoughts are private. But since Ayer wants to treat this doctrine as a thesis about language, it is begging the question to appeal to the doctrine to decide what *must* be the meaning of 'same pain', 'same image', and so on. If he were not captivated by the doctrine, he would see that if someone says, 'He and I get the same pain in damp weather: an intense aching in the joints', then intense aching is counted as one pain. Another pain would be, for example, the searing sting of a pulled muscle.

The confusion about identity can show up in still another way, which Wittgenstein deals with as follows:

> I have seen a person in a discussion on this subject strike himself on the breast and say: "But surely another person can't have THIS pain!"—The answer to this is that one does not define a criterion of identity by emphatic stressing of the word "this" [253].

What Wittgenstein describes here would be exactly analogous to our imaginary philosopher gesturing toward his body and saying: 'But surely another person can't have *this* build!' Although the mistake is more obvious here, it is the same: the word 'this' can be used to refer to a particular pain or build only in accordance with the criterion of identity provided by the use of the general term. The word 'this' does not itself carry a criterion of identity. As we have already seen, to speak of a particular pain would be, for example, to speak of intense aching in the joints, and *that* is something that many people have. How, then, could someone think that by

[20] A. J. Ayer, *The Foundations of Empirical Knowledge*, p. 139; and *The Problem of Knowledge*, p. 199.

stressing the word 'this' he could refer to a pain that he alone can have? Wittgenstein remarks that "what the emphasis does is to suggest the case in which we are conversant with such a criterion of identity, but have to be reminded of it" (253). That is, we might use the emphatic *'this'* to clear up a misunderstanding that has occurred because the general term involved is used at different times with different criteria of identity. To take the stock example, we might clear up in this way a misunderstanding resulting from the type-token ambiguity of the word 'letter'. ('No, I meant that you should count *this* letter, too'.) This will succeed, of course, only if the alternative use of the general term is already well known to us, so that the emphatic *'this'* has only to remind us of it, for as Wittgenstein says, the emphasis "does not define" the kind of identity that is meant. Is there, then, a familiar use of sensation words with a criterion of identity that is reflected in 'But surely another person can't have *this* pain!'?

There is a class of episode words that must be considered here. Such expressions as 'dizzy spell', 'toothache', and sometimes 'pain' are used with a criterion of identity quite different from any described above. Although it makes sense to speak of having had the same sensation or image or dream on several occasions, it does not make sense to speak of having had the same dizzy spell on several occasions, unless this means that one was *still* having the dizzy spell. Similarly, there is a use of the word 'toothache' such that if someone with a toothache should remark that he had one just like it two years ago, it could only be a joke or a confusion to suggest, 'Perhaps it is the same one again'. Toothaches are episodes of pain, just as dizzy spells are episodes of dizziness, so that answering the question, 'How many toothaches have you had?' requires a reference to particular occasions. Moreover, the episodes are counted by reference to particular persons, so that if I were to count the number of toothaches my children had had, and on some date two of them had suffered from toothache, I should have to count two toothaches for that date. This would be like having to keep count of the number of tantrums they have or the number of somersaults they turn in a day. To refer to a particular tantrum or a particular somersault, is to refer to what *one* person did at some time. Thus, if a mother has described one of her children's tantrums, someone else might remark that her child had had a tantrum "exactly like that"; he, too, threw himself on the floor and held his breath until he turned blue. 'Exactly like' is used here in contrast, not with 'same', but with 'rather like', 'rather different', and so forth. That is, it would not be asked: 'Do you suppose they may have had the same one and not just two exactly alike?' This kind of identification question has no place in the grammar of 'tantrum', and so neither do its two answers: 'Yes, they did have the same one' and 'No, they did not have the same one, only two exactly alike'. Now this same point holds for the grammar of 'toothache': the identification question 'Did they have the same one?' has no place and so neither do its answers. That is, it would not make sense to say, as if in answer to that question, *either* 'They had the same toothache' or 'They did not have the same toothache'. Now the relevance of this point can be seen if we bear in mind the inclination to think of sensations as being objects of perception. If we think of first-person sensation statements on analogy with eyewitness reports, the question will arise whether our reports of sensations could be corroborated or denied by other "eyewitnesses." So the question becomes 'Can two people feel the same toothache?' But as between answering that two people *can* feel the same toothache and answering that they *cannot*, we seem to be faced with a Hobson's choice. For the former alternative will seem to be excluded a priori—that is, we will want to say (without knowing quite why, perhaps): 'It can't be the *same* toothache if there are *two* people in pain'. This, of course, is the influence of the criterion of identity (described above) in the use of the word 'toothache'. But with one of the pair of "answers" thus excluded a priori, it will seem that the other one *must* be true, and thus 'No two people can feel the same toothache' comes to be called "a necessary truth." From this one easily concludes that we cannot know anything about another person's toothaches.

This, then, is the complicated story behind the idea that in 'Sensations are private' we have a "necessary truth" or that 'No one can feel another's pain' expresses a "logical impossibility." The notion of "logical impossibility" was meant to be contrasted with "physical impossibility," but borrowing a remark of Wittgenstein's from another context, we might say: it made the difference "look *too slight.* . . . An unsuitable type of expression is a sure means of remaining in a state of confusion. It as it were bars the way out" (339). The "state of confusion" in the present case is that of argument *A*—that of thinking that (as Wittgenstein once imagined it being expressed) "a man's thinking [or dream or toothache] goes on within his consciousness in a seclusion in comparison with which any physical seclusion is an exhibition to public view" (p. 222). It is worth remarking, perhaps, that there is an altogether unproblematic sense in which our sensations may be private: we can sometimes keep them to ourselves. In this sense we often speak of a man's thoughts on some subject being private. No doubt most of our sensations are private in this sense once we passed beyond childhood.

v

In Section I it was mentioned that if argument *A* is taken to be sound, it will be seen to have the following consequence: no one can be taught the names of sensations; each of us must give these words their meanings independently of other people and their use of sensation words, and therefore no one can know what other people mean by them. With argument *A* now disposed of, we can also reject this consequence of it. We were taught the names of sensations by others—by others who knew what our sensations were. So we speak a common language. If one fails to see that Wittgenstein has already established this point before he takes up the question "Can there be a private language?" (256ff.), then one may suppose that what is in question is our actual use of sensation words. As was mentioned in Section I, it has been argued against Wittgenstein that since sensations are private, and since we do have names of sensations in our vocabularies, Wittgenstein could not have exposed any real difficulties in the idea of a private language. This argument has now been sufficiently disposed of in the preceding sections: the requisite notion of 'privacy' is defective. There has recently been published, however, another version of this misunderstanding, which is likely to gain currency, and which I will therefore briefly discuss.

In his recent book on Wittgenstein, George Pitcher has taken the following view of the matter: (*a*) "Everyone acknowledges that sensations are private, that no one can experience another person's sensations, so that the special felt quality of each person's sensations is known to him alone,"[21] so (*b*) it must be acknowledged also that if there were to be genuine names of sensations, they would have to get their meanings by private ostensive definitions, but (*c*) since Wittgenstein rejects the possibility of any word acquiring meaning in this way, he must be taken to be denying that in ordinary language there are any genuine names of sensations.[22] Therefore, (*d*) on Wittgenstein's view, in the language game we play with the word 'pain', for example, a person's "private sensations do not enter in."[23] This means that if we have just seen a man struck down by a car and find that "he is moaning, bleeding, crying out for help, and says he is in great pain," and if we "rush to help him, see that doctors are called, do everything we can to make him comfortable," still that wretched man's sensations "are completely unknown to us; we have no idea what he might be feeling—what the beetle in his box might be like. But this is no . . . stumbling block to the playing of the language-game, for they are not in the least needed. We proceed in exactly the same way no matter what his sensations may be like."[24]

If this reads like an attempted *reductio ad absurdum* of Wittgenstein, it was not intended as such. But one is not surprised to find Pitcher concluding that Wittgenstein's "ideas are obviously highly controversial" and open to "powerful objections."[25] In fact, Pitcher's "exposition" is altogether inaccurate. Wittgenstein, as we have seen, rejects the first step (*a*) in the argument. As for step (*b*), Wittgenstein not only rejects private ostensive definitions, as Pitcher sees, but also explicitly presents an alternative account of how names of sensations are possible (244, 256). But since (*b*) is essential to reaching the conclusion (*d*), how does Pitcher manage to attribute this conclusion to Wittgenstein? The answer is that Pitcher has misunderstood certain passages in which Wittgenstein opposes the idea of "the private object." As can be seen from the above quotation, one of these is the passage in which Wittgenstein

[21] George Pitcher, p. 297.
[22] Ibid., pp. 281–300.
[23] Ibid., p. 299.
[24] Ibid.
[25] Ibid., p. 313.

creates the analogy of the beetle in the box (293). There are several other passages similarly misunderstood (for example, 297), but I will deal with only this one.

Pitcher quotes only the following lines from the beetle-in-the-box passage:

> Suppose everyone had a box with something in it: we call it a "beetle." No one can look into anyone else's box, and everyone says he knows what a beetle is only by looking at *his* beetle.—Here it would be quite possible for everyone to have something different in his box. One might even imagine such a thing constantly changing.— But suppose the word "beetle" had a use in these people's language?— If so it would not be used as the name of a thing. The thing in the box has no place in the language-game at all; not even as a *something:* for the box might even be empty.—No, one can "divide through" by the thing in the box; it cancels out, whatever it is [293].

Without quoting the final, crucial sentence, Pitcher remarks: "The analogy with pain is perfectly clear."[26] By this he seems to mean at least that pains are, as it were, in a box and cut off from public view, so that they have (as Wittgenstein says of the thing in the box) "no place in the language-game at all." But so far from this being Wittgenstein's actual view, it is what he calls a "paradox" (304). What the beetle-in-the-box passage is meant to bear an analogy to is not our use of sensation words but the philosophical picture of that use. Pitcher has reversed the sense of the passage, and he has done so because he takes Wittgenstein to agree that sensations are private objects. But the intention of the passage is clearly shown in the final sentence, which Pitcher does not quote: "That is to say: if we construe the grammar of the expression of sensation on the model of 'object and name' the object drops out of consideration as irrelevant." The word 'if' here is crucial, for it is not Wittgenstein's view but the one he opposes that construes the grammar of the expression of sensation on the model of "object and name," and therefore it is not Wittgenstein, as Pitcher thinks, who is committed to the paradoxical consequence that in the use of the word 'pain', for example, the sensation drops out as irrelevant. The point of the passage, then, is quite the opposite of what Pitcher supposes. Rather

26 Ibid., p. 298.

than showing that sensations cannot have names, it shows that since the view that sensations are private allows sensations to have "no place in the language-game" and thereby makes it impossible to give any account of the actual (that is, the "public") use of sensation words, we must, if we are to give an account of that language game, reject the view that sensations are private. In Wittgenstein's words, we must reject "the grammar which tries to force itself on us here" (304). We have seen that the idea that sensations are private results from construing the grammar of sensation words on analogy with the grammar of words for physical objects. One consequence of this false grammatical analogy is that we are led to think that the names of sensations must get their meanings by private ostensive definitions. Wittgenstein, on the other hand, gives this account of learning the name of a sensation: "words are connected with the primitive, the natural, expressions of the sensation and used in their place. A child has hurt himself and he cries; and then adults talk to him and teach him exclamations and, later, sentences" (244). It is in this way that sensations get their place in the language game.

It is clear that Pitcher cannot have grasped this last point, for although he quotes he does not understand Wittgenstein's remark (246) that it is either false or nonsensical to suppose that no one can know whether another person is in pain. He takes Wittgenstein to agree with him that I cannot "determine that another person feels the same sensation I do: to do that, I would have to be able to feel his pain . . . , and that is impossible."[27] It is not surprising, then, that Pitcher should fail to understand Wittgenstein's reminder of how names of sensations are taught. It is surprising, however, that he should think that the view of sensation words rejected by Wittgenstein is our "commonsensical attitude."[28] Whatever Pitcher may have meant by this phrase, it at least indicates that he has failed to see how very queer is the idea that sensations are essentially private. Could it be that the child who comes crying with a bumped head and who screams when it is touched is giving his peculiar expression to an itching scalp? Or that the giggling child who comes wriggling back for more tickling is really a grotesque creature coming back for more pain? Or that the person who staggers,

---

[27] Ibid., p. 288.
[28] Ibid., p. 283.

gropes for support, blinks, and complains that the room is whirling is exhibiting, not dizziness, but a feeling of bodily exhilaration? No, the idea of the private object is not one that turns up in our common thought and practice; it turns up only in those odd moments when we are under the influence of a false grammatical analogy.

14

"Forms of Life" in Wittgenstein's
Philosophical Investigations

J. F. M. HUNTER

THE expression 'form of life' is
used at five seemingly important junctures in Ludwig Wittgenstein's
Philosophical Investigations, but he was not very helpful as to what
he meant by it. People who write about Wittgenstein often express
themselves with some confidence as to what he meant, but not always with clarity; nor has anyone that I have read produced any
extensive evidence or argument in support of his interpretation. In
this paper I shall defend a novel, but I believe plausible, account of
this matter; and I hope that by doing so, and by carefully canvassing
most of the relevant textual evidence, I may at least map out the
main issues on which a discussion of the matter would center.

The following are all the appearances of the expression 'form of
life' in the *Philosophical Investigations:*

> It is easy to imagine a language consisting only of orders and reports
> in battle. . . . And to imagine a language means to imagine a form
> of life [§19[1]].

Reprinted (with minor corrections) with the kind permission of the
author and the editor from *American Philosophical Quarterly,* 5
(1968):233–43.

[1] Unless otherwise indicated, all references will be to Ludwig Wittgenstein's
Philosophical Investigations (Oxford: Basil Blackwell, 1967), the paragraph sign
(§) referring to sections in Part I, and references to Part II being by page
number. Pages will sometimes be divided for reference into five parts, *a* to *e.*

Here the term "language-*game*" is meant to bring into prominence the fact that the *speaking* of language is part of an activity, or of a form of life [§23].

"So you are saying that human agreement decides what is true and what is false?"—It is what human beings *say* that is *true and false;* and they agree in the *language* they use. That is not agreement in opinions but in form of life [§241].

Can only those hope who can talk? Only those who have mastered the use of a language. That is to say the phenomena of hope are modes of this complicated form of life [p. 174].

It is no doubt true that you could not calculate with certain sorts of paper and ink, if, that is, they were subject to certain queer changes—but still the fact that they changed could in turn only be got from memory and comparison with other means of calculation. And how are these tested in their turn?

What has to be accepted, the given, is—so one could say—*forms of life* [p. 226].[2]

I

I shall now set out four alternative interpretations, each of which seems to me to be antecedently plausible, and the first three of which I find indicated either directly or indirectly in the writings of various people.[3] But to avoid the further difficulty of interpreting the interpreters, I shall not *attribute* these accounts to anyone, but

---

[2] The expression occurs also in Ludwig Wittgenstein, *On Certainty* (Oxford: Basil Blackwell, 1969), where we read:

358. Now I would like to regard this certainty, not as something akin to hastiness or superficiality, but as a form of life. (That is very badly expressed and probably badly thought as well.)

359. But that means I want to conceive it as something beyond being justified or unjustified; as it were, as something animal.

[3] See for example, in *Wittgenstein: The Philosophical Investigations*, ed. G. Pitcher (New York: Doubleday, 1966): A. M. Quinton, p. 13; P. F. Strawson, p. 62; N. Malcolm, pp. 91–92; and S. Cavell, pp. 160–61. See also G. Pitcher in *The Philosophy of Wittgenstein* (Englewood Cliffs, N.J.: Prentice-Hall, 1964), pp. 243–44 and 312.

shall let them ride on their own merits. The fourth of these interpretations will be the one I wish to defend.

Interpretation I

A language game is a prime example of a form of life, and calling it such is saying that it is something formalized or standardized in our life; that it is one of life's forms. It is not necessarily standardized in any permanent way: language games, like any other games, will appear and change and disappear. But at any given time it will be clear enough what the game is, and hence clear enough whether any given utterance counts as "playing the game" or not.

If asked what would be the point or cash value of saying that a language game is a form of life, one could suggest two things: first, that there can't be any *private* language games, that the game must exist as a standard and recognized form before it can be "played"; and second, that unlike most ordinary games, language games are intricately bound up with other aspects of life, with plans and fears and thoughts and activities, and cannot be understood in isolation from these.

On this view a form of life is a distinct something-or-other, and there are a lot of them, at least as many as there are language games. But we had better not inquire right now how one would put a count on language games.

I shall sometimes refer to this as a "language-game account," and also as "an account which holds that forms of life are something shared and standardized."

Interpretation II

A form of life is a sort of package of mutually related tendencies to behave in various ways: to have certain facial expressions and make certain gestures, to do certain things like count apples or help people, and to say certain things. They are "mutually related" in the sense that if we are displaying certain gestures and performing certain actions we are likely to say that we, e.g., pity someone, and also that if we are encouraged to pity someone and do pity them, we shall make gestures and perform actions of the type belonging to the pity package.

The *kind* of relation involved does not follow the typical rational model of, e.g., saying that we pity *on the evidence of* certain actions, gestures, etc. (or alternatively performing those actions, etc., as a result of a logical inference from the meaning of the word 'pity'), but our saying that we pity just comes as part of the pity package. We are jointly inclined to engage in the behavior and (under appropriate circumstances) to say the words. (It might or might not be misleading to call the relation "psychological.")

It would be reasonable and perhaps necessary to connect these behavior packages with language games in some such way as the following: we have the language games we have partly because of certain natural tendencies to smile and frown, to sympathize or to resent, to pursue or to avoid things, etc., but in turn these tendencies are shaped up into patterns or packages by the language games—by our being encouraged and habituated to speak and to connect what we say with behavior in certain *standard* ways.

The above connects behavior packages and language games so closely that a question arises whether it is useful to distinguish them. There is at least this basis of distinction: that one could talk of language games without having the behavior-package view as to the conditions under which they are "played." One could, for example, have a typical rational model according to which we *put on* a smile or a frown as and when the rules provide. The behavior-package view therefore represents one of a number of theories as to the relation between the common language game and the behavior of individual persons.

Like the first interpretation, the behavior-package account holds that to say that something is a form of life is to say there is something formal about it, the formal element in this case being the characteristic relations between the constituents of the package. It also seems to be true that for this interpretation, forms of life are countable: there is a large number of packages, each of which is one of life's forms.

Interpretation III

To say that something is a form of life is to say that it is a way of life, or a mode, manner, fashion, or style of life: that it has something important to do with the class structure, the values, the religion, the types of industry and commerce and of recreation that characterize a group of people. In what follows I shall have little further to say about this interpretation, so let me here explain my reasons both for mentioning it and for not treating it as a serious contender.

It recommends itself in two obvious ways: first, because the expressions 'form of life' and 'way (manner, style, fashion) of life' *can* be used interchangeably; and second, because it probably *is* true that there are interesting relations between the kind of language we have and the manner of life we lead. To have a language with no orders, for example, we would have to have a society with a very different industrial, commercial, military, and family structure.

However, it is not for this reason true that for example (§19) "to imagine a language means to imagine a form (=way) of life." What do we know about the way of life of the builders discussed in §2? More generally, if I imagine a language with, for example, no orders, all I know for certain is that the manner of life of the users of that language would be quite different from ours. I do not know whether they would find ways of training people to do what needs to be done without being told, or whether they would resign themselves to not getting done what we would normally achieve by such measures as giving orders. Even if I could reach some conclusions about this, it is still true that I first imagined the language, independently of the manner of life, and then drew my conclusions as to what manner of life is entailed.

Although §19 is therefore difficult to use for support, it is the *most* promising of the five key passages; and I leave it to the reader to figure out whether there is any sense in which only those can hope who have mastered a complicated way of life, or in which a way of life can be used to settle doubts as to the reliability of paper and ink or memory.[4]

Interpretation IV

The following is the interpretation of 'form of life' which I wish to defend; and as good a clue as any to its outlines might be to say that where Interpretations I and II treat 'form of life' as about equivalent to 'one of the formal things in life' or 'one of life's forms', the sense I am suggesting for it is more like 'something typical of a living being': typical in the sense of being very broadly in the same class as the growth or nutrition of living organisms, or as the organic complexity which enables them to propel themselves about, or to react in complicated ways to their environment. I shall therefore sometimes call this "the organic account."

It is initially difficult to see speaking or language-using, which is what Wittgenstein says is a form of life, as a biological or organic phenomenon, not because anyone would deny that living beings do it, but perhaps because of an inclination to think that it is a person's *mind*, which has its own, nonorganic mode of operation, which is immediately responsible. We do not generally include in the biological what is overt, what is learned, what is done at will or what is intelligent, but only what goes on within us, unaware and without our direction. Yet we can move by easy stages from automatic, unwilled, not-conscious processes like nutrition, through reflex actions, many of which are learned or at least *acquired*, and which, though not done at will, can often be *resisted* at will; then through speaking or writing just insofar as it is forming the words with our mouths or drawing the characters on paper, where, though we may form a word at will, we do not (generally) will the physical manner of our forming it; to, finally, expressing ourselves *in a certain way*, where although it is generally done at will, we do not will the *willing* of it, and we do not know how just this form of words sat-

[4] See Ludwig Wittgenstein, *Lectures on Religious Belief* (Oxford: Basil Blackwell, 1966), p. 58, where a "*way* of life" account is perhaps the only plausible one.

isfies all the various grammatical, social, personal, and intellectual requirements of being something we "want to say." We may by studying it afterwards *find out* how it satisfies such requirements (cf. §82), but the interesting thing is that we generally manage to say things which are just about what we *would* say *if* we had the requirements in mind, but *without a thought* of the requirements. (Not perhaps when we are writing philosophy; but that is not a very typical use of language; and even here it is only a very few of the requirements we have any thought of; the rest comes easily.) Setting the right word in the right sentence construction to serve our purposes is terribly complicated: How do we manage it? Given a certain development of the human organism, we do not *plan and execute* these things, we just do them. They flow from a living human being as naturally as he walks, dances, or digests food: operations of comparable complexity.

I don't know whether to say that Wittgenstein thought there is an interesting *analogy* here, the drawing of which can make certain things about language-using clearer to us, or to say he thought it is *true* that speaking is a biological phenomenon. But this may not matter: what *will* matter is the points about language-using which are brought out by the notion, whichever way it is taken.

II

I would now like to set out three claims about language use which could be said to be the main cash value of an organic account. I shall produce textual evidence that Wittgenstein made these claims, and I shall also discuss some difficulties as I go along.

First, there are a number of passages which taken together express the view that language-teaching is an ad hoc, trial and error process, tailored to the needs and difficulties of each individual, involving *all kinds* of tactics and devices, and designed, not to communicate (indirectly) to the learner some essential thing, some key to the use of an expression, but to mold and shape him until he uses an expression the way we do. The "molding and shaping" process, I suggest, is to be conceived, not on the model of, e.g., programming a computer, but on that of training an organism. It is like teaching a person to dance. Consider for example:

> Whether the word "number" is necessary in the ostensive definition [of "two" by pointing to two nuts] depends on whether without it the other person takes the definition otherwise than I wish. And that will depend on the circumstances under which it is given, and the person I give it to [§29].

Or:

> One might say: an explanation serves to remove or avert a misunderstanding—one, that is, that would occur but for the explanation; not every one that I can imagine [§87].

These remarks, among others (e.g., §§145, 208), suggest the idea of tailoring linguistic instruction to circumstances and to individuals. The idea that there are *all kinds* of tactics may be seen for example, in §69:

> How should we explain to someone what a game is? I imagine that we should describe *games* to him, and we might add: "This *and similar things* are called 'games' " [§69].

Add to this:

> . . . showing how all sorts of other games can be constructed on the analogy of these; saying that I should scarely include this or this among games; and so on [§75].

And:

> . . . I do it, he does it after me; and I influence him by expressions of agreement, rejection, expectation, encouragement. I let him go his way, or hold him back; and so on [§208].

Or again:

> If I wanted to define it at a *single* showing—I should *play-act* fear. Could I also represent hope in this way? Hardly. And what about belief? [p. 188].

The view that the language learner is not supposed to guess something that we cannot communicate to him directly, is expressed in §218:

But do you really explain to the other person what you yourself understand? Don't you get him to *guess* the essential thing? You give him examples, but he has to guess their drift. . . . [Wittgenstein goes on to suggest that anything he could guess, we could have told him] [§218].

Or:

Do we know any more about it ourselves? Is it only other people whom we could not tell exactly what a game is? [§69, also §362].

The view that language teaching is a molding and shaping process is expressed most directly:

For here I am looking at learning German as adjusting a mechanism to respond to a certain kind of influence [§495].

This is also suggested by the description of the process as a kind of *training* (for example in §§6, 189, 208, 630), and by the emphasis (e.g., §208), on the *practice* which is required. These serve to liken language acquisition to learning to dance, which is a matter of conditioning the organism to respond in complex and artful ways, rather than of being provided with the key to, or the system governing, these complex ways of behaving.

In connection with the view I am here trying to put together, it may be interesting to compare what Wittgenstein says about the admittedly rather different matter of learning expert judgment about the genuineness of expressions of feeling:

Can one learn this knowledge? Yes; some can. Not, however, by taking a course in it, but through *experience*.—Can someone else be a man's teacher in this? Certainly. From time to time he gives him the right *tip*.—This is what "learning" and "teaching" are like here. What one acquires here is not a technique; one learns correct judgments. There are also rules, but they do not form a system, and only experienced people can apply them right. Unlike calculation rules.

What is most difficult here is to put this indefiniteness, correctly and unfalsified, into words [p. 227].

One suspects that Wittgenstein thinks it is quite like this with learning language. And I want to suggest that his saying "one learns correct judgments" is an important remark. He seems *not* to be saying that of course a system is necessary for producing such judgments, but it does not matter *what* system (you can have yours and I mine), what is important is that the system should result in correct judgments. He seems rather to be saying that one *just learns correct judgments:* learns to perform correctly.

This last point connects with the second feature of the organic theory I wish to bring out: the view that appropriate language use need not, and does not ordinarily, involve even the most rudimentary mental act of, say, connecting a name to a thing, but comes as an immediate *response* of a person in a situation. It is *like* the way we withdraw our hand from a hot object: we do not think, "Heat only hurts when it is close, therefore keep away," and hence withdraw, but do so immediately and without thought. Not that we have not *learned* this; but the learning has brought it about that we act as it were instinctively. I am suggesting that Wittgenstein thinks it is generally the same with speaking. Not that we generally "speak without thinking," but that in speaking, thoughtfully or otherwise, the words we use come immediately, without thought.

This view is, of course, to be found among his remarks on pain language which, he suggests (§244) can be a natural expression of pain and as such is not *decided on,* but comes as immediately as we cry out or groan.

But he also says the same sort of thing about descriptive uses of language, such as color words:

. . . What is the criterion for the redness of an image? For me, when it is someone else's image, what he says and does. For myself, when it is my image, nothing [§377, see also §381, and cf. §290].

And about expressions of intention:

I reveal to him something of myself when I tell him what I was going to do. Not, however, on grounds of self-observation, but by way of a response (it might also be called an intuition) [§659].

And if pain, color, and intention are in some sense private, this view is not confined to such cases, but applies also, for example, to the naming of physical objects:

First I am aware of it as *this;* and then I remember what it is called.—
Consider: in what cases is it right to say this? [§379].

One doesn't *"take"* what one knows as the cutlery at a meal *for* cutlery; any more than one tries to move one's mouth as one eats, or aims at moving it [p. 195].

I shall now sketch a third feature of the organic theory of language use, a feature which I shall call the theory of linguistic self-sufficiency. It is the theory that, whether in saying things meaningfully, or in understanding what other people say, or what we read, we do not need, and do not generally use, any logical or psychological paraphernalia of any kind: the words themselves are quite sufficient. We do not need to imagine a room to understand a description of a room; we do not need a sample of pain or yellowness to understand what 'pain' or 'yellow' means; we do not need to translate an expression into another expression, and we do not need to guess, or interpret, or apply rules: we understand language just as it stands.

This view is to be found in *The Blue Book*, for example:

We want that the wish that Mr. Smith should come into this room should wish that just *Mr. Smith*, and no substitute, should *come*, and no substitute for that, *into my room*, and no substitute for that. But this is exactly what we said [p. 37].

And at various places in the *Philosophical Investigations*, for example:

"When I imagine that someone who is laughing is really in pain, I don't imagine pain behaviour, for I see just the opposite. So *what* do I imagine?" I have already said what [I imagine he is in pain, that's what] [§393].

Or:

"But mustn't I know what it would be like if I were in pain?"—We fail to get away from the idea that using a sentence involves imagining something for every word. . . . It is as if one were to believe that a written order for a cow . . . always had to be accompanied by an image of a cow, if the order was not to lose its meaning [§449].

Or:

If I give anyone an order I feel it to be *quite enough* to give him signs. And I should never say: this is only words, and I have got to get behind the words [§503].

Also:

> "He measured him with a hostile glance and said. . . ." The reader
> of the narrative understands this; he has no doubt in his mind. Now
> you say: "Very well, he supplies the meaning, he guesses it."—gen-
> erally speaking: no. Generally speaking he supplies nothing, guesses
> nothing [§652].

The part of the self-sufficiency theory that I think many people
would hesitate to attribute to Wittgenstein is the view that we do
not use rules in speaking, or in understanding what people say. I
shall not here go into this difficulty, but I think a careful reading of
§§81 to 84, with help perhaps from §§31, 54, 100, and 102, might
clear it up.[5]

In case it is not very clear what the connection is between an "organic account" and the self-sufficiency theory, I shall suggest two
main connections. The first is that the molding and shaping part of
the organic theory relieves the pressure for rules and other paraphernalia by making it credible that we can get along without them.
The second can best be seen by contrast with a view to which one
is easily inclined: that language is a late development in human evolution, and an artificial and foreign thing (§432) which needs to be
connected with what is natural and human to acquire meaning. On
this view we do not understand language until we translate it into
something non-linguistic—things, feelings, images, sensations, activities. But if instead we regard language as something natural to us,
and so as being itself one of those things into which we would
otherwise want to translate it (§649), then its self-sufficiency may
for the first time be seen as obvious and to be expected. So:

> Commanding, questioning, recounting, chatting, are as much part of
> our natural history as walking, eating, drinking, playing [§25].

A point of considerable general importance in connection with
the organic theory is a suggestion to be found in a couple of places
in the *Philosophical Investigations*, that whatever internal biological
complexities may be involved in certain things we do, *they work*,

---

[5] See also my paper, "Wittgenstein's Theory of Linguistic Self-Sufficiency,"
Dialogue, 6 (1967):367–82.

and to us they are perfectly *simple*. Wiggling my toes involves a marvelous complex of nervous and muscular activity: How do I do it? Well I just wiggle them (cf. §§614, 615). The same thought is expressed:

> I may be able to tell the direction from which a sound comes only because it affects one ear more strongly than the other, but I don't feel this in my ears; yet it has its effect: I *know* the direction from which the sound comes; for instance I look in that direction [p. 185].

This is important because of a possible misunderstanding which might arise from this talk about *organic* theory: one might suppose that it was being suggested that it would be appropriate to inquire into the detail of the organic processes, and thereby *explain* the use of language. But there is a cut-off point here. Language use may be said to be an organic process, but the interesting thing to us about organic processes is that *they work*, and hence to us they are *simple*. To describe what goes on in me when I wiggle my toes is not to further explain *how I wiggle them*, what I do in order to bring it about that they wiggle. That cannot be further explained. I just wiggle them.

Two other pieces of evidence that Wittgenstein held something like the "organic theory" are first that section 4.002 in the *Tractatus* shows that this idea was not not unknown to him:

> Man possesses the capacity of constructing languages, in which every sense can be expressed, but without having an idea how and what each word means—just as one speaks without knowing how the single words are produced.

> Colloquial language is a part of the human organism, and not less complicated than it.

And second, that he explicitly treats "calculating in the head," a thing done by a living being, as something of its own kind, and not necessarily at all like calculation on paper:

> Is calculating in the imagination in some sense less real than calculating on paper? It is *real*—calculation-in-the-head. Is it like calculation on paper?—I don't know whether to call it like. Is a bit of white paper with black lines on it like a human body? [§364, see also §366].

III

If I have now provided reason to believe that Wittgenstein did hold an "organic view," or something like it, I have *not* shown that this is what he meant by a 'form of life'. To do this I shall try to show that this interpretation makes at least as good sense as the other accounts, and sometimes better, of the passages in which that expression appears.

I shall be rather brief about the first three of these passages, and I shall confine myself pretty much to displaying different ways of reading them which would lead to different interpretations. I shall be trying to show less that my own interpretation is strongly indicated, than that it is also a serious contender.

(*a*) . . . to imagine a language means to imagine a form of life [§19].

A great deal hinges here on how we read the word 'means'. If we take it as about equal to 'involves', then Wittgenstein will be saying that to imagine a language the words are not enough, one needs to imagine something more than this: a form of life, whatever that is. And since we know that he thinks that a language may be described by describing the circumstances in which it is used and the actions with which the words are interwoven, it seems safe enough to conclude that either these actions and circumstances, or these together with the words with which they are interwoven (and probably the latter), are what a form of life is.

This reading would strongly support the view that language-games are prime examples of forms of life; and in view of the close connection between the two (see Interpretation II), might with some tolerance support a behavior-package interpretation.

If Wittgenstein *did* mean something like this, it is difficult to see why he would not have just said something like "to imagine a language it is necessary to imagine the game, as part of which the words are used," since the concept of a language-game is particularly clear on this point. However, we cannot assume that he always chose the best way of making his points.[6]

[6] I have already discussed the possibility that imagining a language is being represented as *involving* something a bit different: a *way* of life.

We could also read 'means' in the above passage as about equal to 'is a case of', so that in imagining a language, no matter how that is done (and no doubt it *will* be done by imagining language-games), one is thereby or at the same time imagining a form of life. On this rendering Wittgenstein is not telling us *how* to imagine a language, but something about what the thing imagined is. (Compare "To imagine a composition by Bach means to imagine a piece of baroque music," or "To imagine New York means to imagine a city.")

What is he telling us about a language? Is it reasonable to suggest that part of the answer is to be found in what he immediately goes on to say about the call "Slab!" In considering whether it is a word or a sentence, he says "There is no such sentence as 'Bring me a slab' " in example (2), and "Why should I translate the call 'Slab!' into a different expression in order to say what someone means by it? Why should I not say: 'When he says "Slab!" he means "Slab"!'?" He is saying something about what I have called the "self-sufficiency" of language: that it stands by itself, and needs no further explication. A person in this situation could not say what he means by "Slab!" and yet in the ordinary sense of that expression he knows what it means. How does he know? Well, encouragement, reproof, practice, and examples have brought it about that its use is simply part of the way he functions. A living being now functions that way, as immediately and naturally as he walks or swims, and being simply part of the way a living being functions could be what is meant by being a form of life.

(*b*) There is a comparable option about the interpretation of (§23):

> Here the term "language-*game*" is meant to bring into prominence the fact that the *speaking* of language is part of an activity, or of a form of life [§23].

In what sense is the speaking of language "part of an activity," and what is meant here by 'activity'?

According to the most obvious reading, the uttering of words is interconnected with other behavior, say of builders on a worksite, and the whole composed of utterances and other behavior is what is meant by an activity, and is designated a form of life. This reading would square nicely with a language-game account, and not quite so handily but well enough with a behavior-package account.

But it is also possible that speaking is part of an activity in another sense: not in the sense that *together with other things* it constitutes a whole activity, but in the sense that any given utterance is part of a general competence in using the expressions it contains. On this interpretation, this competence would be what it is that is called a form of life.

How plausible such a reading is will depend a lot on what is understood by the word 'activity'. There are at least two common senses of this word: what one might call an "organized communal affairs" sense, the sense in which the activities at a school are listed as "basketball," "carpentering," etc. (and this is the sense which the first of the above interpretations requires); and the sense in which, when a person is doing something, he is active: the sense in which, not basketball, but *playing* basketball, is an activity. I will suggest two reasons for supposing that Wittgenstein was using the term in the latter of these ways:

1. The fact that he italicized 'speaking' would suggest that he wanted to stress the *doing*, in contrast to the fact that what is done is something organized and communal.

2. He says:

Of course mathematics is a branch of knowledge, but still it is also an *activity* [p. 227].

Mathematics as a branch of knowledge can be likened to basketball considered as an organized activity. But this aspect of it is not identified with, but contrasted with Wittgenstein's sense of "activity," and therefore (here at least) he probably means by an activity, "something that people *do*."

This doing is of course not random or blind, but skilled; and to say that such skilled human activity is a form of life might be a way of likening speaking to the organic skill involved in physical games like basketball: the highly articulated physical artistry necessary to make a ball go where you want it, at the speed at which you want it to go, etc.

This would explain, what it is otherwise difficult to see, why the term 'language-*game*' would bring anything like my view of forms of life into prominence. We tend to think of a game as an organized common activity (in the other sense), but games are also *played*, and the playing of them is an organic human skill.

(*c*) It is what human beings *say* that is true and false; and they agree in the language they use. That is not agreement in opinions but in form of life [§241].

From this it might appear that it is the *language* which is the form of life, and that would lend support to the kind of interpretation according to which a form of life is something shared and standardized. But we could also read "agreeing in the language they use" as about equal to "agreeing in the way they speak" (agreeing in their use of language); and to say that *this* was agreeing in form of life could be to say that training, etc., had brought it about that two or more people simply function the same way.

Hence when a man continues the plus 2 series . . . 1000, 1004, 1008, etc., he and I do not disagree (hold different opinions) as to how it goes: we simply do it differently. The breakdown is not an occasion for *argument*, but for insistence, reproof, encouragement, drill, and all those training devices by which we bring about agreement *in* the way mathematics is done.

If it were the language that was the form of life here, then this *would* be a case of difference of opinion, which could be settled by adducing evidence as to what the convention was in this (or any other) case. But generally there is no convention as to how to continue a series beyond the first few steps, and this is presumably why (in §§185 and 186) Wittgenstein used comparatively *large* numbers as examples.

A further indication that it is language-using, rather than language, which is described as a form of life here is that the wording of §23 marks forms of life as *activities*, and language-*using* can much more readily be seen as an activity than can language.

(*d*) Can only those hope who can talk? Only those who have mastered the use of language. That is to say the phenomena of hope are modes of this complicated form of life [p. 174].

A minor point first: it seems fairly clear that in the above, 'this complicated form of life' refers, not to hope or hoping, but to either the use of language or mastery of the use of language; and perhaps specifically to mastery of the use of the word 'hope'. There *is* a distinction here: one can master the use of the word 'hope' without ever hoping; and there is no such thing as being a masterful hoper. This is important because to say that *hope* was the form of life would lend credence to the behavior-package account, especially if, as might be plausible enough, one said that hope is a package including certain thoughts, gestures, etc., as well as *saying* that one hopes.

But what are "the phenomena of hope," and what is it to be a "mode" of a form of life? Well, on p. 211 "the phenomena of being struck" are said to include one's facial expression and the things one is inclined to say (aloud or to oneself) when one is struck; and they are also said not to be *what it is* to be struck. If one can reason the same way about "the phenomena of hope," these would be the kinds of things one typically notices about oneself *when* one hopes, certain feelings perhaps, and thoughts and facial expressions, and also they would not be *what it is* to hope.[7] (This is confirmed, if I read it correctly, by §545.)

But if the phenomena of hope are not hope, what does it mean to say that they are modes of the use of language, or of the activity which includes the use of language?

We might make some headway by reflecting on what is said (p. 174) about shivering and shuddering. Two points seem to be suggested. (1) When we say "It makes me shiver" as a piece of information, we do not learn this from our sensations (but our saying it is perhaps one expression of revulsion among others?). (2) Saying "It makes me shiver" may thus itself be a shuddering reaction, and may produce the characteristic sensations of shuddering just as physical shuddering does. It is therefore not necessary to conceive the wordless shudder as the ground of the verbal one.

Applying this to hope, one might reckon that Wittgenstein would say that when we say we hope (or have been hoping) as *information*, this is less a report on our thoughts and feelings than another expression of hope, and also that our saying we hope may itself fill

[7] It is more complicated than this (see §§583, 638, 642). One cannot hope for a moment. But this may not matter here.

us with those thoughts and feelings. Either way, saying that we hope is not a secondary or derivative, but a primary thing, at least as basic and natural as any of the other "phenomena of hope." But there is also a sense in which it is prior to any of them: the sense in which, by saying that we hope, we make or show the phenomena of hope to be such. For if the thought that a certain delightful person may come to my party fills me all day with pleasurable feelings, there are no criteria which would decide whether these thoughts and feelings were a case of hoping, yearning, or musing. And if I later say that I have been hoping . . . , I have not *discovered* this, but have *made* what I have been doing hoping (cf. §§557, 653).

To return then to the question what it means to call the "phenomena of hope" (i.e., the characteristic thoughts, feelings, etc., of hoping) "modes of this complicated form of life," we may guess that it means that they are not themselves what it is to hope, but that they may have a sort of secondary status as hope when either they are so marked by our saying that we hope, or they result from our so saying.

We do not say that we hope on the basis of evidence, any more than we have evidence for saying that we promise, but it comes naturally to us in some circumstances to say it. It is one of the stock of human responses, and if this stock were depleted by the loss of the word 'hope' or its equivalents, we would no longer be able to hope. Saying that this use of language is a form of life is saying that it is not derivative, that it is not done on the basis of evidence, that saying the words is itself part of the stock of human responses and is as natural and primordial as an affectionate gesture.

It could not be argued, I think, that either the language-game or the behavior-package account of forms of life is irreconcilable with this passage. I shall therefore confine myself to pointing out the differences between the latter and the account I am suggesting. On my account it is the complicated organic adaptation which enables us to use a word such as 'hope' which is the form of life; and therefore we could, even if we don't often, use the word 'hope' without any of the phenomena of hope occurring, and we could by comparing notes find that there were marked differences in these phenomena from person to person. (Cf. §§33–35, 152, 376, 646, and pp.

181c, 211d, and 218c.) But on the other account the form of life is the package consisting of the "phenomena" and the use of the word, and presumably the constituents of the package could not vary *greatly* from person to person, nor could one rightly use the word in the absence of all the phenomena.

(*e*) We shall now take up the passage (p. 226) where it is suggested that if the paper and ink with which we calculated underwent queer changes this could be discovered by memory and comparison with other methods of calculation, and if we ask how these in turn could be tested the answer is: "What must be accepted, the given, is—so one could say, forms of life."

In what way exactly are forms of life "the given"? Are they some kind of ultimate fact which can be used for testing purposes in the same *kind* of way that, e.g., comparisons with other methods of calculation are used, but which unlike the other methods cannot themselves be tested in turn? Something like this is what one would expect going by the ordinary philosophical use of the expression 'the given'.

But it seems extraordinarily difficult to suggest an example of the operation of this procedure. If forms of life were, for example, customs or conventions, and one were operating in a *milieu* in which paper and ink and memory were thought likely to undergo queer changes, there would appear to be little reason to exempt the sources of information about customs and institutions from the same suspicion.

We might therefore consider the possibility that forms of life are "given" in some odd sort of way (Wittgenstein does say "so one could say"). Consider this example: if, with great care and deliberation, I write a '4' on a piece of paper and something queer happens and it comes out a '5', I might be asked, are you sure that isn't what a four is? I shall be certain that it is not a '4', and yet it may be that when I try to illustrate to myself in imagination what a four is, the same queer thing happens. But I shall know that it has happened, and my inarticulate certainty, even without a token of it, that I know what a four is, could be what is "given," and what is a form of life.

It may be useful to compare this kind of account with one which is often given, and which relies on such passages as:

Our mistake is to look for an explanation where we ought to look at what happens as a "proto-phenomenon." That is, where we ought to have said: *this language-game is played* [§654].

In this account, the fact that we play a language-game in a certain way is what is treated as given; and presumably evidence that the game is so played could be adduced to settle doubts about, e.g., the reliability of paper, ink, and memory. But I suggest it is not something public and common which is the datum here, but something individual. Consider the following passages:

How do I know [how to continue the pattern by myself]?—If that means "Have I reasons?" the answer is: my reasons will soon give out. And then I shall act, without reasons [§211].

If I have exhausted the justifications I have reached bedrock, and my spade is turned. Then I am inclined to say: "This is simply what I do" [§217].

When I obey a rule, I do not choose. I obey the rule *blindly* [§219].

It is not that it is the way *we* do it, but that it is the way *I* do it which is (so one could say) "the given." And on this reading, *however* a person does something, it is his *simply functioning that way* which is a form of life, while on the interpretation which here competes, only the correct way of doing something is a form of life, and it is its correctness, that is its being the standard way, rather than the fact that it is done by a living being, which earns it that title.

IV

I should like finally to consider certain other evidence which might be used in support of one or other of the alternative interpretations we have been discussing. First there is a group of passages where Wittgenstein talks of the "common behavior of mankind" as a guide to the interpretation of a language. For example the quotation from St. Augustine in §1:

Their intention was shown by their bodily movements, as it were the natural language of all peoples: the expression of the face, the play of the eyes, the movement of other parts of the body, and the tone of voice [§1].

Or:

Think of the behaviour characteristic of correcting a slip of the tongue. It would be possible to recognize that someone was doing so even without knowing his language [§54].

Or:

Suppose you came as an explorer into a country with a language quite strange to you. In what circumstances would you say that the people there gave orders, understood them, obeyed them, rebelled against them, and so on?

The common behaviour of mankind is the system of reference by which we interpret an *unknown* language [§206, my italics].

Or:

. . . one human being can be a complete enigma to another. We learn this when we come into a strange country with entirely strange traditions; and what is more, even given a mastery of the country's language. We do not *understand* the people. (And not because of not knowing what they are saying to themselves.) We cannot find our feet with them [p. 223].

This "common behavior of mankind" might be called a form of life, and in §19 Wittgenstein might have been saying that we need to imagine it in order to imagine a language. But there are serious difficulties, for example:

(1) In §21 it is pointed out that gestures, tones of voice, etc., are not essential to the comprehension of a language:

. . . for an order and a report can be spoken in a *variety* of tones of voice and with various expressions of face [§21].

(2) The last of the above passages indicates that one *can* master a language without a knowledge of the traditions associated with it.

(3) Wittgenstein *uses* these observations to make various philosophical points, and does not treat them as being particularly interesting in themselves. For example, in §§1, 32, 206, and 208 he is

making the point (contra Augustine) that the common behavior has nothing to do with our initial learning of language, but only with the learning of a new language (e.g., an Englishman learning French). In §54 he was trying to take care of a difficulty about how one could learn a game just from watching others play; how would he distinguish between mistakes and correct play? And on p. 223 he was trying to make the point that understanding people need not consist in knowing what they are thinking. (But of course it is not impossible that Wittgenstein wanted to do more than one thing with any of these passages.)

The following is a second group of passages that might support alternatives to our interpretation of 'forms of life'. In them, Wittgenstein suggests that certain concepts refer, not to definite experiences, but histories or patterns of thoughts, actions, circumstances.

> . . . Could someone have a feeling of ardent love or of hope for the space of one second—*no matter what* preceded or followed this second?—What is happening now has significance—in these surroundings [§583, also §584].

> Certain antecedents were necessary for me to have had a momentary intention of pretending to someone that I was unwell [§638].

> "At that moment I hated him."—What happened here? . . . If I were to rehearse that moment to myself, I should assume a particular expression, think of certain happenings, breathe in a particular way, arouse certain feelings in myself. I might think up a conversation, a whole scene in which that hatred flared up [§642].

> If I now become ashamed of this incident, I am ashamed of the whole thing [§643].

> "Grief" describes a pattern which recurs, with different variations, in the weave of our life. If a man's bodily expression of sorrow or joy alternated, say with the ticking of a clock, here we should not have the characteristic formation of the pattern of sorrow or of the pattern of joy [p. 174].

Again, it would not be inept to call such patterns—histories—as these "forms of life." Yet I think it is fairly certain they are not what Wittgenstein meant, for the following reasons. (1) It is only some concepts of which this is true at all. It is not true of 'pain', for example. One *can* feel violent pain for a second (p. 174). (2) It is doubtful whether, in all the above passages, Wittgenstein would say, as he says of 'grief', that the concept in question *describes* the pattern or formation. For one thing, 'grief' is (mostly) a descriptive word. We do not use it (much) in the expression of grief. But 'hope' and 'hate' are mostly used in the expression of hope or hatred, and as such *they* do not describe the contexts in which they are used, even if *we* can (as Wittgenstein does in, e.g., §642) describe them. Therefore, in describing them he was probably less interested in what he was affirming than in that he was denying: that 'hate' is the name of a feeling. It is not the name of a feeling but neither is it the name of a history (who would guess that *that* was the history when I say that for a moment I hated him?). It is a word we utter in certain situations for certain purposes. So it is reasonable to read §642, not as reporting what it was to hate him, but as describing a process of recreating the conditions in which I would again be inclined to spit out the words 'I hate him'.

As was suggested earlier about 'hope' and the "phenomena of hope," to say 'I hate him' puts the stamp of hate on the phenomena of hate, which otherwise might be anything or nothing.

It should be noted that §638 goes on to say "But not even the whole story was my evidence for saying 'For a moment. . . .'" And this is presumably not because there was ever so much *more* evidence (more than the whole story?), but because it is not a question of evidence. What *is* it a question of? This is none too clear, but the answer I think is to be found in §§653 and 659; we think we are (in reviewing the history) reading an obscure map, but the fact is that we are *now inclined to say* that we had an intention. We say this to reveal to another person something about ourselves: "Not however on grounds of self-observation, but by way of a response . . ." (§659). Saying that it is "by way of a response" perhaps means that when we cast our thoughts back to a past situation, then just as in one case we are inclined again to spit out the words 'I hate him', so we may likewise be inclined to say 'I did not intend. . . .' This is not a report but a reaction of a person in a situation. He reacts *that* way, using *those* words, not because he recognizes that his situation is an appropriate case for the use of those words, satisfying all the criteria, but as it were blindly, and because this use of words has been built into him, and has become part of the way he functions. (It is a form of life.)

I have now explored the main issues which seem to me relevant to this puzzle, and I shall conclude. For my part I find all this very exciting. I keep wanting to say (cf. §610) that these notes say something glorious, make a powerful gesture. But if at this stage that *needs* to be said, I am sure that neither by saying it nor by saying anything else shall I make the power and the glory any more evident.

15

Privacy and Language

MOLTKE S. GRAM

DISCUSSION of the private language problem has reached a mildly disreputable stage. The pressing problem seems to be not whether such a language is possible, but whether there is any philosophical point in continuing to discuss a problem about which there is little or no agreement concerning even so much as the conditions of its solution. What I hope to contribute to this discussion is a proof that what is defensible in Wittgenstein's arguments against private languages is very different from what those arguments purport to establish. There are, I hope to show, no fewer than four distinguishable arguments in the *Philosophical Investigations* against the possibility of private languages. Only one of them shows something about private languages. What it shows, however, is not that a private language is impossible, but rather that no public language can be constructed out of a set of private languages.

Some philosophers have argued that what we take to be objects which are accessible to more than one observer, which are locatable in public space and time, and which exist even when they are not observed can be replaced by sets of objects which I shall call here essentially private items. An object which is essentially private cannot be observed by more than one observer, is not located in public space and time, and does not exist when it is not being observed. One of the perennial programs in philosophy is to reconstruct our notion of public objects by analyzing them into sets of essentially private objects. Wittgenstein's polemic against private languages does succeed in showing that such a philosophical program cannot succeed. But his polemic fails to show the impossibility of private languages.

1. Wittgenstein's Formation

Wittgenstein states the problem by asking about the possibility of a language in which "individual words . . . are to refer to what can only be known to the person speaking; to his immediate sensations. So another person cannot understand the language."[1] We are asked, in other words, to conceive of a language the vocabulary of which has meaning in virtue of a relation in which its components stand to a certain kind of object. The object in question is one which only one person can observe. This formulation raises two questions which must be answered if we are to understand what Wittgenstein is asking. For one thing, is it essential to a private language that only one person be able to observe the entities which its vocabulary describes? And for another, does Wittgenstein's formulation require merely that it be impossible for two people to *have* the things described by a private language or to *observe* those things? Take these questions in turn.

Wittgenstein's formulation requires that it be logically impossible for more than one person to observe the things described by a private language. This can be shown as follows. Let us assume that the entities to which a private language is applied can in principle be observed by others. This would entail that the language used to describe them could be understood by more than one person. This is merely an immediate consequence of how the words in a private language are said to get their meaning. Wittgenstein says that only one person can understand a private language because the words in such a language refer to things that can be known to only one person. From this I infer that Wittgenstein identifies the meaning of the words here with their referents. If the referents of words in a

---

[1] Ludwig Wittgenstein, *Philosophical Investigations*, §243. All references to this work in the present paper are to the translation of G. E. M. Anscombe, 3rd ed. (New York: Macmillan, 1968).

private language are private, then the meaning of the words used to refer to them must also be private. And so, once one admits that what makes a language private is the privacy of the entities to which words in that language refer, then one cannot hold that it is even a theoretical possibility for more than one person to observe those entities. If you do hold this then you will be admitting—which is contrary to Wittgenstein's formulation of what counts as a private language—that more than one person can understand it. For more than one person could then inspect the objects which confer meaning on the words of a private language.

But this conclusion only gives rise to the second question about Wittgenstein's formulation. What is required for a private language is that only one person can understand the vocabulary in such a language. And this in turn requires that the objects described by that vocabulary be private. But does this very notion of privacy so essential to a private language not rest, after all, on a confusion of two very different kinds of privacy? Don Locke has recently defended a distinction between two senses of privacy.[2] If this distinction is viable, then Wittgenstein's formulation is vitiated by its inability to distinguish between an essentially private and a theoretically public language. The distinction in question separates logical from mental privacy. What is logically private "cannot, logically cannot, be shared with others."[3] What is mentally private can be perceived by only one person.[4] Thus you cannot share my hiccups. Nor can you perform my actions. But you can *perceive* both my actions and my hiccups. The conclusion of this distinction is that the objects of a private language can be logically private without being mentally private.[5] A sensation is the result of a stimulation of the nervous system. It is possible for another person to be joined to my nervous system and, accordingly, to perceive the sensation that activates it. The sensation is logically but not mentally private. If this is true, then what Wittgenstein describes as a private language simply breaks down on a confusion of two very different senses of 'privacy': A language can be private in the sense that its vocabulary

[2] Don Locke, *Myself and Others* (Oxford: Clarendon Press, 1968), 5ff.
[3] Ibid., p. 6.
[4] Ibid.
[5] Ibid., pp. 34-35.

refers to entities that are logically private; but the same language can be public in that the referents of the words in such a language refer to objects that can be observed by more than one person.

The distinction between logical and mental privacy is plausible when it is applied to those things which are conceded to be publicly observable in any case. Thus a hiccup or an action like walking is a public item. And it is obvious that neither is also mentally private. But the issue becomes considerably more complicated when the distinction here is applied to objects like sensations. Can a sensation be logically private without being mentally private? The evidence that it can amounts to the claim that two people can share the same brain messages. And this is precisely what is questionable about the distinction between logical and mental privacy when it is applied to sensations. What has been shown is that two people can have the same physiological stimuli. But from this alone it does not follow that one person can observe another's sensation. But this is not all. To say that sensations can be logically private but not mentally private implies both that they really cannot be logically private after all, and that they can appear to have properties that they really do not have. This can be shown as follows. Suppose that two people stand in a similar epistemic relation—call it simple apprehension—to one and the same sensation. A's simple apprehension of S is qualitatively like B's simple apprehension since both belong to the same epistemic *genre*. The object of A's apprehension is literally the same as the object of B's apprehension. This, I assume, is an illustration of what Locke means when he says that sensations are logically private without being mentally private. But if this is so, then it follows that sensations are not even logically private. If one and the same sensation can form the object of several acts of apprehension, then it follows that the sensation is what it is, independently of the fact that it is the object of A's rather than B's apprehension. What this shows is that the sensation can exist even if either A or B ceases to exist. And from this it also follows that S can appear to have properties that it does not have. If S is independent of any particular act of apprehension, then it is logically possible that S appear to A as f while really possessing the property g. And this in turn obliterates the distinction between sensations and physical objects. For once you admit that an entity can appear to have properties that it lacks, you have already committed yourself to admitting that it can exist unobserved, that it can be observed by more than one person, and that it can endure through time. And this is tantamount to admitting that the entity in question is a physical object.

Thus there are two things that vitiate Locke's distinction between logical and mental privacy. First, since one and the same sensation can be of the object of many different acts of apprehension, then it follows that there is no *logical* tie between a sensation and any person to whom it appears. Thus the mental publicity of sensations implies their logical publicity. If this were not the case, then it would be impossible for B to observe A's sensations; for once A's sensations are tied logically to A's act of apprehension, then it is logically impossible for them to become objects of B's act of apprehension.

The soundness of the foregoing conclusion cannot be impugned by trying to show that the same conclusion follows with respect to *all* logically private items. Consider a hiccup. Somebody might hold that it, too, can be the object of many different acts of apprehension. And yet, it does not cease to be logically private even though it is independent of any particular act of apprehension. But the reason that a hiccup remains logically private while being observed by many different people is that it is no more observed alone than is the proverbial smile of the Cheshire cat. If a hiccup enters my consciousness at all, it enters as a property of an agent. And this is what distinguishes sensations from other things that are alleged to be logically private—to observe A's sensation is not to observe A together with one of A's properties; it is to observe what A observes when he senses something. Thus what is unproblematic about things like hiccups is just what is at issue about sensations: Is a sensation logically dependent upon an act of awareness? To show that it is not permits no inferences about the status of other entities that are obviously *defined* as dependent upon agents possessing them.

Second, permitting one and the same sensation to stand in an epistemic relation to many different acts of awareness destroys the distinction between sensations and physical objects. This would imply that sensations can appear to have properties that they do not in fact have. But whatever else a sensation may be, it cannot be a species of physical object. And so the distinction between logical and mental privacy does not apply to sensations; hence, it cannot be used to show that the vocabulary of a private language can be understood by more than one person. Wittgenstein's formulation of what is to count as a private language is not, accordingly, vitiated by the distinction between logical and mental privacy. It remains an open question whether there are languages that can fulfill Wittgenstein's description.

2. *Wittgenstein's Arguments*

I distinguish four different arguments by which Wittgenstein tries to show the impossibility of a private language. I take them in turn.

1. *The Argument from Reconstruction.* This argument is suggested first in §272, where Wittgenstein suggests that one section of mankind might have one sensation of red and another section quite another sensation of red. The significance of this speculation emerges, however, only in §293, where he argues as follows:

> Suppose everyone had a box with something in it: we call it a "beetle." No one can look into anyone else's box, and everyone says he knows what a beetle is only by looking at *his* beetle.—Here it would be quite possible for everyone to have something different in his box. One might even imagine such a thing constantly changing. . . . The thing in the box has no place in the language-game at all; not even as a *something:* for the box might even be empty.—No, one can 'divide through' by the thing in the box; it cancels out, whatever it is.

What Wittgenstein is claiming here is, I believe, clear. He is saying that, however the word 'beetle' acquires its meaning in our public language, it cannot be said to acquire that meaning by standing in relation to essentially private objects like sensations. It would, he is saying, be possible for everybody to have different sensations of a beetle and still correctly apply the word in the public language (". . . one can 'divide through' by the thing in the box"). Thus the claim is that we cannot account for the meaning of the words we have in our public language by any theory according to which they are given meaning by standing in relation to our sensations.

This much, I think, is clear. What is not clear is Wittgenstein's argument for such a claim.

If we are to interpret Wittgenstein's beetle example as an argument, it would center on one crucial premise: Our sensations can vary, while the public referents of the words we use do not. And this is based on a fact of communication; we can ascertain how another person uses the term 'beetle' without being able to inspect his sensations; hence, we can correctly identify beetles even though we cannot be aware of the sensations others may have when they are perceptually confronted with beetles. The steps of the present argument, then, are these:

1. We can ascertain when a person uses a certain word in public language correctly.

2. We cannot have access to the sensations the person has when he is confronted by the referent of the word he uses.

3. From (1) and (2) it follows that words figuring in our public language do not assume agreement in the sensations we experience.

4. From (3) it follows that the relation a word has to a sensation plays no part in giving that word meaning in a language we all understand.

5. From (4) it follows that the account of meaning associated with private languages is independent of the account given in a public language.

What this argument establishes is, at most, that private languages cannot account for the way in which words are given meaning in public languages. But showing this is very different from showing that private languages are impossible. We can accept, for example, Wittgenstein's claim that the characteristics of sensations of the same object may vary from person to person. But a defender of the existence of a private language is not required to construct a language that more than one person can understand. And it is no objection to such a person to complain that what he has constructed is a private rather than a public language. It is merely a banal reminder that private languages are constructed differently from public languages.

2. *The Argument from Intersubjectivity*. What I am about to outline is not, properly speaking, an argument. It is a collection of similes which might be used to show that a private language is impossible because ascriptions of predicates to others would, on the theory of meaning essential to a private language, have to be declared meaningless. Here two similes are relevant, the first of which occurs in §297:

> Of course, if water boils in a pot, steam comes out of the pot and also pictured steam comes out of the pictured pot. But what if one insisted on saying that there must also be something boiling in the picture of the pot?

The second simile occurs in §350:

> "But if I suppose that someone has a pain, then I am simply supposing that he has just the same as I have so often had."—That gets us no further. It is as if I were to say: "You surely know what 'It is 5 o'clock here' means; so you also know what 'It's 5 o'clock on the sun' means. It means simply that it is just the same time there as it is here when it is 5 o'clock."—The explanation by means of *identity* does not work here. For I know well enough that one can call 5 o'clock here and 5 o'clock there "the same thing," but what I do not know is in what cases one is to speak of its being the same time here and there.

The conclusion of these points occurs in §302, when Wittgenstein says that "if one has to imagine someone else's pain on the model of one's own, this is none too easy a thing to do: for I have to imagine pain which I *do not feel* on the model of the pain which I *do feel*." The significance of these similes for the private language argument is this: If I am restricted to my own sensations in giving meaning to the words in my language, I cannot give meaning to words ascribing predicates to others unless I can apprehend the sensations of others. And this, I take Wittgenstein to be arguing, is precisely what I cannot do. For the only way in which I might be able to accomplish this feat is by imagining the sensations of others on the analogy of my own sensations. And this is what is impossible.

Consider how the similes are prima facie evidence for this conclusion. To imagine that water boils in a pot is pictorially to represent a pot and steam emerging from it. There is no place in such a representation for the boiling water. There are two implicit inferences in this simile. First, there is the inference that the sensations of others occupy the same place in my application of third-person predicates that the boiling water occupies in my representation of a steaming teapot; neither can be imagined. Second, there is the inference that I am unable to give meaning to third-person ascriptions of predicates in a private language by connecting those predicates with any of my sensations.

The simile of time parallels the foregoing exactly. I cannot imagine its being 5 o'clock on the sun on the analogy of its being 5 o'clock on the earth because the very notion of time measurement on earth gets its meaning from the earth's relation to the sun and not conversely. To try to imagine what it is like to be 5 o'clock on the sun, accordingly, is to try to imagine the impossible; it is to try to imagine time coordinates on the sun analogous to those on the earth. And imagining the sensations of others is like imagining what it would be like to be 5 o'clock on the sun; in both cases we are required to occupy a position that we logically cannot occupy.

What I have called the Argument from Intersubjectivity comes, then, to this. If a private language is possible, we must be able to explain the meaning of sensation words as used by others. The only way in which this can be done in private language is to imagine the sensations of others on the analogy of our own sensations. And since this is impossible, there are large classes of sentences that would have to be declared meaningless in a private language. My reconstruction of the argument is this:

1. The meaning of a word in a private language is the sensation to which it refers.

2. One condition for the adequacy of any language is that it gives meaning to third-person ascriptions of predicates.

3. From (1) it follows that meaning can be given to third-person ascriptions in a private language only if we can reproduce to ourselves the sensations of others which give meaning to third-person ascriptions.

4. The condition stated in (3) cannot in principle be met by a private language.

5. From (4) it follows that no private language can give meaning to third-person ascriptions.

6. Hence no private language is adequate.

The Argument from Intersubjectivity is, at first sight, irrelevant to the private language problem. It might be argued that the problem presented by the application of sensation words to other people can be raised quite independently of the problem about private languages. Let us suppose that the predicates of a language get their meaning from the relation they have, not to essentially private objects, but rather to public objects. This would avoid the issue about private languages but would not avoid the issue that arises over whether words referring to sensations of others have the same meaning as they do when they are used to describe one's own sensations. And so it might be thought that the Argument from Intersubjectivity is not properly relevant to the private language issue at all.

This would, however, constitute a misunderstanding of the precise point of the Argument from Intersubjectivity. What that argument purports to show is that the solution to the problem of third-person ascriptions of mental predicates is rendered impossible by the very conditions the solution would have to meet in the context of a private language. To explain how such ascriptions are meaningful would, in the context of a private language, amount to translating them into terms that refer to one's own sensations. And this is a restriction that is not placed on the solution of the problem in the context of public languages. For this reason, then, the Argument from Intersubjectivity, first appearances notwithstanding, must be viewed as an argument against the possibility of a private language.

My concern with the Argument from Intersubjectivity is limited. I do not propose to dispute the soundness of Wittgenstein's argument against analogical representation of the sensations of others. All I wish to show is, first, that the present argument does not render third-person ascriptions in a private language meaningless and, second, that it shows at most the inadequacy as distinct from the impossibility of private languages. Take these points in turn.

What the Argument from Intersubjectivity excludes is that the meaning of third-person ascriptions in a private language be given in terms of the sensations of others. But this consequence does not destroy the distinction between first- and third-person ascriptions in a private language. The distinction can still be maintained by translating third-person ascriptions into sentences describing my sensations of somebody else's behavior. This is, of course, a program of translation for which an argument must be given; I do not propose to argue for it here. My only point is that such a program has not been excluded by the Argument from Intersubjectivity; consequently, the argument does not, as it stands, show the inadequacy of a private language to distinguish between first- and third-person ascriptions.

Even if this problem is waived and we simply concede that no third-person ascriptions would be meaningful in a private language, the present argument still suffers from a serious defect. All it shows is that the sensations of others have no place in a private language. And so far from being an objection to a private language, this is merely a statement of what a private language is; hence, it does not show the impossibility of a private language because it does not show the impossibility of accounting for the meaning of an inventory of noises and sign designs by relating them to sensations.

3. *The Argument from Contrast.* The basis for this argument is a passage in §246:

> In what sense are my sensations *private?*—Well, only I can know whether I am really in pain; another person can only surmise it.— In one way this is wrong, and in another nonsense. If we are using the word "to know" as it is normally used (and how else are we to use it?), then other people very often know when I am in pain.—Yes, but all the same not with the certainty with which I know it myself! —It can't be said of me at all (except perhaps as a joke) that I *know* I am in pain. What is it supposed to mean—except perhaps that I *am* in pain?

The paragraph concludes with the claim that "the truth is: it makes sense to say about other people that they doubt whether I am in pain; but not to say it about myself." Wittgenstein's strategy here is to show the falsity of saying that I know that I am in pain and to infer from this conclusion that my sensations cannot be objects of cognition. A private language would then be impossible because we could never be said to know that any description applies to any sensation at all.

I reconstruct the Argument from Contrast as follows:

1. In a private language I know what words mean by inspecting sensations with which I am acquainted.

2. But in a private language it is impossible for me not to know that I have a certain sensation.

3. Hence it follows that my claim to *know* anything about the sensations I have is false.

4. From (3) it follows that there can be no private language because I cannot be said to know what sensations I am having.

What is problematic here is the step from (2) to (3). Why should Wittgenstein think it wrong to say that I know myself to be in pain if such a claim cannot be false? Here we are left to conjecture from what he means when he says that "I *know* that I am in pain" really means "I *am* in pain." Could he mean to say that it is superfluous to say that I know that I am in pain? If he does mean this, then the argument dissolves immediately; to say that something is pointless or superfluous may be true but does not prove that it is either false or nonsensical. To pronounce something pointless presupposes in fact, not that it is false or nonsensical, but that it is true.

There is a more philosophically respectable interpretation that can be given to Wittgenstein's words. We can make step (3) follow from step (2) by adding the following lemma:

2a. To say that I know *p* (where "*p*" ranges over sentences describing sensations) implies that there are circumstances under which it is logically possible for me to believe falsely that *p*.

If we add step (2a) to the argument, then it is false to say that I know that I am in pain, for there are no circumstances under which I can believe falsely that I am in pain. And if I can never believe falsely that I am in pain, I cannot be said to know that I am in pain.

But even if the argument is understood in this way, it still suffers from a serious defect. The fact on which the argument rests is that it is logically impossible to have false belief about sensations. But the argument can succeed only if this fact can be made to yield the following conclusion: If I cannot specify the circumstances under which I can believe falsely that *p*, then I cannot distinguish between true and false belief with regard to *p*. I do not know whether Wittgenstein intended to draw such a conclusion from (2a). My only point is that such a conclusion must be drawn from (2a) if the argument is to show anything about the impossibility of a private language. If we are content merely to say that it is logically impossible to have false belief about sensations, all we are doing is underscoring a fact about private (as distinct from public) languages. In order to show that private languages are impossible, we must be able to show that we cannot distinguish between true and false belief in such a language. But the fact is that nothing like this follows from the claim that there is no false belief in private languages. To say that I always know *p* when *p* describes a sensation is very different from saying that I do not know when I am correctly (as distinct from incorrectly) applying a description in a private language.

4. *The Argument from Criteria.* This argument turns on the connection between a rule and language. The foundation of the argument is in §258:

> Can I point to the sensation? Not in the ordinary sense. But I speak, or write the sign down, and at the same time I concentrate my attention on the sensation—and so, as it were, point to it inwardly.—But what is this ceremony for? for that is all it seems to be! A definition surely serves to establish the meaning of a sign.—Well, that is done precisely by the concentration of my attention; for in this way I impress on myself the connexion between the sign and the sensation.—But "I impress it on myself" can only mean: this process brings it about that I remember the connexion *right* in the future. But in the present case I have no criterion of correctness. One would like to say: whatever is going to seem right to me is right. And that only means that here we can't talk about 'right'.

A representative statement of the conclusion of this argument occurs in §202:

And to *think* one is obeying a rule is not to obey a rule. Hence it is not possible to obey a rule 'privately': otherwise thinking one was obeying a rule would be the same thing as obeying it.

This argument begins with a description of what it is to apply a predicate and then goes on to ask whether this phenomenon can be explained on the assumption that the words of a language are meaningful because they refer to essentially private objects. To know the meaning of a word is to know the rule governing its application. In a private language, however, knowing the meaning of a word is being aware of the sensation to which it refers. Thus the application of a rule in public language translates into grasping a private object in a private language. And this is what generates Wittgenstein's problem—to apply a rule presupposes an ability to misapply it. Part of what it is to be a rule is to exclude certain classes of things to which it applies. But the notion of direct apprehension essential to the explanation of meaning in a private language does not admit of incorrect apprehension. The inference is that the possibility of misapplication of a predicate cannot be explained by employing the notion of direct apprehension alone. And if a predicate cannot be made to exclude anything from correctly falling under it, then it is meaningless. The words in a private language are declared to be meaningless in this sense. The Argument from Criteria can, accordingly, be stated as follows:

1. A word has meaning because a rule governs its application.

2. In a private language, a word has meaning because I connect it by ostension to a certain sensation.

3. Hence to apply a rule in a private language is just to connect a word with a sensation by ostension.

4. But there is no distinction between correct and incorrect ostension as there is between correct and incorrect application of a rule.

5. Hence there is no distinction between correct and incorrect application of a rule in a private language.

6. From (5) it follows that the user of a private language cannot

know when he is using the vocabulary correctly or incorrectly.

7. Hence a private language is impossible because none of its vocabulary can be correctly applied.

The Argument from Criteria rests on this assumption: The notion of a criterion is essential to understanding the meaning of every word.[6] But the demand for a criterion itself assumes that we can be mistaken about the application of a word. And this in turn implies that the only kind of object to which we can apply criteria is that about which there can be mistakes—an object, in short, which can appear to have properties it really does not have.

The guiding premise of the Argument from Criteria is that words must be associated with criteria in order to have meaning. The argument assumes from the start that the only kind of objects to which we can apply words are those which can appear to have properties that they lack. But all this shows is that criteria are essential to a language in which we talk about public objects. If there are objects which are always as they appear to be, then criteria are not necessary to the explication of the meaning of predicates applied to such objects. The Argument from Criteria does not, as it stands, show the impossibility of a private language. For the argument assumes that there can be no essentially private objects. Given such an assumption, then the conclusion naturally follows that words for which there are no criteria of application cannot have meaning. For as long as language is restricted to public objects, there is a distinc-

---

[6] I ignore here a line of attack on the Argument from Criteria according to which it is possible for us to apply the expressions of a private language correctly without knowing that we are doing so. If we can separate the notion of correct application of a term from our possession of a criterion of correct application, then it would seem that a private language would be possible. This line of attack is vitiated, however, by the distinction between (*a*) having criteria for the application of a word but not knowing what they are and (*b*) lacking all criteria whatsoever. Interpretation (*a*) allows us to apply words without knowing what criteria we are obeying. But this does not show the possibility of a private language. It shows only that we need not know the criteria we obey, not that we can dispense with criteria altogether. Interpretation (*b*) does not succeed, either. If there is no criterion to distinguish when I correctly apply an expression from when I incorrectly apply it—whether I happen to know the criterion in question or not—then it is logically impossible to have a *correct* application at all.

tion between correctly and incorrectly describing these objects—from which it follows that we cannot know when we are correctly applying a word unless we associate it with criteria of application. And this is why the Argument from Criteria does not show that a private language is impossible. It assumes, rather than proves, that there can be no private objects. It awaits an independent proof that there are no such objects in order to establish the impossibility of private languages. And until such an independent proof is given, it remains an open question whether *all* words require criteria of application.

There is, however, an interpretation of the Argument from Criteria which might show that the issue of criteria is as relevant to private as it is to public languages. This is allegedly shown by the dependence of both kinds of language on memorial knowledge. Thus in §265 Wittgenstein makes an implicit distinction that yields a substantially different version of the Argument from Criteria than the one I have so far been considering. The distinction occurs first in §258, where Wittgenstein says that, when I impress upon myself the connection between a sign and a sensation, "this process brings it about that I remember the connexion *right* in the future." This point appears again in §265 when he says that "this process [the process of checking one memory against another] has got to produce a memory which is actually *correct*. If the mental image of the time-table could not itself be *tested* for correctness, how could it confirm the correctness of the first memory?" This point changes the character of the Argument from Criteria as I have stated it. The first version of that argument was formulated independently of memorial knowledge. The issue there was solely whether the present apprehension of an object required a criterion to certify the correctness of the description I may give of it. But the issue has changed now. What is asked is whether we can apply a word unless we are able to remember that we have applied it in that way in the past. And it is argued that the application of predicates in a private language assumes the existence of a way of knowing that we have applied them in the past as we apply them in the present. Since direct awareness alone is incapable of assuring us of this fact, we cannot be said to apply predicates in a private language at all. The revised version of the Argument from Criteria, then, is this:

1. To apply a predicate in any language assumes that we can apply it to a state of affairs in the present of the same kind as those states of affairs to which we have applied it in the past.

2. To know that we apply a predicate correctly, then, is to rely on our memory that we are applying it uniformly.

3. But direct awareness alone will not assure us that we are applying a predicate uniformly. What is presented to direct awareness in memory is not the past situation of application itself but only a memory of that past situation.

4. From (3) it follows that we can have direct awarenesses of memory images that are incorrect.

5. Hence to give meaning to a word in a private language implies giving a criterion by which I can discover that my application of a predicate is uniformly correct.

6. Since direct awareness is the only mode of knowledge in a private language, there can be no distinction between correct and incorrect memory awarenesses.

7. Hence, we cannot know when we are applying a predicate correctly as distinct from incorrectly in a private language.

8. Hence, a private language is impossible.

The distinguishing feature of this version of the Argument from Criteria is the connection between applying a predicate and memory knowledge. What I do when I apply a predicate is, according to premises (1) and (2), to recognize that one object or state of affairs is like another. If I cannot know that the predicate I apply in one context is the same as I have applied in previous contexts of the same kind, then I cannot know that I am applying it correctly to the present context. And so, even if direct awareness is immune to Wittgenstein's attack when we restrict our attention to the present application of a predicate, it is not immune to his attack once it is seen that the application of a predicate assumes memory knowledge and that memory knowledge in turn demands a criterion of correctness.

What the second version of the Argument from Criteria shows is that a private language assumes the reliability of memory knowledge and, consequently, that we cannot know the meaning of a word in such a language merely by connecting a word with a sensation in the present.[7] But does this show the impossibility of a private language? I think not. What it shows is the rather different conclusion that all language, both public and private, assumes memory knowledge to explain the meaning of the words in the language. And this is not the same as showing that a private language is impossible; to show that two things rest on the same assumption is not to show that one is possible and the other impossible, but only that one is as possible or impossible as the other. The issue of memory knowledge is, therefore, irrelevant to the private language issue.

It might be possible to establish that memory knowledge does, after all, affect the private language issue by arguing that there is a distinction between public and private checks on memory knowledge.[8] Thus it could be argued that what militates against the possibility of a private language is not the mere fact of its dependence upon memory knowledge but rather that it is forced to depend upon a certain *kind* of memory knowledge. Thus a speaker of a public language can rely on what might be called independent checks of his memory claims. He can, for example, rely on the testimony of others to check his memory impressions. But this kind of check is denied the speaker of a private language. All he can do is to appeal to his own memory impressions. But this kind of appeal is question-begging in a way in which an appeal to the memory impressions of others is not. The former impressions cannot certify one another just because they are precisely what is subject to check. The latter impressions are different in that your memory impressions are independent of mine and can, accordingly, provide a check for mine that is not question-begging. Since justification consists, as Wittgenstein holds, in "appealing to something independent" (§265), public memory is reliable while private memory is not. It would,

[7] Cf. §199: "It is not possible that there should have been only one occasion on which someone obeyed a rule. It is not possible that there should have been only one occasion on which a report was made, an order given or understood."

[8] Cf. John Turk Saunders and Donald Henze, *The Private Language Problem* (New York: Random House, 1967), p. 36ff.; also C. L. Hardin, "Wittgenstein on Private Languages," *Journal of Philosophy*, 54 (June 4, 1959):520ff.; and N. P. Tanburn, "Private Language Again," *Mind*, 72 (June, 1963):89ff.

accordingly, appear that the issue of memory knowledge *is* relevant to the private language issue. A private language relies on memory impressions that cannot be checked independently and hence merely demonstrate the inability of a speaker of a private language to ascertain when his memory impressions are correct and when they are incorrect.

The putative distinction between public and private memory is not genuine. This can be shown by distinguishing two different senses of memorial independence. The memory impressions of another person are independent just because they are his and not mine. But this does not show that an appeal to his memory constitutes an appeal to something that is any less question-begging than the appeal to my own memory. The only relevant difference here is that an appeal is being made from the memory of one person to that of another.[9] But the mere fact that the impressions in question belong to somebody else rather than to me does not render them any more reliable.

But the appeal in question might have another sense. To say that the appeal to somebody else's memory is an independent check on my own might be taken to mean that there is a difference in the memory impressions themselves and not merely in the fact that they belong to one rather than to another person. This sense of independence is exposed as indefensible as soon as it is pointed out. There is no difference in memory impressions just as impressions. And this implies that no appeal to the memory impressions of somebody else constitutes an independent check on my own in the sense required to distinguish public from private memory knowledge.

[9] Wittgenstein obscures this point when he compares checking memory impressions to the case of a person buying "several copies of the morning paper to assure himself that what it said was true" (§265). The check described here is not unreliable because it is the same newspaper we are examining. The same problem would arise, for example, if somebody were to buy copies of other newspapers in order to check on the reliability of what he reads in a newspaper. The point is that no item with which we are acquainted in the present can assure us of itself that it correctly represents something else with which we are not directly acquainted. This same point applies *mutatis mutandis* to the distinction between checking on my own memory impressions by reference to other impressions that I have and checking on them by reference to those of other people.

3. What Wittgenstein's Arguments Prove

None of the arguments I have canvassed proves the impossibility of a private language. The Argument from Reconstruction shows the irrelevance of private objects to a language by means of which we identify and describe public objects. The Argument from Intersubjectivity shows at most that third-person ascriptions of predicates cannot be made meaningful in a private language by making them refer to the sensations of a third person. The Argument from Contrast breaks down on the false assumption that I cannot believe something truly unless it is logically possible that I believe it falsely. And the Argument from Criteria joins these other arguments by, first, assuming rather than showing that private objects do not exist and, second, making a private language depend as much on memory knowledge as public language. But this, too, fails to show the impossibility of a private language; first, because it leaves an open question whether private objects can be described and, second, because the same problem about memory knowledge can be raised about a public language as well.

The attack on private language does, however, demonstrate a conclusion different from the impossibility of private languages. What it demonstrates is the impossibility of analyzing public objects into sets of essentially private objects. Many philosophers begin with objects that are observable by more than one person, that perdure through time, and that exist when they are not being perceived, and try to show that these objects can be exhaustively analyzed into sets of objects—each of which is essentially private, exists only as long as it is being observed, and lasts only as long as it is being observed. What the private language argument does show is that such an analysis is, in principle, a failure. The main tool of the demonstration is the concept of error. To apply a predicate in a public language is to admit the possibility of applying it incorrectly. Such a language would admit the possibility of applying a predicate to a state of affairs that appears to have properties it does not have. If we abstract from the fallibility of memory knowledge which is endemic to both kinds of language, the problem is how we can reconstruct the possibility of misapplying a predicate in terms of a private language. We must, in short, be able to explain how the explication of what it means to apply a predicate in a private language can reconstruct what it means to apply a predicate in a public language. Part of what counts as succeeding in this enterprise is to explain how we can misapply a predicate. This is always possible and frequently occurs in a public language. But it cannot, in principle, occur in a private language. To apply a predicate at all is to apply it correctly.

The crucial difference between applying predicates in both kinds of language is this: I cannot falsely apply a predicate to a sensation in a private language simply because a predicate applied to a sensation with which it is not associated is meaningless. This is just a consequence of the way in which predicates are endowed with meaning in a private language. To say that a predicate has meaning is to relate it to a sensation of a certain kind. Erroneous application of the predicate would be explicated by saying that the predicate is associated with a sensation different from that which gives the predicate meaning. But this is not erroneous application of a predicate. It makes the predicate in question meaningless. This is why it is impossible to apply a predicate erroneously in a private language. Such an application assumes that the predicate is meaningful as a condition of our ability to say that it is wrongly applied. Anyone using a private language is not in a position to apply a word erroneously.

Although this does not show the impossibility of a private language, it does show that no such language can account for the possibility of erroneous application that is built into a predicate in a public language. Thus what makes it impossible to begin with a private language and to construct a public language out of it is the necessity of making a distinction in a public language between meaningful but false application of the vocabulary in that kind of language. Thus predicates used to describe public objects cannot be constructed out of predicates referring to essentially private objects.

There is of course a classical attempt to meet this objection. Error in a private language allegedly consists, not in erroneously applying a predicate to a public object, but rather in associating a private object with the wrong family or group of private objects. The strategy here is this. Public objects are first reduced to groups or families of private objects. Error in applying a predicate to a public object is explicated as the location of one private object in a family to which it does not belong. But this explication is not open to a user of a private language. While he may make no mistake about the application of predicates to his sensations, he can still make mistakes about the application of predicates according to which he seeks to describe the relation of one of his sensations to a family of sensations. He assumes that there are at least some predicates about which we can say that they are meaningful even though they are falsely applied. And this is precisely what is not open to the user of a private language. He cannot introduce a predicate which describes the relation between one sensation and a family of sensations about which he must be prepared to say that it is meaningful when it is applied erroneously. For this would be a tacit admission that there are some predicates, the meaning of which is not explained by relating them to a sensation. Consider the following illustration of the impossibility of accounting for error in a language describing essentially private objects. Let us begin with

(1) This table is red and round.

The expressions in (1), let us assume, refer to public objects; the proposition expressed by (1) can be both meaningful and false. If we try to reduce (1) to sentences describing essentially private objects, we get

(1′) My table-sensation is red and round.

The move from (1) to (1′) does not constitute a translation. For (1) can be false while (1′) is true. Let us assume that (1) is, in fact, false. The translation of (1) into a language describing essentially private objects would then be this:

(1″) My red and round table-sensation belongs to family x (where in fact the sensation belongs to family y).

Here both (1) and (1″) are false. But (1″) is not a sentence describing an essentially private object. If it were, then the sentence could not be both meaningful and false. And yet the translatability of sentences like (1) into a private language assumes the existence of sentences like (1″) in order to account for one feature of a public language that is not recovered by sentences or classes of sentences like (1′). The feature that is left out by such a translation is error. Thus there must be at least one predicate in a private language that does not derive its meaning by standing in a relation to an essentially private object. The predicate that is involved is ". . . belongs to family *x*" and its synonyms. But if this predicate cannot be meaningful solely in virtue of a relation it has to essentially private objects, then public languages are not reducible without remainder to languages whose vocabulary has meaning in virtue of the relation in which it stands to essentially private objects.

There is, however, a way of apparently countering this objection. Somebody might argue that the plausibility of the foregoing objections depends on an unnecessarily narrow conception of what it is to give meaning to words in a private language. The conception of meaning in such a language necessary to the success of the foregoing argument is this: The meaning of a word in a private language is established by relating a word to one essentially private object. It is thus logically impossible to apply a predicate falsely in such a language just because the only occasion on which it is applied is the occasion on which it is ostensively defined. There cannot be other occasions on which the same predicate is applied to private items that are similar to the item on which the predicate is first applied. For the predicate we apply on such occasions cannot have the same meaning as the predicate we applied on the first occasion of its use. And this is so because the meaning of the predicate is defined by the one item presented on the one occasion it is deployed. Hence, on this conception of meaning, a predicate in a private language can no more be falsely applied than an ostensive definition can be false.

But it might be argued that the foregoing conception of meaning is not an indispensable component of the private language argument. One might, that is, argue that the predicates in such a language derive their meaning, not by a relation to one and only one private item, but rather to a *class* of such items. There is, it will be admitted, the first occasion on which a private item of a certain kind occurs; the meaning of a predicate is established ostensively by relating it, not to the individual private item as such, but rather to the private item as it belongs to a class of such items determined by a common property. This conception of what it is to give meaning to the terms of a private language, unlike the narrower one mentioned above, apparently does permit us to apply a predicate in the language falsely. Although we ostensively define the predicate, let us say, on the first occasion of its use, we can, on later occasions, apply it to an item belonging to a different class without rendering the predicate meaningless. And if this is so, then my claim that private languages cannot reconstruct the notion of error essential to a public language simply collapses.

But very little examination shows that the broader conception of meaning is simply not open to a proponent of a private language. Consider what takes place when the person employing such a language applies a predicate incorrectly to an item of a class. The item in question would have to appear, albeit wrongly, to be a member of one class rather than another. But if an item can appear in this way, it must have properties that it does not appear to have. And if this is so, such an item would not be an essentially private object. Thus as soon as we attempt to make sense of falsely applying a predicate by introducing this broader conception of meaning, we are forced to introduce at the same time the notion of a public object. One thing should, however, be noticed about this way of answering the objection—it does not depend on the distinction between relating a word to a single item and relating it to a class. As long as the class is comprised of essentially private items, the move from a single item to a class does not make it possible to apply a predicate falsely in a private language. As long as the class is composed of essentially private objects, any attempt to make sense of falsely applying a predicate to any item in the class or to the class itself must either surreptitiously depend upon the introduction of public objects or upon the implicit abandonment of the very notion of a false application of a predicate in a private language.

The conclusion, then, is that the present way of explaining the possibility of error within a private language collapses. And this failure merely shows that the predicates which we use in a public language cannot be reduced to predicates of one or more private languages. This is the most valuable lesson of Wittgenstein's argument against private languages. That argument does not show the impossibility of such a language. But it does show that the reduction of the world of public objects to worlds of essentially private objects—whether these objects are called sensa, sense-data, or sensations—is, in principle, impossible.

4. Residual Difficulties

There are three arguments centering on the private language issue which threaten the position I have been arguing so far. The adequacy of that position is bound to remain problematic at least as long as these arguments remain unanswered. There is, first, an argument presented by Ayer to show that all knowledge by criteria implies the existence of a kind of knowledge that does not demand a criterion. If this is right, then the independence of meaning in a public language from meaning in a private language collapses, for a necessary condition of the application of a predicate in a public language will be the application of a predicate in a private language. Second, there is an argument purporting to show that there are rules governing the application of predicates to essentially private objects. Although the motive of the objection is to show the possibility of a private language, what makes the argument troublesome is that it appears to demonstrate that the predicates applied to private objects can be meaningful when they are falsely applied. This, in turn, threatens to vitiate my claim that the distinction between correct and incorrect application of predicates cannot be made in a private language. Finally, there is the argument that there are sentences which are clear cases of rules but which cannot be violated. If this is true, then, once again, my conclusion that a private language is incapable of reconstructing the distinction between correct and incorrect application of predicates would be jeopardized. If there are rules that cannot be violated but remain genuine rules, then the mere absence of rules from a private language would not show the consequent absence of the distinction between correct and incorrect application of predicates.[10]

[10] I take both the second and third arguments from Judith Jarvis Thomson, "Private Languages," *American Philosophical Quarterly*, 1 (January, 1964): 23–24.

Consider the argument that all knowledge by criteria implies as its necessary condition a kind of knowledge that does not require criteria.[11] It runs simply as follows. If we say that the application of a predicate in a public language requires a criterion, we must recognize that the possibility of knowing that the criterion applies demands a kind of knowledge that does not require criteria. If all knowledge required criteria, then no knowledge would be possible. For an infinite regress would develop as we attempt to supply one criterion to make good our claim to know the other criterion; we would have to continue supplying criteria to infinity, unless we recognize that all knowledge by criteria rests on a kind of knowledge that is self-certifying and, hence, does not require criteria.

The first thing to notice about this argument is the consequence it has for my claim that the application of predicates to public objects cannot be reconstructed out of the application of predicates to private objects. If all knowledge by criteria rests on knowledge without criteria, then the former is bound to be a complicated construction out of the latter. For knowing something by a criterion is just to know something by inference from the kind of knowledge we have without criteria. Thus the present argument presents prima facie evidence against my conclusion that predicates in a public language have a meaning that is independent of private languages.

The objection proves that we can have acts of awareness that do not presuppose our having other acts of awareness as a condition of having the former. In this sense, then, what the objection states is right—there must be simple acts of awareness if there is to be any perception at all. What it does not prove, however, is that all such acts must take essentially private items as their objects. To say that I am immediately aware of something, in other words, does not imply that the object of my immediate awareness is mental.

This can be shown by distinguishing between two importantly different senses of 'criterion'. To demand a criterion can be to ask for something which is given in perceptual experience as a way of ascertaining the existence of something that is not so given. This use

[11] I take this from A. J. Ayer, "Privacy," reprinted in *Wittgenstein: The Philosophical Investigations*, ed. George Pitcher (New York: Doubleday, 1966), p. 257ff.

of 'criterion' can be illustrated by the relation between a disease and its manifestations; we know that a person is suffering from a certain disease by our awareness, not of the disease itself, but of the perceptual criteria for the presence of the disease. On this definition of 'criterion', then, we can know something by means of a criterion only if the thing in question is not perceptually given to us. And what *is* perceptually given is not known by a criterion in this sense.

But this does not permit us to infer that what we know without criteria must be an essentially private object. While my knowledge by direct awareness does not demand a criterion in the foregoing sense, it does demand a criterion to decide whether what is presented to me is mental or physical. Therefore, we can know that a description applies to something of which we are immediately aware and still be in doubt about whether what we are describing is a mental or a physical item. Thus direct awareness dispenses with a criterion in one sense but requires one in a different sense. From this it follows that direct awareness alone does not imply that what is thus given is mental. This shows how it is possible to admit that the present objection shows the indispensibility of acts of direct awareness without showing that the only entities given to such acts are essentially private.

There is, however, another claim which threatens the viability of my position. It might be held that it is possible to have rules governing the application of predicates to private objects. And yet, so it is argued, there are violations of such rules; hence, we can genuinely apply rules to private objects. Thus consider a situation in which we are asked to think of *x*. To produce a thought of *x* is to produce an essentially private object. But there is a clear distinction between thinking of *x* correctly and doing so incorrectly; hence there are rules governing the application of predicates to essentially private objects. But this does not make these objects public.

This rests on a misunderstanding of the reason for saying that rules cannot be present in a private language. The reason there can be no rules in a private language is that the vocabulary of such a language derives its meaning from its connection with essentially private objects; hence, a meaningful but false application of a predicate is excluded as a logical impossibility. The reason that rules are involved in thinking of something is just that the predicates involved in describing the thoughts produced have meaning in virtue of their place in a public language. Thus although a thought may be considered an essentially private object, what makes it a thought of, say, a horse rather than a desk is not the result of the relation a word has to an essentially private object but rather the place the word has within a public language. Although the thought itself may be an essentially private object, that it is a thought of one kind of object rather than another is not a fact exclusively about the description of that object but is, rather, a fact about the relation between the description of the private object to what would count as a correct description of the public object that is the object of the thought. The reason that there are rules governing private objects is, accordingly, irrelevant to the issue about private languages. For the sense in which there are such rules is just the sense in which the vocabulary used to describe private objects is derived from a public language.

Another objection is closely allied with the one I have just considered. The preceding objection produced the example of a rule which governs private objects but which can be violated. The present objection produces an example of a rule which cannot be violated but which is nonetheless a rule. This objection threatens my thesis in exactly the way in which the previous objection did. If there are rules governing discourse about private objects that do not rely upon public language for their intelligibility, then it is theoretically possible to construct a public language out of private languages. The present objection purports to give an example of a kind of rule about which it is true to say that thinking one is following the rule implies that one is really following it. And this, it is sometimes argued, violates Wittgenstein's explication of a rule. Something is not a rule, according to Wittgenstein, unless I can think I am following it and in fact *not* be following it. But this explication is allegedly invalidated by the existence of a kind of rule which permits us to infer directly from thinking that we are following it to the conclusion that we are, in fact, following it. Think, for example, of the injunction to think of x whenever you are in circumstances of the kind K. A child might be instructed to think of its mother whenever it is frightened. This is a rule; but it is impossible to think one is following such a rule and, in fact, be violating it. This shows, according to the argument, that there are genuine rules, even though it is logically impossible to violate them. If this is so, then there can be rules governing the use of words in a private language.

The objection does not succeed in producing cases of rules which we cannot violate as long as we think we are following them. The question here is what counts as determining what it means to think of anything correctly. Thus it is quite possible to be convinced that one is thinking of one thing and really be forming a thought of something quite different. This fact is, of course, somewhat obscured by examples like that of thinking of one's mother. It is highly unlikely that I can be convinced that I am thinking of my mother and really be entertaining a thought of somebody else. But this commonplace fact still does not make it logically impossible for me to do so. I can be thinking of a woman with certain characteristics whom I mistakenly take to be my mother. She could in fact be my stepmother, about whose identity as such I have never been informed. This is, to be sure, farfetched. But it is not logically impossible. This shows why the present objection collapses. It presumes that my success in performing a certain act of thought is a matter of my decision. But this is just what it is *not*, as long as the kind of rule in question governs the use of words in a public language applied to my thoughts. And if the words governing my thoughts are not taken from a public language but are expressly identified as belonging to my private language, then the present argument is no better off; following a rule in such a case would be a matter of connecting with the proper sensation. But so far from providing an explication of what it means to follow a rule, the activity of associating a word with a certain *kind* of sensation presupposes the notion of a rule for its own explication. It presupposes, that is, an understanding of what it is to apply the same description to two different cases of the same sensation. Hence the present argument either tacitly relies on public languages to state the kind of rule in question (in which case the thesis of the argument is false), or it relies on the meaning given to a word in a private language (in which case the thesis is question-begging). In either case, then, the argument does not succeed in producing an instance of a rule that you cannot think you are following and really be violating. And from this it follows that one of the claims for which I have been arguing here is not threatened; a private language has no place for the notion of following a rule as it is understood within the context of a public language. For this reason, a private language cannot be used to reconstruct the notion of applying a predicate as it is used in a public language. As long as there is no room in a private language for making sense of what it means to follow a rule incorrectly, there is no hope that such a language can reconstruct the notion of meaning as it is employed in public language.

16

On Language Games and Forms of Life

FARHANG ZABEEH

Geschrieben steht: "Im Anfang war das Wort!*"*

. . .

auf einmal seh ich Rat
Und schreibe getrost: Im Anfang war die Tat!

Faust, 1224–37

Wittgenstein's *Philosophical Investigations* is, among other things, a compendium of poetic, insightful, and thought-provoking metaphors, similes, and analogies which were created primarily in order to exorcise a number of metaphysical ghosts and secondarily to describe in depth the actual structure of our thought.

Instead of arguments and proofs, we are given through these devices an "album" of "philosophical remarks, as it were, a number of sketches of landscapes which were made in the course of these long and involved journeyings," to use the author's words in the Preface.

Such analogies as language game, family resemblance, private language, grammatical joke, language-instrument, word-money, meaning-use, surface-grammar, depth-grammar, forms of life, life of a sign, use of a sign, knowing-mastery of a technique, theology-grammar, and many others are used throughout in order to illuminate some dark metaphysical problems. While some old analogies are singled out as the sources of illusion, e.g., mental mechanism, meaning-process, name-bearer of a name, thought or time as a medium, feeling–inner process.

Among those analogies which play a significant role in the *Philosophical Investigations*, the two interconnected analogies of language games and forms of life are outstanding.

The analogy of a language game is mentioned and made use of numerous times in:

(1) Series of drafts and notes published under *"Notes for Lectures on 'Private Experience' and 'Sense Data' "*[1]
(2) *Preliminary Studies for the "Philosophical Investigations": The Blue Book, The Brown Book*[2]
(3) *Philosophical Investigations*[3]
(4) *Remarks on the Foundations of Mathematics*[4]

It is also made use of (without being mentioned) in:

(5) *Lectures and Conversations on Aesthetics, Psychology and Religious Belief*[5]

Despite the enormous use of this analogy, no explicit formulization of it is given throughout Wittgenstein's work. It lacks "the crystal-line purity" (to use Wittgenstein's own expression) of some old philosophical analogies such as Plato's *The Cave* or *The Divided Line*.

---

[1] "Notes for Lectures on 'Private Experience' and 'Sense Data'," *The Philosophical Review*, 77 (1968). Reprinted in H. Morick, *Introduction to the Philosophy of Mind* (Chicago: Scott, Foresman and Co., 1970). References are to the page numbers of this book, hereafter (*N.*).

[2] Ludwig Wittgenstein, *Preliminary Studies for the "Philosophical Investigations," The Blue Book, The Brown Book*, ed. Rush Rhees (New York: Harper and Row, 1958). References are to page numbers, hereafter (*P.S.*).

[3] Ludwig Wittgenstein, *Philosophical Investigations*, trans. G. E. M. Anscombe (Oxford: Basil Blackwell, 1953). All references in Part I are to paragraph numbers, and in Part II are to page numbers, hereafter (*P.I.*).

[4] Ludwig Wittgenstein, *Remarks on the Foundations of Mathematics*, ed. G. H. von Wright (Oxford: Basil Blackwell, 1956). References are to page numbers, hereafter (*R.*).

[5] Ludwig Wittgenstein, *Lectures and Conversations on Aesthetics, Psychology and Religious Belief* (Berkeley: University of California Press, 1960). References are to page numbers, hereafter (*L.*).

This seems intentional since it is consistent with Wittgenstein's general attitude against what is called 'essentialism', and his specific view that the concepts of language games, and hence of language, are open concepts which lack any natural boundaries, though a boundary may be drawn around them for a specific purpose.

However, it should not be assumed that this analogy, which is used throughout *Philosophical Investigations* (and in other works which were preliminary to this book and were not intended for publication), is used carelessly. The *Philosophical Investigations* is not a carefree and inaccurate expression of ideas and thoughts. It is, on the contrary, a meticulous and guarded work of a man who, as he confesses in the Preface, would have "liked to produce a good book," but produced only "philosophical remarks."

The analogy, form of life, is, as we shall see, intimately connected with the language game analogy. However, the expression 'form of life' as such appears only five times through *Philosophical Investigations;* in an oblique way, though, it is used occasionally in *Preliminary Studies, Remarks,* and *Lectures.*

The first part of this essay is an attempt at a systematization of various descriptions, definitions, and examples of language games given by Wittgenstein. Hence it will be mainly an expository account.

To achieve this I shall discuss:

1. Description and definition of language game
2. Examples of language games
    a. Artificial
    b. Natural
3. Form of life—form of words
4. Why the language game analogy is used
5. The big question: the essence of language.

The second part is an attempt to assess the strength as well as the weakness of the use of this analogy and related ones. We shall show how Wittgenstein's use of these devices led, on one hand, to some conceptual confusions and, on the other hand, paved the way to a more systematic study of actual mechanism of natural language by linguistic philosophers.

I

1. Description and Definition of Language Game

In *Notes for Lectures*, there appears a first hint on what is meant by 'language game':

(a) We call something a language game if it plays a particular role in our human life [*N.*, 177].

This definition appears after a series of questions asked by an imaginary interlocutor, such as "Under what circumstances would we say that he ['Someone painted pictures of the landscape which surrounds him. He sometimes paints the leaves of trees orange, sometimes blue, sometimes the clear sky red, etc.'] did what we call portraying?"

Before remark (a), various linguistic activities such as "description of the picture before one's mind's eye," "showing or telling what one sees," "expressions of feeling," "lying," etc., are called "language games."

The idea that a language game is something that "plays a particular role in our human life" (though vaguely) is important. Since even at this early stage it connects language games with specifiable activities and in an oblique way shows that a mere use of words (or even use of a grammatically well-formed expression in the absence of certain actions, such as informing or warning or referring) is not to be considered as playing a language game. It indicates, for example, that a private language is roughly a language intelligible to its inventor alone for expressing his inner experience; and though it is also called a language game in *Notes*, it is not a language game. It is mentioned later: "Sounds which no one else understands but which I 'appear to understand' *might* be *called* a private language" (*P.I.*, 269, my italics).

In *Preliminary Studies* (which are lectures dictated by Wittgenstein to his students and not merely a series of notes), the idea of a language game takes a clearer shape.

(b) I shall in the future again and again draw your attention to what I shall call language games. These are ways of using signs simpler than those in which we use the signs of our highly complicated everyday language. Language games are forms of language with which a child begins to make use of words. The study of language games is the study of primitive forms of language or primitive languages [*P.S.*, 17].

In the first part of *Preliminary Studies*, i.e., *The Blue Book* in which (*b*) appears, there are other expressions which seem to be similar in some respect or other to 'language game'.

- (*b₁*) "The system of signs" ("The sign [the sentence] gets its significance from the system of signs, from the language to which it belongs. Roughly understanding a sentence means understanding a language" [*P.S.*, 5].)

- (*b₂*) "Ideal language" ("Whenever we make up 'ideal languages' it is not in order to replace our ordinary language by them; but just to remove some trouble caused in someone's mind by thinking that he has got hold of the exact use of a common word. That is also why our method is not merely to enumerate actual usages of words, but rather deliberately to invent new ones, some of them because of their absurd appearance" [*P.S.*, 28].)

- (*b₃*) "Grammatical games" ("Many different grammatical games, resembling each other *more* or *less*, are played with this word ['where']. Think of the different uses of the numeral '1'" [*P.S.*, 50].)

- (*b₄*) "The kind of calculus" ("If someone taught me the word 'bench' and said that he sometimes or always puts a stroke over it thus: 'b̄ench,' and that this meant something to him, I shall say: 'I don't know what sort of idea you associate with this stroke, but it doesn't interest me unless you show me that there is a use for the stroke in the kind of calculus in which you wish to use the word "bench"'" [*P.S.*, 65].)

The *Philosophical Investigations* begins with a quotation from Augustine's *Confessions* in which a speculative account of learning of a language by a child is given. Then a picture of a language, "a system of communication," is produced which fits the description given by Augustine, namely, a language meant to serve as communication between a builder *A* and an assistant *B*. This is called 'language (2)' after the paragraph in which it appears.

Referring to (2) and its extension, a description of language games appears:

> (*c*) I will call these games 'language-games' and will sometimes speak of a primitive language as a language-game. And the processes of naming . . . and of repeating words after someone might be called language-games . . . I shall also call the whole, consisting of language and the actions into which it is woven, the 'language-game' [*P.I.*, 7].

The introduction of *actions* into the fabric of language links the idea of 'language game' with the idea of 'form of life'; it also leads to certain assertions on the multiplicity and contingency of language games.

> (*c₁*) To imagine a language means to imagine a form of life [*P.I.*, 19].
> (*c₂*) Multiplicity of language-games [*P.I.*, 23].
> (*c₃*) New . . . language-games come into existence and others become obsolete and get forgotten [*P.I.*, 23].

Finally, a discussion of these topics led to "the great question that lies behind all these considerations . . . what the essence of a language-game, and hence of language, is" (*P.I.*, 65).

To understand the nature of the question about the essence of language and Wittgenstein's method of showing how the answer to this question should be given, we should try to understand various examples of language games which are produced throughout. We should try to understand also the nature of connection between language games and forms of life and the reason or reasons why this analogy is employed.

2. Examples of Language Games

We shall divide the multitude of examples of language games into two classes of *artificial* (AR) and *natural* (NA) language games.

Though this classification is not Wittgenstein's, it is quite clear that there are at least two distinct classes of language games (hence-forth LG's).

As we already noticed there is a clear indication in *The Blue Book* that to make up an "ideal language" is not "to replace our ordinary language . . . but just to remove some trouble. . . . That is also why our method is not merely to enumerate actual usages of words, but rather deliberately to invent new ones, some of them because of their absurd appearance."

In the *Philosophical Investigations*, he also makes it plain that what he is doing is investigating the formation of concepts by showing "the correspondence between concepts and very general facts of nature." However, he is not doing "natural history, since we can also invent fictitious natural history for our purposes" (*P.I.*, p. 230).

The enumeration of "actual usages of words" or "actual lan-guages" and the description of "the correspondence between con-cepts and very general facts of nature" gives us what we called 'natural' language games, whereas "inventing new usages," or "in-venting fictitious natural history," which often is introduced by "Let us imagine . . . ," leads to the construction of what we called 'artificial language games'.

ARLG's, in contrast to NALG's, are simple, akin to primitive languages, and are like "language with which a child *begins* to make use of words" (my italics). But they are not incomplete in them-selves. That is, they may actually serve the purpose for which they are invented. Our purpose here is to provide samples of LG's with-out going into actual analysis of each.

In *The Brown Book*, various ARLG's are invented (such as: 1. a language game used between a builder and his assistant which con-sists of names for some building materials, etc.; 2. enlargement of (1) by adding to it some numerals; 3. enlargement of (2) by adding to it some pronouns; 4., and 5., and so on, "akin to what in ordinary language we call games"). It is emphasized that they are "not in-complete parts of a language, but as languages complete in them-selves, as complete systems of human communication."

One can imagine "such a simple language to be entire systems of communication of a tribe in a primitive state of society. Think of primitive arithmetics of such tribes."

In contrast, it seems that NALG's are rather complex and complicated, and there exist numerous kind of such LG's. Indeed, it seems that learning more about the world involves learning more NALG's.

> When the boy or grown-up learns what one might call special technical languages, e.g., the use of charts and diagrams, descriptive geometry, chemical symbolism, etc., he learns more language games. (Remark: The picture we have of the language of the grown-up is that of a nebulous mass of language, his mother tongue, surrounded by discrete and more or less clear-cut language games, the technical languages) [*P.S.*, 81].

a. Artificial LG's

The first use of LG appears in *Notes* in connection with "description of the picture before one's mind's eye." He seems to indicate here that when we use such expressions as *description, similarity,* or *identity* of mental images, we should note that such expressions appear within a specific frame which is different from the frame of the language of physical objects. That is, one should be aware that these expressions (when used in such a question, for example, as whether two people can have the same after-image) belong to phenomenalistic language.

Again, it is maintained that a philosophical question on the nature of fact (we know that, in *Tractatus*, it is supposed that facts are combinations of objects, and objects could be named independently of facts), e.g., whether the observer should be included or not from the description of "the fact," is similar to the question whether the picture I paint should contain me. These questions, he says, are not about facts' "nature" but only about "the symbolism."

Next, commenting on the issue of indubitability of sense-data, he states that "the game of 'showing or telling what one sees' is one of the most fundamental language games, which means that what we in ordinary life call using language mostly presupposes this game" (*N.*, 162).

He does not give any reason why this particular language game, i.e., the language game of pointing to objects and calling their names, presupposes other language games. Nor at this point does he mention the subject of multiplicity of language games or name some of its kinds. But to question whether one "can see something without ever saying or showing" or vice versa, he answers that "to the language game which we play with these words it is both essential that the people who play it behave in the particular way we call expressing (saying, showing) what they see and also that sometimes they more or less entirely conceal what they see" (*N.*, 165).

In saying that "he sees red," he "plays a language game," this game, namely, seeing a color and reporting, presupposes the correct application of color word. "If he is to play a language game, the possibility of this will depend upon his own and other people's reactions. The game depends upon the agreement of these reactions, i.e., they must *call* the same things 'red' " (*N.*, 166).

Here and in later passages the issue of private language comes into the focus. The imaginary interlocutor may reply: Is it not possible that some one invent for himself a language and expresses his experience by means of it? "If we describe a game which he plays with himself, is it relevant that he should use the word 'red' for the same color in our sense, or would we also call it a language game if he used it anyhow?" (*N.*, 167). Suppose someone says, " 'Toothache' is a word which I use in a game which I play with other people, but it has a private meaning to me." But then in saying that "it has a private meaning to me," I should note "that the same meaning is kept throughout a game" (*N.*, 167). How can I know what I call 'toothache' always applies to the same private experience?

No doubt one can give a name to his private experience, but giving a name is not playing a language game unless a name could be used throughout. " 'To give a sensation a name' means nothing unless I know already in what sort of a game this name is to be used" (*N.*, 169).

In the next passage, the expression 'private language game' is actually used. "In our private language game we had, it seemed, given a name to an impression—in order, of course, to use the name for this impression in the future" (*N.*, 169).

But then, in the absence of a criterion of a correct use of that name, one cannot know that the name is used later in the same sense. "And all that remains of our private language game is therefore that I sometimes without any particular reason write the word 'red' in my diary" (*N.*, 169).

In the *Notes* the idea of a multiplicity of NALG's is alluded to by saying that "the language games are very much more different than you think," and by an example of how a child may learn to use the expression "I have a toothache" in different and separate language games, e.g., when he has toothache, when he moans on the stage, when he reads out the sentence from a book, and when he lies.

In *The Blue Book*, no specific example of LG is employed as such, though as we observed, a rather detailed definition of LG and the reason why it is invented are given.

At one point an example is given to show that in natural language what are called "referring expressions," such as first-personal pronouns, proper names, and definition descriptions, perform dissimilar functions, though all are used for referring. Hence, to assimilate these expressions into one is to be blind to their distinctive functions. (This remark is developed and elaborated in the *Philosophical Investigations.*)

In *The Brown Book* numerous examples of ARLG's are given. Some of these examples appear in the *Philosophical Investigations.*

Starting with an account given by Augustine of how as a child he learned a language, the remark is made that this account is too simple to be true of learning "our language," though it might be true of learning "a simpler language."[6]

A language is built (language *1*) for which the account given by Augustine holds, i.e., a language used for communication (order and response to order) between a builder and his assistant which consists only of names of some building materials which one can point to and name.

Learning and teaching this simple LG, Wittgenstein seems to say, is compatible with what philosophers call the 'denotation theory of meaning' and 'ostensive definition of words'.

---

[6] Augustine himself criticized the picture of language depicted by him in the *Confessions* in another book, *De Magistro* (see N. Kretzmann, "The History of Semantics," *Encyclopedia of Philosophy*, 7 [1967]:366).

Next, language *1* is developed by introduction of numerals 1–10 which are learned by heart and used for counting building materials, etc., and called language *2*.

The important point is that here

> . . . by introducing numerals we have introduced an entirely different kind of instrument into our language. The difference of kind is much more obvious when we contemplate such a simple example than when we look at our ordinary language with innumerable kinds of words all looking more or less alike when they stand in the dictionary [*P.S.*, 79].

Here teaching the series of these numerals may be done also by pointing not to a specific object but to a group of objects. The difference between pointing to a shape and pointing to a number is blurred if one says, "In óne case we point to a shape, in the other we point to a number" (*P.S.*, 79).

Next, *2* is developed into *3* by introducing a proper name, then into *4* by introducing adverbs 'here' and 'there', into *5* by introducing questions and answers, into *6* by "asking for the name" of a new object. These are all called language games on the ground that they are "akin to what in ordinary language we call games."

The construction of new language games continues by introducing numerous varieties of linguistic expressions, e.g., names of colors, names of cardinals, expressions for recalling, comparing, identifying, etc. There are also varieties of language games which are invented artificially by imagining a tribe in whose language there are expressions used in peculiar situations and in a peculiar manner. (In fact, every number of paragraphs which appears in Part One of *The Brown Book*, from [7] to [73] is also a number of a language game, though not all are called language games.)

In the *Philosophical Investigations*, varieties of ARLG's, some parallel to those appearing in *The Brown Book*, are constructed.

Once again the game of LG's starts with an account given by Augustine of how as a child he learned his mother tongue. This is called 'LG *1*'. This is a language of which one could say that the denotation theory of meaning and teaching by ostensive definition are true. The meaning of each word is identified with "the object for which the word stands," and teaching the meaning of words is done simply by pointing to the objects and uttering some noises, so that a child after associating these noises with their supposed denotata may learn and use this language.

This description, Wittgenstein states, is appropriate—but only for this narrowly circumscribed region. He sees that philosophical theories concerning the nature of meaning or the nature of learning meaning, i.e., the denotation theory of meaning and ostensive teaching of words, are modeled after a speculative and primitive idea of how language functions: "That philosophical concept of meaning has its place in a primitive idea of the way language functions. But one can also say that it is the idea of a language more primitive than ours" (*P.I.*, 2). The primitive idea of the way language functions and the idea of a language more primitive than ours fits perfectly the view once expressed by Russell (which was known to Wittgenstein) on what are called "logically proper names." Russell stipulated that "in strict logical sense" logically proper names are words like 'this' and 'that'. Russell writes: "A name, in the narrow logical sense of a word whose meaning is a particular, can only be applied to a particular with which the speaker is acquainted, because you cannot name anything you are not acquainted with. You remember when Adam named the beasts, they came before him one by one, and he became acquainted with them and named them."[7]

Wittgenstein points out that this assimilation of demonstrative impersonal pronouns to proper names is conducive to confusion.

> If you do not want to produce confusion you will do best not to call these words names at all. —Yet, strange to say, the word 'this' has been called the only *genuine* name, so that anything else we call a name was only in an inexact, approximate sense [*P.I.*, 38].

For he points out various dissimilarities of functions of these linguistic categories.

After commenting on *1*, an LG is constructed for which the description given by Augustine holds. This is a language used for communication between a builder and his assistant. It consists of names of few building materials which are used in the act of responding to a call (language *2*).

---

[7] Bertrand Russell, "The Philosophy of Logical Atomism," in *Logic and Knowledge,* ed. R. C. Marsh (London: Allen & Unwin, 1951), p. 201.

Now if we consider *2* to be the *whole* language of a tribe, we can see that teaching this language could be done by ostensive teaching, i.e., correlating words with objects by pointing to objects and using their names. LG *2* is later developed to *8* by introduction of numerals, singular demonstrative pronouns, and a number of color samples. Now in teaching *8* to a child, pointing to objects and using names will not do, since pointing to a group and using a numeral and pointing to a place and saying "this" and "that" are not like pointing to a slab and saying "slab."

The important point here is this: we distort the heterogeneous functions of different categories of expressions used in these very simple games if we say, for example, that all these expressions are referring expressions, for their uses "are absolutely unlike."

By saying that in *8* "we have different *kinds* of word" we should not forget that speaking of *kinds* "depend[s] on the aim of the classification,—and on our own inclination" (*P.I.*, 17).

In LG *21* (which is an extension of *2*), we have both expression of 'report' and 'command', e.g. 'five slabs'; though here the grammatical form of expression of command and report is similar, the function of each is different.

In §48, another language game is constructed. The language seems to describe combinations of colored squares. The squares form a complex like a chessboard, and to each square is assigned a letter corresponding to the first letter of its color. In constructing this game, the point is to show that a certain metaphysical idea, e.g., that names really signify what is absolutely simple, is an absurd one, since the notion of simplicity is relative to a frame of reference.

b. Natural LG's

As we observed, Wittgenstein in his preliminary works (which led to the composition of the *Philosophical Investigations*), and especially in *The Brown Book*, constructed various language games to serve him in undermining various metaphysical theories. However, in these works sometimes the idea of a language game is used to describe various categories of our natural language.

In the *Philosophical Investigations*, a list of examples of such categories are given. Here, in effect, Wittgenstein shows the inadequacy of the old philosophical tricotomy of factual-conceptual-evaluative which was so long regarded as constituting an exhaustive classification.

To the question, "How many kinds of sentences are there? Say assertion, question and command?" he answers, "There are *countless* kinds." By that he means, "Countless different kinds of use of what we call 'symbols', 'words', 'sentences'. And this multiplicity is not something fixed, given once for all; but new types of language, new language-games, as we may say, come into existence, and others become obsolete and get forgotten" (*P.I.*, 23).

Linking the concept of language game to "kinds of use" of expression is the stepping stone for stating that "speaking of language is part of an activity, or a form of life."

He then points out the multiplicity of language games in the following examples, and in others:

Giving orders, and obeying them—
Describing the appearance of an object, or giving its measurements—
Constructing an object from a description (or drawing)—
Reporting an event—
Speculating about an event—
Forming and testing a hypothesis—
Presenting the results of an experiment in tables and diagrams—
Making up a story, and reading it—
Play-acting—
Singing catches—
Guessing riddles—
Making a joke, telling it—
Solving a problem in practical arithmetic—
Translating from one language into another—
Asking, thanking, cursing, greeting, praying [*P.I.*, 23].

The list serves to throw serious doubt on what logical atomists and metaphysicians have said about the structure of a language, which is supposed to depict the structure of the world.

There are other examples of NALG's in *Philosophical Investigations* which do not appear in the list, such as pretending (*P.I.*, 229), or predicting an event, or predicting an action, or lying. It is said that "lying is a language-game that needs to be learned like any other one" (*P.I.*, 249).

These LG's are all natural since they constitute a large segment of our actual activities. Referring to "the most primitive forms of language—commanding, questioning, recounting, chatting," Wittgenstein points out similarities between such linguistic acts and other nonlinguistic acts. They "are as much a part of our natural history as walking, eating, drinking, playing" (*P.I.*, 25).

Though varieties of NALG's and ARLG's are mentioned and described, it seems that at least two sorts of examples are meant to show that not every use of expressions should be considered to be an LG.

The first example is private language. It is argued here (and also in the *Preliminary Studies*) that a language invented by someone to write down his inner experiences—in such a way that another person could not in principle understand it—is not usable for the inventor himself. This, as we shall see, is an indication that the use of language even in its most primitive form is bound up with the existence of rules which govern the correct use of expressions in that language.

The second example is an imaginary language of a tribe (even though their actions are intelligible). "There is no regular connection between what they say, the sounds they make, and their actions." We cannot understand their speech acts since "there is not enough regularity for us to call it 'language'" (*P.I.*, 207). The example points to what is called by Wittgenstein 'forms of life' or 'frame-work', or more specifically to what may be called semantic regularity pertaining to the use of language.

So it appears that, apart from existence of linguistic rules, to count something as a language, or as an LG, one should establish some connections between linguistic expressions and certain acts which usually accompany them.

This brings us to the issue of connection between LG's and forms of life.

3. Forms of Life—Forms of Words

The expression 'forms of life' (FL) as such appears only five times throughout the *Philosophical Investigations;* however, there are other indirect references to it there and in other works. We should note that an LG is not a mere system of notation, but it is language and action together. Wittgenstein, in speaking of an LG, is not speaking about *langue*, but of *parole*, i.e., *speech*, to use a Saussurian expression; or we may say he is speaking of what of late is called "speech acts," such as making statements, asking, giving commands, referring, etc., and not of words which are items of a *language*.

He is not concerned with questions about the meaning of words or sentences or predicate expressions, or the nature of tautologies or contradictories *as such* (the problems which are stated and answered with finality in the *Tractatus*), but with problems about the use of expressions in varieties of speech situations.

In the *Notes, Preliminary Studies, Lectures,* and *Remarks,* he uses various expressions for his purpose which eventually crystallize into forms of life.

Instead of FL, in *Notes* he talks about "the circumstances" and "the usual consequences" of uttering an expression.

He says, for example,

> But can't the old game lose its point when the circumstances change, so that the expression ceases to have a meaning, although of course I can still pronounce it? He sticks to saying that he has been lying although none of the usual consequences follow. What is there left of the language game except that he says the expression? [*N.,* 181–82].

As we noticed, he also mentioned, in effect, that in using perceptual language it is essential that one behave in a particular way we call expressing (saying, showing) what one perceives.

Closely connected with the issue of specific conditions for the use of an utterance is the important observation that, if we sever an utterance from its particular condition and use it under *any condition* or a condition which does not belong to it, we may produce nonsense.

> It seems, whatever the circumstances, I always know whether to apply the word or not. It seems at first it was a move in a special game, but then it becomes independent of this game. (This reminds one of the way the idea of length became emancipated from any

particular method of measuring it.) We are tempted to say: 'damn it all, a rod has a particular length however I express it.' And one could go on to say that if I see a rod I always see (know) how long it is, although I can't say how many feet, meters, etc.—But suppose I just say: I always know whether it looks tiny or big! [*N.*, 181].

The concept of length, like that of smallness or largeness, is context-bound, as one may say. But we may forget these contexts or conditions and use them in abstraction from their specific LG.

In *The Brown Book*, likewise, the idea of LG is correlated with the idea of certain conditions, or "occasions," or "the role" in which the LG is "played in the whole life." Here the question is: how can one understand and translate a language spoken by a tribe? The answer is: by observing various behavior, action, facial expressions —that is, by observing certain nonverbal behavior and correlating such behavior with verbal expressions we could understand their language.

> Whether a word of the language of our tribe is rightly translated into a word of the English language depends upon the role this word plays in the whole life of the tribe, the occasions on which it is used, the expressions of emotion by which it is generally accompanied, the idea which it generally awakens or which prompt its saying, etc., etc. As an exercise ask yourself: in which cases would you say that a certain word uttered by the people of the tribe was a greeting? In which cases should we say it corresponded to our 'Good-bye', in which to our 'Hello'? In which cases would you say that a word of a foreign language corresponded to our 'perhaps'?—to our expressions of doubt, trust, certainty? You will find the justifications for calling something an expression of doubt, conviction, etc., largely, though of course not wholly, consist in descriptions of gestures, the play of facial expressions and even the tone of voice [*P.S.*, 103].

Since understanding a verbal expression of a tribe ultimately requires observing its nonverbal behavior, it seems here that the principal of the uniformity of human behavior, let us say, is the presupposition for the theory of understanding and translation of a spoken language. It follows that if the behavior of a tribe is quite unlike the behavior of a tribe of the translator, he could not understand their language.

This implication is stated in the *Lectures* and the *Philosophical Investigations*, as we shall see.

In discussing the actual dissimilarities between the use of 'this' and the use of proper names, he points to the fact that the use of certain expressions (such as the demonstrative impersonal pronoun 'this') in speech requires certain actions, such as pointing gestures and something to be pointed at. Without them, the expression loses its meaning:

> But nothing is more unlike than the use of the word 'this' and the use of a proper name—I mean *the game* played with these words, not the phrases in which they are used. For we do say 'This is short' and 'Jack is short', but remember that 'This is short' without the pointing gesture and without the thing we are pointing to would be meaningless.—What can be compared with a name is not the word 'this' but, if you like, the symbol consisting of this word, the gesture, and the sample [*P.S.*, 109].

Instead of the expression 'forms of life', which is used in the *P.I.* in the connection of imagining a language ("to imagine a language means to imagine a form of life" [*P.I.*, 191]), here it is said:

> Imagine a use of language (a culture) in which there was a common name for green and red on the one hand and yellow and blue on the other [*P.S.*, 134].
> We could also easily imagine a language (and that means again a culture) . . . [*P.S.*, 134].

The same point that understanding a concept requires observing the *occasions* of its use, or imagining a language is imagining a culture, or understanding a language game presupposes understanding a form of life, is repeated in the *Lectures* without either the use of LG or FL. He says here, for example, "Imagine an entirely different civilization. . . . where music makes them to do different things . . ." (*L.*, 34). It is also claimed that various philosophical confusions may be attributed to the preoccupation with "form of words" and neglecting the circumstances which occur, and the use of linguistic expressions.

> If I had to say what is the main mistake made by philosophers of the present generation, including Moore, I would say that it is that when

language is looked at, what is looked at is a form of words and not the use made of the forms of words. . . . We are concentrating not on the words 'good' or 'beautiful', which are entirely uncharacteristic . . . but on the occasions on which . . . the aesthetic expression has a place [*L.*, 2].

Suppose someone wished to know what words correspond to 'good' or 'fine' in the language of some tribe which he doesn't understand. He may find his answer by looking "for smiles, gestures, food, toys" (*L.*, 2). That is, to understand a language one needs to look at how the language is used and correlate the forms of words with the form of life.

On the other hand, if the forms of life of a tribe are entirely dissimilar to ours, we shall not be able to carry on any inquiry. "If you went to Mars and men were spheres with sticks coming out, you wouldn't know what to look for" (*L.*, 2).

Unlike Moore and other contemporary philosophers, Wittgenstein says in the *Lectures on Aesthetics* that "we don't start from certain words, but from certain occasions or activities" (*L.*, 3).

In the *Remarks*, where the nature of the laws of logic, inference, and conformity to rules are discussed, the LG analogy and the idea of *activity* are brought forward again. The rules of logical inference are rules of the language game. The LG of arithmetic, like other LG's, is intelligible by reference to some activity.

The concept of the rule for the formation of an infinite decimal is—of course—not a specifically mathematical one. It is a concept connected with a rigidly determined *activity* in human life. The concept of this rule is no more mathematical than of: following the rules. . . . For the expression of the rule and its sense is only a part of the language game: following the rule [*R.*, 186].

In the *Philosophical Investigations*, the FL are used in the following passages:

It is easy to imagine a language consisting of only orders and reports in battle . . . And innumerable others. And to imagine a language means to imagine a form of life [*P.I.*, 19].

Here the term 'language-game' is meant to bring into prominence the fact that the *speaking* of language is part of an activity, or a form of life [*P.I.*, 23].

It is what human beings *say* that is true and false; and they agree in the *language* they use. That is not agreement in opinions but in forms of life [*P.I.*, 241].

Can only those hope who can talk? Only those who have mastered the use of a language. That is to say, the phenomena of hope are modes of this complicated form of life. (If a concept refers to a character of human handwriting, it has no application to beings that do not write) [*P.I.*, p. 174].

What has to be accepted, the given, is—so one could say—*forms of life* [*P.I.*, p. 226].

Apart from these places in which the expression 'forms of life' appears, there are other places in which some allusion to this concept is made.

The point made already, that the interpretation and translation of an unknown language requires a form of life that we share with them, is repeated in the *Philosophical Investigations*. He says here that "the common behaviour of mankind is the system of reference by means of which we interpret an unknown language" (*P.I.*, 206).

Since FL is, so to speak, a superstructure of our concepts, we should not apply these concepts to beings which do not share these forms:

Could one imagine a stone's having consciousness? [*P.I.*, 390] Look at a stone and imagine it having sensations. . . . One might as well ascribe it to a number!—And now look at a wriggling fly and at once these difficulties vanish . . . [*P.I.*, 284].

Why can't a dog simulate pain? Is he too honest? . . . Perhaps it is possible to teach him to howl on particular occasions as if he were in pain, even when he is not. But the surroundings which are necessary for this behavior to be real simulations are missing [*P.I.*, 250].

"A child has much to learn before it can pretend. (A dog cannot be a hypocrite, but neither can he be sincere.)" And if we don't understand a lion's speech ("If a lion would talk, we could not understand him" [*P.I.*, p. 223]) it is not because the forms of words uttered by the animal are unintelligible, but it is because the surrounding circumstances or the form of life connected to it are missing.

Thus forms of words, or "forms of our language" (*P.I.*, 111) as it is sometimes called, is not the key to understanding a language.

> Every sign *by itself* seems dead. *What* gives it life?—In use it is *alive*. Is life breathed into it there?—Or is the *use* its life? [*P.I.*, 432].

Sometimes, instead of FL, some other expressions such as "facts of nature" or "general facts of nature" ("such facts as mostly do not strike us because of their generality") are used.

Wittgenstein then seems to consider a question addressed to him by an imaginary interlocutor. "If the formation of concepts can be explained by facts of nature, should we not be interested, not in grammar, but rather in that nature which is the basis of grammar?" (*P.I.*, p. 230). His answer to this question is simple:

> Our interest certainly includes the correspondence between concepts and very general facts of nature. . . . But our interest does not fall back upon these possible causes of the formation of concepts: we are not doing natural science, nor yet natural history—since we can also invent fictitious natural history for our purposes.
>
> I am not saying: if such-and-such facts of nature were different people would have different concepts (in the sense of a hypothesis). But: if anyone believes that certain concepts are absolutely the correct ones, and that having different ones would mean not realizing something that we realize—then let him imagine certain very general facts of nature to be different from what we are used to, and the formation of concepts different from the usual ones will become intelligible to him [*P.I.*, p. 230].

Here is where Wittgenstein clearly shies away from doing science. He is not interested, as a philosopher, in anthropological inquiry into explanations of concept formation, nor in psychological explanations of the relation of physical movement and expression of thought. For he says that "The question whether the muscles of the larynx are innervated in connection with internal speech, and similar things, may be of great interest, but not in our investigation" (*P.I.*, p. 220). Describing certain general facts of nature and noting correspondence between concepts and these facts, and observing multiplicity of NALG's is all he claims he is doing. However, going beyond that and trying to form a hypothesis in order to explain why certain concepts are the ones we actually use and not others is, it seems, to go beyond the task he sets for himself.

> Our mistake is to look for an explanation where we ought to look at what happens as a 'proto phenomenon'. That is, where we ought to have said: *this language-game is played* [*P.I.*, 654].

At best, we should observe that a certain NALG is played, and in noting that we shall, ipso facto, note FL. "The question is not one for explaining a language-game by means of our experiences, but of noting a language-game" (*P.I.*, 655). To the question raised by an interlocutor: "What is the purpose of telling someone that a time ago I had such-and-such a wish?" He answers, "Look on the language-game as the primary thing. And look on the feelings, etc. . . . as interpretation" (*P.I.*, 656).

Since imagining a language is a tantamount to imagining an FL, noticing a language game of, for example, "expressing the past wishes" is noting the feeling which is part of an FL or surrounding or fact of nature. And this is where the philosophical inquiries end, though a scientific one may very well start. (Note however that what is called 'philosophical anthropology' or 'descriptive metaphysics' [Strawson] is, in effect, a systematic development of Wittgenstein's idea of describing certain general facts of nature and formation of our concepts.)

4. Why the LG Analogy Is Used

There are various reasons (1) why certain ARLG's are invented, and (2) why some NALG's are picked up and described.

There is a clear answer to the first question, i.e.,

> If we want to study the problems of truth and falsehood, of the agreement and disagreement of propositions with reality, of the nature of assertion, assumption, and question, we shall with great advantage look at primitive forms of language in which these forms of asserting appear without the confusing background of highly complicated processes of thought. When we look at such simple forms of language the mental mist which seems to enshroud our ordinary use of language disappears. We see activities, reactions, which are clear-

cut and transparent. On the other hand we recognize in these simple processes forms of language not separated by a break from our more complicated one. We see that we can build up the complicated forms from the primitive one by gradually adding new ones [*P.S.*, 17].

ARLG's are not models which might approximate the actual forms of language or various species of natural language; they are invented for showing similarities and dissimilarities with natural language.

> Our clear sample language-games are not preparatory studies for a future regularization of language—as it were first approximations, ignoring friction and air-resistance. The language-games are rather set up as *objects of comparison* which are meant to throw light on the facts of our language by way not only of similarities, but also of dissimilarities [*P.I.*, 130].

Rush Rhees, editor of *Preliminary Studies*, writes:

> In one of Wittgenstein's *Notebooks* there is a remark about language games—i.e., "When I describe certain simple language games, this is not in order to construct from them gradually the processes of our developed language—or of thinking—which only leads to injustices (Nicod and Russell). I simply set forth the games as what they are, and let them shed their light on the particular problems" [*P.S.*, vii].

Wittgenstein hopes that by inventing various LG's he can dispel persisting metaphysical dogmas which portray language as a picture of the world—dogmas annunciated with finality by some philosophers, including the author of the *Tractatus*.

The invention of LG's seems to be a way to free oneself from "a picture [that] held us captive," e.g., the metaphysical theory that "the general form of propositions is: This is how things are" (*Tractatus* 4.5).

One way to undermine the belief that a certain conceptual frame is necessary for understanding the world is to "imagine certain very general facts of nature to be different from what we are used to, and the formation of concepts different from the usual ones will become intelligible to him" (*P.I.*, p. 230).

For example, if you think that Euclidean geometry is the only possible model of space, imagine a space which curves in (Riemann) or curves out (Bolyai and Lobachevski), and then the non-Euclidean geometry will be intelligible.

There are other reasons why various kinds of NALG's are picked up and described.

One. The idea that the real function of language is to describe facts would lose its hold if we note the multiplicity of NALG's. For example, Wittgenstein's old belief that "there can be no ethical propositions" (*Tractatus* 6.42) or "the tendency of all men who ever tried to write on Ethics or Religion was to run against the boundaries of language. . . . This thrust against the limits of language is ethics." Wittgenstein's "Lecture on Ethics"[8] was based on certain a priori concepts about the nature of the proposition. But as soon as he realized that *fact-stating proposition* is only one category among many other categories of expressions, he dropped his old view on what may be called "the unsayables." In the *Philosophical Investigations* he suggested that abstract questions on meta-ethics or meta-esthetics may be framed and answered if we realize the LG in which they appear. However, it seems that, in the past, philosophical inquiries concerning the meaning of 'good', or 'obligation', or 'beauty'—the very abstract questions—are carried on by supposing that one may find an answer to these questions by neglecting the frame in which these expressions are usually employed. One may question the inquirer by asking, for example, "How did we *learn* the meaning of this word ('good', for instance)? From what sort of examples? In what language-games?" (*P.I.*, 77). Referring to a criticism of his kind of behaviorism, he says, "The paradox disappears only if we make a radical break with the idea that language always functions in one way, always serves the same purpose: to convey thoughts—which may be about houses, pains, good and evil, or anything else you please" (*P.I.*, 304).

Two. It is also an oblique attack on the idea of an ideal language which is assumed to be better and more perfect than our natural language.

If you say that our language only *approximates* to such calculi (which have fixed rules) you are standing on the very brink of mis-

[8] Ludwig Wittgenstein, "Lecture on Ethics," *The Philosophical Review*, 74 (1965):3-11.

understanding. For then it may look as if what we were talking about were an *ideal* language. . . . But here the word 'ideal' is liable to mislead, for it sounds as if these languages were better, more perfect, than our everyday language . . . [*P.I.*, 81].

Commenting on Ramsey's idea that the logic is a "normative science," he said that "in philosophy we often *compare* the use of words with games and calculi which have fixed rules, but cannot say that someone who is using language *must* be playing such a game" (*P.I.*, 81).

The ideal language of logicians is a game with fixed rules, but in using NALG's we do not play a similar game. So the point of using the LG analogy is to show that we should not compare natural language with the ideal language.

Three. Various philosophical confusions can be shown to ensue if one confuses one language game with another.

The confusion of not distinguishing, let us say, perceptual language with the language of physical objects may be removed by realizing that we misinterpret the form of our language. We talk about such things as the location of pleasure, pain, the will, or intention as if they are entities just like heads and stones. We are using words and forgetting the framework in which they appear because they seem alike. "We remain unconscious of the prodigious diversity of all the everyday language because the clothing of our language makes everything alike" (*P.I.*, p. 224).

We are captivated by the form of expressions because their function is not attached to them. And this holds true both when we use ordinary language and when we do philosophy:

> What confuses us is the uniform appearance of words when we hear them spoken or meet them in script and print. For their *application* is not presented to us so clearly. Especially not, when we are doing philosophy [*P.I.*, 11].

Referring to questions concerning the relation of physical objects and sense impressions, he says, "Here we have two different language-games and a complicated relation between them—if you try to reduce their relations to a *simple* formula you go wrong" (*P.I.*, p. 180).

Four. It is an attack on the unreflective use of concepts in abstraction from their proper framework.

Philosophical questions are generally abstract questions. But in raising abstract questions, philosophers often abstract their concepts from the context to which they belong. One of the long-standing philosophical assumptions is simply this: It is thought that in order to answer a first-order question—for example, whether Euthyphro is pious by prosecuting his father—one should know what piety is; and the answer to this turns out then to be dependent on what we mean by 'piety' (the semantic assent). But then it is assumed further that we can answer a meta-linguistic question without considering the actual context in which it appeared—that is, by abstracting the concept we are after from its LG. Whereas if we are searching for the meaning of a concept, we should most certainly observe its use, its function, the surrounding in which it appears, and the reason why it is so used. A Platonic quest for the essence naturally must fall back into the Aristotelian search for the substance.

> When philosophers use a word—'knowledge', 'being', 'object', 'I', 'proposition', 'name'—and try to grasp the *essence* of the thing, one must always ask oneself: is the word ever actually used in this way in the language-game which is its original home?
>
> What *we* do is to bring words back from their metaphysical to their everyday use [*P.I.*, 116].

5. The Big Question: The Essence of Language

We have noticed how the idea of LG is developed, and we have observed why this analogy is employed throughout Wittgenstein's late philosophical investigations. But we have to consider still another question: What is the essence of LG's and hence of language? This seems to Wittgenstein to be "the great question."

Rush Rhees observes,

> The language games there [in the *Investigations*] are not stages in the exposition of a more complicated language, any more than they are in the *Brown Book;* less so, if anything. But they are stages in a dis-

cussion leading up to the "big question" of what language is. . . .
We may want to ask what there is about them that makes us say
that they *are* languages. What makes anything a language, anyway?
[*P.S.*, ix].

After various LG's are discussed in the *Investigations*, an imaginary interlocutor raises a question:

> Here we come up against the great question that lies behind all
> these considerations. For someone might object against me: 'You
> take the easy way out! You talk about all sorts of language games, but
> have nowhere said what the essence of a language-game, and hence of
> language, is: what is common to all these activities, and what makes
> them into language or parts of language. So you let yourself off the
> very part of the investigation that once gave you yourself most head-
> ache, the part about the *general form of propositions* and language'
> [*P.I.*, 65].

Wittgenstein's answer is significant:

> And this is true—Instead of producing something common to all
> that we call language, I am saying that these phenomena have no one
> thing in common which makes us use the same word for all—but
> they are *related* to one another in many different ways. And it is
> because of this relationship, or these relationships, that we call them
> all 'language' [*P.I.*, 65].

Notice the transition which takes place in "the essence of language-game and hence of language" which indicates that the answer
to one is the answer to another.

Again note that Wittgenstein does not say that there is no criterion for identifying something as a language (we observed already
what he said about the so-called "private language"). What he
denies is simply this—that activities we call linguistic activity "have
only one thing in common."

The kind of relationship which holds them together is similar to
the kind of relationship which holds varieties of games together. He
calls this relation 'family resemblance'.

Not only are the things we call games not identical, they are not
similar in any respect. What this boils down to is that relations
among games or, alternatively, among various species of natural

language are nontransitive. *A* may resemble *B* and *B* may resemble *C* and *C* may resemble Z—but *A* does not necessarily resemble Z.

And it is because of this feature, and other features as well—namely, the lack of having one identical feature—that the analogy of language game is used.

Wittgenstein indicates that there are other features in common between language and a game—namely, the fact that both in language and in games one may alter the rules, may create the new ones while using the old, or even break the old rules without necessarily creating a new one.

> Doesn't the analogy between language and games throw light here? We can easily imagine people amusing themselves in a field by playing with a ball so as to start various existing games, but playing many without finishing them and in between throwing the ball aimlessly into the air, chasing one another with the ball and bombarding one another for a joke and so on. And now someone says, the whole time they are playing a ball-game and following definite rules at every throw.
>
> And is there not also the case where we play and make up the rules as we go along? And there is even one where we alter them as we go along [*P.I.*, 83].

Note that Wittgenstein does not deny that games, and hence language, are governed by rules. He denies that the rules are necessarily unambiguous, unbreakable, unalterable, and capable of covering every possible move once and for all. " 'The essence is hidden from us': This is the form our problem assumes. We ask: 'What is language?' 'What is a proposition?' And the answer to these questions is to be given once for all; and independently of any future experience" [*P.I.*, 92].)

But, in fact, the essence of language is not hidden from us. As Wittgenstein points out, one should not say there *must* be something in common; rather, one should look and discover whether there is anything in common to entities covered by a general term.

To the objection that the concept of game or language thus pictured is a concept with "blurred edges," he retorts, " 'But is a blurred concept a concept at all?'—Is an indistinct photograph a picture of a person at all? Is it even always an advantage to replace an indistinct picture by a sharp one?" (*P.I.*, 71).

II

I shall try to explain Wittgenstein's conception of language by using an old but still useful programmatic division of the general theory of language into the threefold categories of Pragmatics, Semantics and Syntactics (Carnap).

We may look at the spoken (or the written) language as sounds (or marks) which are used by the speaker for various ends in such a manner that the hearer may understand the speaker's intentions. The speaker's purpose may be to convey information, to describe a state of affairs, to instigate actions, to greet, to warn, to curse, to refer, to talk about talk, and so on.

Here speaking is likened to a kind of action which could not be performed without the use of language and is called 'speech acts' (Austin).

The speaker could achieve his intention if the sounds he makes possess certain conventional structures, i.e., sounds should be of a certain type which we call 'words', and the strings of words should be arranged in a certain pattern which we call 'sentences', and sentences should be of certain forms which we call 'statements', 'referring expressions', 'prescriptive utterances', and so on.

Not any sound is a word, not any string of words is a sentence, and not any sentence is a statement.

These linguistic instruments are social tools and are available to the speaker. He has learned how to use them from the community of language speakers, though he might create a sentence which was never used before. One may coin a new word and use an expression in a new way and for a specific purpose.

Now if we strip from this picture the *Pragmatic* dimension—the speaker and the hearer, the intention of the speaker and the effects which his words may induce on the hearer—what remains is the corpus of language, i.e., locutions which may be called 'instruments'. The study of these instruments—words, sentences, predicate expressions, statements, referring expressions, greeting expressions, etc., as such—and their relations to things, objects, or to other expressions, or to events and circumstances or occasions of their use falls within the *Semantic* dimension.

If we further delete the relations of linguistic expressions to such things and cast a cold eye solely on linguistic expressions and their internal relations, what remain is called *Syntactics*. Both logic and grammar proper fall within this domain.

Wittgenstein in the period of the *Tractatus*, like Russell and logical empiricists, concentrated on the problems which fall in one way or another within the semantic and syntactic dimensions, e.g., his picture theory of language and theories on tautology, contradiction and the unsayable, to the exclusion of the pragmatic. The picture which was depicted in the *Tractatus*, however, fell when Wittgenstein turned his attention to pragmatics. *Philosophical Investigations* embodies, among other things, a description of various instruments used by him to free himself from the picture which captivated him in the *Tractatus*. That is why he wanted to publish "those old thoughts [*Tractatus*] and the new ones [*Philosophical Investigations*]" together: "that the latter could be seen in the right light only by contrast with and against the background of my old way of thinking" (*P.I.*, foreword).

What freed him from the belief in idea of a necessary and privileged form of language was the invention of ARLG's and description of NALG's or various departments of natural language.

In calling language a game or an instrument (*P.I.*, 569), or by saying that "words are also deeds" (*P.I.*, 549), or in likening the meaning of a piece to its role in the game (*P.I.*, 563), he is trying to look at language from the point of view of the speaker.

Let us then show various respects in which language-game instruments resemble each other. Then we may be able to appreciate the force of these analogies by singling out the most striking features, or "the prerogative instances," of such phenomena.

The following table may illustrate these analogies:

Language	*Game*	*Instrument*
1. Speaker	Player	User
*2. Words	Pieces (board games)	Shapes
*3. Meaning	Role of a piece (board games)	Use function
4. Rules (logical grammer, syntactics)	Rules (for moving pieces, for winning, losing, penalties, etc.)	Rules (for proper use)

Language	Game	Instrument
*5. Multiplicity of linguistic acts (speech acts)	Multiplicity of games	Varieties of instruments
6. Family resemblance of speech acts	Family resemblance of games	Family resemblance of instruments
7. Intentional behavior (designed to satisfy some needs)	Intentional move (designed for amusement, sport, etc.)	Intentional use (designed to satisfy some needs)
8. Mastery of speech (successes and failures)	Mastery of technique (successes and failures)	Mastery of use (successes and failures)
9. Inference (logic)	Calculation (strategy)	
10. Invention of new expressions or new rules	Invention of new games	Inventions of new instruments
*11. Framework (Meaning of words and rules [logical grammar-inference] are bounded by a specific framework or context)	Framework (Determining roles of pieces [board games] and rules [for winning, losing, etc.])	
12. Primary social activity (learned from others and used to address others)	Primary social activity (played with others)	

Let us examine some of these analogies. We begin with some successful ones (numbers 5 and 11) and will offer some comments on the less successful ones (numbers 2 and 3).

Number 5: Multiplicity of linguistic acts. Wittgenstein's invention of ARLG's, the description of some NALG's, and his belief that certain philosophical paradoxes would disappear ("if we make a radical break with the idea that language always functions in one way, always serves the purpose: to convey thoughts—which may be about houses, pains, good and evil, or anything else you please") (*P.I.*, 304), proved to be extremely useful.

One of the crucial points of language game–instrument analogy is simply this: there are numerous types of each, and each type is governed by its own particular rules. Hence assimilating or reducing one LG to another LG (which is tantamount to reducing one department of natural language to another) without noting their differences is to commit mistakes—mistakes which later were labeled 'category mistakes' or 'type violation' or 'descriptive fallacy', etc. (Ryle, Austin).

To commit these logical and semantical blunders, however, is understandable since we look at forms of words. "We remain unconscious of the prodigious diversity of all the everyday language games because the clothing of our language makes everything alike" (*P.I.*, 224), i.e., the language's "surface grammar," and we forget the multiplicity of functions of words and expressions, or their "deep grammar." (No definition of 'deep grammar' or 'surface grammar' is given by Wittgenstein, but only examples.)

Traditionally, philosophers, at least since Aristotle, have made the distinction between fact-claiming sentences (statements), expressions of command or wishes (optatic), and propositions expressing future contingencies. And since Leibniz, Hume, and Kant, the distinction is made between conceptual-factual and those statements which, despite their unexceptionable clothing, are devoid of meaning.

Wittgenstein's use of the LG analogy throws a fundamental doubt both on the truth and the utility of such easily made and aprioristic linguistic classifications. "How many kinds of sentences are there? Say assertion, question, and command? There are *countless* kinds: countless different kinds of use of what we call 'symbols', 'words', 'sentences' " (*P.I.*, 23).

Wittgenstein, however, was not concerned about tabulating or studying manifolds of NALG's.

The lists of examples of the varieties of LG's which appear after the above assertion proceed with the announcement that it is by no means exhaustive, and they are succeeded by the remark that the enumeration was intended for contrasting the multiplicity of kinds of linguistic expressions with what logicians, "including the author of the *Tractatus*," have said about the structure of language.

Wittgenstein's lack of concern with semantics and syntactics as such is reaffirmed by Moore's report. "Wittgenstein stated that he did not discuss such questions . . . because he thought that language was the subject matter of philosophy. He did not think it was. He discussed it only because he thought that particular philosophical errors or 'troubles in our thought' were due to false analogies suggested by an actual use of expressions; and he emphasized that it was only necessary for him to discuss those points about language which he thought led to these particular errors or 'troubles'."[9]

Wittgenstein's view about the multiplicity of NALG's, despite his own misgivings about the relevance of a purely linguistic inquiry into philosophy (Moore's report), led to a more systematic study of the pragmatic dimension under the heading 'speech acts'.

J. L. Austin's tentative classification of speech acts into locutionary, illocutionary, and perlocutionary was an attempt to carry on those positive aspects of Wittgenstein's view on the phenomenon of language.[10]

Norman Malcolm's defense of Anselm's ontological arguments was a new use of Wittgenstein's idea of LG's.[11] It was a relief for theologians to discover that there is such a thing as language of religion so that their unverifiable beliefs could preserve their significance despite the fact that they are devoid of significance in another language game, e.g., "language of science."

In his article, Malcolm invites us "to look at the use of words and not manufacture a priori theses about it." Then he looks around and finds that "in those [Christian and Jewish] complex systems of thought, in those 'language games', God has the status of a necessary

[9] G. E. Moore, "Wittgenstein's Lectures in 1930–33," *Mind*, 63 (1954):5.

[10] J. L. Austin, *How to Do Things with Words* (Oxford: J. O. Urmson, 1965). It is questionable whether Austin was influenced by Wittgenstein; Warnock states "that this has been sometimes suggested, but is certainly untrue" (G. J. Warnock, "John Langshaw Austin: A Biographical Sketch," *Proceedings of the British Academy* [Oxford: Oxford University Press, 1963], p. 345–64).

[11] Norman Malcolm, "Anselm's Ontological Arguments," *The Philosophical Review*, 69 (1960):389–94.

being. Who can doubt that? Here we must say with Wittgenstein 'this language-game is played'. I believe we may rightly take the existence of those religious systems in which God figures as a necessary being to be a disproof of the dogma, affirmed by Hume . . . that no existential proposition can be necessary."[12] No doubt there are some language games in which God has the status of a necessary being. Moslem philosophers often had spoken of God in terms of such an attribute, i.e., Vajeb-al-Vôjod (the necessary being); but then they went out to prove the existence of the necessary being, which indicates their dissatisfaction with playing a conceptual game alone.

However, it is certainly a mistake to believe that Wittgenstein, by opening this Pandora's box of language and discovering varieties of LG's, blurred the lines of demarcation that we draw between truth-claiming assertions and infantile fantasies. To believe this is to assimilate one language game into another, e.g., the language game of astrology to the language game of astronomy.

Throughout his inquiries, Wittgenstein is at pains to show us that such assimilation is a great mistake.

Number 11: The framework. Wittgenstein's LG analogy also illuminates the fact that the meaning of an expression, like a role of a piece in a board game or use of an instrument, is a function of the framework in which it appears; hence understanding an expression requires understanding that framework, or the form of life, or the surrounding belonging to that expression.

If it is absurd to ascribe sensation or consciousness to a stone (*P.I.,* 289), or to a number (*P.I.,* 284), pain simulation to a dog (*P.I.,* 250), speech to a lion (*P.I.,* p. 223), it is simply because "the surroundings which are necessary for (these) behaviors . . . are missing" (*P.I.,* 250).

To this insight philosophers as diverse as Austin and Quine nod with approval. Austin states that

for too long philosophers have neglected this study, [the study of an 'illocutionary' act, "performance of an act *in* saying something as opposed to performance of an act *of* saying something"] treating all problems as problems of 'locutionary usage'. . . . We are now

---

12 Ibid.

getting out of this; for some years we have been realizing more and more clearly that *the occasion of an utterance matters seriously, and that the words used are to some extent to be 'explained' by the 'context' in which they are designed to be or have actually been spoken in a linguistic interchange*[13] [My italics].

Austin points out that the act of merely uttering certain sounds, i.e., the phonetical, should be distinguished from the uttering of certain sounds of a certain type belonging to a certain vocabulary, conforming to a certain grammar, i.e., the phatic act and those from the rhetic act or the performance of an act with a certain more or less definite sense of reference, "for if a monkey makes a noise indistinguishable from 'go' it is still not a phatic act, and hence not a rhetic act."

This, one may say, is an elaboration of Wittgenstein's point of contrasting forms of words and forms of life which are exemplified by such sayings as, "If a lion would talk, we could not understand him."

Likewise Quine, who devised a stimulus theory of meaning (very different from Austin's) with a view toward correlating linguistic expressions with stimulations (a sort of causal explanation), takes into account the contextual frame in which expressions are used. He points out that even onomatopoeia is not an independent form of LG's in which it appears.

> 'Ouch' is a one-word sentence which a man may volunteer from time to time by way of laconic comment on the passing show. The correct occasions of its use are those attended by painful stimulation. Such use of the word, like the correct use of language, generally, is inculcated in the individual by training on the part of society. . . . 'Ouch' is not independent of social training. One has only to prick a foreigner to appreciate that it is an English word.[14]

Now if such seemingly *natural* expressions are words and not mere sounds, and hence one must learn the occasions and the contexts in which they are designed to appear (in the lower bound), obviously understanding theoretical expressions of science (in the

---

[13] J. L. Austin, pp. 91–100.
[14] W. V. Quine, *Word and Object* (New York: John Wiley & Sons, 1959) pp. 5–6.

upper bound) presupposes understanding the structure of the frame of reference in which they appear. Thus writes Quine: "Theoretical sentences such as 'Neutrinos lack mass', or the law of entropy, or the constancy of the speed of light, are at the other extreme. It is of such sentences above all that Wittgenstein's dictum holds true." "Understanding a sentence means understanding a language."[15]

Though the fundamental significance of the framework for understanding linguistic expressions is emphasized again and again by Wittgenstein, the idea itself of the framework or FL is left unexplained.

We know that appearance of an expression extrapolated from all contexts, or interpolated in a wrong context, is conducive to misunderstanding. But there is no indication either about the nature of the framework or about its type. No clear distinction is made between linguistic (semantic-syntactic), institutional, anthropological, or behavioristic frameworks or FL.

This ambiguity led to various suggestions as to what really is a form of life for Wittgenstein.

One author offers what he calls "the organic account" of this concept. He writes, "It is more like 'something typical of a living being', typical in the sense of being very broadly in the same class as the growth or nutrition of living organisms."[16] This seems to hold true of the behavioristic aspects of FL and does not take into account the institutional, or the anthropological, or the linguistic contexts.

Wittgenstein sometimes speaks of *facial* expression or crying as a surrounding, or FL, in connection with the verbal expression of anger or sadness (*P.I.*, 240), but he also talks about institutional frameworks:

> In different surroundings the institution of money doesn't exist either. . . . A coronation is the picture of pomp and dignity. Cut one minute of this proceeding out of its surroundings: the crown is being placed on the head of the king in his coronation robes.—But in different surroundings gold is the cheapest of metals [*P.I.*, 584].

[15] Ibid., p. 76.
[16] J. F. Hunter, "Forms of Life in Wittgenstein's *Philosophical Investigations*," *American Philosophical Quarterly*, 5 (1968):233–43, and reprinted in this volume.

And he even points out the nonmathematical framework of mathematical inquiries:

> Disputes do not break out (among mathematicians, say) over the question whether a rule has been obeyed or not. People don't come to blows over it, for example. That is part of the framework on which the working of our language is based [*P.I.*, 240].

Or,

> Mathematicians do not in general quarrel over the result of a calculation. (This is an important fact.)—If it were otherwise, if for instance one mathematician was convinced that a figure had altered unperceived, or that his or someone else's memory had been deceived, and so on—then our concept of 'mathematical certainty' would not exist [*P.I.*, p. 225].

Philosophical speculation about the origin of the expression 'forms of life' or *Lebnesformen* is irrelevant. Toulmin suggested that since *Lebnesformen* is the title of a book published by Edward Spranger in 1914, "Wittgenstein can hardly have been unaware of its existence when he borrowed the title for his own purpose."[17] (Spranger's book was translated into English under the title, *Types of Men.* The book is a speculative classification of personality into various types, such as economic-theoretic, aesthetic, religious-political-social.)

It seems, however, that this expression is much older and was used in German literature before. Speculation on the origin of the expression 'language game' is also irrelevant. However, we should note that while Wittgenstein was forming his wide view on the nature of language and the frame of reference of linguistic utterance, linguists came upon similar conclusions.

K. L. Pike, a linguist, reports that in 1937 Edward Sapir compared language to a game. "From Sapir in 1937 I first heard language compared to a game of tennis."[18]

More significantly, many linguists came to the conclusion that full understanding of the phenomenon of language requires the study of nonverbal behavior of the speakers and hearers within certain social structures. Already anthropologists such as Malinowski suggested,

---

[17] S. Toulmin, "Ludwig Wittgenstein," *Encounter*, 32 (1969):58–71.
[18] K. L. Pike, *Language in Relation to a Unified Theory of the Structure of Human Behavior* (The Hague, Netherlands: Mouton Co., 1967).

"Language, in its primitive function, [is] to be regarded as a *mode of action*, rather than a countersign of thought."[19]

R. H. Robins comments that "the cardinal principle of linguistics, at least in Great Britain, [is] that language must always, and in every analysis, be studied as a part of social process and social activity, and every utterance must be considered and understood within its context situation . . . and it is contextual function alone that constitutes and guarantees linguistic meaning."[20]

In *Language in Relation to a Unified Theory of the Structure of Human Behavior*, Pike shows that as some human actions are unintelligible without reference to the spoken words which accompany such actions (a farewell banquet or a baptism, for example), so various spoken words are unintelligible without referring to some action or behavior.

> If, for example, one has a tape recording of the word *No!*, with silence for a long period on either side, the incident in which it occurred would not be structurally significant; one needs to know, as well, through a moving picture or a verbal report about the incident, that a child has just reached for a fragile article on a table and his mother has called *No!* to him. Similarly, a tape recording of the phrase *Why, Mommie?* needs an accompanying verbal or pictographic record of the mother gesturing for the child to come, before the incident emerges as a significant behavioral entity.[21]

It thus seems that some linguists viewed language, like Wittgenstein and Austin, as a phenomenon which stands in need of understanding with reference to a set of actions which are intimately connected with *forms of words* or *locutions*.

Numbers 2 & 3. Words and meaning. As is well known, the meaning of a word in the language is likened to a role of a piece in a board game, or the use or function of an instrument.

And as a player moves the pieces across the board in compliance to a certain rule, the speaker makes use of words in compliance to a certain rule in the language.

On this issue, Wittgenstein seems not to be satisfied with produc-

[19] Ibid., p. 33.
[20] Ibid.
[21] Ibid., p. 28.

ing only analogies. He actually comes close to expressing a definition, which is uncharacteristic in his later works.

> For a *large* class of cases—though not for all—in which we employ the word 'meaning' it can be defined thus: the meaning of a word is its use in the language [*P.I.*, 43].

We should note certain key words in this statement. First, the definition is not intended to cover every case; second, it is not claimed that 'meaning' is so-and-so, but only that it "can be defined"; and third, note that if the meaning of a word is its use, it is its use in the language.

I wish to say that Wittgenstein is not defining the meaning of an expression in terms of its use; he is recommending to philosophers that if they look at an expression from the aspect of its use in the language, they would get a clearer picture of it than if they look at it from the aspect of meaning.

In this sense, use and meaning, like Jastraw's duck-rabbit picture (*P.I.*, p. 194), are two aspects of the same thing, i.e., words. Now if we accept this recommendation, we can see the absurdity of some old semantical theories such as the Platonic theory in which philosophers look at meaning as some kind of entity existing by itself "under the aspect of eternity," or the denotation-connotation or the image theories of the classical empiricists in which a supposed causal connection is established between ideas and impressions or objects and words.

This interpretation actually jibes with Ryle's when he refers to a famous slogan (though the slogan does not appear in the *Philosophical Investigations*):

> The famous saying: "Don't ask for the meaning; ask for the use," might have been and I hope was a piece of advice to philosophers, and not to lexicographers or translators. It advised philosophers, I hope, when wrestling with some *aprioria*, to switch their attention from the trouble-making words in their dormancy as language-pieces or dictionary-items to their utilizations in the actual sayings of things —from these words *qua* units of a language to live sentences in which they are being actively employed.[22]

---

[22] Gilbert Ryle, "Use, Usage and Meaning," *Proceedings of the Aristotelian Society*, Suppl. Vol. 35 (1961):223–30.

Ryle here is using the language-speech dichotomy for his purpose (Gardenir's). This interpretation could be further strengthened by noting various passages in which Wittgenstein relates the concept of meaning to the concept of use.

> But can't the meaning of a word that I understand fit the sense of a sentence that I understand? Or the meaning of one word fit the meaning of another? Of course, if the *meaning is the use* we make of the word, it makes no sense to speak of such "fitting." But we *understand* the meaning of a word when we hear or say it; we grasp it in a flash, and what we grasp in this way is surely something different from the "use" which is extended in time! [*P.I.*, 138. My italics.]

> *Let us say that the meaning of a piece is its role in the game.* . . . [*P.I.*, 563. My italics.]

> *Let the use of words teach you their meaning.* (Similarly one can often say in mathematics: let the *proof* teach you *what* was being proved.) [*P.I.*, p. 220. My italics.]

Thus it seems that Wittgenstein is recommending (rather than defining) that one should concentrate on the aspect of use of expressions because he thinks that switching our attention from semantic-syntactic to the pragmatic dimension is conducive to certain desirable results.

To see the duck-rabbit picture as a duck may help a mother to teach a child what a duck looks like if he hasn't seen one. Analogously, to see the aspect of the use of an expression may help a philosopher to see, for example, that he is not missing anything if he did not *experience* the meaning of a word.

> For we want to ask, 'What would you be missing if you did not experience the meaning of a word?' What would you be missing, for instance, if you did not understand the request to pronounce the word 'till' and to mean it as a verb? [*P.I.*, p. 214]. When I pronounce this word while reading with expression, it is completely filled with its meaning. 'How can this be if meaning is the use of the word?' [*P.I.*, p. 215].

Indeed, how absurd it is to look for an object or an experience or a process, as entities or causes which are supposed to supply meaning for linguistic expressions.

To be blind to the aspect of use is to be "aspect-blind" (and not to be color-blind) as in seeing a duck-rabbit and not noting its different aspects, or to lack a "musical ear" while hearing music.

Now many philosophers who are use-blind assumed, and I think wrongly, that Wittgenstein is defining 'meaning' (definiendum) in terms of 'use' (defininens); they provided necessary and sufficient conditions for the definiendum and then went out to produce counterexamples. For example, Pitcher writes:

> Many words have a use in the language, but no meaning—and this is not, of course, to say that they are meaningless, either. Most proper names, for example, have a use, but no meaning. One cannot ask, What is the meaning of 'John Paul Jones' but only 'Who is John Paul Jones'? Wittgenstein's identification of meaning and use leads him to speak of the meaning of proper names and even of their definitions (*P.I.* sect. 40, 49); but in so speaking, he is simply misusing the words 'meaning' and 'definition'. Those two words are not used, as a rule, in connection with proper names. Wittgenstein was mistaken in identifying the meaning of a word with its use in the language. . . . It is quite possible to know the meaning of a word and yet not know its use, and to know the use without knowing the meaning. 'Ultus' means revenge in Latin. . . . (You may) know how to use 'Amen' and the sign 'Q.E.D.', yet few know their meaning.[23]

Here are my comments.

First, there is much doubt that Wittgenstein ever "identified" the meaning of a word with its use in the language. For neither in the quotation cited nor in other quotations which I brought forward is there any assertion concerning the identity of these concepts. The cautious assertion, which is put in this form, "For a large class . . . though not for all . . . it can be defined . . ." rules out the identity assumption. Apart from this (the passage in which so-called definition appears), the various quotations beginning with "Let us say that the meaning . . . ," "Let the use of words . . . ," clearly indicate that Wittgenstein is giving recommendations in order to turn our attention to the pragmatic and not to semantic-syntactic dimensions (which were the subjects of his interest in *Tractatus* and which gave him so much trouble).

[23] G. Pitcher, *The Philosophy of Wittgenstein* (Englewood Cliffs, N.J.: Prentice-Hall, 1925), p. 225.

Pitcher's counterexamples concerning proper names having no meaning is most unfortunate. Indeed, Wittgenstein does talk about the meaning of proper names, and this is by no means strange. Proper names are not just meaningless sounds or signs. They are expressions *purported* in particular context to name only one entity. So if a foreigner or a child asks the meaning of 'John Paul Jones', we may answer that it is a proper name, or (in more detail) that 'John' is a first name, 'Paul' a second name, 'Jones' a surname. And to the question what is the meaning of 'proper name', we might answer that it is an expression purported for *referring* uniquely to entities which *qua* their individuality and not *qua* their *types* are the object of our interest.[24]

To Pitcher's objection that these two words ('meaning' and 'definition') are not used, as a rule, in connection with proper names, we may reply that this does not matter at all. Indeed, some linguists have already attempted to define proper names, and there are books with such titles as H. Sorensen's, *The Meaning of Proper Names*. Pitcher's argument that Wittgenstein "is simply misusing the words 'meaning' and 'definition'. Those two words are not used, as a rule, in connection with proper names" has no force. One may as well argue that, since these words are not used as a rule in connection with numerals, those who speak of the meaning of 'numerals' (and even of their definition) are simply misusing the words 'meaning' and 'definition'. We should not take, as Wittgenstein says, "the familiar physiognomy of words" or the "surface grammar" of 'meaning' or 'definition' seriously.

Concerning Pitcher's other counterexample (that we may use some foreign words such as 'ultus', 'Amen', 'Q.E.D.' without knowing their meaning, or that we may know their meaning without being able to use them), Wittgenstein would probably grant the examples without counting them as counterexamples. After all, the statement, "For large class of cases though not for all" may very well be intended to exclude such cases as (*a*) use of a foreign expression in a language (which does not require grasping its sense in the original

---

[24] Farhang Zabeeh, *What Is in a Name?* (The Hague, Netherlands: Martinus Nijhoff, 1968). For detailed criticism of various views on the nature of proper names and especially on the widespread view that proper names are "meaningless," see this book.

home in which it was used), (*b*) translation of expressions, or (*c*) cases in which we seek the etymological meaning of an expression and not its use in a language.

If there is something wrong in Wittgenstein's attempt in bringing the two aspects of use and meaning of expressions together, it is due to the fact that the use of the concept 'use' is not perspicuous. As Austin remarks, " 'use' is a hopelessly ambiguous or wide word, just as is the word 'meaning', which it has become customary to deride. But 'use', its supplanter, is not in much better case."[25]

Moreover, the use of the expression 'use' and its opposite, 'misuse', regarding linguistic expressions may lead us (as in fact it did) to look at the usage of an expression in the so-called "ordinary language," contrasting it with its philosophical or technical usage and labeling the latter "misuse." (Note the rise [and fall] of the ordinary-language philosophy, which I believe was due mainly to uncritical acceptance of a cliché attributed to Wittgenstein. As if Wittgenstein upheld that ordinary language is the *only language game*, and that any use of any expression outside this framework should therefore be automatically ruled out as misuse!) Finally, the fundamental distinction between use of a word and use of a sentence is simply not made by Wittgenstein. He speaks both of use of words and use of sentences as if it makes no difference:

> There are countless kinds: countless different kinds of use of what we call 'symbols', 'words', 'sentences' [*P.I.*, 23];
> the use of this word 'reading' [*P.I.*, 156];
> the use of the word 'rule' and the use of the word 'same' [*P.I.*, 225];
> example of a useless proposition [*P.I.*, 216];
> when a sentence is called senseless, a combination of words is being excluded from the language, withdrawn from circulation [*P.I.*, 500];
> the sentence only seems queer [*P.I.*, 195].

But drawing distinctions between use of words and use of sentences, or use of words in language and use of sentences in speech is of fundamental importance for constructing a comprehensive theory. Thus Austin writes: "One can clarify the question of sense and meaning of an expression without going into what way the expres-

25 J. L. Austin, p. 100.

sion is used, for example, the meaning of 'Stop' and the use made of 'Stop', i.e., warning."[26]

Wittgenstein makes some oblique reference to the distinction between *teaching* the meaning of words and sentences when he writes:

> We take a sentence and tell someone the meaning of each of its words; this tells him how to apply them and so how to apply the sentence too. If we had chosen a senseless sequence of words instead of the sentence, he would not learn how to apply the *sequence* [*P.I.*, p. 175].

However, from this example it appears that one *could* teach someone the meaning of each word without teaching him how to apply them in a sentence. One could teach, for example, the meaning of words to someone by using a dictionary, but not necessarily the way these words should be used in a sentence. One, for example, may learn the meaning of 'validity' or 'proof' without knowing how to use these concepts in speech acts. He might not know how these concepts are generally used; e.g., to say an argument is valid is to assess a certain formal structure of it. He might know what is a proof but not necessarily how to determine that something is *proven*. This, of course, is not in conflict with Wittgenstein's correlation of use-meaning, since he clearly stated that "the meaning of a word is its use in the language," indicating that outside language (for example in the dictionary, or in random sequences of words) to look for the meaning of an expression is not to look for its use, since, as he says, only in the language game could one learn the use.

Logicians and structural linguists study the formal structure of natural or artificial languages in abstraction from the speaker, the linguistic act in which the speaker engages, the effect of such acts upon the hearer, the occasions in which expressions are used, and the objects or events, if any, to which expressions refer.

Lexicographers are interested in compiling, tabulating, and correlating meanings of words—and not in speech acts, or rules which govern performances of such acts.

In each case, the linguistic inquiries into linguistic materials which fall within syntactics and semantics should be clearly distinguished

---

[26] Ibid.

from the manner in which these materials are used and why they are used if we do not want to commit errors.

Wittgenstein's preoccupation with the pragmatic dimension, which was due mainly to the language game–instrument analogy, led some of his disciples to be dazzled with the analogy—the analogy which in due course made them meaning-blind—as if the deposit of words and rules of grammar or of logic are by themselves of no significance, since they are in the long run tools in the hand of the speakers.

Wittgenstein himself was conscious of the pitfall of his analogy. He points out that if one assumes that "language is an instrument, its concepts are instruments," one may go on and believe "that it can make no *great* difference *which* concepts we employ. As, after all, it is possible to do physics in feet and inches as well as in meters and centimeters; the difference is merely one of convenience. But even this is not true if, for instance, calculations in some system of measurement demand more time and trouble than it is possible for us to give them" (*P.I.*, 569). Obviously one cannot do classical physics with the arithmetical system of some Australian aborigines (a system in which numbers begin with *one* and end with *five* and any number more than *five* is simply called '*many*'), or engage in contemporary legal disputes by using the ancient legal tools, e.g., the Codes of Hammurabi or the *Yasa* of Genghis Khan.

Now if the use of concepts *does* make a great difference, one may study the structure of these concepts and their internal relations as well as their instrumental values in the market place. We may speak both about meaning of a word and use we make of a sentence in which that word is used; for example, that 'good' means, among other things, that which satisfies certain standards, and that in saying that something is good we are grading or commending that thing. We may also use the same expression in countless constructions without violating its dictionary meaning. Analogously, as Wittgenstein suggests, a king in chess may be used to draw lots, or an ax may be used as a hammer, and Wittgenstein's assertion about countless kinds of *uses* of words does not imply that there are therefore countless *meanings* of words. Note that Wittgenstein does not say "words are deeds," but only that "words are also deeds" when they are used in language, though "by themselves seem dead." To put it in Ryle's words: "Words, constructions, etc., are atoms of a language, sentences are what we produce when we say things."[27]

Such distinct inquiries into pragmatics or semantics or syntactics are all in order, unless the practitioners of these disciplines fall into a dogma that theirs are the only bona fide ones. Perhaps in the future the three fields of semiotics could be united through cooperation of philosophers, structural linguists, and anthropologists under a unified general theory.

Wittgenstein's negative (as well as constructive) contribution on the nature of language, his use of the idea of artificial and natural language games, his concept of the framework, and his anthropological observation on the relation of forms of words and forms of life, are without doubt steps toward that goal.

[27] However, it is not clear at all when one should take an expression as an item in speech and when as an item in language—since the distinction between words and sentences is not perfectly clear. A lexicographer who supposedly deals with words in language limits his research if he abandons the search for the usage of words in speech. A dictionary which provides meaning, for example, for an Anglo-Saxon expression for 'love-making', without indicating that the same expression is also used as an obscene word, is not informative enough.

17

Wittgenstein on Meaning and Use

J. F. M. HUNTER

For a *large* class of cases—though not for all—in which we employ the word 'meaning' it can be defined thus: the meaning of a word is its use in the language.

And the *meaning* of a name is sometimes explained by pointing to its bearer [§43].[1]

WE would not go far wrong in assuming that this is an important remark of Wittgenstein's. But although philosophers now refer to it very frequently, and not usually with any expression of uncertainty as to what it means, I do not myself find its meaning in the very least obvious. In the first part of this paper, I will ask a number of questions with a view to making it clear how unclear the passage is; in the second part, I will suggest and defend an interpretation which I believe not only answers with gratifying economy the questions raised in Part I, but also as far as I know provides an altogether new account of the matter. In Part III, I will briefly indicate the bearing this account has on some wider philosophical questions.

[1] All references will be to Ludwig Wittgenstein, *Philosophical Investigations* (Oxford: Basil Blackwell, 1953).

I

There are two main kinds of difficulty one always has in deciding what a puzzling statement means: the difficulty of finding a reading of it that in itself makes some sense or is believable in its own right, and the question whether any proposed reading is in fact what was intended by the statement's author. It is always quite possible that nothing satisfying the former condition will satisfy the latter, but I will assume it as a fundamental principle of the interpreter's art that one should not settle for an interpretation according to which what a man said is unintelligible or unbelievable before making it very clear why no interpretation which is in itself more acceptable can seriously be regarded as what he meant. We could call this the 'principle of charity'. It is a principle that could easily be defended, but I will not attempt that task here.

What is most difficult about §43 from the point of view of charity may be expressed in this question: If the meaning of a word is its use in the language, it can reasonably be supposed that the meaning of the word _____ will be set forth by setting forth its use in the language; but now is there any way of filling the blanks in the sentence form 'The meaning of the word _____ is _____', such that the second blank contains a statement of the use in the language of the word in the first blank, and the resulting sentence at least makes sense and at best is arguably true?

Of course, we do not know right away what 'use in the language' is supposed to mean, and therefore do not know what *kind* of filling to supply for the second blank; but without worrying about their ultimate soundness, let us try out some possibilities, by way of illustrating the difficulty of the question.

First, then, let us suppose (I think probably wrongly) that *commending* could be called a use in the language; then since it is true that 'good' is used to commend, according to the interpretation of §43 we are considering it should be right to say that 'good' *means* [something having to do with commending: there seems no obviously right way of rendering it, and the reader could perhaps choose whatever way is least offensive to him]. But commending does not tell us the meaning of 'good' but its use (in one sense of 'use'). We would talk of the use of 'good' to commend in default of being able to explain what it means; but we would explain its meaning perhaps by saying that it meant *bon* or 'above average', or by indicating some of its different meanings in different constructions. In the expression 'a good man', we might suggest, 'good' means roughly 'morally virtuous', but not in 'a good apple' or 'a good philosopher'.

Again, such descriptions of how we operate with words as "we know numbers by heart and repeat them, putting an apple in a bag for each one until we reach a given number" are (for Wittgenstein apparently) examples of how a word like 'five' is used, and therefore perhaps of its "use in the language"; but if so, what would we say that 'five' means on this basis? The number of items you get when you put one aside for each number up to five? We would not generally say that 'five' *has* a meaning, or if we did we would say that it means *fünf* or *cinq*. And since the number of items yielded by following that little routine is five, we seem on this basis only to be saying that 'five' means 'five'—a conclusion for which the best we can say is that it is not false.

Third, it is a way of describing the use of a word, and one that is probably not foreign to Wittgenstein, to show the ways in which its use is related to that of other words and expressions; for example, to show how we use the word 'know' in cases where a question might arise regarding how or when we have learned, or in cases in which it is possible to suspect or to doubt, etc. (See §§247, 247.) But it would be nonsense to say that 'know' means that we use it in those cases. The most we could say is that it is meaningful only when so used, or that it is not clear whether it has a meaning except in such cases. But to say when a word is meaningful is not to say what it means, even if in some sense we appreciate its meaning better through having our attention drawn to these connections.

What I have said does not demonstrate that there will be no way of explaining the meaning by explaining the use, but I trust it at least shows that what Wittgenstein could have meant by saying that the meaning of a word is its use in the language is very problematic.

One may be led by such considerations as the foregoing to the idea that, contrary to appearances, Wittgenstein is not telling us something about the meaning of words but rather is recommending that we cease talking about meaning and instead talk about use. It is false that 'good' means 'used to commend'; but when asked what 'good' means, one may say, "I don't know, but we use it to commend," thereby declining the question about meaning and offering as a useful substitute something about use. 'Don't ask for the meaning, ask for the use' may therefore seem to be the recommendation.

The following will be a discussion, not just of this case, but of any suggested way of offering something about use as an alternative to an explanation of meaning.

It is, of course, not very charitable to Wittgenstein to suppose that he expressed himself so very ineptly, if something like this is what he meant; but we do not need to rely on the principle of charity to show that this line of interpretation is wrong, since:

(1) There are few words for which we can give the use, in the "human purpose served by" sense that is involved when we say that we use 'good' to commend. (And it is such examples that make this kind of account attractive.)

(2) For other interpretations of the word 'use' it is extremely difficult to give an account of the use of a word *which is a useful alternative to an account of its meaning*—that is, which fills the need expressed by a question as to what it means. If, for example, as suggested above, we offer as an account of the use of 'know' that it comes in a sort of package with (at least) the words 'learn' and 'doubt' and can properly be used only where those words could have been used, we may have a defensible account of at least part of the use of 'know'—but nothing illuminating to a person who does not yet know what it means, and asks.

(3) The only remark of Wittgenstein's that lends any support whatever to this interpretation is:

> But what is the meaning of the word 'five'?—No such thing is in question here, only how the word 'five' is used [§1].

But this would appear to be, according to Wittgenstein, a member of some class of cases in which we *do not* employ the word 'meaning', and therefore the claim in §43 would not apply.

The foregoing are some of the difficulties in charitably interpreting §43. I will briefly indicate some specifically textual difficulties by the following questions.

One. What is the large class of cases referred to? Is it some obvious and briefly definable class, or perhaps just the class, if such there be, of which it is true that the word 'meaning' as it is used in these cases can be defined this way? Does it represent a large proportion of all the cases in which we employ the word 'meaning', or might it be some small proportion, but still of all the classes of case it is a comparatively large one? (It seems very often to be assumed, and I think wrongly, that Wittgenstein means that with rare exceptions the word 'meaning' can be defined as he suggests.)

Two. What function does the inclusion of the clause "in which we employ the word 'meaning'" serve? Does it, for example, confine the application of the definition to cases in which we are ready with an account of the meaning of a word, and exclude the cases of words that do not exactly have a meaning, or of words about whose meaning we do not know what to say? In other words, does it only elucidate accounts of meanings once arrived at, or does it tell us how to arrive at meanings? Or, again, does this clause serve merely to confine us to ordinary (as distinct from philosophical) employments?

Three. In 'it can be defined thus', does 'it' refer to the *word* 'meaning', or to something the word is supposed to stand for or refer to? That is, does the definition simply authorize the substitution of 'use in the language' for 'meaning' in some class of sentences in which the word 'meaning' appears, or does it call for the specification of instances of, or accounts of, uses in the language (whatever they may be) in accounts of the meanings of words? (It is with the latter supposition that we were operating above when we puzzled over the sentence form 'The word _____ means _____'; and yet by far the more natural reading is to say that 'it' refers to the *word* 'meaning', not to its referent.)

Four. The same question arises in connection with the appearance of the expression 'the meaning of a word' *in the definition*. It is very odd that it should appear there, and possibly also misleading, since on the analogy of 'the population of Italy' or 'the height of Mont Blanc', 'the meaning of a word' has the feel of a referring expression. Should we take it that a word has a meaning associated with it but distinguishable from it, and that *what* that meaning is is explained by saying that it is its use in the language? Or might we take it that the appearance here of the expression 'the meaning of a word' is a (somewhat clumsy) way of indicating *which* class of cases is referred to by the first clause of the section—namely the cases in which we explain the meanings of words, for example, by saying 'The word _____ has the same meaning as the word _____'? On the latter supposition, the definition would tell us that in sentences of this form, we can write 'use in the language' for 'meaning'.

Five. What is meant by 'use in the language'? Or better, in view of what has just been said, do we need to be able to *specify* what is meant? On the *de dicto* reading that has just been sketched, §43 merely tells us that in certain sentences in which the word 'meaning' appears, for 'meaning' we may read 'use in the language'; the matter can end there if a person understands the sentence yielded by that substitution. If he does not understand, we may have to explain; but the definition of meaning when taken this way is in no greater need of explanation than is *anything* we ever say—whatever we say, we *may* have to explain further. But on the *de re* reading it is essential to know what 'use in the language' means, because we cannot employ the definition in specifying the meanings of particular words without knowing what is supposed to count as a "use in the language": without knowing, for example, whether it should be a statement of the human purpose served by using the word (commending, relieving our feelings, committing ourselves, etc.), or an account of the difference it makes to the sense of a sentence whether the defined word appears in it, or an account of the grammatical constructions in which the word figures, or an account of the various circumstances in which we would or would not employ the word, or a precise account of the necessary and sufficient conditions for the use of the word.

Six. The words 'in the language' seem idle on *any* line of interpretation; what difference does it make whether we say that the meaning of a word is its use, or that it is its use *in the language?* Can we for most purposes safely omit these words and take it that they were included for some such ancillary purpose as to steer us away from a "use in our lives" interpretation?

Seven. If, as the final sentence of §43 tells us, the meaning of a name is sometimes explained by pointing to its bearer, does this mean that sometimes the meaning *is* the bearer? In view of Wittgenstein's other remarks about names, it would be surprising that he should say this—nor does it seem to be true.

Here let me sketch some background and then offer a suggestion. When asked what 'car' means, we may explain by pointing to cars, but we do not go so far as to say that 'car' means what we point to. When a person understands that 'car' is the name of a type of object, and understands how we use names, and has had some examples of cars and perhaps also some things (like trucks) that might be confused with cars pointed out to him, then we say he knows what 'car' means; that is, he can use the word appropriately and is not puzzled by other people's use of it, and he can perhaps also say such things as that a car is a self-propelled vehicle for transporting people, or that it means 'automobile'. But if he knows the meaning, he has not necessarily been told it, nor can he necessarily say what it is; and if he can say, there is not necessarily any one thing he will or should say. He may say that 'car' means 'automobile', but he may also offer either its equivalent or the equivalent of its equivalent in any other language, including perhaps children's languages, in which cars may be called zoom-zooms.

When we explain the meaning, what we offer by way of explanation is not necessarily itself the meaning. What we do or say is an explanation of meaning as long as it is well calculated to put the person to whom the explanation is given in a position where we would say that he knows the meaning. Now was the final sentence of §43 inserted in the hope that we would see this point and thereby be warned of how the German *erklären* is used in the earlier part of the section? (English readers might not notice that *erklären* is translated 'define' in the first paragraph, and 'explain' in the second.) The point might then be that just as, although we can explain the meaning of a name by pointing to its bearer, the bearer is not the meaning, so also, although we can explain the meaning of a word by explaining the use, the use is not the meaning.

Whether or not Wittgenstein intended us to glean this point, it does seem to be true. There is a sense in which we explain meanings by explaining uses. If we successfully *train* a person in the use of a word, he may afterwards be said to know its meaning; but what he knows in knowing the meaning will not be the use. We say we know the meaning of a word if it is not one of those words we have to pause over, make guesses about, or ask about; but if in so knowing we are in possession of anything that we could call the meaning, it is something that will complete the sentence 'The word _____ means _____', for example, it is 'automobile' or 'zoom-zoom' in the case of the word 'car'. However, there is a difficulty in supposing that the final sentence of the section was intended to alert us to this peculiarity of the use of *erklären*. One could expect that, in that event, instead of saying "the meaning of a word *is* its use in the language," Wittgenstein should have said something like "the meaning of a word may be explained by explaining its use in the language." The way he did express himself is standard for *defining* talk and is not even a loose way of expressing the kind of point that we have suspected may lurk in the final sentence.

Then is the last part of §43 just a point Wittgenstein felt it was important to make somewhere—a point he put here merely for want of a better place? Should we simply regard it as another point, having no particular bearing on the first part of the section?

II

I will now suggest a line of interpretation that may lead us successfully through these puzzles.

A large class of cases in which we use the word 'meaning' is that in which we ask, give, or decline to give the meanings of words using either the verb or the noun form of 'to mean'. We do various things that we are willing to call "explaining the meaning" or "asking for the meaning" without, *in doing them*, using any form of 'to mean': it is an explanation of the meaning of 'car' to say "That is a car," but we do not say, " 'Car' means one of those," or, "*That* is the meaning of the word 'car'." We may explain something about the meaning of the word 'know' by saying that if it would make no sense to ask when or how someone learned something, we should not say he knows it, but as we saw we would not say that 'know' means that we would not use it in those circumstances. When we ask what a word means, it is not exactly an answer, even if it is a very useful substitute, to say, "Well, that is one of them," or, "When someone uses it, you can take it that he is commending what he so describes," or, "We would use the word in these cases, but not in these."

When we use 'to mean' or 'the meaning' *in the course of* asking or giving explanations of the meanings of words, as distinct from using them in talking *about* such explanations, the specific kind of explanation of meaning that we are asking for or giving is an explanation by verbal synonymy: the explicans contemplated or given is another word or stock expression, whether of the same or another language, that is said to have the same meaning. (I say "stock expression" because it offends my linguistic sensitivities to say that 'car' *means* 'a self-propelled vehicle for transporting people'—rather than that a car *is* such an object. The explicans here is not used in conversation. I might offer you the loan of my automobile, but not of my 'self-propelled vehicle for transporting people'. A dictionary might give that account of what a car is, and we could call ascertaining that it did "looking up the meaning," but we would not use the word 'meaning' in giving that explanation of meaning.)

I am treating the class as including both the verb and the noun forms of 'mean'. We say, '(The word) _____ means _____', 'The words _____ and _____ have the same meaning', and 'The word _____ has the same meaning as the word _____'. There are also interrogative forms of such sentences; the class might further be treated as including such sentences as 'The word _____ does not have a meaning', or, 'I don't know the meaning of the word _____'. Such sentences can all be rendered using either the verb or the noun form of 'mean' without significant change of sense, but those using the noun form are better suited to this analysis, since that is the form appearing in §43 and since, there being no comparable verb form of 'use', verb forms of 'mean' must in any case be reduced to noun form before the substitution of 'use' for 'meaning' can be effected.

I am suggesting §43 holds that in sentences in which we use any form of the word 'mean' in the course either of explaining the meaning of a word, or of requesting such an explanation, or of declining such an explanation, for 'means' we can write 'has the same use as', or for 'meaning' we can substitute 'use'. (Here I ignore the words 'in the language'; I will comment later on that fact.)

Before considering whether this is the *correct* interpretation, I would like to point out some answers it implies to questions raised in Part I.

One. We have already seen what it implies as to what the "large class of cases" is. I do not know whether to say that it is part of the definition of this class that in it we explain the meaning of a word by giving verbal equivalents of it, or to say that this is something we discover about the class defined by the fact that we use the word 'mean' in the course of explaining the meaning of a word (or of requesting or declining such explanations); in any case, explanation of meaning by verbal equivalents is characteristic of the class. How large a proportion of all the uses of the word 'mean' this class represents I would not care to estimate, but clearly there is at least one other large class: the class in which the word 'meaning' is used in referring to other ways of elucidating words, for example when we talk of learning the meaning of a word by being trained in its use, or when we talk of looking up the meaning of a word in a dictionary.

Two. It is extremely important that if this *is* the class intended, then the "meaning is use" thesis will not tell us anything that is not already given in any statement that is a member of the class. It will tell us nothing as to how to explain the meaning of a word we are puzzled about, nor will it say anything about words which we are at all inclined to say *haven't* (exactly) a meaning.

Three. It is clearly a *de dicto* and not a *de re* interpretation, and as such it has this very important consequence: It eliminates all those accounts of §43 according to which we should explain the meaning of a word *by* explaining the use, *on whatever interpretation of 'use' one may elect*. For it *starts* explanations of the meanings of words, and these explanations are not supposed to be essentially altered by the substitution of 'use' for 'meaning' in them. It does not tell us *how* to explain what a word means, but instead it tells us the meaning of one of the words we use in explaining meanings.

Four. Since we do not have to explain the use in order to explain the meaning on this line of interpretation, and hence we do not have to decide what is intended to count as a use, it will not immediately be incumbent on us to decide what 'use' means here.

Five. It is implied by this interpretation that the occurrence of the expression 'the meaning of a word' in §43 *is* misleading. Because of its superficially referential character, it wrongly suggests a *de re* account, according to which the definition tells us *what* it is that two words having the same meaning share. There is on our reading no such animal; the function of the expression 'the meaning of a word' has to be treated as a somewhat unfortunate (though not altogether inept) way of indicating *which* class of cases is referred to by the first clause of the section.

A wide swath, therefore, is cut through our difficulties in Part I; but that is not a reason for accepting this interpretation as correct. *Any* interpretation would be likely to do this, and if this one distinguishes itself from others in this regard, it is by doing it so very deftly. To weigh up the question of correctness, I propose to do three things. I will first consider how the account fares from the point of view of the principle of charity—the principle that one should avoid until forced to do so, attributing to someone a view which is false, absurd, implausible, or otherwise low grade. Second, I will consider how well the interpretation squares with §43 itself; third, I will comment on its relation to other remarks in the *Philosophical Investigations* that interestingly connect meaning and use.

One. Is it charitable to Wittgenstein to suppose that he meant something like this?

(*A*) The claim that to say that two words have the same meaning is to say that they are used the same way, while it may not on the face of it be very interesting, appears to be at least intuitively and at least roughly true. When we are given an account of the meaning of a word of the kind under discussion, if we know when to use the explaining word, then we so far know when to use the explained word. We plug in the latter where we would use the former; given that the explanation of meaning on which we are relying is adequate and not in need of extensive qualification, we will use the explained word satisfactorily.

It is true that we do not often hit upon another word or expression that admits of such completely straightforward "plugging in." Although few people would cavil at the proposition that 'handy' means 'convenient', it is in fact only in some cases that where we would say 'convenient' we could equally say 'handy'. We talk of handy gadgets, but were we to use the expression 'convenient gadgets', we would more likely mean that they were immediately on hand than that they were such as to simplify an operation; and we say, "If it is convenient, come around eleven"—but not, "If it is handy." ('Handy', one might say, is more dispositional than 'convenient'.) Generally we might be better to say that one word "has a meaning like (or a use like)" another than that they have the same meaning, and perhaps that is what we are generally understood to mean. Yet this does not serve as an objection to the thesis whose merits we are discussing; if the explanations of meaning are not always as exact as they might be, that is (if anything) an objection to *them* and not to the philosophical claim that when, or to the extent that, two words have the same meaning, they have the same use.

(*B*) To accept this account of a use of the word 'mean' is to reject other accounts, in particular to reject any account that offers an *answer* to this question: 'What is the one thing that two words share when they have the same meaning?' Hence one might, before accepting this account, wish to be shown some reason for supposing that question to be ill-conceived. However, such reasons are not difficult to supply. Two arguments may be suggested for a start:

(1) An answer that is available as to what (if anything) the third thing is, is some further word or expression. If we say that 'five' and *cinq* have the same meaning, and someone asks what it is, an answer will be *fünf;* but then, of course, we can turn around and say that 'five', *cinq*, and *fünf* have the same meaning; it would clearly be a fool's game to persist in asking what that meaning is.

(2) We say every day, readily and without a tremor of doubt, that one word has the same meaning as another, while not having the least idea what any third thing might be that they share. Therefore, we have a choice between saying that we have some utterly mysterious knowledge of this third thing, enabling us to make such judgments, and saying that there is no third thing, but that the grammatical form of our explanation creates that illusion and that what we mean in saying that two words have the same meaning is that one of them serves to explain the other. In the absence of other considerations, the choice should not be difficult.

(C) It might be argued as an objection that so far 'use' has not been defined at all clearly, and that without some quite specific account of how this word should be taken, such complications as the following might arise:

(1) There is a sense of 'can be used' in which, wherever 'hot' can be used, 'cold' can, and therefore on these principles 'hot' might have to mean 'cold'.

(2) It is in one sense of 'use' a use of 'handy' to say that 'handy' is a five-letter word; but it is false that 'convenient' is a five-letter word, and therefore on these principles 'handy' does not mean 'convenient'.

If we try to avoid these complications by saying that the sentences in which we make the substitution must have the same truth value, we will have difficulty accounting for imperatives, questions, evaluations, performatives, etc., while if we say that they must have the same meaning, we proceed in a circle.

However, such difficulties can be avoided satisfactorily by recalling that on the interpretation proposed there is no question of *ascertaining* whether any two words have the same or a different meaning, and therefore just no prospect of 'hot' turning out, through the application of an ill-defined method, to mean 'cold', or any other such absurdities. For Wittgenstein's "large class of cases" being what it is, we *start* with statements of equivalence or non-equivalence of meaning, and they do not stand to be confirmed or revised as a consequence of the explanation of meaning that is given. What is in question is not *perfecting* explanations of meaning, but *understanding* them—for example, understanding whether or not there is some third thing that two words share when they are said to have the same meaning.

Moreover, there is not even any question of our not knowing what to do with such explanations of meaning until we are provided with a clear account of 'use'. For we either do or do not know what to do with them in their analyzed form, and we should not do anything different when provided with Wittgenstein's analysis. If anyone does not know what to do with a statement like " 'handy' means 'convenient'," then it may indeed be of some use to him to say that it means that wherever he would use 'convenient' he could alternatively use 'handy'; but if he does not understand that either, we have no reason to expect that that should be the only or the best way of explaining what to do with these explanations of meaning. We could simply set about training him, letting him make mistakes if he will and correcting him when he does, etc., until he generally does the right thing with these explanations.

I conclude that the principle of charity does not urgently require us to look for another account.

Two. How does our interpretation square with the terms of §43 itself?

It has the merit of taking the first clause of the section seriously: It *finds* a large class of cases; and they are cases in which we do employ the word 'meaning'. Nor does it recommend any changes in the ordinary practice, but (unlike some other candidates) treats these uses of 'meaning' as being quite in order.

In line with the obvious reference of the word 'it' in §43, it defines the *word* 'meaning', rather than something that the word might be supposed to refer to; it does not require any tampering with the word 'define', such as would be required if we were to talk of defining entities or states of affairs or whatever else might be suggested as *what* it is that is shared by words having the same meaning—but it employs 'define' in a very typical philosophical way.

Against it are, first, the fact that (as we have seen) it implies that Wittgenstein expressed himself misleadingly in his use of the expression, 'the meaning of a word'. (That this strongly suggests a *de re* interpretation is verified by the almost universal preference for that kind of account.) But we also saw some justification for this choice of words, in that it served to indicate *which* class of cases was intended.

A second count against the interpretation is that it does not seem to provide any clear role for the words 'in the language'. It is important to say that if we include these words in a statement of the interpretation, if we make it read, 'To say that two words have the same meaning is to say that they have the same use in the language', their inclusion neither makes it nonsense nor a different interpretation. We do not *have* to omit them; the difficulty is only that they seem *idle*.

Of course one can suggest jobs for these words, such as to steer us away from the idea that it is the use in our lives (e.g., for commending) that is meant. But they do not serve that or any other function at all clearly.

Third, it would greatly recommend any interpretation of §43 if it were such as to show right away what we should make of the ever-puzzling second paragraph of the section, and yet as far as I can see this interpretation does not immediately suggest a solution to that problem. In this it is no worse than any other that I am acquainted with; but if it is any better, the way in which it is is somewhat tenuous. It was suggested when this question was raised in Part I that there is a special sense of *erklären* in which the meaning of a word like 'car' is explained by pointing to cars; cars are not themselves the meaning of 'car', but pointing to cars is likely under usual circumstances to bring it about that a person "knows the meaning" of 'car'.

The question was raised whether we were intended to notice this feature of *erklären* and apply it somehow to what had been said in the first sentence of the section, but it was not clear how this might be done, since the language of the first paragraph was fairly clearly that of definition, and not of explanation.

However, it may now be suggested that the second paragraph might alert us to the following feature of the curious "definition" in the first—that just as a car may serve to explain, but is not the meaning of the word 'car', so the idea of using two words in the same way may serve to explain what is meant by saying they have the same meaning, but is not what their having the same meaning means. That is not to say, I hasten to add, that their being said to have the same meaning means *something else*. Rather, it is part of the view suggested earlier, that 'knowing the meaning' is not knowing anything in particular; it is an expression we use when a person has no difficulty with a word, does not have to guess or ask anyone about it. One of the things that is likely to put a person in this position with regard to a given word is being told it has a use like such-and-such a word; but, like pointing to the bearer of a name, this teaches him the meaning without telling him it.

Three. How does this interpretation square with other remarks in the Philosophical Investigations *that interestingly connect meaning and use, and kindred terms?*[2]

It is impossible in a short paper to canvass this question adequately, but let me make some general claims which, albeit with some ingenuity (but ingenuity is always required in the interpretation of Wittgenstein), may be found to be justified.

(*A*) There are not many passages that indicate, or indicate at all clearly, what is meant by 'meaning' or by 'use', or what relation is conceived to obtain between them.

(*B*) Of the few that do give strong indications, a considerable group (§§20, 30, 138; p. 190) supports the interpretation by appearing to treat 'meaning' and 'use' as (often) interchangeable.

(*C*) Many of the remarks can best be seen simply as making related but different points.

(*D*) Perhaps the most awkward groups of remarks are (1) those that suggest the meaning can be *derived* from use (§§10, 29, 119; pp. 200c, 212e), and (2) those that suggest the possibility of an extended account of the use (primarily §§246, 247).

(1) Concerning the former, it may be suggested that remarks like "Let the use teach you the meaning" (p. 212) do not mean anything like "First discover the use, and from that infer the meaning," but rather something like "Remind yourself of some actual uses of a puzzling word, and then you will be in no doubt about its meaning." On this kind of reading, the awkward fact that one must arrive at a statement of the use, which will either *be* the meaning or be something from which the meaning can be derived, is replaced by a suggestion involving the specification of neither the use nor the meaning. One brings a word back from its holidays by thinking of cases of its actual use, and then the problem that one had as to its meaning disappears. On this basis these otherwise awkward passages turn out again merely to be making related but different points.

(2) The possibility of specifying how a word is used, which is at least suggested, e.g., by §246 and §247, may seem to imply (contrary to what the account proposed here holds) that the

[2] §§1, 10, 20, 29, 30, 41, 42, 120, 138, 139, 150, 151, 182, 183, 189, 190, 193, 198, 199, 247, 349, 421, 432, 451, 454, 532, 561, 580; pp. 147, 175, 188, 190, 212, 216.

word 'meaning' does have a referent—namely, the way of using described in any account of the use.

But the principle of charity would give us a strong reason for avoiding interpretations requiring employment of *accounts* of the use, since as we saw above no account of the use of a word will in fact tell us its meaning.

Moreover, although one could perhaps map out the uses of two words said to have the same meaning and find that they do coincide, that fact seems altogether incidental to what is going on when we say, for example, that " 'Handy' means 'convenient'." When we say such things, we are not mindful of the fact that such jobs of mapping could be done, nor have we done them. We are relying on our habitual knowledge of when to use one of the words for explaining when to use the other.

III

I will conclude by outlining briefly some implications of the "meaning is use" thesis as I have interpreted it. It is not very exciting on this reading. It neither tells us how to ascertain the meaning of a word nor what form the statement of its meaning properly should take, nor does it tell us that we should not talk of meanings but of uses. It simply reminds us of the quite commonplace truth that when we say that two words have the same meaning we might alternatively say that where we would use one of them we might equally use the other.

The humdrum character of this point may itself be evidence of the correctness of the interpretation, in view of Wittgenstein's frequent professions (§§109, 124, 415, 599) not to be telling us anything that is not perfectly obvious. But if it is so unexciting, what made it seem to Wittgenstein to be worth saying? I will suggest two implications it may have, which may not be unimportant.

One. It does away with a reason for looking for some third thing that two words (and by extension I should think two sentences, or two statements) having the same meaning share by showing that we are not required to read the expression 'have the same meaning' in such a way that it gives rise to questions about what that meaning is. The superficially referential character of the word 'meaning' in such expressions as 'have the same meaning' is assuredly not the *only* reason for going in search of this third thing. One could no doubt be moved primarily by the idea of the explanatory power of such a third thing, if it could be found. There would then be a very convincing explanation available of how, for example, a bilingual person can tell us what a sentence of one language means in another language; the two sentences share something, and one can proceed by regular means from that something to either of them. Whether the something is the circumstances in which we employ them, the things that stimulate us to utter them, the thought that they express, the facts that make them true, the proposition they express or the statement they make, or something else, is what we have yet to decide. Wittgenstein's point in §43 does not weigh directly against *this* reason for looking for some third thing, but only against the reason, if it is a reason, that the way we express ourselves when we say that two words have the same meaning suggests that we possess an answer to the question what that meaning is that they share.

Two. But I think that the "meaning is use" thesis as here interpreted is closely connected with a theory of Wittgenstein's that *would* weigh against the other suggested reason for looking for this third thing. The theory I mean is the view that linguistic skill is essentially a kind of training—not a training in the deliberate employment of any *procedure*, but a sort of tuning of the human organism until it simply performs well linguistically. It is more like training a child to throw and catch a ball, the result of which is that he does it well without thinking what he is doing, than it is like teaching a person to remember and correctly apply the steps of a method of doing something.

Since I have already argued in two published papers[3] that Wittgenstein held this view, I will not defend that claim here, but I will indicate (*A*) the connection between it and the "meaning is use" thesis, and (*B*) its bearing on the question of the plausibility of programs of explaining identity of meaning by reference to a third

[3] "Wittgenstein's Theory of Linguistic Self-Sufficiency," *Dialogue*, 6 (1967): 367–82; and "'Forms of Life' in Wittgenstein's *Philosophical Investigations*," *American Philosophical Quarterly*, 5 (1963):233–43, and reprinted in this volume.

thing shared by two words (or expressions, or sentences) having the same meaning.

(*A*) The connection lies in the fairly obvious fact that explanations of meaning by word equivalence serve their purpose only when the person to whom they are given already has a mastery of the explaining word, and that he neither needs to be able to say nor generally *can* say how that word is used. If he is simply able to use the explaining word, this established ability may be all that is required to enable him to use the explained word.[4]

If you tell me that 'handy' has the same meaning as 'convenient', I do not think: "Oh, I know what 'convenient' means, it means '————' "—and so understand. If 'convenient' is a word I am familiar with, that is the end of the line. That, and not some further thing, is what I understand 'handy' to mean.

We might call this simple ability to use a word without (in the ordinary case) any reflection or calculation the immediacy of our understanding of language. Neither in deciding how to express ourselves nor in understanding what other people say do we ordinarily perform any operations, apply any rules, arrive at anything further, the seeing of which it is to understand. In the ordinary case we simply have no difficulty. Speak to us in familiar ways and we can go on from there right away, without stopping to tell ourselves, or reckon, what the words mean.

(*B*) The way that the fact of the immediacy of our understanding of language weighs against the plausibility of programs of explaining identity of meaning by means of some third thing is by suggesting that whatever the discovery of such a third thing might do for us, it would not explain either how people arrive at statements of identity of meaning or how they understand such statements. Understanding is not an operation, and hence not the operation of concluding what it is that two words having the same meaning share.

Here I have only been trying to indicate a line of development;

---

[4] Of course, a person may (as we saw he might with 'handy' and 'convenient') apply the explanation too mechanically, and he may have to be corrected at various junctures; but it is nevertheless a useful explanatory measure, just as it is useful to explain the meaning of a name by pointing to one or more of its bearers.

clearly, it would be a lengthy task either to show that this is the kind of importance that Wittgenstein attached to the "meaning is use" thesis, or to show that, if it were, he would have a formidable criticism to offer of the philosophical search for meanings. My main claim in the paper is only as to the correctness of the interpretation offered in Part II.

18

Wittgenstein on Phenomenalism, Skepticism, and Criteria

ANDREW OLDENQUIST

I

INTRODUCTION. Wittgenstein said, according to Moore's notes,[1] ". . . it did not matter whether his results were true or not: what mattered was that 'a method had been found'." Remarks like this plus the obvious employment of a dazzling method and the sheer difficulty of identifying his results have led commentators such as O. K. Bouwsma[2] and M. Lazerowitz[3] to read only meta-philosophy out of Wittgenstein and, inevitably, to cast him as a "therapeutic positivist." I think this distorts Wittgenstein and diminishes his contribution; his results do matter, even if the philosopher himself said No. Von Wright says: "The young Wittgenstein had learned from Frege and Russell. His problems were in part theirs. The later Wittgenstein, I should say, has no ancestors in the history of thought. His work signalizes a radical departure from previously existing paths of philosophy."[4] This view, too, can retard an understanding of Wittgenstein. I am

[1] *Mind*, 1954.

[2] O. K. Bouwsma, "The Blue Book," *The Journal of Philosophy*, 58, no. 6 (1961).

[3] Morris Lazerowitz, "Wittgenstein on the Nature of Philosophy," in *Ludwig Wittgenstein: The Man and His Philosophy*, ed. K. T. Fann (New York: Dell Publishing Co., 1967).

[4] G. H. von Wright, "A Biographical Sketch," *The Philosophical Review*, 64, no. 4 (1955).

morally certain that the later Wittgenstein did not spring full-blown from the head of Zeus and, moreover, that some day he will be acknowledged to have a philosophical position that has a comprehensible location within the history of twentieth-century philosophy. Indeed, before too long, with the benefit of hindsight and when exegetical and interpretative ideas have had longer to marinate, philosophers will dare (although I do not dare) to speak without absurdity of the later Wittgenstein's philosophical system.

I cannot prove the general case, but the rest of this essay should be relevant to it. In this first part, I distinguish two arguments found in Wittgenstein having to do with the notion of privacy. In Part II, I unpack and defend one of those two arguments. Part III develops an argument against skepticism that I think is Wittgenstein's and which depends upon the arguments in Part II. Part IV offers one interpretation of the term 'criteria' that is intelligible and perhaps even plausible in the light of the preceding arguments.

In the 30's and 40's, philosophers debated the truth of different variations on the theme of epistemological idealism. This philosophical theme has as one of its roots what I shall call the Cartesian doctrine of the primacy of self-knowledge. I mean by this the view that what only I can know in the way in which I do know it—my thoughts, ideas, impressions, the given, sense data—is a necessary condition of my knowledge of tables, the colors of things, and other minds. For convenience alone I shall often refer to these views as "phenomenalism."

There is more than one way to characterize the concept of a sense datum or "the given." One characterization is the idea of what is known directly, immediately, or noninferentially; another is the idea of the sense datum as an object of indubitable knowledge; and a third is the idea of an object which *only* I can know in the way in which I do know it, in other words the idea of a private object. Some philosophers who have discussed sense data have rejected or doubted one or another of these characterizations. Moore, for example, quite explicitly explored the possibility that sense data were public objects and that they might be identical with the surfaces of physical objects. But I think that Wittgenstein's conception of the private object of knowledge lies closer to the Cartesian roots of the central idea of the primacy of self-knowledge, from which idealism, phenomenalism, and sense-datum theories spring.[5] It is the idea that all knowledge starts with self-knowledge; it has behooved philosophers, throughout the history of the idea, to refute the objection that if this is where knowledge starts, then this is also where it ends. Wittgenstein's position here is clear enough—his term of convenience for any phenomenalist or sense-datum philosopher is "the solipcist."

The Two Arguments. Wittgenstein sets out to attack the whole phenomenalist and idealist tradition at its root. In the *Philosophical Investigations,* his anti-phenomenalist arguments are found mainly in §§243–315 and 350–411. I want to distinguish two arguments found in these passages, each of them concerned with "private objects" and each anti-phenomenalist. The first is the "private-language argument"; its main presentation is in §§256–69 of *P.I.* The private-language argument maintains that there cannot be a language whose words mean or refer to sensations when sensations are considered to be private objects. It proceeds by challenging the possibility of there being criteria for the re-identification of a private object, and also challenging the intelligibility of private rules for using the name of a private object. The second argument I shall call the "irrelevance argument." It occurs frequently within §§243–315 and 350–411 and maintains that private objects are irrelevant to the meaning of words in our public language.

The private language argument begins with "Now, what about the language which describes my inner experiences and which only I myself can understand?"[6] and proceeds by stating and then rejecting the diary argument of §258, and is left behind when Wittgenstein says:

> Let us now imagine a use for the entry of the sign "S" in my diary. I discover that whenever I have a particular sensation a manometer shews that my blood-pressure rises. So I shall be able to say that my blood-pressure is rising without using any apparatus. This is a useful result. And now it seems quite indifferent whether I have recognized

[5] In "Cartesian Privacy" (in *Wittgenstein: The Philosophical Investigations,* ed. George Pitcher [New York: Anchor Books, 1966]), Anthony Kenny elaborates the connection between private objects, as Wittgenstein conceives them, and Descartes's views.

[6] Ludwig Wittgenstein, *Philosophical Investigations,* 3rd ed. (New York: Macmillan, 1968), §256.

the sensation *right* or not. Let us suppose I regularly identify it wrong, it does not matter in the least. And that alone shews that the hypothesis that I make a mistake is mere show. (We as it were turned a knob which looked as if it could be used to turn on some part of the machine; but it was a mere ornament, not connected with the mechanism at all) [*P.I.,* 270].

When he says "Let us now imagine a use for . . . the sign '*S*,' " he is returning to the question whether private objects have any use or role in our public language. The body of argument surrounding the private-language argument and which I call the irrelevance argument has the broader purpose of denying any role in our public language (that is to say, in the language which other people *can* understand) to what is essentially private. The shift in the argument is this: The private-language argument maintains that a language which by definition could not be public, which could not be understood by others, is not a possible language. §270 resumes the different argument that private objects, whether or not they could be talked about in a private language, are irrelevant to what words mean in our public language. This takes the (admittedly difficult) form in §270 of pointing out that the public term 'feeling of blood pressure rising' does not depend for its use upon any independent re-identifiability of the sensation. There is an obvious difference between saying that private objects are irrelevant to *our* language and saying that they cannot be referred to or meant in any possible language. The conclusion of the irrelevance argument is expressed by means of mechanical analogies in §§270 and 271: When we understand the mechanism of using words meaningfully and of teaching children to use words with meaning, then we see that the private object is a mere ornament, a wheel not connected with the linguistic mechanism.

One can get the impression that some philosophers read this whole central portion of the *Philosophical Investigations* and come away with nothing but the private-language argument, seeing the surrounding sections only as appendages thereto, and consequently find themselves worrying (sometimes secretly) about its point and relevance as well as its soundness. The exegetical points must be made that within this central part of the *Philosophical Investigations* (1) the private-language argument is not the only argument involving the idea of privacy, (2) the private-language argument has a place within a larger pattern of argument, and (3) a main target of the whole pattern of argument is what I variously call the primacy of self-knowledge, sense data, and phenomenalism. Otherwise the private-language argument appears to come out of nowhere and to do nothing, as though Wittgenstein in introducing it had said, "Say, do you want to see something really clever?"

The private-language argument is stronger than the irrelevance argument, for if it is impossible that there be *any* language whose words mean or refer to private objects, it follows that words in *our* language cannot mean or refer to private objects. Thus, if either the private-language argument or the irrelevance argument is sound, phenomenalism is false. But the irrelevance argument can be sound even if the private-language argument is unsound, for it does not follow from the claim that our language cannot contain or depend upon a private language that there cannot be a private language, such as, for example, the diary language of §258.

Commentators have accorded the private-language argument too central a position within his discussion of sensation and privacy, and it is important to show that his critique of phenomenalism does not stand or fall with that argument. I shall neither criticize nor defend the private-language argument, but I think its function within Wittgenstein's strategy against the phenomenalist is roughly as follows: If a philosopher is driven from the view that statements about chairs *mean* sets of statements about private experiences, on the ground that if so the word 'chair' would be unteachable, he may still insist (at least in principle) that there can be words which mean private experiences or sense data. Wittgenstein insists that these words would have to be words in a private language. The private-language hypothesis becomes the last lair of the sense-datum philosopher. But Wittgenstein decides to hunt him there, too; hence the private-language argument.

II

Am I doing child psychology?—I am making a connection between the concept of teaching and the concept of meaning.——Zettel, 412.

Sense Data and Learning 'Red'. It is not the *impossibility* of a private language by which the irrelevance argument refutes phenomenalism, but the very *idea* of one. Put very generally, Wittgenstein argues that we must assume the interpersonal character of language and the public meaning of words in order to intelligibly explain how a child can learn a language in the first place, and that any intelligible explanation of language learning is incompatible with phenomenalism. He describes the target of his argument as follows: "Our teaching connects the word 'red' (or is meant to connect it) with a particular impression of his (a private impression, an impression in him). He then communicates this impression—indirectly, of course—through the medium of speech." (The idea of the private *object* of vision. Appearance, sense datum.)[7]

A child learns the word 'red' by means of examples when he is about two. His parents utter color words while they point to colored objects, and the child gradually learns to utter the words. He often goes through a stage where he recites a string of three or four color words and points to a different colored object for each word, but without very often getting the words right. His parents correct him when he is mistaken and tell him when he is right; they also correct his syntactical errors. The child cannot (as a matter of fact and not of logic) learn the word 'red' unless someone other than himself functions as a source of consistent correction. Otherwise the child will not so much as get the idea that there is a right or wrong to uttering 'red' in the presence of different colors. A child can learn to say words without learning what they mean, and he can also learn to respond correctly to words before he learns to say them. A source of consistent correction constituted by what other people say and do is a necessary condition of his learning what 'red' means in English. On the other hand, if we suppose the possibility that he was learning 'red' as a word in his private language—learning 'red' as the name of a logically private object—he would still require a source of consistent correction, but it would be one which he alone supplied and would not depend upon what other people say and do.

It is Wittgenstein's view that a child has learned the word 'red'

[7] Ludwig Wittgenstein, "Notes for Lectures on 'Private Experience' and 'Sense Data'," *The Philosophical Review*, 77 (July, 1968):279.

when he can use it as other speakers of his language use it; moreover, that if he does use 'red' as his tribe uses it, then he knows what 'red' *means*. And in this case he not only uses 'red' with meaning, but means the same by 'red' as does his tribe.

"We take it as the criterion for meaning the same by 'red' as we do, that as a rule he agrees with us in giving the same names to the colors of objects as we do" (*Notes*, p. 283). From the above we can elicit the principle that if two people (sincerely) use the word 'red' similarly, then it is not conceptually possible that 'red' has a different meaning for each of them. By 'use the word similarly' I mean that they *in general* call the same things red, in general allow the word the same syntactical role, and in general make the same comparisons, e.g., that red is closer to orange than to green, etc.

A child's teachers can knowingly correct his mistakes only if they can know when he has made mistakes, and a child first learns that certain utterances are mistaken only by being corrected. If the child says 'red' of a red picture but nevertheless has a different colored sense datum, this is a "mistake" that is in principle impossible for his teachers to correct. One corrects many sorts of errors in the course of teaching a child the color words, but one "error" it is impossible to correct is his saying 'red' when he has the "wrong" sense datum. And just because one cannot possibly correct a child when he has the wrong sense datum, one cannot possibly *teach* him to call 'red' one kind of sense datum rather than another. So, since the meaning of 'red' is something that can be taught, 'red' cannot mean a particular kind of sense datum. Wittgenstein's argument here is not that there cannot be sense data or private objects, but instead that our words cannot mean sense data. What is claimed is that I have full and complete possession of the meaning of 'red' if and only if I use it in the way my linguistic community uses it.

When a child is learning words from its parents, the idea of a mistake and the idea of what is, in principle, correctable are correlative ideas. That is, at this stage of the argument we must separate the idea of the child having one sense datum rather than another from the idea of his having or doing something which *counts against* the achievement of his parents' aim in teaching him. For let us assume he does have one sense datum rather than another; this is a mistake only if it counts against or defeats his parents' teaching.

But his parents cannot possibly teach him to mean one sense datum rather than another.

It is not that there are possible incorrigible mistakes: Earlier I said that if a child is taught to say color words but is *never* corrected as to which color words go with which colors, he will not so much as have the idea that calling a particular color red is either correct or incorrect. But he cannot possibly be corrected as to which color words go with which sense data, and consequently a child will not so much as have the idea that calling a particular sense datum red is correct or incorrect—any sense datum will be right, or better, it will not matter. And we cannot say here, "Well, he's still either correct or incorrect anyway." Saying *that* is simply to forget the conventional character of language. His parents can never put across the idea that it matters which sense datum he has, and he can never know which sense datum is supposed to be the correct one. What sense datum he has is irrelevant to what they are trying to teach him, and what they are trying to teach him is what 'red' means.

The Contingency of the Connection between Sense Data and Behavior. Before offering some textual support for this interpretation of Wittgenstein, I want to pause to consider an objection. The argument thus far has depended upon the assumption that verbal behavior and sense data can vary independently of one another. For I have attacked the relevance of sense data to meaning by assuming that someone's sense data might be deviant while his verbal behavior is nondeviant, and then arguing that similarity of behavior is a sufficient condition for similarity of meaning, regardless of whether or not his sense data are deviant. The assumption can be challenged by claiming that someone's behavior will be nondeviant only if his sense data are nondeviant. That is to say, perhaps two people will use color words similarly only if they have similar sense data; to support this one might adduce the example that if a man had only red sense data his verbal behavior obviously would be deviant. If this were so, then having similar sense data would be a necessary, although not a sufficient, condition for similarity of meaning just because it would be a necessary condition for emitting similar behavior; and in just this sense it would be false to say that the quality of one's sense data was *irrelevant* to what one meant by 'red'.

Now a peculiarity of this hypothesis is that it rules out, absolutely ad hoc, the skeptical possibility that two people might use color words similarly and nevertheless see colors differently. It appears to be unreasonable to rule out this possibility since, if we admit the notion of the private sense datum in the first place, it appears to be quite possible that my use of 'red' should be standard but my color sense data deviant. The most common hypothesis in this regard is that of spectrum reversal; another is to suppose that I am never aware of "colors" at all and that my central nervous system responds to the visible light frequencies in a radically different way, but with sufficient isomorphism with the normal response that I am able to learn the color words just as normal people do. One of Wittgenstein's less controversial points is that the possibility of this kind of skepticism is built into all sense-datum theories. If a phenomenalist does admit the possibility of such hypotheses, and maintains that having similar sense data is a necessary condition for two people meaning the same by 'red', then he must reject Wittgenstein's principle that two members of a language group mean the same by a word if they use it similarly. Of these two incompatible views, Wittgenstein's seems to be much the more plausible.

Wittgenstein's anti-phenomenalist arguments rely heavily upon the idea that private objects could be different for different people or change within a single person's experience, with our verbal and nonverbal behavior remaining similar. Thus he says:

> Always get rid of the idea of the private object in this way: assume that it constantly changes, but that you do not notice the change because your memory constantly deceives you [*P.I.*, 207].

And in another passage:

> Imagine a person whose memory could not retain *what* the word 'pain' meant—so that he constantly called different things by that name—but nevertheless used the word in a way fitting in with the usual symptoms and presuppositions of pain

and Wittgenstein continues it:

> —in short he uses it as we all do. Here I should like to say: a wheel that can be turned though nothing else moves with it, is not part of the mechanism [*P.I.*, 271].

This presents a difficulty because some philosophers would wish to distinguish verifiable from nonverifiable cases of deviant sense data. For example, spectrum reversal is thought to be a special case in which the deviant condition would never reveal itself in deviant behavior. But Wittgenstein treats the case of the man who sees red things green and green things red as though it were like spectrum reversal—he assumes that the man emits normal behavior. This appears to be mistaken in that it is likely that a man who always saw red things green and green things red would make different comparative judgments—for example, that orange was more similar to green than it was to red.

But Wittgenstein is not mistaken here because his argument does not depend upon the distinction between verifiable and unverifiable cases of deviant color perception. The argument depends instead upon the consequences of conceding that the connection between a private experience and behavior is a contingent connection. If it is contingent, then we always can meaningfully suppose that a man's sense data are wildly different from ours, while his behavior coincides with ours: for example, that he is in great pain but scratches and says it itches, or that he sees red things green and green things red but uses the color words as we do. This is why Wittgenstein so often, and apparently cavalierly, asks us to imagine sense data to be different or to fluctuate. Wittgenstein's point is that the *mere possibility* of his sense data being deviant and his verbal behavior being nondeviant shows the irrelevance of the quality of his sense data to his meaning by 'red' what his language group means. For this reason there is no philosophical point to thinking up ingenious, unverifiable cases of deviant sense data such as spectrum reversal.

Sense data can be relevant to meaning in the way in which gross behavior is only if having a certain kind of sense data is a conceptually necessary, and not merely a causally necessary, condition of using a word with a given meaning. But that can be so only if having a certain kind of sense data is a conceptually necessary condition of emitting standard verbal behavior. But this last is clearly not so. On the hypothesis we are considering, the most one could say is that sense data might have the same kind of relation to verbal behavior as do neurophysiological occurrences or tongue movements. To put the conclusion in Wittgenstein's jargon, the relation between behavior and meaning is criterial while the relation between private experiences and meaning is not (and could not possibly be) criterial. It is worth noting here that for the same reason the relation between neurophysiological occurrences and meaning is not (and could not possibly be) criterial. That reason, again, is that it is a truth (in this case, a contingent truth) that neurophysiological occurrences play no role in the teaching of language and, hence, are at best symptoms and not criteria of what one means by a word. The neurophysiological occurrences are merely contingently related to gross behavior (including verbal behavior) and therefore cannot be a conceptually necessary condition of using a word with a given meaning.

Beetles. The beetle passage in the *Philosophical Investigations* contains a succinct formulation of Wittgenstein's argument for the irrelevance of private objects.

> Now someone tells me that *he* knows what pain is only from his own case!—Suppose everyone had a box with something in it: we call it a "beetle." No one can look into anyone else's box, and everyone says he knows what a beetle is only by looking at *his* beetle.—Here it would be quite possible for everyone to have something different in his box. One might even imagine such a thing constantly changing [*P.I.*, 293].

Up to this point in the passage Wittgenstein hypothesizes, for the sake of argument, that each box owner has his private language in which he names his beetle—i.e., his sense datum,—and knows what it is from his own experience. On this hypothesis it is conceptually impossible for the word 'beetle' to be taught and for the word to have a use or a meaning in an interpersonal language—that is, for two people to know its meaning. Now the passage continues:

> —But suppose the word "beetle" had a use in these people's language?
> —If so it would not be used as the name of a thing. The thing in the box has no place in the language-game at all; not even as a *something:* for the box might even be empty.—No, one can 'divide through' by the thing in the box; it cancels out, whatever it is [*P.I.*, 293].

Now the word has a meaning in a public language, a meaning that can be taught (we are not told what that meaning is). What it meant before in the private language, if anything, is no part of the public meaning, the meaning that can be taught children. The word 'beetle' can be given an interpersonal use only by means of the procedures of teaching and correction already discussed. But the name of a private object is by definition not a word amenable to these procedures of teaching and correction; this is why "the thing in the box" cancels out. The meaning that we can explain and teach cannot be the meaning we fancy the word to have in a private language prior to its having a use. Moreover, it is possible that two persons' use of 'beetle' can be the same—and hence what they mean be the same—and "the thing in the box" be different for each of them. If we admit the bare possibility that the thing in the box can vary independently of the use (and meaning) of 'beetle', it follows that it is irrelevant to the meaning of 'beetle' in an interpersonal language what (if anything) is in the box. It does not rebut Wittgenstein's argument to distinguish what 'beetle' means from what 'beetle' refers to. The kind of thing a word purports to refer to, if it purports to refer to anything at all, depends upon what the word means, and if the nature of the private object is not relevant to a word's meaning it is not relevant to its reference. These are, I think, the arguments behind Wittgenstein's conclusion in the beetle passage that the private object—say, the red sense-datum—"has no place in the language-game at all."

Even if Wittgenstein's argument elsewhere for the impossibility of a private language were unsound, there remains this argument for the irrelevance to our public language of necessarily private objects. The beetle passage does not argue against the possibility of a private language; in fact it assumes for the sake of argument that 'beetle' might be a word in a private language.

Can One Intelligibly Attribute Colors to Sense Data? The irrelevance argument concluded that if two people use 'red' similarly—in general make similar color judgments—then they mean the same by 'red' *even if we suppose them to have different sense data.* Wittgenstein attacks the intelligibility of the rider, "even if we suppose them to have different sense data," maintaining, I believe, that it is unintelligible to so much as speculate about the colors of sense data. I shall attempt to lay out these further arguments, and I should add that these arguments, too, do not stand or fall with the private-language argument. I think that what is important about them is that the earlier argument for the irrelevance of sense data will not be fully convincing so long as one thinks it possible that a man might always see red things green and green things red and nevertheless use color words standardly; that is to say, so long as one still finds it intelligible to hypothesize reversed colors for one's sense data, or to hypothesize reversal regarding how red and green things always *appear* to him.

What does it mean to suppose that two people might have different sense data, given that they mean the same by 'red'? Does it mean that their sense data might be different colors—for example, that my sense data are always green when I see the things that I and everybody else call red whereas other people's sense data are red when they see those things? Saying that makes no sense at all, precisely because it is coupled to the claim that the quality of my sense datum is irrelevant to what I mean by 'green' or by any other color word. In other words, saying that is hypothesizing that the quality or nature of my sense datum is not relevant to what I mean when I assert that, e.g., I might have green sense-data. To hypothesize this is unintelligible.

Could 'red' have two meanings, such that when I mean 'red' one way it is senseless to call a sense datum or other private object red, and when I mean 'red' another way I can intelligibly say that a sense datum or private object is red? Wittgenstein suggests this escape and then attacks it.

> What am I to say about the word "red"?—that it means something 'confronting us all' and that everyone should really have another word, besides this one, to mean his *own* sensation of red? Or is it like this: the word "red" means something known to everyone; and in addition, for each person, it means something known only to him? (Or perhaps rather: it *refers* to something known only to him) [*P.I.*, 273].

> Of course, saying that the word "red" "refers to" instead of "means" something private does not help us in the least to grasp its function; but it is the more psychologically apt expression for a particular experience in doing philosophy. It is as if when I uttered the word I cast a sidelong glance at the private sensation, as it were

in order to say to myself: I know all right what I mean by it [*P.I.*, 274].

If 'green' is a word I use to mean or name my sense datum, it is a word in my private language; it follows at once that I cannot communicate anything to others when I hypothesize that my sense data might be green. Moreover, what do I mean, even to myself, by saying that I might get a *green* sense-datum when I see things that I and everybody else call red? If the word 'green' is doing its old job here, we are back to the first alternative in which 'green' is a word in the public language, and then it cannot be attributed to a sense datum. The 'green' which names a sense datum is not the 'green' which is an English color word. Wittgenstein says, when speaking of the sense datum, "If we say 'he'll tell us what he saw', it is as though he would make use of language which we had never taught him" (*Notes*, p. 279). It would be better to call my sense datum '*S*', for to call it 'green' sets up the pretense that I mean by 'green' something like what I ordinarily mean. This is no more than pretense because we have already established that the quality of my sense datum has absolutely nothing to do with what 'green' means in English.

In summary, the dilemmatic argument is that 'green', in my hypothesis "perhaps I have green sense-data when I see the things I and everybody else call 'red'," is either a public-language word or a private-language word. If the former, I cannot intelligibly say my sense data are green; and if the latter, then I cannot mean anything familiar by 'green', and I cannot communicate what I mean to others.

On How One Can See Red Things Green. However, we have not completely disposed of the hypothesis that a person might see red things green and green things red, for one need not mean that he has green sense-data when he sees the things that everybody calls red and vice versa. One might concede that the hypothesis cannot be about private objects and nevertheless insist that the hypothesis is intelligible. In this form it remains a difficult problem for Wittgenstein because he concedes that *sometimes*, in special circumstances, it makes good sense to say that a man sees red things green and green

things red; and he nevertheless maintains that it is unintelligible to
say that he *always* sees red things green and green things red:

> Now I want to draw attention to one particular difficulty about the
> use of the 'sense datum'. We said that there were cases in which we
> should say that the person sees green what I see red. Now the ques-
> tion suggests itself: if this can be so at all, why should it not be al-
> ways the case? It seems, if once we have admitted that it can happen
> under peculiar circumstances, that it may always happen. But then
> it is clear that the very idea of seeing red loses its use if we can never
> know if the other does not see something utterly different. So what
> are we to do: Are we to say that this can only happen in a limited
> number of cases? This is a very serious situation.—We introduced the
> expression that A sees something else than B and we mustn't forget
> that this had use only under the circumstances under which we intro-
> duced it [*Notes*, p. 316].

The problem is to be able to explain what is intelligible about such
hypotheses without bringing back private objects.

If we know that someone *means* by 'red' and 'green' what his language group means, because he in general calls the same things red
and green that they do, and then on some particular occasion or at
some particular time he *says* that he sees red things green, or simply
begins calling red things green, we can intelligibly say that he sees
green what we see red. We can say, on the basis of what a man says
and does on a particular occasion and against the background that
he in general calls the same things red and green that we do, that on
that occasion he sees red things green. His verbal behavior deviates
from the larger run of behavior which established that he means by
the words what we mean. But just because it is logically impossible
that all of his verbal behavior should be deviant, within his own
ideolect, it is logically impossible that anyone should have *this* kind
of basis for saying that a man *always* saw red things green and green
things red. On this basis red/green reversal could possibly occur
sometimes, but not always.

It is unintelligible to say that a man *always* sees red things green
and green things red, for I cannot mean that his verbal behavior is
deviant, for by hypothesis it is not; and I cannot mean that he has
green sense-data, by the preceding argument. Recourse to his sense
data being different colors is our only option when we try to under-

stand the hypothesis that a man always sees red things green and green things red. The case where he sometimes sees red things green and green things red requires no recourse to sense data because we have verbal behavioral criteria: he says he sees red things green, and he calls red things green, as a deviation from his normal reports.

One point of this discussion of red and green is to show that Wittgenstein's attack on phenomenalism refutes a certain kind of skepticism. It refutes the skepticism which maintains that we can never know whether or not we mean the same by our words as others do. This is very different from the kind of skepticism to be considered next, which maintains that while we might mean the same by our words, we might all be mistaken all of the time in the judgments we use those words to make. But the central point of the preceding arguments is that what refutes phenomenalism is not the impossibility of a private language (though that would do it, too) but the fact that phenomenalism requires a private language. For even if there could be a private language it would be useless; one could not "construct the external world" with the aid of it. And sense data and "the given" can be talked about only in a private language. For example, suppose we took what C. I. Lewis called "terminating judgments" to be about private objects; what Wittgenstein's anti-phenomenalist argument says is that they cannot be part of any meaning analysis of physical object statements or "nonterminating judgments," that Lewis is wrong because they can have nothing to do with what we mean by judgments about tables. This can be maintained even if one has to admit (which Wittgenstein, of course, does not admit) that terminating judgments, by themselves, were meaningful to those who affirm them.

III

If language is to be a means of communication there must be agreement not only in definitions but also (queer as this may sound) in judgments . . . —P.I., 242.

Could We Be Always Wrong about Colors? It is Wittgenstein's view that a child learns the word 'red' by being trained to identify examples, and that this involves being told when he is correct and being corrected when he is mistaken (or, perhaps, appropriately rewarded and punished). A consequence of this is the further view that the members of a language group mean the same thing by 'red' only if they agree substantially in their judgments of what is red. At the very least the child's utterances of 'red' when confronted with examples must be in agreement with his teacher's color judgments about those examples, or else he does not succeed in learning the word. Perhaps, at this early stage, we should hesitate to say the child is *judging;* but he is very soon said to judge, and if later his judgments differ wildly and systematically from those judgments or proto-judgments he made when learning the word, he will have lost the meaning of the word. Now, might *all* of the color judgments people make be false? In particular, is it possible that all of the examples by means of which a whole language group learns the meaning of 'red' are *not* red, but some other color? The kind of skepticism I am considering now has nothing to do with sense data. It is not the skepticism which doubts whether there is a material world that corresponds to our sense experiences, nor is it the skepticism which denies that we can ever know whether two people see the same color when they look at something. I am concerned with the kind of skepticism which asserts the possibility that no one ever judges correctly that a material object is red, and by extension, the possibility that no one ever judges correctly regarding any other properties of material objects.

Consider first the case of a man who is taught the word 'red' by means of examples, none of which are red. If they were all green he would routinely call green things red and, therefore, would not have learned the meaning of 'red'. Or, he might possibly be said to learn *a* meaning of 'red', but not *the* meaning. On the other hand, we might never let a person see red things and teach him the meaning of 'red' by having him identify white things through red-lensed spectacles, or when illuminated in red light. In this case he does know the meaning of 'red' if we accept the hypothesis that were he to see red things he would identify them correctly. "But someone might be taught colour-vocabulary by being made to look at white objects through coloured spectacles. What I teach him however, must be a *capacity*. So he *can* now bring something red at an order; or arrange objects according to colour. But then what is something red?"[8] So while he knows what 'red' means, *all* his judgments are mistaken: everything he calls red merely looks red but is not red. Here then is the possibility, contrived though it is, of someone being fooled all of the time about a color.

Second, it is obvious that, for each and every person, at least some of the color judgments he makes in the course of learning the meaning of 'red' could be mistaken judgments. It is possible that all of the people could be fooled some of the time about a color.

Could everybody be fooled all of the time in their judgments of what is red? For example, could *everybody* be permanently in the situation of the person in the first case, such that all of the things anybody said were red were not red but merely looked red? I think that this is a conceptual impossibility. If *all* English users were taught 'red' (and, perhaps, all German users taught *'rot'*, etc.) by examples all of which were white things illuminated in red light, and no one ever saw what we now call red things, then it would be a contingent truth that red things were white things illuminated in red light. In this possible world, things which merely *looked* red (a distinction we would retain) would be things discoverable by means just like our present means to be specially illuminated. Of course the example is bizarre, since we must employ the skills of Descartes's evil demon to insure that in this possible world red things (as distinct from things which merely look red) continue to look red, as we believe they do, under a wide variety of conditions. That is, the observable distinction between lighting conditions which justify 'red' and those which justify 'looks red' would remain, but with a different factual basis: it would be the distinction between trick lighting conditions which we can discover in the usual way and those we can discover only if the evil demon tips his hand.

The defense of this anti-skeptical claim lies in showing that it is conceptually impossible that all of the examples by means of which we all learn the meaning of 'red' should be false examples, and that therefore it is a conceptual truth that many of our color judgments are actually true. In learning the word 'red' we are taught that *this* and *that* are red. It makes sense for me to say that a learning example is a false example only if I believe it deviates from the general

[8] Ludwig Wittgenstein, *Zettel* (Berkeley and Los Angeles: University of California Press, 1967), 421.

run of such examples. It is the language game played with the teaching examples that defines, in a sense of 'define' yet to be explained, what it is to be red. To say something is red is to say it is like the general run of teaching examples, regardless of what features we might later discover or hypothesize the teaching examples to possess. Moreover, it makes sense to say that all of *my* learning examples merely looked red only if I have in mind a verifiable difference between these examples and the learning examples of the rest of my language group. Wittgenstein writes:

> "What sometimes happens might always happen."—What kind of proposition is that? It is like the following: If "F(a)" makes sense "(x).F(x)" makes sense.
>
> "If it is possible for someone to make a false move in some game, then it might be possible for everybody to make nothing but false moves in every game."—Thus we are under a temptation to misunderstand the logic of our expressions here, to give an incorrect account of the use of our words [*P.I.*, 345].

How are we to understand the hypothesis that all of the teaching examples were really not red but some other color? Children know the word 'red' when they can identify examples correctly. What does 'correctly' mean if they are all always wrong, if none of the examples are red? If they never make correct identifications, then they have failed to learn the word; and if 'correct' means that their identifications agree with those of their parents, then what good reasons have we to say that *this* standard of correctness is insufficient for concluding that what they in general identify as red is red?

There is, I think, nothing intrinsically absurd in saying that red things are white things illuminated in red light. If we discover that this object which looks red is really white and illuminated in red light, we abandon our claim that it is red. If we should discover that *all* the things we are (and were) taught to call red are white and illuminated in red light, we would discover a remarkable *fact* about the physical nature of red things, a fact that logically is on all fours with the fact that red things can appear to have different colors under different lighting conditions, and with the discovery that red things absorb all light frequencies except the red ones.

What I conclude regarding a language group's color judgments is that, whereas Descartes's evil demon could deceive some of the people all of the time, and all of the people some of the time, it is not conceptually possible that it should deceive all of the people all of the time.

Some philosophers believe that the notions of meaning and truth are not so intimately related; they believe that people can learn the *meaning* of a word and use it to make assertions, and that all of those assertions can be *false*. This is not always so; it is true of some words and false of others. The examples we all called red when we were being taught the word must, in general, actually have been red. To suppose they were not red is to suppose that we do not learn the word 'red' through examples but by description (which is how we learn the word 'unicorn').

I am not saying that there are standard or paradigm cases, judgments which we can know with absolute certainty to be true. Although it may be a conceptual truth that not everyone can be mistaken all of the time, it is never a conceptual truth that on *this* occasion I am not mistaken in my judgment that something is red. Even if I should know that *I* could not always be wrong, it does not follow that I could know *when* I was not wrong.

It is because of this possibility that the notion of 'criterion' cannot plausibly be explained in terms of paradigm cases, that is, cases about which one cannot be mistaken. An adequate explanation of criteria must allow the possibility that in any particular case the criterion of *x* can be present and *x* not be the case. The explanation of criteria that I shall propose in Part IV depends instead upon the claim that, *in general,* when the criterion of *x* is present, *x* is the case.

Can it be conceptually possible that any particular judgment that something is red be mistaken and, at the same time, *not* conceptually possible that each and every judgment that something is red be mistaken? I do not see why not. Suppose, for simplification's sake, that the collection of everyone's sincere judgments of the form 'the *x* is red' has just three members, *A*, *B*, and *C*, and let '$-A$' abbreviate 'the assertion "the so-and-so is red" is false'. I wish to affirm

$$(1) \quad \lozenge -A \cdot \lozenge -B \cdot \lozenge -C$$

and

$$(2) - \Diamond (-A \cdot -B \cdot -C).$$

This says that any person's color judgment, whatever the circumstances and evidence, might be false, and also that it is necessary that some of our color judgments be true. My reason for asserting (2) is not, of course, that $-A \cdot -B \cdot -C$ are jointly incompatible, but is the preceding argument about the role of teaching examples. (2) is true on epistemic, not logical, grounds; but even so, (1) and (2) are logically compatible.

On the other hand, the argument does not merely conclude that *some* of our color judgments are actually correct; that trivial conclusion would follow directly from the premise that people sometimes make contradictory color judgments. By saying that our color judgments are generally correct, I mean that most of them are. There is a difficulty here, since the learning cases form a small proportion of the total number of color judgments someone makes during a lifetime, and one might maintain that the judgments one makes after the word is learned could all be mistaken. At the least, however, the judgments an adult makes while teaching children must also be correct in general. Wittgenstein's view is, I believe, that something like the learning process, or reinforcement of it, continues throughout one's life, and that it is equally absurd to suppose that the whole adult population makes only false color judgments.

One of Wittgenstein's themes is that, when a child is learning language, the concepts of doubt and knowledge play no role. Doubting and knowing are language games that are learned at a later stage, after one has learned things like "that's red" and "that is a lovely tree."

"The child, I should like to say, learns to react in such-and-such a way; and in so reacting it doesn't so far know anything. Knowing only begins at a later level."[9] The concept of knowledge is tied to the concepts of reasons and doubt, and of seeking and weighing evidence, and has no role at the earliest stage of learning language. Nonetheless, we cannot always be wrong, for the reasons already given, about the cases by means of which we learned 'red'. The fol-

[9] Ludwig Wittgenstein, *On Certainty* (New York and Evanston: Harper and Row, 1969), 538.

lowing passage does not show Wittgenstein to be repudiating or doubting the line of argument I have presented, but rather, making a point about when the concept of knowing enters our language game:

> So one must know that the objects whose names one teaches a child by an ostensive definition exist.—Why must one know they do? Isn't it enough that experience doesn't later show the opposite?
>
> For why should the language game rest on some kind of knowledge? [*On Certainty*, 477].

Could We Be Always Wrong about Cats? I think that arguments against skepticism similar to the preceding one will work for many property terms. The question arises whether such arguments work regarding assertions about things such as cats and chairs. There is some reason to believe that Wittgenstein employs such arguments and I shall sketch, in an incomplete and inconclusive way, how they might go. Then I shall show how the availability of such arguments contributes to an explanation of Wittgenstein's term 'criteria'.

There are several possible ways of doubting that there ever existed any cats, some of which are (1) doubting one's memory, (2) doubting that there exist physical objects, including cats, in addition to sense data, (3) hypothesizing that cats are always illusions, and (4) hypothesizing that we are tricked, that all the things we call cats are really something else. I shall ignore (1), assume Wittgenstein to have already answered (2), touch briefly on (3), and consider an answer to (4) along lines already suggested. There is a great difference between saying that all cats are illusions and saying that cats (and everything else) are nothing more than sets of sense data. The former claim is an empirical claim and is incompatible with the existence of cats, while the latter is not an empirical claim, and (given some epistemological premises) is compatible with the existence of cats.

It is unintelligible to say that *everything* is an illusion (even if some things are illusions), whereas it is not senseless to say that everything is sense data (if some things can be sense data). It is unintelligible to say that all objects of perception are illusions because it is part of the grammar of 'illusion' that illusions differ from typical objects of perception in certain ways. It is unintelligible for the same kind of reason that it is unintelligible to say that everyone is always selfish (in spite of apparent generosity) or that everyone is really naked (because he is naked underneath his clothes). That is, it would involve altering and extending the concept so as to apply to everything, while retaining some minimal analogy with the original concept, and then going on to use the concept as though it were unaltered.

It does not follow, however, that it is unintelligible to say that all cats are illusions, because we could maintain this while maintaining that other classes of things were not illusions. The anti-skeptical argument which I presented regarding colors, and the one I shall present regarding cats, are not "excluded opposites" arguments, although excluded-opposites arguments are also to be found in Wittgenstein's writings. Perhaps an appropriate name for the argument I am presenting is "conventionalist argument." I shall not attempt to apply the argument to illusion-skepticism; I shall instead confine myself to the fourth kind of skepticism, i.e., to the view that there might be no cats on the ground that all the things we ever called cats might be, say, ingenious machines or thin shells with nothing inside. In other words, this form of skepticism affirms that all the things we call cats might lack some essential property of cats.

The argument is that it is not conceptually possible that all the judgments everybody has made which assert or presuppose that such and such a thing is a cat should be false judgments or contain false presuppositions, on the ground that we succeed in learning (and teaching) the meaning of 'cat' primarily by means of correctly identifying examples. The judgments about the examples are generally correct because they agree with one another, not because they individually agree with some independent standard. This is a bald, and possibly inaccurate, way of putting the matter; but I think it gets at the basis of both the present argument and the very similar one about red. Assuming that my interpretation is not far off the mark, I think that it is in arguments of this sort that the conventionalist strand of Wittgenstein's thought is most apparent.

If we compare how we learn the words 'witch' and 'cat', the procedures appear to be similar; this creates difficulties for the argument. Ostensive teaching plays a role in each case—we teach (or taught) "there is the witch daddy mentioned" and "look at the pretty cat"—but it appears that each word is also taught partly by description: cats are animals with backbones, and witches have made arrangements with the devil. Moreover, both words *could* be taught entirely by description—from pictures and explanations—although 'cat' is not and 'witch' was not taught only in this way. Now there are some important differences between the two cases, but I am not absolutely certain these differences suffice to rescue the argument.

The crucial question is whether or not there is a conceivable discovery we could make about the things we call (and called) cats which would justify concluding that *none* of those things were cats. There certainly is such a possible discovery in the case of witches— namely, that no one has made an arrangement with the devil. It is certainly possible for everyone to imagine evidence which would establish that, on a particular occasion, something he took to be a cat and which looked just like a cat was, in fact, a fake cat. It is also possible to imagine evidence that would justify the claim that a particular person was deceived all his life about cats. For example, in each of these cases one could conceive of discovering that all of the things in question were empty shells or machines, and *for that reason* not cats. But what of the *equally conceivable* hypothesis that all of the things ever called cats by anyone were empty shells or machines? I think that in this case the hypothesis ceases to count as evidence that the things in question were not cats. In other words, the absence of internal organs counts as conclusive evidence that something is not a cat when it is true of only some things we call cats, but does not count at all as evidence that something is not a cat when it is true of all the things we call cats. However, I am not supposing that what we call cat behavior changes—it is, after all, easy enough to imagine that all cats should disappear and be re- placed by something else. On my hypothesis that they are and al- ways were empty shells, they continue to purr, scream when stepped on, and have kittens. Moreover, it may be that the hypothe- sis itself is inconceivable, given the collective experience of the internal properties of cats possessed by veterinarians, anatomists, and others.

The argument is that what we all learn about cats through os- tensive learning is *sufficient* to insure—i.e., render conceptually necessary—that the things we call cats are, in general, cats, and that what we all learn about cats by description can be a *necessary* condition for something to be a cat only in particular cases. If some property of cats that we learned by description subsequently turned out to be false for all cats, it would thereby cease to be a necessary condition for something to be a cat; we would have learned a new contingent proposition about cats. Can we say the same thing about witches? We are (or were) taught ostensively that this or that eccentric crone is a witch, and we are taught by explanation that she has made arrangements with the devil. Does what we learn by ostensive learning render it conceptually necessary that the beings we call witches be, in general, witches; that having made an arrangement with the devil be a necessary condition for someone to be a witch only in particular cases; and that if no one ever made an arrangement with the devil, then the arrangement would thereby cease to be a necessary condition for being a witch? This depends upon the relative importance of the features in question. The concept of a cat is more closely tied to the observed behavior of cats than is the concept of a witch to the observed behavior of witches. People *could* have said, "*Mirabile dictu,* witches have never dealt with the devil" instead of saying, "There are no witches," but we do not, primarily because muttering-crone behavior is a much less interesting and distinctive category of behavior than is cat-like behavior.

IV

When talking about criteria, we must remember that Wittgenstein said that criteria form a family and that if what I am going to suggest accurately picks out one kind of use of the term 'criteria', it surely is not the only kind of use he intends. In *The Blue Book* Wittgenstein says,

> It is part of the grammar of the word "chair" that *this* is what we call "to sit on a chair," and it is part of the grammar of the word "meaning" that *this* is what we call "explanation of a meaning"; in the same way to explain my criterion for another person's having toothache is to give a grammatical explanation about the word "toothache" and,

in this sense, an explanation concerning the meaning of the word "toothache."[10]

First I shall make three interpretative claims about the terminology in the above quotation. (1) The "this" and "this" are *criteria* for someone's sitting on a chair and for another person's having toothache. They are publicly observable states of affairs or events and are capable of being described without mentioning the things of which they are criteria; for example, the "this" which is a criterion of another person's having toothache is described by Wittgenstein in his next paragraph as "holding one's cheek." (2) By saying that some "this" is what we *call* "to sit on a chair" or "explanation of a meaning" or "another person's having toothache," Wittgenstein means that instances like that are the kinds of instances by means of which children were taught to use sentences like 'He's sitting on a chair', 'He's explaining what . . . means', and 'He has a toothache'. That is, one pointed to *this* and trained the child to call it "sitting on a chair," etc. So these instances which are criteria are of the same kind as the instances which were employed in the ostensive teaching of sentences like 'He's sitting on a chair'. (3) By saying that it is part of the *grammar* of 'chair' that this is what we call "to sit on a chair," Wittgenstein means that the criteria have something to do with the meaning of 'chair'. I shall say a little more about grammar shortly; exactly what it is that grammar has to do with meaning will not be intelligible unless we set aside traditional views about meaning and meaning relationships.

If we take the criterial cases to be just like the cases children identified during the course of learning the meanings of 'cat', 'chair', 'toothache', and 'rain', we are able to say two things about criteria which philosophers have wanted to say but have had difficulty rendering mutually consistent. (1) The manifestation of the criteria of X is evidence that X is the case, and not merely in the way in which a symptom is evidence that X is the case. It is a conceptual truth that, in general, if the criteria of X are made manifest, then X is the case. The defense of (1) is the argument of the preceding

[10] Ludwig Wittgenstein, *The Blue and Brown Books* (Oxford: Basil Blackwell, 1968), p. 24.

section. (2) It is never a contradiction or conceptual absurdity to assert, of a particular case, that the criteria are present and X is not the case. This is because there is no meaning relation between the concept of the criterion and the concept of X of a sort which suffices to insure that the case before me is not one of that minority of cases in which I *could* be deceived by my senses or by the evil demon.

So there is no relation of entailment or quasi-entailment between the statement of a criterion and the statement that X is the case, nor is there any particular case in which the criteria, together with certain circumstances, constitute absolutely conclusive evidence that X is the case. Moreover, it is not sufficient to say that criteria necessarily are evidence for X being the case. This view appears to allow the possibility that criteria, while always evidence, are never adequate evidence, and hence the possibility that X is never the case.

On the interpretation of criteria being proposed, there are two levels on which we can state a relation between the criteria and X, the first of which we have just discussed. Each involves a conceptual relation, but of a different sort:

(1) It is a conceptual truth that, *in general*, if the criteria of X are present, then X is the case.

(2) *Without exception*, the concept of the criterion is related to the concept of X.

(2) is harder to explain. The criterial cases are the learning cases and others which resemble them; they are the cases through which one learns the meaning of 'cat', 'chair', 'toothache', or 'rain', and in just this respect the concept of a kind of criterial case is related to the concept that one learned by means of it. But this at best shows that there *is* a meaning relation between the criteria and X, and does not elucidate the nature of the relation.

In *The Blue Book* Wittgenstein speaks of "the criterion, or what we call the defining criterion of angina," and of "the phenomenon which is our defining criterion" (p. 25). The use of the word 'definition' leads us to seek an analytic relation and hence an entailment between sentences about the criterion and sentences about X. But Wittgenstein has abandoned the notion of analyticity, employing the different and broader notion of grammar in its place; in fact he takes the very idea of an analytic *truth* to be nonsense (I shall not defend this interpretation here). And he uses the word 'definition' loosely, or differently; at least it is clear that he does not take definitions to be what generate analytic truths and entailments. So while he says "to explain my criterion" of *X* "is to give . . . an explanation concerning the meaning" of *X* (p. 24), and we should take him at his word, *his* use of 'definition' and *our* notion of 'analytic' will not illuminate the meaning relation between the concept of the criterion of *X* and the concept of *X*.

In the *Philosophical Investigations* Wittgenstein says:

> The fluctuation in grammar between criteria and symptons makes it look as if there were nothing at all but symptoms. We say, for example: "Experience teaches that there is rain when the barometer falls, but it also teaches that there is rain when we have certain sensations of wet and cold, or such-and-such visual impressions." In defense of this one says that these sense-impressions can deceive us. But here one fails to reflect that the fact that the false appearance is precisely one of rain is found on a definition [354].

> The point here is not that our sense-impressions can lie, but that we understand their language. (And this language like any other is founded on convention) [355].

The "certain sensations of wet and cold" and "such-and-such visual impressions" are the criteria of rain—the "this" of *The Blue Book*—and he makes it clear enough that they can deceive us, while *at the same time* claiming that their being a false appearance of *rain* is founded on a definition. He means, I am maintaining, that the concepts of these criteria—the ideas of those kinds of sensations and those kinds of visual impressions—are related to the concept of rain, whereas the concept of the symptom—here, the falling barometer—is not. And this is so because we learned the meaning of 'rain' by being told that it is raining on the occasion of just those sorts of sensations and visual impressions. Because of this, however, it is not conceptually possible that these sensations of wet and cold, and these particular kinds of visual impressions, *never* be accompanied by rain, whereas it is perfectly possible that a falling barometer never be accompanied by rain. If the evil demon has arranged that all our noncriterial beliefs about rain are always false, we would have many factually false beliefs about rain; but there would still be rain.

The obvious objections to this, based on the absence of logical entailments between criterial statements and rain statements, lose their point when we remember that Wittgenstein has radically different views about meaning and related concepts. The jobs done in traditional philosophy by the concept of "meaning" and the auxiliary notions of "analytic," "synthetic," "definition," and "entailment" are accomplished, in Wittgenstein's system of thought, by the central notion of "grammar," with "rule," "use," "meaning," "criteria," and "nonsense" as frequently used satellite notions. Thus: a grammatical explanation of a word is an explanation concerning the meaning of the word (*The Blue Book*, p. 24); "now a definition often clears up the *grammar* of a word" (p. 26); sentences we are inclined to call conceptual or analytic truths are grammatical statements or disguised grammatical statements (p. 30); the propositions '*A* has a gold tooth' and '*A* has a toothache' differ in their grammar (p. 53); "*essence* is expressed by grammar" (*Philosophical Investigations* 371); "grammar tells what kind of object anything is" (373); "asking whether and how a proposition can be verified is only a particular way of asking, 'How d'you mean?' The answer is a contribution to the grammar of the proposition" (353); and Wittgenstein speaks of an expression "whose form makes it look like an empirical proposition, but which is really a grammatical one" (251).

Explaining the grammar of a word is, roughly, explaining how it works. I make no attempt to give an adequate explanation of what Wittgenstein means by grammar (the grammar of 'grammar'); I want instead to indicate the centrality of the idea. So when I say that the concept of the criterion is related to the concept of X, I mean only what Wittgenstein says, that to explain the criterion of X is to explain part of the grammar of X. And given that he is talking about grammar, there is no basis for grinding entailments or analytic truths out of this conceptual relationship.[11]

[11] I am grateful to James Cornman, Peter Machamer, and Wade Robison for helpful comments on an earlier version of this paper.

19

*Tractarian Reflections on Saying and Showing**

DENNIS W. STAMPE

"I⹁ belongs to the essence of a proposition that it should be able to communicate a *new* sense to us" (*Tractatus* 4.027).[1] This should perhaps properly mean that a proposition is essentially capable of communicating something that has not been communicated before. But what Wittgenstein evidently meant was that a proposition is essentially capable of communicating something to us, even though that whereby it is communicated (the propositional sign) is new. So understood, there are two choices. We may take it to be a thesis about what kind of thing is capable of having sense in accordance with 3.3, "Only propositions have sense." This is a thesis refuted by the case of gestures, supposing that having meaning is sufficient for (or the same thing as) having sense; for gestures are typically *not* such as to be intelligible on first seeing, or hearing, and yet gestures do have meaning.[2] Alternatively, we may take 4.027 as part of a complex

* I am indebted to Louis Goble for valuable criticism. I wish also to thank the Institute for Research in the Humanities of the University of Wisconsin, where this work was done, and my colleagues there; particularly the late Julius R. Weinberg. Without his generous help these reflections would play far more uncertainly upon the actual *Tractatus*—and this paper would be a still less worthy object to offer, as I now do, in tribute to his memory.

[1] Ludwig Wittgenstein, *Tractatus logico-philsophicus*, trans. D. F. Pears and B. F. McGuinness (London: Routledge & Kegan Paul, 1961).

[2] We are told that when this fact about gestures was successfully impressed upon Wittgenstein by Sraffa, "it produced in him the feeling that there was an absurdity in the insistence that a proposition and what it describes must have

definition which excludes gestures from among the things to be called *Saetze*. The theory developed to account for the intelligibility of novel "signs" will then be understood, not as a general theory of meaningful signs, but as a theory of sentences, or signs of like capacity and character.

This decision will at least temporarily defend 3.141: "A proposition is articulated." For such gestures as would provide counterexamples to 4.027 are not articulated and do not exhibit the logical segmentation Wittgenstein refers to. A proposition is said to be "articulated" not just in being segmented, but also in setting forth its sense in an articulated way. This comes out in Wittgenstein's speaking of (what would otherwise make no sense) a proposition's being "completely articulated": "Everything that its sense has in common with another sense must be contained separately in the proposition" (*Notebooks*, p. 63e). Ignoring the requirement for *complete* articulation, it seems clear from this that a proposition must have segments which are such that they might recur as segments of another proposition, by virtue of which occurrence the sense of the latter proposition would have something in common with that of the former. Gestures of the kind to be excluded do not have such elements. There is, for instance, no submovement in the gesture of shrugging one's shoulders (expressing indifference) which does or might recur in other gestures, by virtue of which something to do with indifference is expressed (cf. 3.31). There is no submovement or segment of a right-turn hand signal, which means that

---

the same 'form'," or, in a variant of the story that every proposition must have a grammar (Norman Malcolm, *Ludwig Wittgenstein: A Memoir* [London: Oxford University Press, 1958], p. 68). But in 1914 essentially the same point had been dismissed, evidently as irrelevant to the intent of his theory. In the *Notebooks*, he asked (4.10.14), "How is it possible for 'kilo' in a code to mean: 'I'm all right'? Here surely *a simple sign* does assert something and is used to give information to others." The following day (5.10.14) he wrote: "Logic is interested only in reality. And thus in sentences ONLY in so far as they are *pictures* of reality. But how CAN a SINGLE *word* be true or false? At any rate it cannot express the *thought* that agrees or does not agree with reality. That *must* be articulated. A single word cannot be true or false in *this* sense: it cannot agree with reality, or the opposite" (Ludwig Wittgenstein, *Notebooks, 1914–1916*, ed. G. H. von Wright and G. E. M. Anscombe, trans. G. E. M. Anscombe [Oxford: Basil Blackwell, 1961]).

I am going to *turn to* (as opposed to away from) the right, nor one that means that *I* am going to turn right. Gestures tend in this way to be semantically ossified.

Is it necessary at least that those propositions which are such as to be intelligible, even though novel, should exhibit articulation or composite structure? Evidently not. We could devise a code which employed only simple signs which were nonetheless intelligible even when novel. For example, the letters of the alphabet, taken serially, might be correlated with a set of things standing in some fixed serial relation—say, the cities of 100,000 or more situated on U.S. Route 40 going east to west—and certain conventions set up, according to which a letter written in upper case will mean that the object correlated with it is larger than the object preceding it in the series, and written in lower case will mean that the city immediately following its object correlate is more highly industrialized than the three cities preceding the object correlate, and so on. (Call this "Code 40.") We should then be in a position to understand the novel but noncomposite or unarticulated sign 'M'. Its interpretation would require a map and some calculation but no new explanation (cf. 4.026). Of course, here the style in which the letters are written might be counted as if they were elements of the sign. At least there will be something in common between the sense of 'M' and the sense of 'P', which is perhaps "contained separately" in the sign, in their common upper-case "style" as distinguished from what makes them tokens of distinct letters. But we can devise ways to eliminate any semantically significant perceptible differences between signs meaning different things by conventions which, say, make what is meant a matter of the time of day or minute of the hour at which the utterance is produced—e.g., a letter will mean one thing before noon, and another thing between five and six P.M.

In imagining such counterexamples to the thesis that semantically significant articulation is essential to a sign's being intelligible though novel, we imagine devices the expressive power and utility of which are drastically curtailed, limited in the range of things that can be said and by the contingency of what can be said upon aspects and vicissitudes of the objective situation. This must suggest that the hypothesis that intelligible novel signs must be articulated might well be correct if it is limited to propositional signs belonging to languages of utility and expressive power comparable to that of any natural language.[3]

Without such restriction, the claims of the 3.14's come into question, e.g., 3.14: "What constitutes a propositional sign is that in it its elements . . . stand in a determinate relation to one another." It is evidently not necessary that a significant sign, even one that is intelligible though novel, should have even so minimal a syntactic structure as 3.14 is meant to require. Regarding 3.142, "Only facts can express a sense, a set of names cannot,"[4] if we say (as we should in any case) not that "a propositional sign is a fact" (3.143), but that a propositional sign says what it says by virtue of certain facts about it, then this is apparently true. But it is true of any sign whatever, including gestures, if we include facts about the convention or intention underlying the production of the sign. What is meant, however, is that the sensible sign says what it says by virtue of certain *perceptible* facts about it. This can be generally true only of some favored kind of sign.

The Tractarian search for the essence of the proposition can hardly be launched without restricting the search to some rather tightly circumscribed subspecies of meaningful sign. But it is not obvious that the subspecies wanted may not prove to be a reasonably "natural kind," and not merely a contrivance carved out for the theory to fit. Within that class of signs, if not exhausting it, will be included the *sentences* of natural languages; there is no reason to think that there is no interesting rationale to our classifying certain things together as sentences which might serve as the basis for the appropriate classification of signs.[5]

[3] In another connection, Wittgenstein employs the premise that it cannot be a condition of our knowing what a proposition means that we should know whether it is true. (That would, of course, make communication impossible.) In the *Notes Dictated to Moore* this becomes, "The question whether a proposition has sense (*Sinn*) can never depend on the *truth* of another proposition about a constituent of the first" (p. 116, Appendix II of *Notebooks;* cf. also *Tractatus* 2.0211). That formulation is probably too strong. But the tendency in language to minimize such dependency is there, crucial to its expressive capacity.

[4] It is, of course, true that neither gestures nor "Code 40" signs function as names. The existence of a correlation between a sign and an object establishes neither that the sign is being used as a name for, nor that it stands for, an object, nor that without further ado it can be used in such ways.

[5] Compare the analogous situation regarding what is to be counted as a kind

I am inclined to think that there *is* an intuitively distinct sort of sign, central to our concerns, against which a theory with the ambitions of the *Tractatus* theory is properly measured. To delineate the concept of such signs, the intuitive ideas we should have to capture would include the related ideas of a sign which *sets forth* (cf. 2.15) its meaning; of a sign with which we may "make ourselves understood" (4.026) by its making *itself* understood, by its making its meaning *explicit;* thus a sign by means of which one can not merely convey but *say outright* or *make explicit* what one means; and perhaps also the idea of a sign which is an expression of a thought, where it is not sufficient for a thought being given *expression* that one should be able to infer (even in accordance with communicative intentions or conventions) from the sign to the thought.[6]

Wittgenstein speaks of a proposition as *saying* that such-and-such is the case. This I shall take to mean that propositional signs are signs in the uttering of which a person does not merely *mean* but *says* that such-and-such is the case, where the latter involves his making his meaning fully explicit. I shall be arguing that certain facts about the relation of the concepts of saying, showing, and implying make a picture theory of saying unacceptable. But on the other hand, by attending to those same conceptual facts, at least one important thesis of the *Tractatus* can be offered a defense—a thesis crucial to the idea that there is such a thing as what is essential to a sentence which says a given thing, thus some common structure to any sentence which says that thing.

---

of "experience" for the purposes of Kant's deduction, and P. F. Strawson's suggestion that Kant's "thesis of the necessary unity of consciousness" (sc. that it should be such as to permit self-consciousness) "may reasonably be seen as a standard-setting definition of what is to count as 'experience'" (P. F. Strawson, *The Bounds of Sense* [London: Barnes & Noble 1966], p. 25). It is equally permissible for Wittgenstein's deduction, if you will, of the possibility of significant discourse to proceed from a "standard-setting definition" of what shall count as a "proposition." (The obscure and difficult condition which stands over this device is, crudely, that the phenomenon as initially thus defined must occupy such a position that a world which precluded its possibility would somehow fall beyond the pale of conception or expression.)

[6] Wittgenstein's conception of a *Satz* is that of "a thought made manifest," in a phrase of Shwayder's—cf. *Tractatus* 3.1. But I shall not be concerned in what follows with this feature of the conception, but rather with the notion of what is said.

Requiring that propositional signs should be those in the utterance of which one says something, will, in the nonarbitrary way required, exclude gestures from that class of sign. One who shrugs his shoulders, meaning thereby that he is indifferent to the matter in question (that being what that gesture ordinarily or standardly means), does not˙*say* that he is indifferent; nor would he have said anything if the gesture were vocal, like the hiss that means that one disapproves. One may convey information and express thoughts by the means of gestures, but there is still a sense in which he does not make his thought or what he means fully explicit. He does not *say* what he means or thinks. Approaching the matter from the other side, it appears that what a person says, as opposed to what he means, implies, or otherwise conveys, largely has to do with just what words he actually utters, and their syntactic relationships. It is important here that what one says can be reported in direct speech by simply reproducing the same sounds he made. (This is not to say that strictly it can *only* be so reported.) What a person implies, or means, or conveys, on the other hand is not properly reportable in direct speech, or by quotation. Related to this is the fact that the notion of what is said or made explicit is understood in contrast with the notion of what is implied or left implicit: what is implied is implied by, or implicit in, what is said. It is not set forth plainly to the senses.

In some ways it is as if the picture theory had been designed to reflect these aspects of the concept of what is said. There is in particular, answering to the condition of explicitness, the notion of a proposition as *setting forth* its meaning in an articulated manner, and the distinctive thesis that the proposition *shows* its sense in doing so (4.022). A propositional sign must consist of elements which are "expressions" (3.31); it says what it says owing to the fact that these expressions stand in significant relationships to one another. Such relationships are *shown* in the sentence, presented to the senses in such a way that the fluent hearer grasps them without inference or calculation. (Since this is essential to the proposition saying what it says, there is something essential which is not said but rather shown.[7])

----

[7] Cf. "That a *proposition* is a subject-predicate proposition can't be said: but it is *shown* by the symbol" (*Notes Dictated to Moore*, reprinted in *Note-*

Wittgenstein's representation of what is essential to a proposition gave over the significance of the proposition entirely to syntactic facts (3.1432), they being, he said (3.14), what constitute the propositional sign. So the facts which say what is said are facts which show, which are perceptible in the sentence. The sentence does not say that those facts obtain. But if it is the fact that '*a*' stands in a certain relation *S* to '*b*' that says that *aRb*, then it is a short step to the conclusion that the sentence says how things stand, how *a* and *b* stand, by showing how things stand. But no such thing follows immediately. That is, from the fact (1) that one can see (etc.) that in the proposition *p*, '*a*' stands in *S* to '*b*'—and in that sense that *p* shows '*a*' in *S* to '*b*'—and the claim (2) that it is that fact which says that *aRb*, it does not follow (*C*) that *p* shows (or presents) *a* standing in *R* to *b*. That could be made to follow, only if in addition one were to assert (3) that *S* is identical with *R*, and (4) that '*a*' depicts *a* and '*b*' depicts *b*. Thus if *o* depicts a golf ball and *0* depicts an egg, then this: *o0—shows* (is a picture of) a golf ball situated to the left of an egg.[8] (It does not of course *show that* two such objects are so situated.) Now *0*, which *can* depict an egg, can*not* very well *depict* the city of Madison, nor *o* the town of Middleton: that is why *o0* cannot very well depict or show or be a picture of Madison situated next to Middleton. *0* and *o* could, however, be made to *stand for* or *represent* Madison and Middleton respectively: and then *o0* could, supposing it was understood to be a representation of how things stand, *represent* Madison as situated next to Middleton. Thus Wittgenstein:

4.031   Instead of, 'This proposition has such and such a sense', we can simply say, 'This proposition represents such and such a situation'.

4.0311   One name stands for one thing, another for another thing, and they are combined with one another. In this way the whole group—like a *tableau vivant*—presents a state of affairs.

---

books, p. 108). If this had meant merely that that cannot be said in the particular subject-predicate proposition, then, presuming of course the sentence does *not* happen to say that it is a subject-predicate sentence, it would have been true.

[8] Languages are not hieroglyphic; but cf. 4.016.

Wittgenstein held, not (4), but (4w), that the elements of propositions stand for or deputize for objects. And he held, not (3), but (3w), that syntactic relation *S* and the relation being said to obtain, *R*, were identical in *form* (2.17). And this will *perhaps* issue in the conclusion (Cw) that a proposition represents such and such a situation—provided that it can be maintained that the form of *S* shows or is displayed in the proposition. Wittgenstein did maintain this (2.172).

Wittgenstein thought that propositions must be pictures, given, among other things, the "determinateness of sense" that they have. I shall argue that the determinateness of sense which propositions do in fact have is of such a nature that, far from requiring that they should be pictures, it requires instead that they should *not* be pictures. It is possible to make this argument because it is arguable that Wittgenstein misrepresented what that definiteness of sense consists in. I do not, then, merely concede this phrase 'determinateness of sense' to the theoretical lexicon of the picture theory; rather, I accord it a pre-theoretical role, descriptive of something the theory is meant to account for.

Even ordinary propositions have a determinate sense, in Wittgenstein's view. "What a proposition expresses it expresses in a determinate manner, which can be set out clearly" (3.251); and what the propositional sign leaves indeterminate, "what signs slur over, their application says clearly" (3.262). He spoke of it as a "requirement" that sense should be determinate in 3.23—"The requirement that simple signs be possible is the requirement that sense be determinate." The imposition of such a demand derives from the thesis that "a proposition determines a place in logical space" (3.4), or "determines reality" (cf. 4.463) in a definite way. "To understand a proposition means to know what is the case if it is true" (4.024). But its truth or falsity consists in its agreeing or failing to agree with reality as it stands, according to its representation thereof (2.21), its fitting or failing to fit the place in a logical space that it determines. There is no third alternative: "A proposition must restrict reality to two alternatives: yes or no. In order to do that, it must describe reality completely" (4.023).

What threatens such determinateness is generality. For part of what is required is that the sense (as opposed to the truth-value) of a proposition cannot await determination by the truth of other propositions concerning its constituents (3.24)—concerning, e.g., whether what its constituents mention exists. But such indeterminateness arises only when some constituent "signifies a complex"; and "a complex can be given only by its description." A description, however, is necessarily general. Even so, the proposition may have a determinate sense, so long as it is clear *what* is left open by the proposition: "If possibilities *are left open* in the proposition, *just this* must be *definite: what* is left open" (*Notebooks*, p. 63e, q.v.).

The greater problem, however, is that generality tends to infect the sense of ordinary sentences with *vagueness*, so that it is *not* clear just what is left open. Here the theoretical demand that sense be determinate is evidently to be satisfied (at least in the *Notebooks*) by the fact that what we *mean* on a particular occasion may be relatively more highly determinate than what we say, or what is in general meant by what we say. It seemed to Wittgenstein that "it is clear that I *know* what I *mean* by the vague proposition" (*Notebooks*, p. 70e); that "what we MEAN must always be 'sharp'" (p. 68e):

> When I say, "The book is lying on the table", does this really have a completely clear sense? (An EXTREMELY important question.)
>
> But the sense must be clear, for after all we mean *something* by the proposition, and as much as we *certainly* mean must surely be clear.
>
> If the proposition "The book is [lying] on the table" has a clear sense, then I must, whatever *is the case*, be able to say whether the proposition is true or false. There could, however, very well occur *cases* in which I should not be able to say straight off whether the book is still to be called "lying on the table". Then—? [*Notebooks*, p. 67e].

I may be quite clear as to what position I mean to say that the book bears to the table. I may indeed have a definite picture in mind of how things stand—say, the book square in the center of the table, one cover flush against the table's surface—a picture which I want somehow to convey. I may further be clear that at least this situation is one in which the book *is* properly "lying on" the table, despite my being unsure whether certain other positions would be correctly so described (an uncertainty which "shows that I did not know what I meant by 'lying' *in general*" [*Notebooks*, p. 70e], but, so Wittgenstein thought, *not* that I do not know what I mean *here*).[9] But, however, that may be, what I *mean* here by 'lying' cannot be anything so definite or particular as the very particular relationship I may have in mind. At least, it cannot be so *if* what I mean is to be expressed by or intelligible from what I say. Nonetheless, Wittgenstein seems to have thought that what I mean might be as highly determinate as such a picture. Suppose that someone points out that I should be uncertain whether to say the book was lying on the table if it were lying in certain other positions: "If someone were to drive me into a corner in this way in order to shew that I did not know what I mean, I should say: 'I *know* what I mean; I mean just THIS', pointing to the appropriate complex with my finger. And in this complex I do actually have the two objects in a relation."[10]

The representation to which I point serves to represent in a determinate way what I mean. I shall say that it represents in an *over*-determinate way what I can have meant. But first let us trace out this thought as it winds into the picture theory of what I actually said—'The book is lying on the table'. Since what I said also expressed what I meant, albeit without setting it out clearly, what is essential to a sign which expresses that sense must be something common to its sentential expression and to the more perspicuous concatenation of objects I point to. The accidental and dispensable differences include the occurrence in the sentence of the relational term or verb, which has no counterpart in the concatenation of objects, save in the *manner* in which they are concatenated. The two expressions are, in essence, identical; what is essential is that

[9] Wittgenstein at least entertained this thought: "But it may also be that the proposition 'The book is lying on the table' represents my sense completely, but that I am using the words, e.g., 'lying on', with a *special* reference here, and that elsewhere they have another reference. What I mean by the verb is perhaps a quite special relation which the book now actually has to the table" (*Notebooks*, p. 68e).

[10] Ibid., p. 70e. The passage, however, continues, "But all that this *really* means is: The fact can SOMEHOW be portrayed by means of this form too." This perhaps indicates Wittgenstein's awareness of the difficulties that I shall be arguing vitiate the use of such a representation of what I mean.

the elements of the sentence be related as the elements in the situation are being said to be related.

> 3.1431 The essence of a propositional sign is very clearly seen if we imagine one composed of spatial objects (such as tables, chairs, and books) instead of written signs. Then the spatial arrangements of these things will express the sense of the proposition.

Thus what Wittgenstein seems to have required in the end, as a condition of a proposition's being determinate in sense, is that there should exist a possible representation of that sense which is as highly determinate as the sense of the proposition. But since it *is* the proposition that has a definite sense (and given the dubious supposition that the proposition *is* a representation), the proposition must *be*, even if contrary to appearances, such a representation. This requires that the proposition should be a definite picture of a definite situation, which (like any picture) represents a determinate situation by the determinate relations in which its elements stand one to another.

This deduction of the essence of the proposition hinges on the contention that what I mean by a vague proposition can be expressed by what is shown in a pictorial representation—and it falters at just this point. For consider an ordinary picture of a book lying on a table. Such a picture, posing as a representation of what I might have meant when I said, 'The book is lying on the table', will inevitably *over*-define what I meant—if, that is, what I meant is to be shown or depicted in the picture. For the picture will necessarily show the book lying in some particular position on the table (say, with one corner extending over the edge). But I did not likely, much less necessarily, mean that it was lying in just that position when I said what I said, even if I knew or thought that it was. I may (though, equally, I may not) either think that it does lie, or picture it as lying, just so. But that I do is not something that can be known simply by knowing what I *mean*—unless I mean something quite idiosyncratic (not to say private) by what I say.[11]

---

[11] Of course I *might* idiosyncratically have meant that the objects are related in precisely the manner shown. But in that case what I meant will either be unintelligible—whereas "We understand the sense of a propositional sign without its having been explained to us" (4.02)—*or*, it will be intelligible only

This objection turns on insisting upon certain limits to what I can have meant by what I said—limits drawn this side of the picture I may have had, or may present, of the situation I meant to say obtains. What I can have meant cannot be anything other than, including anything more definite than, what I thought could be *understood from* what I said. But I cannot have thought that anyone could understand that by what I said I meant that the book was lying with one corner extending over the edge of the table, or that the book is situated in any particular one of the many determinate relationships that may constitute something's lying on a table.

It cannot rightly be objected that this is to take "literally" features of the picture which require interpretation—like supposing that a stick-figure drawing of a man pictures the man *as* having limbs and trunk of equal thickness (which it does not), or, worse, that it is a picture of such a man. For the picture in question, if it is to serve the purpose for which it was introduced, cannot require interpretation in *this* regard: it must *show* how things stand, and not just that, but show it in such a way that it is perfectly clear exactly how I mean they are related. When Wittgenstein points to the representation of what he means and says, "I mean just this," he cannot be suggesting that he means that the book and the table are related in a manner *more or less* like this. That would hardly go to the point. It would not *show* in a determinate way what definite relation he meant obtains; and so it would not vindicate his claim to know what he means here, if not generally, by the verb. He must surely mean that the two things are related *precisely* as shown. But then the representation is over-determinate.[12]

---

by an ad hoc convention. In the latter case, it cannot be maintained that the relationship between the objects *shows* what I mean in a more highly determinate way.

[12] While this particular employment of the picture model precludes use of the point, a picture may generally leave things open or undetermined, as the stick-figure picture leaves undetermined the relative corpulence of the person depicted; but that this is left open is clear. And this is all Wittgenstein required of a proposition: "If generalizations occur [in a proposition] then the forms of the particular cases must be manifest—and it is clear that this demand is justified, otherwise the proposition cannot be a picture at all, of *anything*. For if possibilities *are left open* in the proposition, *just this* must be definite: what is left open" (*Notebooks*, p. 63e; cf. 4.463). Just this, however, is what is apparently *not* true in the case of the "vague" propositions here in question.

While I cannot intelligibly mean by 'is lying on' anything so particular or determinate as some one of the many determinate relationships which constitute one thing's lying on another, the situation is otherwise with 'the book' and 'the table': here a specification of what I meant might substitute for 'the book' any more specific description of the particular object I meant—i.e., had in mind, or was referring to. If someone should say, "Would you still call the thing a book if it had only five pages, all blank?" or some such thing, trying to persuade me that I did not know what I meant, here I *could* with perfect justice respond, "Perhaps not. But I know what I mean *here:* I mean *this*," throwing the book at him. Of course, here what I mean is the thing I am referring to: and that *is* an object (cf. 3.203).

No such defense will work, however, in defense of Wittgenstein's more questionable confidence that I know exactly what I mean by the verb 'lying'. For what he meant by the verb cannot be identified with the relationship I had in mind, or was referring to.

The fact that I do not know whether I would say that the book is "lying" on the table if it were in some other position does show, I think, contrary to Wittgenstein, that I am *not* entirely clear about what I mean, even on this occasion. It shows that it is unclear, therefore, what it is that would be true, if what I mean were true. But this seems no impediment to its being known to be true that the book is lying on the table, i.e., known that what I mean is true. For this requires only that we should be perfectly clear that the situation that does obtain is sufficient for the truth of what I mean. To know, on the other hand, what I mean by what I say does seem to require that I should know what is *necessary* for the truth of what I mean; cf. 4.024: "To understand a proposition means to know what is the case if it is true." But of course to know what is the case if it is true, it is not enough to know that it would be true if a certain thing were the case.

By contrast, the fact that I do not know whether I would call the thing I am speaking of a book *if* its pages were blank (etc.) does not show that I am not entirely clear what I am saying, or what I mean when I say that the book is lying on the table. It does not show that it would be unclear *what* would be true, if what I mean were true; what I mean, and what would be true, is that *this* particular object is lying on the table. (Had I been saying that what is lying on the table is a book, then uncertainty about what is meant in general by 'book' *would* entail uncertainty about what I now mean.)

Wittgenstein contrived a denotational view of meaning which did not require that there should exist in nature anything general or indeterminate. The masterstroke was to confer the semantic function of general terms, or terms of indeterminate meaning, upon the determinate relations among simple denoting expressions. The failure of the view is in a way as simple as this fundamental idea. The relationships (spatial, temporal, dynamic, etc.) among names or nouns are indeed particular and perfectly determinate; but therefore they cannot supplant the function of terms of indeterminate meaning without rendering the sense of the proposition more highly determinate than what it could mean or say.

There is also a way in which the pictorial representation of sense is *under*-determined, and an aspect of a proposition's determinateness of sense which the picture model cannot be made to represent. Indeed it is at this point that the inadequacy of the model to the notion of what is said becomes particularly instructive. For it involves the inability to capture the contrast between what is said or made explicit and what is merely implied, which, I think, is constitutive of the concept of *saying* something.

Suppose that in uttering a certain sentence a person says and means a certain thing. And suppose the sentence he uttered were replaced with a picture of the situation in which what he said and meant is true. Now this picture will also, necessarily, depict situations the obtaining of which is merely *implied* by the truth of what I said or meant. Thus a picture of a book lying on a table also and eo ipso depicts a book in contiguity with a table, a table positioned below a book, and a book and table temporally coexisting; it depicts two objects standing in a certain relation. But while all these things are equally depicted, it is not the case that I *said* these things when I said that the book was lying on the table. Nor is it the case that what I *meant* when I said that necessarily comprises any or all of them. That is to say, the statement that what I meant was that the book was contiguous with the table, or that the table was below the book, would be a false statement (presuming, as always, that what I meant is intelligible from what I said).

It is obvious that what I *say*, in a strict but familiar ordinary sense, excludes what is implied—since the latter is implied by what I say. It is only slightly less obvious that what I *mean* does not embrace everything that is implied by what I say. One has only to think of recondite implications to see that this could not generally be true.[13]

Thus what a sentence says, and what a speaker means by it as well, is as it were *defined against* what is (logically or otherwise) implied by what is said or meant. The concept of the sense of a proposition, to the extent to which this is identifiable with the concept of what is said in or meant by uttering a sentence, must differ in this regard from the concept of the sense of a picture—if "what a picture represents is its sense" (2.221). For within what a picture presents or depicts there is no one thing discriminated as the thing it depicts in the way that there is, within the totality of what a proposition conveys, a discrimination to be made between what is said (or meant) and what is implied thereby.[14] At the outset, before matters are obscured by refinement, there must appear to be something badly askew in the conception from which the picture theory originated. Wittgenstein conceived of the sense of a proposition as determinate in such a way that the hypothesis that propositions were pictures was required to account for it. But on the contrary, the sense of a proposition is on the one hand not so highly determinate, in one respect, as that of a picture. And on the other hand, and in another respect, the sense of a proposition is determinate or discrete in a way that that of a picture *apparently* could not be. If

[13] It is true, regarding things more transparently implied, that one might ask, e.g., "Do you mean that the book is *touching* the table?" But this is just a manner of speaking—as when I say "Margaret's husband is a junkie," and someone says, "Do you mean that Margaret is married?" Well, yes, she is married, but *no:* that is not what I *meant* by what I said. I meant that her husband is a heroin addict.

[14] There *is* a distinction between what a picture portrays and what is entailed by the obtaining of the situation it portrays, but this is a different distinction from that between what is said or meant and what is entailed thereby. The former distinction has primarily to do with what can be *seen* in the picture (that being roughly what is portrayed) versus what cannot be seen but may be inferred, on the supposition that it is an accurate picture of an actual situation. One may also distinguish the matter of what a picture is a picture of —e.g., Washington crossing the Delaware—and what the picture (let us say) "depicts"—among other things, Washington's boat.

this appearance cannot be made to dissipate, there will be a certain aspect of propositional determinateness which runs strongly counter to the hypothesis that propositions are pictures.

In the *Tractatus* view, propositions are "logical" pictures. This means, among other things, that unlike ordinary pictures, they need not share "representational form" with what they picture. Wittgenstein speaks of the *manner* in which a picture represents what it represents, which he says must be known in order to assess its truth value or accuracy: "The same picture will agree or fail to agree with reality according to how it is supposed to represent" (*Notebooks*, p. 23e). Thus, following Griffin, "The same picture, say '*ab*', can depict a number of states of affairs—even where '*a*' and '*b*' are thought of as having meaning. What more we have to do is determine what one state of affairs this one configuration of the signs, '*ab*', shall picture."[15] But then we shall have to *interpret* what the fact that the names are determinately so related shows, in accordance with a conventional determination of "what one state of affairs this one configuration of the signs . . . shall picture." There is nothing wrong with the supposition that a configuration may show how things stand via certain conventions of representation. The trouble is rather that to the extent that our grasp of what is being shown is mediated by such conventions, we abandon one original attraction of the model, sc., the notion that we see in the essential structure of the proposition a configuration which lays bare to our eyes its perfectly *determinate* sense—"as when in the law-court in Paris a motor-car accident is represented by means of dolls, etc." (*Notebooks*, p. 7e). For the indeterminateness previously lodged in the relational term or verb will now merely reappear as a corresponding indeterminacy in the matter of when and how the conventions are correctly followed. The vagueness implied by one's uncertainty as to whether he should say the same thing had the situation differed in certain ways now becomes one's uncertainty as to whether he would offer the same representation of the situation, had it so differed. For there are correct and incorrect ways of representing a situation, and if the convention dictates that '*ab*' shows *a* lying on *b*, then in any situation in which it is unclear whether *a* is

15 James Griffin, *Wittgenstein's Logical Atomism* (Oxford: Oxford University Press, 1964), p. 97.

to be said to be lying on *b*, it must be equally unclear whether '*ab*' can, in correct accordance with the convention, represent that particular situation, or show how *a* stands to *b*.

> 4.022 A proposition *shows* its sense. A proposition *shows* how things
> stand *if* it is true. And it *says that* they do so stand.

These contentions are at odds with one another, when taken together with the contention that a proposition expresses a definite sense. What a proposition says is some *one* thing, distinct from the several things implied by what it says. Whereas if something shows how things stand, shows *a* standing in *R* to *b*, then if *aRb* implies that *aSb*, *a* is equally shown standing in *S* to *b*. So if a proposition is to say the particular thing it says by virtue of how it shows things standing, it must do so via a conventional determination of what one thing is "shown." But such a picture cannot then pose as a depiction of the same order of determinateness as the situation which would verify it, or with which it is to be compared; in particular, it does not eliminate any vagueness afflicting the general term. While on the other hand, if the relationship between the names were to depict the relationship between their object correlates by dint of the "natural" identity between those relationships (so that '*ab*' might depict this configuration of inscriptions: *CD*), then there is nothing to determine whether what is being said is that the *C* is to the left of, or next to, or printed on the same line as, or spatially related to, the *D*. The result will be, not that '*ab*' is ambiguous—for it is not that it is unclear what it says, or that it might say various things— but rather that there will be no such thing as the thing it says. It will say nothing.[16]

---

[16] I shall not go into the question of how these matters might stand with the elementary propositions out of which ordinary propositions are allegedly built up. The arguments for this thesis are unpersuasive at best, and the related view that ordinary nonelementary propositions are *understood* by virtue of our understanding the elementary propositions of which its sense is a function is incredible—particularly given the depth of our ignorance of what elementary propositions are. But certain points of *Tractatus* doctrine might be deemed relevant. First, no elementary proposition implies any other elementary proposition (5.134). So there would presumably be no distinction between what such a proposition says and what it implies (thus between what it shows and what it says), *so long as* we stay on the level of elementary propositions. Perhaps, accordingly, the relationships among simple objects, referred to metaphorically as concatenation, are supposed to be of such a nature that, if an elementary

Returning now to "logical pictures," let us raise this question: given just the requirement that the relationships among the constituents of pictures should be of the same logical form (not necessarily in any other way the same) as the relationship among the constituents of the situation said to obtain, what situations might the picture '*ab*' represent? Since '*a*' stands to '*b*' in both symmetrical relations (e.g., being next to) and asymmetrical relations (e.g., being to the left of), it would appear that if identity with respect to these formal properties is sufficient, then '*ab*' could picture any two-termed relational situation bearing these same formal properties. I propose here to follow "a guess" of Griffin's, who suggests that in order that '*ab*' should picture a particular fact,[17] as well as the constituents of the situation having to be correlated one-to-one with the constituents of the sentence, it is required further that the latter "also behave as regards combining as the things behave."[18] I shall interpret the notion of the "behavior of names as regards combining" as pertaining to the "syntactic behavior" of these elements and limit my attention to the simple but clear capacity to be transposed without changing the sense of the sentence. Thus, (1) '*a* adjoins *b*' and (2) '*b* adjoins *a*' say the same thing, unlike (3) '*a* precedes *b*' and (4) '*b* precedes *a*'. The fact which in (1) and (2) says that *a* adjoins *b*, is (following 3.1432) the fact that '*a*' stands in a certain relation to '*b*'. That relation is, let us say, the symmetrical dyadic relationship of flanking the verb 'adjoins'. This nicely explains why (1) and (2) say the same thing, since they have in common what is essential to expressing that sense (cf. 3.34, and 3.342). The fact that in (1) '*a*' precedes '*b*' is an accident signifying nothing. But in (3) and (4) it is otherwise. So we may say that in (3) it is the fact that '*a*' is to the left of the verb 'precedes' to the right of which is '*b*',

---

proposition says that *aRb*, there is no relation *S* such that that proposition entails that *aSb*. Finally, certain of the implications of elementary propositions would be nonelementary propositions involving formal concepts, and these might then be held to be things that cannot be said but only shown.

[17] Which requires more than mere "correlation," in order that the sentential constituents "really are representatives of the things" (Griffin, p. 93; *Notebooks* 4.11.14 is cited.) Cf. also Max Black, *A Companion to Wittgenstein's "Tractatus"* (Ithaca: Cornell University Press, 1964), p. 14, on what he calls the "extrinsic conception of logical form."

[18] Griffin, p. 93; cf. *Notebooks* 3.4.15 and 5.11.14.

that says that *a* precedes *b*. This syntactic relationship is asymmetrical, so the hypothesis explains why (4) does not say the same thing. In this we have a formal identity between the relationships of names and the relationships of the objects in the situations said to obtain, and indeed, the demand for such isomorphism seems to be borne out.[19] In this way, then, the behavior of '*a*' and '*b*' as regards combining will mirror, in its logical properties, the relation of their object correlates, where the linguistic "behavior" in question is that of undergoing or declining transposition.[20] (Notice, however, that this is not to say that what the behavior as regards combining [Griffin] or the powers of combination [Black] of names will reflect is necessarily the *behavior* or powers of combination of their object correlates. On the object side, what is being said may have nothing to do with the behavior of objects or their powers of combination.)

I have so far posed the contention that we must be able to distinguish what is said from what is implied as a difficulty for the picture theory. I want now to suggest that the distinction is not a difficulty but an aid to the independent Tractarian thesis (one to which I am sympathetic) that there is something essential to any proposition which says a certain thing "without which the proposition could not express its sense" (3.34), and thus that there is something common to all propositions which say that thing (3.341).

Suppose that it is maintained that this essential feature consists in a common structure, and suppose further that it is held that such

[19] On this interpretation, the relation between '*a*' and '*b*', the obtaining of which (according to 3.1432) is what says that *aRb*, cannot without further information be identified either with the one "that consists in the first standing to the left of *R* and the second to the right of *R*" (Black, p. 105), *or* with the fact "that '*R*' occurs between '*a*' and '*b*'" (*Notes on Logic*, Appendix I of *Notebooks*, p. 99). The former relation is asymmetrical and the latter symmetrical, but we do not know whether *R* is symmetrical or asymmetrical.

[20] Related syntactic behavior occurs in the case of triadic relations, depending on the symmetry or asymmetry of the subordinate relations between respective pairs of the terms of the relation. Thus the relations among donor, donee, and donated are all asymmetrical, so there will be no transposability of terms, whereas with the transitive verb 'marry' ('John and Jill were married by the Parson'), there will be a subordinate relationship between John and Jill which is symmetrical (thus 'Jill and John were married by the Parson' means the same thing), but none between either Jill or John and the Parson (thus 'the Parson and John were married by Jill' says something else).

"structure" consists (in part) in the powers of combination displayed by the nominal elements of the sentence, where this is understood in the way suggested above. (That is, as reflecting formal identity in respect of the logical properties of symmetry or asymmetry, the symmetrical syntactic relation being manifested in the possibility of noun transposition without alteration of what is said, the asymmetrical relation in the impossibility of such transposition.) What 'The book is lying on the table' (bLt) says, implies that what 'The book is contiguous with the table' (bCt) says is true. Consider the position of the essential structure theorist who is willing to say that 'bLt' says (inter alia) that bCt: 'bLt' and 'bCt' are two ways of saying the same thing, though the former says something else as well. Now an antinomy of a familiar sort arises. For, since *lying on* is an asymmetrical and *contiguous with* is a symmetrical relation, the significant relations between the nouns 'the book' and 'the table' must differ in the two sentences. Thus in 'The book is lying on the table' it is significant that it is 'the book' which precedes the verb, whereas in 'The book is contiguous with the table' the same feature is not essential to its saying what it says and signifies nothing. The essential syntactic relation is asymmetrical in 'bLt' and symmetrical in 'bCt'. Now let us raise a question: What is essential to the structure of any sentence which says that the book is lying on the table? The answer cannot very well be that the nominal constituents of the sentence should stand in an *asymmetrical* relation, if we are to say both that there is a sentence which says both that and that the book is contiguous with the table, and also that it is essential to any sentence which says the latter that its nominal elements should stand in a *symmetrical* relationship. The result must be that it is and that it is not essential to a sentence saying that thing that its nominal elements stand in an asymmetrical relationship.

This is a familiar sort of difficulty, or apparent difficulty, plaguing essentialist doctrines, of a piece with the one about the landowning father,[21] or the mathematician cyclist[22] whose two-leggedness and whose rationality are both essential and accidental properties. In such cases, one's first move is to say that his rationality is essential

---

[21] Carnap, *The Logical Syntax of Language* (New York: Humanities Press, 1957), p. 304.
[22] Quine, *Word and Object* (New York: John Wiley & Sons, 1960), p. 199.

only to his being a mathematician and his two-leggedness essential only to his being a cyclist. Similarly, one may try saying that it is essential only to the sentence saying that the book is lying on the table that the nouns should be asymmetrically related and essential only to its saying that the two things are contiguous that they should be symmetrically related. But if, as suggested, these relations are to be manifest in the transposability of the nouns, this will be awkward; for we shall then be saying that '*bLt*' and '*tLb*' say the same thing, viz. that *bCt*. Perhaps this can be tolerated and the conclusion that the proposition is objectionably ambiguous evaded. But it is not necessary to do so, for we may simply allow what is true in any case—that 'the book is lying on the table' does *not* say that the book is contiguous with the table.

It is, of course, the *verb* that has the function of *saying* what relation the book and the table are being said to stand in. And in doing so, it indicates what relationship, whether some symmetrical or some asymmetrical one, between 'the book' and 'the table' is significant, and thus whether the nouns are or are not transposable. Since any sentence the constituents of which are related spatially or temporally (or by pitch or dynamic emphasis or whatnot—i.e., any sentence having a perceptible representation) will necessarily exhibit relationships of both logical forms between such constituents, there must be something in or some fact about the sentence that indicates whether it is their symmetrical or their asymmetrical relationships that are essential to the sentence saying what it says.

Distinguishing what a sentence says from what it implies (or what it says implies) will defend the common structure view against a criticism offered by Waismann. Waismann points out that the two sentences (1) '*A* is north of *B*, and *B* is north of *C*' and (2) '*A* is north of *C*, and *B* is between *A* and *C*' describe the same geographical situation.

Yet the logical form of the two descriptions is entirely different. In Russell's symbolism they would be expressed like this:

aNb.bNc

aNc.B(bac)

In the one case the fact is described by two dyadic relations; in the other case by a dyadic and a triadic relation. And these two expressions have quite different forms. Now which of the two structures is to be called the 'structure of reality'?[23]

But while the two sentences may describe the same situation, they do not say the same thing. Sentence (1) implies, but does not say, that B is between A and C; and (2) implies, but does not say, that B is north of C. So we do not have a counterexample to the claim that two sentences which say the same thing have the same structure. (At the same time, however, we have no warrant for projecting the structure of what is said onto the *situation* which would verify it, or for supposing that the former, even in its essential structure, is a mirror of the latter.) Again, it shows up that what a sentence says, in the strict sense required to maintain the common-structure thesis, turns on just what words actually appear in the sentence, and more particularly, what verb or relational expression relates the nominal expressions. Thus it seems that (1) does not say that B is between A and C for the simple reason that no relational expression synonymous with 'is between' appears in that sentence, relating the expressions 'A', 'C', and 'B'. That is, there is nothing in the sentence which *says* that the relation that obtains between A and C is that B is located between them.

In *Notes on Logic*, Wittgenstein had said, "What symbolizes in '*aRb*' is that '*R*' occurs between '*a*' and '*b*'" (*Notebooks*, p. 99). But *Tractatus* 3.1431 indicates that he came to think that the relational term is inessential. We may agree, of course, that if that term *is* essential, it is not because any proposition that says *aRb* must contain a term which *stands for* or refers to something in addition to *a* and *b*. But to make that point, we need not pretend that we could do without such terms. It is better to understand what the semantical role of the relational term or verb is in fact. Evidently, its role is to *say* what relation obtains. And it is evidently essential that that role should be played by something if the proposition is to say that *aRb*; it is not enough that that relation should be *shown*.

[23] F. Waismann, *The Principles of Linguistic Philosophy* (New York: St. Martin's Press, 1965), p. 315.

PART THREE

Philosophy of Logic and Mathematics

20

Wittgenstein and Logical Necessity

BARRY STROUD

MICHAEL DUMMETT has described
Wittgenstein's account of logical necessity as a "full-blooded conventionalism."[1] On this view, the source of the necessity of any
necessary statement is "our having expressly decided to treat that
very statement as unassailable" (p. 329). Even faced with a rigorous
mathematical proof:

> at each step we are free to choose to accept or reject the proof; there
> is nothing in our formulation of the axioms and of the rules of infer-
> ence, and nothing in our minds when we accepted these before the
> proof was given, which of itself shows whether we shall accept the
> proof or not; and hence there is nothing which *forces* us to accept
> the proof. If we accept the proof, we confer necessity on the theorem
> proved; we "put it in the archives" and will count nothing as telling
> against it. In doing this we are making a new decision, and not merely
> making explicit a decision we had already made implicitly [p. 330].

Reprinted with the kind permission of the author and the editor from
The Philosophical Review, 74 (1965):504–18.

[1] Michael Dummett, "Wittgenstein's Philosophy of Mathematics," *The Philosophical Review*, 68 (1959):324. Page numbers alone in parentheses in the text
always refer to this article. References to Wittgenstein's writings always contain an abbreviation of the title of the book in question. "*PI*" will refer to
Wittgenstein's *Philosophical Investigations* (Oxford: Basil Blackwell, 1953), and
unless otherwise indicated, parenthetical references will be to the numbered
sections of Pt. I. "*RFM*" will refer to *Remarks on the Foundations of Mathematics* (Oxford: Basil Blackwell, 1956).

This implies that it is possible for someone to accept the axioms and the rules of inference and yet to reject the proof, without having failed to understand those axioms or rules. But, Dummett objects:

> We want to say that we do not know what it would be like for someone who, by ordinary criteria, already understood the concepts employed, to reject this proof. . . . The examples given in Wittgenstein's book are—amazingly for him—thin and unconvincing. I think that this is a fairly sure sign that there is something wrong with Wittgenstein's account [p. 333].

Dummett is obviously on strong ground here—it seems impossible to understand this alleged possibility—but I think Wittgenstein would agree. His examples are not designed to show that we do understand this. What is important for the problem of logical necessity is to explain what makes the denial of a necessary truth "impossible" or "unintelligible." It is not enough to say that it is "logically impossible," since an explanation of logical necessity is just what is in question. Dummett appears to agree with this (pp. 328–29). In the rest of this paper I shall try to say what, according to Wittgenstein, is responsible for the unintelligibility in such cases.

In defending the claim that he is not committed to saying that everybody could infer in any way at all, Wittgenstein points out that it is essential to inferring, calculating, counting, and so forth, that not just any result is allowed as correct. If everybody continues the series as he likes, or infers just any way at all, then "we shan't call it 'continuing the series' and also presumably not 'inference'" (*RFM*, I, 116). General agreement among people as to the correct results of inferences of calculations and general agreement in the results that one gets oneself at different times are both necessary in order for there to be inferring or calculating at all (*RFM*, II, 66, 73). The same holds for counting, continuing a series, and so on. These are all activities in which the possibility of different results at different times and places is not left open. It is just here that a calculation differs from an experiment, where people at different times and places can get different results.

These remarks suggest that the source of necessity in inferring or calculating is simply that any activity in which just any results were allowed would not be *called* "inferring," "calculating," and so forth. In the case of drawing logical conclusions:

> The steps which are not brought in question are logical inferences. But the reason why they are not brought in question is not that they "certainly correspond to the truth"—or something of the sort—no, it is just this that is called "thinking," "speaking," "referring," "arguing" [*RFM*, I, 155].

This looks like the standard claim that all necessity finds its source in definitions or in the meanings of words. In inferring, one must write down 'q' after '$p \supset q$' and 'p' because to do otherwise is to cease to infer correctly, and correct inference is just "defined" by the laws of logic. That is what we call correct inference. This would presumably mean that, since it is possible for something else to be meant by 'correct inference', it would also be possible for something else to be the conclusion. Despite suggestions of this "standard conventionalism" in Wittgenstein, I agree with Dummett that he does not hold such a view, although it is not always easy to see how what he says differs from it.

The main target of Wittgenstein's writings on necessity is the Platonism of Frege and the early Russell. In this respect he and the logical positivists are alike. According to Platonism it would be impossible for someone, when given the order "Add 2," to write down all the same numerals as we do up to '1000' and then to go on '1004, 1008, . . .', and still be able to justify his going on in that way. It would be impossible because it is simply wrong, in continuing the series '+2', to write down '1004' right after '1000'; that is not, in fact, the next member of the series. So the pupil must either have misunderstood the instructions or have made a mistake. Anyone who puts anything other than '1002' is wrong and should be declared an idiot or an incorrigible if he persists in his perversity. As Frege puts it: "here we have a hitherto unknown kind of insanity."[2]

The conventionalist's opposition to Platonism consists primarily in showing that our present ways of inferring, counting, calculating, and so forth, are not the only possible ones. But the standard conventionalist would also reject the alleged possibility on the grounds

---

[2] G. Frege, *Grundgesetze der Arithmetik* (Jena, 1903), p. xvi.

that the description of such a state of affairs is contradictory. If the person has understood the instructions, if he has just written down '1000', and if he is to continue following the instructions, then he *must* write down '1002'. Of course, he is free not to continue the series at all, or to claim that he has been following instructions like "Add 2 up to 1000, 4 up to 2000," and so forth, but it is logically impossible (involves a contradiction) for him to have understood the instructions correctly and to write down '1004' right after '1000'. His claiming that '1004' is the correct step is a sufficient condition of his having abandoned the ordinary sense attached to the order "Add 2." That it is correct to write '1002' is already contained in the meaning of those instructions, and once one has agreed to follow them, then because they mean what they do there are certain steps which one logically must take.

The crucial notion in this conventionalistic theory is that of understanding the meaning of a word or a rule, and this is something to which Wittgenstein devotes a great deal of attention. Part of his interest in it is in the sense, if any, in which someone's having understood the instructions somehow logically guarantees that he will write down '1002' right after '1000'. If this is logically guaranteed, then it would seem that his going on '1004, 1008, . . .' could be due only to misunderstanding or to a mistake; in any event, he could not have understood correctly. But what is it to understand correctly? What determines which move is the correct one at a given point? The answer would appear to be that the way the order was meant, or what was meant by the person giving the order, determines which steps are correct. But again, Wittgenstein asks, what shows which way the order was meant? It is not the case that the teacher very quickly thought of each particular step which he wanted the pupil to take, and even if he did, that would not show that "meaning 1002, 1004, . . ." meant "thinking of 1002, 1004, . . ." (*PI*, 692). Rather, what the order means will be shown in the ways we use it, in what we do in following it, in the ways we are taught to use it, and so on (*RFM*, I, 2).

If someone who had learned to continue various series just as we do began to differ from us when he went beyond any point he had reached in his training, would it follow that he simply had not understood the instructions? If he continued to do this, must we say

that he is unintelligent, perhaps idiotic? Wittgenstein tries as follows to suggest negative answers to these questions:

> If my reply is: "Oh yes of course, *that* is how I was applying it!"
> or: "Oh! That's how I ought to have applied it—!"; then I am playing
> your game. But if I simply reply: "Different?—But this surely *isn't*
> different!"—what will you do? That is: somebody may reply like a
> rational person and yet not be playing our game [*RFM*, I, 115].

He tries to show that not all cases of deviating from what we expect or from what we all do in continuing the series can be put
down to simple misunderstanding, stupidity, or deliberate perversity on the part of the pupil. It is almost certain in any particular
case we come across that some discoverable mistake has occurred,
and that the pupil will come to recognize this. But *must* he do so? Is
there no possibility other than those mentioned above? The example
is intended to suggest that there is. But the important, and difficult,
problem is to say exactly what this alleged possibility comes to.
Although Frege said it would be a new kind of insanity, "he never
said what this 'insanity' would really be like" (*RFM*, I, 151). To see
what it would be like is to understand on what our being compelled
in inferring, calculating, counting, and so forth, rests.

The person who continues the series '1004, 1008, . . .' is described
as "finding it natural" to go on in that way; it "strikes him as the
same" as he has done earlier. In trying to get such a person to continue the series as we do it would no longer be useful for us to go
through the training and give him the old explanations over again.
And providing him with a rule precisely formulated in mathematical
terms would not avoid the difficulties, since it is just the possibility
of his understanding such a rule that is in question.

> In such a case we might say, perhaps: It comes natural to this person
> to understand our order with our explanations as *we* should under-
> stand the order: "Add 2 up to 1000, 4 up to 2000, 6 up to 3000, and
> so on."

> Such a case would present similarities with one in which a person
> naturally reacted to the gesture of pointing with the hand by looking
> in the direction of the line from finger-tip to wrist, not from wrist
> to finger-tip [*PI*, 185].

For Wittgenstein, it will not be enough to object that, if we are patient and careful, surely we could eventually get the pupil to see that he is to make the same move after '1000' as before—that he is not to change the size of the steps. He is convinced that he is making the same move, and "who says what 'change' and 'remaining the same' mean here" (*RFM*, I, 113)? One is inclined to reply, I think, that nobody *says* what is the same and what is different; it is just a fact that the pupil is wrong in supposing that going on '1004, 1008, . . .' is doing the same as he was in writing down '2, 4, 6, . . .'. But is there some discoverable fact of which we are aware, and which he is missing? What sort of fact is it, and how could he be brought to acknowledge it? Trying to explain to him that he has not gone on in the same way would be like trying to teach someone how to carry out the order "Go this way" when I point in a particular direction. If that person naturally reacted to the gesture of pointing by looking in the direction of the line from fingertip to wrist, it would not be enough to say to him, "If I point this way (pointing with my right hand) I mean that you should go *this* way (pointing with my left hand in the same direction)." Isn't every explanation of how someone should follow an arrow in the position of another arrow (*BB*, p. 97)?

Or, to choose another example, suppose we come across some people who find it natural to sell wood, not by cubic measure or board feet as we do, but at a price proportionate to the area covered by the pile of wood, and they pay no attention to the height of the pile.

> How could I show them that—as I should say—you don't really buy more wood if you buy a pile covering a bigger area?—I should, for instance, take a pile which was small by their ideas and, by laying the logs around, change it into a "big" one. This *might* convince them—but perhaps they would say: "Yes, now it's a *lot* of wood and costs more"—and that would be the end of the matter [*RFM*, I, 149].

This case is analogous to that of trying to get the deviant pupil to see that the next step after '1000' is really '1002'.[3] But can we de-

---

[3] There are some important features of the two cases as presented which are not analogous. We are imagining a single pupil who makes a single deviant move after having done exactly as we had expected up till now, whereas the example of the wood-sellers is presented from the outset as one in which we

scribe what these people do as "selling wood the wrong way"? Is it a way whose "incorrectness" we could point out to them? And surely it is not logically impossible for there to be such people: the example does not contain a hidden contradiction.

The natural reply to this example is that it shows only that such people mean by 'a lot of wood' and 'a little wood' something different from what we mean by it, and similarly, as Dummett suggests, anyone who agrees with us in accepting all the steps in a proof but who then refuses to accept what we all accept as the conclusion must be blind to the meaning that has already been given to the words in the premises or in previous proofs. It seems as if he could not remain faithful to the meanings of those words and still reject the conclusion. Dummett concludes from this that he is simply *deciding* to accept some particular statement as necessary in complete isolation from everything else he has accepted. This is why Wittgenstein is called a "full-blooded" conventionalist. The strange people Wittgenstein describes differ from us only in having "adopted different conventions." But does it follow from the case which Wittgenstein tries to construct that the deviant pupil simply chooses to write '1004' and that his choice makes that the correct step? Can the people in Wittgenstein's examples properly be said to differ from us only in having adopted different conventions? I think the answer is "No." One thing implied by saying that we have adopted, or are following, a convention is that there are alternatives which we could adopt in its place. But in the case of writing '1002' right after '1000' there appear to be no alternatives open to us. It seems impossible to understand how we could "adopt the convention" that writing '998, 1000, 1004, . . .' is going on in the same way, or taking steps of the same size. Surely if writing '998, 1000, 1002, . . .' is not taking steps of the same size, then nothing is.

come across a whole, flourishing society. Consequently, what appears to be a sudden and inexplicable change, or an individual abberration, in the former case is not present in the latter. Furthermore, and crucially, the society of wood-sellers is not our own, but the strange pupil has apparently sprung up right in our midst. I think that these and other disanalogies can be avoided by presenting both cases in the same way from the beginning, although Wittgenstein never does this. (Some of the difficulties which these differences appear to create for the later stages of my argument were pointed out to me by Professor Stanley Cavell.)

I have been trying to suggest so far that for Wittgenstein such "alternatives" are not inconceivable or unimaginable because they involve or lead to a logical contradiction. Just as there is no logical contradiction involved in the supposition that people might sell wood, and defend their doing so, in the way described earlier, so there is no logical contradiction involved in supposing that someone might agree with us in all uses of words or in all steps of a proof up to the present, and that he should now accept something different from what we all accept as the conclusion, without being simply idiotic or deliberately perverse. Wittgenstein's examples are designed to show this; it is part of the attack on Platonism. But as long as such alternatives are inconceivable in whatever sense, it looks as if Dummett is right in pointing out that "we do not know what it would be like for someone who, by ordinary criteria, already understood the concepts employed, to reject the proof." And if we do not know what this would be like, how can we find at all plausible Wittgenstein's purported examples of someone who "replies like a rational person" and yet is not "playing our game"? So it appears that, as Dummett says, Wittgenstein's examples are "thin and unconvincing," as they presumably must be if they are supposed to be examples of something that is unimaginable or inconceivable.

This seems to present the interpreter of Wittgenstein with a choice between two alternatives. Either Wittgenstein has not succeeded in giving any clear or intelligible examples of people whose ways of calculating, and so forth, are radically different from ours, and therefore he has not begun to support his anti-Platonistic account of logical necessity; or else he has succeeded in giving intelligible, perhaps even convincing, examples which commit him to a "full-blooded conventionalism." And if the latter is the case, then Dummett's successful attack on radical conventionalism will be equally successful against Wittgenstein. But this choice is not an exhaustive one. There can be plausible examples to show the possibility of ways of counting, inferring, calculating, and so forth, different from ours, but which do not imply that our doing these things as we do is solely a result of our abiding by, or having adopted, certain more or less arbitrary conventions to which there are clear and intelligible alternatives. Nor do such examples imply that "at each step we are free to accept or reject the proof" or that "a statement's being necessarily true is solely a result of our having decided to treat that very statement as unassailable." But at one point Wittgenstein says:

> So much is clear: when someone says: "If you follow the rule, it *must* be like this," he has not any *clear* concept of what experience would correspond to the opposite.
>
> Or again: he has not any clear concept of what it would be like for it to be otherwise. And this is very important [*RFM*, III, 29].

If this is true, how can he hope to be successful in giving examples of what it would be like for it to be otherwise, while still maintaining that there is logical necessity in such cases? How can he have it both ways? The solution to this dilemma is to be found in the explanation of why we do not have any clear concept of the opposite in the case of logical necessity, and why Wittgenstein speaks of our not having a *clear* concept here. How could we have any concept at all?

Wittgenstein gives many examples of people whose ways of inferring, counting, calculating, and so forth, are different in significant ways from ours. As well as the wood-sellers mentioned earlier, there might be others who sell wood at a price equal to the labor of felling the timber, measured by the age and strength of the woodsman. Or perhaps each buyer pays the same however much he takes (*RFM*, I, 147). Also, there might be people who measured with soft rubber rulers, or with rulers which expanded to an extraordinary extent when slightly heated (*RFM*, I, 5). Or suppose that people in their calculations sometimes divided by "$(n\text{-}n)$" and yet were not bothered by the results. They would be like people who did not prepare lists of names systematically (for example, alphabetically), and so in some lists some names would appear more than once, but they accept this without worrying (*RFM*, V, 8). Or there might be people who count, but when they want to know numbers for various practical purposes ask certain other people who, having had the practical problem explained to them, shut their eyes and let the appropriate number come to them (*RFM*, V, 14). There are many more such examples, merely mentioned or briefly discussed, throughout Wittgenstein's *Remarks*.[4] They are all intended to be analogous in various ways to the "possibility" that someone might go on '1004' right after '1000' in continuing the series '+2'.

When first presented with these examples it seems that we can understand them, and that we can come to know what such people would be like. We do not happen to do things in these strange ways, but, it seems, we could. If these examples represent clear alternatives, then why doesn't it follow that our calculating, counting, measuring, and so forth, as we do is purely a matter of convention? If this is not a matter of convention, how can these examples be perfectly intelligible to us? In suggesting answers to these questions I will have begun to show how Wittgenstein can escape between the horns of the above dilemma.

When we look more closely at the examples, are they really as intelligible as they seemed at first? For instance, consider the people who sell wood at a price proportionate to the area covered by the pile of wood and who defend their doing so in the way described earlier. Surely they would have to believe that a one-by-six-inch board all of a sudden increased in size or quantity when it was turned from resting on its one-inch edge to resting on its six-inch side. And what would the relation between quantity and weight possibly be for such people? A man could buy as much wood as he could possibly lift, only to find, upon dropping it, that he had just lifted more wood than he could possibly lift. Or is there more wood, but the same weight? Or perhaps these people do not understand the expressions 'more' and 'less' at all. They must, if they can say, "Now it's a lot of wood, and costs more." And do these people think of themselves as shrinking when they shift from standing on both feet to standing on one? Also, it would be possible for a house that is twice as large as another built on exactly the same plan to contain much less wood. How much wood is bought need have no connection with how much wood is needed for building the house. And so on. Problems involved in understanding what it would be like to sell wood in this way can be multiplied indefinitely.

If so, then so far we do not really know what it would be like for us to sell wood, and to try to justify our doing so, in the way Witt-

[4] E.g., *RFM*, I, 136, 139, 152, 168; II, 76, 78, 81, 84; III, 15, 17; IV, 5; V, 6, 12, 27, 29, 36, 42, 43, 44.

genstein has described. And we have already noted the difficulties in trying to understand the example of continuing the series '+2'. I think the initial intelligibility and strength of Wittgenstein's examples derive from their being severely isolated or restricted. We think we can understand and accept them as representing genuine alternatives only because the wider-reaching consequences of counting, calculating, and so forth, in these deviant ways are not brought out explicitly. When we try to trace out the implications of behaving like that consistently and quite generally, our understanding of the alleged possibilities diminishes. I suspect that this would happen with most, if not all, of Wittgenstein's examples, but I do not need to prove this in general, since if my interpretation is right these examples will fulfill their intended role whether or not this point holds.

The reason for this progressive decrease in intelligibility, I think, is that the attempt to get a clearer understanding of what it would be like to be one of these people and to live in their world inevitably leads us to abandon more and more of our own familiar world and the ways of thinking about it upon which our understanding rests. The more successful we are in projecting ourselves into such a world, the less we will have left in terms of which we can find it intelligible. In trying to understand these alleged possibilities, we constantly come across more and more difficulties, more and more questions which must be answered before we can understand them. But this is not to say that we do not understand them because they are "meaningless" or "contradictory," or because what they purport to represent is "logically impossible."

Wittgenstein's examples are intended to oppose Platonism by showing that calculating, counting, inferring, and so forth, might have been done differently. But this implies no more than that the inhabitants of the earth might have engaged in those practices in accordance with rules which are different from those we actually follow. It is in that sense a contingent fact that calculating, inferring, and so forth, are carried out in the ways that they are—just as it is a contingent fact that there is such a thing as calculating or inferring at all. But we can understand and acknowledge the contingency of this fact, and hence the possibility of different ways of calculating, and so forth, without understanding what those different ways might have been. If so, then it does not follow that those rules by which calculating, and so forth, might have been carried out constitute a set of genuine alternatives open to us among which we could choose, or even among which we could have chosen. The only sense that has been given to the claim that "somebody may reply like a rational person and yet not be playing our game" is that there might have been different sorts of beings from us, that the inhabitants of the earth might have come to think and behave in ways different from their actual ones. But this does not imply that we are free to put whatever we like after '1000' when given the instructions "Add 2," or that our deciding to put '1002' is what makes that the correct step. Consequently, Wittgenstein's examples do not commit him to a "radical conventionalism" in Dummett's sense. In trying to explain more fully why he is not committed to this I will return to the sense in which he can be called a "conventionalist."

In several places Wittgenstein describes what he is doing in some such way as this:

> What we are supplying are really remarks on the natural history of man: not curiosities however, but rather observations on facts which no-one has doubted, and which have only gone unremarked because they are always before our eyes [*RFM*, I, 141].

What facts does he have in mind here, and what role do they play in his account of logical necessity? The reason for calling them "facts of our natural history" is to emphasize both what I have called their contingency—that is, that they might not have obtained —and the fact that they are somehow "constitutive" of mankind— that is, that their obtaining is what is responsible for human nature's being what it is.

Part of human behavior consists of calculating sums, distances, quantities, of making inferences, drawing conclusions, and so forth. It is a fact that we engage in such practices: "mathematics is after all an anthropological phenomenon" (*RFM*, V, 26). There are various facts which make it possible for calculating to occur at all. For example, our memories are generally good enough for us not to take numbers twice in counting up to 12, and not to leave any out (*RFM*, V, 2); in correlating two groups of five strokes we practically always can do so without remainder (*RFM*, I, 64); somebody who has learned to calculate never goes on getting different results, in a given multiplication, from what is in the arithmetic books (*RFM*, I, 112); and so on. The inhabitants of the earth might have lacked these and other simple abilities, and if so there would be no such thing as calculating at all. In that way the possibility of calculating depends on such contingent facts. These are examples of what Wittgenstein calls the "physical," "psychological," and "physiological" facts which make activities such as calculating possible (*RFM*, V, 15).

A contingent fact which is responsible for our calculating as we actually do is the fact that we take '1002, 1004, . . .' to be going on in the same way as putting down '996, 998, 1000, . . .'. It is a fact that we naturally go on in this way, but people might not have done so. Since they might naturally have followed the rule in a different way, our rules alone do not logically guarantee that they will not be taken or understood in deviant ways. A rule itself does not make "strange" ways of following it impossible, since a rule is not something which stands apart from our understanding of it, and which mysteriously contains within it all of its future applications. How we naturally understand and follow the rule determines which applications of it are correct, and the way a rule is followed will depend in part on what we take to be "going on in the same way. . . . The use of the word 'rule' and the use of the word 'same' are interwoven" (*PI*, 225). It is because people might not share our natural reactions, or might not be in accord with us in their "judgments of sameness," that their understanding the instructions does not rule out their taking a different step from ours at some point while still finding what they have done to be in accord with the rule. So understanding the rule in the way we do depends on such things as finding it natural to go on to '1002' right after '1000'. That we take just the step we do here is a contingent fact, but it is not the result of a decision; it is not a convention to which there are alternatives among which we could choose. And that we share any such "judgments" at all (whatever they might be) is also a contingent fact, but without this agreement there would be no understanding of any rules at all.

If language is to be a means of communication there must be agreement not only in definitions but also (queer as this may sound) in judgments. This seems to abolish logic, but does not do so [*PI*, 242].

Those described as "not playing our game" are the people who are not in accord with us in the "judgments" on which the possibility of language and communication rests. Wittgenstein's examples of the possibility of people like this serve to bring out the contingency of the fact that, as things are, we are in accord in these "judgments." Anyone who did not go on as we do need not be simply continuing a different series (for example, "Add 2 up to 1000, 4 up to 2000," and so forth), and in that way be "playing a game" different from the one we happen to be playing; nor need he have misunderstood the instructions in a way that can be pointed out to him by more careful explanations. But someone like this would not be fully intelligible to us. Our relation to him would be like our relation to people who naturally reacted to the gesture of pointing by looking in the direction of the line from fingertip to wrist, or who sold wood in the way described earlier. It is not simply that they happen to have chosen to do things one way, and we happen to have chosen to do them differently, but that they would be different sorts of beings from us, beings which we could not understand and with which we could not enter into meaningful communication. They would ultimately be unfathomable to us (compare, for example, *RFM*, I, 34, 61, 66, 152). In order to have a "clear concept" of what it would be like to think and behave as they do we would have to be able to abandon many, if not all, of those "judgments" on which our being able to think or conceive of anything at all rests.

What I have been saying will explain what would otherwise be a puzzling distinction which Wittgenstein makes in a well-known passage:

> I am not saying: if such-and-such facts of nature were different people would have different concepts (in the sense of a hypothesis). But: if anyone believes that certain concepts are absolutely the correct ones, and that having different ones would mean not realizing something that we realize—then let him imagine certain very general facts of nature to be different from what we are used to, and the formation of concepts different from the usual ones will become intelligible to him [*PI*, 230].

The point of Wittgenstein's examples of people who do not "play our game" is only to show that our having the concepts and practices we have is dependent upon certain facts which might not have obtained. They show only that "the formation of concepts different from the usual ones" is intelligible to us; but it does not follow from this that those concepts themselves are intelligible to us. And since the intelligibility of alternative concepts and practices is required by the thesis of radical conventionalism which Dummett ascribes to Wittgenstein, I think that thesis is not borne out by Wittgenstein's examples.

The "shared judgments" (for example, of sameness) upon which our being able to communicate rests, and which are responsible for our calculating, inferring, and so forth, as we do are not properly seen, then, as the results of free decisions in the manner of the logical positivists. They might have been different and, if they had been, then calculating, inferring, and so forth, would have been done differently. But this does not make them conventions in the positivists' sense. In defending the claim that we had made the correct move after '1000' in following the rule "Add 2" we could ultimately get back to something like our "shared judgment" that putting down '1002' is doing the same as we were doing earlier. There is nothing further we could appeal to. These "judgments" represent the limits of our knowledge, and thus they have a role similar to the explicit conventions of the positivists.

From what has been said so far it might still look as if our "sharing judgments" is nothing more than our all agreeing that certain propositions are true or unassailable. But the "agreement" of which Wittgenstein speaks here is not the unanimous acceptance of a particular truth or set of truths.

> "So you are saying that human agreement decides what is true and what is false?"—It is what human beings *say* that is true and false; and they agree in the *language* they use. That is not agreement in opinions but in form of life [*PI*, 241].

This "agreement" is the universal accord of human beings in behaving in certain ways—those "natural reactions" which we all share, or those human practices the engaging in which makes a creature human. Those are the "facts of our natural history" which he is appealing to. The correctness of steps in calculating is not ultimately established on the basis of their agreeing with or being entailed by certain truths which we have accepted without foundation, or which are "self-evident":

> The limits of empiricism are not assumptions unguaranteed, or intuitively known to be correct: they are ways in which we make comparisons and in which we act [*RFM*, V, 18].

This distinguishes Wittgenstein both from the Platonist and from the standard conventionalist. I shall comment on only one other aspect of this difference.

I have said that it is a "fact of our natural history" in Wittgenstein's sense that we agree in finding certain steps in following a rule "doing the same." In some cases we all naturally go on in the same way from the steps which have already been taken. This is what makes it possible for us to follow any rules at all.

> And does this mean e.g. that the definition of "same" would be this: same is what all or most human beings with one voice take for the same?—Of course not.

> For of course I don't make use of the agreement of human beings to affirm identity. What criterion do you use, then? None at all [*RFM*, V, 33].

But if there is no criterion for the truth of assertions of identity, now can we know they are true? Without a proof to the contrary, might not all human beings, for all their agreement, be wrong in supposing that writing '1002' is going on in the same way as writing '1000' after '998'? Wittgenstein replies that "to use a word without a justification does not mean to use it wrongfully" (*RFM*, V, 33). And in this case, at this stage, there is no "justification" of the sort the empiricist seeks. But why not?

The correctness of particular calculations, inferences, and so forth, is decided by appeal to the rules, but can't we also ask whether those rules themselves are correct, whether our techniques of calculation, inference, and so forth, are the correct ones?

> The danger here, I believe, is one of giving a justification of our procedure when there is no such thing as a justification and we ought simply to have said: *that's how we do it* [*RFM*, II, 74].

The ultimate appeal in seeking a "foundation" for our procedures of calculating, inferring, and so forth, can only be to "ways in which we make comparisons and in which we act." That is all that an account of the "foundation" or "source" of logical necessity can achieve. This perhaps helps to explain the point of passages like this:

> What has to be accepted, the given, is—so one could say—*forms of life* [*PI*, 226].

Because these procedures cannot be given a "justification" it does not follow that they are shaky or unreliable, or that we are courting trouble if we decide to engage in them. We do not decide to accept or reject them at all, any more than we decide to be human beings as opposed to trees. To ask whether our human practices or forms of life themselves are "correct" or "justified" is to ask whether we are "correct" or "justified" in being the sorts of things we are.

At the end of his paper Dummett recommends interposing between the Platonist and constructivist pictures of thought and reality an intermediate picture

> of objects springing into being in response to our probing. We do not *make* the objects but must accept them as we find them (this corresponds to the proof imposing itself on us); but they were not already there for our statements to be true or false of before we carried out the investigations which brought them into being [p. 348].

As far as I understand this, it seems to be just the picture to be derived from Wittgenstein if my interpretation is in general correct. Logical necessity, he says, is not like rails that stretch to infinity and compel us always to go in one and only one way; but neither is it the case that we are not compelled at all. Rather, there are the rails we have already traveled, and we can extend them beyond the present point only by depending on those that already exist. In order for the rails to be navigable they must be extended in smooth and natural ways; how they are to be continued is to that extent determined by the route of those rails which are already there. I have been primarily concerned to explain the sense in which we are "responsible" for the ways in which the rails are extended, without destroying anything that could properly be called their objectivity.

21

Negation and Generality

HERBERT HOCHBERG

W<small>ITTGENSTEIN</small> in the *Tractatus*
and Russell in *The Philosophy of Logical Atomism* claimed that
atomic facts exist. But, while Russell also recognized negative and
general facts, Wittgenstein apparently does not. The issue that arises
is one about the ontological status of logical form. Such an issue has
several facets. One aspect of it may be taken as a question regarding
whether or not the logical notions of conjunction, negation, disjunction, and generality have ontological significance. Or, as we will
consider the issue here, are there facts corresponding to true conjunctive, negative, etc., statements? The first step in considering
such a question is to explain what one takes the issue to be. Suppose
it is held that what makes a simple or atomic sentence true is a fact.
Thus, if we consider a miniature universe containing two individuals, one black, one white, and both square, a sentence 'Wa' (with
'a' naming the white square and 'W' standing for 'white') would be
true since the atomic fact which it indicates holds or exists. One
might then put the issue about logical facts in terms of what facts
provide the grounds of truth for sentences like '$\sim Wb$', 'Wa & Bb',
'$(\exists x)Wx$', and '$(x)Sx$' (where 'b' names the black square, 'S'
stands for 'square', and 'B' for 'black'). In short, granted that atomic
facts ground the truth of atomic sentences, are there further facts

Reprinted with minor changes with the kind permission of the author
and the editor from *Nous*, 3 (1969):325–43.

needed to provide the basis for nonatomic sentences being true or will a list of true sentences standing for atomic facts suffice? Here, I will argue that while facts corresponding to true negations of atomic sentences must be acknowledged, only some general facts and no facts corresponding to other true molecular compounds of atomic sentences need be included in an adequate ontology. Thus, negation and the quantifiers differ significantly from the other logical constants in regard to ontological issues.

In terms of the above example we would have the list of atomic sentences

$$(a) \quad \mathrm{W}a, \mathrm{B}b, \mathrm{S}a, \mathrm{S}b$$

ignoring relations and all other simple properties of the objects. With respect to conjunction and disjunction one may reply to the above question immediately and negatively. Given that both 'Wa' and 'Bb' indicate facts, we know that 'Wa & Bb' is true. To put it another way we need only look at the list (a) and the truth table for '&'. The same holds for 'Wa ∨ Wb'. Here one must not be misled by the point that we cannot say that *both* 'Wa' and 'Bb' hold without using 'and'. The issue is not whether the connectives '&' and '∨' can be expressed only by atomic sentences. Of course they cannot. Hence, if one takes the question about whether or not logical facts exist in terms of whether or not some logical signs are primitive, he takes it differently from the way it is being taken here.

Leaving aside any issue about how to take the question, we may note that with negation a difference arises. '∼Wb' is true. Yet we cannot consider any sentence on the list, and hence any facts such sentences refer to, to be the basis for it. One may point out that 'Wb' is absent from the list, and hence '∼Wb' is true. Putting it another way, as Moore and Wittgenstein did, one may speak of the nonexistence of a fact as the ground of truth for '∼Wb'. But this introduces a new notion, for in the case of conjunction and disjunction we didn't need to appeal to absence from the list or speak of nonexistent facts. In a way we have a reflection of the simple point that 'p, q ⊢ p & q' and 'p ⊢ p ∨ q' are valid argument forms but that no corresponding simple form exists for negation. The closest one could come would be 'p ⊢ ∼ ∼ p'. But the point here is that in the cases of conjunction and disjunction the argument forms reflect the fact that if we have certain atomic facts we have, as true, certain compound sentences. By contrast, in the case of negation we have nothing on the list that grounds '~Wb'. The most we could say in the case of negation is that if we have 'Wa' and the truth table for '~' we have the ground for '~ ~Wa'. But this does not help us in the case of '~Wb', and that fact reveals a difference about negation. Consider an expanded list of sentences about our miniature universe:

$$(\beta)\ \ \mathrm{W}a, \mathrm{B}b, \mathrm{S}a, \mathrm{S}b, \sim\mathrm{W}b, \sim\mathrm{B}a.$$

We can now speak of '~Wb' being true simply in terms of what is *present* on the list. In short, if we acknowledge *negative facts*, we do not need to speak of both *presence* and absence from the list, or, alternatively, of existent and nonexistent facts. The dichotomy *fact* and *negative fact* does the same job. By contrast, if we were to add 'Wa & Wb' to the list, all we would have done is enable the phrase 'both are present' to be replaced by 'the conjunction is present'. This simply goes back to the primitiveness of logical constants and does not reflect a symmetry as that between 'presence-absence' and 'positive-negative fact'. The point can be put in another way. Consider two lists: one, (a), a list of true atomic sentences; another, (a'), a list of all possible atomic sentences for our miniature universe. 'Wa' is true since it is on (a). '~Wb' may be held to be true since 'Wb' is on (a') but not on (a). In short '~Wb' is true in virtue of a relation between (a) and (a'). This relation would reflect or ground the truth of negative sentences. One might be tempted to hold that the comparison of the two lists provides the ground for '~Wb' and hence contend that negation is supplied by something we do or think. But this would be misleading since what grounds the truth of '~Wb' is not our comparison of the two lists but the connection between them. In putting the matter in terms of the two lists, (a) and (a'), the covert extension of our ontology is perhaps made more explicit if we consider the matter in terms of possible facts. For, one way of explicitly stating what is involved would be to hold that '~Wb' is true since 'Wb' indicates a *possible fact*, rather than a fact of the sort 'Wa' does. The existence of the two kinds of facts, possible facts and actual facts, would replace the explicit recognition of negative facts and positive facts. In the one case, we would have both atomic sentences and negations of such, if true, referring to facts. In the other case, we would consider only atomic sentences to refer to facts, but they would refer to facts, when true, and to possible facts, when false. Derivatively, a negation of an atomic sentence, when true, would have its ontological ground in that the atomic sentence it negates refers to a possible, and not an actual, fact.[1] In terms of the discussion so far, this alternative might be taken to differ only verbally from the one acknowledging negative facts. But differences may emerge when one considers (*a*) the structure of such facts, (*b*) questions about the ontological status of logical truths, and (*c*) problems of intentionality. (*a*) and (*b*) will be touched on shortly. For the moment we might note how yet another, perhaps only "verbal," alternative may arise. One might hold that *knowing that* 'W*b*' is absent from (*a*) is sufficient for knowing that '~W*b*' is true. But this must not be confused with the question of what is the ontological ground for the truth of '~W*b*'. To use the absence of 'W*b*' from the list as an ontological ground is obviously to make use of 'W*b*' being false as the ground of truth for '~W*b*'. This could be just another way of making use of a possible fact referred to by 'W*b*'. But taking the fact that 'W*b*' is false as the ground of truth for '~W*b*' could also be taken to covertly introduce a false fact that 'W*b*' refers to. Thus, one introduces the categories of facts and false facts. Whether these alternatives are really such is not the concern here. The point is simply that whether one explicitly speaks of negative facts, possible facts, or false facts or attempts to avoid any such category by speaking of absence from a list or by a comparison of lists, two categories of facts are involved. This being so, true negations require an ontological ground.

There is another aspect to the issue of negative facts. When one speaks of a negative fact in the case of '~W*b*' as distinct from the fact which is the basis for 'B*b*' being true, there is a question about the connection of such facts. This raises the issue of synthetic a priori connections which we shall discuss shortly. However one deals with the question, the fact which makes 'B*b*' true would not

[1] For the relevance of the recognition of possible facts to the *Tractatus* see "Facts, Possibilities, and Essences in the *Tractatus*," in this volume. Taken together, the arguments presented in the two papers reveal one sense in which Wittgenstein recognizes negative facts in his ontology.

be the same fact which makes '~W*b*' true in the sense that one and the same fact makes 'W*a*' true and '~W*a*' false. Thus with respect to negation two things are relevant. First, there is the question of negative facts. Second, there is a question about the relations between sentences and facts. One can take care of the question about the truth of '~W*b*' by recognizing negative facts. But the fact that 'W*a*' indicates is literally the fact which falsifies '~W*a*', in terms of the truth table for '~'. This is reflected in the connection between 'not' and 'false' so that we infer that '~W*a*' is false from 'W*a*'. In effect this reflects, in turn, a connection between the sentence '~W*a*' and the fact 'W*a*' refers to. In the case of true negative sentences we have been led to two types of facts; in the case of false sentences one may feel led, in a similar way, to see some ontological significance in there being two types of connections between sentences and facts. This belief may be reinforced if one also thinks that we may either introduce *false facts* so that a pair of sentences like 'W*a*' and '~W*a*' could both be held to stand in the *same type of relation* to *two different kinds of facts* or, alternatively, consider the sentences to stand in *different relations* to one and *the same fact*. In the former case both sentences could be said to refer to the different kinds of facts and would be true or false in virtue of the type of referent involved. In the latter case one sentence would stand in a "true-making relation" while the other stood in a false-making relation to one and the same fact. This way of putting it seems to point up the less obvious ontological roles of truth and falsity, and the connections between sentences and facts, as well as the more obvious ontological role of negative facts. But it would seem extreme, perhaps absurd, to hold that false facts exist *on such grounds* or that any additions are needed to an adequate ontology to provide a basis for sentences being false. For it is precisely the fact referred to by 'W*a*' and the truth table for negation which is the basis for '~W*a*' being false. To put it another way, a complete description of the world need not include a list of false sentences, but need only indicate the factual grounds which make them false. Or, in terms of the above discussion about conjunction and disjunction, 'p ⊢ '~p' is false' is analogous to the simple argument forms for conjunction and disjunction, though containing a meta-linguistic notion. On the basis of the truth tables and the occurrence of 'Wa' and 'Bb' on the list (a) we may infer both 'Wa & Bb' and ''∼Wa' is false'. There is nothing corresponding to this in the case of '∼Wb' being true. Speaking of false facts in this context is quite different from our earlier discussion. There we were considering the referent of a false atomic sentence being the ground for the truth of the negation of such a sentence. Speaking of false facts in that context merely indicated the need for some category of fact to ground the truth of negative sentences; either directly, via negative facts, or indirectly, via possible or false facts. Thus there was no need to consider negations which were false as referring to anything at all or being grounded by anything. Here, the notion of a false fact arises in connection with both false atomic sentences and false negations of atomic sentences. For the question is not one of seeking a ground for the truth of sentences but, given such a ground, seeking a further ground for the falsity of their contradictories. This is what seems needless. Yet there is a question about the ontological significance of the inference from 'p' to ''∼p' is false'. This is a question concerning the ontological ground of logical truth or, if one wishes, of the truth table which codifies the use of 'not' or '∼'. Thus, there are two questions regarding the ontological status of negation. One is whether there is a need to ontologically ground the truth of sentences like '∼Wb'; the other is whether the use of negation, whereby it is necessarily the case that a sentence is determined to be true if and only if its negation is false, requires an ontological ground. One might hold that logical truths, like the law of contradiction, are grounded by necessary facts. Or, one may speak of such truths reflecting the "form" of the world or the form of thought, as opposed to being constituents of the world or contents of thought. This would be analogous to speaking of exemplification as a formal feature of a fact rather than a constituent of it in the way the terms of such a relation would be constituents. Whether such a ground is required and, if so, how it is to be considered are questions that we are avoiding here.

One may seek to find a basis for avoiding negative facts in synthetic a priori connections of incompatibility. In effect one attempts to assimilate the case of '∼Wb' being true to that of '∼Wa' being false. But, as Russell pointed out long ago, such a line fails.[2] On such a gambit one has essentially three options. First, one can hold that the fact indicated by 'B*b*' grounds the truth of '~W*b*' since W is incompatible with B. But this introduces *the fact* that W is incompatible with B as part of the basis for the truth of '~W*b*'. And this may certainly be held to be merely another way of introducing negative facts. Second, one can hold that the generality '(x)(Bx ⊃ ~Wx)' together with 'B*b*' suffices to ground the truth of '~W*b*'. But aside from problems about the necessity of the generalization, the question is begged in that it is not only a generalization, and hence would indicate a logical fact of another kind, but it contains a negation. Third, one may introduce a direct inference from 'B*b*' to '~W*b*' without any appeal to an additional premise stating an incompatibility or generality. Thus one holds that '~W*b*' may be inferred from 'B*b*' just as ' '~W*a*' is false' may be inferred from 'W*a*'. But the grounds for such an inference, as well as the notion of inference itself in such cases, has never been clearly and unproblematically formulated or explicated. Moreover, it would seem that this third case reduces to one of the first two. For, however one attempts to explicate the concept of synthetic a priori necessity, the *inference* from 'B*b*' to '~W*b*' will correspond to the necessary truth that W is incompatible with B or that all B's are not W's, just as the inference from 'p & q' to 'p' corresponds to the tautology '(p & q) ⊃ p'. Thus, as in the previous two cases, the question about negative facts will be begged. This indicates that there is only a verbal difference between the third alternative and either one of the other two.

Acknowledging negative facts poses a problem. One may take a fact as complex or not. Suppose one takes an atomic fact to be a complex of a particular and a property in a relation of exemplification. A negative fact would then seem to be either a complex containing a property, a particular, a tie of exemplification *and* something else—the negative constituent—or a complex of a property and a particular in a different kind of relational tie, say negative exemplification. But the first alternative, as it stands, will not do. For one

---

[2] Bertrand Russell, "The Philosophy of Logical Atomism," in *Logic and Knowledge,* ed. R. C. Marsh (London: Allen & Unwin, 1956), pp. 212–13.

would have exemplification as a tie between a particular and a property in a positive fact *and* as a tie between a particular, a property, and the negative element in a negative fact. Thus we either have a tie playing a double role or are forced to acknowledge an additional tie besides exemplification. Whether one takes this further tie to connect the negative element to the complex composed of the particular, the property, and exemplification or takes it as a three-term relation between the negative element, the property, and the particular makes little difference. On either alternative one recognizes a negative element as well as a negative nexus or tie. Thus, the simple, though awkward sounding, expedient of negative exemplification, without a negative element, seems more economical. Moreover, it puts negation on a par with exemplification as a matter of "form" rather than taking '∼' as some sort of label of an "object." A question may arise regarding the use of negation in molecular sentences like '∼∼p', '∼(p & q)', and '∼(x)[Fx ⊃ Gx]'. All such uses may be regarded as alternative formulations for statements where negations occur only in front of atomic forms. Hence, no problem arises for the ontological accounts of negation, either in terms of a negative nexus or in terms of negative properties. Yet, one may raise a question about the ontological status of the logical equivalences used in such transformations. This, in effect, re-raises the question about the ontological status of logical truths. We may also note that for the issues in this paper it is not necessary to distinguish between the particular white patch and another sense of 'particular' whereby the patch contains a particular substratum or ground of individuation. The latter would be what stands in the exemplification nexus to the properties and thereby constitutes the ordinary particular. Such a substratum would then also be what stands in the relation of negative exemplification to a property. If one holds that an ordinary particular, like the patch, is to be analyzed only in terms of a set of qualities in a relation, then the tie of negative exemplification would be taken to hold between the complex particular (the patch) and a simple property it does not have, i.e., which is not a constituent of it. There would then be a fundamental asymmetry, on such a view, between the analysis of '*a* is white' and '*a* is not black'. In the former case, the predicate would be taken to indicate a property joined with other properties by a tie or nexus to constitute the object; in the latter case, the nexus of negative exemplification would connect the property to the complex particular composed of properties.

The two sentences 'Wb' and '~Wb' then reflect the two possibilities that b is connected to the property W either by exemplification or negative exemplification. That the sentences are contradictories reflects the impossibility of a particular standing in both ties to one and the same property. This way of putting things points to a further difference between the case of 'Wb' and '~Wb', on the one hand, and that of 'Bb' and 'Wb', on the other. For, it would seem that if one held to a synthetic a priori necessity or incompatibility between B and W this would be reflected in the claim that a particular cannot simultaneously stand in the exemplification nexus to two properties that are incompatible, rather than not being able to stand in two relations to one property. But this difference disappears if we accept a third alternative account of negative facts. One may hold that there is neither a negative element nor a negative nexus and seek to account for negative facts by means of negative properties. Thus a negative fact would be analyzed in terms of a particular standing in the exemplification tie to a negative property. On this view both synthetic a priori incompatibilities and logical incompatibilities would involve a particular not (possibly) standing in the exemplification tie to two (or more) properties. Yet, one could hold that the sense of 'possibly' would still be different in the cases of synthetic a priori and logical impossibility, but this difference would be reflected by the distinction between properties and negative properties, rather than by that between exmplification and negative exemplification. For, incompatible properties, like B and W, are not related as are a property and its negative correlate, say B and ~B. This assumes '~B' is not taken as a "simple" sign referring to a "simple" property, but that the former is defined in terms of '~' and 'B' and the latter is taken as complex property having B as a constituent, in some sense. If the negative properties are taken as simple, one abandons the explication of logical necessity propounded by Wittgenstein in the *Tractatus*. For, in effect, one will base logical truths on necessary relations between simple properties, and, consequently, consider logical truths analogously to the way some philosophers have spoken of synthetic a priori truths. It is not the purpose of this paper to explore alternative accounts of negation and negative facts, but analyzing negative facts, either in terms of negative properties or negative exemplification, preserves a distinction between logical incompatibility and synthetic a priori incompatibility. This difference may go along with another. One who adheres to synthetic a priori necessities recognizes an additional kind of fact. Thus, the incompatibility of B and W would be reflected by the addition of something like 'I(W,B)' to the list (a), where 'I' stands for a primitive notion of incompatibility. Here we are not concerned with the question of negative facts nor with whether or not 'I' is a problematic notion. We merely note that holding to synthetic necessities requires a new category of facts. By contrast, one may attempt to speak of analyticity or logical necessity in terms which do not require such an addition. This would involve holding that logical truths like '~(p & ~ p)' do not require an ontological ground, either in the form of logically necessary "facts" or *the fact* that the world has a certain "logical form." If successful such an attempt would reveal a further difference between synthetic and analytic necessities. In this discussion I have merely mentioned but not considered alternatives to the introduction of negative facts, such as possible facts. Hence, questions about the structure of the latter or whether such alternatives differ only verbally are not taken up. The reason for this is simply that the point being argued is that some type of entity, in addition to atomic facts, is needed to ground true negative sentences, and each alternative recognizes such a ground. Moreover, I suspect that, as long as one confines oneself to the issue at hand, no real difference will emerge between the alternatives.

As one argues against the need for conjunctive facts one can seemingly argue against existential facts. What makes a sentence like '$(\exists x)Wx$' true is the fact expressed by 'Wa'. Again, this is reflected in the valid pattern for existential generalization. With universally general facts there seems to be a difference. There is the point of Russell's that

$$\frac{Sa \ \& \ Sb}{(x) \ S(x)}$$

won't do as a valid argument form.[3] Hence, we must add that *a* and *b* are all the objects. This would give us, in effect,

$$(\gamma) \quad \frac{Sa \ \& \ Sb \ \& \ (x) \ (x = a \lor x = b)}{(x) \ Sx.}$$

But then we have a generality as part of the basis of inference. Yet '(x) (x = *a* ∨ x = *b*)' is a special type of generality. For any finite list like (β) all one needs is a generality stating that the individuals listed constitute the totality of individuals. Hence, if we take the valid inference pattern of existential generalization to be the key to the avoidance of existential facts, we can maintain, in view of (γ), that there is only one general fact for a finite universe: that pertaining to how many things (at most) there are. For an infinite domain this pattern will no longer do. In that case we may hold that the very notion of a list is specious. We will consider such a domain shortly. More pertinent for the moment is another type of case. Consider two black crosses against a small white background enclosed by a circular boundary. One sees that there are two black crosses. One also sees that every cross in the circle is black or that no cross in the circle is red. Do these "facts" indicate that there are existential and general facts corresponding to the relevant true existential and universal sentences? One might be tempted to say so if he thought that the experiences in each case were both different from and irreducible to others that could be described by atomic sentences. Since the experiences are not so reducible, what is *meant* or *intended* by (1) 'Every cross in the circle is black' is not the same as (2) '*a* is a black cross in the circle and *b* is a black cross in the circle'. Nor, is it the same as (3) '*a* is a black cross in the circle *c* and *b* is a black cross in the circle *c* and only *a* and *b* are in *c*'. Here the term 'meant' can be taken two ways. First, one can point out that the universal quantifier is not reducible in meaning to a conjunction. Second, one can contend that a thought or intention expressed by (1) is different in kind, from one expressed by either (2) or (3). This latter contention is independent of the issue of the definition or reducibility of the quantifiers. For, even though one defines 'p ⊃ q' as '∼p ∨ q', one may hold that a thought whose

[3] Bertrand Russell, *An Inquiry into Meaning and Truth* (Baltimore: Penguin Books, 1962), pp. 86–87.

content is expressed by one is different in kind from a thought whose content is expressed by the other. Hence, led by the definitional irreducibility of the universal quantifier to a conjunction, one may reject (2) as a transcription of (1); led by the irreducibility of intentional contexts, one may also reject (3) as a suitable transcription. Thus, one could come to hold that (1) indicated a general fact. But this would be a mistake. For the issue, recall, centers around what facts are necessary to ground the truth of (1). The issue is neither whether the meaning of the universal quantifier can be captured by definition nor whether thoughts expressed by a general sentence are different from and irreducible to other thoughts. To point out that 'W*a* or B*a*' does not mean 'W*a*' and that thinking that W*a* or B*a* is not the same, in intention, as thinking that W*a*, is irrelevant to whether or not there are disjunctive facts. Likewise, holding that (1) means neither (2) nor (3) is irrelevant for the question of general facts.

Assume there are four objects, *a*, *b*, *c*, and *d*, and properties referred to by 'C$_1$' for 'cross' and 'C$_2$' for 'circle', in addition to W, B, and S, and a relational predicate 'I' for 'in'. The issue is whether or not a suitable exhaustive list, (δ), of atomic and negative sentences containing 'C$_1$*a*', 'C$_1$*b*', 'C$_2$*c*', 'I*ac*', etc., together with a general sentence stating that there are only four objects or, alternatively, the assumption that the list is complete so that the fact that there are only four objects may be said to show itself, suffices to ground the truth of the generality that all the crosses in the circle are black. Since such a list and such a general sentence do suffice, no general fact is needed to correspond to and ground (1).

Are there then general facts? One who is impressed by the point that generality is required only in the form of a general statement about the number of things there are and by the contrast of this case to that of negation might say "no." He might even feel that this requirement is already taken care of by the specification of the list of atomic and negative sentences. That is, even the general sentence as to the number of things there are is not one that belongs to the list and is, in fact, not even necessary, since this is implied or shown by the list and the stipulation that the list is complete. But this just seems to be a less explicit way of making a claim about the number of things that there are. Hence, one who is impressed by the need to stipulate something in the form of a general sentence, whether added to the list or made about it, might feel forced to acknowledge general facts; i.e., one general fact about individuals for any finite universe. For we cannot explain such generalities away in the manner we employed for conjunctive and disjunctive facts.

An attempt might be made to strengthen the case against general facts by insisting, in Wittgensteinian fashion, that the number of individuals there are is something that cannot be stated but must show itself. Hence, it would be inappropriate to even consider whether there is a general fact corresponding to the true sentence 'There are only four individuals in the universe which is depicted by (δ)'. Being inadmissible, such a sentence could not indicate a general fact. This would put the matter far more strongly than merely holding that such a general sentence is not required. Following such a line, one might insist that if we hold a list like (δ) depicts a model universe, and if we further employ an interpretation rule or, if you will, picturing principle, according to which one sign (name or predicate) represents one thing (individual or universal), it follows from (δ)'s being a picture or representation that there are only four individuals in the universe represented or pictured. One is thus led into holding that there is a general fact only by not realizing what it is to be a picture or representation. But this does not alter the point that no set of atomic sentences will suffice to ground a universal generalization. We may then wonder if it is really crucial whether one adds an explicit premise in the form of a sentence as to there being at most four individuals or holds that this shows itself. Clearly generality has not been eliminated. To meet this objection, one might suggest, following standard logic texts, that in a finite universe a universal quantification can be taken to express a conjunction. Hence, in a universe of two things, '(x)Sx' would follow from 'Sa & Sb' since the former is merely an abbreviation of the latter. Here one would have to acknowledge that the very meaning of the universal quantifier changes depending on the number of things there are, i.e., its sense is relative to the domain we are using it to speak about. But even if there are no objections to this, we could still not express that there would be at most so many things. Hence, one would still have to claim that that "fact" showed itself. Consequently, one might suggest that the peculiarity of a sentence like '(x) (x = a ∨ x = b)', even if admitted in order to derive '(x)Sx' from 'Sa & Sb & (x) (x = a ∨ x = b)', need not commit us to the recognition of a general fact. But this seems more in the nature of announcing a decision than providing an argument. What is peculiar would be the nature of the general fact. For it might not seem amenable to analysis into components as did the atomic and negative facts. Or, to reflect one of Wittgenstein's worries, it is difficult to see how such a fact could be depicted. However, we might consider generality to reduce to a relational property holding among the individuals a and b. That a and b are all the things there are is a relation they exemplify. Hence, the need for only one universally general sentence like '(x) (x = a ∨ x = b)' permits us to consider generality as a property of things. (It is even tempting to speak of a "logical" property.) This would have the advantage of enabling us to consider the structure of a general fact analogously to the structure of atomic and negative facts. One may even speak of the general fact as a kind of atomic fact since it is analyzed in terms of a primitive relation exemplified by particulars. Alternatively, since such a relational property is unlike any ordinary relation, there is a sense in which such a fact is different, in kind, from any atomic fact. Actually, there would be an infinite number of such relations. Each would be an n-place relation, where n would vary according to the size of the domain whose members exemplified the relation. Thus, while each would play the same role in a different possible domain, there would be two aspects involved. To say of a universe of two things that they are all that there are is to say something similar and something different from saying of a domain of three things that the three are all that there are. In a way this simply reflects the varying and the constant sense of the universal quantifier when it is taken as equivalent to a two-term conjunction in a domain of two and a three-term conjunction in a domain of three items. But there is a crucial difference. For, the relations are not taken as "the meaning" of the universal quantifier, since the similar roles played by the various n-term relations is relevant. Thus, the "sense" of *the* quantifier is not given by a specific conjunction or n-term relation but, in part, by the fact that each possible domain involves an n-term relation.

Just as one may feel forced to recognize a universally general fact corresponding to there being only a certain number of individuals, one seems obliged to acknowledge an existential fact corresponding to there being *at least* a certain number of objects. In short, to state that there are exactly two objects, for example, requires both an existential and a universal sentence. Moreover, such an existential sentence will not follow from any set of atomic sentences and negations of such, as '(∃ x)Wx' follows from 'Wa'. Here, one may rehearse the same arguments about certain things showing themselves or being implicit in the notion of a list or representation of facts as were raised about the universally generalized sentence. In fact, one may reinforce the point in the case of the existential sentence by pointing out that accepting '(∃ x)Wx' as a consequence of 'Wa' requires holding that signs like '*a*' must designate. Yet, we would hardly give ontological status to the designation relation. To connect a name to an object requires us to recognize the object, but not the connection, as an entity. Thus, it may be held that if on the list of atomic and negative sentences characterizing the model universe the different names '*a*' and '*b*' occur, and no other names occur, this suffices to "show" that there are two objects. In effect, it is argued that just as one requires that names designate one also requires that different names designate different objects. The second rule should have no more ontological significance than the first. But, while it is true that we may consider both rules to be on a par in that we require a symbolism to conform to them, there is a crucial difference. To require names to name does not state a fact about the world but simply lays down a rule for a language to be used about it. To require that different names name different things can be taken that way also. But that there are two objects rather than three is a fact about a world. Hence, we must not let the rule about different names for different things implicitly assert this fact while pretending that it is simply a rule. In short, there is an existential fact about at least how many things there are just as there is a universal one about at most how many things there are.

Granting such an existential fact we face the question of its structure. Here a symmetry with the purported analysis of the universal fact suggests itself. Difference or diversity has been considered a relation holding between any two different things. But, in a way, to say something is different from something else is to say there are at least two things. That is, there is at least a logical equivalence between the two sentences in that if there are two things, then something will be different from something else, and if the latter is the case it follows that the former is. The same can be said in the case of three or more objects. Just as one speaks of two objects being different one may speak of a three-term, four-term, etc., relation holding among the diverse things that there are. And we may correspondingly hold that the existential fact as to the least number of things that there are is to be analyzed in terms of an n-term relation of diversity among the objects of the model universe. The existential fact thus corresponds, in structure, to the universal one, and the relation involved in the universal fact may be thought of as the dual of the notion of diversity or difference. Or, perhaps better, we might think in terms of two relations, one involved in the existential fact, the other in the universal, and together they reflect the idea of diversity in that both are involved in sentences like 'There are five different things' and 'Consider a universe of five objects'. Like the relation involved in the universal fact, the one in the existential fact is peculiar in that it is not an n-term relation where n can be specified. Speaking of relations corresponding to the general and the existential fact may seem excessively ad hoc. In part, I share the feeling but do not see that it is any more ad hoc than speaking of exemplification as a special kind of relation. Perhaps there is a difference in that one who says exemplification is a special kind of relation does so under the pressure of an argument like Bradley's regress. By contrast, I am suggesting that we consider quantification in terms of certain special relations, not under the pressure of an argument, but to enable us to consider the general and existential facts as basically similar to other facts. But whether such a difference reveals that one "solution" is ad hoc and the other not or that different issues are resolved in different ways is an open question.

A relational property of diversity being involved in an existential fact may seem problematic if we consider a domain of only one individual. For here there would seem to be an existential fact but clearly no relation of diversity to hold among different objects. Thus it appears that one has to treat such a domain as a limiting case. This leads to a few further points. We have been treating the assertion that a is a diverse from b as involving the claim that there are two things. Thus the relational property of diversity is, in effect, a property of existence. This may be thought to be brought out in the limiting case of the domain of one where there appears to be a one-term property rather than a relation. Since such a property is taken to be involved in the existential fact, and this fact is expressed by the use of the existential operator, one might say that the existential operator reflects a property of existence even though it is not a predicate. (Just as one can hold that a relation of diversity may be indicated by the use of different signs for different things rather than by a predicate.) This in turn, would merely reflect the point that such a property, like the relation of exemplification or that of identity, is not an ordinary property or relation.

In the limiting case of a domain of one object, the universal quantifier also reflects a one-term property. But this property would still differ from that reflected by the existential quantifier, for there is a clear difference between the notions of "at least one" and "at most one." That there are two properties rather than one, even in the limiting case, is thus seemingly indicated by the need for both a universal and existential statement. Thus the equivalence of the universal and existential quantifier in a domain of one does not seem to point to the collapsing of the two properties into one in such a domain. However, there is a further problem. To say that there are at least two objects is to employ the existential sentence '$(\exists x)$ $(\exists y)$ $(x \neq y)$' or, perhaps, '$(\exists x)$ $(\exists y)$ $(x = a \,\&\, y = b \,\&\, a \neq b)$'; but to state that there is at least one would involve something like '$(\exists x)$ $(x = x)$' or '$(\exists x)$ $(x = a)$'. Yet, '$(\exists x)$ $(x = x)$', unlike '$(\exists x)$ $(\exists y)$ $(x \neq y)$', is analytic, assuming one does not allow the empty domain as an interpreting domain in validity theory. This may lead one to suggest that the assertion that there is at least one thing is not a fact but a matter of logic, and hence no existential property is involved in the limiting case of a unit domain. To put it another way the very notion of model, domain, or universe involves there being at least one thing. Hence, the fact that separates the unit domain from all others is that there is at most one thing. To put it still differently, the idea of an empty universe makes no sense. Thus the limiting case becomes one in which there is no property of diversity and not one in which the relation becomes a one-term property. In this way the logical equivalence of the quantifiers in the unit domain is reflected in there being only one general fact and one general property in such a universe. To speak of a property of existence, as I did above, is thus misleading, if one holds that '$(\exists x)$ $(x = x)$' is analytic and does not state a fact. (This assumes that one takes '$(\exists x)$ $(x = x)$' to state that at least one thing exists.)

Since the relations of generality and diversity ground the truth of a statement as to the number of things that are in a given universe or model, one might be tempted to think of the ontological ground of elementary arithmetic in terms of such relations rather than in terms of classes of classes. Natural numbers could then be taken to be relational properties holding in possible universes or models. Thus, the facts, or possible facts, indicated by '$(\exists x)$ $(\exists y)$ $[x \neq y$ & $(z)(z = x \vee z = y)]$' and '$(\exists x)$ $(\exists y)$ $(\exists z)$ $[x \neq y$ & $x \neq z$ & $y \neq z$ & $(w)(w = x \vee w = y \vee w = z)]$' would constitute the ontological ground of 2 and 3. Natural numbers would then have a distinct ontological status rather than being construed as the logical fictions (classes) of the logistic reconstruction.[4] To explore this in detail is beyond the scope of this paper, though we may note the bearing of such a possibility on the status of '$(\exists x)$ $(x = x)$' as analytic, and a subsequent question about the number 0.

The above discussion of universal and existential facts has been confined to finite models. Without going into the question of whether the notion of an infinite universe is ultimately a sensible one, we can note certain fundamental differences about infinite and finite model universes. The existential sentence applicable to an infinite world would be of a different kind since, in principle, no set of existential quantifiers over individual variables would suffice. Thus, something like Russell's axiom of infinity would be required. Moreover, one universal fact would no longer suffice. For, together with the sentence used to state that there were at most a denum-

---

[4] Frege took Jevons to be holding something of this sort and criticized such a view on the grounds that one could not construe 0 and 1 adequately. What he had in mind was that numbers were taken to be based on a fundamental relation of diversity and that in the case of applying 0 and 1 no such relation could be involved. The point is whether one is struck more by the difference between the unit domain and all other non-empty domains, in that relational properties are involved in the latter, or by the similarity, in that each existential statement marks out one domain from all others. See G. Frege, *The Foundations of Arithmetic*, trans. J. L. Austin (Evanston: Northwestern University Press, 1968), pp. 56–57.

erably infinite number of objects, no set of atomic (and negations of atomic) sentences would suffice as premises to derive a generality of the form '(x) (Fx ⊃ Gx)'. This is not merely a matter of there possibly being an infinite number of F's but of the possibility of there being an infinite number of F's which are G's without all F's being G's. The point is a simple consequence of the arithmetic of the infinite. Each true generalization would, in effect, require its own fact. Thus what sort of existential and universal facts there are would seem to depend on whether the domain one speaks about is finite or not.

One fundamental objection may be raised concerning the criterion used to dispense with the need for admitting conjunctive and general facts. It can be pointed out that just as one may derive the conjunction 'W*a* & B*b*' from 'W*a*' together with 'B*b*' and derive '(x)S*x*' from 'S*a*', 'S*b*', and '(x)(x = *a* ∨ x = *b*)', we can also derive 'W*a*' from the conjunction and we could derive a sentence indicating an atomic fact from a generalization, as in the case of 'S*a*' and '(x)S*x*', or from a generalization and another atomic sentence, as in the case of '(x)(W*x* ⊃ S*x*)', 'W*a*' and 'S*a*'. Hence, it would appear as if one could hold, in terms of the criterion employed above, either that there is a conjunctive fact but no atomic fact or a general fact but not an atomic fact indicated by the atomic sentence derived by use of the general sentence. But this objection would overlook a crucial point. One could not consistently claim that there was a conjunctive fact without there being an atomic fact. For, one would be forced either to consider the conjunctive fact to be such that it contains atomic facts as constituents or to analyze it into a relation among the constituents of the various atomic facts. In the former case one explicitly acknowledges atomic facts. In the latter case a problem arises. Let the structure of the conjunctive fact indicated by 'W*a* & B*b*' be depicted by 'R(W, B, *a*, *b*)'. One could not then derive that *a* is W while *b* is B. One would have to link the appropriate particulars and universals in the structure of the conjunctive fact. But this would be to acknowledge atomic facts. Thus, the existence of the conjunctive fact would presuppose the existence of the atomic fact it supposedly dispenses with. A similar point can be made against the purported use of a general fact to ground the truth of atomic sentences and hence enable us to dispense with atomic facts. Here, unlike the case of conjunction, one will require atomic sentences in the derivations in those cases where the generalities are like '$(x)(Fx \supset Gx)$', rather than of the form '$(x)Fx$'. Hence, one could not seek to avoid atomic facts altogether. Aside from this, a question arises about the structure of general facts. If one analyzes them in terms of a relation among all the constituent objects and properties involved, the same problem arises that we noted in the case of conjunction. But there is an alternative for generalizations like '$(x)(Fx \supset Gx)$'. One could, for example, take the general fact to involve an asymmetrical relation between the relevant properties. Yet, in both this case and the case of '$(x)Sx$', the existence of the general fact may still be said to imply the existence of atomic facts indicated by the atomic sentences whose truth the general fact is supposed to ground. For, given the distinction between particulars and properties and the consequent tie of exemplification, it would be incoherent to deny that the particular and universal, referred to by the name and predicate of the derived atomic sentence, are tied by exemplification. By contrast, one could deny that the constituents of the supposed general fact do stand in a primitive relation corresponding to the universal operator even though a relevant set of atomic sentences, guaranteeing the truth of the generalization, held.[5] This simply reflects the point that we use the universal quantifier to assert that each particular is tied to a certain property. To put it another way, the basis for the inference from '$(x)Sx$' to 'Sa' is that the universal quantifier is taken to express that every particular, including a, exemplifies S. If '$(x)Sx$', when true, is to be taken as indicating some general fact, a question arises as to the connection between '$(x)Sx$' and 'Sa' whereby the latter is derived from the former. To put it still differently, to take '$(x)Sx$' as indicating a general fact would make no sense unless the existence of that general fact involved or implied that there were atomic facts like that indicated by 'Sa'. But there is nothing comparable to this forcing us to hold that general facts are presupposed by acknowl-

[5] This is not to say that one can consistently deny that the constituents, along with the other individuals of the domain, stand in a relation to constitute the one general fact that I have argued is necessary in any finite domain. The point is that if a generalization like '$(x)Wx$' or '$(x)Wx \supset Sx)$' is true, one can consistently deny that there are general facts corresponding to *those* particular true sentences.

edging atomic facts and the one general fact about the number of individuals in the domain. In dispensing with certain categories of facts the criterion is thus not simply the derivability of sentences purportedly referring to those facts. What one must hold to exist, in order to coherently analyze the facts acknowledged as existents, is also involved.

22

Facts, Possibilities, and Essences in the Tractatus

HERBERT HOCHBERG

I. *The Existence of Facts*

WITTGENSTEIN begins the *Tractatus logico-philosophicus* with the following two claims:

1. The world is all that is the case
1.1 The world is the totality of facts, not of things.[1]

They mean that to state what the world is, or how it is, is to state all the facts that hold or exist. A complete description would be a list of all facts; a partial description, a list of some facts. A list of things does not single out *the* world from other *possible* worlds with the same elements or constituents; a list of facts does. It is not just a question of listing the relations among the things, as well as the things. Consider a painting done in pointillist style. One would not describe it by listing the number and kind of color patches. Nor would one describe it by including the relations that obtain among the patches, if all this meant was including reference to such relations on the list. What one would have to do to describe the picture —to single it out from other possible pictures with the same kinds of patches and relations—would be to specify *which patches stood in*

---

[1] Passages quoted from the *Tractatus* are from the D. F. Pears and B. F. McGuinness translation (London: Routledge & Kegan Paul, 1961) with some slight alterations.

which relations to which other patches. Thus, it would not suffice to know that some patch stood to the left of some other patch, that the relation *left of* held between two patches; one would have to specify, for example, that a green square stood to the left of a blue circle. Consider a collection of three things, *a*, *b*, *c*. Suppose we also know that the relations *R*, *S*, and *C* hold among the things. Consider next the three lists,

(I)	(II)	(III)
a	*a*	*aRb*
b	*b*	*bSc*
c	*c*	*aSc*
	R	*bSa*
	S	
	C	

with the sign combinations on (III) being relational sentences stating that the things referred to stand in the indicated relation. If we take the things to be the objects of a model universe, then only (III) could be said to *characterize* such a universe, to tell us what it is like and how it differs from other possible models *with the same things and the same relations.* (III) may be said to determine a world, if we understand that the list is complete. That is, the list not only tells us what facts hold but that no other facts hold. The very notion of a list may be said to be that of a *complete* listing. Hence,

1.11 The world is determined by the facts, and by their being *all* the facts.

What is involved may be grasped by noting that a list like (III) suffices to uniquely specify, or single out, one possible world from all others that could be described by means of the members of the list (II), and it also completely describes that possible world. In short, (III) serves to *individuate* and to *completely characterize* the world. Taking the sentences of (III) to stand for facts and the set of the sentences of (III) to correspond to a set of facts, one might think of the world, so uniquely and completely characterized, as being a collection of facts—as being composed of or constituted by the facts which are indicated by the sentences on the list. Moreover, given the list (III), with the understanding that such lists are complete, it is apparent just which facts hold. To put it simply, from the totality of facts we can determine the members of the totality; given the list we are given the constituent sentences on it. It is also the case that we can determine which facts do not hold. For example, the absence of the sentence '*aRc*' from the list shows that there is no fact indicated by that sentence.

1.12 For the totality of facts determines what is the case, and also whatever is not the case.

The doctrine is that the list thus reveals what is and what is not the case. But, to see how it does the latter, we must consider the metaphor of logical space.

1.13 The facts in logical space are the world.

We have seen how the facts indicated by the list (III) may be said to determine the world. There is a sense in which the things and relations indicated by the list (II) may also be said to determine something. Given the list (II) and the rule that any of the signs '*a*', '*b*', and '*c*' may be combined with one of the signs '*R*', '*S*', and "*C*" in the pattern '*x* . . . *y*', where any of the small letters may replace the '*x*' and '*y*' and any of the capital letters may replace the '. . .', one may construct a list of all sign combinations permitted by the rule.

(III′)

aRb

aRc

aRa

aSb

aSc

aSa

aCb

. . .

. . .

cCc

For the time, consider each sentence of (III′) to indicate a "possible" fact, by which is meant a fact that may or may not hold, obtain, exist. (III′) thus gives a list of all possible facts. Any list now formed by a selection of sentences from (III') may be taken to determine a possible world in the way in which (III) was earlier said to determine one. (III), of course, is one of the lists that is formed by a selection from (III'). (III) singles out and completely describes a world that is possible; the actual world, if the facts indicated by it obtain or exist. (III') determines the possibilities. Alternatively, one may say that the list (II) and the rule mentioned above determine the possibilities, for *they determine* the list (III'). (III), let us say, describes or characterizes the world; (III') describes or reveals its "logical space."

The metaphor is understandable and suggestive. Each sentence of (III') indicates a possibility, which may be realized or not, just as a place in space may be filled or not. Each sentence of (III), assuming that the list gives a description of the world, indicates a fact—not a possibility, but an existent fact. Just as one may describe which places in an area of space are filled and which are not, (III) tells us which logical spaces (possibilities) are filled (realized) and which are not. Thus, facts may be said to be *in* logical space as one says that physical objects are *in* space. The use of the term 'in' is, nevertheless, analogical. Yet, there is more to it. Before going into what else is involved, another example will aid the analogy. Consider a standard way of characterizing the places or squares of a chessboard:

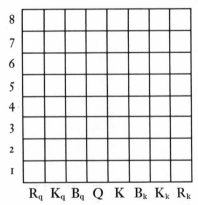

with the subscripts 'q' and 'k' for queen's and king's side, respectively. Each combination of a number sign from the side and a letter sign from the bottom indicates a space or square. We could even arrange a list, like (III'), of all the possible spaces. Suppose one then considered another list, such as:

Black King at K_1
Black Pawn at K_4
White King at K_8
White Pawn at K_5

Such a list could be taken to describe an actual situation, indicating that certain pieces were at certain places and that no other pieces were on the board. It would, in a way, indicate which spaces were occupied by what. (III) also indicates, in its way, which spaces are occupied and thus functions like the list stating which chess pieces are at which places. (III') functions analogously to the matrix formed by the board or the list one may compose from it; only with (III), by indicating the spaces occupied, one also indicates what does the occupying. Perhaps a closer analogy would result from ignoring which pieces were at which places and only considering whether a square was occupied or not. Thus, the list

K_1
K_4
K_8
K_5

would indicate that those, and only those squares, had pieces on them. One would even consider a matrix like

R	x								
S		x		x	x				
C									
	ab	ac	aa	ba	bc	bb	ca	cb	cc

with an '*x*' indicating that the possibility is realized. Such a matrix *with* the *x*'s is another way of writing the list (III). The matrix without any *x*'s would be a way of presenting what is expressed by (III'), the possibilities or the logical space. Thinking in terms of matrices helps bring out something more that is involved in the analogical use of the terms 'in' and 'space'. Showing the location of pieces on a board or the existence of facts by x's on a matrix obviously presupposes the existence of and use of the board and the matrix; for something to be at a place or in a space there must be the place and the space for it to be in. Starting with three objects and three relations, the six signs 'a', 'b', 'c', 'R', 'S', and 'C', and three rules:

Rule 1:   The signs 'a', 'b', and 'c' will stand for objects, while the signs 'R', 'S', and 'C' will stand for relations.

Rule 2:   The sign 'a' stands for the object . . . , 'b' for . . . , . . . , the sign 'C' stands for the relation . . . .

Rule 3:   Any two object signs may be combined with any sign for a relation in the pattern 'x . . . y' where any of the object signs may replace the 'x' or 'y' and any of the relation signs the '. . .',

with the dots in Rule 2 providing a specification of which object and relation the respective signs stand for, we may say the list (II) determines the possible patterns set down in (III'). Taking these patterns as sentences stating possible facts, we may derivatively hold that the objects and relations referred to on the list (II) determine the possible facts indicated by (III'). One may then say that, while (III) *describes* the world, and the facts indicated by the sentences on (III) *determine* how the world is, (II) *reveals* how the world *could be described*, and the objects and relations which are referred to by the signs of (II) *determine* how it *could be*. (II), or (III'), thus shows the logical space which the facts indicated by the sentences on (III) are "in." These facts constitute the world—the world as it actually is, as opposed to the alternative possible worlds.

1.2 The world divides into facts.

In part, 1.2 summarizes what we have just discussed. But there is a further crucial point. Consider the fact indicated by the sentence 'bSc'. The fact is more than the objects that may be called "constituents" of it. Even if we consider the relation which the sign 'S' stands for as a further constituent, the fact is more than the three constituents, a, b, and S. That the fact could not be taken as a class of its constituents would be another way of putting the point.

.

The fact *is* the constituents in a *combination;* the fact is the constituents *joined* together. This is why the fact is indicated by a sentence and not merely by a list of its constituents. The sentence has an order, or structure, or arrangement, and it is this feature of the sentence which is crucial in our use of the sentence to indicate a fact. A mere list would not do.

Consider, (a)

$$c$$
$$b$$
$$S$$

as such a list, and keep in mind that the idea of a list just involves the notion of the occurrence or the absence of something from the list. It does not involve the order, structure, sequence, arrangement, etc., of the constituent items on the list. Thus, (a) and (a')

$$b$$
$$c$$
$$S$$

are the same list, and any other such "arrangement" of the letters 'b', 'c', and 'S' would yield the same list. Recall, forgetting any question of types, that the set signs

$$\hat{x} \ [x = b \vee x = c \vee x = S]$$
$$\hat{x} \ [x = c \vee x = b \vee x = S]$$
$$\cdot \ \cdot \ \cdot \ \cdot \ \cdot \ \cdot \ \cdot \ \cdot \ \cdot \ \cdot \ \cdot \ \cdot$$
$$\hat{x} \ [x = S \vee x = b \vee x = c]$$

all stand for the same class—the class whose members are c, b, and S. But to indicate the fact indicated by the sentence 'bSc', by means of a list like (a) or (a'), we should have to introduce or make use of the order or arrangement of the items. The list is then no longer merely a list; it is an esoteric way of writing a sentence. Just as a fact cannot be taken to be merely a class of its constituents, it cannot be indicated by a mere list of its constituents. This point connects with one of the crucial doctrines of the *Tractatus*, that sentences are not names. There is much to be clarified and some objections to be considered in order to deal adequately with the relevant issues, but we can ignore such questions here. For our purpose, consider a fact to be made up of its constituents connected or structured in a certain way. It thus involves an arrangement of its constituents. A fact does not, therefore, *divide* or *decompose into* its constituents. By contrast, the world *does divide* or *decompose into* facts. The world is not composed of its constituent facts *in* certain arrangements, or relationships, or configurations; it is *merely* composed of its constituent facts.

Suppose one were to hold that facts could or did stand in relation to other facts. Let 'F_1' and 'F_2' stand for relations which facts may stand in, and let a sign sequence like 'bSc F_1 aRb' state that the fact which 'bSc' indicates stands in the relation F_1 to the fact indicated by 'aRb'. In general, let the pattern 'p ::: q' be a further sentence pattern where (1) 'p' and 'q' are replaced by any sentences on (III') and either 'F_1' or 'F_2' replaces the ':::', *or* (2) either 'p' or 'q' is replaced by a pattern obtained according to (1) or by a sentence on (III') and either 'F_1' or 'F_2' replaces the ':::'. Thus we can have new sentences like 'bSc F_1 (bSc F_1 aRb)' as well as simpler ones like 'bSc F_1 aRb'. The number of possible sentence patterns which, recall, stand for possible facts in the model universe, with the relations F_1 and F_2 added to those listed on (II), is now infinite. Therefore, so is the number of possible facts. This means that the number of facts which *could* hold (obtain, exist) in the model universe with the eight constituents a, b, c, R, S, C, F_1, and F_2 is infinite. And this, in turn, means that it is possible that no list of facts would be a complete or adequate one in the sense of containing a sentence for each fact. Prior to the introduction of F_1 and F_2 as relations among facts, *this* type of failure of a list of sentences to "depict" how the model world was constituted was not a possibility. In a world with a finite number of objects and relations, wherein neither objects nor relations have other such things as constituents, but wherein facts are composed of objects standing in relations, there can only be a finite number of facts. A complete list is thus *always* possible, in principle. Concern with this possibility could lead one to be suspicious of relations that purportedly hold among facts.

There are other and much more fundamental reasons for such suspicion. Objects stand in relations to constitute facts. Facts are composed of constituent objects and relations. Relative to each other, facts are complex and structured while objects are simple, without structure. To be complex is to have constituents; to be structured is to be composed of constituents arranged or connected in some way. In a corresponding way, terms which stand for objects are simple as compared with sentences, which are composed of terms arranged in a definite manner. We thus have a basic distinction between terms and sentences, and a corresponding distinction between facts and their constituent objections and relations. If we introduce relations like F_1 and F_2 and acknowledge facts like those that might be indicated by sentences like '*bSc* F_1 *aRb*', we blur the distinction between terms and sentences and, consequently, between facts and constituents of facts. For a sentence may now function like a term, just as a fact may be a constituent of another fact. Thus both facts *and* objects may be constituents of facts, while sentences and names may be "terms" in sentences. However, one might object that, while the distinction may no longer be so clear-cut, it can still be made, since even though a sentence may function like a name (in another sentence), a name of an object cannot function as a sentence. Correspondingly, even if a fact can both have constituents and be a constituent in turn, an object or relation can only be a constituent of a fact. Along this line, one could point out that a distinction between names and predicate terms need not be lost if one allows predicates to function as subjects, since predicate terms can then play both roles while names may be limited to the role of subject terms. This leads to some further points.

Frege had held that a term could not function as both a subject and a predicate term, and Wittgenstein followed his lead in this respect. The governing idea was that there must be one logical role for each linguistic kind of thing. One who thinks along such lines will naturally balk at letting sentences take on the logical role of names. This will be especially so if his account of language and its relation to what it is about depends on the distinction between a name and a sentence. This distinction, as is well known, is of fundamental importance in the *Tractatus*. The point here is that it is connected with the question of whether facts stand in relations to each other or whether the world simply divides into facts.

Aside from any question of the connection of this issue, regarding whether facts can stand in relations, with other themes of the *Tractatus*, there is an obvious problem involved in allowing sentences to function as terms in relational sentences. To get at it, it is necessary to recall some of the features of Russell's theory of descriptions, a view which is behind much of what Wittgenstein says in the *Tractatus*.

A subject-predicate sentence is used to ascribe a predicate to a subject, and a relational sentence like '*bSc*' is used to assert that the two objects named stand in the relation. If they do so stand, the sentence is true; if they do not so stand, it is false. The sentence in question being true or false thus presupposes a condition: the names '*b*' and '*c*' must actually stand for objects. If they do not, then we *neither* have *the* objects *standing or failing to stand* in the relation. What then happens to a sentence when a subject term does not stand for anything? On Russell's theory, a *properly clarified language* would not treat such terms as names but as contextually defined signs as follows:

$$\textbf{(D)} \quad \psi \ (\imath x) \ (\phi x) = \text{def.} \ (\, \exists \, x) \left\{ [\phi x \cdot (y) \ (\phi y \equiv y = x)] \cdot \psi x \right\}$$

with '$\psi(\imath x) \ (\phi x)$' as an apparent subject-predicate sentence pattern, 'ψ' as the predicate terms, and '$(\imath x) \ (\phi x)$' as the subject term. The point is that such a subject term need not stand for an object in order to be used in an *apparent* subject-predicate sentence, for such a sentence will be treated as an existential claim to the effect that one and only one thing has ϕ and that thing also has ψ. Thus the truth or falsity of such a sentence does not presuppose that what the sign stands for has or does not have a certain property, since it does not presuppose that the sign stands for anything at all. But the crucial point is that the sentence '$\psi(\imath x) \ (\phi x)$' is only *apparently* a subject-predicate sentence, for it is construed as being elliptical for a more complicated existentially quantified sentence pattern. This treatment of subject terms which do not stand for anything allows one to retain both the view that a subject-predicate sentence is true if the object which the subject term stands for has the property which is indicated by the predicate term, and that it is false if *it* does not have the property, and the *use* of subject terms which do not stand for anything. It also enables us to retain a fundamental connection between the notions of truth, falsity, and negation. Consider the classic example:

(S₁) The present King of France is bald.
(S₂) The present King of France is not bald.

These sentences present us with the following problem. (S₂) is the negation of (S₁). Thus, if we are to hold (*a*) that an indicative subject-predicate sentence is either true or false, and (*b*) that if a sentence is true (false) its negation is false (true), and (*c*) that a subject-predicate sentence is true or false according to whether or not something has or does not have a certain property, we face a dilemma. For we must hold not only that one of (S₁) or (S₂) is true, but that it is so since something has or lacks a property. But this will not do. Russell's analysis which employs the pattern in (D) points to a solution. Neither (S₁) nor (S₂) is a subject-predicate sentence, when "properly" construed, i.e., analyzed. Treating them along the lines suggested by the use of (D) we may take (S₁) as:

(S₁′) There is one and only one present King of France, and he is bald.

(S₁′) is clearly false, since there is no thing which is presently King of France. It is not false in virtue of the fact that *something* lacks a property which the sentence asserts that it has (or, if you please, which one uses the sentence to assert that it has). It is a false existential statement. On Russell's account, (S₁′) replaces, or is used to analyze, or is the way one construes (S₁). It immediately follows that there are alternative ways of construing (S₂). Two obvious ones are:

(S₂′) There is one and only one present King of France, and he is not bald.

(S₂″) It is not the case that there is one and only one present King of France who is bald.

(S₂′) is false, while (S₂″) is true. Moreover, (S₂″) is the literal negation of (S₁′). But, again, these sentences are not true or false in virtue of something's having or lacking a property, but in virtue of there not being something of a certain kind. They, like (S₁′), are existential statements or denials of existential statements, and not subject-predicate sentences. The grounds of the truth or falsity of such sentences are not facts like those which involve something's having a property or lacking it or something's standing or not standing in a relation to something else. Consider, for example, the sentence '$(\imath x)\ (xRc)\ Sb$', where we have expanded our rules to allow expressions of the form '$(\imath x)\ (..x..)$' to enter into sentential patterns to form additional relational sentences about the model universe which is characterized by (III). Assume we treat such additional expressions in accordance with Russell's theory of descriptions. No object stands in the relation R to c. Thus, as '$(\imath x)\ (xRc)\ Sb$' is an abbreviation for '$(\exists x)\quad [xRc \cdot (y)\quad (yRc \equiv y = x)] \cdot xSb)$', that sentence is false. The sentence 'aRc' is also false. But in this latter case we can say that the sentence is false since the object which the sign 'a' stands for does not stand in the relation R to the object for which the sign 'c' stands. We cannot say this about '$(\imath x)\ (xRc)\ Sb$', though we can say that this latter is false and why it is so. That we cannot speak about '$(\imath x)\ (xRc)\ Sb$' as we do about 'aRc' is crucial, since one notion implicit in the use we are making of sentential patterns like 'aRc' is that they are to be taken to state that an object, here a, stands in a relation, here R, to another object, here c. Where a sign does not stand for an object, we are obviously precluded from using it to state that the object for which it stands is related to another object. Thus, if we allow patterns like '$(\imath x)\ (xRc)\ Sb$' we must either construe them differently from patterns like 'aRc' or take the latter in a different manner than we have so far. Russell's theory involves adopting the first alternative. Here, I must be content to suggest, without any supporting argument, that Wittgenstein's whole view of language requires him to do so as well. Once again, we have come across a fundamental question, or set of such, regarding language and its descriptive role; but we are only concerned presently with the connection of all this to the issue of whether facts may be constituents of further facts and whether sentences may function as terms in further sentences. To see the connection, recall the sentential pattern '$bSc\ F_1\ aRb$'. If it is to purport to state a relational fact, then, like the sentence 'aRb', it is used to state that one "thing," in this case a fact, stands in the relation F_1 to another "thing," in this case another fact. Consider, instead, the sentence pattern '*bSc F_1 aRc*'. Both '*bSc*' and '*aRb*', being true, correspond to facts; '*aRc*' does not, in the model universe which (III) portrays. Thus, '*bSc F_1 aRc*' could not be said to be either true or false depending on whether the fact *bSc* stood in the relation F_1 to *the fact aRc*. Since *aRc* does not exist, *it* cannot be said to stand or fail to stand in the relation F_1 to *bSc* in the same sense in which *aRb* might be said to so stand or fail to. The same sort of question that arises in the case of subject terms which do not stand for anything arises in the case of sentences which do not indicate facts, when such sentences are employed as subject terms.

Three apparent ways of resolving this problem seem rather obvious. First, one might suggest that sentences asserting that relations hold among facts can only be formed if such facts exist. This means that the terms '*a*', '*R*', and '*c*' can be used to form the sentence '*aRc*', when that sentence does not indicate a fact, but that the sentence can only, so to speak, be used *as a sentence* and not as a term in a further relational sentence. But this clearly involves using the notion of a sentence in two ways. A sentence, as opposed to a name or a "label," is a sign sequence that can be used to say "something," i.e., as a sentence, whether or not there is an existent (fact) which corresponds to it. By contrast the name or label is precisely that kind of a sign which must stand for some existent, to be used as a name or label. This is a further cardinal doctrine of the *Tractatus*. To allow some sentences, but not others, as terms of further relational sentences is to turn some sentences into names—to use them in a role that is not that of sentences. To grasp this, consider two points. First, one could introduce further names for facts. Instead of having the sentence '*aRb*' used as a sentence *and* as a name, one could introduce the name 'P_1' for the fact which '*aRb*' corresponds to, and 'P_1' would function exactly as '*aRb*' does when the latter is used as a term. But then we would have a sign without components which are themselves signs, in short a "simple" sign, standing for a fact, which has constituents and, hence, is not simple. This would violate another basic doctrine of the *Tractatus*: the so-called "picture theory of language." That is, without anticipating too much, we can note here that one who takes the connection between descriptive language and what it is about to involve complex things like facts, being connected with complex signs like sentences, cannot admit names of facts. It obviously will not do to suggest that a sign like '*abR*' be used as the name of the fact since such a sign is made up of the signs '*a*', '*b*', and '*R*'. For, *as the name of the fact, it* is not composed of such signs, since such signs do not function as parts of the name '*abR*' as they do as parts of the sentence '*aRb*'. It is beside the point that we know that *a* and *b* are constituents of the fact named by '*abR*', since the signs '*a*' and '*b*' occur in the name. This is something in addition to the use or function of '*aRb*' as a name. As names, '*abR*', '*abababcedR*', and '*P₁*', are all of the same complexity—namely, *simple signs*. As *geometrical patterns*, they differ in complexity. The same holds for taking the "sentence" pattern '*aRb*' as a name of a fact and, hence, using it as a term. Insofar as it functions as a name and term, it is a simple sign.

The second thing to note is that one could introduce signs which are names but name nothing. That is, they would function grammatically as names like '*a*' do, but they would not stand for anything. Along this line, one could say that replacing the '*x*' and '*y*' in patterns like '*xRy*' by such names always results in a false sentence. This clearly changes the notion and "role" of a name. We can easily separate such names from "genuine" names. In a similar way, if we say that sign patterns like '*aRb*' are used *as sentences* in patterns like '*aRb F₁ bSc*' we make use of another sense of 'sentence' than that employed when we say ' '*aRb*' is a *sentence* which is true if it corresponds to a certain fact'.

A second attempt to resolve the problem might be to hold that facts are not related in the sense in which objects are related; hence, a sentence like '*aRb F₁ bSc*' is not to be taken to assert that the fact indicated by '*aRb*' stands in the relation *F₁* to the fact indicated by '*bSc*'. But then, what point is there in saying that facts are related or, for that matter, what could one then mean? In short, if one so changes the notion of "standing in a relation," what is the cogency of the claim that facts stand in relations but in radically different senses? A third attempt would be a variant of the first. It would be to suggest, by analogy with Russell's handling of definite descriptions, that sentences like '*bSc F₁ aRc*' are really elliptical for more complex expressions, involving quantification over variables taking facts as values. But this will not do here in the way in which

Russell's theory of descriptions may well do for the problems regarding names that do not name and descriptive phrases which do not stand for anything. For, again, as a false sentence '*bSc*' would not be construable in terms of some expression analogous to a definite description, but as a purported term in a sentence of the form '*bSc F₁ aRc*' it would be so construed. This double use of nondesignating sentences, if I may so express it, would then match the double use of designating sentences, as sentences and as names, and thus return us to the problem we discussed just above. For the same double use of sentences which do indicate facts would also be involved on this alternative solution, just as on the first one. All this is not surprising when we observe that an alternative to Russell's theory of descriptions has been the suggestion of admitting "names" which do not name, but with the restriction that the simple sentence patterns they enter into be ruled false.

None of the above comments constitute, in themselves, arguments against taking facts as related constituents of further facts. They point to incompatibilities of such a view with certain themes that are central to the *Tractatus*. But insofar as these themes are taken not only as central to Wittgenstein's views but also as cogent theses, they become such arguments.

If there were relations among facts, then some facts would *necessarily be connected* with others. Given that *aRb* stands in F_1 to *bSc*, it *must follow* that *a* stands in *R* to *b*. There is no mystery about the uses of 'necessary connection' and 'follow' here. *Given the way we are treating* sentences and facts of the kind indicated by '*aRb*' and '*aRb F₁ bSc*', if the latter sentence stands for a fact, then so does the former. This does not mean that the latter sentence tautologically implies the former, but that the one sentence *taken in conjunction with statements spelling out the rules* for handling sentences and their connections with facts would tautologically imply the other. In short, 'F_1' does not stand for a truth-function in the standard sense. We thus come across a link of the present discussion with another theme of the *Tractatus:* "relational terms," if they may be so called for the time, which connect sentences into further sentences stand for truth-functional notions.

One who holds that there are no necessary connections between facts must hold, then, that there are no relations among facts. This is one connection of the preceding discussion with the doctrine of logical atomism stated in

> 1.21 Each item can be the case or not the case while everything else remains the same.

But there is a more obvious and more relevant connection, since if there are no relations among facts there can be no necessary connections between them. Wittgenstein is not concerned with the possible necessary connection between purported facts like $aRb\ F_1\ bSc$ and aRb, but with the nonexistence of such connections between facts like aRb and bSc: between facts that do not have other facts as constituents. But if there were necessary connections between facts, then there would be relations among them. One might take this to be obvious, since such connections would be relations; but some further comments seem necessary.

As Wittgenstein puts it, the thesis in question is that each fact can be the case or not, irrespective of any other. Thus any sentence in (III′) could hold, irrespective of whether any other one did or not. Two points are thus involved: to claim that if a fact is the case then some other fact *must be* the case is mistaken; to claim that if a fact is the case then some other fact *cannot be* the case is mistaken. Here we shall only consider the former since, first, it avoids the complication of speaking of negative facts or non-existent facts and, second, it suffices for the matter at hand.

What is it to claim that if a fact is the case then some other fact *must be* the case? One suggestion might be that the sentence expressing the one *implies* the sentence expressing the other. But compare ' '$aRb \cdot bSc$' implies 'bSc' ' with ' 'aRb' implies 'bSc' '. In the former, 'implies' is used in the standard sense of tautologically implies; that is, the sentence '$(aRb \cdot bSc) \supset bSc$' is a tautology or truth of formal logic. In the latter case, we make use of an unexplained sense of 'implies'; unexplained by contrast to the explanations of the former sense that are available in terms of truth-functions, tautologies, identical formulae, and so forth. It will not do to introduce further propositions, whether they be generalities or rules, to ground the "implication" from 'aRb' to 'bSc'. Suppose, to take a simpler case, we are concerned with 'aRb' and 'bSa' and one introduces the generality '(x) (y) $(xRy \supset ySx)$'. He may then note that from this generality and 'aRb' one can "derive," in the standard sense, 'bSa'. But, clearly, to justify the *implication* from 'aRb' to 'bSa', the generality itself must be "necessary." The same would go for any purported generality or rule that would do the same job. Hence the question is merely pushed on to the problem about such a generality, and this is so aside from any question about "general facts" which may also be raised here.

If one attempts to deal with the problem, he must justify the use of 'implies' or talk of a "necessary connection" between facts, keeping in mind that such terms are not used as synonyms for the standard notion of "logical entailment." One way would be to hold that there is some relation which, when it holds between facts, is the ground of truth for the assertion that a sentence indicating one of the facts *implies* a sentence indicating the other. Wittgenstein sought to avoid such relations by grounding the truth of sentences like ' '$aRb \cdot bSc$' implies 'aRb' ' in terms of formal logic and denying any nonformal sense of 'implies'. This avoids an ontological ground for such truths only if logical truths have no such ground. We shall return to the *Tractatus*'s view of the ontological ground of logical truth later. If one does not ground the truth of the implication in question in a relation between the facts, then the only alternative is to ground it in a relation between constituents. If such a relation is held to obtain among the objects a, b, c, then we have another fact of the same "type" as aRb and bSc, i.e., a relation holding among objects. But such a fact is obviously connected with the facts aRb and bSc, since it is in virtue of this fact that they are necessarily connected. Thus, somewhat like the problem associated with F. H. Bradley, the explanatory ground itself requires a further ground. For one must now account for the connection of the newly introduced fact to those it is supposed to "connect."

If the relation in question is held to obtain among the objects a, b, c *and* the relations R and S, then the same problem occurs in addition to a further one. We can see what this further problem is rather easily, if we consider an expression for the fact in question. Let '$\phi_1(a,b,c,R,S)$' stand for such a fact, which, recall, is the basis for bSc holding if aRb holds. Hence, some aspect of the fact in question must connect a and b with R, and b and c with S. If we think of the relation ϕ_1 making such connections, so to speak, we can consider the ordering of the expression '$\phi_1(a,b,c,R,S)$' as revealing that aspect of the relation ϕ_1, holding among the other five constituents of the fact, just as the sentence pattern 'aRb' is taken to express that a stands in the relation R to b and not vice versa. But then, the fact indicated by '$\phi_1(a,b,c,R,S)$' does not seem to differ at all from that indicated by '$aRb\ F_1\ bSc$'. We merely have two ways of linguistically representing that fact. For there is no difference in treating F_1 as a two-term relation holding between aRb and bSc and treating it as a five-term relation holding between a, b, c, R, and S, so long as we take the five-term relation's holding to involve the separation of a, b, and R, on the one hand, and b, c, and S, on the other. In short, whether we write '$F_1(a,b,c,R,S)$' or '$aRb\ F_1\ bSc$' makes no difference. Hence, all we do on such an alternative is hold, first, that there are relations like F_1 between facts *and*, second, that such relations *necessarily hold*, without further explicating the phrase 'necessarily hold'.

Finally, the relation grounding the truth of the implication from 'aRb' to 'bSc' could be taken to hold between the relations R and S. Thus we might think of a relation, represented by the sign 'ϕ_2', which holds between relations. The sentence '$\phi_2(R,S)$' could then be taken to represent the fact that ϕ_2 holds between R and S. Since such a fact would be connected to aRb and bSc, the basic problem of the two alternatives remains. For Wittgenstein, there would be a further problem, since he refuses, for very fundamental reasons, to acknowledge properties like ϕ_2, which are properties or relations of the second type (in Russell's sense), unless such "second-level" properties or relations are "logical" or "internal." Whatever else is involved, this means, first, that to say that R and S stand in the relation ϕ_2 is not to say that there is a fact indicated by '$\phi_2(R,S)$' *and*, second, that the implication holding between 'aRb' and 'bSc' is "logical" in the standard sense. To put it another way, '$\phi_2(R,S)$' would state a logical truth in the standard sense of 'logical truth'. But then, of course, one must show that the connection between 'aRb' and 'bSc' is logical in the standard sense. Whatever problems this engenders, all we need note here is that ϕ_2 could not then be a relation which holds between R and S in the sense in which R is a relation that holds between a and b: '$\phi_2(R,S)$' would not stand for a fact as '*aRb*' does. '$\phi_2(R,S)$', being a logical truth in the standard formal sense, could not then be the basis for the type of necessary connection between *aRb* and *bSc* that we are now investigating.

One could hold, however, that '$\phi_2(R,S)$' stands for a *necessary fact,* and is, therefore, a necessary truth in something like the sense in which philosophers have held that there are synthetic a priori truths. Yet aside from questions that arise regarding (1) the explication and analysis of phrases like 'necessary fact' and 'synthetic a priori truth', (2) taking sentences like '$\phi_2(R,S)$' to stand for facts, (3) acknowledging second-level primitive relational terms like 'ϕ_2', and (4) letting relational terms like '*R*' and '*S*' function both as predicate terms in sentences like '*aRb*' and as subject terms in sentences like '$\phi_2(R,S)$', there remains the basic point that one must still acknowledge relations holding among facts, if one holds that the necessary fact $\phi_2(R,S)$ accounts for the necessary connection between *aRb* and *bSc* or between *aRb* and *bSa.* That is, if one accounts for the implication from '*aRb*' to '*bSa*' in terms of the fact indicated by '$\phi_2(R,S)$', then one still faces the admission of the connection between $\phi_2(R,S)$ and *aRb* and between the former fact and *bSa.* These must be *necessary connections,* in addition to that relation, indicated by the sign 'ϕ_2', which holds between *R* and *S*; as such, they remain unaccounted for unless one recognizes further necessary facts grounding such connections. The introduction of $\phi_2(R,S)$ justifies the *implication* from '*aRb*' to '*bSa*'. But the term 'implication' in the previous sentence does not mean the same thing that it does when I say that there is an implication holding between '$p \cdot q$' and '*p*'. Hence, in addition to the introduction of necessary facts like $\phi_2(R,S)$, we also introduce another sense of 'implication'. This further sense of implication is reflected by connections between the sentences '$\phi_2(R,S)$', '*aRb*', and '*bSa*' and, hence, between the facts indicated by such sentences. Thus, the introduction of facts like $\phi_2(R,S)$ does not avoid having further connections between facts.

We started the above discussion by taking the claim that *if one fact is the case then some other fact must be the case* to state that *a sentence expressing the one implies a sentence expressing the other.* What we have seen is that alternative ways of grounding such an implication require the recognition of connections among facts.

Alternatively, one need not take the claim to involve any talk of an implication holding between sentences but, instead, speak directly of connections among facts, constituent objects, or constituent relations. In so doing one will, as far as I can see, get involved in exactly the same alternatives we have just considered. The point is, then, that holding that there are necessary connections between facts involves holding that facts stand in relations to other facts and, hence, that there are facts which have other facts as constituents. This presupposes that the "necessary connections" involved are not taken to be logical connections, in the standard formal sense, between the relevant sentences.

What we have seen then is that if there are necessary connections between facts, where we are not talking about connections reflected by the standard logical transformations, then there must be relations among facts and this, in turn, means that there are facts which take other facts as constituents. The world could not then divide into or decompose into facts, just as a fact does not divide into its constituents. The world would then be like a fact, with respect to its constituent facts, and not merely a collection of such facts. The doctrine of logical atomism is thus more than the assertion of the "independence" of facts from each other; it is a consequence of the denial that facts may be constituents of other facts, as objects are constituents of facts. Hence it is a corollary of a fundamental theme of the *Tractatus:* the insistence on the basic logical difference between facts and objects and the reflection of this distinction in a corresponding difference between names and sentences.

The denial that facts stand in relations to other facts to constitute further facts also jibes with another fundamental thesis of the *Tractatus.* Wittgenstein holds that any statement about a complex is analyzable into a statement about its constituents, or (as some may put it) such a statement is "really" a statement about the constituents of the complex. A fact like *aRb* is a complex. Hence any statement about it must be taken as elliptical for a statement about *a*, *R*, and *b*. This means that for any statement '. . . *aRb* . . .', where the dots indicate any context for the term '*aRb*', there is another statement '. . . *a* . . . *R* . . . *b* . . .', where the dots indicate a context for the *terms* '*a*', '*R*', and '*b*', such that the latter may be taken as the analysis of the former. Consequently a statement like '(*aRb*) F_1 (*bSc*)', which purportedly indicates a fact having other facts as constituents, is elliptical either for a statement of the form '$\phi_1(a,b,c,R,S)$', which indicates a fact that has only objects and relations as constituents, or for some truth-functional compound of sentences like '*aRb*', '*bSc*', '$\phi_2(R,S)$', etc. Here, one might bring up, as an objection, the reverse of a point made earlier. We noted previously that considering a fact of the form $\phi_1(a,b,c,R,S)$ to ground an "implication" purportedly holding between '*aRb*' and '*bSc*' would not avoid having facts as constituents of other facts, since there didn't seem to be any significant difference between $\phi_1(a,b,c,R,S,)$ and (*aRb*) F_1 (*bSc*). There is, however, a significant difference between the two discussions. In the previous case, the fact purportedly indicated by '$\phi_1(a,b,c,R,S)$' required the grouping of *a* and *b* with *R* and the grouping of *b* and *c* with *S*, in order to ground the implication in question. Here, there is no question of grounding anything; rather, it is a question of holding that what is purportedly a fact of one form is to be analyzed as a fact of a different form. Yet a corresponding question arises, for one might hold that any analysis which purports to replace a statement about a complex with a statement about the constituents of the complex is either inadequate or misleading. It would be inadequate since such a radical replacement must either fail to do justice to what is analyzed or, if it does, then it is misleading in that it is merely an elliptical way of speaking about the complex. We have come across a version of the so-called paradox of analysis applying to the sense in which philosophers purport to give ontological analyses. This "pseudo-problem" we can afford to ignore here.

In a way we have only touched on the doctrine of logical atomism in the preceding discussion, for the point of the doctrine is that facts like *aRb* and *bSc*, as well as the sentences corresponding to them, are *logically independent* of each other. What is meant by this of course depends on the phrase 'logically independent'. The heart of the notion is the standard formal senses of logical "implication" and "logical truth." To say that any two facts are independent is to say that either one *can* hold, irrespective of whether the other does or not. The use of 'can' in the preceding sentence involves the idea that neither the conjunction of the two sentences indicating the respective facts nor the conjunction of either such sentence and the negation of the other is a logical contradiction. Thus, where '*p*' is one such sentence and '*q*' is the other, neither '*p · q*' nor '*p · ~ q*' is a contradiction. Or, to put it another way, the denials of such conjunctions are not *logical truths*. To put the same thing still differently, neither '*q*' nor '*~q*' is *logically implied* by '*p*'. Two themes are involved here. First, there is the claim that notions like 'can', 'necessary', 'implies', etc., are explicated in terms of truth-functions and in the corresponding uses of 'contradiction', 'tautology', etc.; second, there is the claim that there are no other permissible senses of 'necessary', etc. Thus any two sentences on the list (III') are independent of each other in that no two are either logical consequences of each other or contradictories. This assumes that no sentence is a shorthand expression for a disguised, more complicated expression, which is a truth-functional compound of other sentences. That is, it is understood that none of the signs occurring in any of the sentences on (III') is a defined sign in our symbolism. With this understood, then all we need note is that there is nothing in the rules for forming the sentences on (III'), taken together with a standard system of logic, that either precludes any two items from being together on any list like (III) or that necessitates any item being on such a list if some other item is on it. This means that any item on (III') entails an item on (III') only if *they* are one and the same item.

There are other, related, senses of 'independent' involved in the issues that we are dealing with. An object, *a*, may be said to be independent of another object, *b*, if neither is a complex with the other as a constituent. Thus, if the sign '*a*' were taken to refer to the large square below, which has four squares as *spatial constitu-*

ents, and the sign '*b*' was taken to designate one of those smaller squares, then one might say that *a* was *dependent* on *b* in that *a* exists only if *b* does. In short, if a complex (in this case spatial) is taken to consist of its parts, then one might suggest that the complex is dependent on its parts and that certain statements about the complex are true only if certain statements about the parts are true.

A further sense of 'independent' has to do with facts and constituents. One might hold that a fact is independent of an object or relation if such an object or relation is not a constituent of the fact. Thus a fact would be held to be dependent on its constituent objects and relations. This sense of 'independent' is relevant to the notion that for there to be facts there must be things, since facts are composed of things. Facts are thus dependent on things: objects and relations. Finally, if objects and relations were held to exist only as constituents of some fact, then there would be a sense in which one could speak of such things being dependent on facts and on each other. Such a claim raises a further question. We may find it understandable for one to hold that a complex thing is taken to be just those constituents in certain relations. But it may seem problematic to claim that constituents "require" complexes. Moreover, the very meaning of such a claim may itself be problematic on two counts. First, what kind of a claim is it: empirical, analytical (in some sense), philosophical, or what? Second, is it a report of how things in fact are, or how they must be? And if it is a report of how they must be, what is the sense of the phrase 'must be' in such a claim? Once again, we shall have to put off any consideration of such relevant questions.

We may, however, note a connection of the above discussion of the senses of 'independent' with a previous point. Wittgenstein seems to hold that objects are dependent on facts in that they only exist as constituents of facts. If he does make that claim and if he were also to allow facts to be constituents of further facts, then he would face a difficult choice. He can either hold that facts, as constituents, are fundamentally unlike other constituents, objects, and relations, in that they can or that some do exist without being constituents of facts or claim that facts, like objects and relations, must or always do exist as constituents of further facts. Taking the former alternative points to a further difference between facts as constituents and, hence, casts further suspicion on speaking of facts as constituents at all. Choosing the latter alternative points to a sense in which facts would be dependent on other facts, which, at the very least, seems to go against the theme of logical atomism.

Thus taking constituents of facts to be dependent on facts while holding facts to be independent of each other seems to jibe with the denial that facts may be constituents of other facts.

Before proceeding, one point is worth emphasizing. Despite the preoccupation of the first group of statements of the *Tractatus* (1–1.21) with *facts* and in spite of 1.1 and 1.2, Wittgenstein is not offering a fact ontology in the sense that he is denying that things exist and claiming that only facts exist. Such an interpretation would make no sense if one meant by it that in no sense do things, which are constituents of facts, exist. If such a claim is merely a dramatic way of putting points like those involved in (1) the explanation of what it means to say that the world divides into facts, (2) the claim that facts are independent of each other, but that things exist in facts, and (3) one's characterization of a model world by a list of sentences like (III), and not by a list of constituents like (II), then the only harm is an unfortunate overemphasis. Wittgenstein may be said to be offering a fact ontology in that he is claiming that facts do exist and that they are not reducible to their constituents in the way the world is reducible to its constituent facts. In this sense, the world is not an additional entity. Yet, in addition to the constituents of a fact, there is a further entity—the fact.

II. *Possibilities and Essences*

A problem raised by the foregoing discussion of logical atomism is the connection between facts indicated by sentences of the form '$p \cdot q$' and those indicated by the conjuncts 'p' and 'q'. For Wittgenstein this is not a sign of the inadequacy of the doctrine of logical atomism, since he is developing the view that compound sentences, like conjunctions, do not stand for facts. Only sentences like 'aRb' (where, as we noted earlier, it is understood that such a sentence is not to be construed as a more concise way of writing a sentence of a more complex form) are taken as indicating facts. We can see one thing that is behind such a move. Consider the list (III), and think of a conjunction in the standard truth-functional way. The sentences 'aRb' and 'bSc' stand for facts; thus they are true. Since they are so, the conjunction '$aRb \cdot bSc$' is true, without our having to speak of any further facts. It is the existence of the two facts which make '*aRb*' and '*bSc*' true, and those facts alone also make the conjunction true. If one uses the term 'fact' so that *a* fact is taken to make '*aRb · bSc*' true, then Wittgenstein has not been speaking of such facts in 1–1.21. He has been speaking of facts as the correspondents of simple sentences like '*aRb*' and '*bSc*'. This is codified with the introduction of a new, and quite distinct term in

2. What is the case—the fact—is the existence of states of affairs.

There has been some discussion over the translation of the German term *Sachverhalt* as 'state of affairs'. In the Ogden translation 'atomic fact' is used, and the phrase 'possible fact' has also been suggested. 'Atomic fact' has the unfortunate connotation that there are also molecular facts, which does not fit the doctrine of the *Tractatus*. If we understand that the only facts that Wittgenstein admits are composed of constituents, like objects, relations, and properties, and do not have other facts as constituents and, if we further note that such objects, relations, etc., are not composed of other objects, relations, etc., then we can take *Sachverhalt* to be rendered by the term 'fact', so construed. In our model symbolism a *Sachverhalt* corresponds to a sentence on list (III). It is what exists and grounds the truth of such sentences. It is a complex of objects and, in our example, a relation *connected together*. It does not contain a fact, as a purported fact like $aRb\ F_1\ bSc$ would. If we admitted such complex facts, they would not be *Sachverhalten*. In such a context, the notion of an "atomic fact" would be suggestive, since aRb would be an atom of $aRb\ F_1\ bSc$, and the latter would be a complex fact as contrasted with the simple fact aRb. Moreover, facts like aRb would be basic to all other kinds of facts, since they would be constituents of such facts (or even constituents of constituents, etc.) but they would not have facts as constituents. Since there are no complex facts, for Wittgenstein, the notion of an "atomic fact" is redundant, though it has some expository value at points, as we shall see. The phrase 'state of affairs' also seems to pose a problem since, in itself, it does not preclude the existence of complex states of affairs. This is the simple terminological quandry. The phrase 'atomic fact' suggests, by the use of the term 'atomic', the possibility of molecular facts; the phrase 'state of affairs', like the phrase 'fact', suggests the same possibility by the lack of such an adjective. Thus with or without an "appropriate" adjective the same "problem" arises. The point is that one expects too much from the terminology if he expects the term to carry Wittgenstein's meaning. There is really no point in fussing. Any of the terms will do so long as we understand what it is that Wittgenstein is claiming. The term *Sachverhalt* carries the ideas that complex facts are not existents and that the constituents of existent facts are not complexes. In short Wittgenstein, after telling us that facts exist, is now going to tell us what they are like, i.e., of what they are composed and how they are structured.

To sum up, the import of 2. is that only facts of a certain kind are taken as existents. These are what some have called atomic facts and what we may also call simple facts. This might be the point of the phrasing of 2. Wittgenstein speaks of *die Tatsache:*

2. What is the case, *the* fact. . . .

This seems to point up the importance of the comment and its philosophical nature. It is as if he were to say, "The truth is that no fact has another fact as a constituent." In view of the terminological question and the importance of the doctrine involved for understanding the *Tractatus*, I shall adopt the expeditious, if barbarous, practice of retaining the German term *Sachverhalt* in the ensuing discussion in lieu of 'state of affairs', 'atomic fact', 'fact', 'state of things', 'hanging together of things'.[2] (Though, if forced to choose an English expression, I would think either of the latter two would be preferable to the others in that they carry more of the relevant context.)

The point we have been considering emerges quite clearly in

2.01 The Sachverhalt is a combination of objects (things).

A *Sachverhalt* is thus explicitly precluded from being a combination or structuring of facts. With 2.01 we get the first suggestion of one of the problems of interpretation of the *Tractatus*. How extensively are we to take the terms 'object' and 'thing'? Do they apply to relations and properties or only to what may be called individuals (or particulars)? If the latter, does this mean that facts do not contain

[2] This will necessitate ignoring case endings.

relations and properties as constituents? These questions will be ignored in this paper. For our concerns we may safely take 2.01 as making the sharp contrast between facts and constituents that are not facts—as specifying that a *Sachverhalt* does not contain, in any sense, a fact. This is all Wittgenstein seems concerned with in the present passages.

Once the notion of a *Sachverhalt* has been introduced, Wittgenstein turns to a consideration of the constituents of a *Sachverhalt*: objects or things. But early in the *Tractatus* he is not concerned with whether or not they are relations or individuals. Rather, he is merely concerned with the difference between *Sachverhalten* and constituents of such entities, *whatever* these latter may be. Consequently, we shall indiscriminately take the terms 'thing' and 'object' to be synonymous with 'constituent', as we have been using the latter. Constituents of *Sachverhalten* have an *essential* characteristic:

2.011 It is essential to things that they can be constituents of a Sachverhalt.

In one sense the idea is as simple as it is traditional. For something to enter into a relation, or to become characterized in a certain way, it *must have* the possibility (or potentiality, as they once said) of doing so. For a thing to be in relative motion to another, it must be the *kind of thing* that *can* move with respect to other things that have the same potentiality. The italicized expressions in the preceding sentences mark the connection of 2.011 with traditional talk of essences and essential properties. Essential properties have traditionally delineated kinds of things and have been spoken of as necessary characteristics of the things which they characterize. The possibility of being a constituent of a *Sachverhalt* is an essential or necessary property of an object, just as the potentiality of being an oak tree was involved in the essence of an acorn according to a classical philosophical position. For Wittgenstein, objects have essences, and there are two rather important points connected with this theme.

One of the key themes of the *Tractatus* is that the notion of "necessary" is to be explicated in terms of the idea of "logical." Hence, to speak of essential or necessary properties is to speak of logical properties. If it is essential to objects that they may be constituents of *Sachverhalten*, this becomes a matter of logic: it is a logical truth that they are able to be constituents of *Sachverhalten*. We have spoken earlier of the standard notions of logical truth and inference—those associated with the ideas of truth-table tautologies and formal truths. This involves one of the key ideas of what is logical, in the terms of the *Tractatus*. But here, early in the book, we have come across a different notion of 'logical'. Things have essential properties, and these properties are not logical in the standard sense; or (perhaps better) if one thinks that they are, then there is an ambiguity in speaking of the standard or formal sense of logical truth or property. To get at the point, let the sign 'W' stand for a nonrelational property and let the following be an additional rule for the construction of sentences:

Rule 4: 'W' stands for the property . . . and the result of replacing the 'x' in the pattern 'Wx' by any of the object
signs is a sentence ascribing the property to the object.

The sentence 'Wa v $\sim Wa$' is a logical truth. But consider the sentences: (1) The sign 'W' can be combined with the sign 'a' in the pattern 'Wa'; (2) The object a can have the property W. One might either take both (1) and (2) to be alternative ways of stating that 'Wa v $\sim Wa$' is a logical truth, or take (1) to be a condensed version of Rule 4 while (2) is considered as another way of claiming that the disjunction is a logical truth. Neither of these ways of construing (1) and (2) would get at what Wittgenstein is saying. What he is claiming is that (2) is a logical truth, but it is not a re-statement of the claim that 'Wa v $\sim Wa$' is a logical truth; rather, it states something about the essence of the object a, and it is in virtue of *that fact and the truth functions* that 'Wa v $\sim Wa$' is a logical truth. Rule 4, or (1), reflects, as a *formation* rule of our symbolism, that the object a has a certain essential property, *being capable of having* the property W. Thus, there are three "properties" involved in all this: W, *being W or not W*, *being capable of being W*. For the first we have the sign 'W', for the second we might use the sign 'Wx v $\sim Wx$', but for the third there is no sign; that an object has it is "shown" by the kind of sign that stands for the object. An object's having the third is a prerequisite for its having the second, and if it has the third, then in a system with the standard truth-functional signs it also has the second. Both the second and the third may be called logical properties, but the one, so to speak, is a matter of truth-tables and the other is a matter of the formation rules. Or, putting it another way, the formation rules of the symbolism reflect the one while the tautologies reflect the other. The linguistic representative of the third property is a formation rule of the system of signs. Distinguishing between the two types of logical property that an object may be said to have and speaking of one as the essence is not meant to preclude a later development of the following kind. We may see reasons to hold that the notion of essence is used so that *both* of the logical properties we have been talking about are held to belong to the object essentially. Thus, in another sense of the term 'essential', both *being capable of being W* and *being W or not W* may be essential characteristics, and the essence of the object may then be taken as the total set of essential characteristics or as some complex characteristic of which they are constituents, or as some characteristic to which they have some "necessary" connection, etc. Here I am not precluding such a complication but merely noting that the use of 'essential' in 2.011 involves the property of *being capable of being W*, and this involves us in the two senses of 'logical property' that we have been discussing.

The second point that is important to note in connection with the claim that things have essences or that certain possibilities are essential to things is that we are not merely dealing with language. That is, to speak of essential properties, like *being capable of being W*, as logical is not to suggest that we are dealing with a question of language. One might suggest that to say that *being W or not W* is a logical property is to say that it is a matter of language, or merely reflects a "linguistic truth." Such a phrase, of course, requires explication. For the present discussion, we can take "matter of language" to suggest that nothing in the world corresponds to the linguistic feature or expression. Thus, if *being W or not W* is merely a matter of language, the idea is that the expression '*Wx* v ~ *Wx*' does not correspond to anything in the world, in contrast to expressions like '*a*', '*R*', and '*aRb*' which correspond to an object, a relation, and a fact, respectively. In this sense, we must understand that the linguistic representative of *being capable of being W*, namely Rule 4, does correspond to something: an essential characteristic of *a*. To speak of essences or essential characteristics is to speak ontologically: to speak of a feature of the world represented by (III), even though there is no sign or combination of signs on (III), or (III′) for that matter, which by itself stands for it. What stands for it are the rules of the symbolism or certain features of the symbolism rather than certain symbols. One can take these to be reflected by (III′), understood in the context supplied by the rules. That the sign '*a*' can be combined in a certain way with the sign '*W*' to form a sentence, which will be true or false depending on whether the object *a* has the property *W*, corresponds to *the fact* that the object *a* has a certain essence or essential property. This involves a rather special use of the term 'fact', since such facts are not represented by sentences as are those like *aRb*, but by rules and features of the symbolism. But this is merely another way of saying that *the fact* that an object has a certain essence is a matter of logic or necessity and not an ordinary matter of fact, somewhat like one might say that it is a fact that '*p* v ~ *p*' is a tautology while holding that what he was claiming was a necessary truth. Whether such a use of 'necessity' or of 'logical' can be further explicated poses another problem. But a different issue arises, even if we omit any consideration of the explication of such a use of 'necessary' or of 'logical'. One might suggest that *being capable of being W* is best considered, not as a further logical property, but as a distinct *connection* between *a* and *W*. When *a* is *W* there is one connection or tie between the object and the property. The object's being so connected to the property constitutes the fact which makes the sentence '*Wa*' true. Philosophers speaking in this way have considered such a connection to be that of *exemplification*, or *predication*, or *participation*, and so on. Likewise, one may suggest that being capable of having a property indicates a distinct connection between an object and a property other than the connection of *having* or *exemplifying* or *being an instance of* the property. Thus it is misleading to suggest that *a* has the essential property of being capable of being *W*. What one should say is that *a* stands to the property *W*, not in the connection of having it, but in the connection of being capable of having it or of possibly having it. In short, instead of speaking of the properties of *W* and of *being capable of being W*, we should speak of the connections of *being an instance of* and that of *being capable of being an instance of*. The object would stand in the latter connection to the property W *of necessity*, while it may also stand in the former to W *as a matter of fact*. The necessity of the logical connection between the object and its possibly being a constituent of a state of affairs lies in its *necessary connection* to some properties. Thus the connection is what is necessary or logical rather than a property. Instead of saying 'a is (capable of being W)', where the parenthetical expression stands for a property, we should say 'a (is capable of being) W' where the parenthetical expression stands for a unique logical connection parallel to, but different from, exemplification.

In a way we are getting ahead of Wittgenstein's discussion, since we have not considered what he has to say about such "connections" or ties, even in the case of exemplification. Moreover, it is also not clear just how he considers relations and properties. However, such matters, crucial as they are, cannot be taken up in this paper. But we may note that, whichever way one wishes to speak, what is important here is that it is taken to be essential to things that they have certain possibilities, and this sense of essential is tied up with the notions of 'necessary' and of 'logical'. On either alternative, the relevant point here is that the fact that an object has such a possibility is not an ordinary fact but a matter of necessity. Necessary characteristics of objects have sometimes been spoken of as "internal" to the object, as opposed to ordinary properties or relations, like W and R, which are "external" to the object. The idea is that an internal property is one which an object must have, whereas it is possible for an object not to have an external property, even though it in fact does have it. Thus one sometimes says that something could not be the object in question if it does not have such an internal property, but that an object could be one and the same while being without an external property that it in fact has. Such talk sometimes seems to rely on the view that the object contains such internal properties, in some sense, as *constituents*, while external properties are not constituents but further things to which the objects are *connected*. This line could involve one in adhering not only to distinct kinds of properties, *internal* and *external*, but to distinct kinds of connections between the object and such properties, *containing* as contrasted with *being connected to* or *exemplifying*. Thinking of such essential or necessary properties as constituents reinforces the use of the term 'internal', as applied to them. Contrasting such talk of constituents to the earlier discussion of facts having objects and relations as constituents both clarifies the claim and reveals a problem implicit in it. The object a is a constituent of the fact aRb. If a fact does not contain the object a as a constituent, this is a sufficient ground for holding that such a fact cannot be one and the same as aRb. A minimal condition for a fact being *the* fact aRb is that "it" have the same constituents. For any signs for complexes, they will be said to stand for the same complex only if they stand for things with exactly the same constituents. Or, to put it in the problematic way that one must use when he speaks of identity, a complex entity, a, is the same as a complex entity, β, only if "they" have the same constituents. Hence if an essential property is held to be a constituent of an object, say a, then in an analogous fashion we can see what could be involved in claiming that it is necessary or internal to the object, and, hence, any object not having that internal property could not be the object a. The necessity of an object's having an internal property is a simple consequence of the object's being taken to be a complex and of the use of the term 'complex'. In this way, one does not introduce an unexplicated sense of 'necessity' or of 'logical'. But then, one takes the object a to be a complex. In so doing he avoids the need for appealing to an unanalyzed sense of 'necessary' (or 'logical'), but at the price of running into a twofold problem. First, he must explain in what sense objects are complexes as contrasted with facts. This is especially crucial if the original characterization of facts as complexes depended on the contrast of facts with their constituent objects. Second, he must spell out what are the constituents of objects in addition to the essential or internal property we have been talking about, and he must indicate how the constituents "combine" to constitute an object. In attempting this, one not only faces the problem of losing the distinction between facts and objects, but there is the obvious danger of an infinite regress. For will not the constituents of such objects also have essential characteristics determining their combinatorial possibilities? Due to such reasons, one may well prefer to stick with objects as simples, in that they are not taken to be composites which have constituents. He thus gives up the explication of essential property in terms of an internal or constituent property and, in effect, introduces a notion of 'necessary', or 'logical', or 'essential' as a basic concept in the discussion. This is what Wittgenstein does. Yet he will employ the term 'internal' as a synonym for 'essential'; but an internal property, while being necessary or logical, is not to be taken as a constituent of an object. In a sense that will never be explicated, Wittgenstein's objects have essences and are thus *natured* as opposed to *bare*. The introduction of such terms requires some explanation.

Consider three color spots a_1, a_2, and a_3; three sounds or particular auditory sensations b_1, b_2, and b_3; two color properties W and B; and two auditory properties G and D. Suppose one holds that any of the color spots could possibly be an instance of W or of B but could not possibly be an instance of either G or D, while any of the sounds could be an instance of G or of D but could not possibly be an instance of W or B. He might suggest that such possibilities and impossibilities are reflected in the linguistic rules which would permit sentences to be formed from the patterns 'Wx' and 'Bx' by replacing 'a_1' or 'a_2' or 'a_3' for the 'x', but would not permit the replacement in the case of 'b_1' or 'b_2' or 'b_3'. There would be a corresponding rule about 'Gx' and 'Dx'. We might then say that a_1 has the necessary or essential or logical property of being capable of being W or of possibly being W and of not possibly being G. The same sort of thing could be said about each particular. Such properties may be said to determine the nature of the objects. To state that an object has such a property is to state what its nature or essence is (in part, at least), as opposed to stating that it has a property like W, which reports a fact about it. The objects in this example are not bare, being natured. Contrast this with one who holds that the objects may be either color spots or sounds—that no object is essentially one or the other. Thus a_1, while perhaps being an instance of W, could possibly have been an instance of G. He thus admits the sentence 'Ga_1' and holds it to be false, but not necessarily false. His objects, by contrast with those spoken of in the first example, are bare; they are not essentially color spots or sounds. Yet while bare *relative* to the objects of the first example, the objects we are now dealing with may be taken as natured relative to others. In the present case we might have a rule to the effect that in the patterns 'Wx', 'Bx', 'Gx', and 'Dx', any of the signs 'a_1',

'a_2', 'a_3', 'b_1', 'b_2', 'b_3', may replace the 'x' to obtain a sentence, but that none of the signs 'W', 'B', 'D', or 'G' may replace the 'x' to obtain a sentence. This may be taken to reflect the claim that while objects can combine with color or sound properties to constitute facts, such properties cannot combine with each other, just as objects cannot combine merely with each other to form facts. Parallel to the earlier case, we may speak of such objects and properties as having natures in that they necessarily have certain possibilities for combination, but not others. To put it cryptically, one might now say that objects have the essential property of being objects, whereas previously they were essentially colored objects or sounds. Likewise, W, B, G, and D are essentially (or "by nature") properties. By contrast with this sense of taking objects to be essentially just that, i.e., objects as opposed to properties, one might hold that "things" were neither objects nor properties essentially. That a_1 was an object, rather than a property, would be a fact about it, somewhat like its being W rather than B. Along this line one might hold that a_1 could have been a property, just as it could have been an object that had B rather than an object that had W.

A reader who has been patient to this point may at last become exasperated. For while talk of the possibility of a color spot being a sensation of sound may be annoying, to speak of an object's possibly having been a property is outrageous. Yet, to paraphrase, we all know that one man's outrage is another's philosophy. Some philosophers have even balked at speaking of anything possibly being other than the way it is in any manner whatsoever. Whether one takes it to be absurd that Socrates could have been a universal property, or ridiculous to speak of his possibly having been a horse, or inconsistent to assert that he might not have been the teacher of Plato may merely reflect one's philosophical predilections—where one draws the line of the sensible or inconsistent, in a special sense of the term 'inconsistent'. For none of these "claims" amounts to a formal contradiction, in the standard way of understanding a formal contradiction, as the claim that Socrates is both a horse and not a horse is such a contradiction. Once again, we return to that special and unexplained sense of 'logical', and since it is unexplained, there is a certain openness regarding its application by different philosophers. In spite of this openness or vagueness, there is an obvious point to talk of essential properties. Whether we speak of a "felt difference" or "conceptual impossibility" or "absurdity," there is a manifest difference between the suggestion that Socrates might not have known Plato and the claim that he might have been a horse. Aside from the esoteric differences between different philosophers who have spoken of essential properties and the details (and sometimes subtleties) that may be involved, this kind of difference seems to be one thing that they all sought to reflect in speaking of "essential" or "necessary" characteristics of things. Our purpose here is not to enter the dialectics surrounding the notion of 'essential property', but to note that Wittgenstein employs such a notion, as one sense of 'logical property', and that such a use of the phrase 'logical property' is quite distinct from the characterization of the property of either being a horse or not being a horse as a logical property. It is, and will remain in the *Tractatus*, a basic and unexplicated sense of 'logical'.

Even though we need not probe into the question of essential properties, we can see one connection with some previously discussed points. If one holds that an object which is a color patch could have been a sound (or is capable of being a sound) while still literally being one and the same object, he seems required to hold that *the specification of what the object is* must not include a reference to the color property. By 'specification' I do not mean 'identification', but, rather, something like what is involved in the Aristotelian introduction of a substratum underlying change of property, in order to hold that something is literally one and the same both prior to and after the "change." Thus, one could not hold that the color was a part of the object, that an object was a collection of its parts, and that one and the same object could have been a sound instead of a color patch, since we would not then have one and the same collection. By contrast, if one held that the object was something which stood in a relation, say exemplification, to the color, then he could hold that *it* might not stand in that relation to any color but to a sound quality, and yet be one and the same object. Along such a line, he might hold that the object is to be taken as a bare particular or substratum, which in some ways is reminiscent of Aristotle's prime matter. Pushing the line further, we might point to two senses of 'object' that emerge. Consider a color patch, for the moment, as having two properties, a color and a shape. Suppose one also holds that the properties are exemplified by a substratum or particular. Such an entity, the substratum, is an (or *the*) object in one sense. One might also consider the composite or collection of the substratum and the properties it exemplifies to be an (or the) object, in another sense of that term. One might then hold that the substratum is the kind of thing that could have combined with other properties, say a tone and a degree of loudness. But the composite of the substratum, the color, and the shape could not be sensibly said to be capable of being a sound. The specification of what the substratum is does not involve reference to its having a particular color, though it might have reference to the substratum's capability of being colored—to its being the kind of entity that may possibly exemplify a color quality. Such a substratum is not essentially an object that exemplifies a particular color property, though it might essentially be the kind of object that can exemplify a color property. All of this has nothing to do with the question of identifying a substratum or indicating it in terms of properties which it does in fact exemplify—by means of a definite description, for example. To specify what such a thing is is simply to state what kind of a thing or entity it is taken to be on the pattern in question. In so doing one states whether it is simple or complex and, if the latter, of what it is composed. Specifying what the substratum of the color patch is does not involve consideration of the color quality it exemplifies. One may express this by saying that the color is not internal to the substratum, or not essential to it, or not involved in the characterization of it in one's ontological analysis.

In general if we say of anything, a, which is characterized as a ϕ, that *it* need not have been a ϕ but could have been a ψ, then we take a in two ways: once as something, a', for the specification of which ϕ is not relevant, and once as the composite of a' and ϕ in a relation. Suppose one holds that a substratum could have been a universal property and not a particular. He must then hold that the substratum is a composite of something, call it x_1, which would be constant whether it were a particular or a property (that which is the basis for saying that *the* substratum is *the same* thing irrespective of whether *it* is a particular or a property), and something else with which x_1 combines. This latter entity would be the basis for the claim that "it" is a particular or a property, as the case may be, just as x_1 is the basis for the claim that "it" is one and the same. Suppose one takes this latter constituent to be the property of *being a particular* (or that of *being a universal*). The substratum we started with is thus taken to be complex, and we now recognize characteristics like *being a particular* and *being a universal* as well as some more basic kind of *subject* or *substratum*, which may take either of such characteristics. In one sense, such a subject is, in itself, neither a particular nor a universal; for such properties do not enter into its analysis or specification. In another sense, by contrast to the properties of *being a particular* or *being a universal*, it is something of a different kind—a *basic subject* as opposed to a characteristic. If one now takes it to be sensible to hold that such a thing could have been a characteristic, like *being a universal* or *being a particular*, he must then construe a basic subject, x_1 for example, as a composite of something, say x_1', and the characteristic of *being a basic subject*. He must also construe the characteristic of *being a universal* as a composite of something of the new category to which x_1' belongs and of something else which, when combined with an entity of the category of x_1', forms the characteristic of *being a universal*.

Consider yet another case. Suppose one holds it to be sensible to say of the property green that it could have been the property blue. He must then construe the properties blue and green to be complex. They will each contain an entity which is the basis for it being sensible to say "*that* which is the property green could have been the property blue," and they will also contain an entity in virtue of which the first sort of entity is said to be the property green or the property blue, as the case may be. If one also holds it to be sensible to say of two substrata, x_1 and x_2, that they could have been each other, then he holds each of them to be composed of two further entities (at least). Call these further things a subject entity and an individuating characteristic. To say x_1 could have been x_2 is then to say that the subject entity contained in x_1 could have been combined with the individuating characteristic contained in x_2. Thus the characteristics blue and green, as well as the substrata x_1 and x_2, are taken to contain both a subject entity and a characteristic which determines whether the subject entity is part of one of the substrata or of one of the colors. He may also hold that such subject entities combine not only with an individuating characteristic but with one of two further characteristics: *being a particular* or *being a property* (characteristic). Thus x_1 would be composed of a subject entity connected to two characteristics: a generic one such as *being a particular*, which determines that it is a particular rather than a characteristic or universal, and an individuating characteristic, which determines that it is x_1 rather than x_2. (Complex and strange as such a "view" may sound, it seems to be something like what Scotus had in mind in speaking of *haecceitas*. It explains why some of the things he says imply that the *haecceitas* of something is an individuating property, why other things he writes suggest that it is a simple individuating particular, why still other passages indicate that it is a general property of particulars, and, finally, why it sometimes seems to be a composite particular.) The same kind of complexity could be taken to be involved in the case of the colors blue and green. We would then have a subject entity, the generic characteristic of being a universal, and the specific characteristic which determined the resulting combination to be the property green, rather than, say, the property blue. One could continue such a line endlessly, if he now held it to be sensible to raise the same kind of question about the subject entities and the generic and specific characteristics that are involved in the discussion of the particulars x_1 and x_2 and of the properties blue and green.

In a way, all of this is just a reflection of Aristotle's insight concerning the claim that something is one and the same prior to and after a change. It is then not surprising that two familiar points emerge from such considerations. First, if one is to speak of the possibility of something, a, being what it is not, yet remaining one and the same, he is either forced to construe a as a composite or to treat the senses of 'being what it is' and 'being what it is not' in terms of a standing in a relation to something or not so standing. In this latter case the other terms of the relation cannot be involved in the specification of what a is. Hence, if a is taken to be a simple, one can only admit the possibility of its being other than what it is in the latter, relational or nonintrinsic sense. If he then also holds that some characteristics of a simple like a are, in some sense, "intrinsic" in that, first, they do not combine via a relation with a to constitute a fact, second, they are essential characteristics, and third, they are logical characteristics, he introduces unanalyzed senses of 'logical', 'intrinsic', and 'necessary'. For such characteristics neither combine with *a* by some relational tie to constitute a fact, and hence might reasonably be called *extrinsic*, nor are they constituents of simples like *a*, and thus *intrinsic*, in a fairly straightforward sense. On the other hand, if one who acknowledges simples seeks to avoid the absurdities involved in holding that a simple object could have been a characteristic or a relation, he apparently must recognize essential characteristics, such as *being an object*, or *being a characteristic*. He must then also recognize a unique way in which they characterize objects. Whether he does this by holding that there is a unique characterizing tie, or by introducing *necessary facts*, or by proclaiming that for such essential characteristics no tie is needed, or by speaking of what can only be shown and not said, is not crucial for these issues.

But the problem goes a bit deeper, for it is not just a problem faced by one who wishes to hold that some objects could not have certain characteristics and must have others. Suppose one holds that there are simple objects and characteristics, but to avoid acknowledging essential characteristics, he holds that any simple object can combine with any characteristic or property. He still faces the problem due to the difference between *being an object* and *being a characteristic*. If he holds that there are basic simples which become objects when they combine with the characteristic of *being an object* and become characteristics if they combine with an appropriate generic character (*being a characteristic*) *and* an appropriate specific character (that which makes it one property rather than another), then we still have the difference between the basic simples and the unusual characteristics they combine with. Moreover, we seem forced to take such distinctions as essential, in that one can give no sense to the claim that one of the basic simples could have been one and the same as the generic characteristic *being a basic simple object*. One might then seek to hold that there are only basic simple objects, without characteristics, but that talk of characteristics and facts is to be analyzed in terms of configurations of such objects. An object *a* having a property *F* is then to be taken as a set of basic simples, $a_1, a_2, \ldots, a_n$, in a *configuration*. But it is immediately clear that configurations are now constituents of facts, in that a fact is not just a set whose members are a_1, a_2, . . . , a_n, even though configurations are not themselves basic simples like a_1, a_2, . . . , a_n. Consequently, the problem now arises about simple objects and configurations. Also, given talk of configurations we immediately have characteristics, like *being capable* of being in a configuration, which also return us to the distinction between objects and characteristics and, in this latter case, reintroduce essential characteristics. To hold that the problem has disappeared since configurations aren't objects is merely a dodge. It thus appears that to talk of simple objects as constituents of facts forces us to accept essential characteristics.

In presenting the above lengthy discussion engendered by 2.011, I do not mean to suggest that it expresses what Wittgenstein explicitly took to be involved. Rather, I only wish to point out that such questions are involved in his introduction of essential characteristics and that subsequent moves that he will make to render such essential characteristics palatable will tie up with the points raised. The attempt to make essential characteristics respectable involves their being taken as "logical."

> 2.012 In logic nothing is accidental: if a thing *can* occur in a Sachverhalt, the possibility of the Sachverhalt must be prejudged in the thing itself.

Possibilities of things entering into *Sachverhalten* are essential characteristics of things and, as essential characteristics, are to be construed as logical; such possibilities belong to logic where we deal with necessities, not accidents or contingencies.

> 2.0121 It would seem to be a sort of accident, if it turned out that a situation would fit a thing that could already exist entirely on its own.
>
> If things can occur in Sachverhalten, this possibility must be in them from the beginning. (Something logical can not be merely possible. Logic deals with every possibility and all possibilities are its facts.)
>
> Just as we are quite unable to imagine spatial objects outside space or temporal objects outside time, so too there is *no* object that we can imagine excluded from the possibility of combining with others.
>
> If I can imagine objects combined in Sachverhalten, I cannot

imagine them excluded from the possibility of such combinations.

This long passage brings out Wittgenstein's connecting of the logical, the necessary, and the "internal," and also, interestingly enough, his linking them with the quite traditional notion of what is imaginable or what can be thought. The passage also introduces some problems of interpretation. One of these concerns the question of a thing's existing "entirely on its own." The first sentence of 2.0121 could be taken as another way of putting the point that the possible *Sachverhalten* that things can enter into are reflected by an essential or internal property of the things. Such possibilities of combination cannot then be divorced from the things, since they are essential to it—to it being what it is. This line is brought out more explicitly in the second sentence. But the first passage could be taken to suggest that things must exist in some *Sachverhalt* and not "on their own," as a Platonic form might be taken to exist. Every thing *must be* a constituent of some *Sachverhalt* and not merely be capable (essentially) of existing in certain *Sachverhalten*. This is a quite different claim from the more explicit one that possibilities are essential to things. But the remaining sentences seem to deal only with the point that the possibility of combination is necessary. Even the use of the spatial analogy, which might suggest that a thing must be in some fact as a spatial object must be at some place, likens the necessity of a spatial object being in space with the necessity of an object being able to combine with others, and not with the necessity that an object combine with others.

A second and far more crucial problem is introduced with the terms 'possibility' and 'situation' (*Möglichkeit* and *Sachlage*, respectively). In fact, these terms usher in one of the fundamental questions raised by the *Tractatus*. The problem can be put simply. We spoke of "possible facts" in connection with the list (III'). What is the status of such possibilities in the ontology of the *Tractatus?* Does Wittgenstein recognize two kinds of facts, actual and possible ones? Or are we merely dealing with a way of speaking? If the latter, can one cogently develop the views Wittgenstein is expressing without recognizing possibilities, i.e., without giving them some ontological status?

A first approach to the issue might be to suggest that the question of the ontological status of possibilities (possible facts) arises due to a mistake, like the one involved in thinking that there are nonexistent things (possible things) since we talk about "them." One who makes such a suggestion might even point out that we need not consider the term 'nobody' to indicate an entity due to our truly asserting, on occasion, that nobody is in the room. Yet, familiar and obvious as such comments may be, they do not, by themselves, suffice as a solution of the problems, or as an adequate analysis of or ground for the rejection of the issues, or as a rebuttal of Meinongian tendencies. One might buttress such comments, following Russell's lead, with analyses that take the latter statement to be a negation of an existential statement, which thereby does not contain a counterpart to the term 'nobody' as a subject term, and construing statements seemingly employing names or designating phrases for nonexistent objects in conformity with Russell's theory of descriptions. Then one would have, at least, a proposed solution. At this point I do not wish to undertake a defense of Russell's approach, since this has been done in detail on other occasions. Moreover, it is not necessary here, as Russell's approach is obviously acceptable to the Wittgenstein of the *Tractatus,* and we are concerned with the status of possible facts in terms of the doctrines of the *Tractatus.* The key to the Russellian solution lies in the *reconstruing* of certain sentences of one grammatical form in terms of sentences of a quite different grammatical form. In short, he proposes a way of treating certain expressions so that problems associated with their use are dissolved. He does not just assert that there are no problems. In a similar vein, one who takes primitive predicates of a language (or of an ideal schema of a language) to stand for properties might hold that he need not also take defined predicates to stand for properties, since sentences in which the latter predicates occur may be taken as elliptical for sentences in which they do not occur. Such a line also relies on the replacement of one sentence for another to state some matter of fact. Such proposals are like the attempt to dismiss possible facts as entities in that in all these cases the claim is made that some philosophers have given ontological status to entities due to being misled by linguistic forms. But the case of possible facts is radically different. It will help to see what is involved if we recall the traditional talk of propositions, as distinct from both facts and significant sentences, a gambit Russell tried in order to avoid such entities.

One crucial motive for appealing to propositions as the *meanings* of indicative sentences or as being what such sentences *expressed* was an attempt to account for the fact that sentences may be either true or false. Facts could not then be taken as being *the meaning* of sentences, since such things would not exist when the sentences in question were false. *Indicating or referring to a fact* would thus be inadequate as a criterion for a sentence being meaningful in a way that *referring to an object* is not inadequate as a criterion for a sign's being meaningful or acceptable as a proper name. Propositions provide an entity for a sentence to be connected with, irrespective of whether it is true or false, and they thus supply *the meaning* for a sentence even when the sentence is false and the fact in question does not exist. Russell proposed an alternative criterion of meaning for a sentence. An atomic sentence was to be meaningful if all its constituent terms were meaningful—had referents—and if it was grammatically well formed. Such a simple proposal appears to do the job which propositions are introduced to do, but without appealing to such problematic entities. But the appearance is deceptive. The problem is marked by the need to appeal to the grammatical arrangement of the terms. For it is not merely a question of the sentence being meaningful, but one of what it means. This does not mean that I am implicitly smuggling in a presupposition that for a sentence or term to be meaningful there must be something which it means. It is not a question of holding that there must be something which a sentence means, but of noting that a sentence like 'aRb' indicates or is associated with one definite fact. The existence of the fact is the ground of truth of the sentence. If all possible atomic sentences were true, one might then hold that the grammatical arrangement of the terms of the sentence indicated the structure of the corresponding fact. In this sense the existence of the fact with a certain structure would ground the meaningfulness of the sentence. But as such sentences may be false without differing in what they mean or in what they are used to assert about the world, one cannot appeal to the fact as being what is "indicated" by the sentence. The point is that the sentence does indicate or pick out one definite fact, yet the fact may not exist. Hence one may say that what it indicates is a *possible fact* or that the sentence expresses a certain *proposition* or, perhaps, a *thought*. The introduction of such entities merely marks the twofold recognition that the sentence's connection to the world is not reducible to the connections that its constituent terms have to the world and that the connection its constituent terms have to each other in the sentence marks a further tie between language and the world. In the case of definite descriptions and defined predicates, one may successfully hold that sentences containing such terms may be about the world without the respective terms being tied to objects and properties, since the sentences in question are elliptical for other sentences which do not contain the terms at issue. But it is clear that a sentence is not reducible to its terms in the way in which a defined sign is reducible to other signs. For defined signs are reducible in that they are eliminable, but sentence structure is not eliminable. A sentence, like a defined sign, may be called a "complex sign," but it is a vastly different kind of complex sign. It is this feature of a sentence that we are asked to attend to by those who speak of propositions or possible facts. Such entities are the ontological representatives of that most significant feature of atomic sentences. Just as the question 'How is it that a name or a predicate can be used to speak about the world?' requires the partial reply that they stand for objects and properties respectively, the question 'How is it that we can use an atomic sentence to assert something about the world?' seems to require the reply that they stand for, indicate, or express possible facts or propositions. (Another way of putting the last question would be 'Why is it that a sentence is more than a set of terms?') Of course, one can refuse to raise the question and, by so doing, avoid speaking of such entities. But then one does not "avoid" such entities; he merely declines to take up a philosophical issue. Nevertheless, while some such entities appear to be required, propositions or Fregean thoughts are problematic. Russell noticed the problem in "On Denoting,"[3] and it led him to reject propositions and all en-

---

[3] Bertrand Russell, "On Denoting," in *Logic and Knowledge*, ed. R. C. Marsh (New York: Macmillan, 1956). I believe this point may be involved in Russell's complicated and somewhat confusing discussion.

tities belonging to Frege's realm of senses. The problem is easily indicated. Sentences may be about facts or at least purport to indicate facts. If we introduce propositions to solve the problem about sentences indicating nonexistent facts when they are false, such sentences are not about nor do they indicate such propositions. Rather, they are said to *express* or *mean* the relevant propositions. But the propositions themselves then indicate or stand for the facts in question. Moreover, a sentence is then characteristically said to indicate a fact derivatively, in that it does so due to the proposition which it expresses being about the fact. We then face two questions. First, what is the connection between a proposition and the fact it stands for? Second, whatever that relation is, when the fact does not exist how is it that the proposition indicates or singles out one definite fact? In short, irrespective of the answer to the first question, do we not face exactly the same problem that propositions were introduced to solve? We thus have additional entities but no solution. Recognizing this, Russell rejected propositions and proposed the inadequate solution mentioned above. Wittgenstein follows Russell in noting the inadequacy of the gambit which introduces propositions, but he also sees the inadequacy of Russell's attempt to do without any ontological ground for the logical role sentences play in enabling language and thought to be about the world. He thus introduces possible facts and speaks of propositions only as interpreted sign sequences which obey grammatical rules. It is the recognition of the need for such entities that leads to his talk of "possibilities," "possible facts," "possible situations," "situations," "possible states of affairs," "possibility of structure," "pictorial form," and "possibility of existence."

Two questions remain to be answered: "Why is the introduction of possible facts more cogent than the appeal to propositions?" and "How does Wittgenstein fit possible facts into the ontology of the *Tractatus?*"

One can see the cogency of Wittgenstein's alternative when we note that the problem is to state why the structure of a sentence enables a sentence to be linked to a fact. Introducing propositions links the structure of the sentence with the corresponding structure of the proposition but fails to link either of these with the structure of the relevant fact. Introducing possible facts enables one to link the structure of the sentence with the world, irrespective of whether the fact is actual, since one holds *there is* a fact whose structure is represented by the structure of the sentence. The truth or falsity of the sentence is then based on that entity's being possible or actual. The sentence, whether it is true or false, links up with the world since it links up with a fact. By linking a sentence to a proposition, one fails to link it to the facts which make it true or false, and hence to the world, unless one links the proposition, in turn, to the facts. But one can only do the latter by having the structure of the proposition stand for the structure of a fact, irrespective of whether the fact is actual or possible. Thus one introduces possible facts, in addition to propositions. On the other hand, if one introduces possible facts, one does not require propositions in order to ground the connection between a sentence and the world, so that the former can be both about the latter and true or false of it. Both tasks are performed by having the sentence represent one and the same fact. In virtue of this representation, the sentence is about the world: if the fact is possible, the sentence is false; if the fact is actual or existent, the sentence is true.

Speaking as we have makes it appear that Wittgenstein holds to two kinds of facts. Thus one might take him to maintain that atomic facts are of two types. But to speak of actual and possible facts in such a way precludes one from holding that an actual fact is also a possible fact. Yet Wittgenstein characteristically speaks of the possibilities in such a way that it is clear that all of the facts that an object can be a constituent of are possibilities, irrespective of whether such facts exist or not. Moreover, there is another question that arises. What determines the possibilities with respect to an object? Wittgenstein's solution simultaneously avoids literally introducing possible facts as entities, while having the benefits of their introduction, and also provides an answer to the questions just raised. *Possibilities are introduced as essential characteristics of objects.* We have already seen that Wittgenstein's objects are natured. Possible facts are packed, as it were, into the nature of the object. Among such possibilities are those that correlate to actual facts as well.

2.0123　If I know an object I also know all its possible occurrences in Sachverhalten.

(Every one of these possibilities must be part of the nature of the object.)

A new possibility cannot be discovered later.

2.014　Objects contain the possibility of all situations.

This doctrine enables him to recognize only one kind of fact (the actual, existent atomic fact) while grounding the tie between a sentence and what it is about in something—a possibility as part of the nature of the object. Taking objects to have natures thus helps unite several themes of the *Tractatus*. We have already seen how the question of an object's being the kind of thing that it is gets resolved by having objects be natured. Such natures also resolve the problem of how sentences indicate possibilities. In both cases one deals with logical or internal matters. Similarly, the ontological ground of tautologies will also be located in the natures of things. Thus that the object *a* is an object, that it can be a constituent of the possibility expressed by '*aRb*', and that '*aRb*' or '*~aRb*' holds are all based on the nature of the object or, as one may say, on its form. Wittgenstein's notion of form or essence will also cover and ground what others have called synthetic a priori truths like one and the same color spot's not being both red and green (all over simultaneously). Thus such a truth will also be "logical" or "formal." We then have the notions of *essential, logical,* and *formal* covering the five distinct cases of (1) *the kind of thing* that is involved in the sense of an object as opposed to a relation, (2) *the kind of thing* that is involved in the sense of a color spot as opposed to a sound, (3) the combinatorial possibilities involved in the sense of just which possible facts an object may be a constituent of, (4) the tautologies of propositional logic, and (5) the logical truth that nothing is both red and green (all over simultaneously). This is not to say that the five are not related, but they can be and must be distinguished. Insofar as they are all put in the same basket of the formal or logical, they are also features that must be shown by language and not stated in language. The points involved in (1) and (3) are readily understood in this sense, as they are generally reflected by the rules for, and not statements of, the language. For Wittgenstein, that a sign is for a color spot, as opposed to a sound, would also be shown by the sort of sign it is. And, as is generally known, he also held that tautologies and contradictions reveal the limits of language and are not proper sentences of a language (or reflected by sentences of a logically ideal language). Just as all these senses of 'logical' are reflected by, rather than stated in, a proper language, they all have an ontological ground in that they reflect the natures of the constituents of facts. Thus it is a mistake to believe that Wittgenstein did not take the notion of the form of the world to have ontological significance, or that he took logic to be a matter of language alone. What others have considered in terms of essences, propositions, negative facts, synthetic a priori truths (or facts), and logically necessary facts (or truths), he handled under the notion of the nature or form of a constituent.

It is clear that Wittgenstein, in a variety of metaphorical ways, introduced possible facts, as contrasted with propositions.

> 4.031 In a proposition a situation is, as it were, constructed by way of experiment.
> Instead of, 'This proposition has such and such a sense', we can simply say, 'This proposition represents such and such a situation'.

> 4.0311 One name stands for one thing, another for another thing, and they are combined with one another. In this way the whole group—like a tableau vivant—presents the Sachverhalt.

To speak of "situations," as he does, or to talk of presenting a *Sachverhalt* is merely a way of introducing possible facts without explicitly referring to such entities. On the basis of such statements, and others, one might reasonably hold that Wittgenstein recognizes such entities and does not ground possibilities in the natures of the constituents of facts, as I suggested. There would then be two kinds of facts: possible and actual ones. Moreover, the problem mentioned above about a fact not being both actual and possible could be handled by holding that every sentence on list (III′) stood for a possible fact, while every sentence on list (III) stood for an actual fact as well. Thus, the sentence '*aRb*' would be connected with two entities, an actual fact and a possible fact with the same constituents and structure.[4] Talk of the natures of objects would then be taken to be elliptical for reference to the logical relations between the constituents *a*, *b*, and *R*, the possible fact depicted by '*aRb*', and the actual fact that also exists in this case. This would not violate Wittgenstein's dictum that sentences are not names. The sentence '*aRb*' depicts a possible fact in virtue of the structures of the complex sign and of the possible fact. The sentence does not denote by being interpreted or correlated, as does a single sign design. The nature of a constituent would then be given by the possible facts it is correlated with or "in" which it occurs as a constituent.[5] But to fit Wittgenstein's way of speaking, such a correlation would have to hold in virtue of something internal or intrinsic to the constituent. One thus ends up talking about *both essences* of constituents *and possible facts*. In a way it makes no difference which way one chooses to picture such an ontology. The point is that Wittgenstein gives ontological status, on either alternative, to possibilities; he also thinks of constituents as having natures or essences.

It is perhaps interesting to note that the questions he sought to handle in the *Tractatus*, by appeal to natures, are among those he later sought to dissolve by thinking in terms of the essence or nature of language. Some feel that in so doing Wittgenstein abandoned the original questions. Alternatively, one may wonder if the change was so great. Is there much difference between letting such issues rest on the "nature" of things and leaving questions unanswered by appealing to the ordinary context of linguistic use? Both approaches may be taken as either giving up an attempted explanation or as taking us to the point where nothing more could be said.

[4] Alternatively, one may speak in the traditional manner of "actualized possibilities" or of existence being added to essence. Moore was worrying and writing about such matters between 1898 and 1911.

[5] Lest one think that such talk of possible facts is no different from the gambit that introduces propositions, it should be noted that the constituents and structure of possible facts and of actual facts are the same things and properties (or relations). The constituents of propositions are not the same as the constituents of facts. This is precisely why the gambit introducing propositions fails. But then everything rests on the ultimate and unanalyzable difference between a possible and an actual fact or on the *nature* of objects. How one must treat possibilities as essential properties in order to avoid the problem is something sidestepped here. Wittgenstein may have thought of the possible fact that *a* is W in terms of an essential property of *a*, being capable of being W. This, by itself, will not suffice.

23

Arithmetic and Propositional Form in Wittgenstein's Tractatus

HERBERT HOCHBERG

ONE crucial aspect of Wittgenstein's later philosophy, the idea that the logical is not restricted to the tautological, is a simple consequence of his philosophy of arithmetic as presented in the *Tractatus*. According to Wittgenstein, *number* is a formal concept, as are *object, fact,* and *function*. Thus what represents such a concept in a proper symbolism is neither a class sign nor a function sign but a category of sign or kind of variable, just as the notion of an *object* may be represented by the category of individual signs or the occurrence of individual variables in the symbolism. As Wittgenstein puts it:

> 4.1272 Thus the variable name 'x' is the proper sign for the pseudo-concept *object*.[1]

This immediately rules out the Russellian reduction of arithmetic to logic, since (1) there can be no class of natural numbers, (2) a number of statements that can be made on the Russell reconstruction such as '1 is a number' are declared nonsensical, (3) a number cannot be a class, for number expressions must be of a logically different kind than class expressions (just as signs for objects must be of a logically different kind than propositional signs or function signs), and, hence, (4) an adequate symbolism for arithmetic must *show* the logical or internal relations among arithmetical signs,

[1] Quotations from the *Tractatus* are taken from the D. F. Pears and B. F. McGuinness translation (London: Routledge & Kegan Paul, 1961).

while Russell's symbolism purportedly does not do so. In short, that a sign stands for a number must "show itself," and what must show itself cannot be said:

> 4.126 A name shows that it signifies an object, a sign for a number that it signifies a number, etc.

But then, does the ontology of the *Tractatus* encompass numbers as well as objects and facts? If so, what are numbers? If not, what is intended by the assertion that a sign for a number signifies a number?

At places Wittgenstein suggests that a number is what is in the sequences of successors of 0 or reached as the result of some finite number of applications of the successor function; it is, in the familiar way, a member of the posterity of 0 with respect to the successor function. This is what is involved in

> 6.03 The general form of an integer is $[0, \xi, \xi + 1]$.

and in the series of definitions in 6.02, and in

> 4.1273 If we want to express in conceptual notation the general proposition, '*b* is a successor of *a*', then we require an expression for the general term of the series of forms
>
> $$aRb,$$
> $$(\exists x) : aRx \cdot xRb,$$
> $$(\exists x, y) : aRx \cdot xRy \cdot yRb,$$
>
> $$\cdot \ \cdot \ \cdot \ \cdot$$
>
> In order to express the general term of a series of forms, we must use a variable, because the concept 'term of that series of forms' is a *formal* concept. (This is what Frege and Russell overlooked. . . .)
>
> We can determine the general term of a series of forms by giving its first term and the general form of the operation that produces the next term out of the proposition that precedes it.

If 'R' is taken as a variable, then it is clear in what sense the series of forms is "variable." But even if 'R' expresses the relation between any number and its immediate successor in the number series, Wittgenstein holds that we must use a variable to stand for the concept 'being a member of that series'. Only such a sign will reveal the internal or logical connection among the terms: that they are generated from 0 by the successor function. This is "shown" by the sign '$[0, \xi, \xi + 1]$' and not by Russell's definition of natural number. Yet, aside from the somewhat specious declaration that certain things must be shown and not said, Wittgenstein at best seems to be simply offering the Peano postulates as a philosophy of arithmetic. For it seems as if he takes '0' and '$+1$' as primitive notions and holds that 'number' is shown in the symbols for numbers. That is, the sign '$[0, \xi, \xi + 1]$' suggests that correspondents of the Peano primitives are taken as primitive by Wittgenstein. The only *apparent* difference is Wittgenstein's "insight" that the general form of expression, and not another primitive term stands for the formal concept number.[2] Moreover, such a point is rather minor by contrast with a dilemma one now faces. Given that '0' and '$+1$' are primitive, one either takes them as uninterpreted signs in an abstract axiomatic system or as having a definite interpretation. If the former, then we are, so to speak, taken back to the point where Russell and Frege took issue with the "formalists." If the latter, then we face the query regarding what such signs "signify." This is especially pointed for Wittgenstein since, in some sense, arithmetic is a matter of logic:

6.2 Mathematics is a logical method.
The propositions of mathematics are equations, and therefore pseudo-propositions.

6.21 A proposition of mathematics does not express a thought.

6.22 The logic of the world, which is shown in tautologies by the propositions of logic, is shown in equations by mathematics.

It would thus appear that the basic arithmetical signs are in some way to be construed as logical signs, and logical signs do not signify as names signify objects. Wittgenstein must then present an analysis which, first, shows in what sense arithmetical signs are logical signs,

---

[2] The stress on the apparent difference here is twofold. As we shall see, Wittgenstein offers definitions of '0' and '$+1$', and it is not clear that his version of arithmetic is adequate. There are problems regarding the arrangement of parentheses in identity statements, which Rhees reports he later recognized (Rush Rhees, *Discussions of Wittgenstein* [New York: Schocken Books, 1970], p. 35), though I am not sure that Wittgenstein recognizes that '$(1 + 1 + 1 + 1) = (1 + 1) + (1 + 1)$' must be proven or, perhaps better, '$[(1 + 1) + 1] + 1 = (1 + 1) + (1 + 1)$'.

second, avoids the formalist treatment of arithmetic as uninterpreted axiomatics, and, third, avoids the introduction of arithmetical entities.

We can see how Wittgenstein goes about such an analysis by considering his discussion of the general form of a truth function and of a proposition. This he writes as '$[\bar{p}, \bar{\xi}, N\,(\bar{\xi})\,]$', which he explains as:

> 6.001 What this says is just that every proposition is a result of successive applications to elementary propositions of the operation $N(\bar{\xi})$.

The expression for the general form of a proposition stands for (or one may say "shows that") any proposition may be arrived at by applying joint denial to a selection of elementary propositions, and then applying it again to any selection made from the set of elementary propositions or propositions so obtained, and so on. One also gets a sequence of propositions generated by $N(\xi)$ which bears some analogy to the series of propositions generated by 'R' in 4.1273. The elementary propositions can be considered the limiting case where the operation is performed zero times, or as the result of not performing it. Thus,

> 5. A proposition is a truth-function of elementary propositions.
> (An elementary proposition is a truth-function of itself.)

The analogy with the set of statements in 4.1273 or with the number series itself is weak. Anscombe seeks to strengthen it by offering a procedure for ordering the obtainable truth functions of elementary propositions.[3] But that does not really help. What is involved can be seen in terms of the application of joint denial ('$\downarrow$') to a single proposition 'p_1'. The first result is '$p_1 \downarrow p_1$'. If we follow the analogy with either the number series or the propositions of 4.1273, we should then apply the operation to this result. But that yields '$(p_1 \downarrow p_1) \downarrow (p_1 \downarrow p_1)$', which is equivalent to 'p_1'. Hence we do not produce a *new* member of the series. Moreover, there are two other functions of the proposition, '$p_1 \vee \sim p_1$' and '$p_1 \cdot \sim p_1$', which must be generated. We get one of them if we apply the stroke to the two arguments 'p_1' and '$p_1 \downarrow p_1$' with the result

[3] G. E. M. Anscombe, *An Introduction to Wittgenstein's "Tractatus"* (New York: Harper & Row, 1965), Ch. 10.

'$p_1 \downarrow (p_1 \downarrow p_1)$'. We get the other, if we apply the stroke to that result and obtain '$(p_1 \downarrow (p_1 \downarrow p_1)) \downarrow (p_1 \downarrow (p_1 \downarrow p_1))$'. We then have the sequence;

$$p_1$$
$$p_1 \downarrow p_1$$
$$p_1 \downarrow (p_1 \downarrow p_1)$$
$$(p_1 \downarrow (p_1 \downarrow p_1)) \downarrow (p_1 \downarrow (p_1 \downarrow p_1)).$$

There is an analogy to the use of the successor function in the case of the generation of the second line from the first and of the fourth line from the third. But the getting of the third line from the first and second is a different kind of move. Of course one can stipulate a stepwise procedure for getting to all the functions of a set of propositional variables and dropping redundant ones. This Anscombe does, and, in effect, we just did for the case of one variable. But two things are clear. First, the members of such a series could be arranged in several ways, depending on the procedure chosen. Second, one does not, in all cases, get to the $n + 1$st member by applying the operation to the nth member. The natural numbers, by contrast, cannot be "arranged" in several ways via the application of the successor function to 0 and the successors of 0. And, of course, one is getting to each term of the series by applying the operation to the previous one, or, perhaps, applying it a successive number of times to 0. Moreover, there is another distinct and crucial disparity. With one variable the base, in this case 'p_1', can be considered a term of the series and yet every term is generated from previous terms in the series. With two or more variables either the base propositions are not members of the series or, if they are, some members will not be generated from previous members. In the arithmetical case 0 is a member of the series (or mentioned in the first proposition of the series in 4.1273 or 6.02), and every other term comes from applying the operation to a prior term.[4]

Such differences aside, there is a sort of analogy that appeals to

[4] Sometimes Wittgenstein seems to think of the series of forms generated by the successor operation as the series of propositions reflecting what is the successor of what; sometimes he considers the number series itself. The former case strengthens the analogy with the truth-functional sequence, since we deal with propositions in both sequences.

Wittgenstein. Thus arithmetic appears as a matter of form just as propositional logic, based on truth functions, is a matter of form. The relation of 1 to 0 is something like the relation of '$p_1 \downarrow p_1$' to 'p_1', and hence a *matter of logic*. One can then reasonably hold that a postulate (for Peano) like '0 is a number' shows itself just as it shows itself that '$p_1 \downarrow p_1$' is a truth function of 'p_1'. Just as a propositional logic constitutes a "method of logic," so arithmetic may be thought to be a "method of logic." Hence, while arithmetic is not reducible to logic in Russell's sense, it is a kind of logic or a distinct part of logic, somewhat as one may nowadays hold that quantificational logic is a part of logic in addition to propositional logic. But there is more than the analogy between the operations $N(\overline{\xi})$ and $+1$, and their role in generating numbers and truth functions or propositions, behind Wittgenstein's characterization of arithmetic as a method of logic. He seems to see another analogy between the way arithmetical equations function in their empirical applications and the way in which argument patterns and logical truths function. Consider the argument pattern

$$(x) \ (Fx \supset Gx)$$
$$(\exists x)Fx$$
$$\overline{\therefore \ (\exists x)Gx}$$

with 'F' and 'G' as variables. Suppose I know that all men are mortal and that there are men. I may then use the above pattern to conclude that there are mortals. Wittgenstein thinks that we apply arithmetical truths in the same way.

> 6.211 Indeed in real life a mathematical proposition is never what we want. Rather, we make use of mathematical propositions *only* in inferences from propositions that do not belong to mathematics to others that likewise do not belong to mathematics.

Thus, just as the above pattern corresponds to the logical truth '$[(x) \ (Fx \supset Gx) \cdot (\exists x)Fx] \supset (\exists x)Gx$', the arithmetical truth '$7 + 5 = 12$' corresponds to the addition pattern

$$\begin{array}{r} 7 \\ + \ 5 \\ \hline 12 \end{array}$$

which may be applied, in a given case, as

$$
\begin{array}{r}
7 \text{ apples here} \\
\underline{5 \text{ apples there}} \\
\therefore\ 12 \text{ apples altogether.}
\end{array}
$$

This not only links up arithmetic to logic as another method of logic, but also points to a way of holding that arithmetic is a matter of logic, that arithmetical signs do not stand for entities, and that, nevertheless, both Russell's reduction and the abstract axiomatics of the formalist can be avoided. For one does not require the logical signs in the application of tautological patterns to stand for anything. Yet logic is not a question of abstract axiomatics. What logic reflects is the form of the world. Hence, so does arithmetic. Recall here 6.22. Wittgenstein escapes from the crucial questions regarding the ontological ground of arithmetic exactly as he does those of logic itself.[5]

There is yet another link of the arithmetical and the logical. He tells us that

6.021 A number is the exponent of an operation.

Whether we think in terms of some variable operation or in terms of the specific operation $N(\overline{\xi})$, the idea is that we can construe numbers recursively in terms of exponents of operations. Taking the operation to be $N(\overline{\xi})$ gives us another link between "ordinary" logic and arithmetic. The main point, however, is that arithmetical signs do not stand for anything, since they are all defined in terms of '0' and '$+1$', and '0' and '$+1$' are recursively defined by the device of taking them as exponential signs. Of course what Wittgenstein defines is what we might call the null application of an operation. Similarly, he defines the $n + 1$st application of the operation, for, recall, having disposed of the notion of number as a pseudo-concept, he need only define Peano's remaining two primitives, 0 and successor. The $n + 1$st application of an operation yields the same result as the application of the operation to the result of the nth application. The two definitions in 6.02

[5] In a way he doesn't, for all matters of form are grounded in the essences or forms of objects (and perhaps facts). See "Facts, Possibilities, and Essences in the *Tractatus*," in this volume.

$$x = \Omega^{o'} x \text{ Def.,}$$
$$\Omega' \, \Omega^{Y'} x = \Omega^{Y+1'}x \text{ Def.}$$

then yield the series

$$x, \Omega' \, x, \Omega'\Omega' \, x, \Omega' \, \Omega' \, \Omega'x, \, \ldots .$$

Here I am not concerned with questions regarding the adequacy of Wittgenstein's approach: with whether or not his use of the iteration of the operation sign is question-begging, or whether his definition of '0' is so.[6] All we need note is that, as exponents of logical operations, the basic arithmetical notions expressed by '0' and '+1' indicate that arithmetic constitutes a system of logic.[7] As arithmetical truths are not tautologies, but nevertheless logical or formal truths, the stage is set for the idea that the logical is a question of the rules of the "language game" and not to be restricted to the analytic truths of formal logic. Russell accommodated the felt difference

[6] There is a problem corresponding to the one leading to Russell's axiom of infinity, if we are dealing with an operation (ultimately) on elementary propositions.

[7] The phrase 'logical operation' has two senses here. First, there is the idea that we are dealing with what is common to any series of the kind Wittgenstein is concerned with; that is, where we have a null application that yields the same member that is operated on and where the $n + 1$st application yields the same result as operating on the result of the nth application. In this sense we deal with something logical in that we are concerned with the abstract pattern common to all such series. Second, there is the idea that we have a logical operation, joint denial, which generates such a series. The first sense reinforces the idea that arithmetic, like logic, is a matter of *form* applicable to various *content*. It also shows Wittgenstein to hold that we see what arithmetic is when we see what is common to all series of the relevant kind. He thus advocates a mixture of formalist and intuitionist lines. His view is intuitionistic in that everything is based on the fundamental operation generating a series. It is formalistic in that it appears as if we are dealing with an abstract model for such a series with abstract, uninterpreted signs. The twist Wittgenstein introduces is to "define" the operation. But he presupposes an iteration notion as primitive. If the notion of iteration is itself formalized in an abstract system, we have a formalist view. If it is implicitly taken as a basic notion and not treated in terms of abstract sign patterns, then we have a kind of intuitionist view. As Wittgenstein puts it, we have a bit of both. In either case he doesn't really "define" the successor operation; he simply rewrites it. (See n. 8.) A further point may lie behind Wittgenstein's not thinking he is offering a version of the formalism Russell rejected. One naturally speaks of an abstract system as indicating a form common to its various interpretations. Thus, one may think of such a system as standing for a formal property of such interpretations and, hence, as not being merely an abstract system of signs.

between arithmetical truths and empirical ones by attempting to reduce the former to logical truths. Wittgenstein, not holding that all logical or formal truths can be construed as truths of standard logic, will end up by holding that what is logical is a question of a language rule. In a way, then, he will come to hold that the tautologies are merely another kind of reflection of rules of language. One who holds that x is F and not F doesn't understand the language, just as one who holds that 3 equals $2 + 5$ doesn't understand the language of arithmetic. Wittgenstein thus starts out by objecting to Russell's reduction of one kind of statement to another, the arithmetical to the analytic, and he ends by treating the analytical in the same way he treats the arithmetical. What he does is end with the formalist view, which Russell and Frege attacked in arithmetic, in both arithmetic and logic. This is only partly disguised by grafting a contextualist theory of meaning onto the structure of his position under the guise of 'the use' replacing 'the meaning'. In short, the doctrine that mathematics constitutes its own language game and that understanding mathematics is understanding the connection of various statements and procedures within the game, as well as their application in nonmathematical contexts, expresses the core of the formalist view attacked by Russell and Frege. That such a view was already essentially present in the *Tractatus*, we have seen. To clinch the matter, all we need to note is that the construction of arithmetic in the *Tractatus* depends on taking *the exponent (or iteration) of an operation* as a primitive notion.[8] In effect, what Wittgenstein did was cryptically lay down rules for such a notion, as Peano had set down stipulations about number and successor. Later he came to take the contexts of pure mathematics and the application of mathematics to constitute the rules.

[8] See Quine's discussion of iteration in *Set Theory and Its Logic*, pp. 79–80, 95–102. Perhaps *the* point to note is Quine's definition of 'iterates' in terms of 'successor' and, ultimately, in terms of the logical apparatus with iterates as powers of relations.

Selected Bibliography

COMPILED WITH THE ASSISTANCE OF EDWARD NILGES

THE following constitutes only a selective bibliography on Wittgenstein. A complete bibliography may be found in the following works:

Fann, K. T. *Wittgenstein's Conception of Philosophy*. Oxford: Basil Blackwell, 1969, and Berkeley and Los Angeles: University of California Press, 1969.
————. "Supplement to the Wittgenstein Bibliography," *Revue Internationale de Philosophie* (1969), pp. 363–70.

I. *Works by Wittgenstein*
(IN CHRONOLOGICAL ORDER)

"Notes on Logic" (1913). Edited by H. T. Costello, *The Journal of Philosophy*, 54 (1957):230–44. Reprinted in *Notebooks, 1914–16*.
"Notes Dictated to Moore in Norway" (1914). Reprinted in *Notebooks, 1914–16*, pp. 107–18.
Notebooks, 1914–16. Edited by G. H. von Wright and G. E. M. Anscombe, with English translation by G. E. M. Anscombe. Oxford: Basil Blackwell, 1961.
"Letters to Russell, 1912–21." Extracts in *Notebooks, 1914–16*.

Logisch-philosophische Abhandlung (1918). First published in *Annalen der Naturphilosophie*, 14 (1921):185–262.

Tractatus logico-philosophicus, with introduction by Bertrand Russell. English edition of *Logisch-philosophische Abhandlung*, translated by C. K. Ogden. London: Routledge & Kegan Paul, 1922. New English translation by D. F. Pears and B. F. McGuinness. London: Routledge & Kegan Paul, 1961.

Italian edition: translated by G. C. M. Colombo (Milan-Rome, 1954). New Italian translation with *Notebooks, 1914–16*, by Amendo G. Conte (Turin, 1964).

Russian edition: translated by I. Dobronravov and D. Laxuti with introduction by V. Asmus and commentary by D. Laxuti, V. Finn, D. Kuznecov, and I. Dobronravov (Moscow, 1958).

French edition: translated by Pierre Klossowski (Paris, 1961).

Swedish edition: translated by A. Wedberg (Stockholm, 1962).

Danish edition: translated by D. Favrholdt (Copenhagen, 1963).

Chinese edition: translated by Chang Shen-Fu, in *Che-Hsüeh Ping-Lun* (Peking), 1, No. 5 (1927):53–98, and 2, No. 6 (1928):31–80.

Spanish edition: translated by T. Galván (Madrid, 1957).

Yugoslavian edition: translated by G. Petrović (Sarajevo, 1960).

"Some Remarks on Logical Form," *Proceedings of the Aristotelian Society*, Suppl. Vol. 9 (1929):162–71. Reprinted with note by Anscombe in Copi and Beard, eds., *Essays on Wittgenstein's "Tractatus"*.

"A Lecture on Ethics" (1930). *The Philosophical Review*, 74 (1965):3–12. Reprinted in *Philosophy Today*, Vol. 1, ed. Jerry H. Gill (New York: Macmillan, 1968), pp. 4–14.

Philosophische Bemerkungen (1930). Edited by Rush Rhees. Oxford: Basil Blackwell, 1965; Frankfurt: Suhrkamp Verlag. English translation by G. E. M. Anscombe, New York: Barnes and Noble, 1968.

Wörterbuch für Volksschulen. Vienna: Hölder-Pichler-Tempsky, 1926.

"Letter to the Editor," *Mind*, 42 (1933):415–16.

The Blue and Brown Books (1933–35). Edited by Rush Rhees. Oxford: Basil Blackwell, 1958. French translation, Paris: Gallimard, 1965.

"Notes for Lectures on 'Private Experience' and 'Sense Data'," 1934–36. *The Philosophical Review*, 77 (1968). Reprinted in *Introduction to the Philosophy of Mind*, ed. Harold Morick (Glenview, Ill.: Scott, Foresman, 1970), pp. 155–94.

Remarks on the Foundations of Mathematics (1937–44). Edited by G. H. von Wright, R. Rhees, and G. E. M. Anscombe, with English translation by G. E. M. Anscombe. Oxford: Basil Blackwell, 1956.

Lectures and Conversations on Aesthetics, Psychology and Religious Belief (1938). Compiled from notes taken by R. Rhees, Y. Smythies, and J. Taylor; edited by Cyril Barrett. Oxford: Basil Blackwell, 1966.

Philosophical Investigations (Part I, 1945; Part II, 1947–49). English edition of *Philosophische Untersuchungen*, edited by G. E. M. Anscombe and Rush Rhees, with English translation by G. E. M. Anscombe. Oxford: Basil Blackwell, 1st ed., 1953; 2nd ed., 1958; 3rd ed., 1967. French translation by P. Klossowski, Paris, 1961.

Zettel (1945–48). Edited by G. E. M. Anscombe and G. H. von Wright, with English translation by G. E. M. Anscombe. Oxford: Basil Blackwell, 1970, and Berkeley and Los Angeles: University of California Press, 1970.

Notes on Knowledge and Certainty (1950–51). Wittgenstein's last philosophical notes, in preparation.

Schriften. Includes *Tractatus logico-philosophicus, Tagebücher, 1914–16, Philosophische Untersuchungen*. Frankfurt: Suhrkamp Verlag, 1960.

On Certainty. Edited by G. E. M. Anscombe and G. H. von Wright, with English translation by G. H. Paul and G. E. M. Anscombe. Oxford: Basil Blackwell, 1969, and New York: Harper & Row, 1969.

II. *Works on Wittgenstein*

Anscombe, G. E. M. *An Introduction to Wittgenstein's "Tractatus"*. London: Hutchinson, 1959.

Black, Max. *A Companion to Wittgenstein's "Tractatus"*. Ithaca: Cornell University Press, 1964.

Copi, I. M., and R. W. Beard, eds. *Essays on Wittgenstein's "Tractatus"*. New York: Macmillan, 1966, and London: Routledge & Kegan Paul, 1966.

Englemann, Paul. *Ludwig Wittgenstein: A Memoir and Letters*, translated by L. Furtmüller. Oxford: Basil Blackwell.

Fann, K. T., ed. *Wittgenstein, The Man and His Philosophy: An Anthology*. New York: Dell Publishing Co., 1967.

———. *Wittgenstein's Conception of Philosophy*. Oxford: Basil Blackwell, 1969, and Berkeley and Los Angeles: University of California Press, 1969.

Favrholdt, David. *An Interpretation and Critique of Wittgenstein's "Tractatus"*. Copenhagen: Munksgaard, 1964, and New York: Humanities Press, 1966.

Feibleman, James. *Inside the Great Mirror*. The Hague: Martinus Nijhoff, 1958.

Gellner, Ernest. *Words and Things: A Critical Account of Linguistic Philosophy and a Study in Ideology*. Boston: Beacon Press, 1960.

Griffin, James. *Wittgenstein's Logical Atomism*. Oxford: Clarendon Press, 1964.

Hartnack, Justus. *Wittgenstein and Modern Philosophy*. Translated by Maurice Cranston. New York: Doubleday, 1965.

Hudson, W. D. *Ludwig Wittgenstein*. Lutterworth, 1968.

Kielkopf, Charles. *An Investigation of Wittgenstein's "Remarks on the Foundations of Mathematics."* The Hague: Martinus Nijhoff, forthcoming.

Malcolm, Norman. *Ludwig Wittgenstein: A Memoir*. London: Oxford University Press, 1958. Rev. ed., 1966.

Maslow, Alexander. *A Study in Wittgenstein's "Tractatus"*. Berkeley and Los Angeles: University of California Press, 1961.

Mullin, A. A. *Philosophical Comments on the Philosophies of C. S. Peirce and Ludwig Wittgenstein*. Urbana, Illinois: Electrical Engineering Research Laboratory, Engineering Experiment Station, University of Illinois, 1961.

Naess, Arne. *Moderne Filosoffer: Carnap, Wittgenstein, Heidegger, Sartre*. Copenhagen: Stjernebogerne Vintens Forlag, 1965.

Pitcher, George. *The Philosophy of Wittgenstein*. Englewood Cliffs, N.J.: Prentice-Hall, 1964.

Pitcher, George, ed. *Wittgenstein: The Philosophical Investigations*. New York: Doubleday, 1966.

Pears, David. *Ludwig Wittgenstein*. New York: The Viking Press, 1969.

Plochmann, G. K., and J. B. Lawson. *Terms in Their Propositional Contexts in Wittgenstein's "Tractatus": An Index*. Carbondale: Southern Illinois University Press, 1962.

Pole, David. *The Later Philosophy of Wittgenstein*. London: The Athlone Press, University of London, 1958.

Rao, A. Pampapathy. *A Survey of Wittgenstein's Theory of Meaning*. Calcutta, 1965.

Rhees, Rush. *Discussions of Wittgenstein*. New York: Schocken Books Inc., 1970.

Stenius, E. *Wittgenstein's "Tractatus"*. Oxford: Basil Blackwell, 1960.

Van Peursen, C. A. *Ludwig Wittgenstein: An Introduction to His Philosophy*. New York: E. P. Dutton & Co., 1970.

Winch, Peter. *Studies in the Philosophy of Wittgenstein*. London: Routledge & Kegan Paul, 1969, and New York: Humanities Press, 1969.

Index*

* *Compiled by Richard Fleming*

547